Natural Language Processing and
Knowledge Representation

Natural Language Processing and Knowledge Representation

Language for Knowledge and Knowledge for Language

Edited by

Łucja M. Iwańska and Stuart C. Shapiro

AAAI Press / The MIT Press

Menlo Park, California, Cambridge, Massachusetts, London, England

Copublished and distributed by The MIT Press, Massachusetts Institute
of Technology, Cambridge, Massachusetts and London, England.

Library of Congress Cataloging-in-Publication Data

Natural language processing and knowledge representation : language
for knowledge and knowledge for language / edited by Łucja M. Iwańska and Stuart C. Shapiro.
     p.   cm.
  Includes bibliographical references and index.
  ISBN 0-262-59021-2 (pbk. : alk. paper)
  1. Natural language processing (Computer science) 2. Knowledge representation (Information theory). I. Iwańska, Łucja, 1958-. II. Shapiro,
Stuart Charles. III. Title.
QA76.9.N38 N3843 2000
006.3'5—dc21   99-087360
                                                                CIP

Printed on acid-free paper in Canada.

10 9 8 7 6 5 4 3 2 1

For Tomasz — Ł. M. I.
and Caren — S. C. S.

Contents

This chapter presents a novel view of natural language as a powerful, general-purpose knowledge representation system particularly suitable for handling knowledge in not well formalized domains. It discusses a number of highly desirable representational and inferential characteristics unique to natural language. They include great expressiveness combined with computational tractability, rich structure, exploitation of logical contradiction and logical redundancy, inherent underspecificity and context-dependency, and facilitating learning. A formal computational model of natural language that closely simulates these characteristics is presented. Many examples illustrate the computational mechanism of representing and reasoning with meaning of natural language and different types of knowledge, including taxonomic, probabilistic, temporal and some aspects of spatial knowledge. A large-scale implementation of the model is also discussed. The system allows one to automatically acquire and utilize knowledge from large-scale corpora of textual documents.

The authors have argued elsewhere that first order inference can be made more efficient by using nonstandard syntax for first order logic. In this chapter, they define a syntax for first order logic based on the structure of natural language under Montague semantics. They show that, for a certain fairly expressive fragment of this language, satisfiability is polynomial time decidable. The polynomial time decision procedure can be used as a subroutine in general purpose inference systems and seems to be more powerful than analogous procedures based on either classical or taxonomic syntax.

Chapter Three
Issues in the Representation of Real Texts: The Design of KRISP / 77
David D. McDonald

Attempting to understand a journalist's real texts puts special demands on the formalism that a language comprehension system uses to represent what it has understood. KRISP is an experimental representation system that was designed to address these demands: high-speed operation, the ability to accommodate a very wide range of grammatical constructions, and reversibility. Its fundamental motivations stem from investigations over the course of the last decades to try and establish just why it was that other representational systems were always turning out to be awkward when used as the source for the generation of fluent prose. Formally, KRISP is essentially an object-oriented repackaging of a typed lambda calculus, paying particular attention to the representation of partially saturated relations and providing first class objects to represent the binding of a variable to a value. As a representational system, it embodies a theory of how information is structured in a natural language text. This is a hypothesis about the nature of the objects that texts denote and the principles of semantic interpretation that map them to a model comprised of such objects. It is intended to run in close coordination with the SPARSER natural language understanding system.

Chapter Four
Episodic Logic Meets Little Red Riding Hood—A Comprehensive Natural Representation for Language Understanding / 111
Lenhart K. Schubert and Chung Hee Hwang

The authors describe a comprehensive framework for narrative understanding based on episodic logic. This situational logic was developed and implemented as a semantic representation and commonsense knowledge representation that would serve the full range of interpretive and inferential needs of general natural language understanding. The most distinctive feature of episodic logic is its natural languagelike expressiveness. It allows for generalized quantifiers, lambda abstraction, sentence and predicate modifiers, sentence and predicate reification, intensional predicates (corresponding to wanting, believing, making, etc.), unreliable generalizations, and perhaps most importantly, explicit situational variables linked to arbitrary formulas that describe them. These allow episodes to be explicitly related in terms of part-whole, temporal and causal relations. Episodic logical form is easily computed from surface syntax and lends itself to effective inference.

Chapter Five
SNePS: A Logic for Natural Language Understanding and Commonsense Reasoning / 175
Stuart C. Shapiro

The use of logic for knowledge representation and reasoning systems is controversial. There are, indeed, several ways that standard first order predicate logic is inappropriate for modeling natural language understanding and commonsense reasoning. However, a more appropriate logic can be designed. This chapter presents several aspects of such a logic.

Section Two
Knowledge Representation and Acquisition for Large-Scale, General-Purpose Natural Language Processing Systems

Section Introduction / 193
Łucja M. Iwańska and Stuart C. Shapiro

Chapter Six
A Multi-Level Approach to Interlingual Machine Translation: Defining the Interface between Representational Languages / 207
Bonnie J. Dorr and Clare R. Voss

This chapter describes a multi-level design, i.e., a nonuniform approach to interlingual machine translation, in which distinct representational languages are used for different types of knowledge. The authors demonstrate that a linguistically-motivated "division of labor" across multiple representation levels has not complicated, but rather has readily facilitated, the identification and construction of systematic relations at the interface between each level. They describe a model of interpretation and representation of natural language sentences that has been implemented as part of an interlingual machine-translation system called PRINCITRAN.

Chapter Seven
Uniform Natural (Language) Spatio-Temporal Logic: Reasoning about Absolute and Relative Space and Time / 249
Łucja M. Iwańska

In this chapter, uniform spatio-temporal reasoner is presented. Its representational, inferential and computational characteristics closely resemble natural language. It is demonstrated that important inferences about time and space can be captured by a general representation and reasoning mechanism inherent in natural language many aspects of which are closely mimicked by the proposed computational model of natural language. As a result, a uniform representation and inference, and therefore a simple architecture, for temporal, spatial and other reasoning is accomplished. It is also shown that computing logical, context-independent and some nonmonotonic, context-dependent inferences for temporal, spatial and other objects is analogous.

Real-life examples illustrate the representational and reasoning capabilities of the proposed natural language style spatio-temporal reasoner, including many previously unaccounted aspects of temporal and spatial information conveyed by common English temporal expressions, reasoning with information from arbitrary Boolean temporal expressions involving explicit negation, disjunction and conjunction, handling temporal quantifiers, handling infinite number of temporal and spatial relations, handling both absolute and relative temporal and spatial information, and handling nonnumeric qualitative temporal and spatial information.

Chapter Eight
Mixed Depth Representations for Dialog Processing / 283
Susan W. McRoy, Syed S. Ali, and Susan M. Haller

The authors describe their work on developing a general purpose tutoring system that will allow students to practice their decision-making skills in a number of domains. The tutoring system, B2, supports mixed-initiative natural language interaction. The natural language processing and knowledge representation components are also general purpose—which leads to a tradeoff between the limitations of superficial processing and syntactic representations and the difficulty of deeper methods and conceptual representations. Their solution uses a mixed-depth representation, one that encodes syntactic and conceptual information in the same structure. As a result, they can use the same representation framework to produce a detailed representation of requests and to produce a partial representation of questions. Moreover, the representations use the same knowledge representation framework that is used to reason about discourse processing and domain information—so that the system can reason with (and about) the utterances, if necessary. This work is the first (and to our knowledge, the only) implementation of mixed-depth representations for dialog processing.

Appendices

Preface

Why this Book?

THIS BOOK CONTAINS the most recent theoretical and practical computational approaches to representing and utilizing the meaning of natural language. We believe that only such natural-language driven computational models allow the development of truly intelligent computer systems simulating, on a large scale, the critical role of natural language in human information and knowledge processing. Developing knowledge representation and reasoning systems based on natural language constitutes an exciting and, still, quite controversial new research direction in artificial intelligence. Natural language-based knowledge representation and reasoning systems and their large-scale implementations closely simulate the representational and inferential computational machinery of natural language, which, as argued by all the authors in this book, is dramatically different from any other theoretical and practical knowledge representation and reasoning system or automated reasoning system.

New Perspective: Natural Language as Knowledge Representation and Reasoning System, Not Just Interface

The new research direction of natural language based knowledge representation and reasoning systems emerged over the past few years. It grew out of concerns over the efficient handling of large-scale, general-purpose knowledge, reasoning, and the meaning of natural language. One motivation for this line of research was—and still is—the fact that a vast majority of knowledge representation and reasoning systems do not adequately reflect important characteristics of natural language and are representationally and inferentially impoverished relative to natural language. Notable exceptions include natural language motivated knowledge representation and reasoning systems of Schubert, Shapiro, and Sowa. Historically, the goal of knowledge representation and reasoning was to address representational and inferential needs of natural language processing. However, the goals of knowledge representation and reasoning quickly and substantially diverged from that. In the past several years, there has been little interaction and interest between the knowledge representation and natural language processing communities. This book demonstrates that the natural language processing and knowledge representation communities have many common research goals.

The current shape of the natural language-based knowledge representation and reasoning systems direction evolved, in part, from discussions at a number of international symposia, workshops, and journal special issues involving the editors and contributors.

The research direction of natural language-based knowledge representation and reasoning systems constitutes a tremendous change in how we view the role of natural language in an intelligent computer system. The traditional view, widely held within the artificial intelligence and computational linguistics communities, considers natural language as an interface or front end to a system such as an expert system or knowledge base. In this view, inferencing and other interesting information and knowledge processing tasks are not part of natural language processing.

By contrast, the computational models of natural language presented in this book view natural language as a knowledge representation and reasoning system with its own unique, computationally attractive representational and inferential machinery. This new perspective sheds some light on the actual, still largely unknown, relationship between natural language and the human mind. Taken to an extreme, such approaches speculate that the structure of the human mind is close to natural language. In other words, natural language is essentially the language of human thought.

In the natural language-based knowledge representation and reasoning systems, general-purpose information and knowledge are (1) entered in computer systems via natural language in the form of texts or dialogs, (2) represented and combined via algorithms and data structures closely simulating the syntax and semantics of natural language, (3) reasoned about via inference mechanisms, which closely simulate inferences that humans make in natural language, and (4) exited from computer systems via natural language in the form of natural language answers to queries.

This means that all information and knowledge processing tasks supporting the computer system's intelligent behavior take place at the natural language level. The advantage of the natural language-like uniformity of representation and reasoning is a simple and powerful computer architecture. For not well formalized domains, it can be argued that natural language-based knowledge representation and reasoning are more advantageous than knowledge representation and reasoning not motivated by natural language.

Addressing Wide-Spread
Misconceptions about Natural Language

This book sheds new light on the puzzling computational nature of natural language. Not only is natural language algorithmic, but its algorithmic buildup appears very different from both the traditional computer science number-crunching computation and the traditional artificial intelligence symbol-crunching computation. We believe that the research results presented in this book challenge a number of claims about natural language, including its alleged nonalgorithmicity and its remoteness from inference. Despite the fact that such claims have never been substantiated, they remain quite common in artificial intelligence symbol-crunching computation. For example, in his 1990 book *Representations of Commonsense Knowledge* (San Francisco: Morgan Kaufmann, p. 14), Ernest Davis states:

> There is a widespread agreement that AI programs should not use full natural language text as a knowledge representation language. Natural language cannot be easily manipulated algorithmically. It is full of ambiguities. Its meaning is context-dependent. Its syntax is extremely complex, and strongly dependent on semantics. Its connectives (prepositions, articles, and conjunctions) are remarkably vague and unsystematic. There are few powerful rules of inference on natural language strings.

More recently, John McCarthy gave an invited talk at the 1997 AAAI Fall Symposium on Context in Knowledge Representation and Natural Language. He claimed that natural language has little to do with inferencing. His transparency read:

> Language is froth on the surface of thought:
> * A human's basic knowledge of the world is not represented linguistically in the brain. Linguistic expression is often possible.
> * Language is for communication with people who cannot see through your eyes or duplicate your reasoning. Therefore, it cannot express thought directly.

We stress that the exact division of the representational and inferential labor between natural language and other systems such as the human mind, database or knowledge base remains an open research question to be extensively investigated.

Knowledge Representation, Reasoning,
and Acquisition in Large-Scale, General
Purpose Natural Language Processing Systems

In this book, we present contributions concerning the representing of, reasoning with and acquisition of different types of knowledge from large-scale natural language inputs. Some contributions represent the traditional approach in which natural language plays a lesser representational and inferential role and the natural language processing system is supported by a nonnatural language-motivated knowledge representation and reasoning system.

A number of contributors present very interesting methods of automatic knowledge acquisition from medium-to-large-scale natural language inputs. These acquisition methods are based on natural language and incorporate its various algorithmic aspects. They have the potential to replace hand-crafting knowledge from textual documents, a costly and error-prone process. These methods raise hope that we will no longer need humans to postverify and clean-up system-acquired garbage.

Natural language processing researchers and practitioners are constantly faced with the inadequacy of data structures for representing natural language because their syntax and semantics do not fit the syntax and semantics of natural language well. Inference in natural language is not well simulated by traditional reasoning algorithms. This further complicates the task of the natural language processing-required automatic knowledge acquisition.

Computer Science-Style Natural Language Processing: Theory and Serious, Rich-Data Implementation

The authors of this book are computer scientists who focus clearly on the computational, computer science-style aspects of natural language. Most of them have strong interests in and extensive knowledge of such related disciplines as linguistics, psychology, and philosophy. They often incorporate and extend theories which originate in those fields. Some authors present theories of natural language phenomena for which no adequate theory exists in those related disciplines.

Another distinct characteristic is that all the authors view implementation as a necessary and, to some extent, independent piece of evidence of the correctness and generality of their theoretical findings. Their ideas have been implemented in existing, and, in most cases, mature natural language processing systems, which were developed over years at academic and industrial natural language research groups. The scope and scale of implementations vary significantly. Some authors present complete systems capable of a particular type of processing on a large scale. Others discuss a proof-of-concept implementation, which demonstrates a computational feasibility of the proposed theoretical ideas.

The natural language processing systems the authors discuss also differ significantly in terms of their test and development data. Some systems have been designed and tested on artificial, toy examples of English utterances (texts, dialogs and their fragments) illustrating the researched problems. Other systems use plausible simulation data. Finally, some systems are capable of handling large-scale corpora of real data.

Potential for Practical Applications: An In-Depth Processing of Knowledge in Huge Volumes of Internet Texts

The potential for practical applications of the work presented in our book is tremendous. We believe that natural language-based knowledge representation and reasoning systems allow one to uniquely combine the human-like quality of knowledge processing with computer quantitative advantages. Such systems allow computers to process knowledge in the form of natural language similar to people and then to combine it with nonhuman computer capabilities to be precise, fast, systematic and virtually memory-unlimited. We believe that only such human and nonhuman combinations of information and knowledge processing give hope for an in-depth processing of information and knowledge in the huge volumes of natural language inputs. Such huge volumes include documents such as texts and transcribed dialogs freely available on the world wide web. This constantly growing volume is currently estimated to be billions of textual documents.

About this Book

The first part of this book presents natural language based knowledge representation and reasoning systems, or formal, computational models of natural language, whose original motivation was the inherent limitations of the representation of natural language based on first-order classical logic. The second part of the book discusses large-scale approaches to representing reasoning with and acquiring different types of knowledge for general-purpose natural language processing systems.

We have attempted to make this book self-contained text. We provide appendices with basic computational and mathematical concepts needed to successfully follow the material. We discuss the up-to-date utility of first-order classical logic for representing the meaning of natural language. Until very recently, first-order classical logic was a primary non-adhoc computational representation of natural language. Throughout the book, we comment on the inherent limitations of first-order classical logic for capturing the meaning of natural language. We also provide, in

Subject	Professional Activity More Information	Year
Knowledge representation for natural language processing in implemented systems	AAAI Symposium wy.smsu.edu/pub/www/kr_nlp_impl_sys.html	1994
Context in natural language processing	IJCAI Workshop www.cs.wayne.edu/~lucja/context-w1.html	1995
Knowledge representation systems based on natural language	AAAI Symposium www.cs.wayne.edu/~lucja/nlkr-w1.html	1996
Context in knowledge representation and natural language	AAAI Symposium www.cs.wayne.edu/~lucja/context-w2.html	1996
Knowledge representation for natural language	*Minds and Machines* 3(1) Kluwer Academic Publishers	1993
Knowledge representation and inference for natural language processing	*Expert Systems* 9(1) JAI Press	1996
Knowledge representation for natural language processing in implemented systems	*Natural Language Engineering* 3(2) Cambridge University Press	1997
Context in natural language processing	*Computational Intelligence* 13(2) Blackwell Publishers	1997

the appendices, many examples and data illustrating representational and inferential challenges of natural language. These examples and data put to a hard test any general-purpose knowledge representation and reasoning system, natural language-motivated or not, as well as any general-purpose natural language processing system.

Acknowledgments

Many people directly and indirectly contributed to this book. We would like to thank the contributors of the individual chapters as well as the organizers, program committee members and the participants of the professional activities that provided a friendly, but tough discussion forum for many ideas presented here. Our book is a coherent collection largely due to the fact that the editors and the contributors were actively involved in the closely related professional activities, conferences and journal special issues listed in the table above.

- *Łucja M. Iwańska and Stuart C. Shapiro*

Contributors

Syed S. Ali
Department of Mathematical Sciences
University of Wisconsin-Milwaukee
tigger.cs.uwm.edu/~syali/

Karen Ehrlich
Computer Science Department
SUNY College at Fredonia
www.cs.fredonia.edu/~ehrlich/

Bonnie J. Dorr
Department of Computer Science
University of Maryland, College Park
www.umiacs.umd.edu/~bonnie/

Robert Givan
Department of Electrical
& Computer Engineering
Purdue University
dynamo.ecn.purdue.edu/~givan/

Susan M. Haller
Computer Science Department
University of Wisconsin—Parkside
cs.uwp.edu/staff/haller/

Sanda Harabagiu
Department of Computer Science
and Engineering
Southern Methodist University
www.seas.smu.edu/~sanda/

Chung Hee Hwang
Microelectronics & Computer Technology
Corporation (MCC)
hwang@mcc.com

Łucja M. Iwańska
Department of Computer Science
Wayne State University
www.cs.wayne.edu/profs/iwanska.html

Kellyn Kruger
Department of Computer Science
Wayne State University
kkk@cs.wayne.edu

Naveen Mata
Department of Computer Science
Wayne State University
osm@cs.wayne.edu

David McAllester
AT&T Labs Research
www.research.att.com/~dmac/

David D. McDonald
Gensym Corporation
davidmcdonald@alum.mit.edu

Susan W. McRoy
Department of Electrical Engineering and
Computer Science
University of Wisconsin—Milwaukee
www.cs.uwm.edu/~mcroy/

Dan Moldovan
Department of Computer Science
and Engineering
Southern Methodist University
www.seas.smu.edu/~moldovan/

William J. Rapaport
Department of Computer Science
and Engineering
State University of New York at Buffalo
www.cse.buffalo.edu/~rapaport/

Lenhart Schubert
Department of Computer Science
University of Rochester
www.cs.rochester.edu/u/schubert/

Stuart C. Shapiro
Department of Computer Science
and Engineering
State University of New York at Buffalo
www.cse.buffalo.edu/~shapiro/

Clare R. Voss
Information Science and Technology Di-
rectorate, Army Research Laboratory,
Adelphi, MD
voss@arl.mil

Section One

Introduction to Section One

Łucja M. Iwańska and Stuart C. Shapiro

THIS SECTION CONTAINS descriptions of five major knowledge representation and reasoning systems based on natural language: UNO, Montagovian syntax, KRISP, episodic logic, and SNePS. The system that comes closest to natural language *as* knowledge representation and reasoning is McAllester and Givan's Montagovian syntax for first order logic. For example, the sentence of Montagovian syntax corresponding to the English sentence, "Every dog ate some bone" is (every dog (ate (some bone))). Of course, they admit that this close correspondence works only for "simple subject-verb-object sentences" and is "only distantly related to the much richer and more complex syntax of actual natural languages." Their main point, however, is that "the effectiveness of inference is coupled to the selection of the syntax in which formulas are expressed;" that "classical syntax appears to be particularly ineffective," and that a polynominal time inference procedure can be defined for a significant fragment of Montagovian syntax—the "quantifier-free" fragment, which includes the above example.

The Montagovian formula (every dog (ate (some bone))) is quantifier-free, even though it might not look so, because the semantics of Montagovian syntax specifies that all expressions denote sets of individuals, and all atomic formulas are statements that one set is a subset of another or that two sets have a nonempty intersection. Thus, the denotation of (every dog (ate (some bone))) is true if and only if the set of dogs is a subset of the set of individuals each of which has the relation denoted by ate to some member of the set of bones. By discussing sets rather than individuals, Montagovian syntax can express "Every dog ate some bone" without quantifying over individual dogs and individual bones, as the standard syntax of first-order predicate logic would.

The use of sets, either in syntax or semantics, is one of the themes connecting several of these chapters. In Iwańska's UNO, the sentence "Jane is a sick, very unhappy woman" is represented by the type (set)equation

```
Jane  ==  {[woman (health => sick ,
              happy =>(not happy )(degree => very ))]}
```

which says that the set of individuals of type Jane is the same as the "subset of individuals of the type *woman* for which the attribute *health* has the value *sick* and for which the function *happy* yields the value *very unhappy.*"

Shapiro's SNePS uses sets in several ways. First, all the logical connectives of SNePS are functions of sets of propositions, whereas in standard first-order predicate logic they are unary or binary functions of truth values. For example, the SNePS representation of "Squash is an animal, a vegetable, or a mineral" is (in the SNePSLOG syntax) andor(1, 1){animal(squash), vegetable(squash), mineral(squash)}, which says that, of the three propositions, animal(squash), vegetable(squash), and mineral(squash), at least one and at most one are true. A second use of sets in SNePS is that a predicate whose ith argument is supposed to be an individual of some type τ, may be written with a set of τ-individuals in ith position, implying the same predication with any subset of that set in ith position. For example, sisters({Mary, Sue, Sally}) implies sisters({Mary, Sue}), sisters({Mary, Sally}), and sisters{Sue, Sally}).

A second theme connecting several of these chapters is a rich ontology for the domains of discourse. Perhaps the strongest, clearest statement of this in these chapters is McDonald's second principle, "There should be a first-class object type in the representation for every class of syntactic category in the language." A paraphrase of this principle is "Every well-formed expression in the language denotes an individual in the domain." In standard first-order predicate logic, only terms denote individuals of the domain. In Montague semantics and other common theories of natural language where there is a semantic rule for every syntactic rule, most well-formed expressions denote, not individuals in the domain, but functions, whose ranges are, themselves, often functions. Some type of individuals that are recognized by these chapters, but that are seldom recognized by other approaches are propositions, (episodic logic, SNePS, UNO), categories, kinds, or types (UNO, KRISP, episodic logic); partially saturated relations (KRISP); events (KRISP, episodic logic); actions or acts (episodic logic, SNePS); situations (episodic logic). Further recognizing the full range of what is discussed via natural language, none of these chapters use the phrase "objects in the world" when discussing semantics. The chapters on episodic logic and SNePS, in particular, mention intensions, imaginary individuals, and fictional individuals.

A third theme is specialized inference rules. As discussed in the appendix, a logic is specified by syntax, semantics, and an inference method. One could try to build a knowledge representation and reasoning system for natural language interaction by taking a standard logic, specifying particular function symbols, and predicate symbols, and giving meaning postulates for these symbols. An indication that the knowledge representation and reasoning systems discussed here are truly new logics is that the rules of inference are different than those of standard logics. English versions of one-step inferences allowed by several of these systems are shown in the following examples.

UNO: "John doesn't walk. Therefore, John doesn't walk very fast."

Montagovian syntax: "Any child of a bird is a friend of any bird watcher. Therefore, anyone who owns the child of a bird also owns a friend of every bird watcher."

Episodic logic: "Every dress or hood that Little Red Riding Hood wears is pretty. Little Red Riding Hood wears a certain cap or hood, *h*. Therefore, if *h* is a dress or not a cap, it is pretty."

SNePS: "If Hilda is in Boston or Kathy is in Las Vegas, then Eve is in Providence. Hilda is in Boston. Therefore, Eve is in Providence."

The point is not that these inferences cannot be done in first-order predicate logic, but that in first-order predicate logic they would involve several steps, while each is a one-step application of a rule of inference in the listed system.

A final theme connecting these chapters is formal care combined with implementation. The chapters carefully cover the three requirements of defining a logic—syntax, semantics, and inference. Unlike most presentations of logics, the discussions of semantics include discussions of the ontology of the domains, as mentioned above. Yet all five systems are also implemented and really perform. Except for Montagovian syntax, whose purpose differs, all the systems are part of or connected to natural language processing systems. They are excellent examples of knowledge representation and reasoning systems motivated by, and being used for natural language processing.

1 Natural Language Is a Powerful Knowledge Representation System: The UNO Model

Łucja M. Iwańska

OVER THE COURSE OF A DECADE OF RESEARCH and large-scale development, I have reached the conclusion that natural language is a powerful, general-purpose knowledge-representation system. I have developed a formal, computational model of natural language that closely simulates many of its uniquely advantageous representational and inferential characteristics. The model is fully implemented as a large-scale natural language processing system capable of processing knowledge from the real-life corpora of thousands of textual documents in a number of domains.

In this chapter, I present some arguments and primary research results that support the conjecture that natural language is a knowledge representation system. This work provides a novel perspective on the computational nature of natural language and is a significant departure from the traditional view of natural language as an interface, which is widely held in the artificial intelligence, knowledge representation, and natural language processing communities. I must stress that the results herein provide only partial support for the conjecture, and that the traditional notion of natural language as an interface has not been even partially substantiated. The actual computational nature of natural langue in human reasoning, and therefore in intelligent system reasoning, remains an open research problem. After decades of intensive research, the computational nature of natural language remains a puzzling mystery.

Throughout this chapter, I will attempt to separate the arguments about and descriptions of natural language from the description of my model simulating natural language. I hope that this will facilitate comparison of strengths and weaknesses of my model with the other computational models of natural language presented in this book and elsewhere.

The Conjecture: Natural Language Is a Powerful, General-Purpose Knowledge Representation System

My conjecture is that natural language is a powerful knowledge representation system—a representational language particularly suitable for representing and using knowledge in not well formalized domains. Natural language has its own representational and inferential mechanisms, and they are dramatically different from any existing automated reasoning system and knowledge representation system.

1. *Natural language is very expressive and computationally very tractable.* There are two sources of natural language's tractability

(a). Rich structure. Natural language is highly structured. Complex Boolean expressions involving explicit negations, conjunctions, and disjunctions, as well as adjectival and adverbial modifications appear at all syntactic levels, including the sentential (propositional) level. Such complex expressions license systematic, easily-computable inferences whose computation involves a compositional semantic relation of entailment between simple and complex expressions.

(b). A well-defined, close correspondence between the syntactic structure of natural language sentences, their fragments, and the semantic relations (such as entailment, consistency, and inconsistency) among them.

Somewhat similar claims can be found in Hwang and Schubert (1993) and McAllester and Givan (1992). This characteristic of natural language, if fully proven, constitutes a challenge to the widely acknowledged tradeoff between expressiveness and computational tractability of a knowledge-representation system. The structure of natural language has always been a hallmark of linguistic research. However, there does not seem to be any linguistic work that would explain its significance in terms of computability of the inference.

2. *Natural language is general purpose,* which, when combined with its great expressiveness, allows one to achieve a uniformity of representation and reasoning—and therefore a simple and powerful computer system architecture. That same representational and inferential mechanism is capable of taxonomic, probabilistic, temporal, and some aspects of spatial reasoning.

3. *Natural language as a uniform level combining verbal and sensory information.* Verbal and nonverbal sensory (visual, etc.) information can be combined at the level of natural language. Each nonverbal information (knowledge) can be represented as a natural language utterance. Figure 1 illustrates this point.

4. *Logical contradiction and logical redundancy play a central role in natural language.* They serve as a means of identifying knowledge gaps

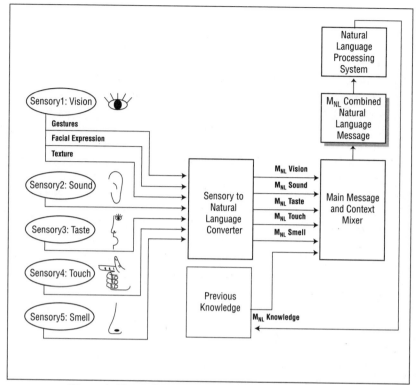

Figure 1. Natural Language as Uniform Representation

It is plausible that verbal and nonverbal sensory information gets combined at the symbolic level of natural language. I hypothesize that this simple computer architecture may reflect a similar simplicity of human brain.

and false beliefs and also as a means of conveying systematic nonliteral meanings. By contrast, virtually all knowledge representation systems consider both contradiction and redundancy as evil twins, most cannot handle contradiction nor do most allow for redundancy—often by design.

5. *Natural language is inherently underspecified and context dependent,* which largely reflects the nature of and the constraints on human knowledge and the process of human knowledge acquisition.

The context dependency of natural language is widely acknowledged and considered as problematic. Some researchers name context dependency as the source of the alleged nonalgorithmicity of natural language, for example, Davis (1990). I agree that current, crisp algorithms that do not take context into consideration do not adequately account for the computational characteristics of natural language. However, natural language-like computation calls for new approaches that inherently involve

context. My preliminary results seem to indicate that such natural languagelike context dependency in information (knowledge) processing is
yet another source of the puzzling expressive-and-tractable characteristics of natural language.

6. *Natural language greatly facilitates learning and knowledge acquisition* by (a) providing an expressive and tractable mechanism for forming or revising hypotheses, and by reducing hypothesis search space, and
(b) providing a number of easily parsable constructions specialized to
convey taxonomic knowledge.

7. *Natural language mixes object-level and meta-level descriptions.* This
is advantageous because the system uses the same representational and inferential mechanism to draw inferences about the environment (object-level) and to reason about its own knowledge and reasoning (meta-level, or
introspection). The drawback of this uniformity is that such a system necessarily involves paradoxes.

This observation about natural language was made a long time ago by
Tarski (1956). Since Tarski's work, virtually all formal reasoning systems,
including various logics proposed in artificial intelligence, were designed
to avoid paradoxes by separating the two representational and inferential
levels. Most currently existing formal knowledge representation and automated reasoning systems do not allow for paradoxes, and therefore do
constitute a truthful computational model of natural language.

Conjecture Validation

Much of my current research and development constitutes a partial validation of the conjecture that natural language is a knowledge representation system. One of the most difficult struggles is to strike a balance between in-depth, necessarily theory-and-idealization-heavy research
investigating a particular unaddressed or an unsatisfactorily addressed
aspect of natural language, and a quantitative and qualitative performance of my natural language processing system on a large volume (200
MB) of real-life textual documents, necessarily involving ad-hoc, "hack
and pretend it is solved" engineering solutions.

To Prove or Not to Prove? How?

Another serious difficulty in attempting to validate the conjecture stems
from the fact that it is not always clear what can or even should be proven
about natural language and therefore about a model simulating natural
language. Some aspects of my validation are, therefore, all too familiar,
lengthy, formal proofs. For example, I have proven that the data structures

and the operations of my model of natural language, motivated by the syntax and semantics of natural language, have Boolean set-theoretic and interval-theoretic semantics (Iwańska 1992a). The soundness of the inference in the model is not proven, but it can be easily done. However, I have not shown the completeness of the inference, because it is not clear that completeness should be considered a desirable formal characteristics, given that it is unknown if natural language itself is complete. It is not even clear that the notion of completeness even applies to natural language.

I also aim at providing a practical "proof" of my conjecture. I am in the process of demonstrating that my natural language-based knowledge representation system, combined with limited-syntax, weak methods, allows one to fully automatically acquire large, general-purpose knowledge bases from test and development data consisting of about twenty-thousands online, multi-domain, multi-source, real-life textual documents—totaling over 200 MB. I show that these knowledge bases can be queried and updated through natural language. I plan to demonstrate that these knowledge bases are particularly attractive for a number of applications utilizing knowledge from textual corpora.

The Representational and Inferential Strengths and Weaknesses of Natural Language Need to Be Intensively Studied

Natural language can be viewed as an extremely intriguing, still fairly unknown, formal representational language whose representational and inferential strengths and weaknesses need to be further intensively studied. A number of computational characteristics of natural language are very attractive, but puzzling. For example, the "very expressive and very tractable" characteristic appears to be in the direct contradiction to the teachings of theory of computation.

I argue that natural language should be in-depth compared with the existing and yet-developed knowledge representation systems with respect to their advantages for representing and utilizing different types of knowledge. I am interested in identifying both the representationally desirable and undesirable characteristics of natural language.

Further on in this chapter, I will elaborate on the representational and reasoning strengths of natural language, in part to counterbalance the biased and unsubstantiated view of natural language as just an interface. However, natural language as a representational language also has weaknesses, including the widely acknowledged inappropriateness of the representation of and reasoning about visual information and computing complex constraints on arbitrary partial orderings.

The Representation of Meaning of Natural Language Does Not Necessarily Involve Some Nonnatural Language Knowledge Representation System

I reject the notion that the representation of meaning of natural language must necessarily involve some nonnatural language knowledge representation system (such as the CLASSIC knowledge representation system) or general theorem prover, present in many natural language processing systems for representing taxonomic knowledge and for drawing inferences. So far, my model of natural language does not involve any non-natural language knowledge representation system—different types of knowledge, including taxonomic, temporal, probabilistic and certain types of spatial knowledge, are all handled by natural language inherent representational and inferential mechanisms. I argued elsewhere—and will restate some of those arguments here—that with respect to a number of important representational and reasoning characteristics, all existing knowledge representation systems that I am aware of are desperately behind natural language in terms of expressiveness and tractability; in other words, they are capable of strictly less than natural language. As such, these systems are virtually useless for representing meaning of natural language.

Knowledge Representation for Natural Language Processing: The Useless and the Useful

My own experience with knowledge representation research and development not directly motivated by natural language for the purpose of natural language processing has been very discouraging. First, knowledge representation systems that are only loosely motivated by natural language or not motivated by natural language at all (the vast majority) are very different from it. When judged from the point of view of natural language, many knowledge representation systems are simply wrong and are virtually always weaker. Second, very few formal knowledge representation approaches discuss real-life or even substantial and plausible, artificial data that motivate and ultimately test their theories. This makes it extremely difficult to determine if these systems indeed capture any aspect of the human knowledge processing reality and, if so, how good a job they do.

However, it is because typical knowledge representation systems are not concerned with natural language that they have the potential to reveal the representational weaknesses of natural language. Being different from natural language could mean better. Such different from but better than natural language knowledge representation systems would constitute a representational alternative to natural language. Only narrow, specialized knowledge representation systems fall into this category. To my knowledge, however, no general-purpose, "better than natural language" knowledge representation systems exist.

In the following sections, I will discusses the UNO model of natural language, its implementation and test and development data. The subsequent sections will discuss the highly desirable representational and inferential characteristics of natural language that I have identified and will provide examples with some further technical details of my model that allowed me to capture these characteristics. The last section contains conclusions.

The UNO Model of Natural Language

My formal, computational model of natural language—the UNO model—offers a solid computational and mathematical framework intact with linguistic theories. Updating the system's knowledge base and automated inferencing is done by the same semantically clean computational mechanism of performing Boolean operations on the representation of natural language input and the representation of previously obtained information (knowledge) stored in the knowledge base.

The UNO model closely mimics the representation and reasoning inherent in natural language because its translation procedure, data structures of the representation, and inference engine are motivated by the semantics, pragmatics, and context dependency of natural language. One payoff of this close correspondence to natural language is its capability of automatically creating knowledge bases from textual documents—limited, of course, by the subset of English covered by the model.

Natural Language Processing as Knowledge Acquisition

I believe that the primary role of natural language is to accumulate, repair, and communicate knowledge. I view natural language understanding as the process of acquiring knowledge conveyed by natural language utterances and updating one's existing knowledge with this new knowledge. This process is always relative to one's existing knowledge, which constitutes one part of context. My formal, computational UNO framework to natural language processing reflects this view.

Viewing natural language understanding as knowledge update calls for revision of some standard linguistic notions. One such notion is the speaker-only based concept of meaning of natural language, which I believe should be changed to a speaker and hearer-based concept, situated in a context. I argue that a number of types of nonliteral meanings, including meaning resulting from implicature, provides a piece of evidence for meaning of natural language utterances to be speaker and hearer-based concept. What the speaker intends to convey and what the hearer actually understands are both equally important aspects of meaning that collectively characterize the *meaning* of an utterance.

Similarly, I do not consider speaker's intention a necessary condition of nonliteral meaning. Hearers often correctly and incorrectly derive some information—a particular aspect of meaning—that was not intended by the speaker. If we assumed the standard notion of meaning as speaker-only concept, then we would have to invent a new name and computational mechanism for the cases we believe to be quite common when a speaker unintentionally implicates something, and the hearer's updated knowledge exactly corresponds to the knowledge when implication is intended. It appears that unintended implicatures are as common as the indented ones, which additionally argues for the meaning to be a speaker and hearer-based concept, and not a speaker-only based concept.

There are some important formal and practical consequences of these theoretical revisions. For example, a formal, computational theory based on such revised notions leaves open a possibility that for the same utterance, a speaker and hearer may arrive at (or compute) entirely different meanings, including contrary, contradictory, or totally orthogonal meanings. I believe that this approach matches well with the reality of natural language human communication.

The Literal Meaning of Natural Language

I equate literal meaning of a given natural language sentence with knowledge that every native speaker is capable of deriving from the sentence in the absence of any explicit or implicit context. Such knowledge can be characterized by the type of questions that a native speaker can correctly answer, based solely on the understanding of the sentence. Inferences that result from understanding literal meaning appear effortless and are universally shared by all native speakers. Such inferences can be characterized and explained in terms of the mathematical and computational aspects of "pure" semantics of natural language. The sources of the universally shared literal meanings are semantics, mathematics, and computability of (1) generalized quantifiers; (2) adjectival and adverbial modification; (3) Boolean modification (negation, disjunction, conjunction) at all syntactic levels; and (4) under-specificity of lexically simple scalars.

Table 1 contains some examples of inferences whose source is universally shared literal meaning of natural language. (Earlier, I characterized

With No Explicit or Implicit Context Literal Meaning of Single Sentence Is Knowledge	Entailed Sentences Reflect Knowledge Gained from Understanding Sentence Literal Meaning
Every student works hard	Every student works
	Every smart student works hard
	Every smart student works
	Every extremely smart student works
	Every not very happy student work
Some very smart students don't work	Some smart students don't work
	Some smart students don't work hard
	Some students don't work hard
	Some students don't work
Some, but not many, people work	Some people work
	Not many people work
	Not very many people work
He is extremely happy	He is very happy
	He is happy
	He is not very unhappy
	He is not very sad
John doesn't walk	John doesn't walk fast
	John doesn't walk very fast
	John doesn't walk his dog
	John doesn't walk late at night
	John or Mary doesn't walk
	John or Mary doesn't walk fast
I love it	I like it
	I don't hate it
	I don't hate it very much

Table 1

In the absence of any explicit or implicit context, single sentences shown in the first column represent knowledge that corresponds to their universally shared literal ("purely" seman-tic) meaning. These sentences entail an infinite number of sentences, including the sentences shown in the corresponding second column. The entailed sentences reflect the knowledge gained solely from understanding literal meaning.

such inferences as logical and context independent. I now revise this characterization to inferences that follow in the absence of any explicit or implicit context.) I am not aware of any other sources of universally shared literal meanings.

Nonliteral Meaning of Natural Language

I equate nonliteral meaning of a given natural language sentence with an explicit or implicit context-dependent knowledge that every native speaker is potentially capable of deriving from the sentence, but depending on a particular context, may or may not derive it or even attempt to derive it. Many types of nonliteral meanings result from exploiting logical redundancy and logical contradiction as well as from context-provided specificity. I will discuss some of the nonliteral meanings later on in this chapter.

Research Problems Motivating the Model

The UNO model of natural language was motivated by both formal, computation theories and weak, engineering solutions. For theories and their implementations, the main goal was to uncover and truthfully capture the largely unknown computational aspects of natural language. For engineering methods, the main goal was to demonstrate that the solutions scale up and work well on large, real-life corpora of textual data. I briefly discuss both types of research below.

Formal Theories and Implementation

The UNO model of natural language was developed after researching a number of independent, yet closely related, open problems. The model's focus was first to provide a complete framework for computing literal meanings of natural language. Recently, this framework has been augmented to account for some of the many nonliteral meanings of natural language, closely related to its general context-dependency.

Three problems have directly motivated the UNO model: (1) a general semantic model of negation in natural language: representation and inference; (2) natural language temporal logic: reasoning about absolute and relative time; and (3) semantics, pragmatics, and context of intensional negative adjectives.

The first problem involves representation and inference for natural language sentences and tiny texts involving explicit negation at different syntactic levels; accounting for the complex interaction between negation and conjunction; disjunction; generalized quantifiers; adjectival and adverbial modification; and formalization of scalar expressions (Iwańska 1992a, 1992b, 1993)

The second problem involves extracting temporal expressions—explicit expressions of different syntactic categories that are references to or descriptions of time—from a large volume of newspaper articles, and automatic generation of their UNO representation, inference, and handling time-related queries (Iwańska 1996).

The third problem to directly motivate the UNO model involves formalization, representation, and inference for context-dependent types created via adjectives *alleged, artificial, false, fake, former,* and *toy*; inferring and computing context-dependent concept (type) definitions; computing concept complements; and disjunctions and conjunctions (Iwańska 1997a).

Weak Methods—Engineering Solutions

I have developed a number of so-called weak methods and provided engineering solutions to three problems: (1) automated processing of narratives written by students in grades 6–12; (2) discourse processing; and (3) the extraction of names, numbers, locations, numeric dates, and numeric values from a large volume of newspaper articles.

The first problem involves preferential sentence-level parsing and extracting prepositional phrases (Iwańska 1989). The second problem involves computing certain common types of discourse structures with nonlinearly distributed knowledge for a large volume of newspaper articles (Iwańska 1991, 1997b; Iwańska et al. 1991). The third problem involves the named entity tasks of the Sixth Message Understanding Conference (MUC-6) (Iwańska et al. 1995) Additionally, I have developed methods for automatically generating the UNO representation of all types of extracted expressions.

Some Technical Aspects of the UNO Model

In this subsection, I will discuss some technical aspects of the UNO model of natural language, including representation of natural language sentences, underspecified terms, and Boolean operations on terms for computing semantic relations.

Representation of Natural Language Sentences

Sentences asserting properties of individuals and sets of individuals, sentences describing subtyping relations as well as sentences that are extensional and intensional type (concept) definitions such as:

1. "John is a neither good nor hard-working nurse."
2. "John is likely, but not very likely, to be HIV-positive."
3. "It is very unlikely that it happened shortly before or after the meeting."
4. "It happened, but not long before the meeting."
5. "Not many students did well."
6. "Dobermans, poodles and terriers are dogs."
7. "Elephant—a huge, thick-skinned, mammal with very few hairs, with a long, flexible snout, and two ivory tusks."

are uniformly represented by the following type equations:

$type == \{<P_1, TP_1>, <P_2, TP_2>, ..., <P_n, TP_n>\}$

The left-hand side of such equations, *type,* is the UNO representation of either a noun phrase, the largest type, or the name of a concept; the right-hand side of such equations is a set of two-element sets:

1. *P,* a property value, the UNO representation of a natural language utterance (a sentence fragment or a sequence of sentences) describing this property;

2. *TP,* a set of two elements $<t, p>$ representing the fact that the property value *P* holds at an absolute temporal interval *t* with the probability *p*. Both *t* and *p* are the UNO representations of natural language expressions that describe this temporal and probabilistic information.

The UNO model uses automatically or hand-created knowledge bases with such type equations bi-directionally:

1. For answering questions about the properties of a particular entity or a concept,

2. For matching particular properties against the properties of an entity or a concept in the system's knowledge base.[1]

Underspecified Terms—Building Blocks of the UNO Representation

Underspecified terms are the building blocks of the UNO representation. Natural language utterances are notoriously underspecified. Some sources of this underspecificity are the unavailability of certain information, its irrelevancy, or the fact that it is context-supplied. Mimicking natural language, the UNO representation is also inherently underspecified, or equivalently, partially specified. If a natural language utterance is underspecified with respect to temporal or probabilistic information, then only property values are shown.

If a property is known to hold for a single temporal interval or if the set of temporal intervals over which the property holds can be described via a single temporal expression involving a temporal quantifier, I flatten the set notation and show the triples $<P, t, p>$ that consist of property value, temporal interval, and probability.

The building blocks of the UNO model, serving as fragments of the representation of property values, temporal intervals and probabilities, are sets $[a_1, a_2, ..., a_n]$ whose elements a_i are terms. These terms are record- and graphlike structures that consist of two elements: (1) a *head,* a type symbol, and (2) a *body,* a possibly empty list of attribute-value pairs *attribute => value,* where attributes are symbols and values are single terms or sets of terms.

For example, a complex noun *sick, very unhappy woman* involving adverbial and adjectival modification is represented by the singleton term

[woman (health =>sick,
         happy $\Rightarrow$ (not happy)(degree $\Rightarrow$ very))]

whose only element has the type *woman* as its head and two attributes: (1) the attribute *health* with the value *sick,* which is a basic type, and (2) the attribute *happy* with the value *(not happy)(degree ⇒ very),* which itself is a term with the complex type *not happy* as its head, and one attribute *degree* with the value *very.*

Semantically, such data structures represent a subtype of the type corresponding to the head noun. For example, the aforementioned term represents this subset of individuals of the type *woman* for which the attribute *health* has the value *sick* and for which the function *happy* yields the value *very unhappy.*

Boolean Operations On Terms for Computing Semantic Relations

The Boolean UNO operations of ⊓, ⊔, and *not,* simulate conjunction, disjunction, and negation in natural language. The intuitively and formally correct results are guaranteed to hold, which allows the model to faithfully simulate inferences in natural language. The Boolean algebra settheoretic semantics of both the terms and the operations on terms is formally proven. These efficient Boolean operations take terms as their arguments and compute the resulting complementary, conjunctive and disjunctive terms with the set-complement, set-intersection and set-union semantics.

Efficient computation of arbitrary Boolean expressions allows the UNO model to compute a number of semantics relations among terms, including (1) entailment (and subsumption, its dual) reflecting set-inclusion, (2) partial overlap reflecting nonempty set-intersection, and (3) disjointness reflecting empty set-intersection.

In the UNO model, these semantic relations are the main vehicle for (1) computing consequences of knowledge expressed in natural language, and therefore for computing answers to various queries of the knowledge base created as the result of processing natural language input; (2) updating system's knowledge base; and (3) identifying system's knowledge gaps and those aspects of knowledge that need repair.

Natural Language Sentences

Simple natural language sentences are represented as knowledge base rules of the form $NP == \{ P_1, \ldots P_n \}$, where NP is the UNO representation of a proper noun, a disjunction of noun phrases, or a quantified noun phrase, P_i are terms representing properties that the denotation of NP is known to possess.

For example, the sentence *John doesn't walk very fast* is represented by the knowledge base rule:

john == { not walk(speed ⇒ fast(adv ⇒ very)) }

This rule encodes the fact that an individual denoted by the proper noun *John* possesses a single property of *not walking very fast*.

The sentence *Every student works hard* is represented by the knowledge base rule

np (det ⇒ every,
    n   ⇒ student) == { [work(adv ⇒ hard)] }

This rule encodes the fact that the set of individuals denoted by the quantified noun phrase *Every student* possesses a property of *working hard*.

Inference

The Boolean operations on terms constitute the essence of the algorithm for representing and updating knowledge derived from actual natural language sentences. The UNO formalism is used to represent natural language sentences and compute their truth-values by computing the entailment relation between the representations of their subject noun phrases and verb phrases. In case of quantified noun phrases, I utilize the fact that the entailment relation on determiners is directly relevant to the entailment of sentences.

Concepts utilized by the inference algorithm include the notion of "NP-stronger than or equal to." Let $S_1 = NP_1$, $Verb_1$ be a sentence, NP_1 and NP_2 be (1) Boolean combinations of proper nouns such that $T(NP_1)$ and $T(NP_2)$ are their UNO representations, or (2) quantified noun phrases $NP_1 = Det_1$, $Noun_1$ and $NP_2 = Det_2$, $Noun_2$ such that $T(Det_1)$, $T(Det_2)$, $T(Noun_1)$, and $T(Noun_2)$ are terms representing Det_1, Det_2, $Noun_1$, and $Noun_2$ respectively.

Then NP_1 is np-stronger than or equal to NP_2 iff

1. NP_1 is left monotone increasing, and
   a. for proper nouns, $T(NP_1) \sqsubseteq T(NP_2)$
   b. for quantified noun phrases, $T(Det_1) \sqsubseteq T(Det_2)$, and $T(Noun_1) \sqsubseteq T(Noun_2)$
2. NP_1 is left monotone decreasing, and
   a. for proper nouns, $T(NP_2) \sqsubseteq T(NP_1)$
   b. for quantified noun phrases, $T(Det_2) \sqsubseteq T(Det_1)$, and $T(Noun_2) \sqsubseteq T(Noun_1)$

For example, (1) in the sentence *Some bright students don't walk* the noun phrase *some bright students* represented by the term

np(det ⇒ [some],
    n   ⇒ [student(adj ⇒ bright)])

is *np-stronger than or equal to* the noun phrase *some students* represented by the term

np(det ⇒ [some],
      n   ⇒ [student])

because

Input:

    a. A true sentence S whose subject noun phrase and verb phrase are represented by the terms *New_NP* and *New_Verb* respectively; if the subject noun phrase is quantified, then *New_NP* is the term $np(det \Rightarrow New\_Det, noun \Rightarrow New\_Noun)$

    b. Existing knowledge base KB, a set of knowledge base rules

Step 1: Check if *S* is entailed by KB

    a. Find a knowledge base rule $NP == \{ P_1, ..., P_n \}$ such that NP is np-stronger than or equal to the New_NP

       i. If one of the properties $P_1 ... P_n$ is v-stronger than or equal to the *New_Verb*, then go to *Step 3* (*S* is entailed by KB)

       ii. If one of the properties $P_1 ... P_n$, say P_i, is relevant to *New_Verb* and $P_i \sqcap New\_Verb =$ [false], then go to *Step 3* (*S* contradicts KB)

    b. If no such rule is found, then

       i. If *New_NP* is quantified, then compute the truth-value of *S* according to the semantics of the determiner *New_Det*:

         A. Compute the denotations of *New_Noun* and *New_Verb*: they are sets of those individuals that possess a property subsumed by the *New_Noun* and *New_Verb* respectively.

         B. If the semantic condition of the determiner is satisfied, then go to *Step 3* (*S* is entailed by knowledge base). Otherwise go to *Step 2*.

       ii. Otherwise go to *Step 2*.

Step 2: Update KB

    a. Find knowledge base rules $R = NP == \{ P_1, ..., P_n \}$ such that (a) NP is np-weaker than or equal to *New_NP*, and (b) one of the properties is relevant for *New_Verb*;

    b. If no such R is found, then add a new rule $New\_NP == \{ New\_Verb \}$ to KB, and go to *Step 3*. Otherwise process each rule R individually:

    Replace each property P_i relevant for *New_Verb* with the result of the updating operation on P_i and *New_Verb*. If for any two rules the updated properties are in the v-stronger-than-or-equal-to relation, then remove the property from the rule whose left-hand side is np-weaker than or equal to *New_NP*.

Step 3: Output Updated KB

Figure 2. Processing a True Sentence: An Algorithm for Updating KB

some is a left monotone increasing determiner,
[*some*] $\sqsubseteq$ [*some*]
[*student*(*adj* $\Rightarrow$ *bright*)] $\sqsubseteq$ [*student*]

(2) In the sentence *Every student walks* the noun phrase *every student* represented by the term

np(det ⇒ [every],
    n   ⇒ [student])

is np-stronger than or equal to the noun phrase *every bright student* represented as

np(det ⇒ [every],
    n   ⇒ [student(adj ⇒ bright)])

because

    a. *every* is a left monotone decreasing determiner

    b. [every] ⊑ [every]

    c. [student(adj ⇒ bright)] ⊑ [student]

Similar notion is defined for verb phrases. Let $S_1 = NP_1\ Verb_1$ be a sentence, $Verb_1$ and $Verb_2$ be verbs with $T(Verb_1)$ and $T(Verb_2)$ as their UNO representations. $Verb_1$ is v-stronger than or equal to $Verb_2$ iff

    1. NP_1 is right monotone increasing and $T(Verb_1) ⊑ T(Verb_2)$, or

    2. NP_1 is right monotone decreasing and $T(Verb_2) ⊑ T(Verb_1)$

For example, in the sentence *Many students don't walk* the verb *don't walk* represented by the term [not walk] is *v-stronger than or equal to* the verb *don't walk fast* represented by the term not walk(adv ⇒ fast) because

    many is a right monotone increasing determiner,
    [not walk] ⊑ *not walk(adv ⇒ fast)*

In the sentence *Not many students walk*, the verb *walk* represented by the term [walk] is *v-stronger than or equal to* the verb *walk fast* represented by the term [walk(adv ⇒ fast)] because

    not many is a right monotone decreasing determiner
    [walk(adv ⇒ fast)] ⊑ [walk]

Given a sentence *S*, the UNO natural language processing system can assign its truth-value:

    True if *S* is entailed by the knowledge base;
    False if *S* contradicts the knowledge base;
    Unknown if the knowledge base does not contain enough information to assign *S* a truth value.

Computing the truth-value of a quantified sentence *Det N VP* can also be done according to the semantics of the determiner *Det*. The denotations of *N* and *VP* are implicit in the knowledge base, and are easily computed. An individual belongs to the denotation of **N** (or *VP*) if some property of this individual is subsumed by this *N* (or *VP*). For example, consider the sentence *Some students walk* and the following knowledge base:

john   ==   { [walk], [student(adj ⇒ smart)] }
mary   ==   { [not walk] }
bob   ==   { [walk(adv ⇒ fast)] }

The denotation of the verb *walk* for this knowledge base is the set { *john, bob* } because John and Bob are the only individuals whose property is subsumed by *walk*. Similarly, the denotation of the noun *students* for this knowledge base is the set { *john* } because John is the only individual whose property is subsumed by *students*.

The semantics of the determiner *some* is such that the sentence *Some students walk* is true if the intersection of the denotations of the noun *students* and verb *walk* is nonempty. For the knowledge base above, this sentence is true because the sets { *john, bob* } and { *john* } have a non-empty intersection { *john* }.

The UNO natural language processing system cannot always determine the truth-value of sentences involving determiners that are not first-order definable because it cannot represent their semantics explicitly. It can, however, account for some inferences. For example, after processing the sentence *Very many students don't walk,* UNO can infer that the sentence *Many students don't walk fast* is true.

The UNO system identifies sentences that contradict the existing knowledge base. This capability is very important because contradictions are learning opportunities. Inconsistencies prompt further investigation that usually results in the revision of one's beliefs. Contradictions can also be exploited for shifting the interpretation of sentences. Consider the sentence *His shirt is red and white.* The knowledge about the properties *red* and *white* being inconsistent combined with the assumption that the sentence must be true if the conversational principles are obeyed, result in a shift of the interpretation of this sentence to something like *One part of his shirt is red, and another part is white.*

Currently the UNO natural language processing system ignores the sentences that contradict the existing knowledge base. However, it is an important feature of the UNO representation that contradictions admitted in the knowledge base remain local. For example, given the contradictory knowledge base below

```
john   ==   { [ walk ], [ not walk ], [ student ] }
mary   ==   { [ not walk ] }
bob  ==   { [ dress(adv ⇒ well) ] }
```

the UNO natural language processing system will be confused about the truth value of the sentence *John walks,* but it will correctly reason about the other properties of John, and about the properties of Mary and Bob.

Full technical details of the UNO representation, the proofs of its mathematical and computational properties, the algorithm behind its inference as well as many detailed examples can be found in Iwańska, (1992a, 1992b, 1993). Later in this chapter, I will discuss examples of natural language expressions representing different types of knowledge, and show their UNO representation and the computation of some of the entailed inferences.

Relation to Other Theories

The Boolean algebra framework of the UNO model—particularly its clean, computable set-theoretic and interval-theoretic semantics—allows one to capture semantics of different syntactic categories of natural language. This is because sets and intervals underlie semantics of many syntactic categories. Common nouns, intransitive verbs, and adjectives can be thought of as denoting sets of persons or objects that possess properties denoted by the words; adjectives and adverbs are functions mapping sets of objects into sets of objects; determiners are functions mapping sets of objects into sets of sets of objects, and the denotations of proper nouns are sets of sets of objects (Dowty, Wall, and Peters 1981; Barwise and Cooper 1981; Keenan and Faltz 1985; Hamm 1989)

In the UNO model, the same representational and inferential machinery is used as a metalanguage for describing and propagating arbitrary Boolean constraints, including dictionary entries describing morphological and grammatical constraints.

The UNO data structures are partially specified, negative constraints are propagated via unification, and the nonmonotonicity of negation (Pereira 1987) is not problematic. In existing unification-based approaches, it is not possible to propagate negative constraints via unification without giving up partiality of feature structures or without admitting some unwanted side effects into the system (Kasper and Round 1986; Moshier and Rounds 1987; Johnson 1988, 1990; Dawar and Vija 1990; Carpenter 1992)

The UNO model shares many computational characteristics with the programming language LIFE (Ait-Kaci et al 1993) because the efficiently computable calculus that underlies LIFE (Ait-Kaci 1986) is extended in the UNO model to handle negation and generalized quantifiers.

Certain aspects of the UNO treatment of scalar expressions, including compositional computation of complex scalars, resembles somewhat the fuzzy logic's linguistic variable approach (Zadeh 1975) while others, such as Boolean algebra structure, are different. For processing natural language, my model offers two advantages over fuzzy logic. First, in the case of linguistic variable, computing entailment between scalars *very old* and *not young* necessarily requires converting these expressions to specific numbers because, as Zadeh put it: "Linguistic variable is not entirely qualitative, but rather it is about numbers." In the UNO model, inference from *very old* to *not young*, and inference from *not many* to *not very many* can be accomplished without involving any numbers. This is

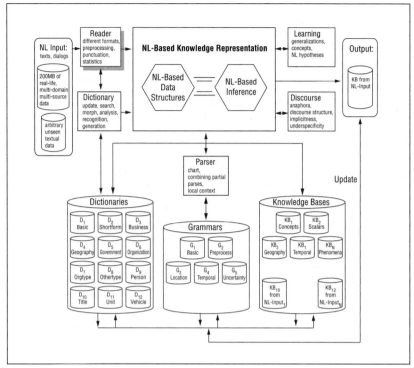

Figure 3. Uniform Architecture of the UNO Knowledge Representation System Based on Natural Language
Modules and resources.

important because numeric values may not be available, one may have no basis for arriving at reasonable estimates, or specific numbers may be unimportant.

Some of the linguistic theories that the UNO model encompasses and extends include Montague semantics of natural language (Montague 1973; Dowty, Wall, and Peters 1981); a Boolean algebra mathematical model of natural language (Keenan and Faltz 1985); the theory of generalized quantifiers (Barwise and Cooper 1981, Hamm 1989); the theory of the pragmatic inference of quantity-based implicature (Horn 1972, 1989); and the theory of negation in natural language (Horn 1989).

Large-Scale Implementation:
The Mature UNO Natural Language Processing System

Figure 3 shows the uniform architecture of the UNO natural language processing system that implements the UNO model. The practical significance of the uniformity of the UNO natural language-based representation and inference is a simple, flexible, nonsequential architecture of the natural language processing system with the following three characteristics.

1. *Uniform representation for all.* All system modules access the knowledge representation module and share its uniform representation.

2. *No external specialists.* There is no need for external specialists such as knowledge representation systems, taxonomic or temporal reasoners. The system uniformly represents and reasons with taxonomic, temporal and some aspects of geographical knowledge.

3. *No interfaces translating between incompatible representations.* With no external specialists, no external interfaces to access them are needed, and therefore there is no need to translate between incompatible representations. A natural language processing system that needs to perform tasks beyond information extraction and to exhibit some in-depth processing such as question answering virtually always calls some external specialists, typically knowledge representation systems. As reported in the literature (for example, Palmer 1993), the necessity to translate between the representation of the natural language processing system and such an external specialist is a difficult task that tremendously complicates control.

Test and Development Data

The UNO test and development data consists of about twenty thousands online, multidomain, multisource textual documents, totaling over 200 MB. Table 2 contains the description of the public-domain and self-collected textual corpora that are utilized in my research.

Qualitative and Quantitative Performance Evaluation

Aside from a standard scientific evaluation, I use recall- and precision-based quantitative measures of the system and human performance. The main basis of the quantitative measures is provided by in-house tagged data—roughly 1,000 textual documents—with tagging encoding challenging problems in knowledge representation, inference, acquisition and use. I plan to compare my automatically acquired knowledge bases with some public-domain hand-crafted ones. One such candidate is WordNet (Miller 1995). Later on in this chapter, I will discuss the uniform UNO representation of different types of knowledge and show the computation of some inferences.

Corpus	Language	Size	Description	Source
books	English	100 pages 100 KB	Excerpts from various books, novels Scanned, typed-in	lucja@cs.wayne.edu
buswire	English	700 texts 1.5MB	Sample of 1990 businesswires Texts classified by 37 industry types	lucja@cs.wayne.edu
definitions	English	100 pages 10KB	Concept definitions from encyclopedias, dictionaries, friends, students Scanned, typed-in, from CD-ROMs	lucja@cs.wayne.edu
law	English	200 texts 5.5 MB	Sample of 1997 Calif. Court of Appeals cases	www.law.emory.edu
narratives	English	40 texts 200 KB	Various narratives	lucja@cs.wayne.edu
papers	English	100 pages	Excerpts from various newspapers, magazines Scanned, typed-in	lucja@cs.wayne.edu
phenomena	English	10 pages 10 KB	Phenomena-based challenging natural language cases for knowledge representation Artificial, plausible, and real examples	lucja@cs.wayne.edu
polish	Polish	10 MB	Donosy-Polish electronic newspaper summaries of major events	donosy@plearn.bitnet
melectro	English	1, 000 texts 3 MB	1990-1991 news wires, articles, communiqués etc. Microelectronics domain Mixed case Tipster data	CD-ROM, Linguistic Data Consortium
terrorist	English	1, 600 texts 4 MB	1988-1990 news wires, articles, communiqués etc. Terrorist attacks domain Mostly upper case MUC data	CD-ROM, Linguistic Data Consortium
time	English	10 MB	1994 issues of Time Magazine	CD-ROM, Softkey Inc.
venture	English	1, 000 texts 4 MB	1980-1991 news wires, articles, communiqués etc. Joint venture domain Upper and mixed case Tipster data	CD-ROM, Linguistic Data Consortium
wsj	English	15, 000 texts 100 MB	Wall Street Journal 1989-1994 issues	CD-ROM, Linguistic Data Consortium

Table 2
Corpora of textual data processed by the UNO natural language processing system.

Natural Language for Representing and Reasoning about Sets

In this section, I discuss basic sets, arbitrary sets, super sets, and flat-context-dependent taxonomies.

Basic Sets: Lexically Simple Common Nouns, Verbs, Adjectives

In natural language, lexically simple common nouns, verbs, and adjectives represent basic sets. Words in these syntactic categories can be thought of as denoting sets of entities (persons, objects, events, and their sets) that possess properties denoted by the words (Dowty, Walland, and Peters 1981; Barwise and Cooper 1981; Keenan and Faltz 1985; Hamm 1989). In this view, the common noun *woman,* the verb *walk,* and the adjective *red* are sets of entities possessing the woman, walk, and red property respectively.

In the UNO model, lexically simple common nouns, verbs and adjectives are represented by singleton terms whose only elements are primitive types. For example, the common noun *woman,* the verb *walk,* and the adjective *red* are represented by the following singleton terms respectively:

$T_1 =$ [woman]
$T_2 =$ [walk]
$T_3 =$ [red]

Subsets (Subtypes): Adjectival and Adverbial Modification

Natural language provides a generative mechanism to refer to arbitrary subsets (subtypes) of the basic sets (types). Adjectival and adverbial modification is a productive, universally understood, and easily computable means of referring to arbitrary subsets of sets denoted by lexically simpler expressions. Adjectives and adverbs are subtyping functions that combine with common nouns, verbs, and adjectives to produce complex expressions extensionally denoting subsets of sets corresponding to the lexically simpler expressions.

For example, the common noun *happy woman* refers to a subset of the set of entities in the extensional denotation of the basic type *woman;* the common noun *very happy woman* is a subset of the set of entities of the type *woman* as well as a subset of the entities in the set referred to as *happy woman.* Similarly, the verb *work hard* refers to a subset of entities with the property *work,* and *walk fast* describes a subset of entities with the property *walk.* The set/subset (subtype) relation expressed in natural language by adjectival and adverbial modification is universally understood by all native speakers and apparently effortless inference. There are no cross-speaker variations in the way this relation is expressed and understood.

Understanding the semantic relation of set/subset is closely tied to the syntactic structural correspondence between the expressions referring to a set and its subset. This close correspondence, in which the distinction between syntax and semantics virtually disappears, is a vehicle for conveying and understanding a large class of sentential entailments. Universal understanding of this type of entailments constitutes one aspect of literal meaning, as illustrated in table 1.

For example, the sentence *Sam is a very happy woman* entails the sentence *Sam is a woman* because the set of individuals of the type *very happy woman* is properly contained in the set of individuals in the denotation of the type *woman*. The sentence *Sam is a very happy woman* also entails the sentence *Sam is a happy woman* because the type *very happy woman* is a subtype of the type *happy woman*.

In the UNO model, complex common nouns, verbs, and adjectives are represented by terms with modifiers, and values are representations of the modifiers. The common noun *happy woman* is represented by the term

T_4 = [woman(happy ⇒ happy)]

The noun *very happy woman* is represented by the term

T_5 = [woman(happy ⇒ happy(degree ⇒ very))]

The operation ⊓ computed on these terms is guaranteed to preserve the subtyping relation between the terms that correspond to the original English expressions:

$T_1 ⊓ T_4 = T_4$, and therefore $T_4 ⊑ T_1$, i.e., happy woman is a woman
$T_1 ⊓ T_5 = T_5$, and therefore $T_5 ⊑ T_1$, i.e., very happy woman is a woman
$T_4 ⊓ T_5 = T_5$, and therefore $T_5 ⊑ T_4$, i.e., very happy woman is a happy woman

This efficiently computed type/subtype relation allows the system to compute the corresponding sentential entailments.

The complex verb *walk fast* is represented by the term

T_6 = [walk(speed ⇒ fast)]

Similar entailments reflecting literal meaning of natural language can be computed for verbs. The subtype relation between the set referred to by *walk fast* and the set referred to by *walk* is guaranteed to be preserved:

$T_2 ⊓ T_6 = T_6$, and therefore $T_6 ⊑ T_2$, i.e. walking fast entails walking.

Establishing this relation allows the UNO system to compute the relation of entailment between the sentences involving the expressions *John walks fast* and *John walks*.

Set-Intersection, Set-Union, Set-Complement: Conjunction, Disjunction, Negation

In natural language, set intersections, set unions, and set complements of the denotations of simple and complex common nouns, verbs, and adjectives are compositionally derived via explicit conjunctions, disjunctions, and negations. The Boolean connectives *not, and,* and *or* are category-preserving functions that take arbitrarily complex expressions of these syntactic, set-theoretic categories as their arguments and generate complex properties (set descriptions) with the set-theoretic semantics.

Understanding semantic relations such as entailment (set-containment), partial overlap (nonempty intersection) and disjointness (empty intersection) between complex and simpler properties is universally shared and easily computed. This is responsible for the universally shared class of entailments and interpretations between natural language sentences involving simpler and composite properties. Understanding this type of entailment and interpretation constitutes another aspect of literal meaning, as illustrated in table 1 Both "positive" (without any explicit negative) and "negative" (with explicit negative) sentences entail an infinite number of sentences.

Conjunction

Let us example conjunction first. For example, the complex common noun *professor and mother* is a complex property obtained via an explicit conjunction of the nouns *professor* and *mother*. This composite common noun—a property—describes a set whose denotation is the intersection of the denotations of the types *professor* and *mother*.

Conjunctive properties result in the entailment relation between sentences with the composite conjunctive property and sentences with simpler properties consisting of some subset of the composite conjuncts. For example, if it is the case that "Sam is a professor and mother" then it automatically follows that "Sam is a professor" and that "Sam is a mother."

The common noun *healthy and happy woman* is a complex common noun, a property that involves an adjectival modification of the common noun *woman* with the complex adjective *healthy and happy;* this adjective is obtained via an explicit conjunction of the adjectives *healthy* and *happy*. This composite property describes a set of entities of the type *woman* whose denotation is the intersection of the sets *healthy and happy* and woman.

Like in the case of common nouns, conjunctive adjectival properties result in the entailment relation between sentences with the composite conjunctive property and sentences with simpler properties consisting of some subset of the composite conjuncts. For example, if it is the case that *Sam is a healthy and happy woman* then it is automatically the case that *Sam is a healthy woman* and that *Sam is a happy woman*.

Negation

Now let us turn to negation. The common noun *not (very happy woman)* is a composite property involving explicit negation of a complex common noun *very happy woman;* this noun is obtained via an adjectival modification of the common noun *woman* with the adjective *very happy,* itself a complex adjective obtained via an adverbial modification with the adverb *very* of the adjective *happy.* This composite property describes a set whose denotation is a set-complement of the set referred to as *very happy woman* and includes three sets: (1) entities with the *not-woman* property, a complex property created via explicit negation; (2) entities with the *(not happy) woman* property, and (3) entities with the *(not very) happy woman* property.

The phrase *a not very happy woman* may be used to refer to entities whose types are consistent with these sets. First, this entity may be of the type *man,* consistent with the type *not woman;* second, it may be of the type *woman that is not happy,* i.e., the type *(not happy) woman;* and third, it may be of the type *woman that is happy, but not very happy,* i.e., the type *(not very) happy woman.*

The sentence *Sam is not a woman* entails the sentence *Sam is not a very happy woman* because *not woman* entails *not very happy woman.* The sentence *John doesn't walk* entails the sentence *John doesn't walk very fast* because the verb phrase *doesn't walk* entails the verb phrase *doesn't walk very fast.*

Disjunction

Now let us turn to disjunction. The noun *dog or large cat* refers to a disjunctive type. It is entailed by the types *dog* and *cat.* Consequently the sentence "It must have been a dog" entails the sentence "It must have been a dog or large cat."

The UNO Model

In the UNO model, representation is compositionally derived via the Boolean operations. The entailments are guaranteed to hold. The common noun *healthy and happy woman* is represented by the term

[woman(health ⇒ healthy,
        happy ⇒ happy)]

The common noun *not very happy woman* is represented by the term

not [woman(happy ⇒ happy(degree ⇒ very))]

This term is equivalent to the three-element term

[not woman,
    woman(happy ⇒ not happy),
    woman(happy ⇒happy(degree ⇒ not very))   ]

This equivalence is automatically established by computing the operation of *not* on the term representing *very happy woman.* The elements of this complement term correspond exactly to the interpretations of the natural language expression *not very happy woman.*

The disjunctive noun *dog or large cat* is represented by the disjunctive two-element term

[dog, cat(size $\Rightarrow$ large)]

Arbitrary Sets, Supersets: Arbitrary Boolean Expressions with Explicit Negation, Conjunction, and Disjunction

In natural language, the combination of adjectival, adverbial, and Boolean modification of basic types (sets) allows one to refer to or describe arbitrary types (sets). All the following expressions are references to such arbitrary types (sets).

very, but not extremely, good candy or good book
neither good nor hard-working nurse
neither short nor very tall
very happy people, tall trees, extremely clear sky

The UNO model mimics this characteristics of natural language. Our natural language-like mechanism for taxonomic reasoning is based on the UNO model capability of handling adjectival, adverbial, and Boolean modifications of common nouns, adjectives and verbs. The UNO representation of such expressions is efficiently, compositionally derived via the Boolean operations. The set-related semantic relations are guaranteed to hold.

Flat, Context-Dependent Taxonomies

Set-related semantic relations of interest (entailment, partial overlap, disjointness etc.) among arbitrary simple and complex types are automatically understood by people, without having to store or remember such relations in one's head. The relations among types such as *dog, dog or cat, but not cow,* and *very small dog with extremely longhair,* are easily computed on the fly. Only the relations between some lexically simple items such as the relation between the type *dog* and *animal* need to be remembered or explicitly represented. Most likely, such relations need to be learned.

Natural language allows one to easily create context-dependent taxonomies that reflect one's life experience and tasks to be accomplished. For example, for Mark, *rusty engines, Teddy bears,* and *the smell of wild roses* may form a coherent type (class) because all these things remind him of his childhood. For him, and very likely only for him, there is a close relationship between the concept of *my childhood* and these things.

With regard to the UNO model, one important consequence of mimicking these characteristics of natural language are flat, context-dependent taxonomies, which tremendously facilitates maintenance of large knowledge bases. Taxonomies are flat because set-related semantic relations among arbitrary simple and complex types are directly computed from the UNO representation of the natural language expressions that represent these types. This fast, on-the-fly computation eliminates the need to store such relations in the system's knowledge base. Only relations between some lexically simple items such as the relation between the types *dog* and *animal* need to be explicitly represented. Just as natural language, the UNO model allows one to define ad-hoc, context-dependent taxonomies with types such as the *my childhood* type above.

Natural Language for Representing and Reasoning about Intervals—Scalars

Natural language offers a large, cross-categorial class of expressions, scalars, that denote quantitative values (Horn 1972, 1989). This class includes determiners, cardinal numbers, evaluative, and gradable adjectives, adverbs, and verbs. The underlying semantics of scalars is interval-theoretic. Lexically simple scalars denote intervals and ordered sets of real numbers. Boolean operations of negation (interval-complement), conjunction (interval-intersection) and disjunction (interval-union) allow one to compositionally refer to arbitrary intervals built out of basic intervals.

Semantic relations such as entailment (interval-inclusion), partial overlap (nonempty interval-intersection) and disjointness (empty interval-intersection) are universally and easily understood by the virtue of universally shared syntactic and semantic characteristics of these operations.

Lexically, scalar Boolean operations are realized by the same words *not, and* and *or.* In natural language, *not, and,* and *or* are polymorphic, multi-type loaded operations. The same adjective and adverb phrases serve as functions that modify scalar and nonscalar expressions. Their intersective semantics remains the same, but for scalars, it reflects interval-containment. For example, the determiner *very many* entails the determiner *many.*

For some scalars, semantic relation of entailment holds between denotations of lexically simple items. The intervals denoted by such scalars are contained one within the other, or equivalently, some scalars have at least meaning. For example, the entailment relation between the frequency quantification adverbs *always* and *sometimes,* the fact that the interval *always* is properly contained in the interval *sometimes* accounts for the fact that when told *John always smiles,* one automatically understands that *John sometimes smiles.* Similarly, it immediately follows that if a person is *stupid,* then this person is *not extremely bright.* The at-least meaning of scalars is exploited for representing incomplete knowledge and for conveying certain information without actually committing to it. If one sees a number of white swans, one forms the belief that *Some swans are white*. This belief should not preclude that all swans may in fact be white. One's knowledge is at this point incomplete and in this case, the sentence *Some swans are white* is equivalent to *At least some swans are white*. Knowing that something is possible is not inconsistent with a possibility that this something is in fact certain. In a situation when one is reluctant to state that *Ann and Mary are lesbian lovers* the sentence *Ann likes Mary* is an understatement that may convey this information without, strictly speaking, admitting it.

Despite the fact that scalar expressions of different categories play different functions in the syntax and semantics of natural language sentences, understanding semantic relations between simple and complex scalars is accomplished via the same representational and computational mechanism between simple and complex scalars, including scalar modal operators. Table 3 gives examples of cross-categorial scalar expressions in the entailment (interval-inclusion) relation. Rusiecki (1985) reports psychological experiments in which human subjects judged logical entailment between pairs of English expressions: one positive (i.e., without explicit negation) and one negative. He found that people were remarkably consistent in their answers and for all of them such judgements appeared effortless.

The UNO Model

The UNO model formalizes scalars as qualitative scales—families of efficiently computable Boolean algebras. These algebras, specific to natural language, capture semantic properties of scalars and allow one to uniformly compute semantic relations of interest between arbitrary scalar expressions of different syntactic categories. The at-least meaning of lexically simple scalars and the fact that two lexically simple scalars may be in the entailment relation is modeled with the notion of directed intervals of real numbers. The lower boundaries of these intervals represent the smallest value denoted by a word and their upper boundaries—the largest.

For example, the lower boundary of the determiner *some* is 0, and its upper boundary is +1, i.e., *some* is the entire interval (0, +1]; the parenthesis signifies the exclusion of the boundary value and the square bracket its inclusion. The direction for lexically simple scalars is either ↑ or ↓. The following are examples of the directed interval-based representations of lexically simple scalars.

1. The determiners *some* and *many* are represented by

Category	Scalar Expression	Entailed Scalar Expression
Cardinal number	two	one
	not one	not two
Determiner	all	some
	none	not all
	not many	not very many
Adverb	always	sometimes
	never	not always
	never	not very often
	not often	not very often
	very often, but not always	sometimes
Verb	know	believe
	not know	not know much
	not know	not firmly believe
	not believe	not know
	love	like
	not like	not love
	not like	not love a lot
Adjective	certain	likely
	not likely	not certain
	not likely	not very likely
	terrible	not very good
	sick	not very healthy
	excellent	good
	not good	not excellent
	stupid	not bright
	stupid	not extremely bright

Table 3
Entailments of cross-categorial scalar expressions.

$[(0, +1], \uparrow]$ $[[l_{many}, +1], \uparrow]$

where $l_{many} > 0$

2. The verbs *like* and *love* are represented by

$[[l_{like}, +1], \uparrow]$ $[[l_{love}, +1], \uparrow]$

where $l_{love} > l_{like}$

3. The adjectives *possible* and *certain* are represented by

$[[l_{possible}, +1], \uparrow]$ $[[l_{certain}], +1], \uparrow]$

where $l_{certain} > l_{possible}$

The representation of complex scalar expressions such as *sometimes, but not very often* is compositionally derived via the Boolean opera-

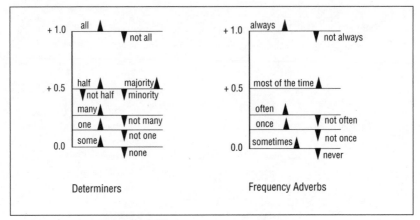

Figure 4. Frequency Quantification Adverbs
Parallel Scalar Semantics of Determiners.

tions on the representation of lexically simple scalars. If arguments are single intervals, adjectival and adverbial modification as well as conjunction always generate a single interval. Negation and disjunction in general produce multiinterval scalars. Figure 4 illustrates two very similar qualitative scales:[2] determiners and frequency quantification adverbs, which reflects the fact that with respect to some inference in the absence of any context, temporal quantifiers behave exactly the same as determiners that give rise to the generalized quantifiers of natural language. A similar distinction between first-order and nonfirst-order definable quantifiers applies: the adverb *always* is like the determiner *all,* and the adverb *often* like the determiner *many.* These similarities allow the UNO system to use the same mechanism for computing temporal and nontemporal quantifiers. Figure 5 illustrates scales with general-purpose scalars.

Natural Language for Expressing and Reasoning with Uncertainty and Incompleteness

Natural language allows one to express uncertainty and incompleteness at all syntactic levels and offers two main ways of doing it: scalar expressions involving probability and beliefs, and explicit disjunction. The sentence *John is likely, but not very likely, to be HIV-positive* expresses the uncertainty about John possessing the HIV-positive property and qualitatively characterizes the probability of this being the case as *likely, but not very likely.*

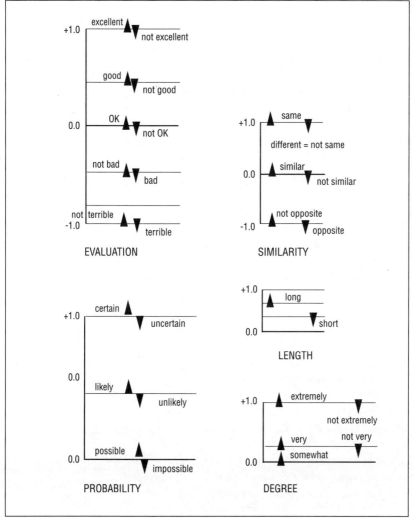

Figure 5. General-Purpose Scalars

The sentence *John or Mary dances well* expresses the uncertainty about the agent of dancing.

The probability scale shown in figure 5 allows the UNO model to capture uncertainty of information. The sentence *John is likely, but not very likely, to be HIV-positive* is represented in the system knowledge base by the following type equation

john == { < [hiv(type ⇒ positive)], [likely(degree ⇒ not very)] > }

The representation of the probability referred to by the natural language expression *likely, but not very likely* is compositionally computed by the UNO natural language processing system as follows:

[likely] ⊓ not [likely(degree ⇒ very)] =
[likely] ⊓ [(not likely), likely(degree ⇒ not very)] =
[likely(degree ⇒ not very)]

The representation of the sentence *John or Mary dances well* is the following type equation

[Mary, John] == { dance(well ⇒ well) }

Natural Language for Representing and Reasoning about Time

Time is an entity whose properties can be expressed in natural language and reasoned about in many ways analogous to reasoning about any other entities. While there are a number of words reserved to refer to time or temporal aspects only, such as *yesterday, frequently,* or *young,* understanding temporal expressions is not really different from understanding nontemporal expressions. Additionally there does not seem to be a difference between expressing and reasoning about absolute and relative temporal information. Figure 5 shows general-purpose scalars relevant for expressing temporal information. One infers from *It took an extremely long time* that *It did not take a long time.* and the falsity of the sentence *It took a very short time.*

The same mechanism accounts for the relevant logical inferences when these adjectives describe nontemporal objects. One infers that if *Pluto has an extremely short tail,* then it is also the case that *Pluto does not have a very long tail.*

Many general-purpose scalars are used to describe time. Entailment between the following pairs of temporal expressions:

< *a very good time,   not a bad time* >
< *a terrible time,   not a very good time* >

works in the exact same fashion as the entailment between their nontemporal versions

< *a very good book, not a bad book* >
< *a terrible student, not a very good student* >

Scalars such as similar, same, and different allow one to express the degree of similarity among entities. One infers from the sentence *X and Y are the same* that *X and Y are very similar* and that *X and Y are not very different.* Understanding logical implications of sentences in which the similarity words describe temporal information is exactly analogous. One infers from the sentence *X and Y happened at the*

same time that *X and Y did not happen at a different time.*
It is important that making inferences does not require any information about the actual times when the events *X* and *Y* took place.

Infinity of Temporal Relations: Adjectival, Adverbial, and Boolean Modifications

Adjectival, adverbial and Boolean modifications work exactly the same for temporal and nontemporal expressions. The following are simple and complex temporal relations with easily understandable semantic relations among them:

"shortly after"	entails	"after"
"not before"	entails	"not long before"
"immediately precede"	entails	"precede"
"long before"	entails	"not immediately after"

Time-Related Uncertainties and Incompleteness

Time-related uncertainties and incompleteness can also be expressed at different syntactic levels. The sentence *It is very likely that X happened shortly before or after Y* illustrates a case of double-uncertainty. The probability phrase *very likely* modifies another uncertainty expressed as adverbial modification of a disjunctive prepositional phrase *shortly before or after*. This ambiguous phrase could mean: (1) *(shortly before) or after* i.e., *X* could have happened either *shortly before Y*, or *after Y*; in the latter case, nothing is known about the distance between *X* and *Y*. (2) The phrase could also mean: *shortly (before or after)* i.e., *X* could have happened either *before Y*, or *after Y*. In both cases the temporal distance between *X* and *Y* is *short*, i.e., the uncertainty pertains the temporal relation only.

The second interpretation contains strictly more information than the first one, i.e., the second entails the first.

The Uno Model

Time-related representation and inference are largely accomplished by our natural language representational and inferential machinery. The general-purpose scalars in figure 5 shown earlier, evaluation, degree, similarity, and length, allow the UNO model to compute time-related entailments involving scalars.

The representation of complex temporal relations is computed analogously to the representation of set-forming categories and the entailment relation is preserved. The relations *shortly after* and *after* are represented as:

T_1 = after(length $\Rightarrow$ short)
T_2 = after
$T_1 \sqcap T_2 = T_1$, and therefore $T_1 \sqsubseteq T_2$, i.e., *shortly after* entails *after.*

The relations *not before* and *not long before* are represented as:

T_1 = not before
T_2 = not before(length $\Rightarrow$ long)
$T_1 \sqcap T_2 = T_1$, and therefore $T_1 \sqsubseteq T_2$, i.e., *not before* entails *not long before*.

The relations *immediately precede* and *precede* are represented as:

T_1 = precede(immediate $\Rightarrow$ immediate)
T_2 = precede
$T_1 \sqcap T_2 = T_1$, and therefore $T_1 \sqsubseteq T_2$, i.e., *immediately precedes* entails "precedes."

The relations *long before* and *not immediately after* are represented as:

T_1 = before(length $\Rightarrow$ long)
T_2 = not after(immediate $\Rightarrow$ immediate)
= [not after, after(length $\Rightarrow$ not long)]
$T_1 \sqcap T_2 = T_1$, and therefore $T_1 \sqsubseteq T_2$, i.e., *long before* entails *not immediately after*

The UNO representation of the phrase *shortly before or after* preserves its ambiguity and the fact that its two interpretations are in the entailment relation. The *(shortly before) or after* interpretation is represented by the term

I_1 = [before(length $\Rightarrow$ shortly), after]

The *shortly (before or after)* interpretation is represented by the term

I_2 = [before, after](length $\Rightarrow$ shortly)
$I_1 \sqcap I_2 = I_2$, or equivalently, $I_2 \sqsubseteq I_1$.

Natural Language for Some Aspects of Spatial Reasoning

It is widely recognized that natural language is not good for spatial reasoning. In general, I agree with this assessment. However, I believe that a large class of space-related inferences can be accomplished with the natural language-inherent representational and inferential machinery. Reasoning about geographical entities with the underlying region-containment semantics appears to be exactly analogous to the taxonomic and temporal reasoning in natural language. Many natural language expressions serve as means to refer to temporal intervals as well as spatial regions. Many prepositions and adverbs are used to describe both temporal and spatial relations. The expression *shortly before or after* applies to both time and space.

My uniform representation motivated by natural language serves us well for representing certain aspects of geographical knowledge. I have encoded a semantic hierarchy of geographical knowledge, for which some aspects of geographical reasoning (for example, region containment) are supported with its general inferencing mechanism. This extensive geographical knowledge base contains major geographical information about all countries, including capital cities, major and important cities, towns, ports, geographical and political regions that divide land such as provinces, islands, major ports and airports, landmarks, money, length, area, and volume systems, official languages, major political organizations, waters, such as oceans, seas, lakes, and rivers, and geographical landmarks and points of interest such as mountains, hills, woods, and national parks.

The system knows that *Detroit is in Michigan* and that *Michigan is in the USA*. This knowledge allows it to infer from *John is in Detroit* that *John is in Michigan* and that *John is somewhere in the USA*. The sentence *John is not in Michigan* automatically implies that *John is not in Detroit*. Similarly the sentence *John is not far from Detroit* is consistent with *John is close to Detroit*.

The Underspecificity and Context Dependency of Natural Language

A general consensus is that natural language is always interpreted in some context (Iwańska and Zadrozny 1997), yet there is no theory of general context in natural language. or computer architecture its context-dependent interpretation. My goal is to rectify this situation. I have developed a computational theory of general context-dependency of natural language, building on my research of some deep and shallow aspects of context.

Top-Down and Bottom-Up Theory Evolution

The top-down theory evolution consists of investigating possible interpretations of natural language utterances in different contexts and their relation to literal meaning. The bottom-up evolution is researching four specific problems.

The first problem is semantics, pragmatics, and context-dependency of intensional negative adjectivals such as *alleged, artificial, fake, false, former,* and *toy* (Iwańska 1997a).

The second problem is processing large textual corpora, including computing discourse structure via heuristics-based definite anaphora resolution (Iwańska 1997b); processing abbreviations (Iwańska, Kruger and Mata 1998); and exploiting local context—for example handling punctuation.

The third problem is reducing underspecificity of negation in natural language.

The final problem is computing context-dependent inference of implicature.

My goal is to make these top-down, uniformity-driven and bottom-up, problem-driven theories fully converge. Currently, I provide two partially overlapping and partially complementary pieces of the context puzzle.

The corresponding aim is to develop a uniform computer architecture that would allow one to process natural language like people do—to represent, reason about, utilize context and be able to automatically compute context-dependent interpretation of natural language utterances. An outline of such an architecture is shown in figure 1.

Underspecificity of Natural Language: Context as Filler, Corrector, Focus

It is my conjecture that natural language is inherently underspecified and context-dependent due to the tension between the needs for expressiveness, limitations of symbolic systems, necessarily incomplete human knowledge, the nature of the outside world that humans deal with, constraints on communication, and social structure.

To accumulate and share knowledge about the outside world, people must refer to an infinite number of entities (objects, individuals, events, and their sets). This infinity is like real-number, Turing-equivalent infinity: any subsets and supersets of sets, any subparts and superparts of entities, time, space, and volume all may be important and may have to be explicitly referred to in order to form and communicate knowledge about them. However, natural language vocabulary and utterances are necessarily very finite—in part due to limited human memory and short human life.

Social structure appears to impose additional requirements on human communication. Social norms of behavior such as politeness and hierarchical dependencies such as employee-employer relation, often lead people to understate their views because they are not in a position to express what they really know or think.

I conjecture that the main role of context is to potentially reduce this underspecificity and act as filler, corrector, and focus. Inherent context-dependency of natural language results in (1) increased information content of natural language utterances, or, equivalently, reduced size of natural language utterances representing particular knowledge, with potentially sacrificed completeness or correctness; and (2) simplified, less precise, computationally cheaper inference. I explain context-dependency of natural language as a computational gamble of achieving conciseness of natural language utterances for representing particular knowledge, risking its completeness, correctness, or precision.

Solution, Not Problem

The tension between the needs for expressiveness, constraints on human communication, and limitations of the symbolic system such as natural language might have jointly resulted in the inherent underspecificity and context-dependency of natural language. In this view, context-dependency of natural language is not a problem[3] but a solution satisfying objective constraints.

One observes the following pieces of evidence of inherent underspecificity of natural language:

The same phrase may refer to uncountably many things and values.

Phrases of all syntactic categories denoting quantitative values may refer to any real number. For example, the word *long* can refer to an arbitrary real number and reflect quantity of time or space. The expression *long time* may mean: one nanosecond, one second, one hour, one century, as well as any temporal interval shorter or longer than these.

Lexically simple common nouns such as *student* may denote infinite sets of objects. Complex common nouns involving adjectival, adverbial and Boolean (negation, conjunction, disjunction) modifications may refer to arbitrary subsets and supersets of sets denoted by lexically simple nouns. For example, the following complex common nouns "very, but not extremely, hard-working students," "not very smart students" "smart students and hard-working students," denote Boolean combinations of different subsets of the set corresponding to the head noun "student."

Referring expressions such as pronouns and definite anaphora are even more underspecified with respect to what they can refer to. Abbreviations are extremely common.

Context Reduces Inherent Underspecificity

The primary role of context is to potentially reduce the inherent underspecificity of natural language. My top-down theory views context as both filler and corrector. Negative contexts result in contradictory and contrary interpretations of natural language utterances and dramatically change knowledge in them. Overwriting contexts result in a significant change of meaning of natural language utterances. Positive contexts result in logically stronger interpretations; they never change information in the utterance, only add new ones. I analyze many nonliteral meanings of natural language as context-reduced underspecificity and the effects of negative and overwriting contexts.

I conjecture that most, if not all, types of underspecificity and context-dependency observed in natural language can be accounted for by a single computational mechanism. My most developed bottom-up theory captures the focusing aspect of context. It formalizes context as a finite set of intensional properties, which allows one to disregard not very relevant knowledge.

Partially Computationally Tested Theory Rooted in Reality

Because of the enormous difficulty and novelty of the research problems involving context, a full-scale implementation performing well on a large-scale, real-life data is not a realistic goal. Some aspects of my theory have been tested on a small-scale, real-life and artificial data such as computing context-dependent interpretation of the sample natural language utterances. Some aspects will be tested on large corpora, several thousands texts, of real-life data, such as, weak methods reliably identifying negative and overwriting contexts in arbitrary texts.

Explicit Representation of Context Is Necessary

To account for the fact that natural language utterances are always interpreted in some context, a model of natural language must explicitly represent context and provide a mechanism for processing it. I distinguish two types of context: explicit and implicit. I represent both types of context as natural language utterances. The choice of natural language to express context is deliberate.

First, context should be handled by the same representational and inferential mechanism that is used to represent meaning of natural language utterances and to compute licensed inferences.

Second, imposing context-provided constraints when interpreting natural language utterances can be accomplished by the same representational mechanism utilized for computing representation of a multi-sentence utterance.

Natural Language as Information (Knowledge) Combining Level

I use natural language to represent verbal and sensory information as well as existing knowledge. This idea of natural language as information-combining and inferencing level (natural language as "mentalese") and the corresponding computer architecture shown in figure 1 are loosely motivated by a plausible hypothesis about human information processing. There is some evidence in psychology that sensory information can be expressed in natural language; for example, Kearney and Mckenzie (1993) use verbalized natural language descriptions of facial expressions in their expert system. The entire multi-modal information processing involves five major steps:

1. Sensory inputs are translated into natural language messages.
2. Decision is made as to which message, an natural language utterance or some nonverbal messages, constitutes the main message and which ones are context.
3. The main message and its context are packaged together.
4. The resulting structured text is processed by a natural language processing system.
5. The results of this processing update the existing knowledge base.

Ferrari (1997) points out that different modalities of human communication (gestures, noddings, facial expressions, intonation etc.) virtually always accompany natural language utterances and often constitute their context. This idea has been incorporated here. Additionally, natural language utterances may serve as context for interpreting information from those other modalities.

Explicit Context

Explicit context includes things usually referred to as "linguistic context" or "discourse context," such as a multi-sentence fragment of text in which an utterance occurs, syntactic constructions involved in the utterance, structure between multi-sentence segments of text and linguistic constraints on referents of the anaphors. The notion of explicit context additionally includes verbalized natural language descriptions of those other modalities accompanying natural language utterances including visual information (gestures, facial expressions, and body movement).

Implicit Context

Implicit context includes things often referred to as "nonlinguistic context." It reflects a general state of an individual, his or her knowledge and beliefs, including beliefs about such general states of other than self individuals, goals, fears and hopes. Implicit context is pictured as a text that constitutes a "core dump" of an individual's mind and the content of his or her memory.

Literal and Nonliteral Meaning of Natural Language

Definition 1 (Utterance)
An ordered set $U = \{ S_1, S_2, ..., S_n \}$ is a natural language utterance, where $S_i \in U$ is a single natural language sentence.

Typically, elements of the utterances (texts, dialogs, and their fragments) are natural language sentences. In dialog, they can also be nonsentential forms that constitute answers to posed questions, such as noun phrases.

Definition 2 (Literal Meaning)
$\mathcal{M}_L(S) = S_L = \mathcal{T}(S)$, literal meaning of a natural language sentence S, is knowledge that every speaker is capable of deriving from S in the absence

of any context and characterized by the set of questions that a speaker can correctly answer based solely on the understanding of S.

Knowledge due to literal meaning can be characterized by the types of questions that a native speaker can correctly answer based solely on the understanding of the sentence.

Definition 3 (Context)

Context $\mathscr{C}$ is the representation of an ordered set of natural language sentences

$\mathscr{T}(\{ S_1, S_2, ..., S_m \})$ computed as follows:

$\mathscr{C} = \mathscr{L}(S_1) \oplus \mathscr{L}(S_2) \oplus ... \oplus \mathscr{L}(S_n)$, where $\oplus$ is left-associative.

Definition 4 (Nonliteral Meaning)

$\mathcal{M}_N(S) = S_N$, nonliteral meaning of a natural language sentence S, is knowledge that in the context $\mathscr{C}$, every native speaker is potentially capable of deriving from S, but depending on further characteristics of $\mathscr{C}$, may or may not derive it or even attempt to derive it. Let $\mathscr{I}$ be information.

Case I. Nonliteral meaning constitutes additional knowledge on top of literal meaning.

$\mathscr{I}(S) = \mathscr{I}(S_L) + \mathscr{I}(S_N)$

> *Case Ia.* It may further specify some aspect of literal meaning, in which case ⊓ is the information combining function:
> If $S_L \sqsubseteq S_C$ then $\mathcal{M}_N(S) = S_L \sqcap S_C$
> *Case Ib.* It may be some meaning orthogonal to the literal meaning
> If $S_L \sqcap S_C = \perp$ then $\mathcal{M}_N(S) = S_L \sqcup S_C$

Case II. Nonliteral meaning may also overwrite literal meaning via a context-dependent function $\mathscr{F}_C$:

$\mathcal{M}_N(S) = \mathscr{F}_C(S_L) = S_N$, $\mathscr{I}(S) = \mathscr{I}(S_N)$

For the nonoverwriting contexts in case I, knowledge grows monotonically. In cases like case II, the growth is nonmonotonic.

Definition 5 (Context of Utterance Participant)

Let P be an utterance participant. $\mathscr{C}_P$ is P's context, a representation computed by the function $\mathscr{T}$ from the structured text that reflects P's knowledge.

Contexts of utterance participants are structured texts that reflect general states of the individuals and include beliefs about such general states of the other than self individuals. For dialogs, we distinguish speakers' and hearers' contexts; for texts— writers' and readers' contexts. Our formalization allows the same utterance to have different meanings for different utterance participants and in different contexts. The same utterance may have identical meanings for different participants if their contexts coincide. Missing some aspect of explicit or implicit context may result in literal meanings being totally different. For some forms of nonliteral meanings, including implicature, they are often quite different.

Definition 6 (Updated Context)

Let S_i be a current, about to be processed element of the utterance U, P an utterance participant, and C_{i-1}^P his or her context.

Then C_i^P, an updated context of P, is $F(C_{i-1}^P, S_i)$, where F is a partial update function. Depending on the nature of both arguments, F differs and the updated context is:

1. For negative contexts, F is consistent with not: $C_i^P \subseteq$ not C_{i-1}^P
2. For overwriting contexts, $F = \mathcal{F}_{\mathscr{C}}$: $C_i^P = \mathcal{F}_{\mathscr{C}}(C_{i-1}^P)$
3. For all other contexts, $\oplus = \sqcap$: $C_i^P = C_{i-1}^P \sqcap S_N$

The updated contexts for the utterance participants reflect their knowledge after processing a subsequent element of the utterance. This change may be monotonic or not. It may involve accommodating a new piece of knowledge without invalidating what was known before or belief revision due to realization of one's incorrect knowledge.

I characterize different contexts as classes of functions affecting the literal meaning of natural language systematically, but differently. For a given natural language utterance, contexts are different in the final understanding of this utterance. They are also quite different in the underlying algorithmic mechanics responsible for the final computation of context-dependent interpretation of natural language utterances. The computational properties of different contexts need to be studied.

For some contexts, computing context-dependent interpretation of natural language utterances can already be accomplished by the efficiently computable UNO operations; for some, it can even be done on a large-scale. The UNO model is particularly well suited to processing negative contexts because the semantics of such contexts is quite similar to the semantics of the general negation in natural language, one the most unique feature of the UNO model.

The computability of other contexts such as contexts triggering implicature, remains an open research problem. Such contexts are characterized as positive, information-adding contexts resulting in logically stronger meaning of the utterance. Computationally, it accounts for identifying a possibility of quantity-based implicatures, and, for some utterances, for the possible range of the implicated meanings. It cannot, however, automatically decide for a given context, if the implicature takes place or to chose among possible implicated meanings.

Context-Provided Further Specificity

Many types of nonliteral meaning result from context-provided further specificity. Examples include (1) underspecificity of explicitly negated verb- phrases with respect to a particular interpretation; (2) common nouns and verbs with respect to attributes and their values; (3) referring expressions with respect to referred entities; and (4) abbreviations with respect to words or phrases they abbreviate. Computing most types of such nonliteral meanings can be accomplished by the meet operation ⊓ on the representation of a sentence and its context.

Underspecificity of Negation

Consider the sentence *John doesn't walk very fast,* which due to the semantics of negation is underspecified with respect to the three mutually exclusive interpretations. These interpretation are (1) *John walks fast, but not very fast;* (2) *John walks, but not fast;* and (3) *John doesn't walk.*

Consider a dialog between Ann, Mark, Mary, and Bill, with Ann stating that "John doesn't walk very fast." If Mark was told a few minutes earlier that "John doesn't walk," then for him, Ann's statement doesn't contain any new piece of knowledge. His implicit context—here his previous knowledge—already contains the representation of a sentence that logically entails Ann's statement. Mark's previous knowledge eliminates one aspect of the underspecificity of Ann's statement.[4] As a result, Mark can correctly compute truth-values of the sentences corresponding to the three possible interpretations of Ann's statement.

This type of underspecificity may be eliminated by some chain of inference. For example, if, the other night, Mary witnessed John breaking both legs, then based on the general knowledge that *people with broken legs don't walk* she may herself infer that in fact *John doesn't walk.*

After interpretation of a natural language utterance, persons who lack context such as relevant knowledge in the above examples will possess strictly less knowledge as compared with those whose context reduces underspecificity. People lacking relevant context will not be able to correctly assign truth-values to the related sentences.[5] For example, if Bill has no knowledge of John's accident, then his context will contain the representation of the sentence uttered by Ann,[6] which is logically weaker than one element of Mark's context. After Ann's statement, Bill will know strictly less than Mark or Mary.

Underspecificity of Common Nouns and Verbs

Common nouns and verbs are often underspecified with respect to the attributes of the referred entities. The sentence *She has two cats* is underspecified in infinitely many ways— it does not specify any attributes of these cats such as color, age, whether they have tails etc. Similarly, verbs that denote actions often do not specify objects, themes, or modes of these actions.

Further Specificity Due to Conventions

Indirect speech acts result in additional nonliteral meaning equivalent to uttering additional explicit statements. For example, the question *Could you pass the salt?* by convention is equivalent to something like *If you can pass the salt, then I want you to do it.* Similarly, the utterance *She is cold* may be an indirect request for an action that would end this presumably unpleasant state, such as closing an open window or appropriately adjusting a thermostat.

Further Specificity Due to Defaults

Another class of fairly productive nonliteral meanings results from generally assumed to be known defaults (types in the object noun phrases or adverbial modifiers) that further specify literal meaning. For example, the unmodified verb *to drink* is often interpreted as *to drink alcohol* because its underspecificity with respect to what one drinks is overwritten by commonly shared defaults.

Overwriting by Negative Contexts

Context may serve as a filter that derives nonliteral meanings of an utterance by performing certain mathematically and computationally well-defined function on its literal meaning. One such example are negative contexts that result in a contrary and contradictory nonliteral meaning of an utterance. Another example are contexts that reduce the certainty about the correctness of knowledge or information expressed in an utterance.

Previous Knowledge as Negative Context

After Paul's statement *He is an excellent student* people with different implicit contexts, here existing beliefs, may understand his message very differently (see figure 6), including the following three interpretations.

1. *He is a bad student* is the meaning that Mark, who believes that *Paul is a liar,* derives from Paul's sentence.
2. *He is not a student* is the meaning that Ann, who believes that *Paul is a terrible liar,* derives from his statement.
3. *He is an excellent student* is the meaning that Maria, who believes Paul, derives from his statement. Her belief exactly corresponds to his statement.

In everyday life, overwriting by negative contexts is not at all uncommon. For example, Detroit's *Free Press* of January 17, 1996, starts the article on page 4 A titled "Jury leader: Fuhrman is a snake" with the following paragraph:

Figure 6. Negative Context
Previous knowledge may constitute an overwriting, negative context. Beliefs resulting from the interpretation of the same utterance may be mutually contradictory, here Mark's and Ann's.

> From the moment the forewoman of the O. J. Simpson jury saw Mark Fuhrman, she thought he was a "snake." After hearing him, she didn't believe what he said.

Nonverbal Messages as Negative Context

After Andrew's statement *He always works extremely hard* people with different explicit contexts, here a gesture and speaker's appearance, may understand his message very differently (see figure 7) including the following two examples:

1. *It is very possible that he never does anything* is the meaning that Bill, who saw Rick's *I don't know about that* gesture and also saw speaker's face when he uttered the statement, derived from the statement.
2. *He always works extremely hard* is the meaning that Ted, who lacked any additional visual clues, believes. Ted's belief corresponds exactly to Andrew's statement.

There are many gestures whose specific purpose is conveying disagreement with presented information. For example, (vigorously) shaking one's head left to right and right to left.

Explicit Negatives as Negative Context

Explicit verbal negative contexts may constitute negative contexts and have a similar overwriting effect. For example, computing knowledge

Figure 7. Negative Context
A nonverbal message, here a gesture and speaker's appearance, may constitute an overwriting, negative context. Beliefs resulting from the interpretation of the same utterance may be mutually contradictory, here Bill's and Ted's.

derived from: *Paul's wife works hard, he told them. This is absolutely not true* is analogous to computing the effect of the nonverbal, implicit and explicit negative contexts discussed earlier.

Arbitrary Overwriting

Both implicit and explicit context may arbitrarily overwrite meaning of natural language, as in the following fragment of Agatha Christie's novel:

> Good old Edmundson. Since all telephones in Ramat had been tapped, Bob and John Edmundson had worked out a little code of their own. A wonderful girl who was "out of this world" meant something urgent and important.

Segments of Discourse Structure as Positive Context

In an earlier paper (Iwańska 1997a), I identified a new type of nonlinear discourse structure very common in English texts and presented a heuristics-based algorithm for computing this structure in large corpora of texts. This structure reflects nonlinear presentation of knowledge in the texts. I observed that the similarities among reported entities and their general characteristics are frequently stated in a separate, multi-sentence, multi-paragraph segment of text, with subsequent segments providing further details about these entities and discussed their unique characteristics. Such nonlinearity is representationally and informationally advantageous because it allows one to create smaller, more compact, knowledge-loaded texts. The segment with similarities and generalities acts as context relative to which subsequent portions of text must be interpreted. The nature of the properties stated up front decides the computational mechanics of these contexts. For distributive properties, such contexts are positive, knowledge adding contexts.

Contexts for Abbreviations, Anaphors

I investigate abbreviations in English, German, and Russian. Abbreviations are universally extremely common[7] because they convey the same amount of information in shorter utterances—another confirmation of the "in natural language, short is beautiful" hypothesis. Implicitly or explicitly full phrases serve as positive context for the abbreviated form.

Processing abbreviations (generation, recognition) is very similar to processing anaphoric expressions. Like definite anaphora, abbreviations can refer to the entities explicitly present in the utterance or to the implicit, assumed to be known entities; *the president* may refer to any explicit or implicit entity whose type is consistent with the type president; similarly, the abbreviation *ACL* may refer to any explicit or implicit phrase with a sequence of three characters *A, C,* and *L; ACL* can (and does) refer to *Association for Computational Linguistics,* and to *Allegro Common Lisp.*

Uniform analysis often renders simpler, smaller code. My weak-method algorithm for computing definite anaphora is very similar to processing abbreviations, the primary difference being the type consistency check. *USA* may refer to any arbitrary phrase as long as this phrase contains a sequence of three characters "u," "s," and "a"; USA may refer to the entity *United States of America,* or to the entity *Unser seliger Adolf,* German for "Our blessed Adolf."

Overwriting Via Interpretation Shifts

In natural language, logical contradiction and logical redundancy play central roles. They allow one to identify and signal knowledge gaps and false beliefs and to systematically convey nonliteral meanings. I have identified a number of systematic alterations of literal meaning of natural language sentences containing logical redundancy and contradiction. The logical redundancy of the expression *John and John* in the sentence *John and John made it happen* conveys information that two distinct individuals named John are referred to. Grading binary properties blocks extensional logical inference and shifts nonliteral meaning to intensional. For example, the sentence *She is very American* does not entail that *She is American* and conveys information that *She* possesses many characteristics typical to individuals characterized as *American*.

Logical contradiction is also exploited to convey nonliteral meaning. This fragment from Jim Aikin's novel *The Wall at the Edge of the World* has a logical contradiction of the form *X is not X:*

> Sunrise was not sunrise, only a dull and ragged reddening, streaked and clotted with yellow and silver, that leaked out beneath the gray.

This contradiction is exploited to convey similarity between the newly observed phenomenon and known concept of a *sunrise.*

Context as Focus: Intensional Negative Adjectives—Context-Dependent Type Builders

Context as focus resulting in less precise, computationally cheaper to handle type definitions has emerged from my research of intensional negative adjectives *alleged, artificial, fake, false, former,* and *toy* (Iwańska 1997a). Many contexts involving such adjectives are negative. I analyze and formalize intensional negative adjectivals as new concept (type) builders, negationlike functions that operate on the values of intensional properties of the concepts denoted by their arguments and yield new concepts whose intensional properties have values consistent with the negation of the old values. Such on-the-fly, type-building functions are representationally desirable because they largely eliminate the need to store context-dependent types permanently, reducing the size of one's knowledge base. These functions fill-in a gap between regular adjectives and negation—they describe a relation between two types that is somewhere between *very similar* reflected by the entailment induced by regular, always restricting adjectives and *very different* reflected by the complement induced by negation. My theory allows one to enhance knowledge representation systems with such unique to natural language functions.

Definition 7 (Intensional Property)
Let *Noun* be a common noun, C_{Noun} a concept denoted by it, $[\![C_{Noun}]\!]$ a set of entities in the extensional denotation of C_{Noun}, $\mathcal{D}_{C_{Noun}}$ an intensional definition of the concept C_{Noun},

a set of conditions of the $[\![C_{Noun}]\!]$ membership.
Then an element $V_p \in \mathcal{D}_{C_{Noun}}$ is a value of an intensional property P
of the concept C_{Noun},
V is a partial function mapping an intensional property of a concept to its
value
$$V : C_{Noun} \times P \rightarrow V_P,$$
where $V_P \in R_P$, R_P is a range of the property P, and $P_{C_{Noun}} = \{ P \mid V_P \in \mathcal{D}_{C_{Noun}} \}$
are intensional properties of the concept C_{Noun}.

The intensional definition of a concept characterizes its current and future instances.[8] An intensional property is a dimension of information in
such definitions. Simple properties are like attributes (slots) in the frame-
based knowledge representation languages (Brachman, Fikes, and
Levesque 1985; Schmolze 1989). These dimensions include those aspects
of information that can be named, such as *size,* and those infinite, unnamed aspects of information described by arbitrary multi-sentence natural language utterances. For example, *never wanting to work hard or
commit to anything* is an unnamed, one-sentence property.

Properties can be binary and multi-valued; the property of *never
wanting to work hard or commit to anything* is binary; the color property takes a range of values (colors) such as blue or red. Values can be numeric and qualitative, for example, the size property can have 2 *feet* or
neither short nor very tall as its value. The number of possible values
may be finite or infinite.

I allow the definitions to be infinite because there does not seem to be
any constraint on their size:[9] when defining a concept, one may provide
a short, one-sentence description or a long, multi-volume one. The
length of a definition interacts with its precision. Roughly, the more one
knows about a concept, the more precise definition becomes and the fewer unwanted or unintended interpretations it admits.

Definition 8 (Context)
Context $\mathcal{C}$ is a partial function $\mathcal{C}: 2^{\mathcal{P}} \rightarrow 2^{\mathcal{P}}$ such that if $\mathcal{P}_1$ and $\mathcal{P}_2$ are sets
of properties and $\mathcal{C}(\mathcal{P}_1) = \mathcal{P}_2$, then:
1. $\mathcal{P}_2$ is finite
2. $\exists P, P \in \mathcal{P}_1, P \in \mathcal{P}_2$

Context focuses on a finite number of properties, deeming the rest irrelevant. The first condition states that context may pick up a subset of
some properties or introduce some additional properties for a consideration. Context cannot, however, disregard all the properties: the second
condition states that at least one property must be preserved.

Definition 9 (Context-Relevant Intensional Property)
Let U be an utterance, $\mathcal{C}$ its context, and C a concept referred to in U.
$\mathcal{P}_C^{\mathcal{C}} = \mathcal{P}_C \cap \mathcal{C} (\mathcal{P}_{\mathcal{C}})$ are $\mathcal{C}$ context-relevant intensional properties of the concept C.

Context-relevant intensional properties of a concept is a finite subset of its intensional properties as defined by the context of an utterance. Context trims down concept intensional definitions and has the effect of directing and restricting inference because context-irrelevant properties and their values are never reasoned about.

Definition 10 (Inherent Intensional Property)
Let $Adjective_{IN}$ be the set of intensional negative adjectives defined extensionally

$Adjective_{IN}$ = { alleged, artificial, fake, false, former, toy },
$Adj_{IN} \in Adjective_{IN}$ be an intensional negative adjective.
Then adjective-inherent intensional properties $P_{Adj_{IN}}$ is a finite set of intensional properties P_i such that for every common noun $Noun$

1. If $P_i \in P_{C_{Noun}}$ then $P_i \in P_{C_{Adj_{IN} Noun}}$
2. $V(C_{Adj_{IN} Noun}, P_i) \neq V(C_{Noun}, P_i)$
3. $V(C_{Adj_{IN} Noun}, P_i) \sqcap (\ not\ V(C_{Noun}, P_i)) \neq \perp$

Inherent intensional property formally captures the fact that some intensional negative adjectives are specialized functions that affect particular properties, regardless of the concept represented by the common noun they modify. The first condition states that the dimension of information represented by an inherent intensional property is preserved in the definition of the new concept. The second condition states that the values of the inherent intensional property in the new and the old concept are different. The third condition further characterizes this difference as consistency of the new value with the negation of the old value.

Definition 11. (Semantics of Intensional Negative Adjectives)
Let C_{Noun} be a concept denoted by some common noun $Noun$,
$\mathscr{P}C_{Noun}$ its intensional properties, and Adj_{IN} an intensional negative adjective.
Then $Adj_{IN} : \mathscr{D}_{Noun} \to \mathscr{D}_{Adj_{IN} Noun}$ is a function such that
1. $\forall P \in \mathscr{P}_{C_{Noun}}, P \in \mathscr{P}_{C_{Adj_{IN} Noun}}$
2. $\forall P_i \in \mathscr{P}_{Adj_{IN}}, V(C_{Adj_{IN} Noun}, P_i) \sqcap (not\ V(C_{Noun}, P_i)) \neq \perp$
3. $\exists P_j \in \mathscr{P}_{C_{Noun}}, V(C_{Adj_{IN} Noun}, P_j) \sqcap (not\ V(C_{Noun}, P_j)) \neq \perp$
4. $\exists P_k \in \mathscr{P}_{C_{Noun}}, V(C_{Adj_{IN} Noun}, P_k) = V(C_{Noun}, P_k)$
5. If $\exists P_j \in \mathscr{P}_{C_{Noun}}$ such that its value is not specified, i.e., P_j can take any value from R_{P_j}, then if P_j is affected by Adj_{IN}, then $V(C_{Adj_{IN} Noun}, P_j) = V_{Adj_{IN}}$, where the value $V_{Adj_{IN}}$ depends on Adj_{IN}.

Intensional negative adjectives are type builders The first condition says that preserving dimensions of information for the new type from the old type. All the characteristics of a *real elephant*—number of legs, having a snout, hairs, etc.—also apply to a *toy elephant*. The second and third conditions state that they affect values of some properties and that these new values are consistent with the negation of the old values. A *toy elephant* may not have any hair. Adjective-inherent properties are always negatively affected. The combination of the second and third conditions allows for some other than adjective-inherent properties to also be negatively affected. For example, *having a snout* is not an inherent property of the adjective *toy*. This is evidenced by the concept *toy car* for which this property is not applicable. Yet a *toy elephant* may have *an inflexible snout*. The fourth condition states that not all the properties in the new concept will have their values negatively affected, and that some of the properties will have the same value in both new and old concepts. This captures the intuition that the new and the old concept always have something in common. Intensional negative adjectives are like general negation, but weaker. The fifth condition states that in case of underspecified properties, those whose original values can take any value from the possible range, their new values may be predetermined by the intensional negative adjective.

Definition 12 (Context-Dependent Concept Interpretation)
Let C be a concept referred to in some utterance U in the context $\mathscr{C}$, $P_\mathscr{C}$ intensional properties of the concept C, Adj_{IN} an intensional negative adjective with inherent intensional properties $\mathscr{P}_{Adj_{IN}}$. Then in the context $\mathscr{C}$, C denotes a concept whose contextual definition $D_C^\mathscr{C}$ consists only of the context-relevant intensional properties $\mathscr{P}_C^\mathscr{C}$ of the concept C.

If C is a concept derived via some intensional negative adjective Adj_{IN}, then its $\mathscr{C}$ contextual definition $D_C^\mathscr{C}$ additionally involves adjective-inherent intensional properties $\mathscr{P}_{Adj_{IN}}$.

Concepts are always interpreted in some context whose main role is to focus on a finite number of their properties. Context allows one to finitely consider, in principle, infinite-type definitions. This captures the intuition that for considering a concept with a particular purpose in mind, one does not need all the available knowledge about this concept but, instead, one needs only some parts of this knowledge. Volumes and volumes have been written about elephants, yet a few-paragraph description of an elephant may be sufficient for carrying out a reasonable discussion. Such context-dependency means disregarding certain aspects of knowledge about concepts. The resulting concept definitions are shorter and strictly subsumed by their full definitions. Focused on particular properties, definitions are less precise and therefore computationally cheaper to handle and cover extentionally larger sets. Less precision means less computational effort needed to handle them. The above definition of a context-dependent concept interpretation applies to all concepts, those derived via intensional negative adjectives such as *toy car* and those that aren't such as *car*. Such context-dependent concept interpretation also allows one to capture the fact that, if needed, the differences among concepts can be disregarded. If one wants a *pet* and has no preferences for *dogs* or *cats,* then a *dog* is equally desirable as a *cat*. Similarly, in the context in which the only thing that matters about *diamonds* is pleasing one's eye, an *imitation diamond* is as good as (indistinguishable from) a *real diamond*.

Context-dependent concept interpretation often results in nonmonotonic information processing. In some contexts, arbitrarily different concepts may appear arbitrarily similar. Note, however, that while consistent concepts may appear different in particular contexts, they always remain consistent with each other. Context may eliminate the differences, but it does not introduce new differences.

Definition 13 (Pragmatics of Intensional Negative Adjectives)
Let $\mathscr{C}$ be some context,
C_1 and C_2 two concepts with $\mathscr{C}$ context-relevant intensional properties P_{C_1} and P_{C_2} respectively.
Then $M_S(C_1, C_2)$ is a contextual similarity between concepts C_1 and C_2:
$M_S(C_1, C_2) = N_c / N_a$,
where
$N_c = |\{ P: P \in P_{C_1}, P \in P_{C_2}, V(C_1, P) \sqcap V(C_2, P) \neq \perp \}|$
$N_a = |\{ P: P \in \mathscr{P}_{C_1}, P \in \mathscr{P}_{C_2} \}|$.

This concept similarity metric is a ratio of the number of intensional properties whose values in both contextual concept definitions are consistent with each other and the total number of the intensional properties present in both contextual concept definitions. $M_S(C_1, C_2) = 1$ and $M_S(C_1, C_2) = 0$ indicate that in the context $\mathscr{C}$, the concepts C_1 and C_2 are extremely similar and extremely dissimilar respectively. This metric applies to any concepts, not only the ones created via intensional adjectivals, for example, it can be used to assess the similarity of the concepts of dog and cat. This formalization allows one to account for the fact that in certain contexts, two different concepts may appear indistinguishable because their similarity is computed with respect to the context-relevant properties only.

In the subsequent definitions, let U be a natural language utterance, $\mathscr{C}$ its context, C a concept denoted by *Noun*, Adj_{IN} an intensional negative adjective, *New* a concept denoted by Adj_{IN} *Noun*, and I an entity characterized by the expression Adj_{IN} *Noun*.

Definition 14 (Special Characteristics of Function "Alleged")
Alleged is a function such that
1. Its inherent intensional properties $\mathscr{P}_{Adj_{IN}} = \{$ probability $\}$; the range of the "probability" property is R_p.
2. It induces
   (a) A context-dependent value $p_C \in R_p$, a probability of I being of the type C,
   (b) A context-dependent distribution function $\mathscr{F}: P \times p_C \to (p_p, V_p)$, where

$p_p \in R_p$ is a probability of the individual I having a property $P \in P_C$ with the value V_p.

Pragmatically, an expression *alleged Noun* attributed to some individual I conveys the information that somebody said, wrote, implied or otherwise expressed an opinion that the individual I possesses a property *Noun*; in other words, *John, an alleged murderer* expresses somebody's opinion that John is a murderer. Pragmatic acts involving *alleged* signal the uncertainty about an individual I characterized by the expression *alleged Noun* possessing properties with value s characteristic to the type *Noun*. It is a metaproperty function because all properties can be characterized by the probability. This function imposes no inherent value. Probability values can be real numbers from the interval [0, 1]; or qualitative values that do not require any numbers: lexically simple such as "possible," lexically complex such as "very, very uncertain, but not impossible." The probability p_p characterizes the degree of hearer's belief that the individual I characterized as "alleged X" is indeed of the type "X." The probability distribution function $\mathcal{T}$ characterizes hearer's beliefs about the individual I possessing different intensional properties of the type "X." Such probabilities may be quite different for speaker and hearer. The order of inducing p_C and $\mathcal{T}$ may be different. From a particular $\mathcal{T}$, given or computed, the value p_C may be concluded, and from a particular p_C, again given or computed, a distribution function $\mathcal{T}$ may be derived.

Definition 15 (Critical Intensional Properties)

Let C_1 and C_2 be concepts.

Then the set $\mathcal{P}^{cr}_{C_1} \subseteq \mathcal{P}_{C_1}$, critical intensional properties of the concept C_1, is a finite set of intensional properties $P \in \mathcal{P}_{C_1}$ such that from the fact that

$V(P, C_2) \sqcap (\text{not } V(P, C_1)) \neq \bot$

it can be concluded that the type C_2 is not of the type C_1, i.e.,

$[\![C_2]\!] \cap [\![C_1]\!] = \emptyset$

Particular values of the critical intensional properties of a concept are critical to the concept. Failure to exhibit these critical values allows one to immediately conclude a consistency with the complement relation between the two types.

Definition 16 (Special Characteristics of Function "Fake")

Fake is a function such that:

1. Its inherent intensional properties are $\mathcal{P}_{Adj_{IN}} \subseteq \mathcal{P}^C_{cr}$
2. For most contexts, $M_s(C, New) \gg 0.5$
3. $\exists P, P \in P^{cr}_C \; V(C, P) \neq V(New, P)$

The adjective *fake* negatively affects some properties critical in the original concept. It creates types similar to the original one, but not infinitely similar. The third condition states that at least one critical property of the original concept will not have the required value. This formalization allows one to account for the fact that the expressions *fake Noun* always denote concepts entailing the negation of *Noun,* i.e.,

⟦ fake Noun ⟧ ⊑ ⟦ (not Noun) ⟧

At the same time, except for some properties, including at least one critical property, the new concept may be arbitrarily similar to the original concept.

For example, in my computational framework, the distinction between linguistic and nonlinguistic context somewhat disappears because we represent knowledge and beliefs with the same mechanism as the meaning of natural language utterances. I show one example of how such adjectives are processed. Processing the appositive *JP, a former president of France* results in the following knowledge base:

JP == { < president(of ⇒ france), past>, <not president(of ⇒ france), now> }

The system can correctly answer the following questions:

Q_1: "Is JP the president of France ?"
Q_2: "Is JP the president of KMart ?"

These questions are represented by the following equations to be matched against the above knowledge base:

JP == { president(of ⇒ france) }
JP == { president(of ⇒ kmart) }

Question Q1 is answered with *No, but in the past, he was the president of France* because for the temporal interval *now,* the property in question one and the property in the knowledge base holding of JP are inconsistent, as revealed by the result of the meet operation on the respective properties:

president(of ⇒ france) ⊓ not president(of ⇒ france) = ⊥

and because the property in question 1 is entailed by a property that holds of JP for the temporal interval *past:*

president(of ⇒ france) ⊑ president(of ⇒ france)

Question Q2 is answered with *I don't know* because while the answer yes is consistent with the current knowledge base, it is not entailed by it:

[president(of ⇒ kmart) ⊓ not president(of ⇒ france) =
president(of ⇒ kmart)
⊓
[not president, president(of ⇒ not france)] =
[president(of ⇒ kmart)] ≠ ⊥

Similarly, the above knowledge base (correctly) does not preclude the possibility that, in the future, JP may become the president of France again.

Natural Language for Learning and Knowledge Acquisition

In this section, I will discuss definite noun phrases, knowledge acquisition via easily parsable natural language constructs that convey taxonomic knowledge, the essence of learning, and filling knowledge gaps.

Definite Noun Phrases Facilitate Knowledge Acquisition

Definite noun phrases are natural language constructs that facilitate acquisition of taxonomic knowledge (Iwańska and Kruge 1996). Definite noun phrases start with the determiner *the*. In the following short text, *A dog was found in our backyard. The animal was dirty, but happy"* there is one definite noun phrase: *the dog*. It is a referring definite noun phrase. Its antecedent, *a dog*, is explicit in the text.

A subset of referring definite noun phrases, we call them indirectly referring, constitutes learning opportunities. Computation of the resolvents of the indirectly referring noun phrases is nontrivial. It often involves a multiple-step reasoning process or an assumption of the existing apriori knowledge. For example, understanding the coreference relation between *a dog* and *the animal* may require an apriori knowledge that dogs are animals, i.e., understanding the relation, in this case set/superset relation, between the concepts of dog and animal; understanding the coreference relation between the expressions *CNN's Capital Gang* and *the show* may involve a three-step inference:

1. "CNN is a network."
2. "Networks have shows."
3. "Capital Gang is a show."

I characterize both of these cases as indirectly referring noun phrases.

If one cannot make such a multi-step reasoning connection or if one does not have such an apriori knowledge, then texts containing such indirectly referring definite noun phrases are learning opportunities. One may assume that a text is coherent and on order to support this assumption, one may further assume that it contains unknown relations and decide to learn it. If one does not know that dogs are animals, i.e., if one's knowledge is incomplete with respect to the relation between the type *dog* and the type *animal,* then the reference *the animal* to an individual characterized as *a dog* allows one to acquire this relation.

If one never heard of *Capital Gang*, then the reference *the show* allows one to acquire knowledge that the entity *CNN's Capital Gang* is an instance of the type *show;* one may additionally make a plausible assumption that other entities of the same type as the entity CNN, network, are in some relation with the entities of the type *show.*

Natural Language Construct	Knowledge Type	Examples, Comments
"X and not Y"	Related types	From "red and not green," system acquires the relation between "red" and "green"
"(At least) X if not Y"	Scalar knowledge	From "possible if not certain," system learns that "certain" is a stronger notion than "possible"
"not only X but Y"	Scalar knowledge	From "not only warm but hot," system learns that "hot" is a stronger notion than "warm"
"X— indeed Y"	Scalar knowledge	From "I've seldom— indeed, hardly ever— smoked cigars," system learns that "hardly ever" is a stronger notion than "seldom"
"NOUN, which BE NP"	Definitional knowledge	From "Colds are caused by viruses, which are extremely small infectious substances," system acquires the definition "viruses are extremely small infectious substances"
"X, or Y,"	Definitional knowledge	From "Your child probably will have more colds, or upper respiratory infections, than any other illness" system learns the definition "colds are upper respiratory infections"
"X such as Y1, Y2, ..."	Definitional knowledge	From "With a young baby, symptoms can be misleading, and colds can quickly develop into more serious ailments, such as bronchiolitis, croup, or pneumonia.," system learns that "bronchiolitis, croup, and pneumonia are serious ailments"

Table 4
Easily parsable on a large scale natural language constructs specialized to express different types of knowledge allow the UNO natural-language processing system acquire vast general-purpose knowledge with extremely high degree of precision, without having to fully understand, and therefore parse at the sentence-level, input texts.

If one doesn't know anything about dinosaurs, then when presented with the following text—*A velociraptor was found in our backyard. The dinosaur was dirty, but happy*—is most likely not going to say *this is incoherent;* one is more likely to conclude that one's knowledge is incomplete and that there are things of the types *dinosaur* and *velociraptor* and that there is some, as of yet unknown relationship between the two types.

Knowledge Acquisition Via Easily Parsable Natural Language Constructs Conveying Taxonomic Knowledge

I simulate "learning from clear cases" knowledge acquisition by exploiting simple, efficiently extractable, parsable and interpretable natural language constructs specialized for conveying taxonomic knowledge. They can be extracted with a high degree of precision, which minimizes post-verification. Table 4 gives examples of such constructs that we have iden-

tified and largely tested for two newspapers corpora. The full details of
the approach and the acquisition results can be found in chapter 10.

Learning Hypothesis Space: Representation and Search

The essence of learning is a mechanism of forming and revising hypotheses, searching hypothesis space and dealing with incomplete and partial
knowledge.

Positive and Negative Knowledge

Natural language utterances allow one to represent learned knowledge,
individual facts and generally true facts, that constitutes positive and negative examples. Disjunction allows one to express possible choices or outcomes, negation allows one to rule them out. Negation also allows one to
state exceptions to general rules as well as correct false hypotheses. *Positive knowledge,* knowing what something is, and *negative knowledge,*
knowing what something is not, are both equally important aspects of
knowledge that equally contribute to learning and knowledge gain.

Forming Inductive Hypotheses

Forming inductive hypotheses in natural language is a reverse of understanding literal meaning. Given a sentence that represents a current hypothesis, natural language offers a well-defined, closely syntactically related spectrum of logically stronger, weaker, or inconsistent sentences that
are candidates for inductive hypotheses. These hypotheses represent inductive generalizations or reflect a strategy to deal with incomplete knowledge. The fact that the candidates for a new hypothesis are closely syntactically related to the current hypothesis has two consequences critical for a
successful learning and computational tractability.

First, the hypothesis space is greatly reduced because only certain syntactically linked natural language sentences are considered; and second,
the hypothesis change is easily computed—if the new hypothesis should
not invalidate the current one, then a logically stronger sentence is considered, otherwise a logically weaker sentence consistent with negation of the
current hypothesis is used.

Natural language offers the following to revise a current hypothesis:

- *Replace a weaker scalar with a stronger one.* For example, from the
  hypothesis *Some swans are white* to the hypothesis *Many swans are
  white* or *All swans are white.* Or, from the hypothesis *He is not very
  bright* to the hypothesis *He is stupid.*
- *Drop some disjuncts.* For example, from the hypothesis *John or Mary
  or Mark did it* to the hypothesis *John did it,* or from the hypothesis *He*

sings or dances well to the hypothesis *He dances well.* Or from the hypothesis *Very many or all participated* to the hypothesis *Very many participated.*

■ *Negate current hypothesis.* For example, from the hypothesis *She works very hard* to the hypothesis *She doesn't work very hard* or to the hypothesis *She works, but not very hard.* Or, from the hypothesis *Every swan is white* to the hypothesis *Not every swan is white.*

■ *Replace complex expression with a logically stronger shorter expression.* For example, from the hypothesis *John was late yesterday and three times last year* to the hypothesis *John is always late.* Or, from the hypothesis *She likes roses and peonies* to the hypothesis *She likes flowers.*

The Boolean UNO operations and the capability of computing a number of semantic relations allow the UNO natural language processing system to generate such spectra of hypotheses from a given natural language sentence.

Filling Knowledge Gaps

Some aspects of the nonliteral, context-dependent meaning of natural language appear to reflect certain strategies to cope within complete knowledge. The mechanics of the quantity-based implicature (Horn 1989) can be viewed as a natural language version of *negation as failure* (Clark 1978), the most celebrated case of default reasoning (Reiter 1985) This type of default reasoning represents the strategy of relying heavily on one's existing knowledge when filling knowledge gaps *If I don't know it, it must be false.*

Quantity-based implicature can be viewed as context-reduced underspecificity due to knowledge of a particular strategy of overcoming the lack of knowledge. This context-dependent inference involves a well-defined syntactically and semantically, easily computable space of defaults. The mechanics of this type of implicature is providing the underspecified boundary for lexically simple scalars via explicit negation. If one knows that *some swans are white* then following the strategy of negation as failure, one assumes that *not all swans are white.*

Natural language allows one to express it concisely as a conjunction at the appropriate syntactic level, here at the level of the determiner in the subject noun phrase *some, but not all, swans are white.* This new sentence represents both the original sentence and the implied sentence.

Conclusion

I have discussed my conjecture that natural language is a particularly attractive knowledge representation system for representing and reasoning with knowledge in not well formalized domains. I have also presented the UNO model of natural language that closely simulates the unique representational and inferential characteristics of natural language and allows one to acquire and use knowledge from large-scale corpora of textual documents. My conjecture, combined with the mature model, shed some light on the puzzling question about the computational nature of natural language. I believe that my research results demonstrate that the currently dominant but unsupported opinion that natural language is just an interface is incorrect.

I have shown that the computational mechanisms of understanding meaning of natural language and the mechanisms for knowledge acquisition and use from texts appear to be essentially the same. Meaning of a natural language utterance is inseparable from the easily computable inference that reveals the implications of the knowledge expressed by the utterance. However, I must stress that much more work needs to be done, particularly in the area of accounting for the general context-dependency of natural language, in order to fully substantiate my conjecture.

Notes

1. The UNO representation as presented in some of the earlier publications had the following form: $type \Rightarrow \{P_1, P_2, ..., P_n\}$ because at that time, I did not account for the temporal or probabilistic aspects; I used $\Rightarrow$, and now the $=='$ sign, because knowledge bases were used in a single direction only.

2. Only lexically simple scalars and their negations can be illustrated by such a picture.

3. Viewing context-dependency of natural language as a problem is common in the natural language processing and knowledge representation communities.

4. The other types of underspecificity of the sentence "John doesn't walk" persist; one such type corresponds to the question "So what does John do?"

5. Their recourse may be to make correct guesses.

6. That it is, of course, if he decides that it is important to remember what she said.

7. I observed, though, that abbreviations seem to be much more common in texts than in dialogs.

8. I am only concerned with the characteristics that can be described in natural language.

9. Except, perhaps, the duration of human life.

2 Natural Language Syntax and First-Order Inference

David McAllester and Robert Givan

THIS CHAPTER PRESENTS A NEW POLYNOMIAL TIME procedure for automated inference. Although no polynomial time procedure can be complete for first order logic, polynomial time inference procedures can often be used as powerful subroutines in general purpose reasoning systems (Constable 1982), (Nelson 1979), (McAllester 1989). The procedure presented here is a significant strengthening of the procedure presented in (McAllester and Givan 1989), which is in turn a significant strengthening of the well known procedure for congruence closure (Kozen 1977), (Downey 1980).

Both the procedure presented here and the one presented in (McAllester and Givan 1989a) are defined by inference rules written in a nonstandard syntax for first order logic. Nonstandard syntax is essential to both the specification and to the implementation of these procedures. The procedure given in McAllester and Givan (1989a) uses a syntax based on taxonomic relations between expressions that denote sets. This procedure can be viewed as an extension of earlier work on knowledge representation languages, for example Bobrow (1977), Fahlman (1979), Brachman (1982), (Brachman 1983). Knowledge representation languages have traditionally been organized around taxonomic relationships between classes. AI researchers often express the intuition that such taxonomic representations facilitate inference. The technical results in McAllester and Givan (1989a) support this intuition. The relationship between the work described here and previous work on knowledge representation languages is discussed in more detail later.

The inference procedure presented here is based on a new nonstandard syntax for first order logic which we call a *Montagovian syntax*. This syntax is based on aspects of natural language syntax under compositional semantics (Adjukiewicz 1935), (Lambek 1958), (Montague 1970a), (Montague 1970b), (Bach,1988). In particular, our Montagovian syntax is centered around *class expressions*, i.e., expressions that denote sets. In the earlier taxonomic syntax we allowed for class symbols, such as the symbol a-person, and class expressions such as (brother-of a-person). The expression (brother-of a-person) denotes the set of all individuals that are the brother of some person. In general, any monadic predicate symbol of classical syntax can be used as a class expression, and for any binary relation R, and class expression s, one can construct the class expression $(R\ s)$ which denotes the set of individuals which are related under R to an element of s. In the new Montagovian syntax we write the class expression $(R\ s)$ as $(R\ (\text{some } s))$ and we allow the construction of the (different) class expression $(R\ (\text{every } s))$. For example, if *loves* is a binary relation symbol, and *person* is a class symbol, then we have the class expressions (loves (some person)) and (loves (every person)).

The former class expression denotes the set of all individuals that love some person while the latter class expression denotes the set of all individuals that love all people. This expansion of the vocabulary of class expressions results in an inference procedure that is, in most respects, more powerful than the one based on taxonomic syntax given in McAllester and Givan (1989a) A precise specification of the syntax and semantics of our Montagovian version of first order logic is presented later in this chapter.

This chapter is intended to provide technical support for two somewhat informal claims: First, the efficiency of inference is sensitive to the syntax used to express statements. Second, natural language is a source of inferentially powerful syntax.

This chapter makes no contribution to the traditional study of the syntax or semantics of natural language. We do not provide any new theory for predicting which strings of words are grammatical natural language sentences (the traditional study of syntax). Nor do we provide any new theory for assigning meaning to natural language utterances (the traditional study of semantics). There is a large literature on these topics with theories far more sophisticated than the ones used here. This chapter addresses a different topic, the relationship between natural language syntax and efficient inference techniques. In studying the relation between syntax and inference we have focused on only the most fundamental properties of natural language.

A Montagovian Syntax for First Order Logic

Our Montagovian syntax is a syntactic variant of first order predicate calculus—every Montagovian formula can be translated to a classical formula, and every classical formula can be translated to a Montagovian formula. However, the quantifier-free fragment of Montagovian syntax is more expressive than the quantifier-free fragment of either classical syntax or our earlier taxonomic syntax. In spite of increased expressive power, the quantifier-free fragment of Montagovian syntax retains most of the nice computational properties of the quantifier-free fragment of classical syntax.

Classical syntax involves terms and formulas. In both taxonomic and Montagovian syntax terms are replaced by class expressions where each class expression denotes a set. The syntax of our Montagovian language is defined as follows.

A class expression is one of the following.

- A variable or constant symbol.
- A monadic predicate symbol.
- An expression of the form (R (some s)) or (R (every s)) where R is a binary relation symbol and s is a class expression.
- An expression of the form ($\lambda x\ \Phi(x)$) where x is a variable and $\Phi(x)$ is a formula.

A formula is one of the following.

- An expression of the form (every s w) or (some s w) where s and w are class expressions. Expressions of this type are called *atomic formulas*.
- A Boolean combination of formulas. Atomic formulas and negations of atomic formulas are called *literals*.

Before giving a formal semantics, it is useful to consider some examples of formulas and their associated meanings. If P and Q are class symbols then (every P Q) is a formula which is true if the set denoted by P is a subset of the set denoted by Q. If man is a class symbol that denotes the set of all men, and runs is a class symbol that denotes the set of all things that run, then the formula (every man runs) is true if every man runs. The formula (some man runs) is true if some man runs.

Constant symbols and variables are taken to denote singleton sets. If John is a constant symbol (or variable) then the formulas (every John runs) and (some John runs) are semantically equivalent and we can use (John runs) as an abbreviation for either formula. Similarly, we write (likes John) as an abbreviation for either of the class expressions (likes (every John)) or (likes (some John)).

If owns is a relation symbol, and denotes the predicate which is true of two objects if the first owns the second, then the class expression (owns (some car)) denotes the set of individuals that own some car. If policeman is a class symbol that denotes the set of all policemen, then the formula (every policeman (owns (some car))) is true if every policeman owns a car.

Unlike Montague, we make no distinction between nouns and verbs. As a result, there are formulas of our Montagovian syntax that do not correspond to grammatical sentences. For example, consider the formulas (every dog mammal) and (every (loves John) (loves Mary)).

The formal semantics for our Montagovian syntax is a (drastic) simplification of Montague's original semantics for English. Just as in classical syntax, a model of our Montagovian language is a first order model, i.e., a domain D together with an interpretation of constant, class, and relation symbols. Any binary relation R can be transformed to a function R' from elements to sets such that y is an element of $R'(x)$ if only if the pair (y, x) is in the relation R. We adopt a superficial modification of the definition of a first order structure so that a binary relation symbol denotes a function from elements to sets rather than a relation. Under our definition, a first order model interprets each constant symbol as an element of its domain, each class symbol as a subset of its domain, and each relation symbol as a function from domain elements to subsets of the domain. If the interpretation of a relation symbol R is clear from context, we will often write $R(d)$ to denote the set that is the result of applying (the value of) R to the domain element d.

If $\mathcal{M}$ is a first order model, and P is a variable interpretation over $\mathcal{M}$, i.e., a mapping from variables to elements of the domain of $\mathcal{M}$, then we write $\mathcal{V}(e, \mathcal{M}, \rho)$ for the semantic value of the expression e in the model under variable interpretation P. If s is a class expression then $\mathcal{V}(s, \mathcal{M}, \rho)$ is a subset of the domain of $\mathcal{M}$. If Φ is a formula, then $\mathcal{V}(\Phi, \mathcal{M}, \rho)$ is a truth value, either **T** or **F**. The semantic evaluation function $\mathcal{V}$ is defined by structural induction on expressions as follows.

- If P is a class symbol then $\mathcal{V}(P, \mathcal{M}, \rho)$ is the set $\mathcal{M}(P)$.
- If c is a constant then $\mathcal{V}(c, \mathcal{M}, \rho)$ is the singleton set $\{\mathcal{M}(c)\}$.
- If x is a variable then $\mathcal{V}(x, \mathcal{M}, \rho)$ is the singleton set $\{\rho(x)\}$.
- $\mathcal{V}((R \text{ (every } s)), \mathcal{M}, \rho)$ is the set of all d such that, for every d' in $\mathcal{V}(s, \mathcal{M}, \rho)$, d is an element of $R(d')$. (Consider the class expression (loves (every child)).)
- $\mathcal{V}((R \text{ (some } s)), \mathcal{M}, \rho)$ is the set of all d such that there exists an element d' in $\mathcal{V}(s, \mathcal{M}, \rho)$ such that d is in the set $R(d')$. (Consider the class expression (loves (some child)).)
- $\mathcal{V}((\lambda x \ \Phi(x)), \mathcal{M}, \rho)$ is the set of all d such that $\mathcal{V}(\Phi(x), \mathcal{M}, \rho[x := d])$ is **T** where $\rho[x := d]$ is the same as ρ except that it interprets x as d.
- $\mathcal{V}((\text{every } s \ t), \mathcal{M}, \rho)$ is **T** if $\mathcal{V}(s, \mathcal{M}, \rho)$ is a subset of $\mathcal{V}(t, \mathcal{M}, \rho)$.
- $\mathcal{V}((\text{some } s \ t), \mathcal{M}, \rho)$ is **T** if $\mathcal{V}(s, \mathcal{M}, \rho)$ has a nonempty intersection with $\mathcal{V}(t, \mathcal{M}, \rho)$.
- Boolean combinations of atomic formulas have their standard meaning.

Although explicit quantification has not been allowed in formulas, the language is rich enough to express quantified formulas. Let THING be an abbreviation for the class expression $(\lambda x \; (\text{every } x \; x))$. Note that in any first order model THING denotes the universal set, i.e., the entire domain of the model. The formula $\forall x \; \Phi(x)$ can be taken to be an abbreviation for (every thing $(\lambda x \; \Phi(x))$). Similarly, the formula $\exists x \; \Phi(x)$ can be treated as an abbreviation for (some thing $(\lambda x \; \Phi(x))$). It is fairly easy to show that any formula in our Montagovian language can be faithfully translated into classical first order logic, and that any formula of classical first order logic can be faithfully translated into our Montagovian language.

Montague gives an independent semantic value to noun phrases such as (some person) and (every person) where these expressions denote functions from sets to truth values. A formula such as (every s w) can then be analyzed as ((every s) w), i.e., the function (every s) applied to the argument w. Montague also gives a compositional meaning to class expressions of the form $(R$ (every s)) in terms of the independent meaning of the expression (every s). Although we have no particular objection to Montague's analysis, we have decided to simplify the exposition of our semantics by avoiding any independent meaning for expressions of the form (every s).

Literal Satisfiability

Since Montagovian syntax is expressively equivalent to full first order logic, it is impossible to construct a procedure which can always determine whether a given formula is satisfiable. However, it is possible to define a fragment of the language for which satisfiability is polynomial time decidable. In constructing a decision procedure we consider only "quantifier-free" formulas. A formula of Montagovian syntax is called quantifier-free if it does not contain any λ-classes. For example, the formula (every woman (likes (some man))) is considered to be quantifier free, while the formula (every man $(\lambda x \; (x \; (\text{likes } x))))$ involves a λ-class and is therefore not considered to be quantifier-free. The quantifier-free fragment of the language has no bound variables and a purely compositional semantics. We view bound variables and noncompositional semantics as the essence of quantification. This notion of quantifier-freeness is motivated, at least in part, by an analogy between the quantifier-free fragment of our Montagovian syntax and the quantifier-free fragment of classical first order logic. The decision procedure for the quantifier-free Montagovian syntax is similar to the decision procedure for the quantifier-free fragment of classical syntax.

The quantifier-free fragment of our Montagovian language roughly corresponds to simple subject-verb-object sentences. For example,

(every dog (ate (some bone)))

or

(every (child-of Sally)
       (married (some (child-of John))))).

Sentences that involve traces or anaphora can usually not be expressed in the quantifier-free fragment of our Montagovian language. For example, the sentence "every man likes himself" involves the anaphora *himself*. Translating this into a Montagovian formula introduces a quantifier—

(every man (λx (x (likes x))))).

As another example, consider the sentence "Mary read some book John bought." Most linguists would agree that the word *bought* in this sentence has an invisible argument called a trace. The following translation of this sentence into a Montagovian formula involves a quantifier.[1]

(Mary (read (some (λx (x book) (John (bought x)))))))

It is difficult to precisely characterize the expressive power of the quantifier-free fragment of Montagovian syntax. The quantifier-free Montagovian formula (every dog (likes (every person))) cannot be expressed in either the quantifier-free fragments of classical or taxonomic syntax.[2] However, because classical and taxonomic syntax allow function symbols and predicates of more than two arguments, the quantifier-free fragments of these languages can express statements that are not expressible in quantifier free Montagovian syntax. If we restrict classical and taxonomic syntax to constant symbols and predicates of no more than two arguments, then quantifier-free Montagovian syntax is strictly more expressive than quantifier-free classical or taxonomic syntax. It seems likely that the basic results of this section can be extended to handle function symbols and predicates of more than two arguments, although the proofs of theorems analogous to those given here are likely to be much more complex.[3] The quantifier-free fragment of Montagovian syntax is expressively incomparable with previously studied knowledge representation languages such as those discussed in a later section.

Although satisfiability is undecidable for unrestricted first order formulas, satisfiability is decidable for quantifier-free Montagovian syntax. Since the quantifier free fragment of Montagovian syntax includes arbitrary Boolean formulas, determining satisfiability is NP-hard and we can not expect to find a polynomial time decision procedure. A more tractable problem is the *literal satisfiability problem*. This is the problem of determining if a given set of literals[4] is satisfiable. In classical syntax, and in taxonomic syntax, the literal satisfiability problems are polynomial time decidable. In Montagovian syntax the literal satisfiability problem is NP-complete. A proof of the NP-hardness of the literal satisfiability problem for Montagovian syntax is given in McAllester (1992). The NP hardness of the Montagovian literal satisfiability problem arises from the fact that, for a given class expression appearing in the input, we may not know whether or not that expression denotes the empty set. If, for each class expression, we know whether or not that expression denotes the empty set then the literal satisfiability problem becomes polynomial time decidable.

To simplify the presentation of the remainder of this chapter we use the notation $\exists s$ where s is a class expression as an abbreviation for the formula (some s s). Formulas of the form $\exists s$ express the statement that there exist elements of the set denoted by s, i.e., s does not denote the empty set.

Definition
We say that a set of formulas Σ *determines existentials* if, for every class expression s that appears in any formula in Σ, Σ contains either the formula $\exists s$ or the formula $\neg \exists s$.

Montagovian Literal Satisfiability Theorem
The satisfiability of a set of quantifier-free Montagovian literals that determines existentials is polynomial time decidable.

The above theorem implies that one can determine whether an arbitrary set Σ of quantifier-free Montagovian literals is satisfiable by searching for a superset of Σ that determines existentials and is satisfiable. If there are n class expressions in then there are at most 2^n extensions of that need to be searched. This also implies that the satisfiability problem for quantifier-free Montagovian formulas is in the complexity class NP—a quantifier free formula Φ is satisfiable if and only if there exists a truth assignment to the atomic formulas in Φ, and a truth assignment to existential statements about the class expressions in Φ, such that the truth assignment is satisfiable according to the above procedure and satisfies the Boolean part of Φ.

The Decision Procedure

We start by transforming the given set of literals Σ into an equi-satisfiable set Σ' which contains no literals of the form (some s t) where s and t are distinct class expressions. We will call such literals *positive intersection literals*. This transformation can be achieved by simply replacing any positive intersection literal (some s t) with the three literals (every w s, every w t and $\exists w$, where w is a new class symbol. Any model of Σ' is also a model of Σ, and any model of Σ yields a model of Σ'. For the remainder of this section we assume that Σ contains no positive intersection literals.

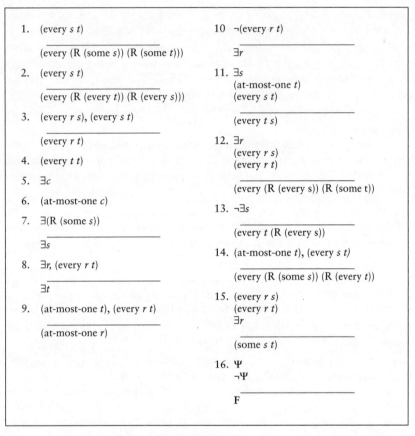

Figure 1. The Inference Rules for Quantifier-Free Literals

In these rules the letters *r*, *s*, and *t* range over class expressions, *c* ranges over constant symbols, and R ranges over relation symbols.

Negative intersection literals, i.e. literals of the form (some *s t*), may still be present.

The literal satisfiability procedure is based on the inference rules given in figure 1. These rules introduce a new formula, (at-most-one *s*) where *s* is a class expression. The formula (at-most-one *s*) is true just in case the set denoted by *s* contains at most one member. Inference rule 15 allows for the derivation of positive intersection formulas—although we can assume that Σ does not contain positive intersection formulas it is convenient to allow such formulas to be inferred. By assuming that Σ does not contain positive intersection formulas we can ensure that whenever we can infer (some *s t*) there exists some expression *w* such that we can infer ∃*w*, (every *w s*), and (every *w t*). We now introduce a restricted inference relation ⊢.

Definition
We write $\Sigma \vdash \Phi$ if Φ can be proven from Σ using the rules in figure 1 such that every class expression appearing in the proof appears in Σ.

The definition of the relation $\vdash$ ensures that to determine whether $\Sigma \vdash \Phi$ we need only consider formulas all of whose class expressions appear in Σ. For a given finite set Σ there are only finitely many class expressions that appear in Σ—the number of class expressions can grow at most linearly in the written length of Σ. The inference rules have the property that they can only be used to infer formulas of the form (every s w), (some s w), or (at-most-one s) (recall that $\exists s$ is actually an abbreviation for [some s s]). If we only consider formulas whose class expressions appear in Σ, then there are at most order $|\Sigma|^2$ such formulas. This implies that by simply enumerating all derivable formulas one can determine, in polynomial time in the size of Σ, determine whether or not $\Sigma \vdash \Phi$.

Satisfiability Completeness Lemma
If Σ is a set of quantifier-free Montagovian literals that determines existentials, then Σ is satisfiable if and only if $\Sigma \vdash F$.

Given that one can determine in polynomial time whether $\Sigma \vdash F$, the above satisfiability completeness lemma immediately implies the Montagovian literal satisfiability theorem of the preceding section. The proof of the above completeness lemma is given in McAllester (1992).

Other Knowledge Representation Languages

Our Montagovian syntax for first order logic is related to a large family of knowledge representation languages known as concept languages or frame-description languages (Schmolze 1985), (Nebel 1988), (Schmidt-Schaub 1991), (Nutt 1991).

Each frame-description language is similar to our Montagovian syntax in that it provides a simple recursive definition of a particular set of class expressions built from constant, predicate, and relation symbols.[5] The class expressions of a particular frame-description language can be considerably different from the class expressions of our Montagovian syntax. For example, all frame-description languages discussed in the knowledge representation literature include intersection operations on class expressions—given any two class expressions s and w the class expression AND(s, w) denotes the intersection of the sets denoted by s and w. A Montagovian syntax that includes a class intersection operation is described in McAllester (1991a).

All languages in the knowledge representation literature also include class expressions of the form $\forall R.C$ where R is a relation symbol and C

is a class expression. An object x is a member of the class expression $\forall R.C$ if, for every y such that the relation R holds between x and y, the individual y is in the set denoted by C. For example, the class expression $\forall$child-of.human denotes the set of all individuals x such that every child of x is human. The statement that every child of a human is human can be expressed as the formula

(every human ($\forall$child-of.human)).

Intuitively, this formula states that every human has the property that every child of that human is human. This same statement can be expressed in our Montagovian syntax (or in our earlier taxonomic syntax) with the formula

(every (child-of (some human)) human).

It is important to note that class expressions of the form $\forall R.C$ are quite different from class expressions of the form (R (every C)). For example, $\forall$loves.human is the class of individuals that love *only* humans, while (loves (every human)) is the class of individuals that love all humans (and possibly other things as well).

Class expressions of the form $\forall R.C$ are not expressible in our Montagovian syntax. In particular, there appears to be no way to express the formula (every ($\forall R.C$) W) in Montagovian syntax. Conversely, there is no way that class expressions of the form $\forall R.C$ can be used to express the class expression (R (some C)). In particular, there appears to be no way of translating the formula (every W (R (some C))) into a formula involving class expressions of the form $\forall R.C$. There does not appear to be any simple relationship between the expressive power of Montagovian syntax and previously studied frame-description languages.

Montagovian Versus Classical Syntax

We have presented a polynomial time inference procedure defined by a set of inference rules stated in a Montagovian syntax for first order logic. These inference rules cannot be stated in classical syntax without resorting to higher order unification. For example, consider inference rule 1.

$$\frac{(every\ s\ t)}{(every\ (R\ (some\ s))\ (R\ (some\ t)))}$$

This inference rule might be written in classical syntax as follows.

$$\frac{\forall x\ P(x) \rightarrow Q(x)}{\forall y\ (\exists x\ P(x) \wedge R(x,\ y)) \rightarrow (\exists x\ Q(x) \wedge R(x,\ y))}$$

Note, however, that to use the rule in classical syntax the predicates P

and Q must be treated as variables that can bind to arbitrary predicates. Theorem provers that instantiate predicate variables have traditionally used higher order unification (Huet 1975). Consider applying the Montagovian version of inference rule 1 to the Montagovian formula

(every (child-of (some bird))
        (friend-of (every bird-watcher))).

This formula states that any child of a bird is a friend of any bird watcher. An application of inference rule 1 allows us to conclude

(every (owner-of (some (child-of (some bird)))))
        (owner-of (some (friend-of
                          (every bird-watcher))))).

This formula says that anyone who owns the child of a bird also owns a friend of every bird watcher. In Montagovian syntax inference rule 1 can be applied using simple (classical) unification to bind the variables s and t of the inference rule to the expressions (child-of (some bird)) and (friend-of (every bird-watcher)) respectively. Now consider the same inference in classical syntax. The premise can be stated as follows.

$\forall x$ ($\exists y$ bird(y) $\wedge$ child-of(y x)) $\rightarrow$
        ($\forall y$ bird-watcher(y) $\rightarrow$ friend-of(y x))

To apply the classical syntax version of the inference rule one must bind the predicate variable P to the λ-predicate

λx $\exists y$ bird(y) $\wedge$ child-of(y x)

and bind Q to the λ-predicate

λx $\forall y$ bird-watcher(y) $\rightarrow$ child-of(y x).

Given this binding of P and Q in the classical syntax rule, the conclusion of the rule must be translated back into classical syntax by β-reducing applications of these λ-predicates. Applying inference rule 1 in classical syntax requires both higher order unification and β-reduction.

The inference procedure described in the previous section has a simple termination condition. Inference is restricted so that all class expressions mentioned by derived formulas must already appear in the input set of literals. This restriction implies that only a finite (polynomial) number of formulas can be derived and hence the inference process must terminate. If the inference rules were expressed in classical rather than Montagovian syntax the termination condition would be much more difficult to state. A similar comparison can be made between classical syntax and other knowledge representation languages such as the frame-description languages discussed earlier.

Conclusions

We have argued that the effectiveness of inference is coupled to the selection of the syntax in which formulas are expressed. If such a coupling does indeed exist then one can speak informally of "effective syntax"—a syntax is effective to the extent that inference processes defined in that syntax can be made effective. Classical syntax appears to be particularly ineffective.

If one accepts the proposition that the effectiveness of inference is coupled to the syntax in which formulas are expressed then it is perhaps not too surprising that natural language is a source of effective syntax. The Montagovian syntax presented here is, of course, only distantly related to the much richer and more complex syntax of actual natural languages. We hope that natural language syntax will continue to be an inspiration for the construction of yet more effective formal languages.

Acknowledgments

This research was supported in part by National Science Foundation Grant IRI-8819624 and in part by the Advanced Research Projects Agency of the Department of Defense under Office of Naval Research contract N00014-85-K-0124 and N00014-89-j-3202. Much of this chapter first appeared in *Artificial Intelligence* 56 (1992): 1–20. It is reprinted here with permission from Elsevier Science.

Notes

1. A more satisfying translation of the second sentence would be an expression of the form (Mary (read (some (book (λx (John (bought x)))))))) where the λ-class is treated as an intersectional adjectival phrase. Unfortunately, our simple Montagovian syntax does not allow for direct intersection of class expressions.

2. The formula (every dog (likes (some person))) can be expressed in quantifier-free taxonomic syntax but not in quantifier-free classical syntax.

3. The use of function symbols in taxonomic syntax greatly increases the complexity of the completeness theorem for the decision procedure for the quantifier-free fragment.

4. As defined above for Montagovian syntax, a literal is either an atomic formula or the negation of an atomic formula where an atomic formula is any formula of the form (every s w) or (some s w).

5. Within the knowledge representation literature a frame-description language is not viewed as an alternative syntax for full first order logic. Rather, the formulas of a frame-description language are restricted to include only subset relations between restricted types of class expressions. These languages are less expressive than full first order logic.

3 Issues in the Representation of Real Texts: The Design of KRISP

David D. McDonald

WHEN A PERSON USES LANGUAGE, there is a relationship between what they hear or say and things[1] in the world. The relationship is not direct, but is mediated by complex mental states and structures—the stuff that is the mental target of the process through which we make sense of what we hear or read, and the source on which we draw as we speak or write. It encompasses a person's knowledge of language and his capacity to communicate given the available words and syntax. It includes a person's semantic conception of the world at large, and his pragmatic appreciation of the particular situation he is in at the time.

Representation

In the cognitive sciences, we typically think of this stuff as consisting of a representation that is acted upon by the processes that are set in motion when we use language. It provides a live model of the person's linguistic capacity, of their conception of the world, of their situation. What this representation consists of in the human mind we do not know. Like the other higher cognitive abilities that people have, it is not accessible to easy experimental manipulation and must be approached indirectly. That the "stuff" even divides neatly into a representation and a set of manipulating processes is only a working hypothesis. All we know for sure is that the knowledge of the language—reality relationship must have some sort of long-term embodiment in the mind and that the nearest thing to that in those entities whose (limited) cognitive abilities we do understand—computers—is a representation.

The most familiar kind of representation to the nontechnical reader is a map. As a representation it indicates to its intended user (a person trying to find out where she is) what is in her world (streets, towns, points of the compass), their properties, and the relationships among them. It has a form (a large sheet of paper with carefully drawn colored lines, shadings, and marks). And it is used in a particular way (trace the lines representing streets with your eyes, read the names indicating towns, etc.). Notably, it also has to be brought into existence (engraved at the printshop), and it has a designer—the person who decides what it should contain, what form it should take, and what level of detail it should include.

Why a New Representation

The thrust of this chapter is to present a new representation of the literal information conveyed by a natural language utterance (which I will refer to from here on as a "text" regardless of whether it is spoken or written). The reader should be suspicious of this. Representational systems (or representation languages) have been studied in artificial intelligence (AI) since the very beginnings of the field forty years ago. Logical systems for formal reasoning date back at least to the work of Frege and the meta-mathematicians that followed him more than a century ago and under some construals back to the ancient Greeks. Reasoning and representation has become a sophisticated field in AI with a rich body of established practice and a dozen or more well characterized systems or methodologies that could be used right off the shelf or easily implemented anew. Why then, given all the options already in existence, should we try to develop yet another one?

If we leave aside the practical issues of access or commercial licensing, the only reasonable answer to this question is that the existing systems are inadequate. A new set of problems has arisen, problems that none of the existing systems were designed to address. This is not to say that they could not be applied to these tasks, and many of them have been, rather that our goal is a well-engineered fitness to the task. Efficiency and explanatory constraints should emerge directly from the structure of the representation rather than stipulated as an after thought or brought about through careful programming.

Areas Addressed

There are three areas where I see problems that must be addressed in research on representations for modeling and manipulating the information in natural language texts. These areas are comprehension of real-world texts, real-time (online) processing speed, and bidirectional representation.

We are long-past the era of working with made-up examples or simple questions. Today we should be studying the comprehension of real texts: texts written by professional writers to be read by people with a serious interest in knowing what they have to say. Similarly, the system should be fast. Formally it should have online time-complexity (i.e. using a limited, constant amount of processing per token), and it should be real-time in the practical sense that it should, for example, be able to read news-wire stories as fast as they come to it over the net. In this the representation should be a plus, not a burden.

A final desideratum, one that is at least as crucial in determining the form of the representation's design as the need for speed, is that the representation of the information that has been comprehended should be the very one from which it later produces (generates) summaries, makes restatements from different perspectives, or translates into other languages. This is the property of a representation being reversible or bidirectional, and it tends to be neglected except for those relatively few places that do research on generation systems. The benefits of having a reversible representation—in the parsimony of stating facts and simple engineering efficiency in moving between the two kinds of language processing—are well known (see, for example, the collection of papers in Strzalkowski 1994), but the examples have been few.

It must also be said at the onset that there is also much that this representation described in this chapter does not do. Its focus, as we shall see, is on what could be called *practical* problems. Its capabilities are weak to nonexistent when it comes to many of the basic issues in representation that concern classical logicians or mathematical linguists.

For example, except for very specialized technical problems in parsing, It has no deductive component. It has no easy way to express a general fact like "all men are mortal." And there is certainly no attempt made to handle the problems that vex linguistic philosophers such as problems inherent in the notorious "donkey sentences" ("If Pedro owns a donkey, he will ride it to town tomorrow"; see Schubert and Pelletier 1989 for an enlightening discussion).

Part of the reason for these lacunae is simply a matter of time and attention: less than one man-year has gone into the development of KRISP (Knowledge Representation In Sparser) to date. But the more substantial reason is that the question of how to even approach issues of deduction and generalization, when applied to the full subtleties of real texts (consider this sentence), remains very much unanswered within the computational linguistics and AI communities. Because I decided long ago that it was no longer going to advance the field to work on small or artificial problems, the complexity of these issues in their real context makes them something I can put on the shelf for another day.

Problems for Representations

Before proceeding to describe the new representation that I have developed—named KRISP—it is important to provide some concrete examples of the problems that prompted its development. In this section, I will look at examples in language comprehension and (informally) at the kinds of representational devices devised in KRISP to deal with them.

First some background. The initial work on KRISP was done in the early 1990s and it was first deployed as part of my work with colleagues at Brandeis University in DARPA's Tipster program (ARPA 1993). Tipster involved (in part) the analysis of a large corpus (1,000 articles) of text in English in the domain of joint ventures—the investment by several companies in some new firm or enterprise that they own together. The corpus was taken from newspapers and newswires presenting straight news (rather than commentary) aimed directly at the business community.

Tipster-1 was an ambitious attempt to develop a serious, exploitable capability to do a very particular and limited kind of language comprehension that goes under the rubric of information extraction. The managers of the Tipster program appreciated that it was virtually impossible today even just to define the range of knowledge that goes into understanding all of the information presented in these texts (as the human businessman would do), and so they defined a specific, limited set of information that systems were to find in the text and then extract it and put into the appropriate fields of a relational database in a well defined format.

Displaced and Nonstandard Constituents

To see the some of the problems for representation KRISP addresses, consider the sentence below; the second sentence in a short article from the Tipster joint ventures corpus.

> The new firm will be 50 percent owned by Takarabune, 45 percent by Merciries, and the rest by a Japanese advertisement concern, Cybac Co., the company said.

Here the information to be extracted is the relative portion of the new joint venture that each of the three participating companies owns. The fact that Cybac is an advertising company, for example, is completely irrelevant to the task. The system doing the comprehension is free to ignore it and needs to know nothing at all about advertising or other types of business activity.

Even with these simplifications, the task remains a daunting one because those sentence poses extremely difficult problems of syntactic and semantic analysis. It is virtually certain that no system developed in the

1970s or 1980s (when most of the fundamental work on language comprehension by machines was done) could have handled it, and few can do so today. If that were not enough, this particular pattern of how joint capitalization is expressed is only one of about a dozen, and is not at all rare.

In this instance the sentence poses two problems. The first is the displaced constituent *50 percent*—displaced because it does not appear in its canonical position, which for this constituent would be in a partitive construction such as *50 percent of the new firm*. If the focus of the author of that article had been on the parent companies rather than the new venture that is how it might have been phrased ("Takarabune will own 50 percent of the new company, Mercires 45 percent, and …"). A generation system might want to do that as well.

The second problem is the nonstandard constituents in the later part of the sentence. As speakers of English, we all know that the phrase *45 percent* refers to a "45% ownership of the new firm," yet that information is not given explicitly but must be inferred from context. The question is how to do that inference in a general and reliable way.

The Standard Approach

The standard means of identifying and populating a domain relationship during the semantic interpretation of a parse is to start with the syntactic head of the phrase as the basis of the type of object or relation to be instantiated, such as *firm* or *owned,* and then to interpret the syntactic arguments to the head as values for the relation's arguments or the object's properties, such as *new* or *by Takarabune.* What makes nonstandard constituents a problem in the standard approach is that a constituent like *45 percent by Merciries* does not permit this kind of analysis. If this phrase is indeed a constituent then its head would be *45 percent,* and there is no sensible way that a company can directly provide an argument to a percentage.

Similarly, the constituent *50 percent* is displaced in the sense that it is not in construction with (roughly speaking, adjacent to) the syntactic argument or head that it would need in order to denote a normal relation. In the era of transformational grammar we would have said it had moved; today we would be more circumspect. The problem for the parser is to identify which of the other phrases in the text is its head and to then arrange for the two to be passed on to semantic analysis as though they had appeared in the canonical partitive construction.

I can summarize these two problems by saying that they arise from phrasal patterns that violate the presumptions of traditional, syntax-driven compositional semantic analysis, presumptions that have been in place since (at least) the work of Montague (1970, or Partee 1984) in linguistic semantics or of Winograd (1972) and Woods (1973) in artificial intelligence.

In the AI version of this tradition (the only option with real parsers and generators), the stuff of the semantic representation of the information in a text consists of terms representing individuals (for example *the four companies*) and predicates representing states, properties, and relations (such as *own*, *be a certain percentage of*, and *new*). Each word or fixed phrase typically has a direct projection onto a term or a predicate, and the syntax of the text, as determined by the grammar that the parser is using, defines how they are composed into larger and larger forms by applying the terms as arguments to the predicates in order to create formulas. In the more recent treatments, the terms and predicates may be typed, structured objects and the information each object represents may actually be distributed across the elements of complex taxonomic or meronymic lattices, but the essence is still the same: a syntactic grammar of adjacency relationships between constituents drives the process of semantic composition and determines the content and format of the final representation of the information in the text.

Given these sorts of representational elements with which to work, the only option for dealing with displaced constituents is either to greatly complicate the machinery of the parser (by introducing transformations that will move the constituent to the correct place) or to add constructions to the grammar that capture the newly observed pattern directly. The same is true of nonstandard constituents, where the problems are so significant that the approach is often to move to a syntactic formalism that is specifically attuned to the problem, such as categorial grammar (Steedman 1987, 1996).

The problem with this approach, which the experience with the Tipster corpus makes plain, is that real texts exhibit a strikingly large variety of phrasal patterns, far more than has been considered a large set in the past when developing grammars for restricted, short-utterance tasks like question answering. I believe that we cannot expect to succeed if what we do is attempt to catalog all the individual syntactic constructions and give each of them their own compositional, rule-by-rule interpretation. The enormous number of constructions and the variations imposed on them by the peculiarities of the semantics of different words will swamp any such effort.

We may be seeing this already in what has become known among the participants in the Message Understanding Conferences (MUC) and Tipster community as the glass ceiling that limits further progress in information extraction. For reasons unknown, to date no one in that community has a combined precision/recall score in their tests on blind texts higher than 60% (which also includes a nontrivial number of mistakes) despite over six years of trying. (See Sundheim 1995, particularly table 4, page 27.) Systems instead climb steadily to about that point as they mature, but then stay there, so far indefinitely. (Intersubject agreement among people in the same task is above 95%.)

If the experience of the Brandeis group is any judge, the source of the glass ceiling lies directly in the central problem of real texts: that there are a great many ways of saying the same thing. Taken as a problem in grammar, identifying and coding all these patterns is a Herculean task. In the tests, groups make mistakes or miss instances simply because they are confronted with constituent patterns that their systems have never seen before.

As the reader probably already expects, I see the answer to the glass ceiling to be to move ever more of the work out of syntax and into in semantics. Keep the grammar and the style of the parser's syntactic analysis relatively simple and move the complexity into the semantics by developing more powerful compositional mechanisms and more expressive and flexible representations. KRISP is offered as a first step in this direction.

Partially Saturated Relations

One of the principles underlying the design of KRISP is that the semantic projection of any grammatically well-formed phrase in a text should be a first-class object. In KRISP the phrase *50 percent* projects to a first class object that is ontologically a partially saturated relation: a function that carries within it information about what kind of thing it combines with and the role that it plays when the composition is finally formed. (The details of this notion are elaborated in the compound types subsection that follows.)

The concept of a first class object comes from the study of programming languages where it refers to those objects that can be returned as the value of functions. Here the focus is on what elements of a representational system can be factored out of the context they are part of and still retain their identity. In the usual notation for the predicate calculus, the letters representing variables cannot be factored out—are not first class—since they gain their meaning only by being in construction with a particularly placed quantifier and appearing at certain positions in a formula. For example, imagine that we have the following formula in the predicate calculus as the representation of "Takarabune owns 50 percent of the firm:"

$\text{Exists}(t) \ \text{Exists}(f)$
   $\text{name}(t, \text{"Takarabune"}) \text{ AND known}(f) \text{ AND company}(f)$
   $\text{AND jointly-owns}(t, f, 50)$

Here the letters t and f have no meaning on their own; the t could just as well be the t in *jointly* for all we know about it outside of that formula. Only by combining these letters with existential quantifiers do we establish their semantic role as variables, and even then only for this particular formula. The same is true of the number 50 in that formula, which takes on its relevant meaning only by being the third argument in a formula with the predicate *jointly-owns*.

In KRISP, we can take information that we know is incomplete ("50 percent of what?") and represent it as a thing that we can pass around and manipulate independently of the larger context. The problem of a displaced constituent then becomes a matter of allowing the parser to carry uncomposable partially saturated relations up the headline (the progressive composition of the denotation of *owned* with its regular arguments) until a binding can be found for it with a suitable type. The movement of the constituent back to its canonical location is thus performed at the semantic level rather than the syntactic.

Dynamically Formulated Functional Types

Using KRISP, the problem of nonstandard syntactic constituents such as the combination in this example of a quantifier *(45 percent)* and a prepositional phrase *(by Mercuries)* is also solved at a semantic level. Linguistically, what we are presented with is the elision of the other constituents of what would have been a full clause had it appeared first in this conjoined sentence rather than second (such as "Merciries owns 45 percent of the new firm"). We can get similarly reduced sets of noncomposing constituents in other syntactic contexts that permit what was once called reduction under identity, such as in answer to a question.

Leaving aside the question of how a parser would determine that the correct syntactic scope of "45 percent by Mercires" is the whole first clause ("The new firm will be 50 percent owned by Takarabune"), the question for the semantic interpretation process is how do we know what was left out from the reduced conjuncts and how do we restore it so that each conjunct will semantically denote an object that carries the same amount of information as the denotation of the original clause. The procedure has to be a dynamic one—formulated on the fly as the analysis is done—since even a cursory examination of a real corpus will show that we cannot do this with any sort of fixed interpretation schema. There are too many possibilities for what can appear as the reduced, nonstandard constituents (equivalently, what can be elided from the first "full" clause of the conjunction) for any such treatment to be possible.

The general formulation of the treatment here is to treat the phrases of the nonstandard constituent as arguments to a function. Applying the arguments yields a complete (fully saturated) relation (i.e. a formula); the question is how to construct the function. With KRISP as the basis of the representation, we can break down any multi-term relation into a set of individual variable bindings. From this perspective the first, full clause of the sentence is a set of three bindings: one for *the new firm*, i.e. the joint venture playing the role of the thing that is (partially) owned; one for *Takarabune*, which is one of the parent companies playing the role of the (partial) owner; and one for *50 percent*, the measurement playing the role of the amount of the partial ownership.

The function is formed dynamically by examining the domain-level types of the constituents in the reduced conjuncts (in this case a measurement and one of the parent companies) and subtracting the equivalent terms from the object denoted by the full clause. This creates a first-class, partially-saturated relation that is underspecified in two of its variables, which can then be applied to the two uncomposed terms in the reduced clauses to form full relations.

Semantic interpretation through the application of complex functions is standard notion in the semantics of categorial grammars. What I am doing here is separating the construction of the function from domain of syntactic parsing. In a syntactically driven approach, I would have needed to have a rule that combined a measurement quantifier and agentive prepositional phrase because I would need a syntactic structure to categorize the roles of the two constituents before I could proceed with a semantic analysis. This has the obvious, possibly insurmountable problem of needing to enumerate and formulate all of the possible combinations of reduced constituents. Using KRISP, all I need at the syntactic level is a segmentation that delimits the scope of the conjuncts, and the substantive work is done at the semantic level. This would not be possible if I had not expanded the number of kinds of semantic stuff allowed in the interpretations and the kinds of operations that were allowed to happen in the course of formulating an interpretation, which is the thrust of the project to develop KRISP.

KRISP and Sparser

The concepts behind KRISP are the result of a long-standing body of work on efficient representations for language generation. If we start from information represented in KRISP, we should get a generation process that is maximally efficient in the sense of McDonald, Meteer, and Pustejovsky 1987—one where the representation of the speaker's situation and its mapping to linguistic resources is organized in a finely modularized, readily recombined network of elements from which the information can be selected and given a linguistic formulation in a way that is easily tuned to the requirements of the focus, perspective, and degree of detail that happen to hold at the time.

At this time, the use of KRISP for generation remains largely just a goal. The substantial development and implementation of KRISP has been instead as the target semantic representation of the language comprehension system SPARSER (McDonald 1992). SPARSER is a fully implemented, mature system for natural language comprehension that was developed during the early 1990s as a commercial information extraction system targeted at the rapid analysis of single subject, information-dense, typically short, business news articles such as one finds on newswire services and in the columns of newspapers such as the *Wall Street Journal* or the *Financial Times* (the primary sources for the Tipster corpus). It has since been applied to a variety of corpora and language-analysis tasks. Substantial grammars have been developed for the articles in the *Wall Street Journal's* "Who's News" column (the source of the texts used in MUC-6 [DARPA 1996]) and for press releases reporting companies quarterly earnings. It has also been applied to the problem of acquiring the concepts of a new domain and their linguistic realizations from large corpora, in particular a set of reference manuals for the Macintosh operating system.

SPARSER produces a full, in-depth, linguistically principled analysis of those parts of the text that it can understand, deliberately ignoring the rest. Its analyses will omit much of the information that (we assume) a person would understand; but in those parts for which it does have a grammar and semantic model, its understanding of the literal content of a text is just as detailed as what a person would arrive at. In this sense it is not a *partial* parser as that term is understood in the parsing literature (see, for example, Bunt and Tomita 1996) but rather a *sparse* parser.

SPARSER is among the very fastest information extraction systems in the literature (compare Appelt et al. 1995). Its speed varies with the percentage of the text that receives an analysis. The article below, for example, is analyzed in every detail and is processed at the rate of 180 words per second (50Mhz Apple Quadra 900 using Macintosh Common Lisp version 2.1); it takes longer to print the words of the text on the screen than it does to process it.

ECONOMIST NEWSPAPER LTD. (LONDON) —- Pierre Vinken, 61 years old, will join the board as a nonexecutive director Nov. 29. Mr. Vinken is chairman of Elsevier N.V., the Dutch publishing group." (*Wall Street Journal*, November 2d, 1989 from the Data Collection Initiative's corpus, ACL/DCI 1991)

By contrast, only about a half of this next text is analyzed (just the elements that are underlined), and it runs at 240 w/sec. (It is excerpted from a *Wall Street Journal* "Who's News" article from February 14, 1991). A text consisting of just a sequence of uninterpreted nonsense words ("aaa") runs at 900 w/sec.

After almost nine tumultuous years, George L. Ball resigned yesterday as chairman and chief executive officer of Prudential- Bache Securities Inc., the nation's fourth-largest securities firm.

Mr. Ball's departure signaled that Prudential Insurance Co. of America, the brokerage firm's parent, had run out of patience with Mr. Ball's quest to turn the unit into a Wall Street powerhouse. Amid mounting losses, Prudential had steadfastly backed the 52- year-old chairman in one failed foray after another.

The output of SPARSER is a stream of event triggers and a domain-level semantic model populated with the individuals, properties, and relations that were detected in the text, all represented using KRISP.[2] The semantic grammar that drives SPARSER's analysis is instantiated as a side-effect of executing KRISP object and category creating expressions. Known objects in the model are looked up when the text refers to them by using automatically created mappings included with the rules of the grammar. New KRISP individuals and (notably) composite categories are created as needed to represent new information found during an analysis. All this will be described in later sections.

Having a Model

The relationship between the text and the representation of its content in SPARSER/KRISP is direct and immediate. It is a denotational relationship of just the same sort as the one between expressions in a mathematical logic (a kind of language) and the model that provides the basis for the truth values of those expressions by providing an interpretation for their terms. In SPARSER's use of KRISP, there is no intermediate language of "logical form" into which the text is first reformulated; no mediating intensional logic. The words in the text and the syntactic objects built from them have an extensional mapping to corresponding objects in SPARSER's internal model of the world.

It is worth taking a moment to make sure that it is clear what I am talking about ontologically when I say "model." There is a tendency, when logicians look at a representation developed in AI, for them to see things of a syntactic sort not unlike their own parentheses and letters; that is, they require an interpretation before their denotations can be established. (Searle [1992] is a good example of this sort of argument. For exceptionally well articulated counter-arguments see Smith [1996].) Models for most logicians are abstract things about which they prove properties; not things that they actually construct. Furthermore, the stuff that populates a logician's model consists of individuals of very simple types such as pure numbers or tuples. The menagerie of types and structures in an AI system is alien to that way of thinking, if only because its complexity makes it virtually impossible to prove theorems about it. Similar considerations lead many within AI to eschew such complex, "scruffy" treatments in favor of the first order predicate calculus.

To understand what a model is like in KRISP it will be helpful to review the usual steps taken by an AI system that can answer questions. What sort of stuff does it manipulate along the way? A question-answering system starts with an expression written in a language, say an English sentence. As it parses the expression and does its semantic interpretation, it typically constructs another linguistic (symbolic) expression, for example a query written in a database access language like SQL. That expression is then passed to the database and is itself parsed and interpreted. The result at that point is something different. We stop making more expressions and start to execute actions against stuff of a different kind: tuples in a database. Expressions were used, off-line, to create those tuples and have them added to the database, but once there and active they became the stuff of a model, not linguistic objects.

Consider another case whose fuzzy edges may make things clearer. In Winograd's classic SHRDLU system (1972), the output of the semantic interpretation phase was also expressions: small programs written on the fly in the programming language MicroPlanner. Suppose, contrary to fact, that the entire range of what SHRDLU could understand had been mapped out and schematized, and that rather than build its MicroPlanner programs from scratch it would just select the appropriate program already compiled down to PDP-10 assembly language, give it some parameters, and execute it. Did it still make an expression requiring interpretation? I think the answer to that question is yes. But again, the blocks world against which those programs would be run was comprised of stuff of a different kind. It was a circumscribed universe of objects consisting of the children's blocks on SHRDLU's table and the spatial relationships among the blocks and with the table.

Let us consider what kind of stuff they consisted of. There actually was a (short) time when one of the experimental pick and place robots at the MIT AI Lab was deployed to manipulate physical blocks under instructions from a reimplementation of SHRDLU. In this case the blocks world was part of our ordinary external reality, which is decidedly not an expression requiring interpretation. In the original implementation there was also the manipulation of nonlinguistic things, namely the display of a simulated robot hand and table with blocks on a computer screen. Ray tracings and excited phosphors are not linguistic stuff, but by the same token they are not, per se, stuff that is isomorphic to the information content of the sentences SHRDLU understood its users to be talking about when they typed in questions for it to answer or commands for it to execute. That connection lay only in the mind of the human viewer of the display.

What then is the ontological status of the stuff inside SHRDLU that it made reference to when it had understood a sentence and was proceeding to set up the directives to drive the display or move the robot arm? It used Lisp symbols such as :B6 to stand for particular blocks, and it used Lisp lists to stand for the relations among them, (on :B6 :B3), all of which were things constructed out of the memory locations and bit patterns of the computer it was running on, and accessible by name or pointer from the Lisp data heap in which they resided.[3] This, I claim, is the stuff of a model in the same sense as a logician would use that term; as are the KRISP units that comprise the content of SPARSER's understanding of the texts it analyzes.

KRISP's Set of Types

As a representational system, KRISP embodies a theory of how information is structured in a natural language text. This is a hypothesis about the nature of the objects that texts denote and the principles of semantic interpretation that map them to a model comprised of such objects. In KRISP the objects lie on two different levels, one realized in terms of the other.

As the interpretation of a text, we have objects that lie at what we might call the *domain* level, where we are representing both the particular instances and the general kinds of people, events, moments, amounts, etc., in profusion that a text can be talking about. Entities at the domain level are in turn constructed out of stuff that resides at the *epistemological* level (following Brachman 1979). At this level lie the fundamental kinds of representational objects—the paper and ink from which the map is assembled. Generalizations about the nature of the mapping from linguistic (text-level) entities to domain level objects are stated here.

I introduce KRISP's epistemological level below. This will include giving part of the rules of formation for domain-level units by discussing how each type of unit is typically realized in English. A full example of a semantic-interpretation will follow in the next section.

Units — the Subrepresentational Level

In a functioning system, every representational level is itself realized (implemented, made operational) by objects and processes at a still lower level. At the lowest level of any semantic interest in KRISP (below it lie the entities of the programming language it is runs in, Lisp in this case), a model consists of a set (technically a heap) of typed objects—the units of information that the model contains. *Units* are the fundamental chunks from which the information in a text is presumed to be composed. Units virtually always refer to other units, but there is a notion of minimality to them. Nothing smaller than a unit carries any information content.

Units are linked together by pointers. The units are first class objects; the pointers are not. Units are structured, with named fields containing pointers from them to other units. The set of fields that a unit has are determined by its type. Every unit is unique; that is, there will only ever be one unit in the model with a given type and given set of units that it points to in its fields. This uniqueness is maintained by the machinery that brings long-term units into existence and manages the semantic interpretation process.

While the notion of a unit having a name is not really sensible (names are themselves entities that need a representation in the model), there still has to be some way to differentiate one unit from the next in an exposition like this (or while debugging a program), and the simplest convention to adopt is to use the word to which the unit would normally correspond as the basis of its name. When necessary, I will use a bracket notation (#<...>) to indicate that I am dealing with model-level objects rather than the words or expressions that realize them in a text.

Primary Epistemological Types

KRISP defines four primary types of units in its epistemological level: individual, category, variable and binding, as well as two types of units that are blends of the primary types: derived categories and partially saturated individuals. Every object (unit) in a KRISP model has one (and only one) of these types.

For concreteness, the discussion here will make use of this sentence, which we have seen earlier, and we will start with the notion of an *individual*, the most ordinary of the six types of units in KRISP.

George L. Ball resigned yesterday as chairman and chief executive officer of Prudential-Bache Securities Inc.

There are 15 individuals in this text. As analyzed by SPARSER's semantic grammar for "Who's News" articles we have one person, one resign event, one day, two titles, one company, two names (one each for the person and the company) and within those names six name elements and one incorporation term. (For a discussion of how proper names are analyzed see McDonald [1996.])

An individual is roughly comparable to Montague's *e* type, KL-One's *nexuses,* or Classic's *individuals* (see respectively Montague [1970], Brachman and Schmolze [1985], and Brachman et al. [1991]). Individuals are used to represent particular things in the world, concrete or abstract. In terms of semantic interpretation, they are the denotations of maximal-projections of the major syntactic categories, such as proper names (designating conventional individuals), referential noun phrases (things anchored in space), and most clauses (things anchored in time; see Talmy 1987).

As a unit, an individual has three fields: one for its type and two for the relationships in which it participates. The nature of these relationships will be taken up below as part of the description of bindings. To define what can appear in (is pointed to by) the type field we must now look at the notion of a category.

Categories represent kinds. They are the denotations of most phrasal heads, such as common nouns and verbs. The type field of an individual contains at least one but possibly several category units that collectively define its domain-level type (for example, transition event, person, being in a state of retirement, title, unicorn). The relationships into which an individual can enter are determined by the categories listed in its type. When the type field contains more than one category, one of them is indicated as primary. It will be an immutable, defining aspect of the individual—person rather programmer—and defines most of the individual's properties. The primary category is central to an individual's semantic identity as the denotation of a natural language word or phrase, hence resign-1 rather than, say, job-event-1. By convention, it is listed first when there are several categories.[4]

Categories are *predicates.* They define relational types with individuals as the corresponding tokens. As a predicate, a category has a specific arity. In a conventional AI frame system we would say that it has a certain set of *slots.* In mathematical logic we would say that a formula based on that predicate would have a certain number of variables. In the lambda calculus—the best reference model for KRISP's epistemological level—we would say that a category is a function open in a certain number of variables. In KRISP we also use the notion of variables and make them first class objects. The number and identity of the variables associated with a category, along with its position in the lattice (below), are what constitute a category's identity and information content; qua unit, they are a category's two fields.

Variables are local to the category that defines them, in the sense that if we were to notate them using names (*x*, agent, members) we could substitute other names without changing their meaning (lambda calculus alpha reduction). Every variable has a value restriction: a category or list of alternative categories that stipulate the kinds of individuals it can be bound to. The two fields on a unit of type variable are the category to which it belongs and its value restriction.

In the example at the start of this section, the verb *resign*, which is the head of its clause, denotes a category. This category is part of SPARSER's a priori knowledge about the domain of "Who's News," and was entered by hand into the model using a category-defining expression as we will see in the next section. It is given the internal name "resign-position" to distinguish it from the other sense of the word that appears frequently in business text, as in "to resign debt." Resign-position has two variables, one for the person resigning and another for the position[5] they resigned from.

Categories are organized into a subsumption lattice on the basis of the variables they define and the restrictions on them. The variables are also linked into this lattice so that the correspondence between the variables of a category and those of its super-category(s) is well-founded.[6] An individual whose domain type includes a relatively specific category, like resign-position, will also satisfy—read: may bind the variables of—all of the categories that resign-position is, for example, a specialization of leave-position, job-change, agentive-event, transition-event, and event.

However subsumption is not a well-developed aspect of KRISP because it has not been designed as a classifier where a set of descriptions would be given to it and it would find the node in the lattice at which they should be placed. Rather KRISP is a source of denotations that are established compositionally through the actions of a parser. Any new, derived categories that a text may refer to are always the daughters (subcategories) of the elements from which they are built. Lexically anchored categories are effectively natural kinds. Derived categories are kept unique through the channeling provided by the variable binding lattice.

Relationships and their components in KRISP are represented by units of type binding. *Bindings* are three-tuples consisting of a unit (typically an individual), a variable, and another unit. They represent facts of the form "unit-1 stands in the relation variable-1 to unit-2." Broadly speaking, bindings are the frame–slot–value structures of standard frame systems, with the difference that binding are first-class objects and exist independently of the units that comprise them. Bindings are sanctioned by the variables defined by the participating individuals' categories. All of the relationships in which an individual participates and all of its attributes other than its categorizations per se are represented by the bindings it is part of.

Bindings provide the denotations for a number of linguistic constructions including most copular clauses and the individual grammatical relationships that tie phrasal heads to their complements and adjuncts (subject, temporal adjunct, etc.). In language comprehension, most semantic relations correspond to the syntactic relationship of a head to its arguments, with the set of relationships (bindings) accruing incrementally from the head outwards in the course of a parse. The head will denote a category, and when all of its required arguments have been determined (those required logically, not just syntactically), the result will be a fully saturated relation, i.e. an individual.

To have the best understand the notion of a binding we should consider what a category like resign-position would look like in the lambda calculus, where it is a function based on a predicate with two arguments. The reference text here is our ongoing example: "George L. Ball resigned yesterday as chairman and chief executive officer of Prudential-Bache Securities Inc."

λ position . λ person .
resign-position(person, position)

If we ignore the question of sense disambiguation for the moment, in our current example the verb *resign* will, given SPARSER's grammar, compose first with the adverb *yesterday*, binding the time variable that resign-position inherits from the category event, and the resulting verb group will then compose with the position constituent *chairman and chief executive officer of Prudential-Bache Securities Inc.* to bind resign-position's position variable. In the lambda calculus, the resulting expression—the denotation of the verb phrase—would look like this:

λ person
((λ position .
(λ time .
resign-position/event
(person, position, time-of-event))
#<date 2/13/91>)
#<position Chairman and CEO, Prudential-Bache Securities>)

This expression shows that we have applied a individual to the variable position, in preparation for doing a beta reduction, and that we have done the same for the inherited variable time, applying an individual of type date, which is one of the subcategories of the type *moment-in-time* that is the value restriction on the generic time variable in SPARSER's model of the world.

In KRISP, unlike the lambda calculus, those argument applications are represented by first class objects: bindings. The equivalent of that aspect of the lambda form above are these two bindings, shown relative to the (partially saturated) individual that is the equivalent of the formula's body, designated "resign-position 16."[7]

```
bindings 105
  :variable #<position>
  :value #<position 1>
  :body #<resign-position 16>
binding 102
  :variable #<time>
  :value #<date 2/13/91>
  :body #<resign-position 16>
```

Compound Types

What are we to say about the epistemological status of the denotation for this verb phrase in this example? ("resigned yesterday as chairman and chief executive officer of Prudential-Bache Securities Inc.") If we accept that it is a unit of information, rather than just something ephemeral in the state of the semantic interpretation of the full sentence, then we have to decide what the unit's type should be. Given the options so far, this unit has some of the properties of a category in that it defines a predicate that is open in the variable *person*. It also has some of the properties of an individual in that it is a particular (if incomplete) thing in the world, being an event anchored to a particular day and involving a particular position, which is sufficient information to make it unique under most circumstances.

To accommodate such objects in a disciplined way, KRISP has the type *partially saturated individual*. Like individuals, such units have a domain type and participate in bindings. Like categories, they define a set of open variables and have positions in the taxonomic lattice. As units they have the fields of an individual plus the field open-in which lists the variables that have yet to be bound. It is suggestive, though not technically accurate, to say that a partially saturated individual that finally gets all of its open variables bound in the course of an interpretation changes its type at that moment and becomes an individual. (Actually a new object is created. The others are retained during at least the life of the analysis as candidate derived categories, as we will see later in the discussion.) Here is the printed form of the denotation of this verb phrase; the bindings are printed in a reduced format since the identity of their body is understood.

```
resign-position 16
  :type ( resign-position past )
  :bindings (   #< time = #<date 2/13/91> >
                #< position = #<position 1> > )
  :open-in ( #<person> )
```

Earlier in this section, single nouns, verbs, and most fixed phrases were described as denoting categories. This is not strictly accurate as it depends on precisely what we call a word. The denotation of the verb is different in *he resigned* versus *he intends to resign*. The first picks out an event that occurred, the second one an event that may or may not occur—more of a type than a token. Moreover, while we don't know from just its spelling-form what would satisfy an instance of the infinitive form of *resign* in the world, we do know something about an instance of *resigned*, namely that it categorizes an event that happened in the past. To deal in a principled way with such differences, KRISP includes units of type *derived category* in its epistemological level.

Simple, primitive categories (natural kinds) are the denotations of uninflected content words. They are primitive in the technical sense that their position in the lattice does not provide necessary or sufficient criteria for their satisfaction. Derived categories are analytic and are the denotations of compositions of linguistic primitives. Most reflect the addition of generic morphological or grammatical elements such as plural, past-tense, modals, negation, etc. Many descriptive *N*-bar level phrases also want to be treated as derived categories since they do not introduce individuals in a text but rather categorize existing individuals or add attributive properties. Something as elaborate as *London-based investment bank* can be reified as a derived category.

In practice there is a fine line between a derived category and a partially saturated individual. Phrases that we want to treat as categories because of their function as predicates and lack of saturation will often incorporate individuals (for example, the city of London). For predefined units, our criteria has been to work from the prototypical denotational patterns, i.e. that head nouns and verbs denote categories and that full NPs and clauses denote individuals. When argument and adjunct phrases are composed onto a head line, if they are more attribute like, rather than more classifying, then to that extent we are more likely to declare the denotation of the new phrase to be a partially saturated individual rather than a derived category.

Thus the word *month* is taken to denote a category, even though it has particular attributes such as being part of a year and being composed of between 28 and 31 days. *December* denotes an individual since it is realized as a proper name and saturates the logically (though not syntactically) apparent variables of months, i.e. the name, the position within the year, and the specific number of days.

Recall the denotation of the verb phrase in this example ("[George L. Ball] resigned yesterday as chairman and chief executive officer of Prudential-Bache Securities Inc."). It is treated here as a partially saturated individual, but would it be useful to think of it as a kind of thing? What about *retire from IBM*? Is that a sufficiently frequent event that a reasoning system would want to give it the status of a category? These are questions of knowledge engineering and design. My criterion when such units are being derived automatically is that any phrase that is syntactically analyzed at less than a maximal *x*-bar level is treated as a derived category if it occurs more than once, and otherwise as a partially saturated relation. As we will see, the mechanics of these two kinds of unit are sufficiently similar that the shift from one to the other is not large.

This section has introduced KRISP's set of epistemological types and illustrated some of their correspondences to particular kinds of words or phrases. However, the denotation of a phrase in isolation explains only part of the process of semantic interpretation. In the next sections we will look at interactions between words and other constituent types, illustrating the kinds of protocols at work as phrases are composed and the denotations of the resulting edges are computed rule by rule in step with the syntactic processes.

Object-Creating Forms

Let us move now to looking at KRISP's equivalent of data base tuple-creating SQL expressions and see some examples of the kind of things a person does when populating a KRISP-based model with objects by hand. Here, for example, is the expression that creates the category *resign-position.*

```
(define-category resign-position
   :specializes leave-position
   :instantiates job-event
   :binds ((person . person)
           (position . position))
   :realization
     (:tree-family intransitive
      :mapping ( (s . job-event)
                 (vg . :self)
                 (np/subject . person)
                 (agent . person))
      :main-verb "resign"
      :additional-rules
        ((:pp-adjunct
          (s (s as-title)
           :head left-referent
           :binds (position right-referent))))))
```

This is an expression in a domain-level language implemented in Lisp. When it is executed it returns a unit of type category with the indicated properties. If such a unit already exists it is accessed and returned rather than another unit being created. This particular category is fit into the lattice as a subcategory of leave-position. It gets an annotation to the effect that for purposes of subsequent reference to individuals of this type in the text they should be classified in terms of a higher category in the lattice, job-event, and instances of it should be recorded as such in SPARSER's discourse history (i.e. leaving and entering a position are considered things of the same kind for that purpose). Two variables are defined, named "person" and "position," and it is indicated that they are restricted to be bound only to individuals whose types include categories that happen to have those same names.

The other field of the expression, realization,[8] takes us to a aspect of KRISP that I have not yet touched on—one that provides the basis for KRISP as a reversible representation that can be used equally well as the source of the production of texts or the target of their comprehension. This field specifies how information belonging to this category (individuals of that type) is expressed in English. Furthermore, the schematization of the information in that field is such that it can be used by either the parsing machinery in SPARSER or the surface structure creating machinery in Mumble-86, the companion system to SPARSER in the bi-directional system I have been developing (see McDonald 1998).

The key to its reversibility is the fact that this specification is based on the use of grammatical constructs that are available in both systems: the tree families of a tree adjoining grammar (TAG) (Joshi 1985, Abeille 1988). Differences in notation aside, the nature of the tree families within the Mumble generator is virtually the same as in a standard TAG and thus need not be illustrated here. Their nature inside SPARSER is another matter, since there they are reconstructed to suit the needs of an efficient parser. (Full details are given in McDonald [1993].) Here is the expression that creates the "exploded tree family" for trees headed by intransitive verbs like *retire*.

```
(define-exploded-tree-family intransitive
   :binding-parameters ( agent )
   :labels ( s vg np/subject )
   :cases
      ((:subject (  s (np/subject vg)
                   :head right-edge
                   :binds (agent left-edge)))))
```

This expression creates a mapping template that is applied to the information in the definition of "resign-position" to create a set of phrase structure rules in SPARSER's semantic grammar, listed here in abbreviated form.

#<PSR1243 job-event → job-event as-title>
#<PSR1347 job-event → person resign-position>

```
#<PSR1343 resign-position → "resign">
#<PSR1344 resign-position → "resigns">
#<PSR1345 resign-position → "resigned">
#<PSR1346 resign-position → "resigning">
```

Let us look at the expression that would have created the second of these rules had we written it by hand. This will give us a sense of how KRISP's facilities are used in SPARSER's semantic interpretation process.

```
(define-cfr job-event (person resign-position)
    :form s
    :referent  (:head right-edge
                :binds (person left-edge)))
```

As its base, SPARSER is a chart parser that creates a set of edges (parse nodes) bottom up in one pass from left to right through the text. All of its edges are binary, and are formed through the operation of a relatively complex control structure that examines selected adjacent pairs of edges, one to the left and one to the right. When a match is found (as in *George L. Ball resigned*, which is parsed as the pair of edges semantically labeled person and resign-position); a new edge is formed; it is given the appropriate semantic label (job-event) and syntactic label (*s*); and its denotation (referent) is constructed. In this case the rule dictates that the referent is to be formed by taking the unit already established as the referent of the head constituent (resign-position, the edge to the right) and adding a binding that assigns the referent of the left-edge (person) to the person variable of the resign-position category. The result is this partially saturated individual:

```
resign-position 13
    :type (resign-position past)
    :binds #< person = #<Ball, George l> >
    :open-in (position)
```

These examples have provided a short look at the machinery that handles the construction of new units. This is only part of the picture however. Any realistic language comprehension system starts with a significant amount of knowledge already built in. To facilitate this, KRISP includes a language for creating individuals and bindings as well as categories and variables. Here, for example, is an expression that creates a individual to represent a particular country, with the side-effect of also adding a rule to the grammar that has a direct pointer to this unit so that the referent of the chart edge can be supplied without needing to do any lookup or object construction. In this analysis, the category *country* has only one logically required variable, *name*, restricted to an object of type name; the name object (an individual) is automatically created as part of the evaluation of this expression. (The fact stated here is of course no longer accurate; however the work in which this individual was used predates the change in geopolitical status.)

(define-individual country
    :name "Hong Kong")

Creating a partially saturated individual is a bit more elaborate. We have to specify the category of the eventual individual and the variable that this unit (psi for short) is to bind. Here is the definition-schema for the class of psi that are percentages.

(define-dependent-term percentage
    :specializes measurement
    :binds ((value . number))
    :governing-relation (amount measurement)
    :realization
        (:tree-family quantity+kind
          :mapping ((np . self)
                    (np-head . ("percent" "%"))
                    (modifier . number)
                    (quantity . value)
                    (result-type . self))

An Extended Example

We can now walk through a relatively complex example where the use of the special facilities of KRISP provides a significant benefit. It will also let us review the basic correspondences between the different types of KRISP units and particular linguistic constructs. We will use the following sentence, which is taken from a short article from the Kyoto News Service about a joint venture by the Yoshinoya D&C Company to set up another of its noodle restaurant chains in Hong Kong.

Hong Kong will be Yoshinoya's third overseas market following 11 outlets in Taiwan and 44 restaurants in the United States.

To make things more realistic, we will imagine that SPARSER does not have any knowledge about the last three head nouns: *market*, *outlets*, and *restaurants*. No language comprehension system today should ever expect to have all the vocabulary it will encounter in its target corpus, and must have facilities for making some sense out of unknown words, especially when they occur in a well-understood context as they do here. It will be as though the text was this:

Hong Kong will be Yoshinoya's third overseas xxx following 11 yyys in Taiwan and 44 zzzs in the United States.

Simple Semantic Interpretation

To SPARSER's lexicalized semantic grammar, the example text looks like the following sequence of preterminal categories:

country + "will" + be + country-possessive + ordinal + location + unknown + "following" + number + unknown/plural + "in" + country + "and" + number + unknown/plural + "in" + "the" + country

The words which have a predefined interpretation in KRISP, such as we saw above for the example of *Hong Kong*, appear in the chart as edges labeled with the category that they have in KRISP. Function words appear as themselves. Words that are outside of SPARSER's (initial) vocabulary are given the label *unknown*, and have annotations that indicate their morphological or orthographic properties (glossed here as part of the name).

Starting at the beginning of the text with *country*, the parsing process proceeds incrementally to the right, where the adjacency of the modal *will* indicates that the verb group has started and that Hong Kong must, correspondingly, be the sentence's subject. *Will* denotes the category *future-time* in my analysis. It combines with any verb or verb group to its right, forming a new edge over those two constituents with the same label as its right neighbor, and imposing the constraint that the denotation of the result include future-time in its domain-type. Here is the expression in SPARSER that creates this rule.

```
(define-form-rule ("will" verb)
    :form verb-group
    :referent  (:head right-edge
                :subtype future-time))
```

This is a rule that mixes syntactic and lexical labels (or in other instances semantic labels). It specifies that the word *will* may combine with an edge of any semantic category to its right so long as that edge has the syntactic (form) label of verb. The result is a new edge with the same label as the semantic label on edge indicated as the head. The subtype directive adds a category to the type field of the unit denoted by the head edge. Note that if this unit is a category (as it will in this instance since the edge to the right is semantically labeled *be*, subsuming differences in the tense of the verb *to be*) and if it denotes a category that is underspecified in the sense of Hobbs et. al 1993), then what we are doing is creating or looking up a derived category. Otherwise we would be adding the category to the type field of an individual or partially saturated individual.

Proceeding onward, a low-level scan will delimit the next constituent after *be*, identifying it as a noun phrase since it definitively starts with the possessive company edge, *Yoshinoya's*, and ends just before the subordinate conjunction *following*. That is enough to infer that the word *market* must be a noun; and since nouns denote categories, we can construct a placeholder category to act as its denotation, giving it the same name as the word. Of course we know nothing about this new category's properties, but we can (1) link all subsequent instances of this word to this same category, and (2) accrue some of its properties by seeing how it is modified by the other words it is in construction with. The chart thus gets an edge over the word *market* with *market* as its semantic label, *head-noun* as its syntactic label, and the new category as its referent.

The preceding three constituents within the noun phrase (Yoshinoya's third overseas ___) can be combined with *market* using default rules of form such as the one shown earlier for *will*. The interesting question is what that combination denotes. Overall the phrase is a description of Hong Kong, the same sort of relationship as if we had said "Hong Kong is a former British colony." Just what form this relationship takes in KRISP depends on the nature of the description. Saying that "Hong Kong is an island" is definitively assigning it to a category, which would corresponding to adding the category *island* to the individual representing Hong Kong, similarly for *former British Colony*. These ascriptions indicate properties of the individual that dictate how it should behave as an object subject to inferences (for example, its residents are probably bilingual in English), and as such should be part of its type field as in any object-oriented system.

On the other hand, what is going on if we read just that "Hong Kong is third" (or "overseas" or "Yoshinoya's")? These are obviously incomplete statements, and they are placing Hong Kong in the sort of relationship where the type of relation is determined by the nature of the missing element (member of a set, geographically separated by an ocean, owned by). In KRISP this corresponds to binding the individual representing Hong Kong to some variable.

As terms in SPARSER's grammar and model, the meanings of the three known constituents (third, overseas, Yoshinoya's) have representations in KRISP. They are partially saturated individuals, and as such they specify the category (domain type) of the individual they would be part of, the variable in it that they would bind, and the variables in that category that remain open, notably including the value restrictions on those variables. Using this machinery, SPARSER is able to construct a denotation for the phrase as a whole that is sufficiently "loose" that all its implicit relationships with the rest of the text can be instantiated using relatively simple compositional mechanisms. We will focus here on what happens with the interpretation of *third*. The other two constituents are handled in virtually the same way.

The ordinal third identifies a position within a sequence and indicates that the thing that it modifies holds that position. Here is its definition, along with the definitions for sequences and for the property of being a member of a sequence. Note that this is a schema that defines the denotations of the whole class of ordinals. The actual instances are defined by substituting a specific word for *self*. Obviously only a few are predefined, just those where the number involved has a name that cannot be evaluated compositionally (i.e. twelfth, billionth, etc., but not twenty second). The others are defined on the fly as needed. As they have so many variations, the realizations of the categories are omitted to save space.

```
(define-dependent-term ordinal
   :binds ((value . number))
   :governing-relation (member-of-a-sequence position)
   :realization (:adjective . self))

(define-category member-of-a-sequence
   :binds ((position . ordinal)
          (sequence . sequence)
          (item . anything)))

(define-category sequence
   :specializes collection
   :binds ((members . collection)
          (count . number)
          (type . category)))
```

At present, the rules that specify the grammatical properties of partially saturated individuals like the dependent term *third* are written by hand since I have yet to devise a comfortable notation by which to derive them as a side-effect of the evaluation of their defining forms as is done with categories. This is not much of a burden, since under a TAG analysis all compositional adjectives and adverbs are auxiliary trees. To the parser, these correspond to simple Chomsky adjunctions and so are naturally captured as form rules:

```
(def-form-rule ( ordinal (n-bar np-head) )
   :form n-bar    ;; This is the syntactic label on the resulting edge.
                  ;; Its semantic label is a copy of the label on the head.
   :referent  (:head right-edge
              :subtype member-of-a-sequence
              :bind (position left-edge))
```

This says that whatever else the unit to the right of the ordinal may be, it is also a member of a sequence, and that with respect to that sequence it is the third item. (In the first line of the expression, the parentheses within the righthand side of the rule are a shorthand for defining two rules.)

Note that the effect of this rule has been to attribute a property to the unknown word *market*, namely that it denotes something that can be a member of a sequence. The composition of the other two premodifiers make similar attributions, and the final result is this unit.

```
market 1
   :type ( #<market>
          #<owned-by-a-company>
```

```
             #<member-of-a-sequence>
             #<has-a-location> )
 :bindings  (   #< relative-location = #<overseas> >
                #< position-in-sequence = #<third> >
                #< owning-company = #<Yoshinoya D and C> > )
 :open-in   (   #<variable sequence>
                #<variable reference-location> )
```

Moving on to the rest of the sentence, a similar process will create denotations for "11 outlets in Taiwan" and "44 restaurants in the United States," attributing to the stand-in categories for the two head nouns (which you may recall we have supposed to be unknown words for the purpose of this example) the categories *collection* and *located-in-a-country*. Note that since neither the numbers or the locations are dependent terms, the denotations for these two phrases will be ordinary (saturated) individuals rather than partially saturated individuals. Conjoined together, these two units form a collection, and when composed with *following* that collection is specialized to be a sequence.

Semantic Composition Via Interior Open Variables

At this point in the exposition I have laid out enough of the representational machinery that KRISP provides to illustrate how it may enable us to break through the glass ceiling of the standard framework for semantic interpretation that I sketched earlier. Within that framework, the construction of denotations is done by rule-by-rule (syntax-driven) composition. Here we are also syntax-driven, but rather than restricting ourselves to operations over patterns of atomic labels, we are working with structured objects and can allow elements of those objects to have interactions of their own. This moves much of the work of forming an interpretation into the semantics, and relieves the syntax of the need to account for every last possible pattern of constituents. In particular, I allow for functionally driven compositions from the interior of those constituents according to the dictates of any unbound variables they may include.

Consider the interaction here of the noun phrase and the gerundive adjunct that follows it ("Yoshinoya's third overseas market following 11 outlets in Taiwan and 44 restaurants in the United States"). I permit them to combine syntactically through a default form rule to the effect that any postnominal qualifier can Chomsky adjoin to the noun phrase proceeding it. As always, we would expect the combination of any modifier and head to involve binding a variable (if that cannot happen then we have a displaced constituent). Default rules, however, cannot in themselves define bindings, since the head unit that would supply the category that would contribute the variables to be bound is by definition anonymous.

To address these cases the compositional process has been loosened so that we can look for the possibility of bindings that are sanctioned by any open variables in the denotations of one or the other constituent, using as our criteria just the domain types specified in the variable's value restrictions. In this instance, the noun phrase is open in a sequence, and the adjunct is just such a sequence. If we gloss the unit denoted by the noun phrase as market-1, which includes the relevant binding *b*-1 as shown in detail below, and gloss the sequence denoted by the adjunct as Taiwan&U.S.-1, then the composition of the noun phrase and the adjunct results in the binding designated *b*-2:

binding *b*-1
:variable #<position>
:value #<individual ordinal third>
:body #<market-1> ; qua its category, "member of a sequence"

binding *b*-2
:variable #<sequence>
:value #<Taiwan&U.S.-1>
:body #<market-1>

Now let us look at what can be done with the last grammatical relationship in this sentence with a denotation yet to be accounted for, the combination of Hong Kong with its predicate nominal (market-1) via the underspecified relation *be*. Again, we would not like to burden the grammar with enumerating every possible category that might be used to describe a city (though some of them, such as population, location, or governance are obvious candidates if one was going to develop a domain model for cities), and we certainly would not want to presume that we have to anticipate that a city can be "a place where a company can market its products" in order to have an adequate information extraction grammar for joint ventures. Anything that we can get through a general rule operating opportunistically through the objects in the semantic model is much to be preferred.

In this case, we can do two things. First we can apply a general rule that given an individual as the denotation of the subject and a derived category as the predicate (the type field of market-1), the verb "be" imposes a substitution relationship between the two. We can then look for what compositions can be made given the type constraints involved (read: additions to #<Hong Kong>'s type or bindings it can be part of). In addition, we can distribute the categories of the predicate and see if there are any rules already in the grammar that specify how they compose.

Following the first procedure, we see that #<market> is just a category that we constructed on the fly, so all that can be done there is to add it to #<Hong Kong> as another category in its type field. #<Owned-by-a-

company> is predefined, but in SPARSER's grammar the only thing that companies can own is other companies so the value restriction precludes any compositions there. Composition with #<overseas> (by way of a rule that combines cities and locations, cf. "Boston is in Massachusetts") yields a partially saturated individual since we don't know what place Hong Kong is being taken to be overseas with respect to. (From the larger context we, as educated people, know it is Japan, since Yoshinoya is a Japanese company and the East and South China Seas lie between the two locations; but it is asking a lot of a system designer to attempt to formalize that inference today in any general way.)

In the case of #<category member-of-a-sequence> we can do a lot. Part of the (presently hand-written) grammar of sequences is the rule:

```
(define-form-rule ( np is-ordinal )
  :form s
  :referent ( :head right-edge
              :binds (item left-edge)))
```

The predicate (market-1) already has the other two variables of the member-of-a-sequence relation bound, and the application of this rule binds the third, yielding the individual:

```
member-of-a-sequence 1
  :type ( member-of-a-sequence )
  :bindings (#< position = #<third> >
             #< sequence = #<Taiwan&U.S.-1> >
             #< item    = #<Hong Kong> > ))
```

This ends the extended example. To summarize the rules of semantic interpretation I have used, the most basic was a direct link between a known word or phrase (Hong Kong, third) and a KRISP unit that was brought into existence when the model was initially populated.[9] The second kind of rule was specified as part of the syntactic rules for combining adjacent, semantically labeled constituents, typically as head and argument. These interpretation rules add bindings or subtypes to the interpretation of the head, interpretations that are then passed up the headline of the syntactic analysis and further compositions are made to it as the syntactic analysis extends.

The final kind of rule is more heuristic and has yet to be properly evaluated through testing on a large corpus. This is to apply general rules of phrasal composition that use the syntactic labels on the constituents and to then look for combinations among the constituent's referents opportunistically on the basis of the semantic types of the constituents and the variables that are open in any partially saturated individuals, the most unusual of the epistemological types supported in KRISP.

Principles

Krisp is fundamentally a semantic network. It is part of the intellectual tradition that began with Quillian (1968) and continues with the KL-One family of languages for knowledge representation (see, for example, Brachman and Schmolze [1985], and MacGregor [1991]). Like them, it permits the representation of actual individuals and the complex categories that describe them, and it entwines them in a net of structured links that enable a reasoning system to efficiently draw conclusions about their properties by following this already built roadmap.

Krisp makes several specific improvements on its predecessors, improvements designed to expedite the only kind of reasoning to which it has so far been applied: the dynamic construction of a model of the information in the text. We can summarize these improvements in terms of three general principles or desiderata that should govern the development of any modern representation. Adhering to these principles facilitates any attempts to achieve the criteria set out at the beginning of this chapter: application to real texts; rapid, efficient processing; and reversibility. This is the first:

> The representation should consist of an inter-connected set of relatively small units.

The smaller the unit, the less often it will have to be torn down and reassembled when we need to express the same information from a different perspective. Consider the example from the last section. It is redundant to have categories for both *sequence* and *member of a sequence* since the one relation can be logically derived from the other. Nevertheless, English provides phrasings for both (which means that having independent semantic projections for both will make for direct, quick interpretations), and given the interconnection of krisp's units and a simple set of copying rules it is virtually no effort to fleshout one form given the other.[10]

More to the point, suppose we had only implemented *member of a sequence* but latter wanted a companion language generation system to say something like "Yoshinoya has three markets overseas: Taiwan, the United States, and Hong Kong." To construct that final conjunction we would have to unpack the three member-of-a-sequence relationships and create a new unit (at least in the state of the generator), whereas if both forms are maintained we get the conjunction as an already packaged unit. Another consideration relevant to this example brings us to the second principle:

> There should be a first-class object type in the representation for every class of syntactic category in the language.

One of the ways of looking at the notion of a first class object is that it provides a *representational term*—something that another term can stand in relation to. Designing the model to supply both a unit for the group and a unit for each company's membership in the group allows those facts to be reasoned about separately (such as for making summaries about the breadth of international markets with the group; summarizing with other investments by Yoshinoya with the membership relation; etc.).

Making the classic concept–slot–value of KL-one a first class object (a binding) simplifies many different activities that in other kinds of representations are problematic or even impossible. For example we can read the relation out (traverse the network) from either direction. If Yoshinoya "has a market in" the U.S., then we can alternatively start from the unit for the U.S. and ask what foreign companies have markets there. A generator can formulate the text "The U.S. is the second overseas market for Yoshinoya" starting with the very same units that were formed when the text with the alternative focus was parsed.

The rule of thumb has been to package no more information into a single unit (binding, category) than corresponds to a single word or a simple one-argument relation. This maximizes the possibilities for rearranging sets of units to best fit the discourse context given what is redundant or salient at the moment. The other side of this coin, however, is to ensure that when we have a particular body of information with an ongoing identity over time or space—something that entails more than one unit to represent it—we must ensure that it retains this identity regardless of how its component units come to be rearranged in the course of linguistic processing. This takes us to our third principle:

All domain entities have a unique representation in the model.

This is the uniqueness principle that was first articulated in the context of the SNePS representational system (see, for example, Maida and Shapiro 1982). Some of its consequences are obvious and could be glossed as the requirement to have a canonical form for the comprehension system's output. The individual we get from analyzing "The new firm will be 50 percent owned by Takarabune" should also be returned for "Takarabune will own 50 percent of the shares in the new firm" or even for "Takarabune's share of the firm" should that phrase appear later in the same text—the very same object, not just the same description (*eq* rather than *equal* in Lisp).

Adherence to this principle has important consequence for the efficiency of the generation process. A generator must always appreciate when it is realizing a second instance of an entity it has already mentioned so that it can deploy the appropriate pronoun or reduced form. By far the easiest way to do this is to notice that the representational entities for the two instances are the identical unit, rather than attempting to match descriptive expressions. Comparing two graphs for equality (which is what matching descriptions comes down to) is a procedure whose time complexity includes the size of the description as one of its factors. It is far better to take up that factor just once when the initial text for the individual is being indexed as it is parsed (at which time it constitutes just a slight increment on the N plus log N factor that is already at play within the parsing process) than to have to experience it time and time again.

A more subtle consequence of this principle comes in an area we have not even touched on in this chapter: the machinery that is needed to ensure that the uniqueness principle is maintained as a matter of intrinsic design rather than deliberate programming. Briefly, the standard taxonomic lattice that organizes the categories and their variables according to sub- and super-classes is extended below the usual level of detail to incorporate a lattice of all of the combinations of bound and unbound variables that could appear in partially saturated individuals. This provides an indexing structure against which to lay out all of the individuals in the model: those that have been predefined and those that are created during the process of comprehending a text, saturated and unsaturated. During a parse, the categories and bindings of each individual are built up gradually unit by unit and indexed to the corresponding nodes of the partial-saturation lattice. This incremental indexing process shadows the syntactic construction of a parse as argument and adjunct constituents are added to a head.

The lattice is so constructed that bindings made in different orders will all lead to the same node for any given combination of variables. Thus a simple collection of the variables and their values node by node suffices to provide a conduit to a common, single representation of any individual or partial individual that the system has ever been informed about.

Concluding Remarks

The design for KRISP has been developed incrementally during the last several years and is still evolving. Its fundamental motivations stem from investigations over the course of the last decades to try and establish just why it was that other representational systems were always turning out to be awkward when used as the source for the generation of fluent prose.

As a practical system in a working parser, KRISP has undergone a goodly amount of revision as new problems in text were tackled. The partially-saturated-individual type, for example, is a recent addition, developed initially to solve the problem of how to represent phrases like *17 vice presidents* that are sometimes descriptions (making them nominally categories), and sometimes names (making them nominally individuals). Once the new type was introduced, it widened the design space available for solving semantic problems in these texts, and lead to cleaner treatments of long-standing problems.

Whenever there has been a question about what direction the design should take, the choice of analysis has always been made by falling back on how the information would look in the lambda calculus. This reinforces the basic distinction between predicates and their arguments, or between saturated relations and the functions that can be abstracted from them. KRISP is essentially just an object-oriented repackaging of a typed lambda calculus, with the insight that the binding of a variable to a value should be given a first class representation.

The evolution of KRISP will continue as improved treatments and alternative analyses are developed. The mechanics of a hook up between SPARSER and my generation systems has just recently begun, and this is likely to prompt many adjustments in the design, small and large, as issues in the combined efficiency of the two very different processes accessing a single representation are considered and solutions found.

One of the problems for generation systems has always been how to assemble a description of how constructions are used in different genres of text—descriptions that could then be used to produce texts that are true to one or another style as required. It is likely that a combination of the indexing structures developed to implement the uniqueness principle and an annotation of the kinds of syntactic constructions used when the component units of an individual are assembled and indexed could lead to just such a style-recording mechanism as a simple side-effect of just having the parser read the text. Should this prove to be true, it will be a significant validation of the design of KRISP as a whole.

Notes

1. The most important of these "things" are the people to whom the person is talking and the community that encompasses them. These are the truly interesting relationships, but unfortunately they are also the most difficult to capture given today's methodology and research.

2. "KRISP" is an acronym for "Knowledge Representation In Sparser," which, if prosaic, does reflect the fact that the two systems were designed to operate with tight integration.)

3. Note that when I write "(on :B6 :B3)" I am writing an expression in a grammar of parentheses, letters, and whitespace that a Lisp program can interpret as directives to identify certain systematically corresponding internal data structures of an ontologically different

sort than we typed in. Do not confuse the expression (a means to an end) with the thing it denotes. In a significant sense the data structure is real and manipulable only to the running computer program in which it resides (i.e. Shrdlu). Any possibility for us, as people, to observe it will require the construction of some external expression or visual configuration such as a print out in a symbolic debugger or a hexadecimal core dump.

4. For the purpose of this chapter, I will designate newly created individuals using a gensym based on their primary category: #<resign-1>, #<person-3>. If the individual is part of Sparser's background knowledge as the denotation of some proper name or the equivalent, then we will just use that English phrase: #<chairman>. If the type of a unit is not clear from context it is included: #<individual 2/13/91>. If the sortal distinction (the domain type) is important and the epistemological type is clear from context, then the individual's primary category is used: #<name-of-a-person "Ball, George L.">.

5. Here a *position* is a category that combines a position proper, as designated by some title or titles, and the company at which the position is held: *chairman and chief executive officer of Prudential-Bache Securities Inc.* Making choices about how information is to be grouped into units is the interesting and substantial work of defining a domain model. In this case it was motivated by the fact that the position and company are invariably realized together in a single constituent.

6. This means that the set of pointers connecting categories/variables in this lattice are effectively organized into "cables," a notion that was originally articulated by Ron Brachman and Brian Smith during the 1970s.

7. Numbers such as this "16" are taken from the actual indices that were used in a run of the example text that was taken while this article was being written. They have no intrinsic significance and just serve to differentiate one unit of a given type from another. They derive from the units' positions in the resource heap of the Lisp implementation.

8. *Realization,* a term adopted from Systemic Grammar, means here the mapping of a body of information in one form, such as values in a system network or in a knowledge base, into another form with different epistemological properties, possible adding or dropping ancillary information along the way according to the differences in the two form as representations.

9. In these cases, the model has more of the trappings of a knowledge base than the interpretation of a text, but this is a necessary state of affairs, since for an information extraction system to have any hope of comprehending real texts it must bring a lot to the table in terms of known individuals and facts before the process even begins.

10. These copying rules are effectively meaning postulates. They have been only sporadically implemented and are ad hoc at the time this is written.

4 Episodic Logic Meets Little Red Riding Hood

A Comprehensive Natural Representation for Language Understanding

Lenhart K. Schubert and Chung Hee Hwang

LANGUAGE UNDERSTANDING is an organic phenomenon, and the various stages or facets of the language understanding process—parsing, computing a representation, making inferences, etc.—should not be considered in isolation from each other. For instance, both during the computation of utterance meaning and upon its completion, a great deal of "spontaneous," input-driven inferencing is presumed to occur, working out plausible interpretations and consequences based on the discourse interpreted so far, and on meaning postulates and world knowledge. This includes computing unique referents for referring expressions, predictions, and explanations which ultimately give a causally coherent elaboration of what has been said. Therefore, an essential requirement is that the representation support such inferences and the knowledge behind them. It should do so in a way that is both intuitively transparent and analyzable in terms of a formal notion of interpretation. The formal interpretability of the representation allows us to examine in detail whether it captures meanings as intended, and whether proposed inference rules are semantically justifiable.

These considerations point to the centrality of the issue of representation. The ease of mapping from syntax to a semantic representation, *deindexing* (amalgamating the context information into the representation of an utterance so that the resulting representation becomes context-independent), and performing inferences all depend on the representation used.

A basic methodological assumption of our work is that these multiple demands on the representation are best met by using a highly expressive logic closely related to natural language itself. The possibility of handling tense, causes, facts, modifiers, propositions, beliefs, etc., simply and directly depends on the expressiveness of the representation. To see the importance of this issue, let us consider the following excerpt from the story of "Little Red Riding Hood."[1]

> The wolf would have very much liked to eat her, but dared not do so on account of some wood-cutters who were in the forest. He asked her where she was going. The poor child, not knowing that it was dangerous to stop and listen to a wolf, said: "I am going to see my grandmother."

This excerpt exemplifies the following interesting syntactic/semantic phenomena: it involves modality *dare* that indicates eating Little Red Riding Hood would have been a substantial risk for the wolf in that particular circumstance; it involves causal relationships—both an explicit one ("on account of") and an implicit one ("not knowing ..."); it contains a relative clause ("who were in the forest"); it contains an indirect wh-question (*"where* she was going"); it is tensed as well as involving perfect and progressive aspects; it involves a possible fact (*"that* it was dangerous...") as object of the attitude "know"; it involves a gerundive ("not knowing") and infinitives ("to stop and listen") whose interpretation is arguably a reified property; it involves the attitude of the narrator ("the *poor* child"); and it involves a purpose clause ("to see my grandmother").

Most natural language processing researchers have shied away from fanciful narratives such as fairy tales in recent years. For all their "childishness," these pose particularly difficult problems in representation and inference. This is not so much because of anthropomorphic animals, magic, and other departures from realism, but because of their open-ended content and their focus on the activities, goals and attitudes of human (or humanlike) characters. To us, this makes fairy tales and other fiction particularly useful as a crucible for testing the adequacy of representational and interpretive techniques for natural language understanding. However, we can attest that even simple task-oriented dialogs pose severe representational and interpretive challenges (Allen and Schubert 1993; Traum et al. 1996)

To provide some sense of what makes our approach distinctive, we should briefly comment on the more usual approaches to semantic representation and knowledge representation in natural language understanding. Typically, the representations employed are either informal or restricted to variants of first-order logic. In the informal approach (for example, Kolodner 1981, or Schank and Leake 1989), representations are proposed that typically include standard logical and AI devices such as predication, Boolean connectives, slot-and-filler structures, inheritance hierarchies, etc., but also freely add further constructs to deal with beliefs, actions, goals, plans, etc., providing only informal, intuitive explanations of these constructs. The advantage of the informal approach is that the practitioner can quickly accommodate a rich variety of concepts and ideas in the representation and proceed with the investigation or modelling of some specific phenomena without being detained very much by intricate foundational and mathematical questions. The price, of course, is uncertainty as to whether the various types of symbols are being used in a coherent and consistent way, and whether or not the proposed inference methods have a rational basis in some sort of consequence relation.

The first-order logic approach (for example, Dahlgren et al. 1989, Hirst 1988, Wilensky et al. 1988) restricts itself to predicates and functions whose arguments are individuals (such as *loves(John,Mary)*, *mother-of(John)*), Boolean connectives ($\land$, $\lor$, $\neg$, $\rightarrow$, ...), equality, and some quantifiers (such as $\forall$, $\exists$), or syntactic forms that can in principle be reduced to those of first-order logic. The advantage is that first-order logic is well-understood syntactically and semantically. But it also has the disadvantage that very little real language is easily expressible in it. For instance, it does not (in any direct way) allow for beliefs, intensional verbs (such as *needing* something), modifiers (such as *very politely* or *possibly*), complex quantifiers (such as "every butterfly along the way"), habituals (such as "she often visited her grandmother"), and many other quite ordinary locutions (we'll discuss nonstandard constructs a little later).

In some approaches to semantic representation, the emphasis is more on mimicking the surface form of certain kinds of natural language phrases than on matching the full expressive power of natural language. To the extent that the proposed logical forms can readily be paraphrased in first-order logic, such approaches can still be classified as first-order logic approaches. For example, McAllester and Givan propose a form of first-order logic with quantification expressed in the manner of Montague (1973) through *generalized quantifiers* (expressions corresponding to noun phrases such as "every man who walks"); but rather than trying to achieve greater expressiveness, their interest is in a subset of their language that allows polynomial-time satisfiability testing (McAllester and Givan 1992). In a similar vein, Ali and Shapiro's ANALOG representation (Ali and Shapiro 1993) renders complex noun phrases (with determiners *all, some,* or *any*) as structured variables in semantic networks. While some devices are also offered for dealing with so-called branching quantifiers and donkey anaphora (for further remarks on the latter see the next section), the representation is for the most part easily translatable to first-order logic.

A few systems do use significantly extended versions of first-order logic as a representation language. Iwańska's UNO language (Iwańska

1993a, Iwańska 1997a) allows for some types of modifiers through the use of functions (such as a *speed* function to express walking speed in "John walks fast"). It also encodes complex quantified noun phrases as second-order predicates (in essence, Montague-style generalized quantifiers), and provides ways of combining first- and second-order predicates (not just sentences) with *and, or,* and *not.* Alshawi and Eijk's Core Language Engine (CLE) (Alshawi and van Eijck 1989) allows for, among other things, event variables, generalized quantifiers, collective and measure terms, natural kinds, and comparatives and superlatives. TACITUS (Hobbs et al. 1987) allows for event variables, sets, scales, time, spaces and dimension, material, causal connection, and so on. But where they go beyond first-order logic, the latter two systems tend to be unclear about semantics. Also, UNO, CLE, and TACITUS still fall short of comprehensive expressiveness; for instance, they lack means to express nominalization, intensional verbs, and generic sentences. As well, the process of mapping syntax to semantics in these systems appears to remain rather ad hoc—perhaps necessarily so, since the representation languages have not been defined to make this mapping as direct and simple as possible. (UNO is perhaps most nearly natural languagelike in form, but since it is an attribute-value logic, it needs to introduce numerous supplementary functions such as role functions for *n*-place predicates, a speed-of-walking function for "walk fast," a mental-attribute function for "bright student," and so on).

A recent trend in natural language processing has been to try to circumvent many of the syntactic and semantic complexities of written and spoken language by aiming to extract only certain predetermined kinds of information from narrowly focused classes of texts or discourse. While such an approach can achieve high *quantitative* returns (large amounts of data extracted from large corpora), it necessarily compromises the *quality* of understanding. We believe that achieving deeper understanding is an important and realistic goal. In fact, some things are made easier by aiming higher. For instance, computing logical forms is easier if the target representation is natural languagelike in expressiveness, rather than being some restricted framelike language. System builders constrained to use restricted languages usually find themselves resorting to "illegal" (and semantically unanalyzed) add-ons, in the effort to deal with real language. As well, certain inferences are made easy by an expressive language which would be at best roundabout, if possible at all, in less expressive representations, such as inferences based on quantifiers like "most" or modifiers like "almost." In fact, we think that the inferences we have obtained experimentally for story fragments are quite beyond the capabilities of virtually all extant knowledge representations.

In this chapter, we report the results of our effort to develop a comprehensive representation for a general natural language understanding system, and describe our conception of the language understanding process based on that representation. *Episodic Logic* (EL) is a highly expressive knowledge representation well-adapted to the interpretive and inferential needs of general natural language understanding. EL serves simultaneously as the semantic representation and knowledge representation, i.e., it is capable of representing both the explicit content of discourse and the linguistic and world knowledge needed to understand it. EL is designed to be easily derivable from surface syntax, to capture the semantic nuances of natural language text, and to facilitate needed inferences.

In the next section, we briefly introduce EL—its syntax, semantics, and inference rules; in the subsequent section, we discuss the natural language understanding process within our framework, with emphasis on inference and understanding. Then, in a further section, we illustrate our natural language processing strategy— from semantic representation to knowledge representation and to the reasoning process. In the penultimate section, we describe the EPILOG implementation and our work on some prototype natural language understanding systems and on story fragments. In the concluding section we summarize the distinctive features of EL and outline future research.

Introduction to Episodic Logic

EL is a natural language-like logical representation whose syntax echoes the kinds of constructs that are available in all natural languages. The adjective *episodic* alludes to the use of explicit terms denoting events and other episodes, and to the fact that narrative texts focus on *time-bounded* eventualities (such as someone being hungry or having a meal), rather than on *timeless* ones (such as wolves being animals, or wage earners having to pay taxes). Our overview begins with a simple example, then enumerates the most important nonstandard constructs, and provides a sketchy outline of semantics and inference.

Basic Sentential Syntax

The following example serves to convey the flavor of EL.

  a. Little Red Riding Hood chased a butterfly
  b. [LRRH ⟨past chase⟩ ⟨∃ butterfly⟩]
  c. (past (∃x: [x butterfly] [LRRH chase x]))
  d. (∃e_1: [e_1 before Now$_1$] [(∃x: [x butterfly] [LRRH chase x]) ** e_1])   (1)

  (1b) is an unscoped logical form. In particular, the angle brackets ⟨ ⟩ indicate that the tense operator *past* and restricted quantifier "∃ butterfly" are still to be moved leftward until they have an entire sentential formula in their scope. The result of this scoping, which also introduces a variable for the quantifier, is the logical form shown in (1c). Note that the meaning of this logical form is still context-dependent, since *past* is an indexical operator, i.e., its meaning depends on *when* the given sentence was uttered. The process of deindexing (removing context dependence) associates an existentially quantified episodic variable e_1 (an episode of Little Red Riding Hood chasing a butterfly) with the sentence in the scope of *past*, and relates the episode explicitly to the time of utterance (denoted by Now_1, a new time constant). The result is the deindexed episodic logical form shown in (1d). Note that we use square brackets and infix syntax (with the predicate in second place) in sentential forms like [LRRH chase x]. This is a "prettified" variant of the underlying prefix form, $((\text{chase } x)$ LRRH$)$, predicating the property of "chasing x" of LRRH.[2] The sentential infix syntax greatly aids readability for complex formulas. The general form of restricted quantification is $(Q\alpha: \Phi\ \Psi)$, where Q is a quantifier such as ∃, ∀, Most, or Few, α is a variable, and restriction Φ and matrix Ψ are arbitrarily complex formulas. $(\forall\alpha: \Phi\ \Psi)$ and $(\exists\alpha: \Phi\ \Psi)$ are equivalent to $(\forall\alpha) [\Phi \rightarrow \Psi]$ and $(\exists\alpha) [\Phi \wedge \Psi]$, respectively. (However, for nonstandard quantifiers such as Many, Most, and Few, there are no such reductions from the restricted form to an unrestricted one.)

The most unconventional feature of the episodic logical form in (1d) is of course the "$**$" operator associating an episode with a sentence. It can be read as *characterizes*, i.e., in this case Little Red Riding Hood's chasing a butterfly characterizes episode e_1; or to put it as we did above, e_1 is an episode of Little Red Riding Hood chasing a butterfly. The ability to associate episodes with sentences is crucial not only for making tense information explicit as in (1d), but also (as illustrated below) for capturing the content of locative, temporal and other adverbials, for enabling anaphoric reference to events, and for making causal relations among events explicit.

We also have a related episodic operator "$*$," where $[\Phi * \eta]$ means "Φ is true in (or, describes some part or aspect of) η." Note that $[\Phi ** \eta]$ implies $[\Phi * \eta]$; for instance, if e is an episode *of* the sun setting, then the sun sets *in* episode e. (The converse does not in general hold: it may be that the sun sets *in* a certain episode, say one where John drives from New York to Chicago, but that does not make the drive an episode *of* the sun setting.) Whereas the operator "$**$" is introduced by English sentences as above, "$*$" is typically introduced by *meaning postulates*, i.e., general axioms about the meanings of classes of predicates or particular predicates. For instance, suitable meaning postulates about "chase," when applied to

[(∃x: [x butterfly] [LRRH chase x]) ∗∗ e_1]

might lead to the conclusions

[(∃x: [x butterfly] [LRRH see x]) ∗ e_1],

and

[(∃x: [x butterfly] [x move]) ∗ e_1].

Note that in any episode of Little Red Riding Hood chasing a butterfly, she surely saw a butterfly, and a butterfly surely moved. Another way to say this would be to introduce subepisodes e_2, e_3 of e_1 characterized by Little Red Riding Hood seeing a butterfly, and a butterfly moving, respectively. (We could use anaphoric variables, briefly discussed in the next subsection, to refer to the same butterfly in all three episodes.) Note that "∗∗" and "∗" are modal operators as they are not truth-functional, i.e., they do not in general allow substitution for their sentential argument of another sentence with the same truth value. For example, [[LRRH sing] ∗ e_1] does not entail

[[[LRRH sing] ∧ [[Granny ill] ∨ ¬[Granny ill]]] ∗ e_1].

In other words, it is not necessarily the case that in any episode where Little Red Riding Hood sings, either Grandmother is ill or she is not, for Grandmother may have no role in that episode, and thus [[Granny ill] ∨ ¬[Granny ill]] may not have a determinate truth value in it.

Our conception of episodes and their connection to sentences has much in common with the situational logics that have evolved from the work of Barwise (1989) and Barwise and Perry (1983). However, while these logics have an operator analogous to "∗," they lack the analogue of "∗∗." We take the latter to be crucial for correctly representing *causal connections* between episodes, which in turn are essential for arriving at coherent interpretations of narratives. For example, suppose that we represent the causal connection in

Little Red Riding Hood chased a butterfly,
and (as a result) lost her way

by writing [e_1 cause-of e_2], where e_1 and e_2 are the episodes associated via "∗∗" with the first and second clauses respectively. This plausibly expresses our understanding that the episode of Little Red Riding Hood chasing a butterfly caused the eventuality of her losing her way. But now imagine that we had connected the clauses to the episodes e_1, e_2 via "∗" rather than "∗∗." Then [e_1 cause-of e_2] would fail to capture the intended causal connection, since it would merely say that a certain episode in which Little Red Riding Hood chased a butterfly caused another episode, in which she lost her way. Such an assertion is perfectly compatible with a state of affairs where, for instance, Little Red Riding Hood chased a butterfly and hunted for mushrooms, and it was her mushroom-hunting, not her butterfly-chasing, which caused her to lose her way. After all, in such a case it is indeed true in a certain episode—namely one comprised of both the butterfly-chasing and the mushroom-hunting—that she chased a butterfly; and this larger episode, via its mushroom-hunting part, is indeed the cause of her losing her way.

Nonstandard Constructs

For space reasons, we limit our further exposition of EL syntax to illustration of some important nonstandard constructs. See Hwang (1992) and Hwang and Schubert (1993b) for formal details and extensive examples.

Modifiers

All natural languages permit the application of modifiers to predicates and sentences. Example (2a) contains several predicate modifiers.

    a. The wolf almost killed two very nice people
    b. (past [Wolf (almost (kill ((num 2) (plur ((attr (very nice))
                                   person))))))])
    c. $(\exists e_1 : [e_1 \text{ before Now}_1]$
        [[Wolf (almost (kill ((num 2) (plur ((attr (very nice))
                                person))))))] ** e_1])   (2)

(2b) is the preliminary (indexical) logical form and (2c) the deindexed episodic logical form corresponding to (2a). Looking at the modifiers from right to left, note first of all the *very* modifier, which applies to a 1-place predicate and produces an intensified version of that predicate, here "(very nice)". Next, *attr* is a higher-order operator that converts a 1-place predicate into a predicate modifier (here, "(attr (very nice))"); as such, it enables us to express the meaning of a predicative adjective phrase that has been placed in attributive (prenominal) position. *plur* is similar to *very* in that it maps a 1-place predicate to a 1-place predicate; however, the resultant predicate is a predicate over *collections* of individuals. In the present case, "(plur person)" is a predicate that is true of any collection of persons (cf., Link 1983). *num* is an operator that converts a number into a predicate modifier, in the present case "(num 2)." This predicate modifier, when applied to a predicate over collections, yields another predicate over collections that is true only of collections of size 2. Finally, *almost* is again a predicate modifier, in particular one whose output predicate entails the falsity of the input predicate; i.e., if the wolf *almost* killed Little Red Riding Hood and Grandmother, then he did *not* kill them. Note that technically *past* is a sentence modifier, though as we saw before it receives a relational interpretation ("before Now$_1$") after deindexing. Adverbial modifiers, which may modify predicates or sentences, are illustrated separately below.

Anaphoric Variables

Consider the following two successive sentences and their logical forms.

a. Little Red Riding Hood chased every butterfly (that she saw)
b. (past ($\forall\ x$: [x butterfly][LRRH chase x]))
c. ($\exists e_1$: [e_1 before Now$_1$][($\forall\ x$: [x butterfly] [LRRH chase x]) $**\ e_1$])   (3)

a. *It* made her tired
b. (past [*It* (make2 tired) LRRH])
c. ($\exists e_2$: [e_2 before Now$_2$] [[e_1 (make2 tired) LRRH] $**\ e_2$]))   (4)

As before, (3b) and (4b) are preliminary, indexical logical forms (omitting the relative clause for simplicity), and (3c) and (4c) are deindexed episodic logical forms. In (4b) and (4c), *make2* is a 2-fold predicate modifier, mapping the 1-place predicate *tired* into the 2-place predicate "(make2 tired)." (Note the distinction between 2-fold predicate modifiers and ordinary ones such as *very*, which produce 1-place predicates.) Observe that *It* in (4b) has been resolved to e_1 in (4c), so that e_1 now occurs outside the scope of its $\exists$-quantifier in (3c). Such anaphoric variables are allowed in EL, thanks to a parameter mechanism that does much the same work as dynamic binding in DRT (Kamp 1981) or dynamic predicate logic (Groenendijk and Stokhof 1991). Intuitively, we can think of the existential quantification in (3c) as binding some value (viz., an episode of Little Red Riding Hood chasing every butterfly she saw) to the variable e_1, where this binding persists to (4c). The effect is that the conjunction of (3c) and (4c) is interpreted as if the $\exists$-quantifier binding e_1 had maximally wide scope.

The parameter mechanism is also crucial for dealing with donkey anaphora (Geach 1962) in sentences like "Every man who owns a donkey feeds it" or "If I have a quarter I'll put it in the parking meter." Sentences of this sort provided much of the impetus behind the development of DRT and dynamic predicate logic. The difficulty in the examples lies in the fact that an existentially quantified variable (for "a donkey" in the first sentence and "a quarter" in the second) is referred to by a pronoun ("it") lying outside the scope of the quantifier. The situation is thus much as in the pair of (c)-sentences above, and is handled by the parameter mechanism in much the same way. Semantically, the second sentence (from Schubert and Pelletier [1989]) in our treatment is logically equivalent to "If I have a quarter, then I have a quarter that I will put in the parking meter." This differs from the standard DRT treatment in not asserting that I will put *all* quarters that I have into the meter; for some further discussion of these issues (see, for example, Chierchia [1995] and Schubert [forthcoming]).

Attitudes

We think that the objects of attitudes such as *believing, telling, hoping,* etc., are propositions. These are abstract individuals formed from sentence intensions (which in our case are truth-valued partial functions on situations) by applying the operator That, as illustrated in example 5.

a. Mother told Little Red Riding Hood that Grandmother was ill
b. (past [Mother tell LRRH (That (past [Granny ill]))])
c. $(\exists e_1: [e_1 \text{ before Now}_1]$
$\quad [[\text{Mother tell LRRH (That}$
$\quad\quad\quad (\exists e_2: [e_2 \text{ at-or-before } e_1] \; [[\text{Granny ill}] ** e_2]))]$
$\quad ** e_1])$ (5)

We take propositions as subsuming possible facts. Possible facts are just consistent propositions. There are self-contradictory propositions (and these may, for instance, be objects of beliefs, etc.), but there are no self-contradictory possible facts.

Actions

Actions are distinguished from events or episodes in that they have well-defined agents—thus, one may perform an action, but not perform an episode or event; likewise, there are intentional actions, wicked actions, etc., but not "intentional events" or "wicked events." In EL, actions are represented as agent-event pairs; i.e., to specify a particular action is to specify both the agent of the action and the event brought about through the action. Here is an example.

a. The wolf gobbled up Grandmother
b. *It* was a very wicked deed   (6)

a. (past [Wolf gobble-up Granny])
b. (past [*It* ((attr (very wicked)) deed)])   (7)

a. $(\exists e_1: [e_1 \text{ before Now}_1] \; [[\text{Wolf gobble-up Granny}] ** e_1])$
b. $(\exists e_2: [e_2 \text{ before Now}_2] \; [[[\text{Wolf} \mid e_1] ((\text{attr (very wicked)}) \text{ deed})] ** e_2])$ (8)

Notice that *It* in (7b) is resolved to the ordered pair [Wolf | e_1] in (8b), namely, the wolf's action of gobbling up Grandmother. "|" is a pairing function applicable to individuals and tuples. (As in Lisp and Prolog, an individual paired with an *n*-tuple gives an $(n + 1)$-tuple headed by the individual.)

Kinds of Actions and Events

Our approach here is inspired by Carlson (1982) and Chierchia (1985). We start with a basic kind-forming operator K applicable to predicates like "dog" (for example, (K dog) represents dog-kind, whose instances are dogs), and then posit analogous operators for forming kinds of actions and kinds of events. For example, "to visit Grandmother" is a kind of action, and example (9a) says that Little Red Riding Hood likes to do that kind of action. (Compare with "Little Red Riding Hood likes animals," which is about her liking a particular kind of thing, viz., animals.) On the other hand, "for Little Red Riding Hood to talk to a stranger" is a kind of event, and example (10a) asserts that this kind of event is not unusual. (Compare with "Gray wolves are not unusual," which makes a generic claim about the kind of thing, gray wolves. To be more accurate, we should perhaps use *gpres* (generic present) tense below.)

a. Little Red Riding Hood likes to visit Grandmother
b. (pres [LRRH like (*Ka* (visit Granny))])
c. ($\exists e_1$: [e_1 at-about Now$_1$] [[LRRH like (*Ka* (visit Granny))] ** e_1])   (9)

a. For Little Red Riding Hood to talk to a stranger is not unusual
b. (pres (¬[(*Ke* ($\exists x$: [x stranger] [LRRH talk-to x])) unusual]))
c. ($\exists e_2$: [e_2 at-about Now$_2$]
[(¬[(*Ke* ($\exists x$: [x stranger] [LRRH talk-to x])) unusual]) ** e_2])   (10)

In these representations, *Ka* maps 1-place action predicates into kinds of actions, and *Ke* maps sentences into kinds of events. *Ka*- or *Ke*-constructs can be equivalently written as constructs headed by the *K* operator.[3]

Probabilistic Conditionals

We use probabilistic conditionals of form $\Phi \rightarrow_{p, \alpha_1, \alpha_2, ..., \alpha_n} \Psi$, where α_1, α_2, ..., α_n are *controlled variables,* to represent extensionally interpretable generic statements. Intuitively, the meaning is that at least a fraction p of the tuples of values of α_1, ..., α_n that satisfy Φ also satisfy Ψ. Let us consider the following example. (Here *non* is a predicate modifier with the property that [x (non π)], for π a monadic predicate, entails ¬[x π].)

a. If a predatory animal finds a nonpredatory creature of modest size, he may attack it.
b. ($\exists e_1$ [($\exists x$: [x ((attr predatory) animal)]
    ($\exists y$: [[y ((attr (non predatory)) creature)] $\wedge$
        (¬[y big-rel-to x]) $\wedge$ (¬[y tiny-rel-to x])]
    [x find y])) ** e_1])
    $\rightarrow_{.2, e_1}$ ($\exists e_2$: [e_1 immed-cause-of e_2] [[x attack y] ** e_2])   (11)

This formula says that in at least 20 percent of the situations e_1 in which the antecedent is true, the consequent will also be true. This statistical probability becomes the epistemic probability of the consequent, when we detach the consequent for some true instance of the antecedent. For instance, given that "a wolf found a rabbit" (and background knowledge to the effect that a wolf is a predatory animal, that a rabbit is a nonpredatory animal that is neither big nor tiny relative to a wolf), the above conditional allows us to conclude that the wolf may have attacked the rabbit, with minimum epistemic probability (degree of confidence) .2.

The fact that only e_1 (and not x and y) are controlled in the conditional means that in a situation where multiple predators (such as a pack of wolves) encounter multiple potential prey (such as a herd of deer), we do not predict an attack by each predator on each prey, just some predator-prey attack.[4] Probabilistic conditionals are very convenient in representing generic world knowledge, and as will be seen in a later section, are used extensively in our implementation.[5]

Adverbials

We focus on verb phrase adverbials here such as temporal, locative and manner adverbials, since these are the most common. We interpet such adverbials in a two-stage process. First, in forming the preliminary (indexical) logical form, we map adverbials that intuitively modify actions (including manner adverbials such as *politely*) into predicate operators applied to the interpretation of the verb phrase; and we map adverbials that intuitively modify episodes (including temporal and locative adverbials such as *in the forest*) into sentential operators applied to the interpretation of the sentence. In the second, deindexing stage, we recast the action-modifying operators as explicit predications about actions, and episode-modifying operators as explicit predications about episodes. This is made possible by the introduction of explicit episodic variables in the deindexing process that produces the final episodic logical form. For example, consider the following sentence, involving two adverbials.

a. The wolf politely greeted Little Red Riding Hood in the forest

b. (past (The x: [x wolf] (The y: [y forest]
        ((adv-e (in-loc y))   [x ((adv-a (in-manner polite))
                                      (greet LRRH))])))))

c. ($\exists e_1$: [e_1 before Now$_1$]
        [[[e_1 in-loc Forest1] $\land$ [[Wolf | e_1] (in-manner polite)] $\land$
        [Wolf greet LRRH]]
        ** e_1])   (12)

In (12a), "in the forest" modifies the episode described by "the wolf greet Little Red Riding Hood," or, more specifically, its spatial location; "politely," on the other hand, modifies the action of the wolf's greeting Little Red Riding Hood (by specifying the manner in which the action was performed). In the indexical logical form, an episode-modifying adverbial assumes the form (adv-e π), where π is a predicate over episodes, and an action-modifying adverbial takes the form (adv-a π), where π is a 1-place predicate over actions (more generally, over "attributes," allowing for static verb phrases). That is, adv-e is an operator that uniformly maps 1-place predicates into sentence modifiers, and adv-a is an operator that maps 1-place predicates into predicate modifiers. Additional examples are (adv-e (during Yesterday)) for "yesterday," (adv-e (lasts-for (K ((num 1) hour)))) for "for an hour," and (adv-a (with-accomp LRRH)) for "with Little Red Riding Hood."

Note that the scope of $**$ in (12c) extends leftward over a conjunction of three formulas, so that e_1 is asserted to be an episode of the wolf greeting Little Red Riding Hood politely in the forest. Certain general axioms allow us to narrow the scope of $**$ to exclude atemporal formulas like $[e_1$ in-loc Forest$_1]$ and $[[$Wolf $|$ $e_1]$ (in-manner polite)]; in the present case, this brings out the fact that an episode of the wolf greeting Little Red Riding Hood politely in the forest is necessarily an episode of the wolf greeting Little Red Riding Hood. With this scope-narrowing, and after Skolemizing e_1 to E_1 and separating conjuncts, we obtain

   a. $[E_1$ before Now$_1]$
   b. $[E_1$ in-loc Forest$_1]$
   c. $[[$Wolf $|$ $E_1]$ (in-manner polite)]
   d. $[[$Wolf greet LRRH] $**$ $E_1]$

This makes plain how adverbials in EL ultimately provide conjunctive information about the described episode.[6] It is also worth noting that this ultimate format is quite similar to a Davidsonian one (Davidson 1967). However, while Davidson introduced event variables as "extra arguments" of verbs, our approach (following Reichbach [1947] and the more recent situation-theoretic tradition) associates episodic variables with arbitrarily complex sentences. This has the important advantage that it allows us to make formal sense of such notions as "a three-day episode of the wolf not eating anything" (involving negation), "an episode of John drinking and driving" (involving conjunction), and "the lengthy process of each graduate ascending to the podium and taking receipt of his or her diploma" (involving quantification). In other words, we contend that not only atomic predications, but arbitrary sentences, can be used to characterize episodes; several of our examples (such as 10c and 12c) have illustrated this point.

Some linguistic phenomena whose representation in episodic logic is still somewhat up in the air are quantifier modifiers (as in "very few," or "all but five"), comparatives (such as "ran as fast as his feet would carry him," or "the better to hear you with"), and Wh-questions ("Why are your ears so large?"). Jumping ahead a little, we should mention that our EPILOG system (the computational system for EL; [Miller et al. 1991]) is able to answer many yes-no and Wh-questions, for instance "Who met whom?" expressed as

   (W? x: [x person] (W? y: [y person] ($\exists e$ [[x meet y] $*$ e]))).

However, the analysis of questions we currently favor calls for some modification of this format, involving the use of intension and exten-

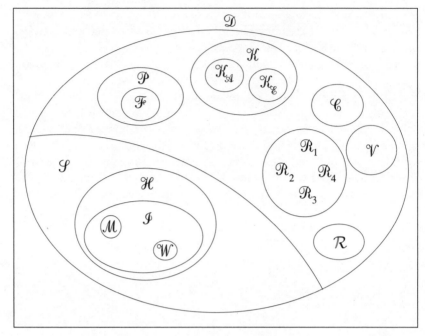

Figure 1. Ontology of Basic Individuals

sion operators.[7] Despite these open issues, we believe that EL is the most expressive knowledge and semantic representation yet to be brought to bear on the problem of natural language understanding.

Ontology and Glimpses of Semantics

Our syntactic examples involved not just ordinary individuals such as people and butterflies, but also events (episodes), collections, actions, propositions, kinds of things, and kinds of events and actions. Correspondingly, the semantics of EL is based on an ontology of possible individuals $\mathcal{D}$ that includes all of these sorts of things (and some others), as shown in figure 1. As Hobbs (1985b) argues, it is better to expand one's ontology to allow more kinds of entities than to complicate the logical form of sentences, or the interpretive process. *Possible* individuals are meant to include not only real or actual individuals but also imaginary or fictitious ones, such as those denoted by the phrases "Sherlock Holmes, the fictitious detective" and "the cancelled lecture" (from Hirst [1991]).

The most distinctive aspect of our semantics concerns the ontology of possible situations $\mathcal{S}$ (the lower left portion of figure 1), their special subclasses, and their part-of structure. We use the term *situation* rather than *episode* when discussing denotational semantics, in deference to custom in situation semantics and also to avoid the implication that we are limiting ourselves to time-bounded situations. We discuss situations and their sub-classes in greater detail below. Disjointly from $\mathcal{S}$, we have not only ordinary individuals of our experience, but also propositions $\mathcal{P}$, possible facts $\mathcal{F}$ (which as mentioned are consistent propositions), kinds of individuals $\mathcal{K}$ (including kinds of ordinary individuals, kinds of actions $\mathcal{K}_A$, and kinds of episodes, or situations, $\mathcal{K}_E$), the real numbers $\mathcal{R}$ (augmented with $-\infty$ and $+\infty$), and n-dimensional regions $\mathcal{R}_n$ ($1 \leq n \leq 4$), containing subsets of $\mathcal{R}^n$. $\mathcal{R}_4$ contains space-time trajectories that may not be connected. These are important since we regard situations as occupying times and places, or, more generally, spatiotemporal trajectories (regions). Finally, there are collections $\mathcal{C}$ and n-vectors (i.e., tuples) $\mathcal{V}$, $n = 2, 3, \ldots$, of all of these.

Situations, Times, and Worlds

Possible situations subsume what we might ordinarily (informally) call specific events, states of affairs, and circumstances or eventualities. Unlike situations in situation semantics (which are deemed to be real), possible situations in EL are "partial possible worlds," in that predicate symbols are assigned partial extensions (argument values for which they are true) and antiextensions (argument values where they are false) relative to them. Indeed, we get from arbitrary situations to possible worlds by maximizing over space, time, and information: among the possible situations $\mathcal{S}$ are the informationally maximal exhaustive situations $\mathcal{H}$, and among the exhaustive situations are the spatially maximal possible times $\mathcal{I}$ (intervals), conceived of as "everything that happened or was the case over a particular clock-time interval"; possible times in turn include the spatiotemporally maximal possible worlds $\mathcal{W}$ and the spatially maximal, temporally minimal moments of time $\mathcal{M}$. Thus the usual indices of semantic evaluation, worlds and times, are here collapsed into one, viz., situations.

The treatment of times and worlds as certain kinds of situations is unusual but quite plausible. Consider, for instance, "This week has been eventful," or "the present moment is the outcome of the entire history of the universe," suggesting that times such as *this week* or the *present moment* have episodic content.[8] Note that actions or activities are not included in $\mathcal{S}$. Actions are regarded as events paired with their agents, as illustrated in the earlier subsection on Actions.

Part-of Structure of Situations and Persistence of Information

The notion of maximizing along spatiotemporal and information dimensions presupposes a *part-of* ordering among situations. The particular part-of structure we assume is motivated by certain intuitively warranted entailment patterns (or truth persistence patterns). These can be observed when we evaluate sentences relative to ever-more-inclusive situations, or conversely, relative to ever-smaller subsituations. We briefly illustrate some of the phenomena at issue, using mnemonic abbreviations for certain sentences and for episodes characterized by those sentences:

> [WalkToCottage ** EntireWalk], [WalkThroughForest ** ForestWalk], [MeetWolf ** Meeting], [Alone ** AloneEp].

Here WalkToCottage stands for the (formalized, tenseless) sentence "Little Red Riding Hood walks to Grandmother's cottage," and EntireWalk stands for an *episode* characterized by that sentence, i.e., it is an episode of Little Red Riding Hood walking to Grandmother's cottage. WalkThroughForest stands for "Little Red Riding Hood walks through the forest" and correspondingly ForestWalk is an episode of Little Red Riding Hood walking through the forest, specifically the part of EntireWalk that is located in the forest on Little Red Riding Hood's way to Grandmother's cottage. We will also use MeetWolf to abbreviate "Little Red Riding Hood meets the wolf," and Alone to abbreviate "Little Red Riding Hood is alone."

Given this, we note the following entailments and nonentailments. (Here ⊨ and ⫤ mean "entails" and "is entailed by," and the crossed-off versions deny the corresponding entailments.)

> a. [MeetWolf * ForestWalk] ⫤̸ [MeetWolf * EntireWalk]
>
> b. [Alone * ForestWalk] ⊭ [Alone * EntireWalk]}
>
> c. [(¬MeetWolf) * ForestWalk] ⊭ [(¬MeetWolf) * EntireWalk]
>
> d. [(¬Alone) * ForestWalk] ⊭ [(¬Alone) * EntireWalk]

Here (a) illustrates what we call *outward persistence* of *telic* formulas; i.e., if a telic formula Φ—one that describes an inherently time-bounded, culminating episode such as meeting or greeting someone, walking to Grandmother's cottage, etc.—is true in a temporal segment of a larger episode, then it is also true in the larger episode. The converse does not hold, i.e., knowing only that Little Red Riding Hood meets a wolf in her walk to Grandmother's cottage, we cannot say that she meets him in her walk through the forest—the meeting might take place in another part of the walk. Thus we do not have *inward persistence* for telic formulas. We have the opposite situation for the *atelic* formula in (b) (asserting that Little Red Riding Hood is alone)—an inherently homogeneous description, not entailing a particular culmination or termination within the described episode. Clearly if Little Red Riding Hood is alone in her walk to Grandmother's cottage, she is alone in any temporal segment of that walk, in particular in her walk through the forest, while the converse need not hold. So for atelic formulas, we have inward, but not in general outward persistence. (As just indicated, inward persistence is sometimes called *homogeneity* in the literature.) In (c) and (d), we see that negated formulas behave like atelic ones, whether the original formula was telic or atelic. In both cases, we have inward, but not outward persistence.[9]

Situations can be part of one another in both a temporal sense and in an informational sense. For example, Little Red Riding Hood's walk through the forest is a temporal segment of her walk to Grandmother's cottage. On the other hand, if Little Red Riding Hood was alone and carefree in her walk to Grandmother's cottage, then the situation of her being alone, and that of her being carefree, are *coextensive* (simultaneous) parts of the "more informed," cumulative situation of her being alone and carefree in that walk.

The coextensive subepisode ordering is written $s \leq s'$ and relates a "less informed" situation s to a "more informed" coextensive situation s', i.e., one with the same temporal location but with more situational content. This basic ordering supports full persistence of information: whatever is true (false) in s is also true (false) in s'. We call this form of persistence *upward persistence* (imagining more informed situations as being "higher" in the $\leq$-ordering). There is also a *subsegment relation* $\unlhd$, where $s \unlhd s'$ means that s is a temporal segment of s' (or a multi-segment, consisting of multiple disjoint segments). Only telic and atemporal (eternal) sentences are guaranteed to have persistent extensions through the $\unlhd$ ordering. For instance, if [LRRH meet Wolf] or [5 integer] is true in s, then it is also true in s', for $s \unlhd s'$. This is what we called "outward persistence" above. But for an atelic sentence like [LRRH alone], its truth in s does not guarantee its truth in s', for $s \unlhd s'$. This is what we called "outward persistence" earlier. But for an atelic sentence like [LRRH alone], its truth in s does not guarantee its truth in s', for $s \unlhd s'$.

We can combine $\leq$ and $\unlhd$ by forming the transitive closure of their disjunction, i.e. the transitive closure of

$$\{\langle s, s' \rangle \mid s \leq s' \text{ or } s \unlhd s'\}.$$

We write the resulting relation as $\sqsubseteq$, and refer to this as the (general) *subepisode* relation. In this partial ordering, a subepisode can be both informationally and temporally "smaller" than the situation of which it is a part. Note that telic and atemporal sentences are outward/upward persistent in the $\sqsubseteq$-ordering. Atelic sentences are inward persistent in the $\unlhd$-ordering, but not in general inward/downward persistent in the $\sqsubseteq$-ordering.

A transitive, reflexive relation *Actual* $\subset \mathcal{D} \times \mathcal{S}$ determines what individuals are actual with respect to a given situation. The *Actual* relation extends $\sqsubseteq$, since we would like to regard any part of a situation as actual relative to it. As well, there is a relation *Nonactual* $\subset \mathcal{D} \times \mathcal{S}$, disjoint from *Actual*, determining the possible but nonactual individuals involved in a situation. We assume that an individual that is nonactual with respect to a given situation is also nonactual with respect to any more inclusive situation.

Interpretations

A *model* $\mathcal{M} = (\ \mathcal{D}, I\ )$ in EL consists of a domain of individuals $\mathcal{D}$ (structured as outlined above, with various additional constraints) and an interpretation function I that partially interprets individual constants and variables,[10] function and predicate constants, predicate modifiers, and several other kinds of atoms (again subject to various constraints).

The most important aspect of any type of situation semantics is the semantics of predication, and how this provides the basis for truth-in-situations relative to a model $\mathcal{M}$. For our purposes, there are two alternative ways we could conceptualize predicate interpretations: as determining *characterizations* of certain basic situations in terms of atomic predications, or as directly determining *truth / falsity* in situations, for atomic predications. In the first approach we would say, for example, that $I(\text{sneeze})(d)(s) = 1, 0$, or is undefined respectively if s is a situation (episode) of individual d sneezing, a situation of d not sneezing, or neither. The notion of truth / falsity in a situation would then be derivative—for instance, if $I(\text{sneeze}\})(d)(s) = 1$, we would say it is true in all situations s' more inclusive than s (i.e., $s \sqsubseteq s'$) that d sneezes. Note that this would assure outward persistence of telic sentences.

Though the notion of interpretation in the first approach is intuitively very natural, we opt for the second approach, since this simplifies (and makes more nearly "conventional") the connection between interpretations and truth. Thus we say, for example, that $I(\text{sneeze})(d)(s) = 1, 0$, or is undefined respectively if s is a situation (episode) *in which* individual d sneezes, one in which d doesn't sneeze, or one where d's sneezing or not sneezing is not determinate. Here s need no longer be an episode *of d* sneezing in order for $I(\text{sneeze})(d)(s)$ to be 1—rather, s might consist of many subepisodes, only one of which happens to be an episode of d sneezing. So in this case, persistence properties are presumed to be "built into" the interpretations of predicates. To begin with, we assure upward persistence of all predications (whether telic or atelic) by assuming that if a predication is true in s, then it is also true in s', for $s \leq s'$. In addition, to ensure outward persistence of a predication like [Mary sneeze], we would assume that whenever $I(\text{sneeze})(d)(s) = 1$ holds, $I(\text{sneeze})(d)(s') = 1$ holds for any more inclusive situation s' (i.e., for $s \sqsubseteq s'$). In the same way we assume that the inward persistence of atelic predications and of negated predications is built into the interpretations of the relevant predicates. For instance, if we have $I(\text{alone})(d)(s) = 1$ (individual d is alone in situation s), this no longer means that s is a situation *of* d being alone, but only that it contains such a situation as a *coextensive part;* in other words, we assume that there is an $s' \leq s$ which is a situation of d being alone and all of whose temporal segments are also situations in which d is alone (for all $s'' \trianglelefteq s'$, $I(\text{alone})(d)(s'') = 1$). Similarly, if we have $I(\text{alone})(d)(s) = 0$ (individual d is not alone in situation s), then we assume that there will also be a coextensive part $s' \leq s$ (intuitively, that part or aspect of s which is the situation *of* d not being alone) all of whose smaller parts are also situations in which d is not alone.

Note that we have assumed above that we can apply the interpretation of a monadic predicate successively to an individual and a situation to obtain a truth value in $\{0, 1\}$. So the interpretations of *meet* and *alone,* for example, are "curried" partial functions of type $\mathscr{D} \rightarrow (\mathscr{S} \rightarrow 2)$ (writing 2 for $\{0, 1\}$).[11] Upon applying such a function to an individual, we obtain a *sentence intension*—a partial 0, 1-valued function on situations. In the same way, we interpret 2-place predicates as elements of $\mathscr{D} \rightarrow (\mathscr{D} \rightarrow (\mathscr{S} \rightarrow 2))$; etc. For instance, *greet* denotes an element of $\mathscr{D} \rightarrow (\mathscr{D} \rightarrow (\mathscr{S} \rightarrow 2))$, (greet Mary)} denotes an element of $\mathscr{D} \rightarrow (\mathscr{S} \rightarrow 2)$, and ((greet Mary) John) (also written in "flattened," infix form as [John greet Mary]) denotes an element of $\mathscr{S} \rightarrow 2$.

With this approach to predicate interpretation, it is the notion of characterization that becomes derivative. In other words, we need to specify the semantics of the "∗∗" operator in terms of truth *in* situations, since predicate interpretations no longer provide characterizations of situations in any direct way. We indicate in the next subsection how we do this. Before proceeding, we should say a few words about the interpretation of atoms other than predicates. Two examples of nonstandard constructs for which our ample ontology provides direct interpretations are those for nominalizing (reifying) actions and sentences. In particular, if π is an action predicate (for example, $\pi = $ (greet Mary)), with a denotation in $\mathscr{D} \rightarrow (\mathscr{S} \rightarrow 2)$, then (Ka π) denotes an element of $\mathscr{K}_A$ (a kind of action—in the example, the action of greeting Mary). Similarly if Φ is a sentence, then (That Φ) denotes an element of $\mathscr{P}$ (i.e., a proposition). The abstract individuals obtained in this way can be "talked about" in EL like any others.

Truth Conditions

As was seen above, sentences are assigned denotations of type $\mathscr{S} \rightarrow 2$, i.e., a sentence may be true, false or truth-valueless in a given (possible) situation. The sentences which are true or false in a situation can be thought of defining its "information content." A well-known advantage of this type of partial semantics is that it avoids the assumption of omniscience in the logic of knowledge, belief, and other attitudes; i.e., believers are not presumed to believe all the consequences of their beliefs.

Let's indicate briefly how we arrive at truth values of sentences in situations, relative to a model $\mathcal{M} = (\mathcal{D}, I)$. First, given our truth-based (rather than characterization-based) semantics of predication, the truth conditions for an atomic sentence (where π is an n-place predicate and τ_1, ..., τ_n are terms) are simply

$$[\pi(\tau_1) \ldots (\tau_n)]^s_{\mathcal{M}} = \{^1_0\} \text{ iff } I(\pi)([\tau_1]_{\mathcal{M}}) \ldots ([\tau_n]_{\mathcal{M}})(s) = \{^1_0\}$$

where s is an arbitrary situation in $\mathcal{S}$ and the $[\tau_i]_{\mathcal{M}}$ are the denotations of the τ_i in model $\mathcal{M}$. (We omit the semantics of terms, except to mention that terms may have undefined denotations, but are rigidly interpreted, i.e., their values, if any, are independent of particular situations.)

As was seen in the section on basic sentential syntax, the "∗" operator allows the truth of an EL sentence relative to a situation to be expressed within EL itself, and this is what enables us to explicitly describe events, circumstances, etc., through sentences that hold in them. That "∗" does indeed correspond to truth in a situation can be seen from its semantics, which says that (for Φ a sentence, η a term, and s a situation in $\mathcal{S}$),

$$[\Phi * \eta]^s_{\mathcal{M}} = 1 \text{ iff Actual}([\eta]_{\mathcal{M}}, s) \text{ and } [\Phi]^{[\eta]_{\mathcal{M}}}_{\mathcal{M}} = 1 ;$$
$$= 0 \text{ iff Nonactual}([\eta]_{\mathcal{M}}, s) \text{ or } [\Phi]^{[\eta]_{\mathcal{M}}}_{\mathcal{M}} = 0.$$

The requirement that $[\eta]_{\mathcal{M}}$ must be actual in order for Φ to be true in it makes "∗" (and indirectly, "∗∗") a *factive* operator; i.e., if $[\Phi * \eta]$ holds then η, and hence a subepisode of type Φ, must in fact have occurred. For instance, though we can in principle talk about a fictitious episode E, as soon as we assert [[Mary sneeze] ∗ E] we are committed to the reality of E and the actual occurrence of a subepisode of Mary sneezing in E.

The meaning of [Φ ∗∗ η], ("Φ characterizes η") is similar to that of [Φ ∗ η] but requires that η *as a whole,* rather than just some part of it, be of type Φ. Instead of giving a direct truth-conditional definition we treat "∗∗" as syntactically defined as follows. The definition says that η is either a minimal episode in which Φ holds, or it is comprised of temporal segments in all of which Φ holds, but none of which have coextensive proper parts in which Φ holds.

$$[\Phi ** \eta] \equiv_{def} [[\Phi * \eta] \wedge (\forall e : [e \sqsubset \eta] \neg[\Phi * e])] \vee$$
$$(\forall e: [e \trianglelefteq \eta] [[\Phi * e] \wedge (\forall e' : [e' < e] \neg[\Phi * e'])])$$

(For conciseness we have used the metalinguistic ordering relations "⊏," "⊴," and "<" here, where in our implementation we would use object language predicates like "proper-subep-of," "subsegment-of," and "proper-coexten-subep-of.") For telic formulas, the definition simplifies to the first disjunct, and for atelic ones to the second. Many formulas—though not all—can be classified as telic or atelic. Without going into details, we assume that atomic predicates are dichotomized in this way, and that certain operators produce a telic or atelic result. For instance, activity predicates such as "walk" and "sit" are atelic, but when we include a destination adverbial such as "to Grandmother's cottage" or a duration adverbial such as "for an hour" in sentences based on atelic predicates, the result is telic. This is because a modified sentence such as "Little Red Riding Hood walked to Grandmother's cottage" implies a culminated action, whereas "Little Red Riding Hood walked" does not.[12] On the other hand, application of the *progressive* operator "prog" to a telic sentence (formula) produces an atelic result; for example, "Little Red Riding Hood was walking to Grandmother's cottage" is atelic. Probabilistic conditionals (which as explained are used for certain kinds of generic sentences) likewise produce an atelic result. A conjunction of a telic and atelic sentence is telic. Negation produces an atelic result, as does application of the "$*$" and "$**$" operators. In fact formulas of form $[\Phi * \eta]$ or $[\Phi ** \eta]$ are atemporal—they are true at all situations where they have a truth value, or false at all such situations.[13]

The semantics of logical connectives have a rather familiar look (modulo partiality), and we mention only two examples:

$$[\neg\Phi]^s_{\mathcal{M}} = \{^1_0\} \text{ iff } [\Phi]^s_{\mathcal{M}} = \{^0_1\};$$
$$[\Phi \vee \Psi]^s_{\mathcal{M}} = 1 \text{ iff } [\neg\Phi]^s_{\mathcal{M}} = 1 \text{ or } [\Psi]^s_{\mathcal{M}} = 1;$$
$$= 0 \text{ iff } [\Phi]^s_{\mathcal{M}} = 0 \text{ and } [\Psi]^s_{\mathcal{M}} = 0.$$

We omit the truth conditions for conjunction ($\wedge$) and the material conditional ($\rightarrow$) since these involve some small complications to allow for the possible presence of anaphoric connections. These in turn depend on our slightly unconventional approach to $\exists$- and The-quantification. ($\exists\alpha\colon \Phi\ \Psi$)} has the expected semantics (intuitively, "Some value of α satisfying Φ satisfies Ψ") only if α does not have a value under the current interpretation I. If α does have a value, ($\exists\alpha\colon \Phi\ \Psi$) is equivalent to $[\Phi \wedge \Psi]$. Analogous remarks apply to (The $\alpha\colon \Phi\ \Psi$). Consequently, certain $\exists$- or The-quantified variables of a formula, called its *parameters,* can have their values "externally" supplied, and this allows us to deal with anaphora in the DRT-like manner we previously illustrated.[14]

Our semantics of $\forall$, Most, Many, etc., together with the semantics of "$**$", leads to a conception of episodes with quantified characterizations as the *join* of a set of subepisodes of the type quantified over. For instance, in the sentences, "On her way to Grandmother's cottage, Little Red Riding Hood chased every butterfly she saw. *That* took up half the trip," the quantified episode consists of the join of chasing subepisodes, which may be separated by breaks of various lengths; that is what makes it possible for the second sentence (about the proportion of the time taken up by butterfly-chasing) to be true even if the time-stretch from the first to the last butterfly-chase covers the entire trip. Still, the truth conditions for $\exists$, $\forall$ and standard connectives do not differ radically from "standard" ones (for example, as in Barwise [1989] or Devlin [1991]).

We leave matters of ontology and formal semantics here, and proceed to our inference rules. For further details on semantics, see Hwang- and Schubert [1993b] and Hwang [1992], with the caveat that we have significantly altered our semantics for "$*$" and "$**$."[15]

Inference Rules

We should begin by mentioning certain normalizing rules that we apply whenever possible:

1. Minimize the scope of negation. For instance, change

    $\neg(\forall x: [x\ \text{person}]\ [x\ \text{afraid-of Wolf}])$

    to

    $(\exists x: [x\ \text{person}]\ \neg[x\ \text{afraid-of Wolf}])$.

2. Skolemize top-level existential variables (i.e., replace them by new constants). For instance, change

    $(\exists x: [x\ \text{person}]\ \neg[x\ \text{afraid-of Wolf}])$

    to

    $[[C\ \text{person}]\ \wedge\ \neg[C\ \text{afraid-of Wolf}]]$.

3. Separate top-level conjuncts. For instance, change

    $[[C\ \text{person}]\ \wedge\ \neg[C\ \text{afraid-of Wolf}]]$

    to

    $[C\ \text{person}],\ \neg[C\ \text{afraid-of Wolf}]$.

4. For formulas involving the atomic sentences $\top$ (truth) or $\bot$ (falsity), apply a set of simplifying rules. For instance, change $\neg\top$ to $\bot$, $\neg\bot$ to $\top$, $\Phi \vee \top$ to $\top$, $\Phi \wedge \top$ to Φ, $\Phi \vee \bot$ to Φ, $\Phi \to \bot$ to $\neg\Phi$, $(\forall\alpha : \bot\ \Phi)$ to $\top$, etc.

The main inference rules of EL are *rule instantiation* and *goal chaining*. These are generalizations of what are commonly referred to as "forward chaining" and "backward chaining" in AI terminology. Rule instantiation is heavily used in input-driven inference, i.e., the process of elaborating the meaning and discourse significance of a new input sentence, in the light of meaning postulates, world knowledge, and prior discourse context. Goal chaining predominates in goal-driven inference, such as would occur during question-answering or discourse planning. It is also used in support of input-driven inference, typically to satisfy antecedents of input-triggered rules. We first illustrate the use of rule instantiation and goal chaining and then state them more precisely.

Rule Instantiation

Rule instantiation consists of two variant rules, each of which allows arbitrarily many minor premises to be matched against arbitrarily deeply embedded subformulas of a complex major premise. Though there are no formal constraints on the syntactic forms of the premises, the major premise will usually be an implicative and/ or quantified formula. Such formulas are often called "rules" in the AI literature, hence the term *rule instantiation*. This creates some ambiguity in speaking of rules, since these may be inference rules or general formulas (rulelike knowledge), so in the following explanation of rule instantiation, we adhere to the "major/minor premise" terminology.

Rule instantiation is related to the well-known rules of *modus ponens, modus tollens,* and *resolution,*[16] but besides allowing for matching of arbitrarily many, arbitrarily deeply embedded subformulas, it can also instantiate probabilistic conditionals. The following (nonprobabilistic) example illustrates the main features of rule instantiation. We first state the sample inference in English, and then in its logical format.

Every dress or hood that Little Red Riding Hood wears is pretty;
Little Red Riding Hood wears a certain cap or hood H

Therefore, if H is a dress or not a cap, it is pretty

$(\forall x: [[[x \text{ dress}] \vee [x \text{ hood}]] \wedge [\text{LRRH wears } x]] \, [x \text{ pretty}]);$
$[H \text{ cap}] \vee [H \text{ hood}], [\text{LRRH wears } H]$

$[[H \text{ dress}] \vee \neg[H \text{ cap}]] \to [H \text{ pretty}]$

The inference is obtained by two matching operations and several substitutions, as follows:

1. We match part of the first minor premise, namely its disjunct $[H \text{ hood}]$, against the embedded clause $[x \text{ hood}]$ of the major premise, recording the substitution $\{H/x\}$ (a substitution of a constant for a universally quantified variable).

2. We apply the substitution to the major premise, obtaining

   $[[[H \text{ dress}] \vee [H \text{ hood}]] \wedge [\text{LRRH wears } H]] \to [H \text{ pretty}].$

   Note that in the process of substituting for the universal variable, the restrictor and matrix of the universal formula become the antecedent and consequent respectively of a conditional formula. We will refer to this formula as the *converted major premise.*

3. We now form the negation of the minor premise we used, after replacing the matched portion by $\bot$ (falsity): $\neg([H \text{ cap}] \vee \bot)$, which is the same as $\neg[H \text{ cap}]$. We call this the *converted minor premise.*

4. We substitute the converted minor premise for the matched portion $[H \text{ hood}]$ of the converted major premise, obtaining

   $[[[H \text{ dress}] \vee \neg[H \text{ cap}]] \wedge [\text{LRRH wears } H]] \to [H \text{ pretty}].$

We refer to this formula as the *intermediate result*. It is in fact a valid inference, but we are only half-way, since we also want to use the second minor premise.

5. Proceeding as in step 1, we match the second minor premise, [LRRH wears *H*], against the embedded clause [LRRH wears *H*].

6. Since no substitution is required, the analogue of step 2 is trivial, and the converted intermediate result is the same as the intermediate result.

7. We again form the negation of the minor premise we used, with the matched portion replaced by ⊥: ¬⊥, which is ⊤ (truth). This is the new converted minor premise.

8. We substitute the converted minor premise (⊤) for the matched portion [LRRH wears *H*] of the (converted) intermediate result, obtaining

[[[*H* dress] ∨ ¬[*H* cap]] ∧⊤] → [*H* pretty].

This simplifies to

[[*H* dress] ∨ ¬[*H* cap]] → [*H* pretty],

which is the inference delivered by rule instantiation.

One constraint tacitly observed in the above procedure is that in matching a part of a minor premise against a part of the major premise, these parts must occur *positively* and *negatively* in their respective formulas. A formula occurs positively in another if it is embedded within zero or more operators that create a positive embedding environment, and within an even number of operators that create a negative embedding environment. For instance, consider

[[*H* dress] ∨ ¬[*H* cap]] → [*H* pretty].

The subformula [*H* dress] occurs negatively, since it lies within the scope of "∨" (which creates a positive embedding environment) and within the antecedent of "→" (which creates a negative embedding environment for its antecedent and a positive environment for its consequent). Similarly ¬[*H* cap] occurs negatively, while [*H* cap] occurs positively, since it is embedded by two operators that create a negative embedding environment, namely the conditional antecedent and the negation. [*H* pretty] occurs positively, since it lies in the consequent of the conditional, which is a positive environment. Additional relevant operators are conjunction (∧) and ∃-quantification, both of which create only positive environments, and ∀-quantification, which creates a negative environment in the restrictor and a positive environment in the matrix clause. Premises of rule instantiation may also involve probabilistic conditionals and quantifiers like Most, but we postpone discussion of probabilistic inference.

Steps 1-4 above for obtaining a conclusion from a major premise and a single minor premise can be concisely summarized as follows, writing

$MAJ^-(\Phi)$ for a major premise with a negative occurrence of subformula Φ, and $MIN^+(\Phi')$ for a minor premise with a positive occurrence of subformula Φ', where Φ and Φ' are matchable (unifiable):

$$\frac{MAJ^-(\Phi),\ MIN^+(\Phi')}{MAJ^-_\sigma(\neg(MIN^+_\sigma(\bot)))}$$

Here σ is the substitution that unifies (matches) Φ and Φ'. Steps 1-4 correspond to (1) forming unifying substitution σ, (2) forming the converted major premise $MAJ^-_\sigma(\Phi_\sigma)$, (3) forming the converted minor premise $\neg(MIN^+_\sigma(\bot))$, and (4) substituting the converted minor premise for the matched subformula Φ_σ in the converted major premise to obtain the conclusion, $MAJ^-_\sigma(\neg(MIN^+_\sigma(\bot)))$.

One point needing further clarification is the mechanics of matching (unification). A variable in a major or minor premise is matchable (i.e., we may substitute a term for it) if it is bound by a positively occurring universal quantifier or negatively occurring existential quantifier. For instance, substitution of w for x is legal in a positively embedded subformula $(\forall x:[x\ \text{P}][x\ \text{Q}])$, yielding $[[w\ \text{P}] \rightarrow [w\ \text{Q}]]$, and the same substitution is legal in a negatively embedded subformula $(\exists x:[x\ \text{P}][x\ \text{Q}])$, yielding $[[w\ \text{P}] \wedge [w\ \text{Q}]]$.

The variant of rule instantiation we have been discussing turns out to be *sound* (yielding only true conclusions from true premises) if the matched subformula Φ' in the minor premise contains no unmatchable free variables which are bound in $MIN^+(\Phi')$ as a whole. So in particular, the rule is sound if $MIN^+(\Phi')$ contains only constants and top-level universal (hence matchable) variables. In certain cases where the condition for soundness is violated, we can apply another variant of rule instantiation which interchanges the roles of the major and minor premises in the conclusion, as follows:

$$\frac{MAJ^-(\Phi),\ MIN^+(\Phi')}{MIN^+_\sigma(MAJ^-_\sigma(\top))}$$

This variant is sound if the matched subformula Φ in the major premise contains no unmatchable free variables which are bound in $MAJ^-(\Phi)$ as a whole.

Suppose, for instance, that our disjunctive minor premise in steps 1-4 above had been existentially quantified:

$(\exists y\ [[y\ \text{cap}] \vee [y\ \text{hood}]])$.

In this case if we attempt to match $[y\ \text{hood}]$ against $[x\ \text{hood}]$ in the major premise, we observe that y is free in $[y\ \text{hood}]$ but is unmatchable since it is bound by a positively occurring existential quantifier at the top level. Thus we are not allowed to apply the first variant of rule instantiation. However, we can apply the second variant, and the reader can verify that the result at step 4 is

$(\exists y \; [[y \; cap] \vee [[LRRH \; wears \; y] \rightarrow [y \; pretty]]]])$.

Goal Chaining

Goal chaining is a pair of very general goal reduction rules, analogous to the two variants of rule instantiation; however, instead of deriving a conclusion from a major premise and one or more minor ones, we derive a subgoal from a major premise, possibly some minor premises, and a given goal. Chaining from consequents to antecedents of quantified or unquantified conditionals is a special case. An example that closely parallels the rule instantiation example would be the following. Note that the goal is to prove that H is pretty, which we write as ?[H pretty]:

> Every dress or hood that Little Red Riding Hood wears is pretty;
> Little Red Riding Hood wears a certain cap or hood H
> Goal: Is H pretty?
> ___
> Subgoal: Is H a dress or not a cap?

$(\forall x: [[[x \; dress] \vee [x \; hood]] \wedge [LRRH \; wears \; x]] \; [x \; pretty])$;
$[H \; cap] \vee [H \; hood], [LRRH \; wears \; H]$
?[H pretty]
___
?[[H dress] $\vee \neg[H \; cap]]$

In essence, what we are doing here is to match the goal ?[H pretty] to the consequent [x pretty] of the universal conditional, chaining back to the intermediate subgoal

?[[[H dress] $\vee$ [H hood]] $\wedge$ [LRRH wears H]].

But in this backward chaining, we are also allowed to use any number of minor premises to reduce the new goal. In the present case we can use the first minor premise to replace [H hood] with $\neg[H$ cap] in the intermediate subgoal, and the second minor premise to delete [LRRH wears H] from it (technically, replacing it with T). This gives the final subgoal shown above.

A point of difference from rule instantiation is that in matching a (part of a) goal to a part of a premise we use different notions of "matchable variables" in goals and premises. In premises, the matchable variables—the ones we are allowed to substitute for—are defined as before; but in a goal, the matchable variables are those that are bound by positively occurring existential quantifiers or negatively occurring universal quantifiers. This plays no role above since the goal contains no variables; but it is easy to see that an existential goal like

?($\exists y \; [y \; pretty])$

should be satisfiable by a premise like [H pretty], and this involves unifying the existential variable y with the constant H.

For completeness we give the formal statements of the two goal chaining rules for the nonprobabilistic case, with no minor premises. We will then go through another detailed example.

$$\frac{MAJ^+(\Phi),\ ?GOAL^+(\Phi')}{?\neg(MAJ^+_\sigma(\neg(GOAL^+_\sigma(\top))))} \qquad \frac{MAJ^+(\Phi),\ ?GOAL^+(\Phi')}{?GOAL^+_\sigma(\neg(MAJ^+_\sigma(\bot)))}$$

where σ unifies Φ with Φ'. The first rule is *sound* if Φ' contains no unmatchable free variables which are bound in $GOAL^+(\Phi')$ as a whole (for example, a variable bound by a top-level universal quantifier). The second rule is sound if Φ contains no unmatchable free variables which are bound in $MAJ^+(\Phi)$ as a whole (for example, a variable bound by a top-level existential quantifier).

We have so far suppressed episodic variables in explaining rule instantiation and goal chaining. In view of the importance of such variables in our semantic representation of natural language sentences, we now give a detailed illustration of goal chaining (with use of supplementary premises) based on episodic formulas. Consider the following general "explanatory" axiom:

$(\forall x: [x\ ((attr\ predatory)\ animal)]\ (\forall\ y: [y\ creature]$
$\quad (\forall e_1: [[y\ near\ x] ** e_1]$
$\qquad (\forall e_2: [e_2\ during\ e_1]$
$\qquad\quad [[[x\ attack\ y] ** e_2]$
$\qquad\qquad \rightarrow (\exists e_3: [e_3\ same\text{-}time\ e_2]$
$\qquad\qquad\quad [[[x\ hungry] ** e_3] \vee [[x\ enraged] ** e_3]])])))))$

A predatory animal attacks a nearby creature only when it is hungry or enraged.

Note that x, y, e_1 and e_2 are matchable variables. Suppose we want to know if the wolf was ever enraged. Then this goal can be posed as

$?(\exists e_4: [e_4\ before\ Now]\ [[Wolf\ enraged] ** e_4])$

where we observe that e_4 is a matchable variable. Since the goal has no unmatchable variables, we use the first goal chaining rule. Note that the matrix of the goal matches the second disjunct in the consequent of the general axiom, with substitution {Wolf / x, e_3 / e_4}. So applying the first goal chaining rule, we obtain the following new goal (after simplifying and distributing negation):

$?[[Wolf\ ((attr\ predatory)\ animal)] \wedge$
$\quad (\exists y\,[[y\ creature] \wedge$
$\qquad (\exists e_1\,[[[y\ near\ Wolf] ** e_1] \wedge$
$\qquad\quad (\exists e_2\,[[e_2\ during\ e_1] \wedge$
$\qquad\qquad [[[Wolf\ attack\ y] ** e_2] \wedge$
$\qquad\qquad\quad (\forall e_3: [e_3\ same\text{-}time\ e_2]$
$\qquad\qquad\qquad [[e_3\ before\ Now] \wedge \neg[[Wolf\ hungry] ** e_3]])])])])].$

Suppose now that our knowledge base contains the axiom

$(\forall\ x: [x\ wolf]\ [x\ ((attr\ predatory)\ animal)])$

as well as the particular fact [Wolf wolf].Then the initial conjunct [Wolf ((attr predatory) animal)] of our goal formula will be reduced via the first axiom to [Wolf wolf] and this in turn will immediately be eliminated via the second axiom. Thus, we are left with subgoal

$?(\exists y\,[[y \text{ creature}] \wedge$
$\quad (\exists e_1\,[[[y \text{ near Wolf}] ** e_1] \wedge$
$\quad\quad (\exists e_2\,[[e_2 \text{ during } e_1] \wedge$
$\quad\quad\quad [[[\text{Wolf attack } y] ** e_2] \wedge$
$\quad\quad\quad\quad (\forall e_3\!:\![e_3 \text{ same-time } e_2]$
$\quad\quad\quad\quad\quad [[e_3 \text{ before } Now] \wedge \neg[[\text{Wolf hungry}] ** e_3]])]])])]).$

The new goal asks, "Did the wolf attack a nearby creature sometime in the past, but was not hungry?"[17] Suppose now the knowledge base contains facts: [[Wolf attack Fox] ** E], [[Fox near Wolf] * E], and [E before Now]. Then the question could be further simplified to

$?\,(\forall e_3\!:\![e_3 \text{ same-time } E]\;\neg[[\text{Wolf hungry}] ** e_3]).$

If this cannot be answered, then we would go back to the previous goal and attempt to prove it using other facts.

The probabilistic version of rule instantiation produces conclusions that are annotated with a lower bound on the certainty (degree of belief) of those conclusions. The bounds are computed as a product of the bounds associated with the minor premises used and, if the major premise is a probabilistic conditional, with the numeric strength of that conditional. This is not quite as crude as it sounds, since some provision is made to avoid repeated use of the same evidence to strengthen (or weaken) belief in the same conclusion. (This is done by keeping track of support sets in the inference process.) Also for linear inference chaining using a nonrepetitive sequence of simple probabilistic conditionals, the computed probability bounds conform to the probabilistic semantics in Bacchus et al. (1996). When multiple proofs or disproofs are found for the same proposition, with various lower bounds on the probabilities that the conclusion is true/ false, these probability bounds are combined through a multiple-evidence scheme essentially like the noisy-OR technique in Bayes nets (Pearl 1988). (This involves some rather crass independence assumptions.)

Forward inference chaining using rule instantiation is terminated when the *expected interestingness* of the conclusions being drawn falls below a threshold value. Thus, for instance, we would tend to pursue the consequences of Little Red Riding Hood being attacked, but would be unlikely to reason that Little Red Riding Hood is a person and therefore has a head, and also must have a mother who also has a head, and so on. The expected interestingness of a proposition is the product of its interestingness and its lower bound on certainty. Predicates, individuals (constants), and propositions (sentences) all have interestingness ratings. Those of predicates are currently pre-set; for instance action predicates are generally rated as more interesting than atelic ones, and of course some actions, like marrying or attacking someone, are rated higher than others, such as walking or resting. Among atelic predicates, being a person is more interesting than being a rock, and being terrified is more interesting than being comfortable. The ratings of individuals and propositions evolve as information accumulates. The idea is that an individual is interesting to the extent that we know a lot of interesting facts about it; and in turn, a proposition is interesting to the extent that it involves interesting individuals and predicates. This may sound circular, but in fact can be implemented consistently. We also allow for inheritance of interestingness from premises to consequences, and from effects to their causes (i.e., causes of interesting effects are apt to be interesting themselves). Salience in context might be expected to be important as well, but some preliminary experiments suggested this may not be particularly important for inference termination.

Rule instantiation and goal chaining do most of the work needed to generate immediate consequences of new inputs and to answer questions. However, for question-answering there is also another class of goal-directed methods consisting of standard natural deduction rules such as proving a conjunction by proving the conjuncts, proving a conditional by assuming the antecedent and proving the consequent, and proving a disjunction by proving one of the disjuncts while assuming the negation of the others. These rules are used for breaking down a given goal, forming a goal tree whose leaves are then tackled by using goal chaining. For rules that use assumption-making, the assumptions may be used to trigger forward inferencing via rule instantiation; assumptions (and their consequences) are retracted once a proof attempt has terminated.

With the kinds of EL inference rules described so far, EPILOG is able to make some quite complex inferences and to answer questions based on logically represented simple narratives or telegraphic messages (Namioka et al. 1992). The control structure for question answering (for questions presented as logical goals) may be sketched as follows. For a given question, simultaneous attempts are made to prove the corresponding goal and its negation. (For *Wh*-questions, variable bindings are tracked in these attempts.) An agenda containing potential knowledge-access actions and goal-chaining actions for subgoals at the leaves of the current goal trees is used to prioritize the steps of the proof and disproof attempts. Knowledge-access actions are guided by a systematic, automatically maintained classification of all formulas in terms of keys consisting of (predicate, argument) or (predicate, argument type) pairs (with an indication of the argument's role), and by "climbing" *type hierarchies* in which these arguments or argument types participate. (We will show some sample classifications in the section on implementation status and test scenarios.) Multiple factors are taken into account in the prioritization of agenda items; in the case of goal-chaining actions these include: the location (including depth) of the subgoal in its goal tree; whether the proposed goal-chaining action matches an antecedent or consequent clause of the selected major premise; and the interestingness and complexity of the subgoal.

In addition, an important feature of the inference process is the use of multiple *specialists* to provide fast inferences about taxonomies, times, parts, sets, etc. These can greatly accelerate proof attempts by evaluating and simplifying certain kinds of terms and formulas in derived clauses or goals, and by directly detecting inconsistencies between certain kinds of subformulas (such as incompatible types in a type hierarchy, or cycles in a set of temporal ordering relations), where we might otherwise need lengthy disproofs. These remarks bring us close to implementation issues, about which we will have a little more to say in the Implementation Status and Test Scenarios section.

Simulative Inference

Stories are often not just about physical events, but also about what goes on in people's minds, i.e., about mental events and processes. Now it seems that the easiest and most natural way to think about someone else's thinking is to try to *simulate* their thought processes, rather than reasoning purely axiomatically. The point is this: to simulate someone's thinking only requires that one have (and be able to "run") a mental apparatus similar to theirs. But to reason axiomatically about someone's thinking, one needs a detailed theory of their mental apparatus—a requirement extremely unlikely to be met. Therefore, we need to develop ways of enabling a story understanding system to make inferences about mental processes by simulation. In other words, the system should be able to temporarily treat the beliefs of another agent as if they were its own, then "observe" what further beliefs it would derive from those assumed, and then ascribe those additional beliefs to the other agent.

This appealing idea has a considerable history in AI, with some studies aimed at developing logically rigorous models of sound simulative inference (for example, Creary 1979, Haas 1986, Konolige 1986), and others leaning more toward practical goals (for example, Moore 1977, Ballim and Wilks 1991, Chalupsky and Shapiro 1996). Kaplan and Schubert (1997) and Kaplan (1998) offer a thorough formal analysis of simulative inference in a computational setting. The model is based on viewing belief retrieval and augmentation in terms of an ASK-TELL mechanism that operates on an agent's belief store (which can take any form, not necessarily a set of formulas). ASK is an algorithmic query mechanism that returns *yes* or *no* for any query formula, indicating respectively that the formula is believed or not believed. (A formula that is not believed need not be disbelieved, i.e., it may be that neither the formula nor its negation is believed.). TELL is an algorithmic belief augmentation mechanism that attempts to add a formula to the agent's beliefs. (This may fail, for example, if contradictions are encountered.) The main results in the cited references concern the conditions on ASK and TELL under which simulative inference is sound, and there are also restricted completeness results.

We will not discuss simulative inference in detail here, since its implementation for EL remains largely a research issue. We merely mention that we envisage an implementation in two parts, one relying on a goal-driven ASK mechanism and the other on an input-driven TELL mechanism. ASK and TELL would be much like the goal-driven and input-driven inference mechanisms we have already described, except that they would make only very simple inferences, to assure fast termination. (Keep in mind that ASK is intended as a model of belief retrieval, not problem solving.) Goal-driven simulative inference would be triggered by goals of form $[[\alpha \text{ believes } \beta] * \eta]$ (i.e., in a certain situation η, agent α believes proposition β), and would consist of an attempt to "evaluate" the goal to truth or falsity, by running ASK on query β within a *belief space* for agent α in situation η. (More accurately, the query would be a formula Φ, assuming that proposition $\beta = (\text{That } \Phi)$). It may also be feasible to have the simulation return subgoals (such as beliefs to be proven by ordinary inference) in cases where the result is neither truth nor falsity. In a system that reasons about beliefs, a belief space for another agent is a way of configuring or clustering the known beliefs of that agent so as to facilitate reasoning about them. Belief space mechanisms have been incorporated into many knowledge representation systems, including our EPILOG system. For the purpose of simulative inference, the crucial computational requirement is that running ASK or TELL in the belief space of another agent should yield precisely the same results as if the beliefs of the other agent were the system's own, i.e., as if they had been stripped of the belief-wrapper [α believes ...] and integrated into the system's own belief space.[18]

Input-driven simulative inference would be triggered by storage of formulas of form $[[\alpha \text{ learns } \beta] ** \eta]$, i.e., there is some event η that consists of some agent α learning (coming to believe, from some external source) proposition β. In this case simulative inference would consist of an attempt to add β (or more exactly Φ, as above) to the belief space for α, using the TELL mechanism. In general this will trigger a cascade of further inferences, and the output of the simulation would consist of significant inferences observed in this simulative use of TELL. For instance, if upon asserting (TELLing) Φ in α's belief space, Ψ is inferred and this is rated as a sufficiently "interesting" inference, then something like the formulas

[[α infers (That Ψ)] ** η_i],
[η cause-of η_i],

would be included among the outputs of the simulation. This expresses the prediction that α infers that Ψ holds (and thus will believe that it holds) as a result of learning β (i.e., that Φ holds).

We think this sort of prediction is particularly important in story understanding. When humans learn new information, they often become instantly aware of certain significant consequences of that information, and potentially act on those consequences. For instance, a person encountering a dangerous animal in the woods (thus learning about its proximity) would immediately think of the possibility of being attacked, and hence might take some appropriate action (freezing, fleeing, etc.). So to anticipate and understand the behavior of story characters, we need to actively anticipate their thoughts, and this would be greatly facilitated by input-driven simulative inference.

We should emphasize that simulative inference, though potentially extremely useful, cannot be a stand-alone method of reasoning about beliefs. Observe, for instance, that we cannot apply simulative inference to premises [[A believes P1] $\bigvee$ [A believes P2]], ¬[A believes P2] to obtain [A believes P1], even though this is a trivial deduction. So the way to view simulative inference is as special "attachment" techniques (in the terminology of Konolige [1986]) that are integrated into the regular goal-driven and input-driven inference mechanisms, reducing certain formulas to truth or falsity (or to subgoals), and adding many belief inferences that would be very difficult to obtain by ordinary logical inference.

Many theoretical and practical difficulties will need to be dealt with in further work on simulative inference in EL. One is that the theory of propositions in our situational logic does not quite fit with the computational model of belief in Kaplan and Schubert (1997), or other sentence-based theories. For instance, in EL, a compound (but quantifier-free) sentence is semantically indistinguishable from logically equivalent sentences built up out of the same constituents (for example [¬Φ $\bigvee$ Ψ] is semantically indistinguishable from [[Φ $\bigwedge$ ¬Ψ] $\rightarrow$ [¬Φ $\bigvee$ Ψ]]). So belief in one is the same as belief in the other. While it is easy to particularize the computational model to conform with such a constraint, we may not want this, and in that case our situation theory would require significant changes. Another problem is the time-dependence of beliefs. On the one hand, we want an understand-

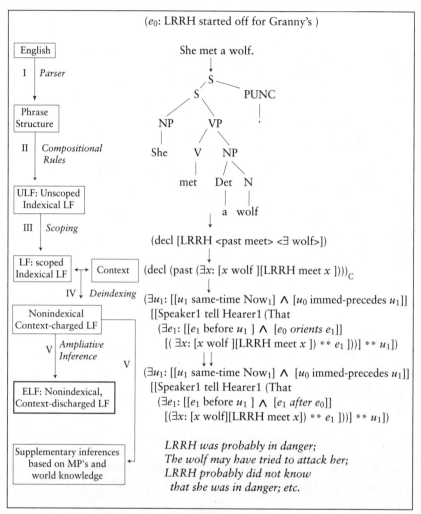

Figure 2. The Conceptual Stages of Natural-Language Understanding

ing system to be able to "time-stamp" beliefs (or in our case, "situation-stamp" them), since beliefs can and do change. On the other hand, we want to assume by default that a belief is still held if there is no reason to think it has been abandoned. In essence, this is the *frame problem* for beliefs. It is also unclear under what conditions simulative inference in a logic as expressive as EL will be sound; or even for the first-order subset of EL, how we can ensure that ASK and TELL (goal-driven and input-driven inference) will satisfy the conditions for soundness identified in Kaplan and Schubert (1997). From a practical perspective, the main problem is how to make ASK and TELL belief-space independent in the sense required by simulative inference.

On the other hand, we think that rough-and-ready versions of ASK and TELL could fairly readily be implemented as variants of the goal-driven and input-driven inference mechanisms in EPILOG, and employed to support useful (even if not always sound) simulative inferencing.

A View of the Language Understanding Process

Figure 2 depicts our current view of the stages of the understanding process, at a theoretical level. The first three stages in this view are fairly conventional, though the details are eclectic, incorporating ideas from GPSG, HPSG, DRT, and from prior work on mapping English into logic, in particular, Schubert and Pelletier (1982, 1989). At the procedural level, these stages are intended to be interleaved, with on-line disambiguation based on syntactic, semantic and pragmatic principles and preferences.

Let us now consider each of the stages shown in figure 2. Suppose we have the following short passage.

> Little Red Riding Hood started off for Grandmother's
> with a cake in a basket. (13)
>
> In the forest, she met a wolf who had not eaten for three days. (14)

Stages I and II:
Obtaining Phrase Structure and the Unscoped Logical Form

In stage I, we obtain parse trees from English, i.e., initial phrase structure trees, using a GPSG-like parser. We will trace the processing of sentence (14) in this section. See the sample parse tree on the right-hand side of the figure. (See Hwang [1992] and Hwang and Schubert [1993b] for some grammar fragments. For space reasons, the adverbial and the relative clause are omitted in figure 2.) From the semantic rules paired with phrase structure rules, we obtain the preliminary, unscoped indexical logical form (unscoped logical form) in stage II, as shown below.

$$(\text{decl }((\text{adv-}e \ (\text{in-loc } \langle \text{The forest}\rangle)))$$
$$[\text{LRRH} \ \langle \text{past meet}\rangle$$
$$\langle \exists \ \lambda w[\ [w \ \text{wolf}] \ \wedge$$
$$\langle \text{past (perf }((\text{adv-}e \ (\text{lasts-for } (K \ ((\text{num } 3) \ (\text{plur day}))))))$$
$$(\neg[w \ \text{eat}])))\rangle]\rangle]))) \quad (15)$$

This preliminary unscoped logical form is in general ambiguous—for example, with respect to the scopes of quantifiers and other operators—and context-dependent—for example, involving indexical operators like *past*, whose interpretation depends on the utterance time. The top-level *decl* operator is obtained from the sentence mood and punctuation, and signals the type of surface speech act (to be made explicit in stage IV). As before, predicate infixing is used for readability, and angle brackets indicate unscoped operators that are to be raised to some sentence-level position. The above unscoped logical form involves four operators that need be scoped: ∃, The, and two *past's*. The subsequent processing stages are aimed at removing ambiguity and context-dependence.

Stage III: Scoping

Scoping quantifiers in stage III involves introduction of variables, i.e., x and y in this case, and conversion of the restriction predicate to a restriction formula:

(decl (past (The y: [y forest]
    ((adv-*e* (in-loc y))
    (∃x: [[x wolf] ∧
        (past (perf ((adv-*e* (lasts-for (K ((num 3) (plur day)))))
                                                    (¬[x eat)))))]
    [LRRH meet x]))))), (16)

Also, tense operators and coordinators are scoped at this stage; *past* and *perf* are considered sentence-level operators. In general, tense has a strong, though not absolute, wide-scoping tendency (right below the sentence mood indicator *decl* and some definites); like quantifiers, however, it is "trapped" by scope islands, such as embedded clauses. Note the positions of the ∃-quantifier and *past* operator in the scoped logical form (16). The subscripted C indicates the explicit context structure with respect to which the scoped logical form is to be interpreted. Among other things, this consists of a *tense tree,* whose purpose is to facilitate context-dependent tense-aspect interpretation, a *clock* which generates a succession of *Now*-points for speech times, and hearer and speaker parameters.

Stage IV: Deindexing

The scoped, indexical translation is deindexed with respect to this context C in stage IV, so as to obtain a nonindexical logical form usable for inference. The computation of the nonindexical episodic logical form from the logical form is driven by a simple, recursive deindexing mechanism that makes use of the tense tree in context structure C. The deindexing rules handle tense, aspect, and many temporal PP-adverbials and their interaction; their effect is to bring the context information into the logical form, removing context dependency. In particular, tense and aspect operators are replaced by relationships among episodes, and explicit episodic variables are introduced into the formula on the right-hand side.

Note that u_0 in figure 2 (stages IV and V logical forms) is the utterance episode of the previous sentence, i.e, sentence (13), and e_0 is the episode introduced by it, i.e., that of Little Red Riding Hood's starting off for Grandmother's cottage. $Now1$ is the speech time of sentence (14). Application of appropriate deindexing rules transforms logical form (16) into episodic logical form (17) as shown below.

$$(\exists\, u_1\!: [[u_1 \text{ same-time } Now_1] \wedge [u_0 \text{ immediately-precedes } u_1]]$$
$$[[\text{Speaker1 tell Hearer1 (That}$$
$$(\exists e_1\!: [[e_1 \text{ before } u_1] \wedge [e_0 \text{ orients } e_1]]$$
$$[[[e_1 \text{ in-loc Forest}] \wedge$$
$$(\exists x\!: [[x \text{ wolf}] \wedge$$
$$(\exists e_2\!: [e_2 \text{ at-about } e_1]$$
$$[(\exists e_3\!:[e_3 \text{ impinges-on } e_2]$$
$$[[[e_3 \text{ lasts-for (K ((num 3) (plur day)))}] \wedge$$
$$(\neg[x \text{ eat}])] ** e_3])$$
$$** e_2])]$$
$$[\text{LRRH meet } x])]$$
$$** e_1)))]$$
$$** u_1]). \tag{17}$$

While producing this deindexed formula, the deindexing process also modifies the tense tree component of the context by adding branches and episode tokens as a side effect.

This deindexing mechanism is compositional in the sense that operators *pres, past, futr, perf,* etc., contribute separately and uniformly to the meanings of their operand formulas, driving the generation and traversal of tense trees in deindexing. We cannot include a detailed introduction to tense trees here. Instead, we will have to confine ourselves to a sketchy intuitive exposition, an example of the notation we use for deindexing rules, and pointers to our prior writings on the subject (Hwang and Schubert [1992], Hwang [1992], and Hwang and Schubert [1993b]).

Tense trees grow downward, though one tree can "embed" another via certain horizontal links. They can be thought of as being generated as a byproduct of a depth-first traversal of the (indexical) logical form of a sentence (viewed as a nested list structure), in the course of deindexing that logical form. In fact they reflect the tense-operator structure of the logical form: each branch signifies the embedding of some clause of the logical form by an operator; and the direction of a branch indicates the "temporal orientation" of the corresponding operator. In particular, the branches generated by *past, perf,* and *futr* operators point down to the left, straight down, and down to the right respectively. (Imagine time as progressing from left to right.) The tense tree for a single sentence is typically just a zig-zag path; it is the layering of such paths on top of each other for successive clauses or sentences that may lead to multiple branches at a single node, particularly as a result of tense changes.

What's the use of a tense tree? In the course of its generation and subsequent re-traversals *episode tokens* are generated and placed at the tree nodes, and temporal relationships among tokens are automatically asserted, capturing the deindexed meaning of the tense operators as well as interclausal and intersentential connections. The actual work is done by a set of deindexing rules, one for each operator, named *Pres, Past, Futr, Perf,* etc., accordingly. Each rule can be viewed declaratively as consisting of an equivalence and an equation. The following deindexing rule for *past* is the only one we will look at:

Past: $(\text{past } \Phi)_T \leftrightarrow (\exists e_T : [[e_T \text{ bef}_T \text{ Emb}_T] \wedge [\text{Last}_{\nearrow T} \text{ orients } e_T]] [\Phi_{\bigcirc \nearrow T} ** e_T])$
Tree transformation: $(\text{past } \Phi) \cdot T = \uparrow (\Phi \cdot (\bigcirc \nearrow T))$

The equivalence specifies what (past Φ) means, in terms of the episode tokens in a given tense tree T. (Note the introduction of the characterization operator "$**$"!) $[e_T \text{ bef}_T \text{ Emb}_T]$ says that the new episode e_T characterized by Φ is *at* or *before* ("bef$_T$") Emb$_T$, the episode at the nearest node embedding T (dominating the root)—usually this is the speech (or narration) event. $[\text{Last}_{\nearrow T} \text{ orients } e_T]$ says that the last event that was stored at the past-node (before e_T was placed there) provides a "point of orientation" for e_T (cf., Leech [1987] and Webber [1988]). We comment further on the *orients* relation below.

The equation in the *Past* rule states a structural constraint that a tense tree T must satisfy if it is generated by the logical form (past Φ). But we can equally well view it as a recursive tree-modification rule, reading the right-hand side "inside-out, right-to-left," like a Lisp expression: the arrow operators indicate tree traversal in the direction of the arrow, and the open dot dictates the placement of a new episode token e_T at the node reached. More exactly, the equation prescribes a left downward traversal from the current node (generating a new branch if necessary), followed by placement of new episode token e_T at the node reached, followed by letting Φ have its effect on the tree (this is guaranteed to bring us back to the same node), followed by return to the start node.

Only four operators actually induce downward branching in tense trees, viz., *past, perf, futr* and *fpres* (future present, as in "Little Red Riding Hood won't recognize the wolf when she *arrives* at Grandmother's"). *pres* adds an episode token but does not cause branching. Horizontal embedding branches are generated for the surface speech act (the act of telling the hearer something, asking something, etc.) and for subordinate clauses (for example, ones headed in the logical form by the proposition-forming operator *That*). For most other operators (such as *prog* and *predicates*), deindexing simply means moving the dependence on the tense tree T inward to their operands—there is neither a syntactic transformation nor an effect on the tense tree. However, as we have seen, ad-

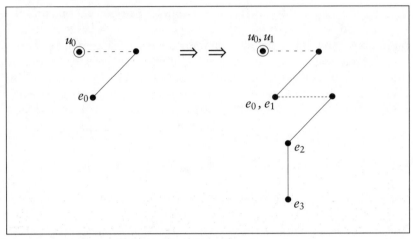

Figure 3. Tense Tree Transformation

verbials of certain sorts (such as temporal and locative ones) are an important exception; they are syntactically transformed into conjoined predications about episodes (much as in traditional approaches, such as Reichenbach [1947], Davidson [1967], and Dowty [1982]). For details on the interpretation and deindexing of temporal and other adverbials, see Hwang (1992) and Hwang and Schubert (1993c and 1994).

We conclude our look at tense trees with figure 3, showing how the tense tree resulting from processing sentence (13) is extended when logical form (16) (the logical form for sentence 14) is deindexed.

The left diagram of figure 3 shows the tense tree induced by sentence (13); the right one shows the final tree after logical form (16) has been completely deindexed, yielding (17). The dashed link corresponds to the two embedding speech acts (the "telling that" implicit in the two narrative sentences (13) and (14)), and the dotted link corresponds to the syntactic embedding of the relative clause "who had not eaten for three days."

Stage V, Part 1: Narrative Inferences

Let us return to the *orienting* relation $[e_0$ orients $e_1]$ in (17). This is generated by the *Past* rule, and asserts that e_0, the event of Little Red Riding Hood starting out, is the "point of orientation" for the subsequently described event e_1 of Little Red Riding Hood meeting a wolf. (Note that e_0, e_1 were placed next to each other in the tense tree above; this is what enables the generation of the orienting relation.) Orienting relations contribute to narrative coherence, and their automatic derivation is one of the most important benefits of the tense tree mechanism. However, *orients* does not quite have the status of a logical predicate; rather, it is what we call a *context-charged* relation. Such relations suggest various possibilities (such as various possible temporal or causal relations), and the idea is that their meaning is to be discharged through *narrative inferences*. These are nondeductive (probabilistic or default) inferences comprising part of stage V of the understanding process, the ampliative inference stage. Narrative inferences hypothesize alternative meanings for context-charged or otherwise ambiguous expressions in the logical form using various features of the current logical form and previous episodic logical forms to assign a priori likelihoods to these alternatives. Other inference processes, termed "implicit question-answering" in the next subsection, are assumed to perform the final adjudication among various alternatives so as to arrive at an overall sentence interpretation coherent with the already interpreted prior discourse. In that sense, the meaning of context-charged relations still depend on discourse context, though not on the explicit context structure C.

In our example, $[e_0$ orients $e_1]$ suggests among other possibilities that e_1 (immediately) follows e_0 (in e_0's "consequent" or "result" phase, in the terminology of Moens and Steedman [1988]). Given the telic characterizations of e_0 (Little Red Riding Hood's starting off) and e_1 (her meeting a wolf) and the circumstances described, this hypothesis would be deemed the most probable, but in other cases the most probable particularization of the orients relation may be a subepisode relation, a causal or explanatory relation, or any of the discourse relations that have been discussed in the literature.

Note that besides the *orients* relation, (17) contains another context-charged relation, namely $[e_3$ impinges-on $e_2]$. This is generated by the deindexing rule for the *perf* operator, and is intended to be particularized into either *until* or *before* through narrative inferences. It relates the episode e_3 of the wolf's not eating for three days (reported in past perfect tense) to the past reference point e_2 (which coincides temporally with the meeting event e_1). The fact that the characterization of e_3 is negative and hence atelic is taken to provide strong evidence for the *until* interpretation of *impinges-on;* i.e., the not-eating episode lasts until the reference time, and hence until the meeting. Thus, taking for granted the final adjudicative process (or assuming that the feature-based evidence is in this case already decisive), the context-charged logical form (17) would be particularized to

$$(\exists u_1 \colon [[u_1 \text{ same-time Now}_1] \wedge [\, u_0 \text{ immediately-precedes } u_1]]$$
$$[[\text{Speaker1 tell Hearer1 (That}$$
$$(\exists e_1 \colon [[e_1 \text{ before } u_1] \wedge [e_1 \text{ } after \text{ } e_0]]$$
$$[[[e_1 \text{ in-loc Forest}] \wedge$$

$$(\exists x: [[x \text{ wolf}] \wedge$$
$$(\exists e_2: [e_2 \text{ at-about } e_1]$$
$$[(\exists e_3: [e_3 \text{ until } e_2]$$
$$[[[e_3 \text{ lasts-for } (K ((\text{num } 3) (\text{plur day})))] \wedge$$
$$(\neg[x \text{ eat}])] ** e_3])$$
$$** e_2])]$$
$$[\text{LRRH meet } x])]$$
$$** e_1]))]$$
$$** u_1]) . \qquad\qquad (18)$$

Note that $[e_0 \text{ orients } e_1]$ has been particularized into $[e_1 \text{ after } e_0]$, and $[e_3 \text{ impinges-on } e_2]$ into $[e_3 \text{ until } e_2]$.

Although we assumed at the beginning that the referent of the pronoun *she* in sentence (14) had been resolved to Little Red Riding Hood in the unscoped logical form (15), in actuality it would be resolved in stage V, simultaneously with the discharging of context-charged relations. In fact, we conjecture that reference resolution could naturally be accomplished in a manner paralleling the derivation of temporal relations. First we would add a kind of anaphora deindexing to the temporal deindexing in stage IV, consisting of augmenting anaphoric expressions (terms corresponding to pronouns and definite descriptions) with lists of readily accessible antecedents. Accessibility would be determined from the structure of the logical form of the current sentence and the episodic logical forms of prior sentences. Then in stage V, narrative inferences aimed specifically at reference resolution would assign prior probabilities to the accessible antecedents based on features of the current logical form and prior episodic logical forms, and implicit question answering would perform the final adjudication.

Stage V, Part 2: Adjudication through Implicit Q-A

The narrative inferences posited above should be viewed as part of a broader stream of input-driven inferences, triggered by the information in the current logical form and prior episodic logical forms in conjunction with meaning postulates and world knowledge. These more general inferences are indicated by the second branch of stage V indicated in figure 2, leading to "supplementary inferences"; some sample inferences we would expect to obtain are indicated at the bottom right of the figure.

However, the problem is that in general the inference stream is not univocal. Rather, there will be various alternative ways to extrapolate inferentially from the current logical form and prior episodic logical forms, depending both on alternative ways of discharging context-charged relations, and alternative kinds of world knowledge that can be brought to bear. For example, the pronoun *she* in sentence (14) could theoretically refer to Grandmother rather than Little Red Riding Hood, and such an interpretation would lead to very different inferences. Also, instead of conjecturing that the hungry wolf was a hazard to Little Red Riding Hood, we might alternatively conjecture that he would take an interest in the cake in Little Red Riding Hood's basket. In fact, such an inference would be essential for making sense of a continuation such as "the wolf slyly inquired whether he could help Little Red Riding Hood carry the basket."

While we need not sort out all such alternatives immediately to achieve understanding (and may never need to sort out some of them), we do clearly need to adjudicate among alternative forward inferences in order to achieve a coherent interpretation of a narrative. We think that our earlier description of the EL inference mechanisms provides a reasonably clear and specific picture of how forward inferencing might work; but we have so far offered few clues about how to do the sorting-out that achieves global coherence. We suggest that this cannot be primarily a matter of deciding what global picture is most plausible in terms of our world knowledge, since coherence is in a sense a contractual matter between narrator and reader (or speaker and hearer), not just a matter of how the world is. In other words, the narrator is under a conventional obligation to make the story cohere, and the reader relies on this convention in choosing among alternative inferences.

Of course, some a priori biases will be introduced by the more or less likely particularizations of context-charged relations and the more or less likely conclusions based on world knowledge in the form of probabilistic conditionals. As well, the mechanisms we have mentioned for combining probabilistically weighted evidence for or against a conclusion reached via multiple inference pathways will cause some belief shifts. However, in general such processes will merely lead to adjustment of degrees of belief in various alternatives, not to a "crystallization" of a particular global interpretation. The following is a speculative discussion of a process we call "implicit question answering," which we regard as the key to arriving at a coherent interpretation.

The idea is that a text (or discourse) raises certain questions, and new inputs are preferentially interpreted so as to answer these implicit questions. We identify "raising a question" with inferring a prediction or explanation with less than complete certainty by inference chaining. The question raised is answered when the next input sentence, or one of its (more or less certain) consequences via inference chaining, is found to confirm or disconfirm it (to some degree). The assumptions and inferences that provided the confirming or disconfirming answer are then considered correct. The key point for us (and the reason for our question-answering terminology) is that the narrator is free to answer the tacitly raised questions either positively or negatively, regardless of how unexpected the answer may be. In fact, a story in which all expectations are confirmed would be utterly uninteresting.

A Positive Example of Implicit Question Answering

We begin with an illustration of the positive case:

    a. John dropped the glass on the floor.
    b. It broke.   (19)

Inference chaining based on sentence (19a), along with axioms about "dropping," "glasses," and about fragile objects striking hard surfaces would quickly lead to a rather probable (but not certain) prediction that the glass broke. In our terminology, therefore, the question of whether the glass broke is raised. Now in (19b), the pronoun may a priori refer to either the glass or the floor. If it refers to the floor, then (19b) neither confirms nor disconfirms any predictions triggered by (19a). But if it refers to the glass, then (19b) directly supports the predicted breakage of the glass. Thus according to the implicit question answering principle, the latter interpretation is chosen. Note also that a tentative inference from the orienting relation computed for (19a) and (19b), namely, that the breaking was right after, and caused by, the dropping will thereby be confirmed as well (assuming that such an immediately following causal consequence was predicted from [19a]).

So far this will sound rather familiar. What is happening, in effect, is that inferences from successive sentences are being matched and unified. This is quite similar to what would happen in an ACT-based (or script or MOP-based, etc.) understanding system, where the expectations implicit in an evoked script are matched against subsequent inputs (for example, MARGIE [Schank et al. 1975] and SAM [Cullingford 1981]). Also, this view of interpretation is closely related to the abductive approaches of Charniak (1988), Charniak and Goldman (1988) and Hobbs et al. (1993) in which a new input is interpreted so that it is derivable from what is already known with a minimal set of supplementary assumptions.

However, the other half of our proposed principle is that *disconfirmation* of a prior inference (a negative answer to the question raised) can play the same role in determining the interpretation of new material as its affirmation. In this respect our proposal seems quite different from previous ones.[19]

A Negative Example of Implicit Question Answering

A suitable illustration is sentence (19a) plus the denial of (19b):

    a. John dropped the glass on the floor.
    b. It didn't break.   (20)

In this case, it is the *denial* of a prediction from (20a) that the glass broke, i.e., that the glass didn't break, that is supported by (20b), with the pronoun resolved to "the glass." Again, resolving the pronoun to "the floor" neither confirms nor disconfirms any questions raised by (20a), and hence that possible way of resolving the pronoun is not confirmed. By contrast, approaches like those of Charniak and Goldman or Hobbs et al. which insist on interpreting new inputs as logically supported by prior inputs (and background knowledge) would get the wrong interpretation here. In particular, since general knowledge certainly supports the conclusion that the *floor* didn't break, the pronoun would be resolved to refer to the floor.[20]

A Final Example of Implicit Question Answering

The examples above are simpler than anything likely to be encountered in real narratives. The (a)-sentence forcefully suggests a particular prediction (breakage of the glass), and the (b)-sentence directly confirms or disconfirms that prediction. More commonly, narrative sentences tend to evoke a variety of possible explanations for the reported situation or event, and a variety of possible predictions. So implicit question-answering in general involves searching for corroborative or antagonistic connections between tentative explanations and predictions evoked by a new sentence and those evoked by prior sentences. The following example is more realistic.

    a. John heard steps behind him.
    b. He began to run.   (21)

A spontaneous explanatory inference from sentence (21a) is likely to be that there was someone behind John, quite close to him (and he knew this). In turn, this leads to the (possibly very tentative) conjecture that John may believe himself in danger, and may try to get away from the person behind him. Other, more benign possibilities are that the person behind John wishes to catch up and communicate with him, or simply intends to walk past him. If the latter are the most likely possibilities in John's mind, we would not expect any special actions from him, except perhaps to attend to the approaching walker. (Of course, prior context may disable one or another inference chain, or suggest less conventional ones. Also, the inference of danger from (21a) seems to have something to do with expectations based on what typically happens in stories, as opposed to world-experience. But that is not the issue here.)

Now sentence (21b) also suggests multiple alternative explanations, considered in isolation: John (the only possible referent for *he* in this case) may simply be in a hurry, or he may be trying to get away from someone or something near him, or catch up with someone or something, or he may be exercising. (These seem like the most probable explanations.) Once again, only one of these possible inferences, namely the second, bears on any of the questions raised by (21a). In particular, this inference confirms that John is trying to get away from someone near him, and hence that inference, and everything leading up to it, and the relevant interpretation of (21b), are deemed correct.

We leave the discussion of implicit question-answering here. Developing the details of such a theory, and implementing it in EL, remains a major challenge for the future.

To conclude the discussion of the stages of understanding, we emphasize again that though the stages have been described as if they ran sequentially, and the start-up implementations in which EL has played a role were in fact sequential (viz., the TRAINS system [Allen and Schubert 1993], [Traum et al. 1996] and the message processing application [Namioka et al. 1992]), the intention is to interleave them eventually. The sequencing is feasible only as long as structural disambiguation, scoping, referent determination and discharging of context-charged relations can be adequately "guessed," based only on syntactic preferences and crude semantic checks.

Implementation Status and Test Scenarios

While there is as yet no complete story understanding system that includes all of the modules and processes described in the previous sections, the EL knowledge representation along with the input-driven and goal-driven inference mechanisms have been fully implemented in the EPILOG system (Miller et al 1991). Also, various aspects of our approach have been incorporated into two complete prototype natural language processing systems: the TRAINS91-93 systems (Allen and Schubert 1993 and Traum et al. 1996) and a message processing application at Boeing company (Namioka et al 1992). In addition, we have carried out detailed analyses of several story excerpts, and verified that EPILOG is able to perform many of the inferences necessary for understanding.

We begin with an overview of EPILOG, continue with brief descriptions of the two prototype systems, and then discuss our work on story fragments at some length, concluding with a note on the frame problem in narratives.

The EPILOG System

The EPILOG system is the practical knowledge representation and inference system for EL, and represents the culmination of many years of im-

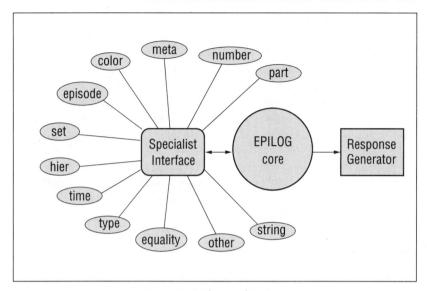

Figure 4. Epilog Architecture

plementation work on a succession of natural language-oriented representations. It allows for the full EL syntax, and besides the input-driven and goal-driven inference mechanisms, deploys an array of specialist subsystems to help with both of these inference modes (see Miller and Schubert [1988], Gerevini and Schubert [1995], and further references therein). As shown in figure 4, there is a type specialist for efficiently handling facts such as that wolves are animals, using a preorder numbering scheme on tangled type hierarchies; a part-of specialist, also based on numbered hierarchies; a time specialist using a "timegraph" structure for fast transitive inference; a color specialist based on a cylindrical color space; specialists for efficient string and set manipulation, arithmetic, etc. The specialists are used for immediate simplification of terms and formulas when these are stored, and for "generalized resolving," such as the detection of inconsistencies between simple formulas such as [x wolf] and ¬[x animal], or [H red] and [H green]. Some of these specialists, such as the time and set specialists, are dynamic in the sense that they accumulate information in their own specialized data structures as new inputs are presented. The specialists are uniformly tied into the general inference mechanisms via a specialist interface, making it easy to add new specialists. This interface also enables indirect communication between specialists, so that they can help each other without knowing of each other's existence. Note also the response generator indicated in the figure, which is able to give rough-and-ready verbalizations in English of EL formulas.

An important design goal for EPILOG was to assure efficient use of *relevant* knowledge in an inference task even if the knowledge base is very large. This is accomplished by two kinds of knowledge indexing, one based on *predicate-argument* pairs and the other on *topic-argument* pairs. Predicate-argument indices are the primary means of accessing relevant formulas in both input-driven and goal-driven inference. They are based on classifying formulas in terms of the more interesting atomic subformulas occurring within them, using as keys the predicates in those subformulas paired with one argument or argument type. For instance, a formula describing what happens when a predator attacks another creature might contain a subformula [*x* attack *y*], where *x* is typed as a predator and *y* as a creature, through quantifier restrictions. In that case, the formula as a whole would be hash-indexed under (predator attack subj) and (creature attack obj), indicating that the formula involves predicate *attack* with a subject of type *predator* and an object of type *creature*. EPILOG classifies input formulas automatically in this way, and then uses this classification to find formulas to match against subformulas in rule instantiation and goal chaining. The restriction of the classification to the more interesting atomic subformulas is important in that it prevents triggering an excessively broad inference process; for instance, we do not want to classify the formula about predators attacking other creatures using the subformula [*y* creature], as this would cause EPILOG to think of attacks by predators whenever *any* creature is mentioned.

Predicate-argument indexing for belief formulas of form [α believe (That Φ)] uses extended key lists, obtained by adding key words corresponding to α and *believe* to those extracted from Φ; similarly for other modal predicates, such as *hope, say*, etc. (We also regard fictional tales as lying within the scope of a modal predicate; for example, [LRRH-story has-it (That ...)].) This facilitates uniform inference about the beliefs (etc.) of other agents, in a manner paralleling inference based on its own beliefs. (However, it is not clear whether the parallelism is sufficiently exact to provide a basis for simulative inference.)

Topic-argument indices consist of an individual or type paired with a topic, for example, (LRRH tp.appearance), or (wolf tp.feeding). They provide a way of generating descriptive output, as an end in itself or when a question cannot be answered exactly. For instance, they allow EPILOG to access and output everything it knows about Little Red Riding Hood's appearance or emotional attitudes, or about a wolf's feeding habits. If a question like "Does Little Red Riding Hood like the wolf?" cannot be answered exactly, the related information "Little Red Riding Hood likes animals," "Little Red Riding Hood loves Grandmother," etc. (if previously supplied) could in principle be returned. Topic-argument indexing is based on user-supplied *topic indicators* for nontype (i.e., non-nounlike) predicates. There is a predetermined (but extensible) hierarchy of several dozen topics under which facts about any given thing or type of thing can be classified, such as appearance-related topics (color, shape, texture, etc.), behavior-related topics (such as feeding, locomotion, etc.), function/ use (for artifacts), and so on. Topic indicators specify what topic a predicate indicates with respect to each of its argument positions. For instance, *eat* indicates tp.feeding with respect to the subject and tp.existence with respect to the object (since eating something terminates or at least threatens its existence).

In the course of its development, EPILOG has been tested on numerous simple deduction and probabilistic inference problems, some of which will be mentioned in the subsections that follow. Though it was designed for shallow inference on large knowledge bases rather than for deep reasoning, EPILOG can handle some quite challenging theorem proving problems, including the Steamroller (Stickel 1986), when the hierarchy information in this problem is placed in a type hierarchy.

Two Prototype Systems

The first prototype system we will describe made use of EL as a semantic representation, but not directly for inference. The second system emphasized the use of the EPILOG inference engine, adhering only very loosely to our conception of how to derive a semantic representation from English.

TRAINS91-93 (Allen and Schubert 1993; Traum et al. 1996) helped a user solve simple problems in transporting goods by rail (including simple manufacturing steps like having a factory produce orange juice from oranges) in a small simulated railroad network. The 1991 system used a GPSG-like grammar and parser and semantic rules associated one-to-one with phrase structure rules to derive unscoped logical forms from user inputs (and also from the system's own responses); these were then scoped to obtain indexical logical forms, and deindexed with the aid of tense trees to obtain final nonindexical episodic logical forms. Since there was a pre-existing framelike knowledge representation for domain problem solving, episodic logical forms were not employed directly for inference in this system, but rather were used as sources of information for subsequent modules aimed at speech act analysis, dialogue management, and planning. TRAINS-93 was similar in its architecture, but used an integrated scoping, referent determination and tense deindexing module, and improved modules further "downstream." For a discussion of the various knowledge representations used, the pros and cons of a nonuniform approach, and further references, see Traum et al. (1996). From our EL perspective, a particularly gratifying aspect of the TRAINS experience was that EL as a semantic representation of natural language, and our method of deriving episodic logical forms, proved readily applicable in an interactive problem solving domain very far removed from the story understanding scenarios that motivated us originally. We take this as evidence for the generality and domain-independence of our approach to semantic representation.

The Boeing message processing application was developed for the Boeing Commercial Airplane Reliability and Maintainability (R&M) division (Namioka et al. 1992). The goal was to partially automate the process of extracting information from the thousands of telexes received monthly by the division, reporting problems and repairs on the Boeing fleet. The start-up system used a GPSG parser, originally developed by P. Harrison and subsequently adapted for use on the telegraphic messages (Jenkins et al. 1990). The phrase structure rules used were well-adapted to computing approximate episodic logical forms, though there was not a full-fledged version of a semantic interpreter. The features of EL that made it particularly suitable for this application were its expressiveness, its direct connection to language, its natural handling of causation, and its probabilistic rules, allowing expert system-like knowledge encoding. For example, EL made it easy to represent such notions as "reporting that ..." (i.e., modal operators), "severe wear" (i.e., modifiers), "an impact by some object causing formation of a crack" (causation), and rules (generalizations) such as

If an aircraft that is less than 3 years old has a crack,
usually the crack is not due to corrosion. (22)

Moreover, the input-driven and goal-driven inference mechanisms of EPILOG were well-suited to extraction of the desired information from messages.

The ultimate limitations of both the TRAINS-93 system and the R&M prototype system were the fact that large amounts of linguistic and world knowledge are needed to deal with even a small set of dialogues or messages. Particularly gaps in linguistic knowledge are apt to cause failure, leading to very brittle systems. Recent natural language processing systems have striven to overcome brittleness through partial parsing and partial interpretation. In addition, the world knowledge bottleneck is often finessed by specializing systems so that they seek out particular kinds of information from texts or dialogues in very restricted domains. To the extent that the kinds of information sought are highly predictable and schematized, many syntactic and semantic details can be ignored. Such approaches can be practically rewarding, but it seems to us that genuine, domain-independent language understanding ultimately depends on dealing successfully with those syntactic and semantic details. We expect that the problem of acquiring many of the details will ultimately yield to automated learning techniques—but a framework as rich as EL will still be required to accommodate them.

Story Fragments

Since our primary interest is in the use of EL in story understanding, we have examined several story fragments in detail, to determine how readily the inferences that seem to be made spontaneously by people in the comprehension process could be generated by EPILOG from EL representations of the fragments.[21]

Most of these tests were carried out without the benefit of a natural language front end that could handle all of the grammatical, semantic, scoping and deindexing issues (not to mention ambiguities) involved in the chosen examples, and so the episodic logical forms used as inputs to EPILOG were hand-constructed. In the initial trials, these episodic logical forms were not exactly the forms we would expect to obtain mechanically, for various reasons: our conception of the episodic logical form was still evolving; in some cases the *frame problem* posed difficulties (for example, an exploding bomb ceases to be a bomb, but most static properties persist; knowing which ones do can be crucial); some involved simulative inference, which was unimplemented; and in some cases more accurate representations would have required extensive use of schematic meaning postulates involving predicate variables, sentence variables, etc., and the mechanisms for applying such schematic meaning postulates were still under development. We will discuss three examples, two of them very sketchily since they were based on inaccurate episodic logical forms, and the third, whose representation is faithful to our theory of logical form, in a little more detail.

A principle we firmly adhered to in working out these examples is to specify the requisite knowledge at the most general level possible. This is extremely important, since it is all too easy to invent highly specific rules that will appear to deal successfully with any given, small example, or even with certain narrow classes of examples. For instance, it would be a "cheat" to have a rule (conditional formula) for the Little Red Riding Hood story that says that if a child encounters a wolf, the wolf will make plans to eat the child. A more defensible rule would be one that says that if a predator encounters a nonpredatory creature no larger than itself, and is either hungry or enraged, it may try to attack (and perhaps subdue and eat) that creature. Many semipractical systems that extract semantic content from certain types of stories (such as reports on business mergers or terrorist incidents) depend heavily on using rules that work only for those types of stories. Our interest, however, is in domain-independent language understanding.

Terrorist Story Excerpt

As a first example, we briefly discuss an excerpt from a *Wall Street Journal* news item:

> An explosives-laden car blew up near the office of an [Afghan] guerrilla group in a crowded Shiite Moslem neighborhood in Beirut.   (23)

Simplifications we allowed ourselves here were the treatment of *explosives-laden* and *Shiite Moslem* as single lexical items; conjunctive interpretation of *explosives-laden car* (i.e., as a quantifier restriction [[x explosives-laden] $\wedge$ [x car]] rather than [x ((attr explosives-laden) car)]) and similarly for *crowded Shiite Moslem neighborhood;* and the temporal linking of the episode of the car being explosives-laden with the episode of the office existing as such, and the latter episode with the episode of the neighborhood being crowded.

Some inferences that are indicative of understanding example (23) are the following:

> A car was destroyed, and so (probably) was an office, and some furniture;
> Probably someone was killed, and hence was dead.

EPILOG made these inferences, among others, based on one meaning postulate and 12 general facts, including the following:

> Anything in a location where a bomb explodes is probably destroyed.
> Anyone who is destroyed is killed.
>
> Anyone who is killed becomes dead.
>
> If something is an office, there is a good chance that some furniture, a computer, and documents are in it.

Besides drawing the obvious conclusions by input-driven inference, EPILOG also was able to answer questions framed in terms of quantifiers such as "Was there something near the location where the explosion took place?" "Was no-one killed?" etc., posed as episodic logical form query formulas. With additional rules, EPILOG's understanding of the excerpt could have been deepened; for instance, EPILOG could have inferred the target organization with a rule to the effect that detonation of an explosive device at or near the premises of some individual, group or organization indicates that some hostile agent or agency intended this as an attack against the individual, group or organization.

The Wolf and the Woodcutters

One fragment of the Little Red Riding Hood story that we studied at length is the following.

> In the forest, Little Red Riding Hood met a wolf.

The wolf would have very much liked to eat her,
but he dared not do so on account of some woodcutters nearby.

(24)

Fully processing this fragment requires extensive reasoning including inferences based on meaning postulates, predictive inferences, explanatory inferences and simulative inferences. For example, genuine understanding of the third sentence entails being able to explain why the wolf decided against eating Little Red Riding Hood, and how the presence of woodcutters nearby affected the wolf's decision. In particular, one has to know that when some agent dares not do something, he must think it possible that his attempt to do it would have adverse consequences for himself; then one has to simulate his reasoning process to guess what unpleasant consequences he anticipates. Since we had not implemented simulative inference, we did not aim at full comprehension of the passage but rather at generating a set of plausible inferences under the hypothesis that the wolf attempts to eat Little Red Riding Hood, with the woodcutters nearby. In addition to this hypothesis, EPILOG was given several dozen pieces of general knowledge. Among the inferences it generated in input-driven mode were ones leading to the conclusion that the wolf may be severely punished. The following summarizes the relevant inference chain (consisting of about 30 inference steps) in words (Schubert and Hwang 1989). We state major intermediate conclusions, with parenthetical indications of the steps leading to them.

> The wolf's attempt to eat Little Red Riding Hood is an instance of the action type, "trying to eat Little Red Riding Hood" (based on a meaning postulate about the relation between action instances and action types).
>
> Trying to eat Little Red Riding Hood involves attacking her (because trying to eat a living creature involves attacking it in order to subdue it).
>
> There will be an instance of the wolf attacking Little Red Riding Hood during his attempt to eat her (from an axiom about what it means for one action to involve another).
>
> The wolf's attack on Little Red Riding Hood is an extremely wicked action (because for any creature to attack a child is extremely wicked).
>
> The attack is conspicuous for a nearby woodcutter (because there are some woodcutters nearby, and woodcutters are human, and neither the wolf nor Little Red Riding Hood are tiny relative to the woodcutter, and for a sizable creature to attack a sizable thing is conspicuous to a human being).
>
> The woodcutter may notice the attack (because if a person is near something, that thing is likely to be within plain sight of the person, and a conspicuous action within plain sight of a person is apt to be noticed by the person).
>
> The wolf may be severely punished (because if a human being notices something extremely wicked going on, the wrongdoer may eventually be severely punished).

A simulative inference process would now ascribe this reasoning to the wolf, and conclude that he anticipates possible punishment if he were to act on his desire to eat Little Red Riding Hood, thus explaining why he dared not eat her. Of course, we do not claim that the above inference chain is somehow uniquely correct. Changes to the knowledge base could have produced other variations, but we suggest that *something* like the above is needed.

We do think it is possible to understand the passage at a more superficial level with a less elaborate inference chain. We could just reason that the wolf must perceive some hazard from the proximity of the woodcutters, if he were to attempt to eat Little Red Riding Hood, and leave it at that. But it is our sense that most human readers of the story "fill in" a more detailed scenario, and so it is important for an automated system to be able to do likewise. Imagine asking a reader, "Why do you suppose the wolf feared the nearby woodcutters?" The answer would surely be something like, "Well, the woodcutters might go after the wolf and perhaps kill him," which presupposes much of the reasoning above.

The Wolf Enters Grandmother's Cottage

The story excerpt for which we have performed the most nearly complete analysis and knowledge base construction is the following:

> The wolf drew out the peg and the door flew open. Then he sprang upon the poor old lady and ate her up in less than no time, for he had been more than three days without food. (25)

We should also provide the immediately preceding sentence, since we use some facts from it (without doing a full analysis): "The worthy grandmother was in bed, not being very well, and cried out to him, 'Pull out the peg and the latch will fall.'" We will first outline a set of inferences needed for understanding, then present the logical forms of the sentences in the fragment and the representations of a few bits of background knowledge needed to produce those inferences.

Again the above excerpt may be explained in various ways by humans. Similarly, the system could in principle explain the story in several ways, depending on the kind of background knowledge supplied. The following is a clause-by-clause outline of the inferences enabled by the knowledge base we built. EPILOG was able to make most of the inferences mentioned, except for those based on the implicit question answering principle, which (as we explained) are beyond the system's current capabilities. Since implicit question answering is needed to resolve references, we helped the system along by manually supplying the equations that resolve the referring expressions, at the point of need. In this way we were able to "walk" the system through the passage.

1.1. "The wolf drew out the peg, ..."

The latch will fall (since Grandmother said so).

The door will then be ready to be opened, and the wolf could push it open (causing it to become open) and enter the cottage.

The wolf's reason for drawing out the peg was to bring about the above events. (We assume the system already knows that the wolf wanted to enter the cottage as the story mentioned earlier that the wolf knocked on the door.)

1.2 . "...and the door flew open."

This confirms that the door became open, as anticipated. By the implicit question answering principle, this also confirms that the wolf pushed it open, though the narrator's failure to mention this tends to undercut the inference (i.e., it may have opened spontaneously).[22]

It is very likely that the wolf entered the cottage when the door opened (since the wolf had wanted the door to open so that he could enter the cottage).

When he entered the cottage, he was near Grandmother and alone with her in the cottage, and she was weaker than he (being old and ill), and he knew this.

Since the wolf was probably wicked, he would probably use the opportunity to do something bad to Grandmother, in particular, attack her (knowing she was weaker than him).

2.1 "Then he sprang upon the poor old lady ..."

His "springing upon" her suggests—if we view him as a person—that he will assault and perhaps kill her, since this is one way of initiating an assault. But since this is also an instance of a predator springing upon a weaker creature, he may be preparing to subdue, kill, and eat her. In either case, the expectation that the wolf will do something bad to Grandmother is confirmed, and the assessment of the wolf as very wicked is strengthened.

2.2. "... and ate her up in less than no time ..."

His eating her confirms one of the previous predictions. By the implicit question answering principle, this also confirms he first subdued and killed her, though the narrator's failure to mention this tends to undercut the inference.

Furthermore, his eating Grandmother very quickly suggests that he was either very hungry or in a great hurry.

2.3. "... for he had been more than three days without food."

No one can eat if he has no food, and a creature will be very hungry if he hasn't eaten for a day or more. That confirms one of the alternative explanations of the wolf's haste.

We now know that the wolf is extremely wicked, and that Little Red Riding Hood is likely to arrive at the cottage shortly, and that the wolf knows this, and that he may therefore want to do something bad to Little Red Riding Hood upon her arrival, and hence may stay at the cottage to await her.

After having been walked through the excerpt, EPILOG is also able to answer the following kinds of questions with very little effort. (Questions are shown in EL, followed by English glosses of the EL questions and answers).

? (Wh e: [e episode] (The e': [e cause-of e'] [[Wolf pull-out Peg] ∗∗ e']))
Why did the wolf pull out the peg?
Because he wanted to enter Grandmother's cottage.

?($\exists e$: [[Wolf hungry] ∗∗ e]
(The e': [e right-after e'] [[Wolf eat-up Granny] ∗∗ e']))
Was the wolf hungry right after the episode of his eating up Grandmother?
Probably not.

Note that the answer to the second question is qualified with an epistemic probability (for example, .75), as it is based on an uncertain inference. That is, the system predicts that the wolf was probably not hungry after eating Grandmother, since we have an axiom stating that if a creature eats a large portion of food, it is likely to be full immediately afterwards, with minimum degree of certainty .75.

We now show how the excerpt is translated and give a small sampling of the background knowledge required for understanding the story as above. We conclude with some remarks on the frame problem. Readers not interested in technical details may safely skip the rest of this subsection.

Story Representation. We show the initial, unscoped logical forms, scoped but still indexical logical forms, and completely deindexed episodic logical forms, in that order. We omit speech act operators.

1. *The wolf drew out the peg and the door flew open.*

⇒⟨ ∧ [⟨The wolf⟩ ⟨past draw-out⟩ ⟨the peg⟩]
[⟨The door⟩ (⟨past fly⟩ open)]⟩

⇒[(past (The x_1: [x_1 wolf] (The x_2: [x_2 peg] [x_1 draw-out x_2])))) ∧
(past (The x_3: [x_3 door] [x_3 (fly open)]))]

⇒[($\exists e_{21}$: [[e_{21} before Now$_{11}$] ∧
[E_{10} orients e_{21}]] [[Wolf pull-out Peg] ∗∗ e_{21}]) ∧
($\exists e_{22}$: [[e_{22} before Now$_{12}$] ∧
[e_{21} orients e_{22}]] [[Door (fly open)] ∗∗ e_{22}])]

2. *Then he sprang upon the poor old lady and ate her up in less than no time, for he had been more than three days without food.*

⇒[⟨ ∧ ((adv-e at-time-Then)
[He ⟨past spring-upon⟩⟨The ((attr poor2) ((attr old) lady))⟩])
[He ((adv-a (in-manner (very quick)))⟨⟨past eat-up⟩ Her)]⟩
because ⟨past (perf((adv-e (lasts-for (K ((num 3) (plur day)))))
[He without (K food)])))]

$\Rightarrow$ [[(past (The x_4:[x_4 ((attr poor2) ((attr old) lady))]
    ((adv-e at-time-Then) [He spring-upon x_4]))) $\wedge$
    (past [He ((adv-a (in-manner (very quick))) (eat-up Her))])])]
    because (past (perf ((adv-e (lasts-for (K ((num 3) (plur day)))))
    [He without (K food)])))]

$\Rightarrow$ [[($\exists e_{23}$: [[e_{23} before Now$_{13}$] $\wedge$ [e_{22} orients e_{23}]]
    [[[e_{23} right-after e_{22}] $\wedge$ [GM poor2] $\wedge$
    [Wolf spring-upon GM]] $**$ e_{23}])$\wedge$
    ($\exists e_{24}$: [[e_{24} before Now$_{14}$] $\wedge$ [e_{23} orients e_{24}]]
    [[[[Wolf | e_{24}] (in-manner (very quick))] $\wedge$
    [Wolf eat-up GM]] $**$ e_{24}])]
    because ($\exists e_{25}$: [[e_{25} before Now$_{15}$] $\wedge$ [e_{24} orients e_{25}]]
    [($\exists e_{26}$: [e_{26} impinges-on e_{25}]
    [[[e_{26} lasts-for (K ((num 3) (plur day)))] $\wedge$
    [Wolf without (K food)]] $**$ e_{26}])
    $**$ e_{25}])]

In the above, x_1, x_2, x_3, and x_4 are resolved to Wolf, Peg, Door and GM, respectively. We take "in less than no time" as an idiom and translate it as "very quickly," and simplify "more than three days" into "for three days." Note that "draw out" is translated into *pull-out* (the lexical rule for "draw" with subcategorization feature *out* translates the phrase as such). *poor2* indicates the narrator's attitude of feeling sorry for an individual (this seems inferrable from the fact that the qualifier *poor* is redundant for identifying the referent of the description, and was not previously given or implied); and this new information about Grandmother being poor in situation e_{23} is left in the final, deindexed formula in conjunction with other descriptions of e_{23}. [e_{23} at-time-Then] is replaced by [e_{23} right-after e_{22}] at the deindexing phase once the orienting episode of e_{23} is determined to be e_{22}.

At this point, the final, deindexed episodic logical forms are ready to be entered into the knowledge base. Note, however, that they still involve context-charged relations, i.e., *orients* and *impinges-on*. Note also that when these formulas are asserted in the knowledge base, simplifications like distributing negations (not needed in this example), splitting conjunctions, and top-level Skolemization are performed.

The following 10 axioms are selected from the 50-or-so used in the inference process, and are intended to give some idea of the variety and forms of knowledge involved. (For a more comprehensive listing, see Hwang and Scubert [1993a].)

Narrative Axioms. Two narrative axioms that particularize the *orients* relation are the following. We assume here that narrative axioms are applied before all others.

Narr 1. Two successive telic sentences in a text usually indicate that events occurred in that order.

For Φ, Ψ telic,

$(\exists e_1: [\Phi ** e_1] (\exists e_2 : [\Psi ** e_2] [e_1 \text{ orients } e_2])) \rightarrow_{.5, e_1, e_2} [e_2 \text{ after } e_1]$

Narr 2. When a telic sentence is followed by a stative sentence in a text, this often indicates that the (telic) event ends at a point where the state holds.

For Φ telic, Ψ stative (atelic),

$(\exists e_1: [\Phi ** e_1] (\exists e_2: [\Psi ** e_2] [e_1 \text{ orients } e_2])) \rightarrow_{.5, e1, e2} [e_2 \text{ at-end-of } e_1]$

Some Meaning Postulates About "cause-of" and "because"

MP1. $(\forall e_1 (\forall e_2 (\forall e_3 [[[e_1 \text{ cause-of } e_2] \wedge [e_2 \text{ cause-of } e_3]]$
$\rightarrow [e_1 \text{ cause-of } e_3]])))$

MP 2. $(\forall e_1 (\forall e_2 (\forall e_3 [[[e_1 \text{ coexten-subep-of } e_2] \wedge [e_1 \text{ cause-of } e_3]]$
$\rightarrow [e_2 \text{ cause-of } e_3]])))$

MP 3. $(\forall e_1 (\forall e_2 [[[\Phi ** e_1] \text{ because } [\Psi ** e_2]]$
$\leftrightarrow [[e_2 \text{ cause-of } e_1] \wedge [\Phi ** e_1] \wedge [\Psi ** e_2]]]))$

Some Meaning Postulates About * and **

MP 4. $(\forall e_1 [[\Phi * e_1] \rightarrow (\exists e_2: [e_2 \text{ coexten-subep-of } e_1] [\Phi ** e_2])])$, for Φ atelic

MP 5. $(\forall e_1 [[\Phi * e_1] \rightarrow (\exists e_2: [e_2 \text{ subep-of } e_1] [\Phi ** e_2])])$, for Φ telic

A Meaning Postulate about Monotone Predicate Modifiers

MP 6. For α a monotone predicate modifier (such as "very") and π a monadic predicate, $(\forall x [[x (\alpha \pi)] \rightarrow [x \pi]])$

Two Pieces of Relevant World Knowledge

WK 1. If a predatory animal springs upon a nonpredatory creature, that probably is part of an attack intended to subdue the creature, allowing it to be killed and eaten.

$(\exists x: [x ((\text{attr predatory}) \text{animal})] (\exists y: [[y \text{ creature}] \wedge (\neg[x \text{ predatory}])]$
$\quad (\exists e_1 [[x \text{ spring-upon } y] ** e_1])))$
$\rightarrow_{.85, e_1} \quad (\exists e_2: [[e_2 \text{ involves } e_1] \wedge [[x \text{ attack } y] ** e_2]]$
$\qquad [[x \mid e_2] \text{ done-with-intention}$
$\qquad (\text{Ka } ((\text{adv-a } (\text{for-purpose } (\text{Ka } \lambda z (\text{seq } [z \text{ kill } y] [z \text{ eat } y])))))$
$\qquad\qquad (\text{subdue } y)))])$

% *seq* is an operator that maps *n* formulas, $n \geq 1$, into a sequence of formulas.

WK 2. Creatures are very hungry when they have not eaten for more than a day.

$(\exists n: [[n \text{ number}] \wedge [n \geq 1]]$
$\quad (\exists e_1: [e_1 \text{ lasts-for } (K ((\text{num } n) (\text{plur day})))]$
$\qquad [(\exists x:[x \text{ creature}](\neg[x \text{ eat}])) ** e_1]))$
$\rightarrow_{.9, n, e_1} \quad (\exists e_2: [[e_2 \text{ at-end-of } e_1] \wedge [e_1 \text{ cause-of } e_2]]$
$\qquad [[x (\text{very hungry})] ** e_2])$

A Note on the Frame Problem

One problem that arises quite frequently in narratives is that we need to assume the persistence of certain properties or relationships, in the absence of explicit or implicit information to the contrary. As mentioned before, this is a version of the well-known *frame problem* in AI.

For instance, at a point in the story prior to the excerpt about the wolf entering Grandmother's cottage, we are told that the wolf knocked on the door. From this we would make the inference that he probably wanted to enter. When the narrator says "the door flew open," we are quite sure that the wolf still wanted to enter, and so infer that he did so. (Note that the story does not say this!)

Dealing with the frame problem has generally been treated in AI as a matter of designing the right logic, rather than as a matter of having the right knowledge. In fact, this has been a major impetus behind the development of nonmonotonic logics. We think, on the contrary, that persistence is not a matter of logic, but something to be inferred from the right sorts of knowledge about the world, about one's own knowledge, and about narration. One of us has made specific proposals about the relevant world knowledge in a non-narrative setting (Schubert 1990, 1994), but this is not the place to pursue the matter. We want to suggest, however, that in a narrative setting persistence inferences hinge on certain narrative conventions, to the effect that the narrator is expected to let the reader know about changes in relevant properties and relationships, either explicitly or by providing a basis for inferring the changes. For instance, coming back to the wolf's evident intention to enter Grandmother's cottage, if the wolf had dropped that intention after knocking (for example, because no one answered), the story would have given us a basis for inferring this. Since it did not, we infer that the wolf's intention persists.

We have formulated this idea as a narrative axiom. For a formal statement of the axiom, we refer the reader to Hwang and Schubert (1993a); here we just state the idea in words:

A state evoked by a narrative and characterized by an atelic sentence extends temporally to any given later episode unless I (the reader of the story) have been led to disbelieve this.

An *evoked episode,* in the context of a narrative, is one for which a token has been generated as a result of input-driven inference chaining. In particular, all episodes occurring in orienting relations are considered evoked episodes. Like *orients,* the property of being evoked is context-charged, i.e., it is a property that a thing has in virtue of its role in the narrative, rather than its role in the "world." The question of whether the reader has been led to believe or disbelieve a particular claim is settled simply by introspection: if at a certain point in the story the reader can verify with minimal inference effort (and with reasonably high probability) (That Φ), where Φ concerns entities or events in the story, then that's what the reader has been led to believe.[23] Disbelief is just belief in the negation.

We have not implemented belief introspection as a means of evaluating formulas that assert beliefs of the system, and so we have not used the above axiom. It plays no direct role in the excerpts we have discussed because of their brevity. However, note that we made a number of assumptions in the reasoning process for the final excerpt that would require persistence inferences from earlier parts of the story in a more complete system. They include the supposition that the wolf is wicked, that he wants to enter Grandmother's cottage, that Grandmother is in the cottage and is ill and alone, that drawing out the peg on the door will make the latch fall, that Little Red Riding Hood is on her way to the cottage, and that the wolf knows all this.

Conclusions and Future Work

The main concern of our research has been to develop an adequate semantic representation and knowledge representation for general natural language understanding systems, especially ones aimed at understanding narratives. As a logic, EL is in a state analogous to that of various nonmonotonic, conditional and probabilistic logics whose semantics remains an active area of research. In other words, the syntax is better worked out than the semantics. We have, however, specified the semantic types of all EL expressions, adding various constraints on the structure of situations and other classes of domain entities and on the intepretations of the basic operators, predicates and functions of EL (Hwang [1992] and Hwang and Schubert [1993b]). We also have (unpublished) proofs of the validity of various axiom schemas, the soundness of rule instantiation and goal chaining, and the persistence of (certain kinds of) information through the situation ordering. However, revisions are needed because of our recent revisions to the semantics of "∗∗" and "∗," and we need to demonstrate that there exist (nontrivial) models of the most general sort we have posited.[24]

There are two extreme views about the deployment of knowledge representations whose semantics is not fully understood. One extreme is to reject such deployment altogether, on the grounds that there will be no guarantee that all reachable conclusions are justifiable and all justifiable conclusions are reachable, and this may be disastrous in certain critical applications. The other extreme is to reject formal denotational semantics altogether, on the grounds that the design of representations and inference mechanisms (especially in language understanding) is a cognitive modeling task in which the correspondence between symbols and the world has no role to play.

We think both extreme views are harmful and account in part for the rift that remains within knowledge representation and reasoning as practiced outside and within natural language processing. We firmly believe that the most effective strategy for arriving at a representation adequate for general natural language understanding and commonsense reasoning is one of progressive refinement and theoretical deepening, starting with a representation that allows us to express linguistic meaning and commonsense knowledge easily and directly, fits with a conceptually modular view of the language understanding process (in the spirit of "divide and conquer"), and readily supports all the sorts of inferences that people are apt to make. The refinement and deepening should be driven by concurrent theoretical investigations and experimental implementations.

The EL representation meets many of our desiderata. It does so by combining ideas from Montague grammar, situation semantics and DRT, and adding a number of new ideas concerning the semantics of situations, actions, propositions and facts, times, quantification and tense and aspect. The deindexing of indexical logical forms with the aid of tense trees is a crucial stage in our approach, systematically deriving episodic logical formulas that can then be used for inference.

EL has been implemented and tested on small but realistic text samples, including ones from the particularly challenging genre of fairy tales, and also has been incorporated into complete prototype natural language processing systems. The results so far are encouraging, suggesting that it is indeed possible to grapple simultaneously with a wide spectrum of problems in natural language understanding. More specifically, the following are the contributions of EL to knowledge representation for natural language processing.

First, EL is an *expressive* semantic representation / knowledge representation that allows the content of most English sentences and most world knowledge to be represented in an intuitively comprehensible, computationally usable and formally analyzable manner. It makes implicit time and situation dependencies explicit through the use of episodic variables, and admits unbound anaphoric variables and the representation of (extensional) generic conditionals, as well as restricted quantifiers, modal operators, predicate and sentence nominalization operators, and predicate and sentence modifiers. These features have been brought together for the first time in a logic for narrative understanding. Also, the mapping from English to EL is transparent and modular, handling many combinations of tense, aspect and adverbials (this was not discussed in detail here for space reasons, but see Hwang [1992] and Hwang and Schubert [1994]).

Second, in theory and in practice, EL allows linguistic and domain knowledge to be strictly separated from parsing and inference control structure, so that the former can be expanded and revised independently of the latter.

Finally, the main rules of inference in EL, rule instantiation and goal chaining, provide input-driven and goal-driven inference modes, and are able to combine multiple premises in one fell swoop. Since the rules allow the use of probabilistic conditionals, they support expert system-like combination of evidence in the derivation of probable explanations or predictions. Furthermore, these rules have been successfully implemented in EPILOG, and integrated uniformly with an array of specialized inference techniques.

Although we think that EL and the associated interpretive and inference mechanisms provide a good "first draft" of a comprehensive foundation for language understanding, many formidable challenges remain. The following are among the most important issues for future work.

First, the representation and semantics of several linguistic phenomena remains unclear. This includes quantifier modifiers ("almost all"), comparatives, questions and *Wh*-nominals ("why she left"), clausal adverbials ("even though she left"), various uses of "except" and "only," etc. A particularly important area for further investigation is the semantics of *generic passages* (Carlson and Spejewski 1997)—extended passages that describe typical or habitual patterns of events or relationships. We believe that much of our world knowledge consists, in effect, of such generic passages. (Scripts and frames can be viewed as representations of such passages; see Schank and Abelson [1977], Minsky [1975], Schubert, [forthcoming].)

Second, as we have already discussed, we need to extend and deepen the semantics of EL itself, fully justifying various basic axioms and the rule instantiation and goal chaining rules, and demonstrating the existence of models.

Third, the probabilistic constructs and inferences need to be put on a firmer theoretical foundations. Ideally, we would like to develop an analogue of Bayes net reasoning within a logical setting, resting on analogous conditional independence assumptions (i.e., something like independence of a conclusion of all knowledge-base hypotheses other than ones derived from the conclusion, given the truth or falsity of just those hypotheses that support a one-step probabilistic inference to the conclusion or its negation).

Fourth, inference control needs to be further improved. In particular forward inference termination through "interestingness" and probability criteria is not always intuitively satisfactory.

Fifth, we need to gain a better understanding of both simulative and *introspective* inference in EL, and to implement these important modes of reasoning.

Sixth, closely related to this is the need for further work on the *frame problem* in the context of narratives; as we indicated, we think this depends on introspective (autoepistemic) reasoning.

Seventh, we need to develop in detail a computational theory of *implicit question answering* as outlined earlier, as a means of arriving at a coherent interpretation of extended texts.

Eighth, some of the EPILOG specialists need further development, and some new ones are needed, most importantly a specialist for "imagining" objects interacting and in motion (including complex deformable objects like people, plants, clothing, newspapers, etc.). For instance, when we're told "John tossed the umbrella in the trunk of his car," how do we infer that the umbrella was probably folded up?

Ninth, a major long-range goal in the development of EPILOG is to equip it with a goal-directed component, so that it will be capable of exhibiting independent initiative, for example, by asking questions. Of course, EPILOG (like many other inference engines) already does goal-directed inference, but these inferences are aimed at answering questions, not guiding action. We are thinking in terms of a set of overarching "drives," such as cooperativeness and curiosity, guiding a behavioral component consisting primarily of a conversation and reasoning manager.

Tenth, we are eager to link up EPILOG with a broad-coverage, preference-seeking parser for English. In the shorter term, we are planning to experiment with available parsers, and in the longer term we expect to employ an ambitious parser of our own, one particularly well-suited to our interpretive goals, that has been under sporadic development for many years (based on ideas in Schubert [1984, 1986]).

Last and perhaps most importantly, we need ways of breaking through the "knowledge bottleneck," both in linguistic and world knowledge. One approach to this problem is *knowledge bootstrapping* through linguistic input. This presupposes a certain minimal linguistic competence and basic world knowledge to begin with. The basic grammatical knowledge can be hand-coded (automated grammar acquisition so far does not lead to grammars capable of supporting semantic analysis). However, this leaves the task of disambiguation, which is knowledge-intensive and a major obstacle to getting off the ground. Some work we are currently undertaking is aimed at the accumulation of *head patterns* from linguistic corpora, for use in disambiguation. In essence, head patterns are patterns of co-occurrence of predicates and other operators (such as modifiers) with particular arguments or types of arguments. (As such they are related to the knowledge indexing scheme we use.)

To help accumulate some basic world knowledge, we intend to avail ourselves of (and extend) work that has been done in extracting semantic information from lexicons, especially type hierarchy information and part-of information. We also think that text corpora, particularly fictional ones (because of the everyday minutiae they touch on), are a potentially rich source of knowledge about the properties various kinds of entities are likely to have, the actions and relationships they participate in, and ultimately the causal and habitual patterns of events they tend to be involved in. We think that large amounts of such knowledge can be extracted by observing patterns of predication in large corpora, with only very shallow semantic analysis.

With a reasonably comprehensive grammar, pattern-based disambiguation, and some rudimentary world knowledge in place, and presupposing the solution of some of the more important remaining representational problems (particularly the representation of comparatives and generic passages), we would be ready to provide further knowledge by telling it to the system in English. This would be an effective way to continue the bootstrapping process, provided that the system had some capacity to detect its own knowledge gaps, and could muster the initiative to ask.

Acknowledgments

We are grateful to Phil Harrison for his insights and suggestions during much of the development of Episodic Logic and to James Allen for many useful comments in the context of the TRAINS project. We also owe a large debt of gratitude to Stephanie Schaeffer, who implemented EPILOG, happily accepting and actualizing ever more ambitious specifications and giving us continuous and crucial feedback on how our ideas were working out (or not working out) in practice.

This research was supported in part by NSF Research Grants IRI-9013160 and IRI-9503312, ONR/DARPA Research Contract No. N00014-92-J-1512, the Boeing Company in Seattle under Purchase Contracts W278258 and W288104, and a Killam Memorial Scholarship (CHH).

Notes

1. In our later discussion of test scenarios, the wording is slightly different, as we were rather haphazardly using several children's books. One source was Perrault (1961).

2. Observe that in this underlying prefix form we are applying the predicate to one argument at a time. In this so-called "curried" form of predication (associated with the names of Curry, Schoenfinkel and Church), an n-place predicate is interpreted as a function that can be applied to a single argument to give an $(n-1)$-place predicate (and finally a truth value, when $n = 1$).

3. In particular, $(Ke\ \Phi)$ is equivalent to $(K\ \lambda e[\Phi ** e])$, i.e., the kind of event that is characterized by Φ; and $(Ka\ \pi)$ is equivalent to $(K\ \lambda a[[(\text{fst } a)\ \pi] ** (\text{rst } a)])$, i.e., the kind of action

such that the event this action brings about ((rst a), the second element of a) is characterized by the sentence [(fst a) π], where (fst a) is the agent of the action (the first element of a).

4. Controlled variables thus allow us to address the "proportion problem" (Kadmon 1987). If we made x an additional controlled variable in the example, we would be quantifying over individual predators, even in situations where several predators simultaneously find some nonpredatory creature(s).

5. The topic of generic sentences is a complex one (for example, Carlson and Pelletier [1995]), and "genericity" cannot in general be equated with statistical preponderance. For instance, Carlson's sentence "Alligators die before they are 20 weeks old" seems false even if survival chances for baby alligators are very poor. Nonetheless, statistical generalizations are very useful, and cover more ground than might be thought (see Cohen [1997] for some interesting points).

6. See Hwang and Schuber (1994) for an extensive discussion of our treatment of temporal and other kinds of adverbials. However, since writing that paper we have made some significant adjustments in our conception of the connection between episodes and sentences, leading to a simpler episodic logical form for sentences with adverbials.

7. In the above example, the embedded question would be prefixed by an extension operator "$\vee$"; and a question like "Which book did each child read?" would involve both an intension and an extension operator: $^\wedge(\forall x\colon [x \text{ child}] \vee(\text{W?} \ y\colon [y \text{ book}] \ (\exists e \ [[x \text{ read } y] \ast e])))$. We cannot discuss question semantics here, except to mention that we view questions as functions on episodes, where the value of a question at an episode, if defined, is a full and true answer to the question (and thus is a sentence intension). Our reliance on full answers in the semantics is something of a departure from more standard approaches (for example, Chierchia [1993]).

8. *Clock times* are distinguished from *times* in the episodic sense: clock times are formally modelled as multi-intervals on the real numbers, and as such have no "information content."

9. In expanding out (d) to "Little Red Riding Hood is not alone in her walk through the forest," we have to be careful not to misunderstand the negation as having wide scope; i.e., the intended reading is that Little Red Riding Hood is unaccompanied in her walk through the forest, rather than that "It is false that Little Red Riding Hood is alone in her walk through the forest." In fact, for the wide-scope negative reading, the entailments are obviously reversed: $\neg[\text{Alone} \ast \text{ForestWalk}] \nRightarrow \neg[\text{Alone} \ast \text{EntireWalk}]$.

10. I.e., we do not separate variable assignments from interpretations.

11. Refer to footnote 2.

12. More precisely, we take the *basic* reading of "Little Red Riding Hood walked" to be nonculminated. There is also a culminated reading, tantamount to "Little Red Riding Hood took a walk," but we take this reading to involve tacit application of a certain "episode-bounding" operator.

13. Formulas like [[LRRH greet W] $\vee$ $\neg$[LRRH silent]] or ($\forall x\colon [x \text{ person}]$ [[x die] $\vee$ $\neg$[x die]]) are neither telic nor atelic. Still, if they are true in a given situation, they will satisfy the first or second disjunct of our definition for some part η of that situation. Which disjunct is satisfied depends on whether or not there is a telic fact among the atomic facts in virtue of which the formula is true in the given situation.

14. It may also allow us to account for the dual existential/ referential character of indefinites (cf. Fodor and Sag [1982]).

15. The main change is that we have abandoned the notion that the situations character-ized by natural language sentences support the truth of just those sentences (and certain equivalent ones) and are atomic (have no parts). Rather, we regard those situations as po-tentially having an arbitrarily fine-grained part-structure and as supporting arbitrarily large amounts of information. This seems like a much more naturalistic notion of situa-tions. For instance, we can now say that an extended episode such as an episode of Little Red Riding Hood being alone can have many (temporally smaller) parts, and all those parts are also episodes of Little Red Riding Hood being alone. (Previously we had to stip-ulate that an extended episode of Little Red Riding Hood being alone entails the existence of shorter episodes of Little Red Riding Hood being alone, at all times during the given episode.) We can also say now that *in* an episode of Little Red Riding Hood greeting the wolf, Little Red Riding Hood and the wolf are near of each other, instead of having to say that such a being-near episode exists at the same time as the greeting episode (but not as a part of it).

16. In particular see the embedded form of resolution employed in Traugott (1986); how-ever, rule instantiation avoids Skolemization.

17. The fact $(\forall e\, (\forall e_1\, (\forall e_2\, [[e_2 \text{ same-time } e_1] \rightarrow [[e_2 \text{ before } e] \leftrightarrow [e_1 \text{ before } e]]])))$ would also be needed eventually.

18. One issue that arises is how to treat self-references by the other agent.

19. The proposals in Lascarides and Asher (1991) and Lascarides et al. (1992) do invoke discourse conventions to sort out interpretations of narratives, instead of making this a matter of world knowledge (alone), but as far as we can tell would not deal properly with negative examples.

20. It might be countered that the resolution of the pronoun in both (19) and (20) is the re-sult of centering, where the verb object in (a) is the preferred center. However, this is dis-confirmed by "John accidentally dropped the cutting-board on the glass. Fortunately, it didn't break."

21. For some further details see http://www.cs.rochester.edu/research/epilog/

22. We do not at present deal with this "undercutting" phenomenon.

23. In contrast with the perspective taken in autoepistemic logic (Moore 1985), we regard it as crucial that an agent should need only a very small computational effort to check whether it believes something or not (as in Kaplan and Schubert [1997] and Kaplan [1998]).

24. We have recently clarified and fully formalized the semantics of "∗" and "∗∗" in an ex-tension of first-order logic called FOL∗∗ (Schubert forthcoming). This logic reconciles many of the (apparently conflicting) ideas about the connection between events and sen-tences in Reichenbach (1947), Davidson (1967), and Barwise and Perry (1983).

5 SNePS: A Logic for Natural Language Understanding and Commonsense Reasoning

Stuart C. Shapiro

MY COLLEAGUES, STUDENTS, AND I have been engaged in a long-term project to build a natural language using intelligent agent. While our approach to natural language understanding and commonsense reasoning has been logic-based, we have thought that the logics developed for metamathematics (Kleene 1950) are not the best ones for our purpose. Instead, we have designed new logics, better suited for natural language understanding and commonsense reasoning. The current version of these logics constitutes the formal language and inference mechanism of the knowledge representation and reasoning system, SNePS 2.4 (Shapiro and the SNePS Implementation Group 1998). SNePS is a constantly evolving system (Shapiro and Rapaport 1992) that implements our evolving theory of how to build a computational, natural language using, rational agent that does commonsense reasoning.

In this chapter, I will survey several ways in which the SNePS logic has been designed to be more appropriate for natural language understanding and commonsense reasoning than the standard first order predicate logic.[1] In each section, I will present a commensense reasoning problem in English. Then I will discuss the difficulties involved in representing and solving the problem in first order predicate logic, and will show how it is represented and solved in SNePS. For some subtle problems, I will first show the SNePS solution before revealing the difficulties it presents to first order predicate logic solutions. SNePS examples will be in SNePS-LOG, (Shapiro et al. 1981, Shapiro and The SNePS Implementation Group 1998, Chapter 7) a first order predicate logiclike user interface to SNePS.

This chapter is about SNePS logic per se, rather than the way we have used it for representing particular entities and relations important to natural language understanding and commonsense reasoning. For some of these discussions, see Peters and Shapiro (1987), Peters et al. (1988), and Peters and Rapaport (1990) for basic- and superordinate-level categories; Chun (1987) and Shapiro and Rapaport (1991) for possessives; Almeida (1995) for tense and aspect; and Rapaport et al. (1997) for proper names and beliefs about knowledge and belief.

What is Represented in the Knowledge Representation Formalism

As said above, we view our long-term project as developing a natural language using intelligent agent, who we tend to refer to as Cassie (Shapiro 1989, Shapiro and Rapaport 1991). At any point in Cassie's operation, the material represented in SNePS constitutes the contents of Cassie's mind (Shapiro 1993). We are not interested in representing the "meaning" of words, phrases, clauses, or sentences, rather we are interested in the changes to Cassie's mind that result from her understanding natural language utterances in the context of a conversation or of reading a book or article. In the discussion that follows, I will be interested in the logic of the representation of beliefs that result from understanding utterances in certain ways. It might be that some of the sentences I cite might be understood differently in contexts other than the ones I am considering. That is beside the point. What is to the point is my claim that there are contexts in which a natural language understander would understand the utterance in the way I suggest, and that in that case SNePS logic is more appropriate for representing that understanding than standard first order predicate logic. Certainly a transducer is needed that can take an English utterance as input and use the entire relevant state of Cassie's mind to modify her mind to register an understanding of that utterance. That transducer, however, is not the subject of this chapter. (Although see Shapiro [1982], Shapiro [1989], Shapiro and Rapaport [1987], Neal and Shapiro [1987], Neal and Shapiro [1991], Neal and Shapiro [1994], and Shapiro and Rapaport [1995].)

There are four types of expressions in SNePS logic, denoting propositions, rules, acts, and individuals. Propositions are the sorts of entities that agents can believe or disbelieve. We say that a proposition expression representing a proposition that Cassie believes is "asserted." Rule expressions are proposition expressions whose syntax is recognized by the SNePS inference routines. If the proposition P is asserted and the rule $P \Rightarrow Q$ is asserted, then the SNePS inference routines may cause Q to be asserted. Acts are the sort of entities an agent may perform. Act expressions use a syntax recognized by SNeRE, the SNePS rational engine (Shapiro and The SNePS Implementation Group 1998, Chapter 4), but are beyond the scope of this chapter (but see Kumar [1996]; Kumar and Shapiro [1994]; Shapiro [1998]). Individuals are everything else. However, all expressions are terms (Shapiro 1993, Chalupsky and Shapiro 1994), and may be used as arguments of functions.

Set-Oriented Logical Connectives

Consider the following problems:

Everything is an animal, a vegetable, or a mineral.   (1)
(a)   Squash is a vegetable.
      Is squash an animal? A mineral?
(b)   Marble is neither an animal nor a vegetable.
      Is marble a mineral?

For every object, the following statements are equivalent: (2)
      It is human.
      It is a featherless biped.
      It is a rational animal.
(a)   Socrates is human.
      Is Socrates a featherless biped? A rational animal?
(b)   Snoopy is not a featherless biped.
      Is Snoopy a rational animal? A human?

Consider formalizing problem (1). The first order predicate logic wff

$$\forall(x) [Animal(x) \lor Vegetable(x) \lor Mineral(x)] \qquad (3)$$

is wrong because $\lor$ is the inclusive or, and we want to be able to conclude that squash is neither an animal nor a mineral.[2] Neither is

$$\forall(x) [Animal(x) \oplus Vegetable(x) \oplus Mineral(x)]$$

correct, where $\oplus$ is the exclusive or, because that is satisfied by something that is an animal, a vegetable, *and* a mineral.

In English, utterances of the form "Either P_1 or ... or P_n" are often understood as saying that exactly one of P_1, ..., P_n is true, but such an understanding is not easily formulated in first-order predicate logic. We have implemented a logical connective for this and similar problems in SNePS (Shapiro 1979b, pp. 189ff., Shapiro and Rapaport 1992, p. 250, Shapiro and The SNePS Implementation Group 1998, section 3.1). The SNePSLOG wff

$$andor(i, j)\{P_1, ..., P_n\}$$

is true if and only if at least i and at most j of the wffs in the set $\{P_1, ..., P_n\}$ are true. Using andor, problems 1 and 1a can be solved in SNePSLOG as shown here:

```
: all(x)(andor(1, 1) {animal(x), vegetable(x), mineral(x)}).
  all(X)(andor(1, 1) {ANIMAL(X), VEGETABLE(X), MINERAL(X)})
```

```
: vegetable(squash)!
VEGETABLE(SQUASH)
~ANIMAL(SQUASH)
~MINERAL(SQUASH)
```

(The ":" is the SNePSLOG prompt. Input is shown after the prompt in lower, and, occasionally, mixed case. Output is shown in all upper case (except for logical constants such as all and andor). Input terminating in a period (".") is stored and echoed, but in the rest of this chapter, the echo will not be shown to conserve space and enhance readability. The terminal "!" means store and perform forward inference. The output lines following inference commands report all wffs inferred and stored as a result of the inference. SNePSLOG interactions have been edited only to conserve space and to fit the format of this chapter. The character strings shown, however, are actual input and output.) andor(0, 0) serves as a generalized nor, so that problem 1b can be solved as follows:

```
: andor(0, 0){animal(marble), vegetable(marble)}!
~ANIMAL(MARBLE)
~VEGETABLE(MARBLE)
MINERAL(MARBLE)
```

andor can also be used to represent the inclusive or. For example,

all(x)(andor(1, 3){animal(x), vegetable(x), mineral(x)})

is the SNePSLOG version of the first order predicate logic wff 3.

Novice logicians would probably try to formalize problem 2 as

$\forall(x) [Human(x) \Leftrightarrow Featherless\text{-}Biped(x) \Leftrightarrow Rational\text{-}Animal(x)]$

However, this is not correct because, for example, it is satisfied by something that is human, but neither a rational animal nor a featherless biped. The correct way to formalize problem 2 in first-order predicate logic is

$\forall x[(Human(x) \Rightarrow Featherless\text{-}Biped(x))$
$\wedge(Featherless\text{-}Biped(x) \Rightarrow Rational\text{-}Animal(x))$
$\wedge(Rational\text{-}Animal(x) \Rightarrow Human(x))]$

However, this does not capture the style of the original, which more simply asserted a relation among three propositions.

Problem 2 can be done in SNePSLOG using nested andors as

```
all(x)(andor(1, 1) {andor(3, 3){Human(x),
                         Featherless-Biped(x),
                         Rational-Animal(x)},
            andor(0, 0){Human(x),
                         Featherless-Biped(x),
                         Rational-Animal(x)}})
```

In other words, the three propositions are either all true or all false. However, this also fails to capture the simple relation among the three propositions. Therefore another connective has been included in SNeP-SLOG. The wff thresh(i, j){P_1, ..., P_n}

is true if and only if either fewer than i of the wffs in the set {P_1, ..., P_n} are true or more than j are true. Using thresh, problem 2 can be solved in SNePSLOG as shown here:

```
: all(x)(thresh(1, 2){human(x), featherless-biped(x), rational-animal(x)}).
: human(Socrates)!
  HUMAN(SOCRATES)
  FEATHERLESS-BIPED(SOCRATES)
  RATIONAL-ANIMAL(SOCRATES)
: ~featherless-biped(Snoopy)!
  ~RATIONAL-ANIMAL(SNOOPY)
  ~FEATHERLESS-BIPED(SNOOPY)
  ~HUMAN(SNOOPY)
```

When, in previous talks, I have suggested that *or* in English usually means exclusive or rather than inclusive or,[3] one common rejoinder is that in sentences like "If Hilda is in Boston or Kathy is in Las Vegas, then Eve is in Providence" (Rips 1983, p. 63) we would certainly not want the inference to be blocked if Hilda were in Boston and Kathy were also in Las Vegas. This is cited as evidence that the or in this sentence is the inclusive or. The logical form of the sentence is taken to be $(P \lor R) \Rightarrow Q$, and the steps of reasoning from P to Q are taken to be

1. $(P \lor R) \Rightarrow Q$ *Hyp.*
2. P *Hyp.*
3. $P \lor R$ $\lor$ *Introduction*
4. Q $\Rightarrow$ *Elimination*

with the $\lor$ an inclusive or, and the rule of $\lor$ Introduction being truth-functional.

Rips (1983), however, studied the reasoning of subjects not trained in formal logic to assess how available certain logical rules of inference were to them. He found that the rule of $\lor$ Introduction was virtually not available at all, but that instead the rule of "Disjunctive Modus Ponens"

$$\frac{P, P \lor R \Rightarrow Q}{Q}$$

was among the most available rules. Thus, $(P \lor R)$ is not a subformula of $P \lor R \Rightarrow Q$ whose truth value is assessed. It is as if $\_ \lor \_ \Rightarrow \_$ were a single propositional connective with its own rule of inference.

A generalization of this connective is included in SNePS. It is called *or-entailment*. The SNePSLOG wff

{P_1, ..., P_n} v $\Rightarrow$ {Q_1, ..., Q_m}

is true if and only if Ai, $j[P_i \Rightarrow Q_j]$. The SNePSLOG elimination rule for this connective is the appropriate generalization of disjunctive modus ponens:

```
: {in(Hilda, Boston), in(Kathy, Las_Vegas)} v => {in(Eve, Providence)}.
: in(Hilda, Boston)!
```

Since {IN(HILDA, BOSTON), IN(KATHY, LAS_VEGAS)}
    v => {IN(EVE, PROVIDENCE)}
and IN(HILDA, BOSTON)
I infer IN(EVE, PROVIDENCE)
    IN(HILDA, BOSTON)
    IN(EVE, PROVIDENCE)

In the preceeding run, I turned the inference trace on, so the reader can see the firing of the generalized disjunctive modus ponens rule.

The Unique Variable Binding Rule

When setting up some example in a talk, a philosophy professor said[4]

"If someone votes for X and someone votes for Y, one of them will be disappointed"

(or something very close to that). Let us formalize our understanding of this sentence in SNePSLOG:

(4) all(u, v, x, y)({votesfor(u, x), votesfor(v, y)}
            &=> {andor(1, 1){disappointed(u), disappointed(v)}})

(Here I again interpreted "or" to mean exclusive or, and I used the SNeP-SLOG wff

$\{A_1, ..., A_n\}$ &$\Rightarrow$ $\{C_1, ..., C_m\}$

which means that the conjunction of $\{A_1, ..., A_n\}$ implies the conjunction of $\{C_1, ..., C_m\}$.) To complete this example, we should note that anyone who votes for the winner is not disappointed:

all(u, x)({votesfor(u, x), wins(x)} &=> {~disappointed{u}})

Now let's try these rules in a specific example:

: all(u, v, x, y)({votesfor(u, x), votesfor(v, y)}
            &=> {andor(1, 1){disappointed(u), disappointed(v)}}).
: all(u, x)({votesfor(u, x), wins(x)} &=> {~disappointed{u}}).
: votesfor(Hillary, Bill).
: votesfor(Elizabeth, Bob).
: wins(Bill).
: disappointed(?x)?
    DISAPPOINTED(ELIZABETH)
    ~DISAPPOINTED(HILLARY)

(Free variables in queries are indicated by a prefixed "?," which is also used as termination punctuation to start backward inference. The response to a query consists of all positive and negative instances of the query that can be derived.) The conclusion is that Elizabeth is disappointed, but Hillary isn't. The surprising aspect of this example is that in first order predicate logic, an instance of statement 4 is

{votesfor(Hillary, Bill), votesfor(Hillary, Bill)}
&=> {andor(1, 1){disappointed(Hillary), disappointed(Hillary)}}

From which, given the specific example, disappointed(Hillary) follows.

The problem is that in first order predicate logic, one is allowed to replace two universally quantified variables by the same term, but in normal understanding of natural language utterances such as the above quote, it is assumed that different noun phrases in one sentence refer to different entities (unless one of the noun phrases is marked as an anaphoric reference to another). A first order predicate logic representation of such a natural language utterance usually requires a judicious inclusion of $\neq$ predicates. However, this inclusion is unintuitive, makes the formalized statement more cumbersome, and the transduction process error-prone. For example, in presenting an example of a KLONE definition of an arch, Brachman says that "any example of this type of object has two UPRIGHTs, " (Brachman [1979], p. 37) and goes on to explain the structural description, $S2$, by saying, "$S2$ specifies that no two UPRIGHTs touch each other" (Brachman 1979, p. 37) but in the actual figure being described, the first order predicate logic sentence attached to $S2$ is

$$\forall X \in \text{UPRIGHT } (\exists Y \in \text{UPRIGHT. } \sim\text{TOUCH}(X, Y))$$

and this can be satisfied by two touching uprights neither of which touches itself.

Our approach to this issue has been to modify the rule of universal instantiation so that two variables in one wff cannot be replaced by the same term. This restriction is called the "unique variable binding rule," (Shapiro 1986). It was the unique variable binding rule that allowed statement 4 to be the formalization of our understanding of the "disappointed" quote.

Set Arguments

Consider the statement, "Mary, Sue, and Sally are sisters." The usual way to formalize this in first order predicate logic would be

$$sisters(Mary, Sue) \wedge sisters(Sue, Sally)$$

along with statements that $sisters$ is symmetric

$$\forall(x, y)[sisters(x, y) \Leftrightarrow sisters(y, x)]$$

and almost transitive

$$\forall(x, z)[x \neq z \Rightarrow (\exists(y)[sisters(x, y) \wedge sisters(y, z)] \Rightarrow sisters(x, z))]$$

Because of the cumbersomeness of this formalization compared with the English statement, we have introduced set arguments into SNePS (Shapiro 1986). If P is an m-ary predicate, and τ is a set whose members are of the appropriate type for the ith argument of P, then the following two inference rules are included in SNePS logic.

$$\frac{P(s_1, ..., s_{i-1}, \tau, s_{i+1}, ..., s_m), \tau' \subset \tau}{P(s_1, ..., s_{i-1}, \tau', s_{i+1}, ..., s_m)} \qquad \frac{P(s_1, ..., s_{i-1}, \tau, s_{i+1}, ..., s_m), t \in \tau}{P(s_1, ..., s_{i-1}, t, s_{i+1}, ..., s_m)}$$

These are versions of what we have called *reduction inference* (Shapiro [1991], Shapiro and The SNePS Implementation Group [1998], Chapter 2.5.1). Thus sisters({Mary, Sue, Sally}) implies sisters({Mary, Sue}), sisters({Mary, Sally}), and sisters({Sue, Sally}) (as well as the admittedly peculiar sisters(Mary), sisters(Sue), and sisters(Sally)[5]).

The usefulness of set arguments (combined with the unique variable binding rule) may be seen in an inference from "Mary, Sue, and Sally are sisters" and "Sisters like each other":

  : sisters({Mary, Sue, Sally}).
  : all(x, y)(sisters({x, y}) => {likes(x, y), likes(y, x)}).
  : likes(?x, ?y)?
    LIKES(SUE, MARY)
    LIKES(MARY, SUE)
    LIKES(SALLY, SUE)
    LIKES(SUE, SALLY)
    LIKES(MARY, SALLY)
    LIKES(SALLY, MARY)

Notice that not only are all six combinations found, but the three instances of likes(x, x) are avoided due to the unique variable binding rule.

"Higher-Order" Logic

If a relation, R, is transitive, then whenever any x is in the R relation to some y, and y is also in the R relation to some z, then x is in the R relation to z. That statement is not expressible in first order predicate logic, because it requires quantifying over predicates. Nevertheless, it is useful, so we have allowed users of SNePS to express themselves in higher-order logic (Shapiro et al. 1981):

  : all(R)(Transitive(R) => all(x, y, z)({R(x, y), R(y, z)} &=> {R(x, z)})).
  : Transitive(bigger).
  : bigger(elephant, lion).
  : bigger(lion, mouse).
  : bigger(elephant, mouse)?
    BIGGER(ELEPHANT, MOUSE)

It is really only the user language that is higher order. The representation formalism is only first order. User-language predications such as bigger(elephant, lion) are stored using a variety of the "Holds" predicate, such as, *Holds(bigger, elephant, lion)*. Thus, the rule about transitive relations is really stored looking more like

$$\forall(R)[Transitive(R)$$
$$\Rightarrow \forall(x, y, z)[Holds(R, x, y) \wedge Holds(R, y, z)] \Rightarrow Holds(R, x, z)]$$

than like a higher-order rule. Nevertheless, the ability to express rules in a higher-order language is very useful.

Another aspect of higher-order logic is the ability to quantify over formulas. Consider the argument

Anything Bob believes is true.
Bob believes anything Bill believes.
Bill believes whatever Kevin's favorite proposition is.
Kevin's favorite proposition is that John is taller than Mary.
Therefore John is taller than Mary.

SNePS wffs such as Taller(John, Mary) are not actually sentences, but functional terms that denote propositions (Shapiro 1993; Chalupsky and Shapiro 1994). Therefore, using them as arguments and quantifying over them does not take us out of first order logic. Here is this example in SNePSLOG:

```
: all(p)(Believes(Bob, p) => p).
: all(p)(Believes(Bill, p) => Believes(Bob, p)).
: all(p)(Favorite-proposition(Kevin, p) => Believes(Bill, p)).
: Favorite-proposition(Kevin, Taller(John, Mary)).
: Taller(John, Mary)?
  TALLER(JOHN, MARY)
```

Notice that "higher-order" is in quotes in the heading of this section because, while the SNePSLOG wffs in this section look like higher-order formulas, the underlying SNePS logic is really first order.

Intensional Representation

Natural language sentences contain what are known as *opaque contexts,* in which one denoting phrase cannot necessarily be substituted for another even though they denote the same object. An example due to Russell is, "George IV wished to know whether Scott was the author of *Waverly*" (Russell 1905, p. 485) because *Waverly* was published anonymously. One obviously cannot replace "the author of *Waverly*" by "Scott" in that sentence even though Scott was, in fact the author of *Waverly*. Verbs such as *know* and *believe* put their complements in opaque contexts. The standard terminology is that the denoting phrases *Scott* and *the author of* Waverly denote different intensions, but the same extension. In SNePS, all terms represent intensions only (Maida and Shapiro 1982; Shapiro and Rapaport 1987), and the entire SNePS network is considered to be an opaque context. Thus, there is no built-in equality predicate in SNePS because no two terms are taken as denoting the same entity (the uniqueness principle).

An example from the AI literature is due to John McCarthy (1979):

> the meaning of the phrase *"Mike's telephone number"* in the sentence *"Pat knows Mike's telephone number"* is the concept of Mike's telephone number, whereas its meaning in the sentence *"Pat dialled Mike's telephone number"* is the number itself. Thus if we also have *"Mary's telephone number = Mike's telephone number,"* then *"Pat dialled Mary's telephone number"* follows, but *"Pat knows Mary's telephone number"* does not. (McCarthy 1979, p. 129-130, italics in the original).

Notice that *knows* creates an opaque context, whereas *dials* does not, so McCarthy is making the same point as above—*Mary's telephone number* cannot replace *Mike's telephone number* in the sentence "Pat knows Mike's telephone number, " even though they have the same extension, but it can in the sentence "Pat dialled Mary's telephone number."

Although there is no built-in equality predicate in SNePS, we can introduce one to mean that two entities have the same extension[6], and explicitly specify which contexts are not opaque. A SNePSLOG example of applying this technique to McCarthy's telephone problem is:

```
: all(R)(Transparent(R) => all(a, x, y)({R(a, x), =({x, y})} &=> {R(a, y)})).
: Transparent(Dial).
: =({Telephone(Mike), Telephone(Mary)}).
: Know(Pat, Telephone(Mike)).
: Dial(Pat, Telephone(Mike)).
: ?what(Pat, ?which)?
  DIAL(PAT, TELEPHONE(MARY))
  KNOW(PAT, TELEPHONE(MIKE))
  DIAL(PAT, TELEPHONE(MIKE))
```

Note the use of set arguments in the = predicate, and the use of a second order query.

The Numerical Quantifiers

Consider the following problems:

> No one has more than one mother.　　　　　　　　　　　　　　　　(1)
> Jane is John's mother.
> Is Mary John's mother?

> The committee members are Chris, Leslie, Pat, and Stevie.　　　(2)
> At least two members of the committee are women.
> Leslie and Stevie are men.
> Is Pat a man or a woman?

To facilitate such "reasoning by the process of elimination," SNePS logic includes the numerical quantifiers (Shapiro 1979a).

$$\text{nexists}(i, j, k)(x)(\{P_1(x), ..., P_n(x)\}: \{Q(x)\})$$

means that there are k individuals that satisfy $P_1(x) \wedge ... \wedge P_n(x)$, and, of them, at least i and at most j also satisfy $Q(x)$. There are two elimination rules of inference for the numerical quantifiers:

1. If j individuals are known that satisfy $P_1(x) \wedge ... \wedge P_n(x) \wedge Q(x)$ then it may be inferred that every other individual that satisfies $P_1(x) \wedge ... \wedge P_n(x)$ also satisfies $\tilde{} Q(x)$.

2. If $k - i$ individuals are known that satisfy $P_1(x) \wedge ... \wedge P_n(x) \wedge \tilde{} Q(x)$ then it may be inferred that every other individual that satisfies $P_1(x) \wedge ... \wedge P_n(x)$ also satisfies $Q(x)$.

If one expects to use only one of these rules of inference, one may use either abbreviated form nexists(_, j, _) or nexists(i, _, k).

The following interaction shows the above two problems solved in SNePSLOG.

```
:  all(x)(Person(x) => nexists(_, 1, _)(y)({Person(y)}: {Mother(y, x)})).
:  Person({John, Jane, Mary}).
:  Mother(Jane, John).
:  Mother(Mary, John)?
   ~MOTHER(MARY, JOHN)
:  Member({Chris, Leslie, Pat, Stevie}).
:  nexists(2, _, 4)(x)({Member(x)}: {Woman(x)}).
:  all(x)(Member(x) => andor(1, 1){Man(x), Woman(x)}).
:  Man({Leslie, Stevie}).
:  ?What(Pat)?
   WOMAN(PAT)
   MEMBER(PAT)
   ~MAN(PAT)
```

Since the numerical quantifier elimination rules count individuals, we had to decide how to count. The current version of SNePS counts each distinct term as different. We are considering the possibility that in future versions of SNePS, coextensional terms will be counted only once.

Contexts

When doing natural language understanding and commonsense reasoning, some kind of context mechanism is needed to keep different domains separate. For example, when reading a fictional narrative, it is important to be able to use background knowledge from the real world to understand the narrative, while accepting fictional information even if it contradicts real-world beliefs (see Rapaport and Shapiro 1995).

SNePS contains a context mechanism as part of its assumption-based belief revision system (see the section on belief revision that follows). SNePS contexts are defined both extensionally and intensionally. Extensionally, a context is a set of assumptions or hypotheses—propositions asserted to Cassie by the user. A new hypothesis cannot be added to an existing context, extensionally defined, just as a new element cannot be added to a set, extensionally defined. Intensionally, a context is a named structure that contains a set of assumptions (referred to as "assertions" in the sample run below). A new assumption can be added to a context, intensionally defined.

Some SNePSLOG commands take an intensional context as an optional argument. Otherwise, all SNePSLOG commands are taken as referring to the default context, which by default is the one named DEFAULT-DE-FAULTCT. The following run demonstrates reasoning in two overlapping contexts, the real-world and the world of mythology.

```
:   ;;; Create the real-world context with an empty set of assertions.
set-context real-world ()
:   ;;; Make real-world the default context.
set-default-context real-world
:   ;;; Animals are partitioned into birds and beasts.
all(x)({Bird(x), Beast(x)} v => {Animal(x)}).
:   all(x)(Animal(x) => andor(1, 1){Bird(x), Beast(x)}).
:   ;;; Horses are beasts.
all(x)(Horse(x) => Beast(x)).
:   ;;; Pegasus is a horse.
Horse(Pegasus).
:   ;;; A rider travels by ground or air depending on
    ;;; whether what (s)he is riding has wings.
all(x, y)(Rides(x, y) => andor(1, 1){Travelsby(x, air), Travelsby(x, ground)}).
:   all(x, y)(Rides(x, y) => thresh(1, 1){Winged(y), Travelsby(x, air)}).
:   ;;; Bellerophon rides Pegasus.
Rides(Bellerophon, Pegasus).
:   ;;; Show the context. (The set of restrictions is used by belief revision.)
describe-context
((ASSERTIONS (WFF1 WFF2 WFF3 WFF4 WFF5 WFF6 WFF7))
(RESTRICTION NIL)
(NAMED (REAL-WORLD)))

:   ;;; Create the mythology context, initialized to agree with the real-world.
set-context mythology (WFF1 WFF2 WFF3 WFF4 WFF5 WFF6 WFF7)
:   ;;; Still in the real world, birds and only birds have wings.
all(x)(Winged(x) <=> Bird(x)).
:   ;;; How does Bellerophon travel?
Travelsby(Bellerophon, ?what)?
    TRAVELSBY(BELLEROPHON, GROUND)
    ~TRAVELSBY(BELLEROPHON, AIR)

:   ;;; Change the default context to be mythology.
set-default-context mythology
:   ;;; Here, Pegasus has wings.
Winged(Pegasus).
:   ;;; How does Bellerophon travel here?
Travelsby(Bellerophon, ?what)?
    ~TRAVELSBY(BELLEROPHON, GROUND)
    TRAVELSBY(BELLEROPHON, AIR)

:   ;;; List all beliefs in the mythology context.
```

list-asserted-wffs mythology
all(X)({BIRD(X), BEAST(X)} v => {ANIMAL(X)})
andor(1, 1){TRAVELSBY(BELLEROPHON, GROUND),
TRAVELSBY(BELLEROPHON, AIR)}
WINGED(PEGASUS)
WINGED(PEGASUS) <=> TRAVELSBY(BELLEROPHON, AIR)
ANIMAL(PEGASUS)
BEAST(PEGASUS)
andor(1, 1){BIRD(PEGASUS), BEAST(PEGASUS)}
~BIRD(PEGASUS)
all(X)(ANIMAL(X) => (andor(1, 1){BIRD(X), BEAST(X)}))
~TRAVELSBY(BELLEROPHON, GROUND)
all(X)(HORSE(X) => BEAST(X))
HORSE(PEGASUS)
all(X, Y)(RIDES(X, Y) => (andor(1, 1){TRAVELSBY(X, AIR),
TRAVELSBY(X, GROUND)}))
all(X, Y)(RIDES(X, Y) => (WINGED(Y) <=> TRAVELSBY(X, AIR)))
RIDES(BELLEROPHON, PEGASUS)
TRAVELSBY(BELLEROPHON, AIR)
:   ;;; List all beliefs in the real-world context.
list-asserted-wffs real-world
all(X)({BIRD(X), BEAST(X)} v => {ANIMAL(X)})
TRAVELSBY(BELLEROPHON, GROUND)
andor(1, 1){TRAVELSBY(BELLEROPHON, GROUND),
TRAVELSBY(BELLEROPHON, AIR)}
WINGED(PEGASUS) <=> TRAVELSBY(BELLEROPHON, AIR)
ANIMAL(PEGASUS)
BEAST(PEGASUS)
andor(1, 1){BIRD(PEGASUS), BEAST(PEGASUS)}
~BIRD(PEGASUS)
~WINGED(PEGASUS)
all(X)(ANIMAL(X) => (andor(1, 1){BIRD(X), BEAST(X)}))
~TRAVELSBY(BELLEROPHON, AIR)
all(X)(HORSE(X) => BEAST(X))
HORSE(PEGASUS)
all(X, Y)(RIDES(X, Y) => (andor(1, 1){TRAVELSBY(X, AIR),
TRAVELSBY(X, GROUND)}))
all(X, Y)(RIDES(X, Y) => (WINGED(Y) <=> TRAVELSBY(X, AIR)))
RIDES(BELLEROPHON, PEGASUS)
all(X)(WINGED(X) <=> BIRD(X))

Notice that Cassie believes that Bellerophon travels through the air
in the world of mythology, but on the ground in the real world.

Belief Revision

AI systems that get their input from normal people (as opposed to pro-
grammers or knowledge engineers) will certainly occasionally get contra-

dictory information. To deal with this, the system needs two facilities. First, the ability to recognize and trap explicit contradictions so that something can be done about them; and second, the ability to retract stored information inferred from information that is later retracted. SNePS 2.4 includes SNeBR (Martins and Shapiro 1988), a belief revision system that has these two abilities.

When some proposition is entered or inferred that directly contradicts one that is already stored, SNeBR opens a dialogue with the user:

```
: all(x)(Bird(x) => Flies(x)).
: all(x)(Penguin(x) => Bird(x)).
: all(x)(Penguin(x) => ~Flies(x)).
: Bird(Opus)!
  BIRD(OPUS)
  FLIES(OPUS)

: Penguin(Opus)!
  A contradiction was detected within context DEFAULT-DEFAULTCT.
  The contradiction involves the newly derived proposition:
      ~FLIES(OPUS)
  and the previously existing proposition:
      FLIES(OPUS)

  You have the following options:
      1. [C]ontinue anyway, knowing that a contradiction is derivable;
      2. [R]e-start the exact same run in a different context which is not
         inconsistent;
      3. [D]rop the run altogether.
      (please type c, r or d)
  =><=...
```

If the user chooses option 2, the system will help her to identify and re-move the proposition(s) that caused the contradiction.

The system keeps track of the hypotheses that underly inferred propo-sitions. (An hypothesis is a proposition that was told to the system, as opposed to one that the system inferred.) So if an hypothesis is retracted, the system retracts every inferred proposition that was derived from it:

```
: all(x)(Bird(x) => Flies(x)).
: all(x)(Flies(x) => Feathered(x)).
: all(x)(Canary(x) => Bird(x)).
: Canary(Tweety)!
  CANARY(TWEETY)
  BIRD(TWEETY)
  FLIES(TWEETY)
  FEATHERED(TWEETY)

: Canary(Clyde)!
  FLIES(CLYDE)
  FEATHERED(CLYDE)
  CANARY(CLYDE)
  BIRD(CLYDE)
```

: list-asserted-wffs
all(X)(BIRD(X) => FLIES(X))
FLIES(CLYDE)
FEATHERED(CLYDE)
all(X)(FLIES(X) => FEATHERED(X))
all(X)(CANARY(X) => BIRD(X))
CANARY(TWEETY)
BIRD(TWEETY)
FLIES(TWEETY)
FEATHERED(TWEETY)
CANARY(CLYDE)
BIRD(CLYDE)

: ~Feathered(Clyde)!
A contradiction was detected within context DEFAULT-DEFAULTCT.
The contradiction involves the proposition you want to assert:
    ~FEATHERED(CLYDE)
and the previously existing proposition:
    FEATHERED(CLYDE)
You have the following options:
    1. [c] to continue anyway, knowing that a contradiction is derivable;
    2. [r] to revise the inconsistent part of the context
    3. [d] to discard this contradictory new assertion from the context
    (please type c, r or d)
=><=r

In order to make the context consistent you must delete at least
one hypothesis from each of the following sets of hypotheses:
    (WFF1 WFF12 WFF2 WFF3 WFF8)
In order to make the context consistent you must delete at least one
    hypothesis from the set listed below.
An inconsistent set of hypotheses:
1 : all(X)(BIRD(X) => FLIES(X))
            (5 supported propositions: (WFF1 WFF10 WFF11 WFF6 WFF7))
2 : ~FEATHERED(CLYDE)
            (1 supported proposition: (WFF12))
3 : all(X)(FLIES(X) => FEATHERED(X))
            (3 supported propositions: (WFF11 WFF2 WFF7))
4 : all(X)(CANARY(X) => BIRD(X))
            (7 supported propositions: (WFF10 WFF11 WFF3 WFF5 WFF6
                                        WFF7 WFF9))
5 : CANARY(CLYDE)
            (4 supported propositions: (WFF10 WFF11 WFF8 WFF9))
Enter the list number of a hypothesis to examine or
[d] to discard some hypothesis from this list,
[a] to see ALL the hypotheses in the full context,
[r] to see what you have already removed,
[q] to quit revising this set, or
[i] for instructions
(please type a number OR d, a, r, q or i)
=><= d
Enter the list number of a hypothesis to discard,

[c] to cancel this discard, or [q] to quit revising this set.
=><= 5

The consistent set of hypotheses:
  1 : all(X)(BIRD(X) => FLIES(X))
          (5 supported propositions: (WFF1 WFF10 WFF11 WFF6 WFF7))
  2 : ~FEATHERED(CLYDE)
          (1 supported proposition: (WFF12))
  3 : all(X)(FLIES(X) => FEATHERED(X))
          (3 supported propositions: (WFF11 WFF2 WFF7))
  4 : all(X)(CANARY(X) => BIRD(X))
          (7 supported propositions: (WFF10 WFF11 WFF3 WFF5 WFF6
                                      WFF7 WFF9))

  Enter the list number of a hypothesis to examine or
  [d] to discard some hypothesis from this list,
  [a] to see ALL the hypotheses in the full context,
  [r] to see what you have already removed,
  [q] to quit revising this set, or
  [i] for instructions
  (please type a number OR d, a, r, q or i)
=><= q

  The following (not known to be inconsistent) set of hypotheses was
  also part of the context where the contradiction was derived:
    (WFF4)
  Do you want to inspect or discard some of them?
=><= no

  Do you want to add a new hypothesis?
=><= no
  ~FEATHERED(CLYDE)

: list-asserted-wffs
  all(X)(BIRD(X) => FLIES(X))
  ~FEATHERED(CLYDE)
  ~CANARY(CLYDE)
  all(X)(FLIES(X) => FEATHERED(X))
  all(X)(CANARY(X) => BIRD(X))
  CANARY(TWEETY)
  BIRD(TWEETY)
  FLIES(TWEETY)
  FEATHERED(TWEETY)

Notice that after retracting Canary(Clyde), the propositions that were
inferred from it, FLIES(CLYDE), BIRD(CLYDE), and FEATHERED(CLYDE) were
also removed.

SNeBR tells the user how many propositions are supported by each hypothesis in case she wants to remove the hypothesis that makes a minimal change to the knowledge base (Alchourrón et al. 1985). However,
since we assume that there is more to be learned, this may not be the
definitive criterion, and, in fact, in this example, the removed hypothesis
was not the one that made the minimal change.

Relevance Logic

In first order predicate logic, a contradiction implies anything whatsoever, but most people would say that just because you believe that Opus does and doesn't fly, that's no reason to believe something totally unrelated to Opus and flying, such as that the Earth is flat. SNePS logic is a version of Relevance Logic (Anderson and Belnap 1975; Anderson et al. 1992; Shapiro 1992b), a "paraconsistent" logic in which the so-called "paradoxes of implication" such as $(A \wedge \neg A) \Rightarrow B$, are not valid.

```
:  all(x)(Flies(x) => Feathered(x)).
:  all(x)(~Flies(x) => Swims(x)).
:  Flies(Opus).
:  ~Flies(Opus).
```
A contradiction was detected within context DEFAULT-DEFAULTCT.
The contradiction involves the proposition you want to assert:
    ~FLIES(OPUS)
and the previously existing proposition:
    FLIES(OPUS)

You have the following options:
1. [c] to continue anyway, knowing that a contradiction is derivable;
2. [r] to revise the inconsistent part of the context
3. [d] to discard this contradictory new assertion from the context
(please type c, r or d)
```
=><= c
~FLIES(OPUS)
```

```
:  Feathered(Opus)?
```
A contradiction was detected within context DEFAULT-DEFAULTCT.
The contradiction involves the newly derived proposition:
    FLIES(OPUS)
and the previously existing proposition:
    ~FLIES(OPUS)

You have the following options:
1. [C]ontinue anyway, knowing that a contradiction is derivable;
2. [R]e-start the exact same run in a different context which is not inconsistent;
3. [D]rop the run altogether.
(please type c, r or d)
```
=><= c
FEATHERED(OPUS)
```

```
:  Swims(Opus)?
```
A contradiction was detected within context DEFAULT-DEFAULTCT.
The contradiction involves the newly derived proposition:
    ~FLIES(OPUS)
and the previously existing proposition:
    FLIES(OPUS)

You have the following options:
1. [C]ontinue anyway, knowing that a contradiction is derivable;

2. [R]e-start the exact same run in a different context which is not inconsistent;
3. [D]rop the run altogether.
(please type c, r or d)
=><= c
  SWIMS(OPUS)

: Flat(Earth)?
: list-asserted-wffs
  all(X)(FLIES(X) => FEATHERED(X))
  all(X)((~FLIES(X)) => SWIMS(X))
  FLIES(OPUS)
  ~FLIES(OPUS)
  FEATHERED(OPUS)
  SWIMS(OPUS)

(Remember that when a question *A*? is asked, if *A* can be derived from the stored information, it is printed, and if ~*A* can be derived, it is printed. If neither can be derived, nothing is printed, which is the case here, indicated by nothing being shown between the query, Flat(Earth)?, and the next prompt.)So the contradiction allows the system to infer related contradictory information, specifically SWIMS(OPUS) and FEATHERED-(OPUS), but not irrelevant information such as Flat(Earth).

Another paradox of implication is that anything whatsoever implies a truth, $A \Rightarrow (B \Rightarrow A)$. First notice that SNePS can derive implications:

: all(x)(Canary(x) => Bird(x)).
: all(x)(Bird(x) => Flies(x)).
: Canary(Tweety) => Flies(Tweety)?
  CANARY(TWEETY) => FLIES(TWEETY)

Now, let's try $A \Rightarrow (B \Rightarrow A)$:

: Penguin(Opus).
: Canary(Tweety) => Penguin(Opus)?
:

The implication is not derived.

Circular and Recursive Rules

Above I said that normal people occasionally give contradictory information. They also tend to give circular definitions, which get formalized as recursive rules. The SNePS inference mechanism was designed to work without getting into infinite loops in the face of recursive rules without regard to: the order of entry of rules or ground propositions; the order of predicates within rules; whether recursive rules are left- or right-recursive, or both; what predicates are used in ground propositions. (Shapiro and Mckay 1980; Mckay and Shapiro 1981) An example of using a circular definition is

```
:  all(x, y)(thresh(1, 1){North-of(x, y), South-of(y, x)}).
:  North-of(Seattle, Portland).
:  South-of(San_Francisco, Portland).
:  North-of(San_Francisco, Los_Angeles).
:  South-of(San_Diego, Los_Angeles).
:  North-of(?x, ?y)?
NORTH-OF(SEATTLE, PORTLAND)
NORTH-OF(SAN_FRANCISCO, LOS_ANGELES)
NORTH-OF(LOS_ANGELES, SAN_DIEGO)
NORTH-OF(PORTLAND, SAN_FRANCISCO)
```

A more traditional example of a recursive rule is

```
:  all(x, y)(parent(x, y) => ancestor(x, y)).
:  all(x, y, z)({ancestor(x, y), ancestor(y, z)} &=> {ancestor(x, z)}).
:  parent(John, Mary).
:  ancestor(Mary, George).
:  ancestor(George, Sally).
:  parent(Sally, Jimmy).
:  ancestor(John, ?y)?
ANCESTOR(JOHN, JIMMY)
ANCESTOR(JOHN, MARY)
ANCESTOR(JOHN, GEORGE)
ANCESTOR(JOHN, SALLY)

:  ancestor(?x, Jimmy)?
ANCESTOR(SALLY, JIMMY)
ANCESTOR(JOHN, JIMMY)
ANCESTOR(GEORGE, JIMMY)
ANCESTOR(MARY, JIMMY)
```

Of course, SNePS will infinitely loop if it is asked to forward chain through a rule of the form $\forall(x)[P(x) \Rightarrow P(f(x))]$ or back-chain through one of the form $\forall(x)[P(f(x)) \Rightarrow P(x)]$.

Summary

SNePS has been and is being designed to be a knowledge representation and reasoning system for a computerized natural language using, common-sense reasoning rational agent. SNePS is founded on logic, but on a logic that has been (and is being) designed specifically to support natural language processing and commonsense reasoning. Several aspects of this logic have been summarized in this chapter. We may categorize them as follows.

First, those that differ from first order predicate logic in syntax (with appropriate semantics and inference rules), including set arguments, set-oriented logical connectives, numerical quantifiers, and "higher-order" logic.

Second, those that differ from first order predicate logic in some inference rule(s) (with appropriate semantics), including the unique variable binding rule and relevance logic.

Third, those that differ from first order predicate logic only in semantics, including intensional representation.

Fourth, we summarized those that rely on an appropriate inference mechanism, including contexts, belief revision, and the use of circular and recursive rules.

More recent developments, that have not yet been incorporated with the other features of SNePS 2.4, are "structured variables" (Ali 1993; Ali and Shapiro 1993; Ali 1994b) and using simulative reasoning to reason about the beliefs of other agents (Chalupsky and Shapiro 1994; Chalupsky 1996; Chalupsky and Shapiro 1996).

Acknowledgments

This chapter is a revised version of Formalizing English, *International Journal of Expert Systems* 9(1) (1996): 151–171 (Shapiro 1996). The original portions are reproduced here with the kind permission of JAI Press. Previous versions were presented at the Third Golden West International Conference on Intelligent Systems (GWIC), Las Vegas, NV, June 6–8 1994, and the AAAI Fall Symposium on Knowledge Representation for Natural Language Processing in Implemented Systems, November 1994. Developments described in this chapter were carried out in conjunction with William J. Rapaport, Donald P. McKay, João P. Martins, and other members of the SNePS Research Group of the Department of Computer Science and Engineering, State University of New York at Buffalo (UB). The SNeBR dialogue shown here was programmed by Frances L. Johnson as a modification of a previous version. I appreciate the help provided by Rohini Srihari and Jean-Pierre Koenig, the comments of Syed Ali and Łucja Iwańska on earlier drafts of this chapter, and the general intellectual support of the University at Buffalo's Center for Cognitive Science and its Research Group on Discourse and Narrative. The work reported here was supported in part by Equipment Grant No. EDUD-US-932022 from SUN Microsystems Computer Corporation, in part by NASA under contract NAS 9-19335, and in part by the U.S. Army CECOM through a contract with CACI Technologies.

Notes

1. In this chapter "first order predicate logic" will always refer to the standard, classical, first order predicate logic, using its standard syntax.

2. Some might argue that the *or* of problem (1) means inclusive or, and that we already have background knowledge that the categories of animals, vegetables, and minerals are mutually disjoint. In that case, it is that background knowledge I want to represent, and that is not captured correctly by the proffered first order predicate logic wff.

3. Notice that I am no longer making that claim—I am making no claims about the mean-

ing of words. Rather, my claim in the previous section is about the pragmatic understanding of certain utterances.

4. Deborah Johnson, Department Colloquium, Department of Computer Science, State University of New York at Buffalo, March 17 1994.

5. A method of restricting such implications is included in SNePS 3, currently being implemented.

6. This predicate has been called EQUIV in previous papers.

Section Two

Introduction to Section Two

Łucja M. Iwańska and Stuart C. Shapiro

THE SECOND PART OF THIS BOOK is devoted to the problems of knowledge-related issues for large-scale, general-purpose natural language processing systems. Two main themes are presented in this section. The first theme is uniform versus nonuniform knowledge representation and reasoning. The second theme is automatic knowledge acquisition from natural language inputs.

Uniform Versus Nonuniform Knowledge Representation and Reasoning

It has been long-known that natural language processing systems that interpret or generate natural language must represent and use many different types of knowledge, such as world knowledge, knowledge due to meaning of natural language utterances, and knowledge about natural language processed.

World knowledge includes domain knowledge, common or shared knowledge, and relevant knowledge. Such knowledge is often expressed as if-then rules; for example *If the patient's temperature rises above 103 degrees, give him extra-strength Motrin.* Such knowledge must be correctly handled for many specific tasks.

Another type of knowledge is knowledge due to the meaning of natural language utterances. Part of the natural language meaning is reflected in the universal capability of answering questions based solely on understanding natural language utterances. For example, after being told that *Every student works hard,* a native English speaker can correctly and easily answer related questions, such as *Do students work? Is it true that every good student works? Does anybody work?*

Here, cognitive knowing is based on understanding the semantics of the determiner *every* and the natural language-inherent type-subtype relation between the pairs of phrases *student* and *good student,* i.e., that a good student is a student, and between *works hard* and *works,* i.e., that working hard means working. Natural language processing systems must simulate gaining such knowledge through the in-depth understanding of natural language utterances.

Another type of knowledge is knowledge about natural language processed. This includes knowledge about natural language morphology, the structure of words and its implications for their meaning, and knowledge of natural language syntax—the structure of sentences. Such knowledge is required to compute the meaning of natural language utterances.

It has also been long-known that general-purpose natural language processing systems must be capable of reasoning. Computing inferences must be done efficiently, with near real-time performance for many tasks. For a general-purpose (as opposed to domain-specific or task-specific) natural language processing system, one must choose the approach to knowledge representation and reasoning. Existing approaches fall into one of the two major categories: (1) nonuniform approach to knowledge representation and reasoning and (2) uniform knowledge representation and reasoning.

The Nonuniform Approach to Knowledge Representation and Reasoning

A nonuniform approach to knowledge representation and reasoning advocates different representational languages for different tasks and different architectural components. Examples are some nonnatural language-motivated knowledge representation and reasoning system for representing and reasoning about world knowledge and unification-based formalism for representing the meaning of natural language utterances. Currently, the nonuniform knowledge representation and reasoning approach is the common one.

The primary problem with the nonuniform approach is its necessity to translate between different representations to exchange or combine knowledge. This translation task is extremely difficult, particularly when processing large-scale, real-life data. Such translations invariably involve information loss because the semantics of the representations (that is, if such a semantics exists—frequently, it simply doesn't) and inference engines are quite different. Knowledge representation and reasoning languages often have different formal power. One knowledge representation and reasoning language may have modalities, λ–expressions, generalized quantifiers and other higher-order constructs. The other knowledge representation and reasoning language may be roughly equivalent to the standard first-order predicate logic or a restricted, vivid representation such as a relational database.

The Uniform Approach to Knowledge Representation and Reasoning

A uniform approach to knowledge representation and reasoning advocates the same representational language for every task and component. A typical choice is an extension of standard first-order predicate logic. Currently, the uniform knowledge representation and reasoning approach is less common than the non-uniform knowledge representation and reasoning. The main problem with existing uniform knowledge representation and reasoning approaches is that available knowledge representation and reasoning systems do not adequately reflect important characteristics of natural language. Relative to natural language, such knowledge representation and reasoning systems are representationally and inferentially impoverished.

The authors in this section address a wide range of the natural language processing research and development problems. They resolve differently the uniform versus nonuniform knowledge representation and reasoning dilemma. We caution readers against any premature conclusions about the absolute advantages and disadvantages of either approach. We stress that the uniform versus nonuniform knowledge representation and reasoning choice remains an open research and development problem. The work presented in this book provides the essence of rich material ripe for discussions about the pros and cons in both knowledge representation and reasoning approaches.

Natural Language-like and Nonnatural Language-like Computation: Representational and Inferential Division of Labor

We vigorously pursue the problem of the representational and inferential division of labor in the natural languagelike and nonnatural languagelike computation. We have asked the authors for specific technical explanations as to why they consider certain processing tasks such as reasoning about concepts (types) and computing their similarities to be nonnatural languagelike computation. We also requested the justification for their particular choices of the existing knowledge representation and reasoning software. In the editorial guidelines we sent to the authors, we included the following directions:

> First, discuss how your knowledge representation and reasoning is similar to/different from existing knowledge representation and reasoning systems not motivated by natural language.

Second, discuss how you reconcile the needs for representing natural language meaning and the needs for the nonnatural language knowledge that supports processing natural language.

Third, discuss what belongs in the nonnatural language knowledge representation and reasoning.

Finally, if you employ existing knowledge representation and reasoning system(s), briefly explain your choice. Be specific about the motivations behind your choice, both technical and nontechnical.

We have not obtained clear technical justifications for the representational and inferential division of labor chosen or for the specific choice of the existing knowledge representation and reasoning software. In most cases, the authors felt that the required specific reasoning tasks were too remote from the focus of their own research and, pragmatically, chose some existing nonnatural language-motivated knowledge representation and reasoning system. Frequently, the logical choice was simple: the in-house developed software.

In our personal and informal discussions, some researchers admitted that a seemingly technical decision is sometimes "politically" motivated. Funding agencies and companies heavily invested in the development of particular knowledge representation and reasoning systems, both financially and academically. They are happy when others use their tools. Sometimes they insist. We, therefore, caution readers not to automatically draw a conclusion that just because a certain knowledge representation and reasoning system is utilized by some natural language processing system, that this system is good or the best for this kind of knowledge representation and reasoning needs. In fact, we are aware of one natural language-motivated knowledge representation and reasoning system that was not used because politically-motivated funding pressures overshadowed technical considerations.

Summary of Chapters

In the first chapter addressing the nonuniformity of knowledge representation and reasoning, Bonnie Dorr and Clare R. Voss argue for the traditional nonuniform knowledge representation and reasoning approach in their machine translation natural language processing system. The main advantage for handling knowledge-related processing is the efficiency of the specialized representations. Dorr and Voss argue that this advantage justifies the increased complexities of system design and implementation, having to provide an interface enabling interaction between different knowledge representation and reasoning levels.

The linguistically-motivated knowledge representation and reasoning level is geared toward capturing syntactic structural mismatches in different natural languages. Dorr's representation closely resembles the classical Schankian conceptual dependency. Some widely acknowledged problems of semantic primitives representations are unclear semantics (sic !), and the inability to correctly reflect rich semantic structure of natural language such as generalized quantifiers and negation.

The knowledge representation level referred to as nonlinguistically-motivated resolves structural mismatches by computing concept similarities such as is-more-general-than and partially-overlapping relations on concepts. Dorr's and Voss's natural language processing system is a serious implementation. For the knowledge representation and reasoning-related processing tasks, it utilizes the existing taxonomic reasoner of the LOOM knowledge representation and reasoning system. The system primarily processes artificial, small-scale linguistic data.

In the second chapter addressing the nonuniformity of knowledge representation and reasoning, Łucja M. Iwańska argues for the uniform knowledge representation and reasoning approach. She proposes a uniform, temporal-and-spatial reasoner with representational, inferential and computational characteristics that closely resemble natural language. Iwańska argues that her natural language-motivated representation can be applied to handle many aspects of temporal and spatial reasoning. Numerous examples of inferences for a wide spectrum of temporal and spatial expressions in English illustrate the representational and reasoning capabilities. Iwańska further discusses methodology for collecting hundreds of real-life test and design examples which allow one to quantitatively evaluate system performance in terms of recall and precision.

Iwańska's natural language processing system is a serious implementation. It processes artificial, small-scale linguistic data as well as real-life, large-scale multi-source, multi-domain corpora of textual documents.

In the third chapter addressing the nonuniformity of knowledge representation and reasoning, Susan W. McRoy, Syed S. Ali and Susan M. Haller advocate the uniform knowledge representation and reasoning approach in their tutoring natural language processing system. They demonstrate how in their system, a propositional semantic network representation is used to encode, reason about and reason with different types of knowledge, including knowledge about English syntax, domain, structure of dialogs and plans. Their uniform knowledge representation and reasoning eliminates the distinction between the object-level and meta-level processing. The same structures encode and are used to reason with knowledge derived from the utterances (object level) as well as knowledge about the utterances (meta level).

Another argument for the uniform knowledge representation and reasoning is the efficient handling of resource-based computation such as disambiguation and maintaining appropriate levels of specificity and relevancy of knowledge, as required by different stages of dialog processing. McRoy's, Ali's, and Haller's implementation is currently under development. Their system utilizes some of the existing tools of the SNePS and ANALOG natural language processing/knowledge representation and reasoning systems. The linguistic data to be processed is mostly small-to-medium-scale real-life.

Automatic Knowledge Acquisition
from Natural Language Inputs

Obtaining knowledge required for a general-purpose natural language processing system is a real problem. After decades of hand-crafting knowledge from textual documents, it became painfully obvious that this time-consuming, costly and error-prone acquisition process is entirely inadequate for all but "toy" systems. The only hope appears to be in the success of the automatic knowledge acquisition from texts. However, no fully satisfactory automatic knowledge acquisition methods from texts have been proposed. Virtually all existing methods involve humans (large number of humans) in the loop as a method for the post-verification and clean-up of the system-acquired garbage.

The chapters addressing the knowledge acquisition theme presented in this part contain some very interesting results on fully automatic methods for knowledge acquisition from medium-to-large-scale natural language inputs. The natural language processing specificity in this line of research stems from two facts. First, knowledge source is in the form of natural language inputs, such as corpora of textual documents or transcribed dialogs; and second, the acquisition methods are based on natural language and incorporate its various algorithmic aspects.

Some of these methods have already been shown to be capable of fully automatic, large-scale, knowledge acquisition from natural language inputs. Some methods demonstrate a strong promise to accomplish this.

Natural language processing researchers and practitioners are constantly faced with the problem of inadequate for natural language knowledge representations with data structures and reasoning algorithms, whose syntax and semantics that do not fit natural language well. This further complicates the task of the natural language processing-needed automatic knowledge acquisition.

Aside from the new exciting ideas for automatic knowledge acquisition, the methods presented here were chosen because they involve semantically clean or rather clean representations geared toward correctly reflecting natural language meaning. Both of these aspects are very important. Hundreds of millions of on-line texts, including web pages and on-line versions of traditional publications such as books and journal articles, remain incredible, but largely unused, sources of knowledge. Furthermore, we believe there is a strong possibility that the same representational and inferential natural language-like mechanisms can underlie both knowledge acquisition and its utilization. This would simplify the architecture of an intelligent system enormously.

Summary of Chapters

In the first chapter addressing the knowledge acquisition theme, Sanda Harabagiu and Dan Moldovan propose an ambitious method for fully automatic enriching large-scale, hand-crafted lexical taxonomy with system-selected fragments from crawler-obtained texts. The resulting enriched taxonomy represents knowledge in a more natural language-like fashion than the traditional taxonomies. Enriched with some contextual information, the combined representation more closely reflects the meaning of natural language sentences. It resembles Sowa's natural language-motivated conceptual graphs. The proposed acquisition algorithm is quite complex, partly formal and partly heuristic. The main acquisition idea is to look for certain predefined patterns. The authors discuss their approach validation for a number of the in-depth natural language processing tasks involving context. For a small number of texts, their experiments show improved precision for these tasks.

Harabagiu's and Moldovan's system is a serious implementation that uses a number of existing tools and resources. Their system processes small-to-medium scale, real-life, multi-domain textual data, including publically-available corpora and data from the world wide web. The system's performance is evaluated in terms of recall and precision for a small number of concepts in a small number of texts.

In the second chapter addressing the knowledge acquisition theme, Lucja Iwańska, Naveen Mata, and Kellyn Kruger propose another ambitious method for fully automatic acquisition of taxonomic knowledge, including concept (type) definitions from large-scale, real-life textual corpora. The algorithm is based on processing simple, easily extractable, parsable and interpretable constructs of natural language conveying taxonomic knowledge. Their experiments show that the system acquires hundreds of general-purpose concept definitions from thousands of multi-domain, multi-corpora texts with a high degree of recall and precision. The authors argue that their approach practically eliminates human preprocessing, such as hand-tagging, and human post-processing, such as knowledge verification.

Iwańska's, Mata's and Kruger's system is a serious, stand-alone implementation. The system processes medium-to-large scale, real-life textual data, including public-domain, private and self-collected corpora of texts. The system's performance is evaluated in terms of recall and precision for a large number of texts. The authors discuss human experts' qualitative evaluation of the system-acquired concept definitions.

In the third chapter addressing the knowledge-acquisition theme, William J. Rapaport and Karen Ehrlich proposes a psychologically-motivated method for acquiring dictionarylike definitions of new words, their different senses and novel uses. In its full scope, it is the most ambitious of the three knowledge acquisition chapters. The acquisition method is based on reconciling known selected properties relevant for a given concept (word) with the new pieces of evidence from the natural language input processed. Preliminary, small-scale experiments show that this system is capable of acquiring new knowledge by bootstrapping what it already knows. Rapaport's and Ehrlich's implementation is currently under development. The system processes small-scale data extracted from real narrative texts and dialogs. Quantitative system performance is not discussed.

6 A Multi-Level Approach to Interlingual Machine Translation

Defining the Interface between Representational Languages

Bonnie J. Dorr and Clare R. Voss

TO PRODUCE AN APPROPRIATE TRANSLATION of a source-language sentence, a machine translation system must have access to several different representation types. Some examples of these are: lexical, for lexicon-based information; syntactic, for defining phrase structure; interlingual for sentence interpretation; and knowledge representational for filtering out interpretations that are incompatible with facts in the machine translation system's knowledge base. This chapter examines the interface between the interlingua and other representation types in an interlingual machine translation system. We adopt a multi-level design (Dorr and Voss 1993), i.e., a nonuniform approach, in which distinct representational languages are used for different types of knowledge. In our research and machine translation system construction, we have found that a linguistically-motivated "division of labor" in the translation task across multiple representation levels has not complicated, but rather has readily facilitated, the identification and construction of systematic relations at the interface between each level. We argue that our specific natural language processing application, the task of machine translation, is not hindered by a nonuniform approach.

Figure 1 illustrates the multi-level approach to interlingual machine translation. We adopt three different representational levels—syntactic, interlingual, and knowledge representation—each corresponding to a different processing phase in the system: First, an analysis/synthesis phase in which a source-language sentence is parsed into a syntactic structure or a target-language sentence is generated from a syntactic structure and associated lexical items; second, a composition/decompo-

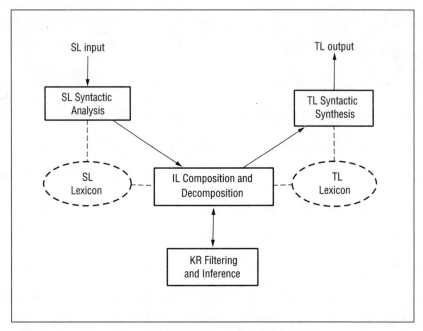

Figure 1. Multi-Level Approach to
Interlingual Machine Translation: Processing Phases

sition phase in which a source language syntactic structure is composed into an interlingual representation or an interlingual representation is decomposed into a target language syntactic structure and lexical items; and third, a knowledge representation phase that checks the interlingual representations, filtering out those forms incompatible with known facts and, as needed, coercing or augmenting interlingual forms with logically inferred knowledge in order to resolve an incomplete interlingual composition. The model assumes that the source language and target language lexicons are each accessed, respectively, during the composition and decomposition of the interlingual form.[1] Figure 2 illustrates, for one sense of the intransitive verb *stand,* the static forms stored at the syntactic and interlingual levels and the primitives from within the interlingual form that are concepts grounded at the knowledge representation level.

As Dorr and Voss (1993) argue, the field of machine translation research lacks a consensus on what an interlingua is and how it is defined. Machine translation system developers in building their individual interlinguas have selected from among a variety of semantic formalisms as the basis for their interlingual. For example, the Rosetta system (Rosetta 1994) used an interlingua based on **M**-grammar, a representation derived from Montague grammar. In the machine translation system

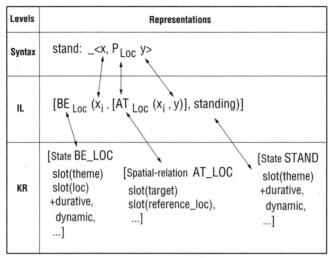

Levels	Representations
Syntax	stand: $\_\!<x, P_{Loc}\ y>$
IL	$[BE_{Loc}\ (x_i\ ,\ [AT_{Loc}\ (x_i\ ,\ y)],\ standing)]$
KR	[State BE_LOC slot(theme) slot(loc) +durative, dynamic, ...] [Spatial-relation AT_LOC slot(target) slot(reference_loc), ...] [State STAND slot(theme) +durative, dynamic, ...]

Figure 2. Multi-Level Approach to
Interlingual Machine Translation: Static Forms

Mikrokosmos, Levin and Nirenburg (1994) have been developing an interlingua based on their own text meaning representation language. Rupp, Johnson, and Rosner (1992) have worked with Situation Schemata, inspired by the Situation Semantics of Barwise and Perry (1983), for their semantic representation language. Recently Mani (1995), following insights from Zwarts and Verkuyl (1994), has proposed a "layered" interlingua whose forms contain discourse representation structures (DRSs of Kamp [1981]) at one level and lexical conceptual structures (LCSs of Jackendoff [1983; 1990]) at another level of representation.

Our approach assumes an interlingua derived from the lexical semantics and predicate decomposition approaches of Jackendoff (1983; 1990) and Levin and Rappaport-Hovav (1995a; 1995b). We describe a model of interpretation and representation of natural language sentences which has been implemented as part of an interlingual machine translation system called PRINCITRAN. This system combines the syntactic processing design of PRINCIPAR (Dorr, Lin, Lee, and Suh [1995]) with the syntax-interlingual interface originally developed in the UNITRAN system (Dorr 1993) and the interlingual-knowledge representation interface from the LEXITRAN system (Dorr and Voss 1993; Dorr et al. 1994).

Throughout this chapter we aim to demonstrate the utility of a linguistically-motivated division into distinct representational languages in a multi-level interlingual machine translation design. The next section describes our framework for interlingual machine translation, citing examples from the spatial domain in support of our nonuniform representational approach. The third section describes our framework for defining an interlingual representation. The final two sections describe how the basic units of the interlingual representation serve as the mediating structures at the syntax/interlingual interface and at the interlingual/knowledge representation interface.

Framework for Interlingual Machine Translation

We adopt a nonuniform approach to machine translation in that knowledge is represented at different levels using distinct representational formalisms. First, we give an example of translation data that led us to explore this nonuniform or "division of labor" approach. We then spell out the assumptions inherent in our machine translation system design. Next, we present the problem space and the subset of natural language that we have been working with. Finally, we describe our modularization of knowledge encodings into different machine translation components.

Motivation for Nonuniform Approach

The separation of knowledge into different representational levels is motivated by cases such as the following German example:

Die Kirche liegt im Süden der Stadt (1)

which may have either of the following interpretations:

a. The church lies in the south of the city (2)
b. The church lies to the south of the city

In the first interpretation, the church is located in the southern part of the city (i.e., within city limits), whereas in the second case, the church lies south of the city (i.e., outside its limits).

In sentence 1, the ambiguity is not readily noticeable in the words of the German sentence, yet the conceptual distinction underlying the ambiguity (i.e., lying inside of , versus lying outside of) is strikingly clear. That is, this translation data enables us to see that the German phrase *im Süden der Stadt* maps to two distinct representations: south-and-internal corresponding to the southern region of the city and south-and-external corresponding to the region south of the city.[2]

If sentence 1 referred to a mountain rather than a church, the machine translation system should be able to use default knowledge in the knowledge representation that mountains are physical entities that are typically distinct and external to cities (thus choosing the second translation 2b); yet, the system should also take advantage of specific facts in the knowledge representation, for example, that a particular mountain is in the city, in order to override default knowledge as needed (thus choosing the first translation 2a). We take this to be a knowledge representation filtering function that is independent of particular lexical knowledge. The need to translate such sentences accurately presents a clear case of where general as well as specific real world knowledge should assist in eliminating inappropriate translations. In the model we adopt, it is the knowledge representation, not the interlingua, that provides this capability.

The nonuniform approach alleviates many of the problems that might be encountered if one were to adopt a machine translation system design with only one representational language to assign interpretations to natural language input. In particular, the separation of the interlingua from the knowledge representation allows us to build a machine translation system in which we need not represent the "full" meaning for each word in a sentence being translated.[3] Furthermore, with the multilevel approach we can let the choice of interlingual structures be driven by the limited demands of the syntax-to-interlingual mapping, rather than by the full complexity of conceptual categories for events and states that properly belong in the knowledge representation system. This design consideration protects our system from becoming unnecessarily brittle as the knowledge representation system grows or changes with the domain of translation. It also reflects our bias toward maintaining the advantages of assumptions made by Dorr (1993) over those of Nirenburg et al. (1992) in interlingua-based machine translation system design when the two have different consequences for PRINCITRAN.

Assumptions

We assume processing to be sentence-level only (i.e., no discourse analysis) and we take the output of the PRINCIPAR system (the parser used in PRINCITRAN as described by Dorr, Lin, Lee, and Suh [1995]) as our input. A source language sentence is analyzed into a set of parse trees representing all possible syntactic interpretations, within the government-binding theory of syntax upon which our parser is based. It is then the job of interlingual and knowledge representation components to interpret the source language phrase structure and provide an appropriate interlingua for the generation of the target language. Thus, there are two types of interfaces that we define between our three knowledge levels: one that relates interlingual representations to corresponding syntactic forms by means of lexical entries; and one that checks the interlingual representations in the knowledge representation, filtering out those forms incompatible with known facts and, as needed, coercing or augmenting interlingual forms with logically inferred knowledge in order to resolve an incomplete interlingual composition. (See figure 1.)

The interlingual forms themselves are defined in terms of those two types of interfaces. As can be seen in the example of a lexical interlingual form in figure 2, the interlingual forms retain linguistically-relevant information from both interfaced levels: first, structural components of lexical knowledge such as predicate-argument relations (for example, that spatial verbs such as *stand* and *lie* involve an ordered binary relation on a located object and a location) and second, conceptual content such as predicate primitives and prototypical constants (for example, that spatial zero-related verbs[4] such as *shovel* in *she shoveled the snow from the driveway* include generic event-type concepts such as removal activities and object-type concepts such as shovel). Thus the interlingua serves as an interfacing level that mediates between the knowledge representation and its corresponding syntactic realization.

Defining the Problem Space: Translation Mismatches

We seek to address issues concerning translation mismatches. This is a problem area that has received increasingly greater attention in recent literature (Dorr and Voss 1993; Barnett et al. 1994; Beaven 1992; Kameyama et al. 1991; Kinoshita, Phillips, and Tsujii 1992; Lindop and Tsujii 1991; Whitelock 1992) as well as related discussion in Melby (1986) and Nirenburg and Nirenburg (1988). In particular, Barnett et al. (1994) identify two categories of differences between the source language and the target language: translation *divergences,* in which the same content is overtly conveyed in the source and target texts, but the structures of the sentences are different (as also defined in previous work by Dorr [1994]); and translation *mismatches,* in which the content that is conveyed is different in the source and target languages (as in Kameyama et al. [1991]). Both types of distinctions must be addressed in translation, yet most machine translation researchers have attended to one or the other.

Researchers investigating divergences (see Dorr and Voss 1993) are more inclined to address the mechanism that links the interlingual representation to the syntactic structure of the target language, whereas investigators of the mismatch problem (see Barnett et al. 1994; Kameyama et al. 1991; Wu and Palmer 1994; Palmer and Wu 1995) are more inclined to focus on the details of the conceptual representation underlying the interlingua. The novelty of our approach is that it addresses the problem of mismatches through access to the knowledge representation while retaining enough of the structure in the interlingua to resolve the divergence problem.

We have examined the problem space within the domain of spatial predicates; we view the range of lexical mismatches in this domain as a set of equivalence classes. Figure 3 shows a sample of lexical mismatch class-

Gaps in lexicalization for zero-related verbs[7]
no English word for go by vehicle
but *bus, train, jet* (go by bus, train, jet)

no German word for go
but *gehen, fahren* (go on foot, go by vehicle)

Lexical synonymy
English *lift, raise*
French *lever, hausser*

Differential lexicalization of caused/noncaused events
English noncausative *fall* and causative *fell*/make fall
but noncausative and causative *break*

French noncausative *tomber* and causative *faire tomber*
but noncausative and causative *casser*

Figure 3. A Sample of Lexical Mismatch Classes Within the Spatial Domain

es.[5] This partitioning is designed to provide a framework within which a solution for one example in a partition or problem class will work on all the examples in that class. Operationally in interlingua-based machine translation, the mismatches occur during generation, when matching an interlingual form in the target language lexicon, but finding no target language lexical entry (a gap in lexicalization), or when matching on more than one target language entry (by lexical synonymy or differential lexicalizations). We do not attempt here to cover the full space of lexical mismatches; rather, we restrict our attention to a few of those that occur at the syntax-interlingual and interlingual-knowledge representation interface. In particular, we have left aside those that must be resolved by reference to broader contextual knowledge of transactions.[6]

At generation time, we make the assumption that, for each source language word, there exists at least one target language word that is closest in meaning. From this it follows that, when an exact target language word match is missing (a gap), there are three possible relations between the closest target language word and the source language word: subsumes, subsumed-by, and overlapping, i.e., the closest target language word is over-general, over-specific, or overlapping in meaning with respect to source language word's meaning.[8] In later sections we will examine examples in each of these classes and show that in our approach, although the target language word that is initially selected does not exactly match the meaning of the corresponding source language word, a full-coverage meaning match is ultimately obtained by ensuring that some combination of target language words matches the overall source language concept.[9]

Domain of Inquiry: Spatial Predicates

The primary focus of our investigation is in the domain of simple spatial expressions, with specific attention to spatial verbs and prepositions that, collectively at the interlingual level, we label *spatial predicates*. Such predicates are used to describe relations between physical objects in real 3-dimensional space (such as a cup on a table). We take this to be a critical area of inquiry for interlingual machine translation since this is where a very high level of cross-linguistic diversity has been shown to exist. Consider the following English/French translations:[10]

a. English: The car roared down the street (3)
b. French: La voiture descendit la rue en vrombissant
   "The car went down the street (in) roaring"

a. English: The truck rumbled into the yard (4)
b. French: Le camion entra dans la cour dans un grand fracas
   "The truck entered in the yard in a big din"

English permits spatial directional predicates in phrases such as *down the street* and *into the yard* to compose readily with verbs of sound emission such as *roar* and *rumble*. In such constructions, we understand that the car and truck are moving as they make these noises even though there are no words that overtly refer to the motion. French, by contrast, does not permit such compositions: the motion and sound emission each must be lexicalized separately, as two verbs (in example 3b or as a verb and an extra modifier phrase as in example 4b). Thus, there is a mismatch in translating from English into French. Compared to English, French has a gap in its lexicalization space: French has no words equivalent to *roar* and *rumble* in the sentences above, meaning go with a roaring or rumbling noise. Consequently, in the analysis phase of translations, the machine translation system must identify the motion implicit in these English sentences, encode this in the interlingual representation, and then in the generation phase, make the motion lexically explicit when the target language is French.[11] Recent linguistic research indicates that Hebrew patterns like English in this regard while Japanese patterns like French.

In addition to such sentential structural distinctions found cross-linguistically, there also exists wide variation in the language-specific canonical surface location of spatial relations among the lexemes and morphemes of a sentence. For example, the spatial relation expressed in a preposition in English may appear in the combination of a verbal prefix and an overt preposition in a Russian translation, or as a postfix on the head noun of an NP in a language such as Korean. Or the equivalent of the English preposition may not actually appear as an overt distinct surface element in a Spanish translation, but instead be incorporated into the meaning of a verb.

One last note concerning this domain. While natural language predicates in the spatial domain may need, for operational reasons, to be reduced to mathematical relations (for example, described by Cartesian coordinates or topological models) for nonmachine translation applications (for example, as a natural language front-end to a virtual reality system), it is not the case that mathematical formalizations predict the specific combinations of spatial relations within natural language spatial predicates. Talmy (1983) captures this fact nicely in his detailed description of the meaning of the English word *across*.

Modularization of Knowledge Encodings

To talk about the encoding of spatial relations, we need to clarify which encodings appear in which part of the machine translation system. The following terms are used to classify the encoding of spatial relations on the basis of the evidence we have for them:

Lexically explicit: a spatial relation encoded explicitly in a word.[12]

Lexically implicit: a spatial relation encoded implicitly, or internal to the structure representing the meaning of a word.

Logically inferable: a spatial relation logically inferred from lexically explicit or implicit relations, but not itself part of the structure representing the meaning of a word.

In the first two cases, the relation appears in the lexical entry for the relevant word; in the third case, the relation does not appear in the lexical entry.

An example of the first case is the direction SOUTH as an abstract concept, which is lexically explicit in the word *south*.[13] An example of the second case is the direction *up* as a lexically implicit component of the word *raise*. The implicit presence of this constituent is apparent in tests for synonymy: "they raised the platform one and a half feet, they raised the platform up one and a half feet." Finally, as an example of the last category, the direction FROM and a location that is distinct from his home are logically inferable in the sentence "John arrived home," where the verb's lexically implicit relation PATH contains the explicit DESTINATION home, and where we can infer logically that in a PATH ending at home, there was also a place from which the arriver, John, came.

The definition of these categories is tied to the way we have modularized PRINCITRAN into components. In table 1, the X's mark which types of encoding of a spatial relation may appear in which of the components in our machine translation system.

Following up on the examples above, the relation SOUTH in *south* will be represented at all levels in PRINCITRAN, whereas UP in *raise* will only be represented at the interlingual and knowledge representation levels, and

Spatial Relation	Component of PRINCITRAN		
	Syntax	Interlingua	KR
lexically explicit	X	X	X
lexically implicit		X	X
logically inferable		X	

Table 1. Encoding of Spatial Relations in the Components of PRINCITRAN
The logically inferable relations can be broken out into the "logically explicit" facts explicitly encoded in the knowledge representation system and the "logically implicit" facts that are derived from other facts and inference rules in the system.

FROM in *John arrived home* will only be represented at the knowledge representation level (as the result of inferencing).

We can readily see that the syntax-interlingual mapping requires tracking which elements in the spatial predicates (at the interlingual level) appear in the surface source language and target language sentences and where in the sentence syntax they will be positioned. The knowledge representation-interlingual relation is not of this nature; rather, the knowledge representation system serves to verify the appropriateness of the spatial information that appears in the interlingual representation. One must not confuse the spatial information contained in the interlingua and that which is inferred by the knowledge representation system. To clarify this point, consider the following English sentences:

a. He took the book to Tanya's table   (5)
b. He took the book from Florence's floor

If the sentences are translated into German, the *take-to* component of the first sentence translates to *bringen* whereas the *take-from* component in the second sentence translates to *nehmen*. In both sentences there is an implicit PATH relation where a book moves from one location to another. The FROM direction is logically inferable in the first sentence but lexically explicit in the second sentence. The situation is reversed with a TO direction: the TO is lexically explicit in the first sentence, but only logically inferable in the second sentence. If our interlingual representation of the first sentence were to include the FROM relation by using a general PATH predicate with an inferred source location (here, not at Tanya's table)—and similarly if our interlingual representation of the second sentence were to include the TO relation by using a general PATH predicate with an inferred goal location (here, not at Florence's floor)—then at the point in translation where the system must generate a German sentence, it would have the added step of having to rederive what had been inferred (here, the negated locations) and what had been in the source language lexicalization in order to select between the two German verbs.

This last example and the chart above help illustrate the double set of justifications that are required in a theory of the interlingua. In particular, the syntax-interlingual mapping provides one set of constraints on the interlingual, whereas the the interlingual-knowledge representation relation provides another set. Currently no theory of the interlingua defines these constraints and addresses the criteria to be used in evaluating them, yet it is clear from the above discussion that a nonuniform model does not hinder and indeed may actually facilitate capturing the types of distinctions (such as between sources and destinations in spatial paths) required for successfully translating diverse language pairs.

Defining an Interlingua

This section provides a specification for the interlingua. We start by outlining the resources that have contributed toward the development of an interlingual representation. We then define and illustrate the structure of the interlingual. Finally, we describe our use of the interlingual representation in interlingual machine translation, addressing issues of lexicon development and implementation status of PRINCITRAN.

Contributions to the LCS-derived Representation Language

Our interlingual representation derives from the lexical conceptual structures (LCSs) of Jackendoff (1983, 1990, 1991).[14] The lexical conceptual structures framework consists of three independent subsystems: fields, conceptual constituents, and boundedness and aggregation properties. Only the first two are currently a part of our interlingual framework.

The LCS fields (i.e., Loc(ational), Temp(oral), Poss(essional), Ident(ificational), Perc(eptual), and others) are motivated by well-known observations of lexical parallelism, where the same lexical item has parallel or related meanings in two or more semantic fields. The conceptual constituents in the second LCS subsystem are variants on predicate-argument structures. These include primitive predicators (such as GO, BE, and CAUSE) and their arguments and modifiers, each of which has an ontological type (for example, Thing, State, Event, Place, Path, and Property); the internal structure of each constituent may decompose into another conceptual constituent. The primitive predicators are subscripted by field in addition to being typed by category.

As an example of how the primitive predicator GO (of ontological type Event) is used in representing the sentence semantics of a spatial expression (i.e., in the Loc(ational) field), consider the following case:

a. The ball rolled toward Beth. (6)

b. $[_{Event} GO_{Loc}([_{Thing} BALL],$
$[_{Path} TOWARD_{Loc}$
$([_{Thing} BALL], [_{Position} AT_{Loc}([_{Thing} BALL], [_{Thing} BETH])])])]$

Roughly, this representation means "The ball went locationally toward Beth."[15] Predicators (enclosed in square brackets "[]") can take zero or more arguments (enclosed in parentheses "()"). In the lexical entry for the sense of *roll* in example 6, the predicator GO takes two arguments: the first is a thematic (affected) object and the second is either a directional path or a means/manner by-phrase.[16]

Jackendoff makes the claim that the conceptual structures generalize across fields. In particular, he adapts a localist view, claiming that the formalism for encoding constituents in the spatial field at some level of abstraction, generalizes to other fields. A localist, or localist-related, approach to lexical semantics is by no means unique to Jackendoff. See, for example, among many others, Anderson (1971), Heine, Claudi, and Huennemeyer (1991), Langacker (1987), and Schank (1975). In particular, early translation approaches used the spatially oriented conceptual dependency representation as the basis for interlingual machine translation (Schank 1975; Schank and Abelson 1977; Lytinen and Schank,1982). The conceptual dependency-based interlingua is a decompositional representation based on a small set of primitives that revolve around basic spatial notions such as motion, location, and direction. However, the conceptual dependency-based framework for machine translation does not provide a systematic relation between the interlingua and its corresponding surface realization. For example, there is no uniform mechanism for handling even simple translation divergences such as argument reversal cases (for example, translation of the English sentence "I like Mary" into the Spanish sentence "me gusta Maria"—"Mary pleases me"). Our approach differs in that it provides a systematic syntax-interlingual interface geared toward providing a uniform treatment of translation divergences.[17]

Although Jackendoff addresses the problem of defining a mapping between the semantics (i.e., the interlingua) and its corresponding syntactic realization, his work does not address the computational issues associated with representing or processing LCSs.[18] In particular, although Jackendoff writes that thematic relations (i.e., the roles in predicate-argument structure) depend crucially on an enriched knowledge representation, he leaves open to interpretation what that knowledge representation ought to look like and what would constitute an adequate scheme for grounding the primitives of the LCS representation in the knowledge representation.

Another resource for the development of our interlingual representation is the linguistically motivated notion of *lexical semantic template* (LST) as defined in the work of Levin and Rappaport-Hovav (1995a; 1995b).[19] The lexical semantic template framework provides a decomposition of verbs into predicate structure and nonpredicate constants, where a verb with many meanings reflects the pairing of one constant with several different predicate structures. To illustrate this point, consider the following sentences:

a. The soldiers marched. (7)
b. The soldiers marched to the barracks.
c. The soldiers marched clear of the falling rocks.
d. The soldiers marched the soles of their boots flat.
e. The general marched the soldiers to the barracks.

In each of the sentences above, the verb *march* introduces a single constant, denoted with angle brackets, the manner-of-motion constant <MARCH>. It is the predicate structure that distinguishes the verbs in each of these examples—respectively, simple manner of motion, directional motion, state-change resultative, "fake" reflexive resultative, and causative directional motion.[20]

This framework also allows the same predicate structure to be associated with different constant names; each predicate-constant combination is realized as a different verb in the surface form, but the argument-taking properties are identical:

a. They funneled the mixture into the jar. (8)
b. They ladled the mixture into the jar.
c. They shoveled the mixture into the jar.
d. They spooned the mixture into the jar.

In all of the cases above, there is an affected object within a directional resultative, but the constant underlying each case, the instrument of the action, is different— respectively, <FUNNEL>, <LADLE>, <SHOVEL>, and <SPOON>. Note that such constants cannot be specified in isolation, but must be found in some knowledge representation.

It is precisely this lexical semantic template-style systematic use of the constant in our representations that allows us to transcend Jackendoff's framework. For example, we have adapted his representation given previously in example 6 to include the constant <ROLL>, thus providing a means for grounding the representation in the knowledge representation:

a. The ball rolled toward Beth. (9)

b. $[_{\text{Event}} \text{ GO}_{\text{Loc}}([_{\text{Thing}} \text{ BALL}],$
$[_{\text{Path}} \text{ TOWARD}_{\text{Loc}}$
$([_{\text{Thing}} \text{ BALL}], [_{\text{Position}} \text{ AT}_{\text{Loc}}([_{\text{Thing}} \text{ BALL}], [_{\text{Thing}} \text{ BETH}])])],$
$[\text{BY} <\text{ROLL}>])]$

Roughly, this representation means "The ball went locationally toward Beth by rolling." Note that the primitive GO has two arguments in example 6 but three arguments in example 9. In the spirit of the lexical semantic template framework, we adopt the former two-argument representation for lexical items and the latter three-argument representation for the interlingual form associated with the full sentence. In the lexical entry for roll, as used in the sentence above, the two arguments in the GO predicate are the thematic (affected) object and the means/manner by-phrase. The directional path predicate in the full sentential interlingual form above does not originate in the lexical representation for *roll*. It appears in the form above as the result of analyzing the phrase *toward Beth* within the verb phrase.

By adapting this representation, we retain the benefits of the interlingual-syntax interface, while addressing the computational issue of associating the interlingual primitives with concepts in the knowledge representation. Furthermore, we are able to preserve the structural constraints on the Loc(ational) field that hold in other fields. For example, in the Ident(ificational) field, sentence 10 will still have a structure parallel to the adapted one in sentence 9.

a. The snowman melted into a puddle. (10)

b. $[_{\text{Event}} \text{ GO}_{\text{Ident}}([_{\text{Thing}} \text{ SNOWMAN}],$
$[_{\text{Path}} \text{ TO}_{\text{Ident}}$
$([_{\text{Thing}} \text{ SNOWMAN}],$
$[_{\text{Position}} \text{ AT}_{\text{Ident}}([_{\text{Thing}} \text{ SNOWMAN}], [_{\text{Thing}} \text{ PUDDLE}])])],$
$[\text{BY} <\text{MELT}>])]$

A third resource for our interlingual development is the semantic classification scheme of Levin (1993), which was developed as a foundation for determining shared syntactic behaviors across different English verbs. In Levin's terms, a semantic class is a set of verbs where each member participates in the same set of surface alternations (i.e., syntactic behaviors). Levin suggests that members of a set share components of meaning; however, the predicate structures corresponding to meaning components are not identified. Levin's subsequent work with Rappaport-Hovav on the LSTs, already described above, also provides a more extensive linguistic analysis of verb behaviors. The semantic categories in this later work are more general than the semantic classes of Levin (1993). For example, the semantic category verbs of motion subsumes more than one of Levin's classes (manner of motion, inherently directed motion, etc.).

Decompositional/Predicate-Based Representation: RLCS

The combination of the three resources described above forms the basis for our lexical interlingual structure—called RLCS (root word LCS). Each RLCS is language-specific and is associated with one root form (for example, uninflected form for verbs) in its language's machine translation lexicon. Consistent with the lexical semantic template approach, verbs sharing a semantic class from Levin (1993) have the same predicate structure and differ only in the constant within that structure. All verbs within a given class are subject to the same set of linguistic constraints in syntax. Our interlingual structures diverge from Levin and Rappaport-Hovav's lexical semantic templates in terms of the particular primitive predicators and in our inclusion of semantic fields (Jackendoff 1983). As our interest is in the area of spatial predicates, we have investigated verbs of motion, removal, and placement; however, the same linguistic constraints apply to verbs in other seemingly unrelated domains (such as sound).

As outlined informally above, we distinguish among the three types of primitives within our RLCSs:

Constants: within-class identifiers (for example, <ROLL>) which are distinct from predicate structure, but are attached within an interlingual form.

Situation-Level Predicators: a small set of nonconstant primitives corresponding to primary relations (for example, GO, ACT, BE, CAUSE).[21] These primitives are associated with a small set of fields denoted by subscripted labels (for example, Loc(ational), Temp(oral), Poss(essional), Ident(ificational), Perc(eptual)).

Situation-Internal Predicators: primitives (for example, TOWARD, AT) dominated by situation-level predicators.

Both Situation-Level and Situation-Internal predicators (enclosed in square brackets "[]") can take zero or more arguments (enclosed in parentheses "()"). With respect to constants, each word sense uses a constant to encode information that is idiosyncratic to (but not necessarily unique to) that particular word. The constant is also grounded as a concept of the knowledge representation system.

We note that the constant in a word's RLCS serves as a link between that word's lexical-semantic structure, which maps systematically to syntax, and conceptual knowledge that is required for logical inferencing. This is consistent with the work of Levin and Rappaport-Hovav (1995b), where *semantic structure*—the structural component of meaning which maps systematically to syntax—is distinguished from semantic content—the idiosyncratic component of meaning which has its underpinnings in conceptual knowledge. These terms readily extend to our framework: the interlingual predicates are a part of the semantic structure, serving as a link between the interlingua and the syntax, and the constants such as <ROLL> are a part of the semantic content, conveying idiosyncratic knowledge necessary for distinguishing this word from others within the same semantic class. At generation time when the machine translation system accesses the *interlingual lexicon*—a reverse index into target language lexicons (as discussed in a later section)—the constants are critical to handling translation mismatches such as lexical gaps in the target language.[22]

The systematic use of constants here is an improvement on earlier work (see, for example, Dorr [1993]) where manner constants such as *runningly* were viewed on a par with primitives such as GO and CAUSE; these constants were proliferated, without linguistic justification, throughout the lexical interlingual representations. Typically, such usage was accompanied by a footnote indicating that further investigation into the nature of lexical-semantic structure would be necessary. We attempt to remedy this shortcoming by developing our current representations in terms of lexical interlingual templates so that they conform to structural constraints invoked by the lexical semantic template framework.

Within this lexical interlingual template approach, lexical entries adhere to a small set of structural requirements that divide verbs into *result verbs* such as *clear,* which incorporate a resultant state, and *manner/means verbs* such as *shovel,* which incorporate manner or means. The result versus means/manner dichotomy is a basic distinction in the verb lexicon that has been carefully studied and characterized by Levin and Rappaport-Hovav (1995a; 1995b). The distinction cuts across verbs in the spatial domain in our investigation as well as across verbs from seemingly unrelated semantic classes.[23]

The reason the result versus means/manner distinction is important is that it correlates with a difference in syntactic behavior. As an example, consider the removal category. Within this category, the behavior of verbs in one class, such as *clear,* contrasts syntactically with verbs in another class, such as *shovel.* Only in the case of *shovel* is the change-of-state resultative construction allowed:[24]

a. *I cleared the table clean   (11)
b. I shoveled the driveway clean

On the other hand, an "of" phrase can be used for *clear,* but not *shovel:*

a. I cleared the table of dishes   (12)
b. *I shoveled the driveway of snow

Table 2 shows five broad semantic categories (taken from Levin and Rappaport-Hovav [1995b]) and, for each, two example verbs along with their associated RLCS representations in the lexicon. Specifically, each

Category	Verb	Class	RLCS	Template
Motion	leave	51.2	$[GO_{Loc}$ (Y, ([<AWAY-FROM> (Y, [AT (Y, Z)])])]	13a(ii)
	run	51.3.1	$[ACT_{Loc}$(X, [BY <RUN>])]	13b(i)
Removal	clear	10.3	[CAUSE (X, $[GO_{Ident}$(Y, ([TOWARD$_{Ident}$ (Y, ([AT$_{Ident}$ (Y, ([<CLEAR>$_{Ident}$ (([<OF>$_{Poss}$ (*HEAD*, Z)])])])])])])]	13a(i)
	shovel	10.4.2	$[ACT_{Loc} [ON_{Loc}$ (Y)], [BY <SHOVEL>])]	13b(i)
Placement	fill	9.8	[CAUSE (X, ($[GO_{Ident}$(Y, ([TOWARD$_{Ident}$(Y, ([AT$_{Ident}$ (Y, ([<FULL>$_{Ident}$ ((([<WITH>$_{Poss}$ (*HEAD*, Z)])])])])])])])]	13a(i)
	pour	9.5	$[ACT_{Loc}[ON_{Loc}$(Y)], [BY <POUR>])]	13b(i)
Sound	say	37.7	[CAUSE (X, ($[GO_{Ident}$(Y, ([TOWARD$_{Ident}$(Y, ([AT$_{Ident}$ (Y, ([<SAID>$_{Ident}$])])])])])]	13a(i)
	shout	37.3	$[ACT_{Perc} [ON_{Perc}$ (Y)], [BY <SHOUT>])]	13b(i)
Killing	kill	42.1	[CAUSE (X, ($[GO_{Ident}$(Y, ([TOWARD$_{Ident}$(Y, ([AT$_{Ident}$ (Y, ([<KILLED>$_{Ident}$ ((([<WITH>$_{Instr}$ (*HEAD*, Z)])])])])])])])]	13a(i)
	stab	42.2	$[ACT_{Perc} [ON_{Perc}$ (Y)], [BY <STAB>])]	13b(i)

Table 2. RLCSs Based on Levin's Verb Classification

broad category includes one result verb entry (for example, *leave*) and one means/manner verb entry (for example, *run*). Class numbers from Levin's 1993 book are provided for each verb example. The distinction between these two types of verbs is reflected in the constant of the RLCS representation. For result verbs, the constant corresponds to a resulting state (as in *clear* and *fill*) or location (as in *leave*). For manner/means verbs, the constant may specify a manner (as in *run* and *pour*) or means (as in *shovel*). We use the following basic templates, cross-referenced in table 2, to characterize the result vs. manner/means dichotomy:[25][26]

a. Result Verbs: (13)
  i [CAUSE (X, $[GO_{Ident}$(Y, [TOWARD$_{Ident}$ (Y, [AT$_{Ident}$(Y, [<STATE>])])])])]
  ii [CAUSE (X, $[GO_{Loc}$(Y, [<DIRECTION>$_{Loc}$ (Y, [AT$_{Loc}$(Y, Z)])])])]
  iii [CAUSE (X, $[GO_{Loc}$ (Y, [TOWARD$_{Loc}$ (Y, [<POSITION>$_{Loc}$])])])]

b. Means/Manner Verbs:
  i $[ACT_{Loc/Perc}$(X, [ON$_{Loc/Perc}$ (Y)], [BY <MEANS/MANNER>])]
  ii [CAUSE (X, $[GO_{Loc/Perc}$ (Y, [TOWARD$_{Loc}$ (Y,[AT$_{Loc}$(Y, Z)]), [BY <MEANS/MANNER>])])]

The underlining in example 13 is a shorthand notation to condense the presentation of multiple templates. Note that these basic templates vary along a number of different dimensions, for example, the name of the situation-level predicator, the number of arguments associated with the predicator, the allowable fields, and the position of the constant. In addition, certain primitives are interchangeable with others, for example, AT_{Loc} can be replaced with other static spatial relations, such as the static UP_{Loc}(meaning "at the top of") in the RLCS of the transitive verb *climb* (as we will see in the next section).

In short, these basic templates show how the full space of RLCSs vary predictably and capture the result versus means/manner distinction, thus enhancing our approach to defining a systematic interface between the interlingual and the syntactic structure. This interface is the topic of the syntax/interlingual interface section that follows.

Use of the RLCS in Interlingual Machine Translation

The representations and constraints described above serve as the foundation of a large-scale, RLCS-based lexicon for interlingual machine translation of English, Arabic, French, Korean, and Spanish. We have built a database of English RLCS representations for the 3,828 verb entries in Levin (1993), where an entry is a semantic class/verb sense pair, for example, *42.1/kill* from table 2. These RLCSs were automatically derived from a manually-encoded set of templates for all 192 of Levin's semantic classes.[27] The classes consist of a total of 2,775 unique verbs distributed across the 3,828 Levin-based entries (some verbs occur in multiple classes). In addition, we have developed RLCS representations for 3,500 non-Levin verbs,[28] by associating with each verb a semantic class and then instantiating the RLCS template associated with that class in order to build that verb's lexical entry. For details of experiments in the automatic construction of an RLCS-based lexicon for other languages such as Arabic, see Dorr, Garman, and Weinberg (1995).

The full set of RLCS's has now been ported to Arabic and Spanish; these are being used in a large-scale analysis component of an implemented foreign language tutoring system (Dorr et al. 1995). The analysis component of this tutoring system, coupled with the RLCS lexicon, serve as the core components of PRINCITRAN. A prototype version of the generation component has been constructed for complete end-to-end translation (Dorr et al. 1994).

Our interlingual model assumes that the analysis phase (from source language input to interlingual form) involves the source language lexicon and the generation phase (from interlingual form to target language output) involves the target language lexicon. The role of the RLCS's in each of the lexicons is slightly different, as the task in each direction is inherently distinct: during analysis, the appropriate RLCSs are selected from the source language lexicon, as a function of syntax, and the interlingual is constructed compositionally from the predicate/constant information in the RLCSs; during generation, the RLCS's of the target language are accessed from a larger interlingual lexicon (described in a later section) and the target language words are selected such that their RLCSs semantically cover the predicate/constant information in the interlingua. The next section examines each of these two tasks more closely, at the interface level, where the RLCS serves as the primary mediating structure.

The Syntax/Interlingual Interface

As illustrated in the previous section, our investigation into the nature of spatial mismatches has led to a better understanding of what must necessarily be included in the interlingua. This section describes the interface between the interlingual representation and the syntax, and in particular, discusses the allocation of information in the RLCS-based lexicons and the rules that operate on RLCSs to produce the full (sentential) interlingual form.

Information Allocation in RLCS-Based Lexicon

In the spatial predicates subsection we argued that, in order to provide adequate cross-linguistic coverage, a machine translation system must address cases where languages differ with respect to their patterns of lexicalization, for example, which arguments may be incorporated into a lexical item (Talmy 1983; Talmy 1985). An interlingual formalism that identifies incorporated information will provide a greater variety of lexicalization options for mapping between the source and target language. The decompositional nature of our RLCS representation provides a means for capturing incorporated information.

Consider, for example, the English verbs *lift, ascend,* and *climb* as used in the following sentences:

    a. Mary lifted the baby.   (14)
    b. The plane ascended.
    c. John climbed the stairs.

All three verbs hide (or incorporate) the semantics of another word, *up.* This incorporated information is encoded in each verb's lexicon entry (i.e., in the RLCS) either as its own constant or as part of the meaning of a conceptually more complex constant:[29]

a. lift: [CAUSE (W, [GO$_{Loc}$(Y, [BY <LIFT>])])]   (13a[i])   (15)
b. ascend: [GO$_{Loc}$(Y, [TOWARD$_{Loc}$(Y, [<UP>$_{Loc}$])])]   13a[iii])
c. climb: [GO$_{Loc}$(Y, [TOWARD$_{Loc}$(Y, [UP$_{Loc}$(Y, Z)])]), [BY <CLIMB>])]
(13a[ii])

During sentence analysis, the constants in *lift, ascend,* and *climb* encode our notion of inherent upward motion in distinct ways.[30] In the *lift* RLCS, the constant encodes that motion. It is the <LIFT> constant that allows the *lift* RLCS to be composed with the particle up. That the semantics of upward motion belongs in a constant that in turn is grounded in the knowledge representation may seem too well hidden in the representation. We note here only that for many native speakers of English there is no strict requirement that a lifting motion necessarily be upwards; for example, one person could be on a ladder removing items from the top shelf of a kitchen cabinet and be lifting down those items to someone standing on the ground beneath them.

The *ascend* RLCS differs from the one for *lift* in two ways. First, *lift* in the sentence above is a causative verb, requiring an external cause; it contains the primitive CAUSE and an argument W. The verb *ascend* is not grammatically causative: in English, we cannot say that "X ascends Y" means "X caused Y to go upward." Second, unlike *lift, ascend* may not co-occur with a spatial direction such as down: "*he ascended down the hill." Thus, we say *ascend* is inherently directed with TOWARD and the constant <UP>.

The RLCS for *climb* differs from that of *lift* and *ascend* in that there is an UP predicator with two arguments, the second of which must be lexicalized. The particular meaning of *climb* that comes with an obligatory argument as theme incorporates UP as its own primitive. That is, climbing any object entails upward motion on that object. The UP is disjoint from the <CLIMB> constant which is reserved for the clambering manner of motion that defines climbing in English. It is interesting to note that in languages as distinct as German and Turkish, one cannot use the same *climb* word for expressing climbing a mountain (inherently upward) and climbing down a mountain. That is, where we have two RLCSs for two distinct uses of the one English word *climb,* other languages have two separate words.[31][32]

Composition of the Interlingual

As we noted above, the constants and primitives in the interlingual forms corresponding to *lift, ascend,* and *climb* are all retained into their composed interlingual forms. This illustrates a key benefit of our formalism: the substructure and constant information of the source language input is preserved and so the decision process on lexicalization into the target language is not prematurely foreclosed. By leaving the lexicalization decision open into the target language phase, our machine translation system allows for target language-specific pragmatic information to be used and for stylistic choices to be made in the final generation steps[33]—after the target language lexical options have been identified from the interlingual form.

We are now prepared to describe the composition process that derives the interlingual representations. During the analysis phase of translation, the RLCSs are composed, producing what is called a *composed LCS* as the interlingual form. This process is governed by linguistic rules that are associated with the RLCSs of the source language sentence. We assume that verbs, or more accurately verb senses, sharing a semantic class have the same RLCS template and that all RLCSs in a given class are subject to the same set of constraints on possible compositional operations. An example of a compositional operation is one that derives the change-of-state resultative construction illustrated in example 11; this operation applies to verbs like *shovel* (in class 10.4.2 of Levin [1993]) but not verbs like *clear* (in class 10.3 of Levin [1993]).

Recall that our motivation for adhering to certain restrictions of the lexical semantic template framework was that they provide a means for defining a systematic interface between interlingual forms and their possible syntactic realizations. In particular, we exploit the constraints inherent in the lexical semantic template framework for distinguishing between different syntactic behaviors as exemplified in examples 11 and 12. There are two advantages to using the lexical semantic template framework for defining the RLCS lexicon: templates may be freely augmented by composition with other templates, subject to certain constraints; and constants in the templates are systematically related to surface lexical items and arguments in the templates are systematically related to syntactic argument positions.

To illustrate these two points, consider the different syntactic distributions of *clear* and *shovel* again. The lexical entry for *clear* directly incorporates the resultant state <CLEAR> whereas no such state is available in the *shovel* entry. (These entries are shown in table 2.) Thus, there is no way to further augment the *clear* template through a change-of-state resultative composition operation as in the sentence *I cleared the table clean*. In the case of *shovel,* this option is open: "I shoveled the driveway clean." The operation that derives this sentence yields the following composed LCS representation:

I shoveled the driveway clean.   (16)
   [CAUSE
      ([ACT$_{Loc}$ (I, [ON$_{Loc}$ (DRIVEWAY)]), [BY <SHOVEL>])],
   [GO$_{Ident}$

(DRIVEWAY,
[TOWARD$_{\text{Ident}}$ (DRIVEWAY,
[AT$_{\text{Ident}}$ (DRIVEWAY, [<CLEAN>$_{\text{Ident}}$])])])])]

Optionally, we could add an *of* phrase, as in the sentence "I shoveled the driveway clean of snow." The word *of* corresponds to constant <OF>, which is available as an inherent argument of <CLEAN>:

I shoveled the driveway clean (of snow).   (17)
  [CAUSE
    ([ACT$_{\text{Loc}}$ (I, [ON$_{\text{Loc}}$ (DRIVEWAY)], [BY <SHOVEL>])],
    [GO$_{\text{Ident}}$
    (DRIVEWAY,
    [TOWARD$_{\text{Ident}}$ (DRIVEWAY,
    [AT$_{\text{Ident}}$(DRIVEWAY, [<CLEAN>$_{\text{Ident}}$([<OF>$_{\text{Poss}}$ (*HEAD*,
    SNOW)])])])])])]

Implicit in the machinery described here is the assumption that all overt lexical items in the surface sentence must necessarily be related to a constant, whether inherent or compositionally introduced. This assumption rules out certain syntactic realizations for *shovel* that are available for verbs like *clear*. For example, *clear* allows a bare *of* phrase to be used, as in "I cleared the table of dishes," because this option is available in the lexical entry. This option would produce the following representation:

I cleared the table of dishes.   (18)
  [CAUSE
    (I,
    [GO$_{\text{Ident}}$
    (TABLE,
    [TOWARD$_{\text{Ident}}$(TABLE,
    [AT$_{\text{Ident}}$(TABLE, [<CLEAR>$_{\text{Ident}}$([<OF>$_{\text{Poss}}$ (*HEAD*, DISHES)])])])])])]

The words *clear* and *of* in the surface sentence are mapped into the constants <CLEAR> and <OF> in this representation.

The same is not true of *shovel,* i.e., it would not be possible to introduce a bare "of" phrase, as in *I shoveled the driveway of snow:*

I shoveled the driveway clean (of snow).   (19)
  [CAUSE
    ([ACT$_{\text{Loc}}$(I, [ON$_{\text{Loc}}$(DRIVEWAY)], [BY <SHOVEL>])],
    [GO$_{\text{Ident}}$
    (DRIVEWAY,
    [TOWARD$_{\text{Ident}}$(DRIVEWAY,
    [AT$_{\text{Ident}}$(DRIVEWAY, [<???>$_{\text{Ident}}$([<OF>$_{\text{Poss}}$ (*HEAD*, SNOW)])])])])])])]

Here, the structure is ruled out because there is no word in the surface sentence to map onto a state constant in the underlying representation. Note that this constraint is inherent in the machinery of the lexical semantic template framework; it falls out from restrictions on the representation itself, not from the application of explicit constraints. This is precisely the benefit we seek to gain in adapting this framework to the the RLCS framework described above.

In short, the lexical representation of a verb in the composed LCS, i.e., after composition, does not differ from that of its original form in the RLCS, i.e., before composition. In other words, the substructures within a verb are retained, thus (monotonically) preserving the predicates for the later target language generation phase.

Cross-Linguistic Application of the RLCS Framework

We turn now to the use of this representational approach in an interlingual machine translation system. It is clear that there would be no benefit to basing our RLCS representations on the lexical semantic template framework unless there were some way of accounting for cross-linguistic variation with respect to the applicability of composition operations. For example the change-of-state resultative construction, as in "I shoveled the driveway clean," is not available in a language like Spanish; thus, the same meaning must be conveyed either as a paraphrase with two clauses or as a single clause with some omitted or redistributed information:

a. Traspalé el garaje para que esté limpio (20)
   "I shoveled the driveway so that it is clean"

b. Limpié el garaje (con una pala)
   "I cleaned the driveway (with a shovel)"

The approach we adopt to handling such a distinction is to parameterize the interlingual/syntax mapping so that the change-of-state resultative operation is applied in English, but not in Spanish. For each natural language, we identify allowable sets of composition operations in that language, and then we identify, more narrowly, the classes of lexical items to which these operations apply. The parameterization permits each language to have its own idiosyncratic syntactic realization while sharing the same underlying interlingual representations.

The first sentence above most closely reflects the meaning of the English change-of-state resultative construction; thus its composed LCS will be identical to that of the English sentence. The second sentence, on the other hand, will map to a different composed LCS. The two respective composed LCS representations are given here:

a. [CAUSE (21)
   ([ACT$_{Loc}$(I, [ON$_{Loc}$(DRIVEWAY)], [BY <SHOVEL>])],
   [GO$_{Ident}$
   (DRIVEWAY,
   [TOWARD$_{Ident}$(DRIVEWAY, [AT$_{Ident}$(DRIVEWAY,
   [<CLEAN>$_{Ident}$])])])])]

b. [CAUSE

(I,
    [GO$_{Ident}$
    (DRIVEWAY,
        [TOWARD$_{Ident}$(DRIVEWAY, [AT$_{Ident}$(DRIVEWAY,
            [<CLEAN>$_{Ident}$])])])],
        [<WITH>$_{Instr}$(*HEAD*, <SHOVEL>)])]

Interestingly, the difference between the two translations is one of style; in Spanish, the first is much more awkward than the second.[34] Yet it is the first one that fits our translation scheme, in going from English to Spanish. Given that the parameterized scheme disallows the change-of-state resultative construction in Spanish, the syntactic realization of the first structure would result in the two-clause realization, "Traspalé el garaje para que esté limpio."

The second composed LCS, on the other hand, would never be the result of analysis of the original English sentence, "I shoveled the driveway clean." The question of whether we could view this alternate structure—which actually contains the main subcomponents of the first structure—as an adequate match for translation into Spanish depends heavily on whether it is possible to omit or redistribute different pieces of information based on the context of the sentence. For example, if one can determine from the setting of the sentence that the activity causing the clean state of the driveway involves a shovel, then perhaps this piece can either be dropped or moved into an instrumental position. Such an issue has been discussed at length by Slobin (1996), where English and Spanish are distinguished by their inclusion of context information. In fact, according to Slobin, Spanish translators often make changes that *reduce* the amount of information conveyed in the English sentence in order to produce the Spanish sentence. Currently, our system opts for the more awkward translation—as long as it is syntactically realizable—over a loss or redistribution of information in the final output. However, it is clear that, with a richer theory of context, we have enough machinery to generate a target language sentence that corresponds to the second structure rather than the first one.

Note, by contrast, that a translation in the other direction (from Spanish to English) would most likely involve the second structure as the source-language sentence since a native speaker typically would not start off with the more awkward choice. In this case, perhaps it would be reasonable to redistribute or even *augment* the information (if the instrument is omitted) in the interlingua in order to produce an English output. According to Slobin, English translators sometimes do add a bit of information, but in most cases, they follow the original Spanish sentence in producing the English sentence. This is fortunate for us because, as can be seen in the structures in example 21, it would be a simple task to map the first to the second, assuming the instrument can be dropped (since this would require reduction of information), but not the other way around (since this would require addition or redistribution of information). On the other hand, if we were to couple a rich theory of context with our rules of composition (which, for example, would allow change-of-state resultatives to be expressed in English), then we could perhaps identify cases where a more elaborate English sentence could be produced from a simpler composed LCS form.

The RLCS scheme described here has the added benefit that these very same structures are well-interfaced with the knowledge representation module as described in the next section.

The Interlingual–Knowledge Representation Interface

The previous section described the relation between the interlingua and the syntax, showing that the machine translation task is not hindered by taking a nonuniform approach to defining the representational languages at these two levels. This section further demonstrates this point by describing a systematic relation between the interlingua and the knowledge representation: the interlingual primitives in the interlingual forms are grounded as knowledge representation concepts, making deeper conceptual knowledge stored in the knowledge representation accessible in processing the interlingual forms. As above, we show that the division into levels is both linguistically motivated and applicable to diverse languages.

Here we present the interlingual/knowledge representation interface in terms of three machine translation system processing steps where the interlingual and knowledge representation "meet" at runtime: during interlingual filtering, interlingual composition in the analysis phase, and interlingual decomposition in the lexical selection of the generation phase. Our goal is to convey broadly the distinct range of issues that arise in defining the "meeting" at the interface in each of these steps. In the first subsection, we consider object-specific knowledge in the knowledge representation and its role in the filtering phase, eliminating interlingual forms that were composed during the analysis phase but that are incompatible with known spatial properties of objects. In the following subsection, we examine the role that event knowledge in the knowledge representation can play when interlingual composition fails during the analysis of the source language input. In the final subsection, we focus on the generation phase and the role of the knowledge representation system in holding the interlingual lexicon, a reverse index for retrieving lexical entries from target language lexicons.

For the examples in the first two subsections, the meeting of the inter-lingua and knowledge representation arises when the machine transla-tion system examines an interlingual primitive in an interlingual form (for example, in comparing two interlingual forms for type matching during interlingual composition) and then looks into the knowledge rep-resentation ontology for its grounded version of that primitive. In these cases, the leap, as it were, by the machine translation system from the in-terlingual primitive to the knowledge representation primitive may be done solely by looking up that term in the knowledge representation on-tology. There is no structured connection or link between the interlingual primitive in the interlingual form composed at runtime and the knowl-edge representation primitive with further knowledge about that inter-lingual primitive. By contrast, in the third subsection, the meeting of the interlingual and the knowledge representation primitives takes place within the knowledge representation system itself: the interlingual lexi-con, a structure accessing all lexical interlingual forms, or RLCSs, is con-structed as its own hierarchy within the knowledge representation sys-tem, enabling the primitives within those entries to be defined in terms of the knowledge representation primitives in the knowledge representation system's separate knowledge representation ontology.

Although we have placed the interlingual lexicon operationally within the knowledge representation system, as will be described below, we need to reiterate here that the interlingual and knowledge representation are, nonetheless, two distinct levels of representation. The syntax of the inter-lingual forms differs from that of expressions in the knowledge represen-tation system and the set of primitives in the interlingual forms is a proper subset of the concepts in the knowledge representation. We take the inter-lingual lexicon to be the lexicalization space of the machine translation system, delimiting the set of possible lexical interlingual forms. By con-trast, we take the knowledge representation ontology—a data structure in the knowledge representation component that is distinct from the interlin-gual lexicon—to be the concept space of the machine translation system, establishing the set of ontological terms in which the interlingual lexicon's primitives may be grounded. While all primitives in lexical interlingual forms correspond to knowledge representation concepts, not all knowl-edge representation concepts have a corresponding entry in the interlin-gual lexicon.

We should note that, not being the developers of the knowledge repre-sentation systems we have worked with, but rather knowledge represen-tation consumers, we found that, as our machine translation system evolved, so did our knowledge representation needs. Our initial choice for a knowledge representation system, PARKA, was adequate for the problems we tackled in the filtering phase and in the analysis phase during composition failures.[35] For the generation phase, however, we moved to LOOM with its more developed user interface, documentation, and its classifier, an option not available in the earlier system. At this point our work has taken the form of developing experimental knowledge representation ontologies in PARKA and LOOM, and most recently, the testing of the interlingual lexicon within LOOM.

During the Interlingual Filtering Phase

We make the assumption that object-specific knowledge, i.e., nonlinguistic information about physical objects in the real world, belongs at the conceptual level in the knowledge representation component of the machine translation system. Given this division of labor, here we will look at an example where object knowledge is used after the full interlingual form for the source language input has been composed.

First consider the translation of the following English sentence into German:

> English: The mouse ran under the table   (22)
> a. German: Die Maus ist unter dem Tisch gelaufen
>   "The mouse ran (about in the area) under the table."
>
> b. German: Die Maus ist unter den Tisch gelaufen
>   "The mouse ran (to a place somewhere) under the table."
>
> c. German: Die Maus ist unter dem Tisch durch gelaufen
>   "The mouse ran (past a place somewhere) under the table"

During sentence analysis, two syntactic structures are created, capturing the fact that the phrase under the table, can attach either as an adjunct (in case 22a) or as an argument (in cases 22b and 22c to the verb). At the semantic interpretation step, the analysis creates another split in the interpretation, differentiating between two senses of the PP argument as a PATH (cases 22b and 22c). From the three interlingual forms created in the analysis phase, the machine translation system then in the generation stage, outputs a distinct German sentence.

Now consider the translation of a slight variant on the English sentence:

> The mouse ran under the fence   (23)

The change from *table* to *fence* in sentence 23 does not alter the processing steps in the machine translation system's analysis phase from those described above for sentence 22. However, since the difference between tables and fences is only captured at the knowledge representation level in our system, it is consistent with our division of labor that the machine translation system should use this knowledge during its filtering phase when knowledge representation-based information is synthesized up through the interlingual form. In particular, the system must filter out the interpretations, paralleling cases 22a and 22b above, of the mouse running about in the area under the fence and the mouse running to a place under the fence.

The key to solving this problem is developing representations for tables and fences that are adequate for differentiating their prototypical spatial properties when it comes to motion of an object on a horizontal plane under them. Our first-pass approach to this problem was to use the feature-based notation developed by Jackendoff (1991). This choice was most attractive because the features were defined within his LCS framework and his examples provided clear starting points for our own test sentences. We were able to apply the feature system to capturing prototypical boundedness properties of physical objects, including tables and fences, and path types and places. Then, by extending the features as well as to physical motions, the features in the different knowledge representation concepts were available across the relevant interlingual types (THING, PATH, PLACE, and EVENT). Rules for synthesizing the features up through the interlingual forms were developed so that conflicting values signaled an invalid interlingual form that was not acceptable for translation. For example, the bounded 2-dimensional spatial relation of *under* type PLACE conflicted with the unbounded 1-dimensional schematization of a fence, in synthesizing the knowledge representation feature values grounding interlingual primitives in the interlingual predicate for *under the fence* in the PP adjunct analysis. With these adjustments, the filtering phase eliminated two of the three interpretations in the sentence 23 as needed.

This test effort also pointed out several limitations to the feature system in our task. We found it difficult to agree among ourselves on the features for an object independent of any spatial relation. For example, when coding the features we needed to designate one of the several schematizations of the object as primary. When we knew which spatial relation was going to be evaluated on that object, as was the case in our test work, the selection of the primary schema was straightforward. Without that information, our approach led only to an arbitrary ordering of one schema over another, an unsatisfactory engineering decision at best. Of equal concern was the restricted notation available in Jackendoff's approach to physical motion. In particular, while the features—developed for capturing linguistic aspect—differentiated bounded paths from unbounded ones, as in case 22b versus case 22c, they were not expressive enough to contrast the wider range of spatial motions, as found in the manner of motion and directed verb classes of Levin (1993).

Despite the limitations of this specific object representation system, the test experiment did show that filtering in our machine translation system based on knowledge representation-based object information was possible. With further work now underway in integrating natural language and vision research, the field of AI may provide us with a more adequate formalism in the near future for further testing our system.

During Interlingual Composition

When interlingual composition for a syntactic parse succeeds, the analysis phase is complete for that parse and the filtering phase begins. However, when the interlingual composition fails in certain well-defined ways on a particular interlingual form under construction, the machine translation system can recover the semantic interpretation by accessing information stored in knowledge representation concepts. This section looks at one such situation, when a type mismatch occurs between an adjunct and the site at which it attaches.

We make the assumption in the lexical interlingual forms, or RLCSs, for verbs that the type of the argument position(s) is coded on a verb-by-verb basis, but that the adjunct position is always of type PLACE. That is, in the interpretation of our interlingual forms, the adjunct position corresponds to the spatial location, or frame location, of the event represented by the verb. For example, in sentence 24, the PP *on the bed* may be attached as the verb's argument in which case the sentence refers to the specific manner of motion meaning in case 24a. When the PP is attached as the verb's adjunct, it may only have the static locational reading, paraphrasable as in case 24b.

The child jumped on the bed. (24)
a. The child jumped onto the bed.
b. The child was on the bed jumping (on it).

With the strict requirement that the adjunct phrases be of type PLACE, a noncanonical sentence such as sentence 25 will cause a type mismatch failure at the interlingual composition step.[36] The PP *through the tunnel* will be syntactically parsed as an adjunct because the lexical syntactic form for the verb *sleep* has no arguments and so, from the parser's point of view, it must be attached as an adjunct. When the interlingual composition step attempts to attach the PATH-typed interlingual form for this adjunct PP to the PLACE-typed adjunct position in *sleep's* interlingual form, a mismatch is detected. Indeed we find that, in German, this sentence cannot be translated literally. The spatial sense of *durch,* a German equivalent of *through,* is not acceptable as head of an adjunct phrase and so an alternate paraphrase is required.

a. English: She slept through the tunnel. (25)
b. German: Sie schlief waehrend sie durch den Tunnel ging.

"She slept while she through the tunnel went."

Operationally, the composition fails because the intransitive verb has no argument position and the PP "falls" into the adjunct position. But the general question concerns how to treat PATH interlingual forms when they appear in adjunct PLACE-typed positions. Note that sentence 25a is indeed grammatical and needs to be interpreted by the machine translation system. Furthermore, following our principle for division of labor, we have sought a solution to the processing of this noncanonical sentence that reflects the logical inferencing required for its interpretation. We have been guided in our solution to interpreting this sentence both by our interlingual syntax that permits factoring a verb's meaning into a predicator with a constant modifier and by the German translation of the sentence. Given a durative verb, i.e., one whose knowledge representation concept refers to a situation that lasts over some period of time, when encountering a PATH-typed adjunct spatial relation, the machine translation system may augment the interpretation of the sentence in order to recover the logically inferable spatial motion (here introduced in English by the PP). In particular, the subject's interlingual form and the PP's interlingual form are composed into a newly introduced GO_{Loc} general spatial motion interlingual form while the constant in the verb's interlingual form is attached as a modifier of the GO_{Loc} predicate.

The analysis here for sentence 25a contrasts with that of the sentence "the truck rumbled into the yard" given earlier in example 4. In both cases a directional PP appears following an intransitive verb (i.e., whose lexical syntactic form has no argument position available at which to attach the PP). The difference between the *sleep* and the *rumble* analyses is as follows. In the latter case we argue that the semantics of the verb's event entitles us to encode, as *lexically implicit,* both the sound and the motion within the single lexical form: the rumbling sound and the rumbling motion are necessarily concommitent within the same event. By contrast, in the former case, it is the knowledge representation-based properties of the verb's event that entitles us to *logically infer* when it is compatible with a concurrent motion event. We are able to capture this semantic distinction in the machine translation system by virtue of the separate levels of representation.

During Interlingual Decomposition

Once a full interlingual form for the source language input sentence has been analyzed and checked in the filtering phase, the machine translation system begins the first step in generating the target language output by determining the range of target language lexical interlingual forms that can cover the full interlingual form. In our approach using predicate decompositional structures for the interlingual level of representation, the full interlingual form is the guiding structure out of which lexical interlingual forms are extracted or decomposed. The lexical interlingual forms must then be found in the target language lexicon and the associated target language word (or phrase) can be retrieved. In this section we discuss our work building an indexing data structure for organizing the machine translation system's lexical interlingual forms and retrieving a target language entry given such a form.

Interlingual Lexicon: An Example

As an example of our approach, consider a small portion of an interlingual lexicon, as shown in figure 4, that consists of seven lexical-semantic forms (RLCS's without language-specific annotations) and their respective lexicalizations in English and German. (We have placed "****" in the figure where no word for the particular language exactly matches the forms listed.) The German words are *veranlassen, bewegen, transportieren,* and *fahren,* and the English words are *cause, move, transport,* and *bus.* Prior to translation runtime, the lexical entries are classified and the interlingual lexicon in figure 4 is produced. Note that, if we were to classify the three verbs used earlier in example 14 as part of this structure in figure 4, *lift* would be aligned with $[\text{CAUSE}(\_,[\text{GO}_{\text{Loc}}(\_,\_)])]$ and *ascend* and *climb* would be aligned with $[\text{GO}_{\text{Loc}}(\_,\_)]$.

The organization of the interlingual lexicon is guided by the syntax of the lexical interlingual forms held in the nodes of the data structure itself. Our goal here is to be able both to delimit the space of lexical interlingual forms available in the machine translation system(what was referred to above as the lexicalization space) and to efficiently retrieve lexical interlingual forms that correspond to the substructures found within a composed interlingual form.

With respect to the first goal of delimiting the lexicalization space, we have found this is critical to developing RLCSs for a new language to be added to the machine translation system. When a nonnative speaker of English begins building the RLCSs for lexical items in their native language, difficulties arise immediately as they attempt to understand the interlingual predicators that are given English labels. By having the interlingual predicators ground in the knowledge representation ontology, the deeper conceptual knowledge stored in the corresponding knowledge representation concept is also available as another source in defining the basic interlingual terms.

The second goal of retrieving lexicalized substructures for a given interlingual form is motivated by the decomposition task and the specific

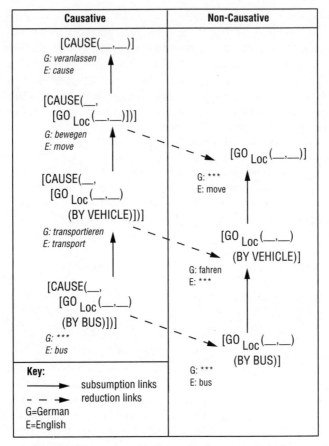

Figure 4. RLCS's with Directed Subsumption Links and Crossover Reduction Links in Semantic Ontology

way in which the interlingual forms are constructed and lexicalized. Here we will examine the structures of a few causative verbs and their noncausative counterparts to clarify this relation between the interlingual structures and the decomposition task.

Consider the verb *wash* in example 26.

a. The storm washed the ship ashore. (26)
b. The ship washed ashore.

The English verb *wash* has a causative reading in sentence 26a that is also conveyed in the paraphrase, "the storm caused the ship's being washed ashore." *Wash* also has a noncausative reading, as in sentence 26b. From this minimal pair, it is clear that the lexical semantics of this noncausative sense is contained within the lexical semantics of the causative sense. In the predicate decompositional form of our interlingual, this semantic containment relationship is captured by having the lexical interlingual form of the noncausative sense as a substructure in the lexical interlingual form of the causative sense.

Now consider this relation as represented in the interlingual lexicon: a *reduction link* connects the lexical interlingual form of a causative form to its noncausative counterpart. This type of link is used in the interlingual decomposition process when no causative form can be found in the target language lexicon. By following a reduction link, the search algorithm in the decomposition process will seek an alternate translation using the noncausative form together with a lexicalization for the cause predicate. In figure 4, the reduction links (dashed arrows) run from left to right, connecting individual entries in the column of lexical interlingual forms for causative verbs with their noncausative counterparts.

Figure 4 also contains a second type of link relevant to the interlingual decomposition process, *subsumption links* shown by solid arrows. For example, the interlingual form for the English word *move* (in the left-hand column, this refers to externally caused motion) stands in a subsumption relation with (i.e., is more specific than) the English word *cause*. On the other hand, the RLCS for the English word *move* (left-hand column) stands in a reduction relation with its noncausative English counterpart *move* (right-hand column, this refers to motion that is not externally caused or whose actual cause is linguistically unspecified). This latter link is nonstandard as knowledge representation schemes go—in fact, the left-hand *move* is neither more specific nor more general than the right-hand *move*; rather, there is the linguistically-relevant structural relation between the causative and noncausative interlingual forms of the same verb that is logically distinct from subsumption relations. The causative interlingual form will contain substructures corresponding to its causing and its resulting subevents. Thus, the reduction links serve to partition verbal meaning into subcomponents where each part has its meaning preserved. The subsumption links lead to structures that have a narrower, more specific sense than their subsumers and that bear a well-defined structural relation to those of their subsumers. While these links do not preserve meaning subcomponents, by virtue of their structural relation, they provide another search path for the decomposition algorithm to follow and an alternative resource in lexicalizing an interlingual form.

Recall from the translation mismatches subsection that there are three mismatch cases between source language and target language words that we are attempting to handle: subsumes, subsumed-by, and overlapping.[37]

Consider the case of translating from English to German. In figure 4 in the RHS column, we can see first that the noncausative English verb *bus* has no German lexical equivalent. However, since German does have a slightly more general noncausative verb *fahren*, the translation algorithm can opt for a *subsumes relation* to resolve the mismatch and select *fahren* as the translation of *bus*. Suffice it to say here that the selected verb, *fahren* becomes the head of the target language phrase and the information dropped in the move up the ontological hierarchy (from noncausative *bus* to *fahren*) becomes the restrictive modifier phrase to that head. (The information for the phrase is readily identifiable from a structural comparison between subsumer and subsumee.) This procedure is the verb phrase analog to the approach taken by Sondheimer, Cumming, and Albano (1990) with noun phrases. The translations for the sentences in example 27 show the result of this procedure. As with *bus*, translating the noncausative verb *train* to German also requires using a combination of partial matches with German words to achieve the full coverage matching of the English verb's interlingual form: a subsuming verb becomes the main verb, *fahren,* and a modifier phrase, *mit dem Zug,* restricts the sense of the more general subsuming verb.[38]

    a. They bused into town.   (27)
    b. Sie fuhren mit dem Autobus in die Stadt.
       "They vehicled by bus into town"

    a. They trained into town.   (28)
    b. Sie fuhren mit dem Zug in die Stadt.
       "They vehicled by train into town"

A subsumes relation is not always available to resolve lexicalization gap mismatches. The noncausative English verbs *go* and *move* are very general and do not exist as a simple lexical entry in German.[39] At that level in the ontology, there is no more general noncausative concept to tap for the translation. For example, in sentence 29, the common English verb *go* is translated into the German equivalent of *run, laufen,* a verb whose sense is subsumed by that of *go.* That is, in this case the selection algorithm must opt for a subsumes-by relation by translating the source language word as a target language word that is lower down in the ontology. In translating verbs, this selection depends crucially on finding a target language verb whose constraints are met by both the source language verb and its arguments.

    a. Because of the dog, the cat went away.   (29)
    b. Wegen dem Hund lief die Katze weg.
       "Because of the dog, ran the cat away"

Finally an *overlap relation* occurs in translating the causative English verb *bus* where again we find no corresponding German lexical entry in the ontology, as in sentence 30. One option needed for translating this verb in a formal style of speech (such as in a legal document) involves decomposing its meaning into the comparable phrase "to cause to go by bus." While the cause concept (for *veranlassen*) subsumes that of the causative *bus,* a reduction link relation (see lowest dashed arrow in figure 4)—not a subsumption relation is needed to capture *go by bus.*[40]

a. The man bussed the animals to the zoo.   (30)
b. Der Mann veranlasste, dass die Tiere mit den Bus zum Zoo gefahren wurden.
  "The man caused/made (that) the animals by bus to the zoo vehicled were"

Sketch of Lexical Selection Algorithm

We now describe our lexical selection algorithm. The role of this algorithm is to return the target language (target language) lexical entries whose interlingual forms cover the interlingual form submitted as input.[41] A key point about the algorithm is that the classifier, which is used prior to processing time, is also a main driving component of the lexical selection scheme in the Lookup step.

The details are given here:

Input Interlingual Form Lookup: Search the interlingual lexicon on the basis of the algorithm's input: a composed interlingual form (i.e., the composed LCS of Dorr, [1993]) or part thereof, in order to determine its hierarchical position. If no corresponding form is found, return to calling program (input is not a syntactically valid lexical interlingual form).

RLCS Retrieval: Retrieve, from the target language lexicon, instances of target language words indexed from the current entry, i.e., interlingual lexicon entry in current hierarchical position.

Match Detection: If there exists one or more target language RLCS for the current entry, return the associated target language lexical items(s) and entry form.

Overlapping Case: In the absence of an exact match, first follow a reduction link, if available,[42] to a substructure entry and then follow subsumption link to a root entry.[43] If the substructure entry has target language RLCS, return the root and substructure target language RLCSs and entries. If the substructure entry does not have a target language RLCS, return the root RLCS and entry and then recursively call this algorithm with the substructure entry as input.

Familial Information Return: In the absence of structural coverage (the match or overlap cases above), return, where available, the ontological parent (subsumer) and list of ontological children (subsumed-by) and current entry.

Note that the overlap reduction has a higher standing than subsumption. This is because our research goal has been to experiment with retrieving the fullest possible exact structural coverage of the interlingual input; if we attempt subsumption before reduction, the calling process must derive the structural difference between the interlingual forms of the subsumer or subsumee and the current entry, and then generate the modifying phrase that best approximates a structural cover—and the reduction option will never be reached. Nothing in principal however preempts revising the algorithm to run both the reduction and subsumption options. This adds to the set of lexicalization options available at the next processing stage in the generation phase.

Implementation and Related Approaches

We have implemented this approach in LOOM (MacGregor 1991), a KL-ONE-like term classifier and its concept definitions. (Other details are given in Dorr et al., [1994].) LOOM and other frame-based systems (for example, KL-ONE and knowledge representation) have also been used by a number of other researchers, including Brachman and Schmolze (1985), MacGregor (1991), Woods and Brachman (1978). As mentioned above, our goal in developing the interlingual lexicon in LOOM was to test the feasibility of having this data structure within a knowledge representation system with a classifier where the interlingual primitives in the interlingual lexicon entries would also be established as concepts in the knowledge representation system's ontology, maintaining the consistency in the grounded terms at the interlingual/knowledge representation interface. As part of this feasibility experiment, we built only a small knowledge representation ontology for the purposes of supporting the primitives in the interlingual lexicon and the inferences in the composition and filtering phases.

Our approach is similar to the approach of DiMarco, Hirst, and Stede (1993), which also uses the LOOM classifier, but with the complementary goal of handling fine-grained, stylistic variations. There are also similarities between our approach and that of Nirenburg et al. (1992), in that we seek a single unifying data structure to establish a range of semantic relations among words.[44] Because our primary focus is on the development of the interlingua and the interlingual lexicon, our knowledge representation entries are driven by our lexicalization needs and the interlingual primitives in the interlingual syntax. (By contrast, in many large-scale knowledge-base machine translation projects, the knowledge-base concepts in the large ontologies drive the definitions of lexical entries.)

Alternative knowledge representation formalisms have been explored by a number of researchers including Wu and Palmer (1994), Palmer and Wu (1995), Ali and Shapiro (1993), Iwańska (1993), Quantz and Schmitz (1994), Schubert (1991), Sowa (1991). In the approach of Wu and Palmer (1994) and Palmer and Wu (1995), lexical mismatches are resolved through the use of a conceptual lattice based on an adapted version of Levin (1993). While this approach is similar in spirit to our method of mismatch resolution, Palmer and Wu propose an approximate matching scheme based on semantic closeness as determined by numerical distances between semantic classes, whereas our scheme relies on a full structural coverage matching as determined by alignment among lexical-semantic components that systematically map into syntactic structure. We argued in the section defining an interlingua that we must necessarily preserve substructure information (i.e., LCS descriptions) in order to provide an adequate translation into a target language surface structure; thus, a numerical measure of semantic closeness would not be adequate for our purposes. Moreover, the structural coverage matching scheme is a prerequisite for recursive instantiation of substructures that are not necessarily aligned with the full structure of the interlingual during the translation process. We have already seen examples of such cases the interlingua lexicon example subsection. Finally, the classification system of Levin (1993) has been refined in later work (Levin and Rappaport-Hovav 1995a; Levin and Rappaport-Hovav 1995b), where regularities in lexical representations—and the (parameterized) rules that operate on these representations—can be exploited for a more economical approach to machine translation. We saw several cases where we could benefit from this economy in the syntax or interlingua interface section. Such regularities would be lost if we were to adopt a numerical closest match scheme.

Other approaches have different objectives or address deeper conceptual issues. One example out of many is the work of Iwańska (1993), which is concerned with notions such as logical inferences, entailment, negation, and quantification. The primary concern in Iwańska's work is the population of a knowledge base and the provision of a framework for truth maintenance and queries. While this work has certain elements in common with our approach (for example, the representation of entailment, which is similar to our notion of classification), the framework is more applicable to a discourse analysis system than to the problem of mismatch handling in machine translation.

Conclusions

We have described a nonuniform approach to interlingual machine translation, in which distinct representational languages are used for different types of knowledge. The key contribution of this work is that it provides a linguistically-motivated "division of labor" across multiple representation levels. We have shown that this multilevel approach has not complicated, but rather has readily facilitated, the identification and construction of systematic relations at the interface between each level.

The novelty of our approach is that the interlingual representation is designed to preserve the semantic structure of the source language and target language sentences while still retaining the semantic content by means of conceptually grounded primitives. The preservation of semantic structure allows us to readily map between the interlingua and the syntax; the preservation of semantic content allows us to readily map between the interlingua and knowledge representation. Approaches that ignore the structural nature of lexical items and their combination stand to lose the benefit of regularities that exist within a language (in the lexicon) as well across languages (in the surface syntactic form). By decomposing verbs into predicate structure and nonpredicate constants, we exploit such regularities.

We have cited examples from the spatial domain in support of our nonuniform representational approach, and we have demonstrated the cross-linguistic applicability of the multi-level machine translation design in this domain. We have implemented this design in the PRINCITRAN system, which handles a wide range of cross-linguistic mismatches. Areas of future investigation include development of a framework for handling multiple sentences; in particular, a rich theory of context coupled with our rules of composition might allow us to identify cases where the interlingual underlying the source language sentence must be either reduced or augmented in order to produce an appropriate target language sentence.

Notes

1. Throughout this chapter source language and target language lexicons will refer to the natural language-specific lexicons of the machine translation system that include interlingual forms. These lexicons are also accessed for their syntactic structures. For further details about the syntactic processing mechanism, see Dorr, Lin, Lee, and Suh (1995).

2. Note that the French translation "l'église est au sud de la ville" has the same ambiguity. For readers not versed in German or French, consider the ambiguity in English: "he drove to the south of the city" has distinct readings for south-and-internal corresponding to the southern region of the city and south-and-external corresponding to the region south of the city. We will not address here the problem of lexical allocation, i.e., determining whether to allocate the ambiguity lexically to *Süden* or *in dem* in the phrase.

3. Thus, we keep the fine-grained semantic distinctions that are specific to particular languages and poorly motivated by conceptual categories, separate from the interlingual level of representation. We hold the view that a mapping from all possible lexical semantic distinctions, fine-grained and otherwise, to the conceptual categories of the knowledge representation amounts to a strong version of the Whorfian hypothesis and, thus, we reject the notion of such a mapping.

4. We take the term *zero-related verb* from Levin (1993) for verbs either derived from nouns or out of which nouns have been derived.

5. Some of these examples are taken from related work by DiMarco, Hirst, and Stede (1993). Their research addresses many of the same questions we are examining.

6. To give the reader a sense of what these knowledge representation level mismatches entail, consider the case of how the British, Swiss French and Swiss Germans lexicalize the same transaction during a bus ride: *punch the ticket, validate the ticket,* and *invalidate the ticket* (Kay, Gawron, and Norvig 1994). Each focuses on a different aspect of the overall transaction, one on the action itself (the punching), one on the state of the ticket during the ride (a valid ticket), and one on the state of the ticket after the ride (an invalid ticket). These are more properly labeled transaction-focus knowledge representation mismatches.

7. A reviewer points out that many vehicle names do not have zero-related verbs, such as *car, truck,* and *fiacre,* etc. We are not assuming that all vehicles names have a verbal counterpart; rather, our intention is to cover the cases where a zero-related verbal counterpart does exist. Note that the class of such verbs is larger than one might expect: *balloon, bicycle, bike, boat, bobsled, bus, cab, canoe, caravan, chariot, coach, cycle, dogsled, ferry, gondola, helicopter, jeep, jet, kayak, moped, motor, motorbike, motorcycle, parachute, punt, raft, rickshaw, rocket, ship, skate, skateboard, ski, sled, sledge, sleigh, taxi, toboggan, tram, trolley, yacht,* and so forth.

8. It has been argued in fuller detail elsewhere that these three relations span the full range of possible meaning mismatches (Barnett et al. 1994).

9. By allowing a combination of target language words to be generated, we account for compounds such as *lift up, climb down,* etc.

10. These examples are taken from Levin and Rappaport-Hovav (1995a). For other examples, also see the extensive discussions in Talmy (1983, 1985).

11. We discuss our use of the terms lexically implicit and lexically explicit further in the next subsection.

12. We use *word* here to refer to lexicon entry "names."

13. The words in capital letters refer to the spatial relation, i.e., the abstract term.

14. See Dorr (1993) for details of a machine translation system whose interlingual is LCS-derived. Recently the LCS framework has been used by others for French, for example, Pugeault, Saint-Dizier, and Monteil (1994) and Verrière (1994).

15. Given that the ontological type is uniquely determined by the name of the primitive predicator, examples in later sections use a short-hand notation where the type is omitted.

16. If the second argument is a means/manner by-phrase, it is still possible to instantiate a directional path in the interlingual representation, although this would not appear in the verb's lexical entry. We will clarify this point further shortly.

17. If we dig a bit deeper into the reasons behind the difficulty of using the conceptual dependency representation as an interlingua, we find that the fundamental problem is that the conceptual dependency framework subscribes to the notion that every imaginable component of meaning must be captured in a single representational formalism. Indeed, the conceptual dependency formalism is one of the most developed representations in the field of AI, with care given to including information beyond the scope of the LCS formalism, (for example, concerning short-term and long-term memory). However, the conceptual dependency approach pays a high price for incorporating deeper knowledge in a single representation without preserving structurally defined information. In addition to missing linguistic generalization in the interlingual-syntax mapping, the conceptual dependency representa-

tion is difficult to bound: the decomposition process on which it is based may lead to deep recursion. As noted by Schank himself (1973, p. 201), this is particularly a problem with instrumentality: "If every ACT requires an instrumental case which itself contains an ACT, it should be obvious that we can never finish diagramming a given conceptualization. For [the] sentence [John ate the ice cream with a spoon], for example, we might have "John ingested the ice cream by transing the ice cream on a spoon to his mouth, by transing the spoon to the ice cream, by grasping the spoon, by moving his hand to the spoon, by moving his hand muscles, by thinking about moving his hand muscles," and so on."

18. He points this out explicitly in response to criticism from some in the computational linguistic community.

19. The name lexical semantic template is taken from Levin and Rappaport-Hovav (1995a, p. 24).

20. While *march* may appear in an indefinite number of distinct semantic contexts, here we are only distinguishing among its structural frames for which there are syntactic diagnostics.

21. The primitive ACT has been borrowed from the lexical semantic template framework in order to characterize certain activities (such as *shovel*) which could not be adequately characterized by Jackendoff's GO primitive. In his more recent LCS specification, Jackendoff (1990) augments the thematic tier of his earlier work (1983) with an action tier which serves to characterize activities using additional machinery. We choose to simplify this characterization by using the ACT primitive rather than introducing yet another level of representation.

22. Note that the constant is not always identified by the word itself, but by some form that is semantically related to the verb.

23. To simplify the discussion here, we have restricted our examples to verb senses that fall into one of the two categories, either result or means/manner. There are also some verbs that have both elements of meaning, such as *cut*.

24. Occasionally it is possible for a result verb to participate in a resultative construction, but only if the result phrase further specifies the verb's inherent result as in "I drained the tub dry." In such noncanonical examples, we would expect human judgments to vary with respect to grammaticality.

25. For the purpose of this discussion, we restrict our attention in these templates to non-stative verbs. States, however, are also allowed through the use of the BE situation-level predicator. The *HEAD* symbol is a place-holder that points to the root, event-level node of the overall lexical entry. Modifiers, such as instrumental phrases, typically include this symbol. See Dorr (1993) for more details of this notation.

26. Templates 13a(iii) and 13b(ii) are not included in table 2; examples of these will be given in the Information Allocation in RLCS-Based Lexicon section.

27. Levin's classes are labeled with numbers ranging from 9 to 57. However, the actual number of semantic classes is 192 (not 46) due to many class subdivisions under each major class.

28. By non-Levin verbs, we mean verbs or individual verb senses that do not appear in Levin (1993).

29. These are cross-referenced with the corresponding templates from (13).

30. For a more detailed examination of the computational lexical semantics of *up* in English and Turkish, see Voss, Dorr, and Sencan (1995).

31. If the target language were German, for either a *lift* or *lift up* source language input,

there would be a *heben/anheben* choice (where the German prefix an corresponds loosely to the English *up* in this case). For *climb* with direct object in the source language input, there would be a *steigen/aufsteigen* choice (among a few others). And finally for an *ascend* source language input, there would be a *steigen/ersteigen* choice (among possibly a few others). These choices correspond to the lexical synonymy case in figure 3.

32. A reviewer points out that one needs to allow for different verb-particle realizations: (a) *John climbed/ascended the rope.* (b) *John climbed/*ascended up the rope.* The mechanism that achieves this distinction lexically is the star-marker, described in (Dorr 1993). The star-marked constituents would be <LIFT> in 15a and UP_{Loc} in example 15c. By contrast, the UP_{Loc} would not be star-marked in example 15b.

33. For example, the target language discourse may be informal and call for a *go up* in lieu of an *ascend*.

34. We have been informed by native speakers that climate differences make shoveling a driveway a rarity in many Spanish-speaking countries. Thus, the second sentence is also somewhat awkward, but for different reasons; the same sentence with the word *broom* (instead of *shovel*) is much more natural sounding.

35. PARKA is a research knowledge representation system under development at the University of Maryland.

36. This sentence often causes readers, on a first reading, to pause. Had the sentence been about sleeping through the night, i.e., had the word *through* been used in a strictly temporal sense rather than as in (25)(i), the reading would have been unproblematic. It appears, though we have seen no psycholinguistic research on this, that the *through* phrase in sentence (25)(i) requires some extra processing by readers and they are aware of this.

37. We note briefly here that without a mismatch, the runtime processing is straightforward. Consider the translation of the German word *bewegen* into the English word *move*. First the RLCS for the German word is retrieved and composed with other sentence elements to form the full interlingual form in the analysis phase. Then, during generation, the same term classifier that placed RLCSs (lexical interlingual forms) for English and German entries into the interlingual lexicon pre-runtime, now determines where the relevant portion of the full interlingual form falls among the English RLCSs in the interlingual lexicon. Since *bewegen* is synonymous with one sense of the word *move,* the classifier will match that portion of the composed interlingual form with the RLCS entry for that synonymous sense; this will then be realized in English as *move*.

38. Not all speakers of English accept verbs of this form. As with all acceptability judgements, we find variation among native speakers. Once a word such as *bus* is listed in the dictionary (here Webster's Ninth), as a transitive verb along with both definitions "to travel by bus" and "to transport by bus", i.e., precisely the noncausative and causative readings, then we treat it as acceptable.

39. German *sich bewegen* is the closest, nonsimple equivalent to the noncausative English *move*.

40. The careful reader will note both within a language and cross-linguistically, that in general, when paraphrasing a single verb with a periphrastic, or multiple word expression, some subtle event-level changes in meaning will occur.

41. The task of identifying the input interlingual form is based on the fully composed interlingual form for the source language input and is carried out by a lexical options generator that calls this algorithm.

42. If no reduction link is available, the overlap case does not apply.

43. *Substructure entry* refers to the interlingual lexicon entry at the end of the reduction link and *root entry* refers to the interlingual lexicon entry for the root predicate of the current entry. All root predicate entries in the interlingual lexicon have target language RLCSs.

44. Strictly speaking, the lexicons in interlingua-based machine translation systems are not restricted to word-level entries. For the purposes of this chapter however we will refer to "words" in the lexicons, setting aside the details about other types of lexical entries. See (Levin and Nirenburg 1993) for further discussion on extending the range of lexical entries in machine translation systems.

7 Uniform Natural (Language) Spatio-Temporal Logic

Reasoning about Absolute and Relative Space and Time

Łucja M. Iwańska

VIRTUALLY ALL REAL-LIFE PROBLEMS involve handling spatio-temporal information. In this chapter, I will show that reasoning about time and space is a problem in which natural language general reasoning capabilities mix in a very interesting way with the capabilities specific to understanding space and time. Time and space are objects whose properties can be expressed and reasoned about via natural language in many ways analogous to reasoning about other objects.

In this chapter, I discuss many English temporal expressions that illustrate the complexity of the general spatio-temporal reasoning. I show how these examples are handled by my theory and implementing it natural language processing system in order to substantiate my main claims that spatio-temporal reasoning can be handled by a natural language logic, and the UNO model is a novel spatio-temporal reasoner.

I have tried to make this chapter as self-contained as possible, without overloading the discussion with too many formal details reported elsewhere; for example, I do not discuss full technical details of the UNO model—my rather complete spatio-temporal grammar and translating English utterances into the UNO representation; I provide only some details of the inferencing algorithm; chapter one provides further details and includes references to the publications containing full formal definitions, constructions, and proofs of the mathematical and computational properties of the UNO model.

Throughout this chapter, the expressions UNO system and system are deliberately ambiguous between the formal, computational UNO model of natural language with its proven set-theoretic and interval-theoretic semantics, and its implementation, the UNO natural language processing system.

This chapter is organized as follows. The first section briefly discusses a uniform approach to many types of knowledge. The second section then discusses my spatio-temporal reasoner. The third section briefly presents my framework for natural language processing, and contrasts it with some existing frameworks; the fourth section discusses natural language inherent reasoning about time and space, including context-independent and context-dependent processing of spatio-temporal information; The fifth section discusses time-specific knowledge and inference, including some spatio-temporal taxonomies; The sixth section sketches my ongoing and future work; The last section sums up the chapter and provides some concluding remarks.

Uniform Approach to Handling Many Types of Knowledge

Lenat and Guha (1990a) and Davis (1990) argue that a designer of a general-purpose knowledge representation system capable of handling large knowledge bases and supporting taxonomic, deductive, nonmonotonic, probabilistic, temporal, commonsense and other inference does not really have a choice, but to chose a uniform representational language. They point out that given the requirement that the representation have clean semantics and be computationally efficient, this choice basically boils down to some version of the first-order predicate logic, typically quite restricted. Often sacrificed aspects of the expressiveness general negation, general disjunction, and generalized quantifiers other than those involving determiners *some* and *every*. Specifically for spatio-temporal reasoning, Guha and Lenat argue that specialized representations and inference schemas for capturing only a particular aspect of spatio-temporal reasoning, and not relating it to handling the other types of knowledge and inference, are not very useful for a designer of a general knowledge representation system.

Natural Language-like Representational Language

In the course of my research and development, I reached the same conclusion—that the uniformity of the representational language is both theoretically and practically critical. My research results advocate a uniform approach for a number of types of knowledge and reasonings that were previously believed to be involving different representational languages. First, while addressing the problem of representing and reasoning with explicit negative information in natural language utterances, I have proposed a Boolean algebra framework for natural language processing, the UNO model of natural language (Iwańska 1992b, 1992a, 1993); it is also discussed in chapter 1 of this book. This model closely simulates representational and inferential characteristics of natural language. In its handling of negation, it surpasses all knowledge representation and reasoning systems available then and today. For the phenomena and the subset of natural language that were considered, this model demonstrates that in order to account for meaning and licensed inferences of natural language utterances, one does not need different representational languages.

Taxonomic Reasoning

My natural languagelike mechanism for taxonomic reasoning is based on the UNO model capability of handling adjectival, adverbial and Boolean modifications of common nouns and verbs. Its distinct features are flat, context-dependent taxonomies, which tremendously facilitates maintenance of large knowledge bases. Taxonomies are flat because only relations between lexically simple items such as the relation between the type *dog* and *animal* need to represented. Complex types such as *dog or cat, dog and not cat, very small dog with long hair* do not need to be explicitly stored in a knowledge base; subsumption relation between arbitrary types, simple and complex, is computed directly from their representation. Proven mathematical and computational properties of the UNO representation and its Boolean operations guarantee computing correct subsumption relation. Taxonomies are context-dependent because the model allows one to define arbitrary types. For example, for Mark, *rusty engines, Teddy bears,* and *the smell of wild roses* may form a coherent type (class) because all these things remind him of his childhood. For him, and most likely only for him, there is a close relationship between the concept of *childhood* and these things.

Spatio-Temporal Reasoning

Second, I extended the UNO model to handle temporal reasoning (Iwańska 1996). I have produced some further evidence that the choice of the representational language for a general knowledge representation and reasoning system should not be some version of the first-order predicate logic, but a natural language logic, a logic that I believe underlies natural language. I have also demonstrated that so-called in-depth reasoning, for example, spatio-temporal reasoning with negative and disjunctive information, can be accomplished for a large number of real-life textual documents without performing sentential-level parsing.

In this chapter, I present my unified natural language-based spatio-temporal reasoner. The generality of my theoretical and practical results is largely assured by the methodology of designing and testing the algorithms on large-scale, real-life independently produced data.

We collected several hundreds of real-life English examples from the UNO corpora, including *Wall Street Journal* corpus and *Time Magazine* corpus. We marked all the occurrences of explicit spatial and temporal expressions with the SGMLlike <te> and </te> tags for temporal expressions and <se>, and </se> tags for spatial expressions. For example, consider the following original two-paragraph fragment in the 891005-0059 *Wall Street Journal* document:

> Mr. Montgomery was ousted a few weeks later by Mr. Talmo, who is the bank's controlling shareholder, and replaced by Palm Beach investor John E. Nicolo. Then, Mr. Nicolo quit shortly afterward to make room for William W. Landa, a Miami real estate developer. Last month, Mr. Billmeyer resigned after only nine months as president.

> The bank agreed to a first administrative order in late 1987, after the bank began suffering big losses under Mr. Talmo's much-criticized policies toward investing in big real estate ventures. The bank tried changing its strategy to a more traditional, conservative operating mode, but was unable to stem the losses. Its stock has plummeted from a high of about 15 in 1986 to a low of about 87.5 cents earlier this year.

When marked, the resulting document is as follows:

> Mr. Montgomery was ousted <te> a few weeks later</te> by Mr. Talmo, who is the bank's controlling shareholder, and replaced by <le>Palm Beach</le> investor John E. Nicolo. <te>Then</te>, Mr. Nicolo quit <te>shortly afterward</te> to make room for William W. Landa, a <le>Miami</le> real estate developer. <te>Last month</te>, Mr. Billmeyer resigned <te>after only nine months</te> as president.

> The bank agreed to a first administrative order <te>in late 1987</te>, <te>after</te> the bank began suffering big losses under Mr. Talmo's much-criticized policies toward investing in big real estate ventures. The bank tried changing its strategy to a more traditional, conservative operating mode, but was unable to stem the losses. Its stock has plummeted from a high of about 15 <te>in 1986</te> to a low of about 87.5 cents <te>earlier this year</te>.

I also consulted other sources such as medical records, magazines, novels, excerpts from books, transcripts of various dialogs, and reference materials on English grammar; categorized the collected examples and developed two comprehensive grammars: temporal and spatial. I have also hand-encoded in my uniform UNO representation a semantic hierarchy of geographical knowledge, for which some aspects of geographical reasoning (such as region containment) are supported with its general inferencing mechanism. This extensive geographical knowledge base contains major geographical information about all countries, including capital cities, major and important cities, towns, ports, geographical and political regions that divide land such as provinces, islands, major ports and airports, landmarks, monetary, length, area, and volume systems, official languages, major political organizations, waters such as oceans, seas, lakes, and rivers, and geographical landmarks and points of interest such as mountains, hills, woods, and national parks.

The grammars and the geographical hierarchy allow my natural language processing system to extract spatial and temporal expressions from arbitrary unmarked texts.

I analyzed all the examples collected with respect to their information content and licensed inferences. Part of this analysis consisted of generating by hand plausible spatio-temporal queries to the sentences in which the expressions occurred.

Originally, I had planned to accomplish the extension of my UNO model by incorporating an existing spatial reasoner and temporal reasoner. However, after a close examination of the collected examples, I came to three conclusions.

1. I could find no existing theoretical or implemented spatio-temporal reasoner that is capable of supporting the space-time-related inferences these examples illustrated.

2. Temporal reasoning is a problem of natural language because virtually all its important aspects can be accomplished by a general, natural language inherent representation and inference mechanism. Temporal reasoning reveals previously unknown representational and inferential strengths of natural language.

3. Spatial reasoning is only partially a problem of natural language because only some of its important aspects can be accomplished by natural languagelike reasoning. Spatial reasoning demonstrates representational and inferential limitations of natural language for handling all aspects of spatial reasoning.

The Computational Nature of Natural Language

Many questions about a computational nature of natural language remain widely open, including the following four: (1) Is natural language algorithmic? (2) Can natural language be considered a formal language and, if so, what is its computational complexity? (3) What is its computational complexity? (4) What is the relation between a representation of the meaning of natural language utterances and the semantics of a representational language capturing general human knowledge? Should they be the same or different?

In the course of developing my UNO model of natural language, I have produced a number of pieces of evidence that support my answers to these questions: *Definitely yes* to the first question; *yes, and it appears quite tractable* to the second and third questions; and *they should be the same* to the third and fourth one.

My model of natural language can be viewed as a knowledge representation system closely resembling natural language in terms of representation and inference. The advantages of such a natural language-based knowledge representation system are enormous and widely acknowledged: the ease of use because people express, share, and acquire new knowledge through natural language, the need for an easy to use interface eliminated, hard to match expressiveness and precision of natural language, particularly in not well formalized domains, and a close resemblance of commonsense reasoning concepts to natural language form.

I believe that my research provides a strong piece of evidence that natural language-based knowledge representation systems are theoretically and practically realistic, that natural language does not merely interface some knowledge representation system, but is a knowledge representation system with its own representational and reasoning mechanism. My research partially substantiates a claim that there is a logic behind natural language, a logic that appears quite, but not entirely, different from first-order predicate logic. I argue that the mathematical and computational properties of this natural language logic need to be further studied. I believe that such theoretically and computationally sound natural language logics like mine offer a designer of a general-purpose knowledge representation system a new, exciting spectrum of choices of the representational language.

Spatio-Temporal Reasoner, Natural Language Style

My spatio-temporal reasoner automatically extracts explicit temporal expressions from on-line textual documents and creates their representation. This representation allows the natural language processing system to compute entailed logical, context-independent, deductive inferences and facilitates computing context-dependent, nonmonotonic inferences, including implicature, specialization, and generalization.

For any set of English spatio-temporal expressions, their information content can be computed and compared, which allows the system to compute answers to the yes-no questions about various aspects of space and time, answers to the *when? where? how far? how long?* and *how often?* queries of the resulting knowledge base, and spatio-temporal relations described in the documents.

Logical inferences capture knowledge and information that virtually all people gain after reading such textual documents. Computing logical entailments allows my natural language processing system to compute answers to all kinds of questions that people can answer after reading the same document. Implicatures and other nonmonotonic inferences capture those additional aspects of knowledge and information that some people in certain contexts may understand or try to convey. Computing some nonmonotonic inferences allows my natural language system to compute answers to additional questions.

Novel Characteristics

My spatio-temporal reasoner is novel in a number of important ways, which I will discuss in the following subsections.

Uniform Representation, Inference, and Architecture for Spatio-Temporal and Nonspatio-Temporal Reasoning

I demonstrate that important inferences about space and time can be handled by a general representation and inference mechanism inherent in natural language. This quite unexpected, interesting result shows a complicated nature of the natural language versus mind division of reasoning labor, and demonstrates that more representational and reasoning power is "built into" natural language than previously believed.

The practical significance of this result is a simple architecture with a uniform representation and inference for both spatio-temporal and non-spatio-temporal reasoning. For example, spatio-temporal and nonspatio-temporal taxonomies are represented and reasoned with uniformly.

Natural Expressiveness

The spatio-temporal reasoner allows one to automatically represent and compute absolute and relative informativeness of a wide spectrum of English spatio-temporal expressions describing various aspects of space and time. Like Kahn and Gorry (1977) and Allen (1983 1984), I strive to account for the spatio-temporal information conveyed through natural language.

Negative and Disjunctive Information, Uncertainty

I account for understanding and reasoning with information from arbitrary Boolean temporal expressions involving explicit *and, or, not* at different syntactic levels such as *not very often; not very close; not in the immediate future; and it did not happen far from here.*

I am not aware of a spatio-temporal reasoner capable of handling general case of explicit negative information. Representing and reasoning with explicit negation in a semantically clean fashion is a fairly unique characteristic of my model. Limited forms of negation have been addressed by a number of researchers, including Allen (1983), Beek (1992), and Hwang and Schubert (1993).

Temporal reasoners often inherit problems with negation from the assumed representation. For example, Dean and McDermott (1987) implemented their temporal reasoner in Prolog (Sterling and Shapiro 1986), which allows them to represent propositional (sentential) negation only and offers, lacking semantics, negation as failure. A number of temporal reasoners are capable of handling disjunctive information, usually in limited forms (Allen 1983; Shoham 1987; Beek 1988; Schrag, Buddy, and Carciofini 1992; Gerevini and Schubert 1993).

For the texts and domains I considered, I could not justify the typical idealization of eliminating processing general negative or disjunctive information. It is simply a fact of life that people's knowledge is incomplete and uncertain, even when critical for assessing and treating their own health problems. People often do not exactly remember when an event or a situation took place, but often remember that it did not take place during certain time intervals such as holidays or important events.

Rusiecki (1985) discusses the results of his psychological experiments in which human subjects judged logical entailment between pairs of English expressions: one positive (i.e., without explicit negation) and one negative. He found that people were remarkably consistent in their answers and for all of them such judgements appeared effortless. Rusiecki's experiments support the claim that many aspects of reasoning with explicit negative information, the kind of negative information that is so problematic for virtually all automated reasoning and knowledge representation systems, is quite easy for people.

I provide a number of real-life examples with complex Boolean expressions involving negative and disjunctive temporal information that for people appears and for my natural language processing system is easy.

Temporal Quantifiers

I handle temporal and spatial quantifiers such as *sometimes, somewhere, very often,* and *everywhere.*

Many More Spatio-Temporal Relations

I handle many more temporal relations observed in natural language than any other spatio-temporal reasoner. Due to the adjectival and adverbial modifications and Booleanity of natural language, the number of spatio-temporal relations is in principle infinite. Examples of complex temporal relations that I can handle include *shortly before or after, five or six days before, five or six blocks before, not very far from* and *not long before.*

Schubert and Hwang (1994) investigate a number of temporal adverbials and treat them as sentence-level modifiers, which does not always correspond well to the structure of the English language because many temporal modifiers appear at the level of verb phrases, and not sentences. Schubert and Hwang do not account for modifications of the lexically simple temporal relations. For example, in their representation, the symbol *immediately precedes* presumably represents a temporal relation expressed by the English expression *immediately precedes.* In this expression, the adverb *immediately* modifies the verb *precedes,* and should be compositionally derived from the lexically simple *precedes* relation. This gap in the compositionality combined with the availability of the propositional (sentential) negation only, results in their inability to represent such complex relations as *not immediately after* and to compute logical entailments among different relations such as the fact that the *not immediately after* relation is logically consistent with *long before.*

Nonnumeric Qualitative Information and Absolute and Relative Temporal Information

My system is capable of reasoning with qualitative information such as *very long* or *an instant,* even when no numeric value specifying how long is *long* is available.

Absolute and Relative Spatio-Temporal Information

Based on my investigation of a large number of real-life texts, I consider handling absolute and relative spatio-temporal information as equally important and equally common. This is in contrast with reasoners that give priority to relative temporal information such as Allen (1983), and those that consider absolute information as more important, such as Dean and McDermott (1987). In some cases, my system can automatically express absolute spatio-temporal information with relative one, and vice-versa.

Boolean Algebra Framework for Natural Language Processing

In this section, I will discuss three topics: (1) representational language; (2) existing frameworks to natural language processing as representational language; and, finally, (3) the UNO model as a representation language.

Representational Language

The UNO model is a representational language (see the definition below) closely simulating representational and inferential characteristics of natural language.

> **Definition 1. (Representational Language)**
>
> Representational language $\mathscr{L}$ is a formal language with a Boolean algebra structure defined by the tuple $<\mathscr{T}, \mathscr{A}, \sqcap, \sqcup, not \sqsubseteq, =, \perp, \top>$, where
>
> 1. $\mathscr{T}: \mathscr{L}_{N} \to A$ is a polynomially computable translation function mapping natural language utterances onto A, a set of typed data structures, in such a way as to maximally preserve information present in natural language and minimally introduce information absent from natural language.
> 2. $\sqcap, \sqcup, not$ are computable operations of meet, join, and complement on A and simulate conjunction, disjunction and negation in natural language at different syntactic levels.
> 3. $\sqsubseteq$ is the ordering (entailment) relation induced by $\sqcap$ and $\sqcup$.
> $a_1 \sqsubseteq a_2$ iff $(a_1 \sqcap a_2 = a_1$ or $a_1 \sqcup a_2 = a_2)$.
> 4. $=$ is a computable equality relation.
> 5. $\perp$ is the smallest (zero) element of A.
> 6. $\top$ is the largest (one) element of A.

Existing Frameworks to Natural Language Processing as Representational Language

There are a number of natural language processing frameworks and systems that to various degree satisfy the above requirements of a representational language. I will discuss these frameworks briefly in the following paragraphs.

Introduce Information Not Present in Natural Language

One of the most common problems with introducing information not present in natural language is a standard first-order logic representation of sentences with quantified noun phrases involving determiners *all* or *every*. For example, the sentence *All ravens are black* is represented by the formula $\forall x \; raven(x) \to black(x)$, which, as Horn (1989, page 466) puts it,

> ... is not about ravens at all. It is in fact about everything: it states of every individual x that if x is a raven, then x is black, that is, everything is either black or a nonraven.

Even logics whose goal is to closely mimic the expressiveness of natural language such as the logic proposed by Hwang and Schubert (1993), suffer from this problem with no easy fix. The very few logics that do not suffer from this problem include the representation proposed by Ali and Shapiro (1993) and Iwańska (1992a, 1993).

Information Present in Natural Language But Not Captured.

Natural language exhibits structure that allows communicating and understanding certain information. Adjectival and adverbial modification and complex Boolean expressions occur at all syntactic levels, and without accounting for this structure, additional information, particularly negative information, cannot be represented and properly reasoned with.

For example, the fact that negation of determiners and verb phrases in natural language sentences reverses sentential entailment cannot be accounted for. The problem of handling general explicit negation also lacks an easy fix, as evidenced by the difficulties with negation in virtually all areas of computer science, including databases, logic programming, and artificial intelligence.

A rule of thumb for identifying potential problems of a representational language stemming from an insufficient or no account of the modification in natural language is the presence of hyphenated or underscored multi-word symbols such as the discussed earlier symbol *immediately-precedes* disguising a complex temporal relation.

Complex expressions invariably license additional inferences whose computation is either obscured or plain impossible in representational languages that do not fully mimic the structure of natural language.

For example, if it is true that X *happened immediately after Y,* then it is also true that X *happened after Y,* simply because there is a logical relation between *immediately after* and *after.*

It is probably possible, and maybe even already done, to make up for this potential problem with the completeness of the logic of Hwang and Schubert (1994) by throwing additional formulas or axioms. Such an approach, however, would almost never work for modification of determiners such as *very many* or negation such as *not very many* and *very few people didn't understand the problem.* If the representation only offers propositional (sentential) negation corresponding to the *it is not true that* and *it is not the case that* operators, then it is incapable of correctly and closely representing natural language utterances.

Disjunction in natural language often represents uncertainty and incompleteness of knowledge. For example, the sentence *most or all people hate taxes* communicates the uncertainty about the quantity of people that hate taxes. It is not even clear how to represent in the first-order predicate logic such natural language sentences involving disjunction of determiners.

UNO Model as Representational Language

$\mathscr{L}_{UNO}$ closely mimics the representation and reasoning inherent in natural language because its translation procedure, data structures of the repre-

sentation, and inference engine are motivated by the semantics and pragmatics of natural language. One payoff of this close correspondence to
natural language is the capability of automatically creating knowledge
base's from textual documents.[1]

Sentences asserting properties of (sets of) individuals, sentences describing subtyping relations, including extentional type definitions, as
well as intensional definitions of concepts such as

1. "John is a neither good nor hard-working nurse"
   "Not many students did well"
2. "Dobermans, poodles and terriers are dogs"
3. "Elephant—a huge, thick-skinned, mammal with very few hairs, with a
   long, flexible snout, and two ivory tusks"

are uniformly represented by the following type equations:

type == {< P_1, TP_1 >, < P_2, TP_2 >, ..., < P_n, TP_n > }

Their left-hand side, *type,* is the representation of a noun phrase, the
largest type, or the name of a concept; the right-hand side is a two-element set: a property value *P, TP*—a set of < *t, p*> elements representing
the fact that the property value *P* holds at a temporal interval *t* with the
probability *p*.[2] If spatio-temporal or probabilistic information is unavailable or irrelevant, I only show property values. If a property is known to
hold for one temporal interval or the set of such intervals is described via
a temporal quantifier, I flatten the set notation and show the property
value, temporal interval and probability triples < *P, t, p*>.

Individual property values, temporal intervals and probabilities are
represented by the sets [a_1, a_2, ..., a_n] whose elements a_i are terms, record-
like structures consisting of a head, a type symbol, and a body, a list of
attribute-value pairs: attribute ⇒ value. For example, a complex noun
sick, very unhappy woman is represented by

[woman(health ⇒ sick,
          happy ⇒ (not happy)(degree ⇒ very))]

whose only term has the type *woman* as its head and two attributes: the
attribute *health* with the value *sick,* and the attribute *happy* with the value *(not happy)(degree ⇒ very).*

Semantically, these data structures represent a subtype of the type corresponding to the head noun. For example, the above term represents
this subset of individuals of the type *woman* for which the attribute
health has the value *sick* and the function *happy* yields the value *very un-*
happy.

The computable Boolean operations ⊓, ⊔, and not, in the UNO model
take such terms as arguments and automatically produce the resulting
term, including complementary terms with the set-complement semantics. Computing various relations among terms such as entailment and

its dual subsumption (set-inclusion) or partial overlap (nonempty set-intersection) involves performing these operations on these terms. These Boolean operations simulate conjunction, disjunction and negation in natural language. The intuitively and formally correct results are guaranteed to hold, which allows the system to closely simulate inferences in natural language.

The UNO natural language processing system uses type equations bi-directionally: for answering questions about the properties of a particular individual, and for matching particular properties against the properties of individuals in its knowledge base[6].

The UNO representation offers a solid computational and mathematical framework in tact with linguistic theories. Updating knowledge base and automated inferencing is done by the same semantically clean computational mechanism of performing Boolean operations on the representation of natural language input and the representation of previously obtained information stored in the knowledge base.

The underlying knowledge representation formalisms with the computable Boolean algebras with set-theoretic and interval-theoretic semantics allows one to capture semantics of different syntactic categories because sets and intervals underlie semantics of many syntactic categories: common nouns, intransitive verbs, and adjectives can be thought of as denoting sets of persons or objects that possess properties denoted by the words; adjectives and adverbs are functions mapping sets of objects into sets of objects; determiners are functions mapping sets of objects into sets of sets of objects, and the denotations of proper nouns are sets of sets of objects (Dowty, Wall, and Peters 1981; Barwise and Cooper 1981; Keenan and Faltz 1985; Hamm 1989).

The same machinery is used as a metalanguage for describing and propagating arbitrary Boolean constraints, including dictionary entries describing morphological and grammatical constraints. The data structures are partially specified, negative constraints are propagated via unification, and the nonmonotonicity of negation (Pereira 1987) is not problematic. In the existing unification-based approaches, it is not possible to propagate negative constraints via unification without giving up partiality of feature structures or without admitting some unwanted side effects into the system (Kasper and Rounds 1986; Moshier and Rounds 1987; Johnson 1988, 1990; Dawar and Vijay-Shanker 1990; Carpenter 1992).

The UNO model shares many computational characteristics with the programming language LIFE (Aït-Kaci 1986, Meyer and Van Roy 1993) because the efficiently computable calculus that underlies LIFE (Aït-Kaci 1986) is extended in the UNO model to handle negation and generalized quantifiers.

Some of the linguistic theories that the UNO model encompasses and (or) extends include insights of the Montague semantics of natural language (Montague 1973; Dowty et al. 1981), the Boolean algebra mathematical model of Keenan and Faltz (1985), the theory of generalized quantifiers (Barwise and Cooper 1981; Hamm 1989), the theory of the pragmatic inference of quantity-based implicature of Horn (1972, 1989), and the theory of negation in natural language of Horn (1989).

UNO Natural Language Processing System

The practical significance of the uniformity of the UNO natural language-based representation and inference, is a simple, flexible, nonsequential architecture of my natural language processing system. This architecture has three characteristics. First, all UNO modules access the knowledge representation module and share its uniform representation. Second, there is no need for external specialists such as knowledge representation systems or spatio-temporal reasoners. My system uniformly represents and reasons with taxonomic, temporal and geographical knowledge. Third, with no external specialists, no interfaces to access them are needed, and therefore there is no need to translate between incompatible representations.

A natural language processing system that needs to perform tasks beyond information extraction and to exhibit some in-depth processing such as question answering virtually always calls some external specialists, typically knowledge representation systems. As reported in the literature, (for example, Palmer et al. [1993]) the necessity to translate between the representation of the natural language processing system and such an external specialist is very hard to do and it tremendously complicates control.

Natural Language Inherent Reasoning about Space and Time

In this section, I will discuss seven topics: logical, context-independent inference; the scalar nature of spatio-temporals; uncertainty and incompleteness; comparison with fuzzy logic's linguistic variable; nonlogical, context-dependent inference, absolute time and space, and relative time and space.

Logical, Context-Independent Inference

If one is told that *Long before the crash, Sam lost a lot of money,* then one automatically understands that it is also the case that *Sam lost a lot of money before the crash* because one understands that the expression *long before* contains more information than the expression *before*.

Understanding and reasoning with natural language references to time is exactly analogous to the human understanding of natural language expressions describing properties of and referring to various objects.[4] For example, the sentence *Sam is a sick, very unhappy woman* entails the sentence *Sam is a woman* because the noun *sick, very unhappy woman* contains more information than the noun *woman;* or equivalently, the set of individuals of the type *sick, very unhappy woman* is properly included in the set of individuals in the denotation of the type *woman;* $\mathcal{L}_{UNO}$ preserves and automatically computes this relation:

T_1 = [woman(health $\Rightarrow$ sick,
            happy $\Rightarrow$ (not happy)(degree $\Rightarrow$ very))]
T_2 = [woman]
$T_1 \sqcap T_2 = T_1$, and therefore $T_1 \sqsubseteq T_2$

The same representation and inference mechanism can be used to utilize information from and compute referents of such complex references to time as *It was an extremely difficult and unhappy time.* For example, the UNO system can infer that *It was a difficult time* because *extremely difficult and unhappy time* entails *difficult time,* which is paralleled by the UNO representation:

T_3 = [time(difficult $\Rightarrow$ difficult(degree $\Rightarrow$ extremely),
            happy $\Rightarrow$ (not happy)(degree $\Rightarrow$ extremely))]
T_4 = [time(difficult $\Rightarrow$ difficult)]
$T_3 \sqcap T_4 = T_3$, and therefore $T_3 \sqsubseteq T_4$

It can also infer that *it was not a very happy time* because *extremely difficult and unhappy time* entails *not very happy time:*

T_5 = not [time(happy $\Rightarrow$ happy(degree $\Rightarrow$ very))]=
[(not time), time(happy $\Rightarrow$ not happy), time(happy $\Rightarrow$ happy(degree
                                              $\Rightarrow$ not very))]
$T_3 \sqcap T_5 = T_3$, and therefore $T_3 \sqsubseteq T_5$

Reasoning with explicit negative information is also no different. The sentence *Sam is not a woman* entails the sentence *Sam is not a sick, very unhappy woman* because *not woman* entails not *(sick, very unhappy woman).* Exactly analogously, the sentence *Sam lost a lot of money, but not before the crash,* entails the sentence *Sam's lost a lot of money, but not long before the crash* because *not before* entails *not long before.*

Scalar Nature of Spatials and Temporals

One understands that the sentence *He is never sick* logically entails the sentence *It is not very often that he is sick* because the quantification frequency adverb *never* logically entails *not very often.* Such logical entailments are due to the scalar nature of the quantification frequency adverbs.

Scalar predicates, a large, cross-categorial class of expressions of natural language that denote certain quantitative values, also includes cardinal numbers, determiners, evaluative and gradable adjectives, modals, and epistemic verbs. For scalar predicates, semantic relation of entailment holds between denotations of lexically simple items. It is this entailment relation between *always* and *sometimes* that accounts for the fact that when told *John always smiles*, one automatically understands that *John sometimes smiles*.

$\mathscr{L}_{UNO}$ improves upon Horn's (1972, 1989) theory of quantity-based implicature by providing a formal, computational model allowing for the representation and comparison of complex Boolean predicates, particularly negated and nonnegated values, by defining the operators of negation, conjunction, and disjunction, and by computing relations like contradiction given by him in terms of geometric properties of a picture.

Hirschberg (1985), and Hobbs, Croft, Davies, Edwards, and Laws (1986) represent scalar predicates as partially ordered sets (posets). I argue that their semantics should be modeled with the stronger notion of Boolean algebras because posets do not guarantee the existence of the greatest lower boundary (and least upper boundary), and therefore posets do not guarantee the distributivity of meet and join. Without the distributivity of these operations, complex scalar predicates cannot be given appropriate semantics. As the result, one cannot represent or compute entailment between expressions such as *not extremely bright* and *stupid,* or between *very often, but not always* and *sometimes*.

I capture semantic properties of scalar predicates and allow one to uniformly compute logical entailments between arbitrary scalar expressions of different syntactic categories. Lexically simple scalars, for example, the determiner *some* or verb *like*, have an "at least" meaning that can be exploited for representing incomplete knowledge and for conveying certain information without actually committing to it.

If one sees a number of white swans, one forms the belief that some swans are white. This belief should not preclude that all swans may in fact be white. One's knowledge is incomplete and in this case, the sentence *Some swans are white* reads as *At least some swans are white*.

I model the "at least" meaning of lexically simple scalars, the fact that two lexically simple scalars may be in the entailment relation, with directed intervals of real numbers. The lower boundaries of these intervals represent the smallest value denoted by a word, and their upper boundaries the largest. For example, the lower boundary of the determiner *some* is 0, and its upper boundary is +1, i.e., *some* is the entire interval

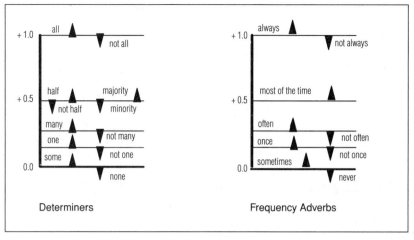

Figure 1. Frequency Quantification Adverbs
Parallel Scalar Semantics of Determiners

(0, + 1]; the parenthesis signifies the exclusion of the boundary value and the square bracket its inclusion. The direction for lexically simple scalars is either ↑ or ↓.

The following are examples of the interval-based representations of lexically simple scalars:

1. The determiners *some* and *many* are represented by
   $[(0, +1], ↑]$ and $[[l_{many}, +1], ↑]$, where $l_{many} > 0$
2. The verbs *like* and *love* are represented by
   $[[l_{like}, +1], ↑]$ and $[[l_{love}, +1], ↑]$, where $l_{love} > l_{like}$.

The representation of complex scalar expressions such as *sometimes, but not very often* is compositionally derived via the Boolean operations on the representation of lexically simple scalars. Computing entailment between complex adverbs *never* and *not very often, close* and *not very far,* and between complex adjectives *terrible* and *not very good,* or *sick* and *not very healthy,* is accomplished by the same mechanism.

Figure 1 illustrates two very similar qualitative scales:[5] DETERMINERS, and FREQUENCY ADVERBS, which reflects the fact that with respect to some logical inference, temporal quantifiers behave exactly the same as determiners that give rise to the generalized quantifiers of natural language. A similar distinction between first-order and non-first-order definable quantifiers applies: the adverb *always* is like the determiner *all,* and the adverb *often* like the determiner *many.* These similarities allow the UNO system to use the same mechanism for computing temporal and nontemporal quantifiers.

Some scalar predicates such as *young, old, early* and *late* convey tem-

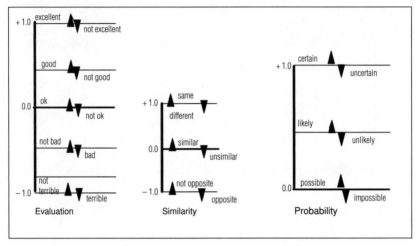

Figure 2. Scalar Predicates Relevant for Expressing Temporal Information

poral information only. They allow the UNO model to account for the entailments between pairs of sentences such as *John is very old* and *John is not young,* and to represent and reason with the information from exchanges like

"Was John late for the last checkup ?"
"No, this time, he showed up very early."

Many general-purpose scalar predicates (see figure 2) are used to describe both space and time. The EVALUATION and DEGREE scales allow the UNO model to account for the entailment between spatial and temporal noun phrases such as

<a very good time, not a bad time> <a terrible time, not a very good time>
in the exact same fashion as for the entailment between their nonspatiotemporal versions

<a very good book, not a bad book>
<a terrible student, not a very good student>.

The SIMILARITY scale relates words describing degree of similarity among objects. This scale allows the UNO model to infer from the sentence *X and Y are the same* that *X and Y are very similar* and that *X and Y are not very different.*

Understanding logical implications of sentences in which the similarity words describe temporal information is exactly analogous. The UNO system infers from the sentence *X and Y happened at the same time* (plxw) that *X and Y did not happen at a different time* (place). It is important that computing such inferences does not require any additional information about the times or places when the events X and Y took place.

The LENGTH scale allows the UNO system to infer from the sentence *It took an extremely long time* the falsity of the sentences *It took a very short time* and *It did not take a long time.*

The same mechanism accounts for the relevant logical inferences when these adjectives describe nonspatio-temporal objects. For example, the UNO system infers that if *Pluto has an extremely short tail*, then it is also the case that *Pluto does not have a very long tail.*

Uncertainty and Incompleteness

The PROBABILITY scale shown in figure 2 allows $\mathcal{L}_{\text{UNO}}$ to capture uncertainty of information. The sentence *John is likely, but not very likely, to be HIV-positive* describes the uncertainty about John possessing the *HIV-positive* property; the representation of *likely, but not very likely* is compositionally computed by the UNO natural language processing system as follows:

[likely] ⊓ not[likely(degree ⇒ very)]=

= [likely] ⊓ [(not likely), likely(degree ⇒ not very)]=

= [likely(degree ⇒ not very)]

and the above sentence is represented in the system knowledge base by the following type equation

john == { < [hiv(type ⇒ positive)], [likely(degree ⇒ not very)] > }

Space and time-related uncertainties and incompleteness can also be expressed at different syntactic levels, often involving disjunction and various ambiguities. While some of these expressions are quite complex, they are by no means unusual, as illustrated by the sentence *It is very likely that X happened shortly before or after Y* in which the likelihood phrase *very likely* modifies another uncertainty expressed by the disjunctive prepositional phrase *shortly before or after.* This ambiguous phrase could mean *(shortly before) or after* i.e., X could have happened either *shortly before Y*, or *after Y*; in the latter case, nothing is known about the distance between X and Y; this interpretation is represented by the term

I_1 = [before(length ⇒ shortly), after]

The ambiguous phrase could also mean *shortly (before or after)* i.e., X could have happened either *before Y*, or *after Y*, but in both cases the temporal distance between X and Y is *short*; i.e., the uncertainty pertains the temporal relation only; this interpretation is represented by the term

I_2 = [before, after](length ⇒ shortly)

This ambiguity and the relationship between the interpretations is truthfully captured by the UNO representation. In the above example, one interpretation is entailed by the other, in other words, I_2 contains strictly more information than I_1:

$I_1 \sqcap I_2 = I_2$, or equivalently, $I_2 \sqsubseteq I_1$.

In a conservative-reasoner mode, [6] the UNO natural language processing system prefers logically weaker interpretations, and I_1 gets stored in its knowledge base as the temporal relation described in the above sentence. In a nonconservative-reasoner mode the system prefers logically stronger interpretations and represents this temporal relation as I_2.

Comparison with Fuzzy Logic's Linguistic Variable

For processing natural language, $\mathcal{L}_{UNO}$ offers two advantages over fuzzy logic's linguistic variable (Zadeh 1975). First, in case of linguistic variable, computing entailment between *very old* and *not young* necessarily requires converting them to concrete numbers because, as Zadeh put it, linguistic variable is not entirely qualitative, but rather it is about numbers. In my model, inference from *very old* to *not young* can be accomplished without involving any numbers. This is important because numeric values may not be available or may be unimportant, which is not at all uncommon. For example, Shelov's 1991 reference guide (pages 535-536) describes cold and ear infections and uses many scalar predicates without any indication of their numeric values, including *extremely small, slightly, usually, few, often,* and *tiny.* When numeric values are available or desirable, I also use them. In such cases, the uncertainty aspect of my representation resembles that of Schubert and Hwang (1989) in that expressions such as *very likely* are replaced with specific numbers such as "0.8."

Second, the meaning of the $\mathcal{L}_{UNO}$ entailment relation closely corresponds to the semantics of natural language and reflects relative informativeness of natural language expressions—the entailed expression contains less or equal information than the expression by which it is entailed; *excellent* contains more information than *good,* and therefore the sentence *He is excellent* logically entails the sentence *He is good.*

In case of the linguistic variable, the entailment relation between *excellent* and *good,* if any,[7] means that for each possible value of the relevant variable, one expression is more compatible with it than the other, which does not correspond well to the information that people convey via natural language.

Schwartz (1989) adopts Zadeh's linguistic variable approach to reasoning with qualitative linguistic information and incorporates quantity-based implicature into his logical deduction scheme. It follows from the meaning of his elementary terms that the conjunction of two distinct elementary terms is contradictory. There is no entailment between *very short* and *short* because these two terms are contradictory. For Schwartz, the sentence *Ann is short* contradicts the sentence *Ann is very short* and logically implies the sentence *Ann is not very short*. Schwartz's approach makes it impossible to represent incomplete knowledge. The most striking problem with Schwartz's approach, however, is the proliferation of negations in natural language; for example, Schwartz defines five different negations, each for different types of elementary terms.

Nonlogical, Context-Dependent Inference

Spatials and temporals also engage in quantity-based implicature, a context-dependent, pragmatic, nonmonotonic inference extremely common in natural language (Horn 1972, 1989; Iwańska 1992a, 1993). In certain contexts, logically weaker statements may convey information of logically stronger statements, due to, in part, incomplete knowledge and social norms of behavior.

The sentence *Sometimes he looks very healthy* is logically consistent with *He always looks very healthy,* but may nonlogically implicate a logically stronger sentence *It is not always that he looks very healthy.* The sentence *She is not very young* may be a polite way of saying that *She is old,* and the sentence *He rarely washes dishe*s may be an understatement nonlogically implicating that actually *He never washes dishes.*

Such implicatures are extremely common in everyday communication, scientific and otherwise. Even doctors recording observations of their patients who presumably strive to be as specific and unambiguous as possible implicate information, instead of directly stating it. For example, a psychologist treating a child recorded the following after a session with parents *The child does not relate very well to his mother.*

It was absolutely clear from the following description of the child's behavior, hitting the mother and yelling at her, that this sentence was an understatement whose real information content was something like *The child was terrible to his mother.*

It is critical to capture information conveyed via such implicatures. Understanding and computing this kind of implicatures depends on the capability of understanding and computing logical entailments; one cannot possibly obtain the information implicated by *not very young* if one does not understand the logical relation of entailment between *not very young* and *old.*

Currently the UNO system is not capable of fully automatically computing such implicated meaning because it does not represent or reason about contexts that license and cancel this type of implicature. For now, this type of context-dependency is controlled by yet another rigid external parameter.

Absolute Time and Space

Temporal information can be given in absolute terms as a description of temporal intervals. One very common example of such a description is a date. In factual reporting such as newspaper articles or medical records, a date typically consists of three elements: a day, a month, and a year. In the UNO system, dates are represented by the following term:

D = [date(day   ⇒   day,
            month ⇒   month,
            year   ⇒   year)]

For example, the date April 22, 1992 is represented by the term

D_1 = [date(day   ⇒   22,
            month ⇒   April,
            year   ⇒   1992)]

I account for different date conventions. In Europe, the date *6.05.95* refers to the sixth day of the fifth month of 1995, but in the United States, the same date refers to the fifth day of the sixth month of 1995.[11] These different conventions are taken into consideration during parsing and generating natural language, but the internal UNO representation is order-independent. I do not account for the implicit in calendar dates such as AD, BC or BCE.

The date on the instructions obtained in a hospital emergency room or in a military application such as combat zone simulation may be more specific, for example, *April 22, 1992, 1:09* or *April 22, 1992, 1309*. The representation of such more detailed dates is exactly analogous, and the only difference is that a few more attributes have specified values (i.e., fewer attributes are underspecified):

D = [date(day   ⇒ 22,
            month ⇒ April,
            year   ⇒ 1992,
            hour   ⇒ 1,
            minute ⇒ 9)]

Geographical Regions

Geographical regions such as villages, cities, states, and continents are spatial equivalents of dates. The typical convention is to show smaller regions first as in *Detroit, Michigan, USA*. My representation of geographical regions mimics that of dates. For example, the above region is represented by the term

R_1 = [region(city   ⇒ Detroit,
              state   ⇒ Michigan,
              country ⇒ USA)]

Representing, Combining, and Reasoning with Partial Information

Partiality of any information, including temporal information, is represented in the UNO model as underspecificity of attributes and their values. For example, the representation of a partial date *April, 1992* is

D_3 = [date(month ⇒ April,
            year   ⇒ 1992)]

It immediately follows from this representation that D_1 has more information than D_3: $D_1 \sqcap D_3 = D_1$, and therefore $D_1 \sqsubseteq D_3$.

In my model, combining partial information from various sources is automatic. For example, if one person told the UNO natural language processing system that *X took place sometimes in April or May, 1992* and another person informed it that *X did not happen in early May* then the system automatically puts the two pieces of information together and infers that it must be the case that either *X happened in April, 1992* or *X happened in May, but not early May, 1992.*

This is computed as follows. The temporal information from the first expression is represented as

D_4 = [date(month ⇒ [April, May],
            year   ⇒ 1992)]

preserving the uncertainty about the month, expressed as a disjunctive two-term element; the temporal information from the second expression is represented as

D_5 = date(month ⇒ not May(early ⇒ early))=
    date(month ⇒ [not May,   May(early ⇒ not early)])

The Boolean operation of meet ⊓ combines the information from both terms in the most general way:

$D_4 \sqcap D_5$ =   [date(month ⇒ [April, May(early ⇒ not early)],
                  year   ⇒ 1992)]

The resulting disjunctive value of the *month* attribute corresponds to the above conclusion.

Holidays also constitute absolute references to time. Temporal intervals corresponding to holidays are important because they are often used as reference intervals. I represent such intervals referred to by the names of various holidays by their date. For example, the temporal interval referred to by the expression *Christmas* is represented by the following partial date

D_c = [date(day   ⇒ 25,
           month ⇒ December)]

Absolute time is also frequently described by the expressions such as *late afternoon* and *very early morning*.

Quantified and Non-Quantified "At Time" and "At Place" Operators

In the UNO model, nonquantified noun phrases such as *John* and quantified noun phrases such as *very many students* are represented uniformly. The same uniformity is preserved for nonquantified and quantified absolute temporal information. Natural language sentences involving *at time operators* (Davis 1990), references to absolute time and space, often a single, but in general, a set of spatio-temporal intervals, are represented by the type equations whose spatio-temporal component corresponds to the explicit or inferred spatio-temporal information.

For example, processing the sentence *On April 22, 1992, John did not feel well* results in the following type equation added to the system's knowledge base:[12]

john == < not feel(good ⇒ well), date(day   ⇒ 22,
                                   month ⇒ April,
                                   year   ⇒ 1992)
                                   state   ⇒ Michigan)
                                   region (city ⇒ Detroit) >

Processing the sentence *John very often does not feel well* results in this type equation added to the knowledge base:

john == < not feel(good ⇒ well), often(degree ⇒ very) >

Note that the system handles underspecified information: it is given no indication how often is often.

Other Nonmonotonic Inferences: Inductive Specialization and Generalization

The uniform representation of nonquantified and quantified information facilitates computing nonmonotonic inferences due to inductive, deductively unwarranted generalizations and specializations that people are not only capable of, but seem to be doing all the time. Subsequently, people's actions, beliefs, and relevant inferences are based on such unwarranted conclusions.

For example, it is enough for most people to catch somebody lie on two or three different occasions, say, last year and on Thursday, in order to conclude, quite possibly incorrectly, that he is a liar, i.e., that he always lies. This corresponds to generalizing some set of temporal intervals over which some property is known to hold to a strictly larger, usually much larger, temporal interval. In the above example, the property of *lying* known to hold at the temporal intervals denoted by the expressions *last year* and *on Thursday*, is generalized to hold over a much larger interval referred to by the expression *always*. Spatial generalizations are similar. For example, seeing flowers in three or four places results in

spatiotemporal relation	==	[some overlap, no overlap]
some overlap	==	[overlap, when, where] .
overlap	==	[begin, end, during, coincide, concurrent, inside, simultaneous, since, until] .
no overlap	==	[after, before, follow, precede, prior, later, earlier, between].

after	== follow.	after	== ater.				
before	== precede.	before	== earlier.	before	== prior .		
begin	== since.	end	== until .	overlap	== when .		
same time	== coincide.	same time	== overlap fully	same time	== simultaneous .		
same time	== begin and end.	same time	== concurrent .	between X and Y == after X and before Y .			

Figure 3. Hierarchy of Basic Spatio-Temporal Relations and Their Equivalences

the falsity preserving generalization *Flowers are everywhere.*

Computing entailments (specializations) and subsumptions (generalizations) of temporal and nontemporal information is quite similar. In both cases, the process of deciding whether these relations obtain is inferentially and computationally heavy, and in both cases, a correctly computed relation gives the system lots of additional information and therefore inferential power:

Inductive entailment (specialization) allows the UNO natural language processing system to use general knowledge for specific instances. If one inductively, though correctly, concludes from knowing that a property holds for *very many students,* that this property also holds of *John,* the one can correctly answer some additional questions involving unavailable knowledge. Similarly, an inductive leap from knowing that a property holds *very often* to assuming that this property also holds *on April 22, 1992,* increases the number of questions one correctly answers.

Inductive subsumption (generalization) allows the UNO natural language processing system to use specific knowledge for predicting unknown or future instances. The gain from being able to inductively, though correctly conclude from knowing that a property holds for *John,* that this property also holds of *very many students* is very similar to the gain from being able to inductively, though correctly conclude from knowing that a property holds *on April 22, 1992* that that this property holds *very often.*

Relative Space and Time

Temporal information is often given in relative terms. There are a number of lexically simple natural language expressions that allow one to relate temporal intervals of different events. Figure 4 shows my hierarchy of basic temporal relations arranged with respect to the extent of the

Relation	Examples of Basic Temporal Relations
same-time	(1) The meetings took place at the same time (2) These simultaneous events surprised many (3) The same basic machines will be sold simultaneously in the United States, Europe and Japan (4) He named ambassador to New Zealand Takeo Iguchi to serve concurrently as ambassador to western Samoa (5) The announcement of the pact coincided with the release by Volkswagen of its second-quarter earnings report
start	(1) His talk starts the conference (2) The conference starts with his talk
end	(1) His talk ends the conference (2) The conference ends with his talk
during	Operations came to a halt during the Cultural Revolution
after	(1) Dancing was after singing (2) After singing they danced (3) My house is after the red barn
before	(1) Singing was before dancing (2) Before dancing, they sang (3) Monroe is before Toledo
follow	(1) Dancing followed singing (2) First it was singing; then dancing followed
precede	Singing preceded dancing
prior	Singing was prior to dancing
later	First it was singing; dancing was later
earlier	Now they dance; singing was earlier
between	(1) He was born sometime between the First and Second World Wars (2) Monroe is between Detroit and Toledo

Table 1

Times and locations of different events can be related by lexically simple natural language expressions.

Basic Relation	Modifiers	Examples of Complex Temporal Relations
after	five months or so	Five months or so after the treatment, he was fully recovered
after	five miles or so	Five miles or so after the woods, you will see a meadow
	a few minutes	It happened a few minutes after their conversation
	a few kilometers	It happened a few kilometers after Toronto
	not, very long	He fell asleep not very long after the meeting
follow	immediately	The arrest immediately followed his confession
before	five or six days	Five or six days before the trial, he confessed
after, before	or, shortly	He gave me these papers shortly before or after the meeting
after	not, immediately	It didn't happen immediately after the exam
earlier	not, much	John came home not much earlier than Mark
	this month	The announcement was made earlier this month
later	two years	Two years later, she was married
follow	shortly	Dancing followed shortly
during	not	It didn't happen during the party

Table 2.

Times and locations of different events can be related by complex expressions of natural language compositionally derived from basic temporal relations via modifiers, Boolean connectives and, or, not, and cardinal numbers.

overlap of the intervals. Some relations, such as *after, before,* and *between,* are like in Allen (1983), but apply to both intervals and their end points (boundaries). Others are quite different: my *overlap* relation is underspecified with respect to the extent of the overlap; the *begin* and *end* relations are similarly underspecified.

This underspecificity of temporal relations allows us to capture incomplete knowledge. If one is only told that *The time of these events overlaps,* then this information is incomplete: the overlap may be partial only, or full. Similarly, if some event X started another event Y, then both outcomes, that they end at the same time, and that they end at different times, may be possible.

Some basic relations such as *after* and *follow* convey similar, if not identical, temporal ordering information.[9] I encode such equivalences via type equalities also shown in figure 3.

The number of possible spatio-temporal relations that can be expressed in natural language appears infinite because basic temporal relations, most of which are lexically simple items, can be further specified via complex expressions involving adverbial modifiers, Boolean connectives and, or, not, and cardinal numbers; tables 1 and 2 and give examples of natural language sentences with basic and complex spatio-temporal relations.

If the system is told that X *happened, but not (long before Y),* where X is some event and Y an event, temporal interval, or region, then this spatio-temporal information is processed as follows: First, the representation of this expression

not(before(length $\Rightarrow$ long))

is computed to the equivalent

[not before, before(length $\Rightarrow$ not long)]

by computing the negation operation *not* on the representation of *long before;* with the resulting term in its knowledge base, the system is correctly open to the possibility that X *happened many years after* Y or to the possibility that X *happened before, but not long before,* Y.

Special Knowledge about Time and Space

When reasoning about time and space, people use spatio-temporal domain knowledge, which does not appear language-inherent, but instead is reflected in natural language. This specialized spatio-temporal knowledge interacts interestingly with the semantics and pragmatics of natural language.

Spatio-Temporal Units

One example of such temporal domain knowledge is knowledge about different units of time such as *day* or *month,* their qualitative semantic relations, for example, that the unit of *month* is larger than the unit of *day,* and quantitative relations such as the fact that a given month consists of a particular number of days. Such quantitative and qualitative relations between different units of time are encoded in the UNO model by the type equations of the following form

1Larger_Unit == Number Smaller_Unit.

for example,

1 century == 100 year.
1 year == 12 month.

Analogous equations encode quantitative relations for particular months and days.

The UNO system uses such equations for numerical conversions between different units and for inferring qualitative ordering relation on temporal units, both contributing to computing entailments of sentences. For example, the system computes that the sentence *it took him one week* entails the sentence *it took him two days* because the denotation of *one week* entails the denotation of *two days,* where the word *two* is not subject to implicature and purely semantically means *at least two.* This is computed as follows. First the representations of these temporal expressions

$$Dur_1 = dur(\text{week} \Rightarrow true(\det \Rightarrow one,$$
$$n \Rightarrow week))$$
$$Dur_2 = dur(\text{day} \Rightarrow true(\det \Rightarrow two,$$
$$n \Rightarrow day))$$

are converted to the normal form with identical temporal units. The system does it according to the type equations relating different units. For the resulting representations

$$Dur_1 = dur(day \Rightarrow true(\det \Rightarrow seven,$$
$$n \Rightarrow day))$$
$$Dur_2 = dur(day \Rightarrow true(\det \Rightarrow two,$$
$$n \Rightarrow day))$$

the meet operation ⊓ correctly computes the above entailment because the number *seven* entails the number *two.*

Conversion to such normal form assures computing correct relations between complex temporal units specified in terms of different basic units such as *month* versus *week.*

With regard to complex temporal units, modifiers, numbers, and Boolean connectives allow the UNO natural language processing system to create and understand arbitrary units of time and refer to temporal intervals of arbitrary length. For example, the expression *one year, three weeks, and five hours* refers to a complex unit of time, which in my UNO model is compositionally derived via the Boolean operation of meet, ⊓:

$$Dur_3 = dur(\ year \Rightarrow true(det \Rightarrow one,$$
$$n \Rightarrow year))$$
$$Dur_4 = dur(\ week \Rightarrow true(det \Rightarrow three,$$
$$n \Rightarrow week))$$
$$Dur_5 = dur(\ hour \Rightarrow true(det \Rightarrow five,$$
$$n \Rightarrow hour))$$
$$Dur_3 \sqcap Dur_4 \sqcap Dur_5$$
$$= dur(\ year \Rightarrow true(\ det \Rightarrow one,$$
$$n \Rightarrow year),$$
$$week \Rightarrow true(\ det \Rightarrow three,$$
$$n \Rightarrow week),$$
$$hour \Rightarrow true(\ det \Rightarrow five,$$
$$n \Rightarrow hour))$$

Temporal containment and precedence relation of different temporal units and of certain special intervals is encoded by the temporal type equations $==_t$. For example, knowledge that every year, week, and day consists of named months, days, and parts that always come in a fixed order is encoded by the following temporal type equations:

year $==_t$ [January, February, March, April, May, June, July, August, September, October, November, December]

week $==_t$ [Monday, Tuesday, Wednesday, Thursday, Friday, Saturday, Sunday]

day $==_t$ [predawn, dawn, sunrise, morning, noon, dusk, sunset, evening, night]

The UNO natural language processing system automatically generates from these equations some of the quantitative equations described earlier.

Temporal stages are also encoded by such temporal precedence equations. For example, knowledge that mammals' life consists of certain developmental stages is captured by the following equation

life(animal $\Rightarrow$ mammal) $==_t$
[babyhood, youth, puberty, adolescence, prime, middle aged, elder]

Knowledge of such stages allows the UNO system to associate each stage with relevant or important information such as typical health problems, common diseases, patterns of behavior, goals, physical development etc. Such knowledge facilitates reasoning about development of an individual and facilitates medical diagnosis.

Knowledge encoded via these temporal containment and precedence equations allows the UNO natural language processing system to compute time-related logical inferences. For example, if told that *it happened in the morning*, the system automatically infers that *it did not happen in the evening* and that *it happened during the day*. Notice that for computing these inferences the referents do not have to be resolved (decontextualized): neither for the pronoun *it,* nor for the definite anaphora *the day.*

Next let us examine arbitrary subintervals and subregions. Natural language allows one to refer to arbitrary subintervals via adjectival, adverbial and Boolean modification as well as expressions such as "the { *beginning, middle, end* } *of*" and "{ *first, second, nth, small, large* } *part of.*" For example, the sentence *X happened early in the morning* refers to the initial part of the interval referred to by the word *morning.* This temporal expression is represented as follows:

morning(part ⇒ early)

It automatically follows from this representation that *X happened in the morning* and that *X did not happen in the evening.* Representation of other similar expressions such as *Very early summer, the beginning of the second quarter, Late May* is exactly analogous.

Context-Dependent Grain Size

Golding, Magliano, and Hemphill (1992) found that in some contexts, particular units of time may be most appropriate when answering questions about future events. In their experiments, human subjects in response to the question *When is the meeting on salary increases?* produced answers that included such units of time as *hour* and *minute;* units like *milliseconds* or *centuries* were never produced.

However, given incomplete knowledge and therefore wrong or no expectations, a spatio-temporal reasoner must be capable of understanding exchanges involving arbitrarily different grains of spatio-temporal units such as the following exchange in which the question *How long does it take for an electron to travel through the channel?* is answered by a careless physics student with *two months* instead of the expected *two nanoseconds.* To a limited extent, I handle such differences in grain, as illustrated by the earlier examples.

Intensionally Defined Spatio-Temporal Units

Some words such as *instant* and *while* denote very small time units; others such as *eon* and *eternity* refer to very long intervals. The meaning of such intensional units is represented in the UNO model as type equations created automatically from their natural language definitions. For example, Guralnik (1982, page 730) defines *instant* as *a point or very short space of time,* which is represented in the UNO system as

instant== [point, time(length ⇒ short(degree ⇒ very))]

This knowledge base allows the system to conclude that if some event took *an instant,* then this event did not take a long time because

[time(length ⇒ long)] ⊓ instant = ⊥

Comparison of Spatio-Temporal and Nonspatio-Temporal Taxonomies

In the UNO model, spatio-temporal and nonspatio-temporal taxonomies are very similar in that the underlying ordering relations, for objects, entailment reflecting set containment, and for temporal intervals, entailment reflecting interval containment, license logical inferences. For example, based on knowledge encoded in the following equations:

dog == [doberman, poodle, terrier]
day ==$_t$ [predawn, dawn, sunrise, morning, noon,
       dusk, sunset, evening, night]

computing inference from *X is a doberman* to *X is a dog* and *X is not a poodle* and computing inference from *X happened in the morning* to *X happened in the day* and *X did not happen in the evening* is absolutely analogous. Similarly analogous is computing inference from *X is not a dog* to *X is not a doberman* and computing inference from *X did not happen during the day* to *X did not happen in the morning.* The main difference between temporal and nontemporal taxonomies is that temporals additionally involve precedence relation. The order of temporal types in the right-hand-side of the type equations matters, whereas for nontemporal objects it does not.

Propagating Spatio-Temporal Constraints

Propagating spatio-temporal constraints often amounts to computing some transitive closure, and also appears not to be about natural language, or at least, not entirely about natural language. Obviously, inferences discussed in the previous sections result from computing (propagating) spatio-temporal constraints. Interestingly, such inferences seem quite easy for people. Computing spatio-temporal anaphora, not discussed here, is also very obviously about propagating temporal constraints.

But equally obviously, computing consistency of complicated partial temporal orderings (Allen 1984; Davis and Carnes 1991; Dechter, Meiri , and Pearl 1991) takes computation outside natural language. Interestingly, such problems are very difficult for most people.

Limitations, Ongoing and Future Research

There are still very many things that a general spatio-temporal reasoner should do, but I currently do not. A few of the major ones include combining explicit temporal information with tense and aspect, computing temporal anaphora, handling context dependency, and expressing qualitative and quantitative temporal information one with another. I'll discuss these tasks further in the following paragraphs.

First, let me examine the task of combining explicit temporal information with tense and aspect. There is an extremely large body of linguistic research on tense and aspect; for some computational approaches, see, for example the special issue of *Computational Linguistics* edited by Bonnie Webber (volume 14, issue 2, 1988), and more recently the paper by Hwang and Schubert (1994).

Full understanding of temporal information in natural language utterances involves combining information from explicit temporal expressions with the information about tense and aspect. For example, explicit temporal information often helps disambiguating the order of events described by the sentences with the notoriously ambiguous *when* temporal conjunction. One difficulty with approaching this problem for a large number of textual documents stems from the fact that the reliability of the morphologically and lexically marked tense and aspect information critically depends on highly correct, sentential-level parsing. However, for a large amounts of textual data such as the *Wall Street Journal* corpus, not a single academic or industrial natural language processing system can deliver significantly more than chance (50 percent) performance in correct sentential-level parsing.

Next, consider computing temporal anaphora. The capability of computing logical relations between different temporal expressions facilitates computing temporal anaphora. I am currently adopting my rather standard anaphora resolution algorithm to computing temporal anaphora.

As for handling context-dependency, I plan to further identify and handle context-dependent, nonmonotonic aspects of spatio-temporal reasoning. Implicatures and, most likely, other context-dependent inferences critically depend on understanding logical entailments. I feel that only now, with my experimentally verified research of the logical, context-independent aspects of spatio-temporal reasoning mostly accomplished, I am ready to seriously address context dependent, nonlogical inferences.

Finally, with regard to expressing qualitative and quantitative temporal information one with another, I plan to further investigate converting qualitative temporal information into quantitative, and vice versa. Such mutual conversions necessarily involve handling intensionality and context-dependency of natural language: a 25 year old man may be a very young professor, but a somewhat old scout; in the context of the Big Bang theory, one year is an instant, but in the context of a medical emergency, one minute may be an eternity.

Conclusion

I have presented a novel spatio-temporal reasoner whose representational, inferential and computational characteristics closely resemble natural language. This close resemblance assures its ease of use by people, eliminates the need for an interface accessing knowledge stored in a computer knowledge base, offers hard to match expressiveness and precision of natural language, and facilitates computing commonsense reasoning. These characteristics make the proposed spatio-temporal reasoner particularly attractive for a domain-independent processing of temporal information.

I have demonstrated that important inferences about spatio-space and time can be captured by a general representation and reasoning mechanism inherent in natural language, many aspects of which are closely mimicked by my UNO model of natural language. I have shown that reasoning about space and time is a problem in which natural language general reasoning capabilities mix in a very interesting way with the capabilities specific to understanding space and time, and that separating the two is extremely difficult. As the result, I offer a uniform representation and inference, and therefore a simple architecture, for spatio-temporal and nonspatio-temporal reasoning. I have also shown that computing logical, context-independent and some nonmonotonic, context-dependent inferences for spatio-temporal and nonspatio-temporal objects is almost exactly analogous.

I have discussed a number of real-life examples from existing textual documents that illustrate novel representational and reasoning capabilities of my natural language style spatio-temporal reasoner, including many previously unaccounted aspects of temporal information conveyed by common English temporal expression, reasoning with information from arbitrary Boolean temporal expressions involving explicit negation, disjunction and conjunction, handling temporal quantifiers, handling infinite number of temporal relations, handling both absolute and relative temporal information, and handling nonnumeric qualitative temporal information.

Acknowledgments

I thank Syed Ali, Mary Croll, Paul Nielsen, Stuart Shapiro, and Wlodek Zadrozny for their insightful comments on the earlier drafts. This chapter is based on earlier work that was published in the *International Journal of Expert Systems* 9(1): 113–149. Those portions that were retained from that journal are reprinted here with the permission of JAI Press.

Notes

1. Needless to say, limited by the subset of English covered by the model.

2. Such intervals represent absolute temporal information. The UNO representation of the relative temporal information is shown later in the chapter.

3. The UNO representation as presented in Iwańska (1992b) had the following form: type $\rightarrow \{ P_1, P_2, ..., P_n \}$ because at that time, I did not account for the temporal or probabilistic aspects; I used a pointed arrow, and now the "==" sign, because knowledge bases were used in a single direction only.

4. Properties are often described by complex adjectives, common nouns, and verbs, but in general, they can be described by arbitrary multi-sentence utterances.

5. Only lexically simple scalars and their negations can be illustrated by such a picture.

6. Users are free to define or not define this relationship.

7. In some European countries, slashes and not dots are used as separators.

8. At this point, this is a logical representation because the system has not decided yet whether implicature took place.

9. This is not to say that these temporal-order-equivalent expressions are redundant. For example, their discourse-level functions are quite different.

8 Mixed Depth Representations for Dialog Processing

Susan W. McRoy, Syed S. Ali, and Susan M. Haller

WE DESCRIBE OUR WORK on developing a general-purpose tutoring system that will allow students to practice their decision-making skills in a number of domains. The tutoring system, called B2, supports mixed-initiative natural language interaction. The natural language processing and knowledge representation components are also general purpose—which leads to a tradeoff between the limitations of superficial processing and syntactic representations and the difficulty of deeper methods and conceptual representations. Students' utterances may be short and ambiguous, requiring extensive reasoning about the domain or the discourse model to fully resolve. However, full disambiguation is rarely necessary. Our solution is to use a mixed-depth representation, one that encodes syntactic and conceptual information in the same structure. As a result, we can use the same representation framework to produce a detailed representation of requests (which tend to be well-specified) and to produce a partial representation of questions (which tend to require more inference about the context). Moreover, the representations use the same knowledge representation framework that is used to reason about discourse processing and domain information—so that the system can reason with (and about) the utterances, if necessary. This work is the first (and to our knowledge, the only) implementation of mixed-depth representations for dialog processing.

A *mixed-depth representation* is one that may be shallow or deep in different places, depending on what was known or needed at the time the representation was created (Hirst and Ryan 1992). Moreover, shallow and deep are a matter of degree. *Shallow representations* can be a surface syntactic structure, or it can be the text itself (as a string of characters). *Deep representations* might be a conventional first-order (or higher-order) AI knowledge representation, taking into account such aspects of language understanding as lexical disambiguation, marking case relations, attachment of modifiers of uncertain placement, reference resolution, quantifier scoping, and distinguishing extensional, intensional, generic, and descriptive noun phrases. Unlike quasi-logical form, which is used primarily for storage of information, mixed-depth representations are well-formed propositions, subject to logical inference. Disambiguation, when it occurs, is done by reasoning.

Other systems that represent sentence meaning at multiple levels (such as syntactic, semantic, and pragmatic) build separate complete structures for each level. So, for example, when processing an utterance, a parser must either defer all semantic processing or resolve semantic ambiguities without the full knowledge necessary to do so correctly. The mixed-depth approach opportunistically builds semantic constituent structures as soon as enough information is available. (Minimally, this will be information about the syntax of the utterance but it may include some semantic information about properties of discourse objects introduced by the utterance). This allows us to do as much semantic interpretation as possible, as soon as possible.

In our work, we use a parser with a linguistically based grammar to process the student's typed inputs and produce a structure that captures syntactic marking and bracketing, along with some conceptual information. Encoding decisions that require reasoning about the domain or about the discourse context are left to the knowledge representation and discourse processing components, respectively. The primary benefits of this approach are generality, expressiveness, and uniformity.

In generality, the representation language and conceptual structures that are built during the initial parsing phase are not specific to any one domain.

In expressiveness, the representation language is very expressive; our grammar covers a wide variety of syntactic constructions including fragments and sentences with embedded sentences (such as relative clauses and clause complements). For example, students can request a diagnostic exercise using a variety of forms including "give me a story problem," "I want you to describe a case for me," "tell me a story," "a story please," or "another case."

Finally, in uniformity, the structures that are built by the parser are all subject to inference; they use the same conceptual framework that is used by the other components, including discourse processing, planning, and plan recognition. For example, students can request a diagnostic exercise by mentioning any step of the tutoring plan including "tell me a story," or "quiz me," or by mentioning the overall tutoring plan with "tutor me."

This mixed-depth approach allows us to use the same representation framework to produce a detailed representation of requests (which are often interpreted through plan recognition without considering the context) and to produce a partial representation of questions (which tend to require more inference). Moreover, these representations use the same knowledge representation framework that is used by the system to reason about the discourse and the domain—so that the system can reason with (and about) the utterances, if necessary.

This chapter gives an overview of our tutoring system, B2. It describes the knowledge representation components of B2 and our approach to the representation of questions and requests. The domain that we have developed most thoroughly helps medical students learn a statistical model for medical diagnosis. Many of the examples will be taken from this domain. According to B2's plans for tutoring, the system does this by generating story problems that describe a scenario and then asking the student about conclusions that might be drawn. B2 also supports requests to explain its reasoning and questions about facts.

Overview of B2

The B2 system performs three distinct, but interrelated, tasks that rely on a variety of information sources. The tasks are managing the interaction between the user and B2, including the interpretation of context-dependent utterances; reasoning about the domain, for example, the relation between components of a medical case history and diseases that might occur; and meta-reasoning about the reasoner and its conclusions, including an ability to explain the conclusions by identifying the factors that were most significant.

The tasks interact by addressing and handling queries to each other. However, the knowledge underlying these queries and the knowledge needed to generate a response can come from a variety of knowledge sources. Translating between knowledge sources is not an effective solution.

The information sources that B2 uses include the following: (1) linguistic knowledge—knowledge about the meanings of utterances and plans for expressing meanings as text. (2) Discourse knowledge—knowledge about the intentional, social, and rhetorical relationships that link utterances. (3) Domain knowledge—factual knowledge of the medical domain and the medical case that is under consideration. (4) Pedagogy—knowledge about the tutoring task. (5) Decision-support—knowledge about the statistical model and how to interpret the information that is derivable from the model. In B2, the interaction between the tasks is possible because the information for all knowledge sources is represented in

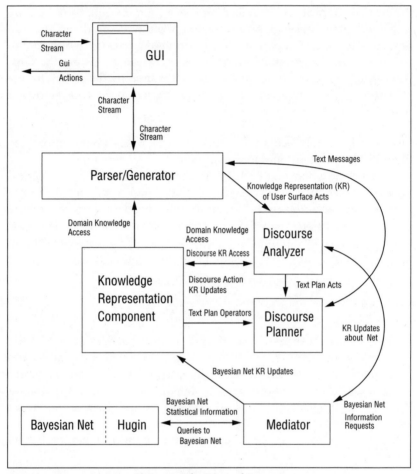

Figure 1. The B2 Architecture

a uniform framework. The knowledge representation component serves as a central blackboard for all other components.

The B2 system consists of seven components (see figure 1). In the diagram, solid, directed arrows indicate the direction of information flow between components. The system gets the user's input using a graphical user interface that supports both natural language interaction and mouse inputs. The *Parser* component of the Parser/Generator performs the first level of processing on the user input using its grammar and the domain information from the Knowledge Representation Component. The Parser interprets the user's inputs to form propositional representations of surface-level utterances for the Discourse Analyzer. The *Generator* produces natural language outputs from the text messages (propositional descriptions of text) that it receives from the Discourse Planner.

The system as a whole is controlled by a module called the Discourse Analyzer. The *Discourse Analyzer* determines an appropriate response to the user's actions on the basis of a model of the discourse and a model of the domain, stored in the knowledge representation component. The Analyzer invokes the Discourse Planner to select the content of the response and to structure it. The Analyzer relies on a component called the Mediator to interact with the Bayesian network processor. This Mediator processes domain level information, such as ranking the effectiveness of alternative diagnostic tests. The Mediator also handles the information interchange between the propositional information that is used by the Analyzer and the probabilistic data that is used by the Bayesian network processor. All phases of this process are recorded in the knowledge representation component, resulting in a complete history of the discourse. Thus, the knowledge representation component serves as a central "blackboard" for all other components.

The Knowledge Representation Blackboard

B2 represents both domain knowledge and discourse knowledge in a uniform framework as a propositional semantic network. A propositional semantic network is a framework for representing the concepts of a cognitive agent who is capable of using language (hence the term semantic). The information is represented as a graph composed of nodes and labeled directed arcs. In a propositional semantic network, the propositions are represented by the nodes, rather than the arcs; arcs represent only non-conceptual binary relations between nodes. The particular systems that are being used for B2 are SNePS and ANALOG (Ali 1994a, Ali 1994b, Shapiro and The SNePS Implementation Group 1992) which provide facilities for building and finding nodes as well as for reasoning and truth-maintenance. These systems satisfy the following additional constraints. First, each node represents a unique concept. Second, each concept represented in the network is represented by a unique node. Finally, the knowledge represented about each concept is represented by the structure of the entire network connected to the node that represents that concept.

These constraints allow efficient inference when processing natural language. For example, such networks can represent complex descriptions (common in the medical domain), and can support the resolution of ellipsis and anaphora, as well as general reasoning tasks such as subsumption (Ali 1994a, Ali 1994b, Maida and Shapiro 1982, Shapiro and Rapaport 1987, Shapiro and Rapaport 1992).

We characterize a knowledge representation as uniform when it allows the representation of different kinds of knowledge in the same knowledge base using the same inference processes. The knowledge representation component of B2 is uniform because it provides a representation of the discourse knowledge, domain knowledge, and probabilistic knowledge (from the Bayesian net). This supports intertask communication and cooperation for interactive processing of tutorial dialogs.

The rule in figure 2 is a good example of how the uniform representation of information in the semantic network allows us to relate domain information (a medical case) to discourse planning information (a plan to describe it). This network represents a text plan for describing a medical case to the user. Text plans are represented as rules in the knowledge representation. Rules are general statements about objects in the domain; they are represented by using case frames[1] that have FORALL or EXISTS arcs to nodes that represent variables that are bound by these quantifier arcs.

In figure 2, node $M13$ is a rule with three universally quantified variables (at the end of the FORALL arcs), an antecedent (at the end of the ANT arc), and a consequent (at the end of the CQ arc). This means that if an instance of the antecedent is believed, then a suitably instantiated instance of the consequent is believed. $M13$ states that if $V1$ (which is at the end of the CASE-NUMBER arc) is the case number of a case, and $V2$ and $V3$ (which are at the end of CASE-INFO arcs) are two pieces of case information, then a plan to describe the case will conjoin[2] the two pieces of case information. Node $P1$ represents the concept that something is a member of the class case and $P2$ represents the concept that the case concept has a case number and case information. For more details about the knowledge representation, see McRoy et al. (1997).

The Representation of the Discourse

The discourse model has five levels of representation, shown in figure 3. These levels capture what the student and the system have each said, as well as how their utterances extend the ongoing discourse. Unlike many systems, B2's model of discourse will include a representation of questions and requests, as well as statements of fact. (Systems that do not represent questions and requests typically give these utterances a procedural semantics, interpreting them as operations to be performed.) Having an explicit representation of questions and requests simplifies the inter-

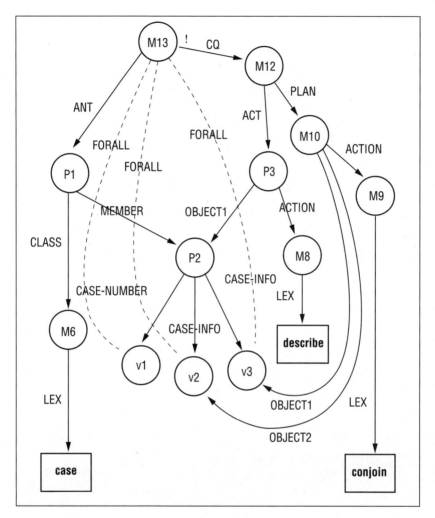

Figure 2

A rule stating that if V1 is the case number of a case, and V2 and V3 are two pieces of case information, then a plan for generating a description of the case will present the two pieces of information in a coordinating conjunction.

pretation of context-dependent utterances such as *Why?* or *What about HIDA?* (Haller 1996).[3] It also allows the system to recover from misunderstandings, should they occur (McRoy 1998, McRoy 1995, McRoy and Hirst 1995).

We will consider each of these levels in turn, starting with the utterance level, shown at the bottom of figure 3.

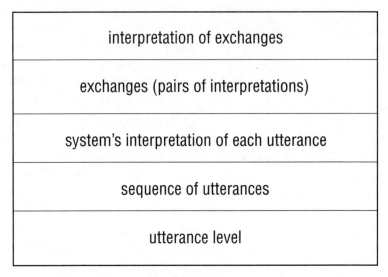

Figure 3. Five Levels of Representation

The Utterance Level

For all inputs, the parser produces a representation of its surface content, which the analyzer will assert as part of an occurrence of an event of type *say*. The content of the user's utterance is always represented by what she said literally. In the case of requests, the student may request a story problem directly, as an imperative sentence—*Tell me a story*—or indirectly, as a declarative sentence that expresses a desire—*I want you to tell me a story*. The complete representation of the imperative sentence *Tell me a story* is shown in figure 4.

For the system's utterances, the utterance level representation corresponds to a text generation event (this contains much more fine-grained information about the system's utterance, such as mode and tense.) The content of the system's utterance is the text message that is sent to the language generator.

Sequence of Utterances

The second level corresponds to the sequence of utterances. (This level is comparable to the linguistic structure in the tripartite model of Grosz and Sidner [1986]). In the semantic network, we represent the sequencing of utterances explicitly, with asserted propositions that use the BE-FORE-AFTER case frame. The order in which utterances occurred (system and user) can be determined by traversing these structures. This representation is discussed in detail in McRoy et al. (1997).

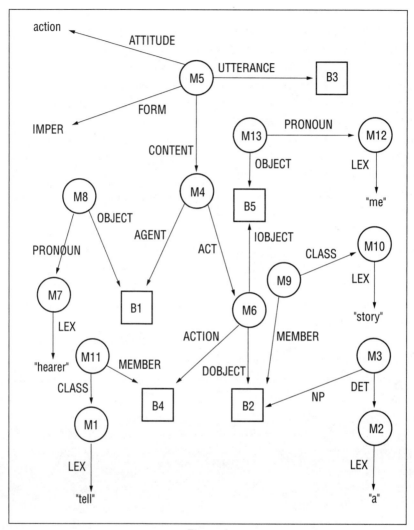

Figure 4

Node *B*3 represents an utterance whose form is imperative, and whose content (*M*4) is the proposition that the hearer (*B*1) will tell a story (*B*2) to the speaker (*B*5).

The Interpretation Level

In the third level, we represent the system's interpretation of each utterance. Each utterance event (from level 1) will have an associated system interpretation, which is represented using the INTERPRETATION_OF—INTERPRETATION case frame. For example, consider the interpretation of the

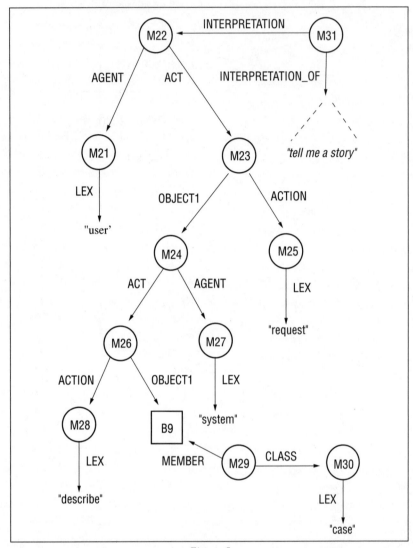

Figure 5

Node *M*31 is a proposition that the interpretation of *Tell me a story* (which is glossed in this figure) is *M*22. Node *M*22 is the proposition that the user requested that the system describe a case to the user. (Describing a case is a domain-specific action; the pronouns from the utterance level have been interpreted according to the context.)

utterance *Tell me a story* (as well as *I want you to tell me a story*), shown in figure 5. (Every utterance has one or more interpretations; at any time, only one is believed and a justification-based truth maintenance system is used to track changes in belief.)

The Exchange and Exchange Interpretation Levels

The fourth and fifth levels of representation in our discourse model are exchanges and interpretations of exchanges, respectively. A *conversational exchange* is a pair of interpreted events that fit one of the conventional structures for dialog (such as QUESTION—ANSWER). Figure 6 gives the network representation of a conversational exchange and its interpretation. Node $M113$ represents the exchange in which the system has asked a question and the user has answered it. Using the MEMBER-CLASS case frame, propositional node $M115$ asserts that the node $M113$ is an exchange. Propositional node $M112$ represents the system's interpretation of this exchange: that the user has accepted the system's question (i.e. that the user has understood the question and requires no further clarification). Finally, propositional node $M116$ represents the system's belief that node $M112$ is the interpretation of the exchange represented by node $M113$.

Interaction Among the Levels

A major advantage of the network representation is the knowledge sharing between these five levels. We term this knowledge sharing *associativity*. This occurs because the representation is uniform and every concept is represented by a unique node (see the knowledge representation blackboard section). As a result, we can retrieve and make use of information that is represented in the network implicitly, by the arcs that connect propositional nodes. For example, if the system needed to explain why the user had said HIDA, it could follow the arcs from the node representing the utterance that User said HIDA to the system's interpretation of that utterance, node $M108$, to determine that the user's utterance was understood as the answer within an exchange (node $M113$), and the user's answer indicated her acceptance and understanding of the discourse, up to that point $M112$. This same representation could be used to explain why the system believed that the user had understood the system's question. This associativity in the network is vital if the interaction starts to fail.

An Example: Mapping Utterance Level to Interpretation Level

In this section we illustrate the advantages of a uniform, mixed-depth representation in more detail. We do so by showing the interpretation of a question (which parses into a mixed-depth representation) and the derivation of its answer. This example (shown in figure 7) illustrates the use

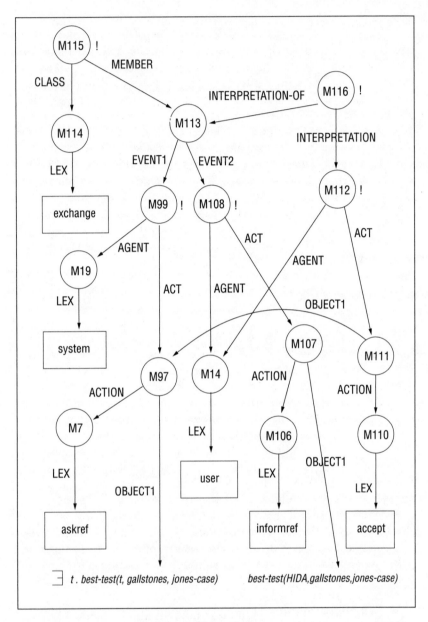

Figure 6

Node M115 represents the proposition that node M113 is an exchange comprised of the events M99 and M108. M108 is the proposition that The user answered "HIDA is the best test to rule in Gallstones." Additionally, node M116 represents the proposition that the interpretation of M113 is event M112. M112 is the proposition that the user has accepted M96. (M96 is the question that the system asked in event M99.)

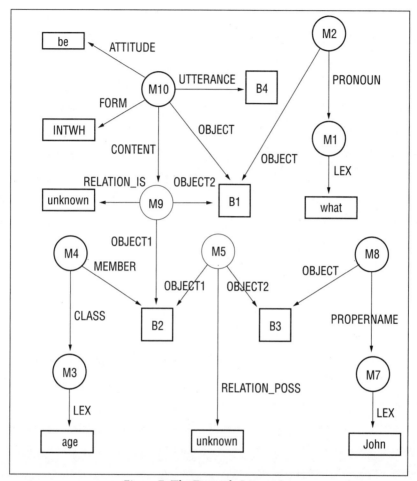

Figure 7. The Example Interaction

of domain knowledge and interpretation rules from the interpretation level, as well as the planning and acting subsystem.

The initial sentence is parsed into a mixed-depth representation corresponding to an interrogative "be" question. The content of this question is that there is an unknown RELATION_IS relation between *John's age* and What. In addition, there is an unknown possessive (RELATION_ POSS) relationship between an individual whose proper name is John and age. These relationships are, initially, unknown because their interpretation may be domain dependent, or require reasoning to disambiguate. (For example, the possessive relationship could be a kinship one, as in *John's mother.*) Figure 8 shows a portion of the representations produced after parsing.

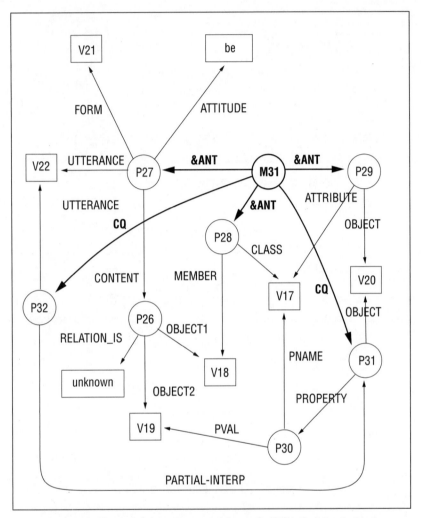

Figure 8. The Level One Representations for What Is Mary's Age?

The base nodes (those labeled *Bn*) correspond to the various discourse entities. Node B4 is the utterance itself, *B1* is the pronoun *what*, *B2* is *age*, and *B3* is *Mary*.

After the parse, interpretation rules (some of which are domain dependent) are applied to determine, first, that the possessive relation between *John* and *age* (age is an attribute of objects in the domain); and second, that the unknown RELATION_IS is about the age attribute of John. The possessive-relation interpretation-rule is not shown here, for space reasons, but it interprets the mixed-depth representations of figure 8 (specifically node M5) as an attribute specification (an ATTRIBUTE-OBJECT node). Figure 9 shows the interpretation rule (node M31) that interprets

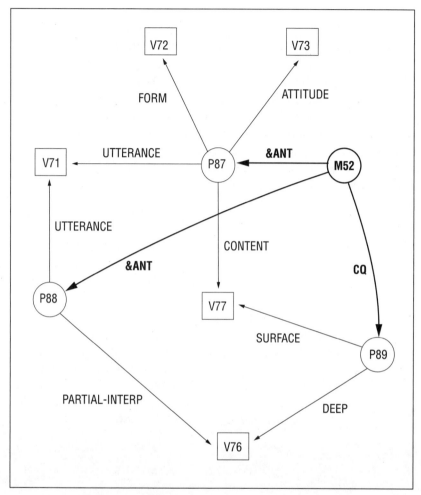

*Figure 9. The Level One Interpretation Rule for Copula
Utterances with Attributive Objects, Such as* What Is Mary's Age?

The antecedents of this rule (nodes at the end of &ANT arcs) require that there be an utterance with attitude be (P27) whose content is an unknown RELATION_IS (P26) between an
object (V19) and an attribute (V18). When these antecedents are satisfied (as are in the example utterance), a suitably instantiated instance of node P31 is believed.

copula utterances with attributive objects as OBJECT-PROPERTY utterances. The rule of figure 9 applies if an utterance (such as *B4* in figure 8)
expressed an unknown "is" relation between an object (such as *what*)
and a (domain-specific) potential attribute (such as *age*). This rule would
also apply to sentences such as *Is Mary's age 42? Mary's age is 42,* or
Mary's blood pressure is high.

In level three, this partial interpretation is then further interpreted as an ASKREF[4] speech act by the user. This interpretation is done by three rules. The first is a general interpretation rule that says that whenever there is an utterance with surface form f, attitude a, and content c and there is a plan that says that a speech act s with deep-content d could be expressed using a surface expression of content c, with attitude a and form f (that is, the surface expression would match the utterance) then speech act s with content d is an interpretation of the utterance. The second is a rule for generation that says that if the deep content d is expressed by a surface form c, then an ASKREF about d can be performed by uttering the surface expression c with form INTWH (a *wh*-question) and attitude "be." The third is an interpretation rule that says that for any utterance, the partial interpretation (derived while processing the level 1 form) corresponds to the deep-content expressed by the content (a mixed-depth representation) of the utterance.

As a result of this interpretation, the system will do inference to determine if this question is reasonable (given the prior context) and to determine an appropriate response. The recognition of a question triggers an action by the system to find an answer. Finding that it does indeed know the answer, the system will adopt the goal that the hearer know the answer and adopt the plan of performing an INFORMREF to achieve this goal. Finally, there is a generation rule that says that an INFORMREF can be performed by uttering a declarative surface expression that corresponds to the answer (the deep-content). (For the current example, this surface content might include the pronoun "her" instead of "Mary.")

The Current Status of the Work

B2 is being developed using the Common Lisp programming language. We are using the SNePS 2.3.1 and ANALOG 1.1 tools to create the lexicon, parser, generator, and underlying knowledge representations of domain and discourse information (Shapiro and The SNePS Implementation Group 1992, Shapiro and Rapaport 1992, Ali 1994a, b). Developed at the State University of New York at Buffalo, SNePS (semantic network processing system) provides tools for building and reasoning over nodes in a propositional semantic network.

An Internet-accessible, graphical front-end to B2 is being developed using the Java 1.1 programming language. It can be run using a network browser, such as Netscape. The interface that the user sees communicates with a server-side program that initiates a Lisp process.

Summary

The goal of our work is to give students an opportunity to practice their decision making skills where the primary modality of interaction is English. We give students the opportunity to ask the system to explain what factors were most influential to its decision and why.

The natural language processing and knowledge representation components of B2 are general purpose. It builds a five-level model of the discourse that represents what was literally said, what was meant, and how each utterance and its interpretation relates to previous ones. This is necessary because students' utterances may be short and ambiguous, requiring extensive reasoning about the domain or the discourse model to fully resolve. We have shown how our mixed-depth representations encode syntactic and conceptual information in the same structure. This allows us to defer any extensive reasoning until needed, rather than when parsing. We use the same representation framework to produce a detailed representation of requests and to produce a representation of questions. The representations use the same knowledge representation framework that is used to reason about discourse processing and domain information—so that the system can reason with (and about) the utterances.

Acknowledgments

This work was partially funded by the National Science Foundation, under grants IRI-9701617 and IRI-9523666, Intel Corporation, and by gifts from the University of Wisconsin Medical School, Department of Medicine.

Notes

1. Case frames are conventionally agreed upon sets of arcs emanating from a node that are used to express a proposition. For example, to express that A isa B we use the MEMBER-CLASS case frame which is a node with a MEMBER arc and a CLASS. arc(Shapiro et al. 1994) provides a dictionary of standard case frames. Additional case frames can be defined as needed.

2. "Conjoin" is a technical term from Rhetorical Structure Theory (Mann and Thompson 1986); it refers to a co-ordinate conjunction of clauses.

3. HIDA stands for radio-nuclide hepatobiliary imaging, a diagnostic test.

4. ASKREF is used to denote a wh-question that is intended to express that the speaker does not know the referent of some description, that the speaker intends to know the referent, and intends that the hearer should tell the speaker what the referent is (by performing an INFORMREF.) (McRoy and Hirst 1995, Hinkelman 1990).

9 Enriching the WordNet Taxonomy with Contextual Knowledge Acquired from Text

Sanda M. Harabagiu and Dan I. Moldovan

RECENTLY, A NEW VERSION of the WordNet lexical database (Miller 1995) developed at Princeton has become publicly available (www.cogsci.princeton.edu/~wn). WordNet~1.6 contains 126,520 English words grouped into 91,595 synonym sets, called *synsets.* Words and synsets are entangled by 391,885 lexico-semantic relations, making WordNet a useful resource for natural language processing systems. WordNet has recently been used in conjunction with annotated corpora (like Treebank, described by Marcus et al. [1993]) for applications such as word-sense disambiguation (Ng and Lee 1996), information extraction (Bagga et al. 1997), text summarization (Robin and McKeown 1995), conversational implicature (Harabagiu et al. 1996), and probabilistic world wide web search engines similar to those presented in Ackerman et al. (1997). Most of these applications rely implicitly on linguistic and/or discourse contexts, and the integration of contextual objects in the WordNet taxonomy is beneficial and can lead to novel, more performant processing techniques.

WordNet covers the majority of English nouns, verbs, adjectives and adverbs, but it implements only fourteen types of lexico-semantic relations, thus providing with a small connectivity between nodes, desired to be enriched. The meaning of each synset of WordNet 1.6 is defined by a textual gloss, which can be considered also as a minimal contextual definition. Contextual representations in lexical databases have been considered before as important indicators of word senses in WordNet (Miller and Charles 1991). The problem was to find an empirical solution to the representation problem. Furthermore, information about the context in which a concept is used brings knowledge about the world, transforming the lexicon into an approximation of common-sense knowledge.

The codification of human knowledge using contextual representations was also attempted in the CYC project (Lenat 1995), (Lenat and Guha 1990). CYC covers 10^5 concepts, spanned by 10^5 hand-crafted common-sense axioms and thousands of semantic relation types. The only role of contexts in CYC is to support the validity of factual assertions, constituents of the propositional common-sense knowledge base. Lexical ambiguity was just recently asserted in CYC as an important problem, and its handling is still in progress.

Most of the on-going linguistic theories do not define precisely the concept of linguistic context. Many performing methods of word-sense disambiguation account for context by using windows of surrounding words. The same representation is insufficient for discourse theories, that need to produce higher-level pragmatic inferences using elaborate information pertaining to the situation conveyed by the text. Discourse-based theories rely on the logic and coherence of a text, thus needing a representation of the context from which complex implications can be derived. In this chapter, we employ such a representation, provided as a byproduct of finding lexico-semantic paths from texts. The lexico-semantic paths surrounding a text unit account for the logical implications derived by the text situations and furthermore, correspond to the contextual objects proposed by McCarthy (1993).

McCarthy, and then Buvac (Buvac et al. 1995), treat contexts as formal objects, and have developed a quantificational logic of context. Their proposed content logic is a declarative knowledge representation derived from the experience of managing large encyclopedic knowledge bases, specifically the CYC project (Guha 1991). Their studies focus on the logical properties of contexts, disregarding the actual content of the context object. We take here the reverse perspective, trying to grab the structure of context objects, knowing their logical features. We show that the contextual structures containing webs of WordNet lexical paths support also Grice's (1975) maxims for conversational implicatures. Gricean implicatures have been recognized by Thomason and Moore (1993) as important indicators of the capabilities of a context model to handle nonliteral inferences, as part of the complex discourse phenomena they have to accommodate. A computational model capable of handling Gricean implicatures can indicate whether sufficient contextual information is used, as it is known that Gricean implicatures are highly dependent on the text context. These implicatures bring forward information used to perform coreference resolution.

The extensions of WordNet considered here follow the same design principles as the initial database: economy and wide coverage of lexical

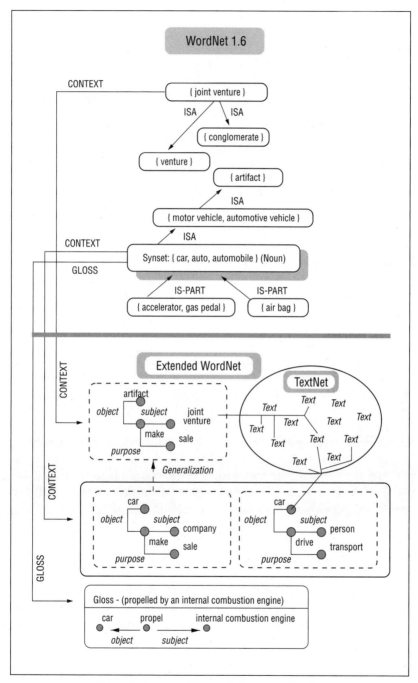

Figure 1. Enriching WordNet with Contextual Information

relations. The relational semantics of the dictionary, proven to be a viable alternative to compositional semantics, is extended with novel types of lexical relations, acquired from the corpus of conceptual glosses provided by WordNet. The existing semantic network is maintained and enriched with more relations.

The original WordNet semantic network of nodes and lexical relations can be conveniently formalized as $KB_{WNextended} = (N, R, N_G, R_G)$, where N is the current set of nodes representing words or concepts, R represents the existing lexico-semantic relations, while N_G and R_G are the gloss nodes and relations. The gloss nodes are actually place holders for regular WordNet concepts that are used in gloss definitions. The R_G are novel semantic relations, derived from the gloss texts. Their validity is restricted to the scope of the gloss, and thus any logical property they entail is true only in the context of the gloss. Next, we extend WordNet to $KB_{WNcontextualized} = (N, R, N_G, R_G, N_C, R_C)$, encompassing also context nodes N_C and context relations R_C associated with every WordNet concept. The context nodes and relations are organized as a frame where, similarly to the gloss transformations, the context nodes are place holders of regular WordNet synsets, and the context relations are produced from semantic paths.

More than one context frame is characteristic for one WordNet concept, as it is illustrated in figure 1. To determine what part of the lexico-semantic paths derived from a text is representative for the general contextual usage of a WordNet concept, we have developed a classification mechanism. The context frame results from generalization and specialization processed over fragments of semantic path. In this way WordNet is enhanced in two ways. First, the contextual structures provide with an alternate definition of a concept, targeting automatic processing instead of human understanding and second, the network of words is attached with a web of contextually related texts, that we have coined TextNet in one of our 1997 papers (Harabagiu and Moldovan 1997).

Acquisition of Contextual Structures from Text

Semantic connections retrieved from a linguistic knowledge base are the means for finding information that is not directly stated in textual documents, but rather it is implied. Networks of concepts and lexical relations interconnect words in texts, providing for the information space upon which textual inferences (known also as implicatures, cf. Grice [1975]) can be drawn. As the context of a text is assumed to contain all the information that is drawn from lexico-semantic paths, we have de-

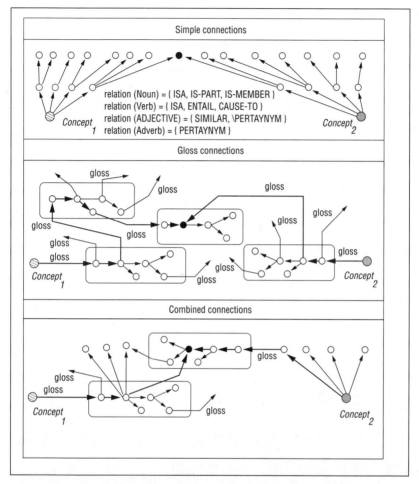

Figure 2. Search Primitives Between Two WordNet Concepts

veloped an algorithm that returns an approximation of the context as a structure of WordNet concepts and relations.

The path-finding algorithm was designed to find intra- and intersentential semantic paths in a text, while building the contexts of sentences. The algorithm consists of four steps that successively perform searches in WordNet and consolidate the contextual structures.

The search mechanism uses three types of primitives, illustrated in figure 2. Each primitive constructs a semantic path between a pair of concepts by using a different set of knowledge base relations. The simple primitive uses only some regular WordNet relations, the gloss primitive uses only gloss relations, and the combine primitive uses both types of relations.

A Path-Finding Algorithm

In this subsection, we will describe the four steps of the algorithm.

Step 1: Find Paths that Explain Textual Lexical Relations

In a large knowledge base there are many possible connections between the concepts used in the text, however, only some of these are relevant for the text on hand while others are relevant in other contexts. Our approach to reduce the number of irrelevant inferences is to find only those paths from the knowledge base that relate directly with the textual lexical relations.

There are several ways in which one can take advantage of the textual lexical relations. For a given lexical relation linking two concepts, the search strategy is to look for the same lexical relation in the glosses of nearby concepts. We have investigated three methods that have different search strategies. In what follows, a lexical relation r between $concept_i$ and $concept_j$ is denoted as $r(concept_i, concept_j)$. Furthermore, $concept_i$ is the source and $concept_j$ is the destination of relation.

The first method, illustrated in figure 3a, searches for relation r first in the gloss of $concept_i$ and then in the glosses of concepts that connect with $concept_i$ via simple/gloss/combined paths. When relation r is found in such a gloss, connections are sought between the destination concept of that relation and $concept_j$.

The second method, illustrated in figure 3b, is used when there are two adjacent relations $r_1(concept_i, concept_j)$ and $r_2(concept_j, concept_q)$. This method searches for relation r_1 in the glosses of concepts that connect to $concept_q$ via a simple/gloss/combine connection. If relation r_1 is found in the gloss of one of the concepts, a path can be established if simple/gloss/combine connections also exist between the destination concept of r_1 and $concept_j$.

Finally, the third method, illustrated in figure 3c searches first for all glosses that contain $concept_i$ and marks the concepts in these glosses as gloss_$concept_i$. Then, the method searches for relation r in the gloss of some concept that connects to any of the gloss identified before. When relation i is found, then simple/gloss/combined connections are sought between $concept_j$ and the destination concept of relation r is performed.

Step 2: Determine the Local Context of a Sentence

The role of this step is to merge the paths found in step 1 for all lexical relations of a sentence into a graph where common concepts are not repeated. This consolidated graph is considered to represent the context of that sentence. Regarding the sentence as a collection of lexical relations $\{r(concept_i, concept_j)\}$ the approach of building the contextual graph consists of the five steps depicted in figure 4.

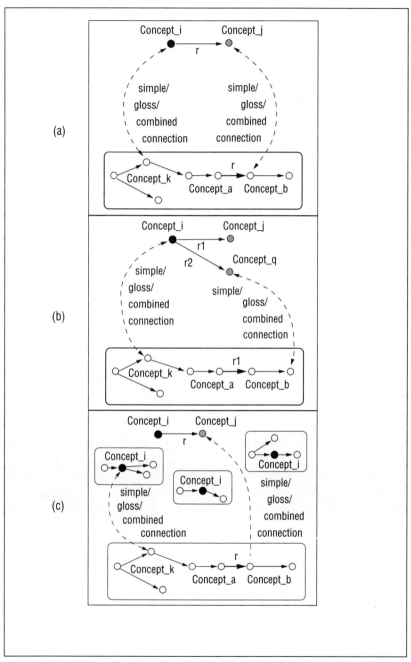

(a)

(b)

(c)

Figure 3. Three Methods of Path Search in WordNet

---

1   Length-based sorting of paths corresponding to every $r(concept_i,$ $concept_j)$;

2   Search every $concept_n$ from any $path_m$ in all the other paths that are longer than $path_m$;

3   For every $concept_n$ found in $path_{m+x}$

       3a   Add the incoming link of $concept_n$ in $path_{m+x}$ to the list of incoming links of $concept_n$ in $path_m$;

       3b   Same as 3a for outgoing links;

       3c   Delete $concept_n$ in $path_m$;

4   Search every $concept_p$ from $path_{q(r)}$ of $r(concept_i, concept_j)$ in the paths corresponding to the other lexical relations of the sentence;

5   For every $concept_p$ found in $path_{q(r)}$

       5a   Add the incoming link of $concept_p$ in $path_{s(r')}$ to the list of incoming links of $concept_p$ in $path_{q(r)}$;

       5b   Same as 5a for outgoing links;

       5c   Delete $concept_p$ in $path_{s(r')}$;

Figure 4. Building the Contextual Graph

The result of this procedure is a web of concepts connected through relations that were building the paths detected at step 1.

Step 3: Find Paths Between Sentences

Step 3 takes advantage of the collective meaning of all sentences in the text by finding connections between their local contexts. We have developed three different ways of retrieving connections between the concepts of different sentences. One way is to find knowledge base paths between the verbs of one sentence and the verbs of the other sentence. This method is illustrated in figure 5a. For linguistic reasons, we select only verbs since they are the dominant words of any sentence. The second way, illustrated in figure 5b is to find paths between the verbs of one sentence and the nodes of the local context of the other sentence. A third way is to pair the nodes from the local contexts of one sentence with the nodes from the local context of the other sentence. As figure 5 suggests, for each sentence, all possible connections to previously processed sentences are explored.

Step 4: Structuring the Global Context of a Text

The global context of a sequence of sentences is achieved by building a

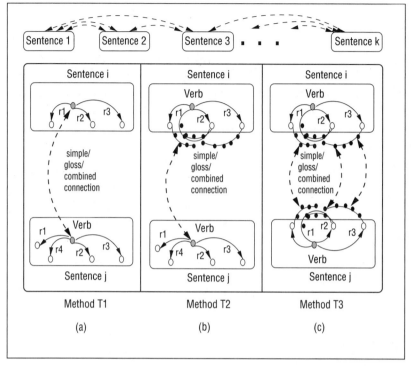

Figure 5. Establishing Intersentential Paths Building the Local Contexts

structure that eliminates repeating concepts throughout textual paths and local contexts. First, the common concepts between the textual connections are reduced by applying the same procedure as the one used in step 2 for building the local contexts. Then this new structure is matched against each local context, and common concepts are further reduced.

Contextual Objects

McCarthy (1993) has introduced contexts as formal objects for artificial intelligence by investigating their logical properties from a purely mathematical point of view. A classical propositional logic of contexts was developed, extended now to the quantificational case (Buvac 1996). The theory is based on the *ist* modality: $ist(c, p)$ is true iff p is true within the scope of the context c. The usage of the *ist* as a validity measure corresponds to Guha's proposal of context semantics, motivated by the CYC knowledge base.

As WordNet 1.6 does not represent contextual information, and furthermore, its relational semantics is context-independent, we find appropriate to try to model the context structures by making use of the WordNet knowledge and regardless of the representation principles used in CYC, to make use of the contextual-logic assumptions. In McCarthy's and Buvac 's theory, the context objects are known entities of unprecise content, which validate the truth value of some atoms. In the context model presented here, several classes of atoms are assumed, known to be true in the contexts whose structure we seek. Therefore, a context object is defined by all the WordNet knowledge that verifies the truth of the atoms it associates with. This assumption is enforced when proof is made that such contextual structures behave similarly as the formal objects from the first-order theory of contexts.

The extension of WordNet with contextual information considers only four types of context objects: conceptual atoms, lexical relation atoms, sentence atoms, and text atoms. We assume some inclusion principles between the contexts of these atoms, i.e. we expect that the context of a lexical relation between two concepts includes information from the contexts of the two concepts. Similarly, the context of a sentence includes the contexts of its lexical relations, and the context of a text includes the contexts of its sentences.

Given a WordNet concept, we define its context to be the set of WordNet concepts chained to the given concept through WordNet or gloss relations, and the corresponding connections. Similarly, the context structure associated with a lexical relation is defined by the results returned by the three methods from the first step of the path-finding algorithm when applied to that relation. For example, figure 6 illustrates the contextual structure corresponding to the lexical relation (make—*object*→car). A gloss connection relates synset {make, produce} to the synset {create} whose object, the synset {product, production}, is linked through a gloss connection to synset {car, auto, automobile, machine, motorcar}. Other contextual concepts brought forward by the path-finding algorithm are {industry, manufacturing} and {commodity, goods}.

The context of (make—*object*→car) contains only those paths from the context structures of the concepts *make* and *car* that correspond to assertions that are true in the situation of making cars. For example, the context of car contains such concepts as *license plate, car seat, passenger, chauffeur* or *jeep*. Although they are connected to the concept *car,* they are discarded because they are not contained in any paths connecting *make* and *car* to the arguments of another object relation.

Filtering out from the context of a textual relation the concepts that belong to the context of the argument concepts which are no longer valid

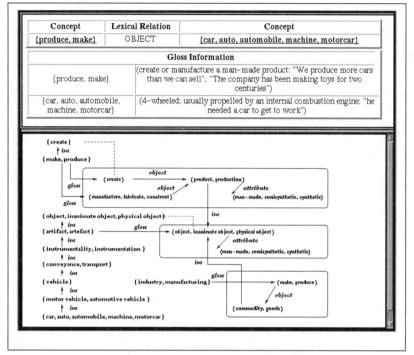

Concept	Lexical Relation	Concept
{produce, make}	OBJECT	{car, auto, automobile, machine, motorcar}

	Gloss Information
{produce, make}	(create or manufacture a man-made product: "We produce more cars than we can sell"; "The company has been making toys for two centuries")
{car, auto, automobile, machine, motorcar}	(4-wheeled; usually propelled by an internal combustion engine; "he needed a car to get to work")

Figure 6. Example of Context Structures Associated with a Lexical Relation

in the new context complies with the enter and the exit axioms of Mc-Carthy.

(Enter)

$ist(context_0, ist(context_1, p))$
$ist(context_0, p)$

(Exit)

$ist(context_0, p)$
$ist(context_1, ist(context_0, p))$

These axioms grant derivability between the contexts. The Enter axiom states that a property evaluated in a $context_0$ as being true in $context_1$ is also true in $context_0$. For example, the property of an object to be man-made as derived from the gloss of artifact, illustrated in figure 6 is also true in the context of (make—*object*→car). This entails that this property is inherited by all the hyponyms (i.e. subsumers) of object from this context as well, comprising the synsets {commodity, goods} or {product, production}. Conversely, the exit axiom states that every property that is true in some context will maintain its evaluation in any outer

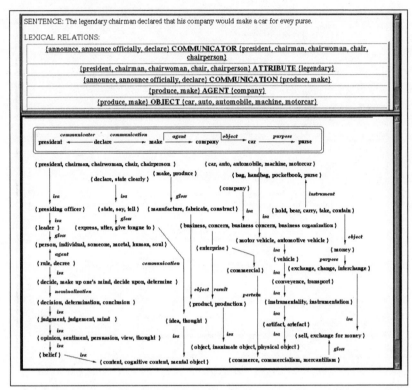

Figure 7. Example of Context Structures Associated with a Sentence

context. This means that all properties from the context of (make—*object*→car) are valid properties of the contexts of the concepts *make* and *car* as well, assumption upon which relies the path-finding algorithm.

The context structure corresponding to a sentence is the result of the second step of the path-finding algorithm. An example of the context structure of a sentence is illustrated in figure 7. A communication regarding the production of cars is made in this sentence, and the sentence context contains information from the context of the lexical relation (make—*object*→car), already presented in figure 6. Only one of the two semantic paths of the lexical relation context is retained, because it has more common concepts with the contexts of the other lexical relations of the sentence.

The selection of the appropriate path in the context of the sentence complies with the context attributes defined by Buvac's *contextual omniscience axiom*:

$$ist(context_1, ist(context_2, p)) \lor ist(context_1, \neg ist(context_2, p))$$

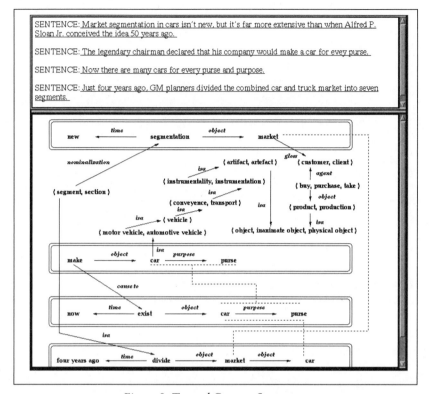

SENTENCE: Market segmentation in cars isn't new, but it's far more extensive than when Alfred P. Sloan Jr. conceived the idea 50 years ago.

SENTENCE: The legendary chairman declared that his company would make a car for every purse.

SENTENCE: Now there are many cars for every purse and purpose.

SENTENCE: Just four years ago, GM planners divided the combined car and truck market into seven segments.

Figure 8. Textual Context Structures

This axiom captures the fact that any model of contexts has to "know" whether a property of one of its objects is valid or not in another context. The incremental method of deriving contexts induced by the path-finding algorithm implements this capability of the context model we consider here.

The context of the text is assembled by the fourth step of the path-finding algorithm, by eliminating the common concepts from the paths between sentences derived at step 3. Figure 8 illustrates the context of a text fragment from a *Wall Street Journal* article containing the sentence previously discussed.

The illustration of the semantic paths bridging the discourse representations of the sentences shows the connections between the concept *market* from the first sentence and the lexical relation [(car for every purse)] of the second sentence. Semantic connections link the concept segmentation and the concept *divide,* as well as *make* and *exist.* The context representation from figure 8 highlights the semantic paths that exist between the first two sentences. Most of the concepts and relations were present in the context of the second sentence already. This complies with Buvac's axiom:

$$ist(context_1, ist(context_2, p)) \leftrightarrow (ist(context_2, p),$$

which tells us that every context looks the same, regardless from which context it is viewed. For the context structures we use, this axiom follows the intuition that the context of any sentence should be viewed in the same way, either from the context of the text or from the context of any of its constituent lexical relations. Therefore, we found that the path-finding algorithm builds context structures that are in accordance with the properties of the context logic. Next we show that these structures also cover Grice's principles of conversational logic.

Context and Gricean Implicatures

The notion of implicature, originated in the work of H. P. Grice, is often invoked to demonstrate the indispensability of pragmatic and contextual information in discourse understanding. Implicatures were introduced by Grice to account for those inferences suggested by texts or conversations that rely on extra-linguistic knowledge, and thus are different from the usual inferences derived from discourse.

Masuko (1996) indicates that conversational implicature is amenable to a lexical solution. Using persistent default unification as a computational tool and incorporating defeasible information into the lexical entries of Pustejovsky's qualia structure (Pustejowsky 1995), Masuko demonstrates that conversational implicatures can be derived through lexical semantics. Her work extends the method of Briscoe, Copesake, and Lascarides (Briscoe et al. 1995) that employ lexical rules formalized in the common-sense entailment logic (Asher and Morreau 1991).

Similarly, the contextual structures derived from WordNet can be used to derive conversational implicatures. In Harabagiu et al. (1996) a system that uses Gricean constraints to evaluate text coherence is presented. Grice's maxims provide conditions to test coherence, while the semantic paths drawn from WordNet provide the space upon which these conditions are tested. The incorporation of conversational implicatures in the model of contextual objects based on the interpretation of the results of the path-finding algorithm entails an interpretation of Grice's maxims from WordNet semantic paths.

There is a controversial attitude among computational linguists regarding Grice's maxims. Although many researchers find the Gricean approaches necessary for the detection of important discourse phenomena

(Kronfeld 1996, Iwańska 1996, Horacek 1996, Green and Lehman 1996, Dale and Reiter 1996, Marcu and Hirst 1996), Grice's maxims are accused of being hopelessly vague (Frederking 1996) or too restrictive (Joshi 1996). Our reformulation of the maxims in the spirit of the quantificational logic of contexts eliminates the object of these criticisms.

The key idea behind the relation between context and conversational logic presented here is expressed by the connection between Grice's maxims and the high-level inferences drawn from the semantic paths derived from WordNet. The semantic paths account for the logical connections of the text, expressing the contextual properties and information regarding text coherence. Testing the Gricean constraints posed by the maxims of conversational logic provides information for granting or discarding inferences. The interpretation of the maxims using the analysis of the semantic paths derived from the WordNet knowledge base is the venue considered here. This interpretation determines rewriting the Gricean maxims as axioms for contextual logic, based on the characteristics of WordNet semantic paths.

Frederking (1996) argues that Grice's taxonomy of conversational implicatures is inadequate for discourse phenomena, as Grice acknowledges to borrow the classification principles from a prelinguistic philosophical classification of statements, developed by Kant (1992) in his theory of categories. His claim is that taxonomies cannot be transferred from one domain to another and still retain any usefulness.

The fact that Grice's principles have been used successfully in implementing systems that capture discourse implicatures, like Green and Carberry's (1994) reasoning model for indirect answers, shows that Grice's theory, like many other discourse logic models, is too informal rather than inadequate. In contrast with Grice's logic, the quantificational logic of contexts developed by Buvac (1996) is a clear, precise formal theory. Therefore, a reformulation of Grice's principles via Buvac-like axioms meets the requirements set by Frederking: correct, detailed mathematic descriptions, preceded by a correct general theory.

The axioms presented here were suggested by the study of the contextual structures relying on lexico-semantic paths and on the tests that were described previously as corresponding to Grice's maxims.

Quantity Maxim 1

Make your contribution as informative as required. This maxim refers to informational adequacy. We observed that a conversation respects quantity maxim 1 when given a contextual structure, there are concepts that are connected to many of the other concepts from the context. We call such nodes *context foci* (such as *car* or *market* in the context of the text illustrated in figure 8). In addition, as the text unfolds, new statements connect to the previous concepts via one of the context foci.

The quantity maxim 1, requiring to make a contribution to a discourse as informative as possible, can be formalized based on the interpretation of the "informative" notion. Intuitively, we consider that a contribution is informative if the new discourse brings about information that (a) is true in the context derived from the previous discourse and (b) was not present in the previous context. Therefore, the evaluation of the validity of a proposition p in context k_1 performed in the space of context k_0 is equivalent with the evaluation of the validity of the proposition p in both contexts.

This intuition is enforced by the fact that there are some context foci that are going to have properties valid in the context of several sentences as well as in the context of the overall text. If such properties are referred by variable p, then the maxim can be formalized as:

$$ist(k_0, ist(k_1, p)) = ist(k_0, p) \wedge ist(k_1, p)$$

Quantity Maxim 2

Do not make your contribution more informative than necessary. This maxim suggests the elimination of redundant information that can be inferred quickly otherwise. The system checks if semantic paths traverse repeatedly the same concepts. The maxim can be formalized as an implication that when a proposition p is true in k_0, which is the context of the previous discourse, if the novel contribution reaffirms p or another proposition q, then the new context should incorporate only facts assessing q. The formulation of the axiom is:

$$ist(k_0, p \wedge ist(k_1, p \vee q)) \Rightarrow ist(k_0, p) \vee ist(k_0, q)$$

Quality Maxim 1

Do not say what you believe to be false. This maxim suggests that intentions revealed by the utterances of the conversations should not contradict themselves. This implies that the evaluation of a proposition p in the new context should be false if it is true that $\sim p$ (non-p) is valid in the previous context. The formalization is

$$ist(k_0, ist(k_1, \neg p)) \Rightarrow \neg ist(k_0, p)$$

Quality Maxim 2

Do not say that for which you lack evidence. This maxim suggests that statements should introduce information that supports previous and future intentions of the conversation participants. A lack of evidence may be reflected by contradictions or paths that connect at very general concepts in the WordNet noun or verb hierarchies. This is equivalent to the implication that if in the new context, the assertion that p is true in the initial context k_1 is false, then p should not belong to the new context either. The axiom formalizing this maxim is:

$$ist(k_0, \neg ist(k_1, p)) \Rightarrow \neg ist(k_0, p)$$

Relation Maxim

Be relevant. This maxim suggests that any statement should introduce information that connects with as many previously activated concepts as possible. The system may count the number of new concepts along a path and decide whether or not the statement is relevant by checking if its paths are established in different areas of the knowledge base, are dispersed and the inferences they produce do not converge. The relation maxim, requesting for the contribution to be relevant, is formalized by an axiom that implies that the addition of irrelevant (or already known) facts to a context should be discarded.

$$ist(k_0, p \lor ist(k_1, p)) \Rightarrow ist(k_0, p)$$

Manner Maxim 1

Avoid obscurity of expression. Clarity of expression is reflected in a small number of gloss concepts and gloss relations along the paths. The more obscure a discourse is, the more glosses are needed to retrieve defining information. A clear discourse results in a rich set of semantic connections among input concepts, not among concepts that are vague generalizations of the input words.

The manner maxims, unlike the previous maxims, have more to do with how something is said rather then with what is said. The manner maxim 1, urging to avoid obscurity of expression, is formalized by an implication that discards the import in the new context of those facts that were not true in the former context:

$$ist(k_0, ist(k_1, p \lor \neg q)) \Rightarrow \neg ist(k_0, p)$$

Manner Maxim 2

Avoid ambiguity. An ambiguity is detected whenever the path-finding algorithm cannot bridge sentences with paths connecting textual relations, but rather the majority of the paths link concepts from the local contexts of the sentences. Furthermore, some of those paths bring about contradictory concepts.

The manner maxim 2 discards contradictory facts brought by the novel context, implying that a property valid in a context but invalid in another inner context should be invalidated in the outer context as well:

$$ist(k_0, p \land ist(k_1, \neg p)) \Rightarrow \neg ist(k_0, p)$$

Manner Maxim 3

Be brief. Brevity testing can be done by checking whether or not the activated concepts along semantic paths were already activated earlier. The more new relevant concepts, the briefer the discourse is.

Manner maxim 3, asking for brevity, disregards the information brought by the new context, if it relied on facts that were already known. The axiomatic formalization is:

$$ist(k_0, p \land ist(k_1, p)) \Rightarrow ist(k_0, p)$$

Manner Maxim 4

Be orderly. In an orderly discourse, semantic paths between succeeding sentences may be established, whereas in an unorderly discourse, many critical paths are formed between sentences that do not follow each other. This manner maxim corresponds to an axiom that transfers the order of implication along transcending contexts:

$$ist(k_0, ist(k_1, p) \to ist(k_2, q)) \Rightarrow ist(k_0, p \to q)$$

Discussion

Contextual structures rendered by lexico-semantic paths contain information that is relevant for the conventional or conversational implicatures derived from a text. Therefore, paths that fail the test of Grice's maxims should be discarded, and this action needs to be reflected in an extension of the logic of contexts, that covers this class of inferences.

Quantity maxim 1 discards the paths that do not contain contextually informative concepts. Quantity maxim 2 discards the paths that establish connections between concepts that are already related. The quality maxims eliminate paths that bring contradictory information. The relation maxim discards paths containing concepts that are semantically distant from the context foci. Manner maxim 1 selects the shortest paths that connect two concepts. Manner maxim 2 discards paths containing concepts with large level of abstraction. Manner maxim 3 scans all paths to find considerable chunks of interrelated concepts that repeat along multiple paths. Manner maxim 4 checks if the semantic paths provide for coherence of the text.

The sequence of sentences in a text is considered coherent if the logical flow of information is accounted for. Several models that capture this phenomenon have been proposed (Hobbs 1985, Mann and Thomson 1988). Like these models, our semantic path connectivity method relies on plausible inferences that can be drawn when processing a text. But unlike these models, which operate on a finite set of coherence relations or rhetorical structures, we do not constrain the possible connections between sentences to a prefixed set. We consider that anytime a path satisfies all linguistic constraints imposed by the text and does not violate Grice's conditions, that path indicates a coherence relation.

It is known that the interpretation of the coherence relations spanning a text is not unique. The text from figure 8 can be interpreted as an example of elaboration as defined in either Hobbs's or Mann and Thomson models. Moreover, the same text informs about Mr. Sloan's intentions to manufacture cars for more than one market. Intentions are not captured by this model of contextual structures, but they can be considered via the coherence relations that can be recognized. Moore and Paris (1993) have discussed the mapping of rhetorical relations in speakers' intentions, but did not relate these ideas to context.

There have been other important formalizations of special types of implicatures, that can be easily incorporated in this proposed system. The most notable is Hirschberg's (1985) theory of scalar implicature, which defines the characteristics of scalar implicatures, arising from the violation of quantity maxims. The scalar implicature inference rules from Hirshberg's theory introduce, besides the contextual information, a belief system that validates predicates, logical or epistemic operators, connective or quantifier symbols of a proposition p, or any wff that is a subformula of p.

An excellent contribution to the computational usage of Grice's maxims has been done by Marilyn Walker (1992, 1996). Her work comprises a computational transformation of Lewis's shared environment model of common knowledge (Lewis 1969), explaining how implicatures can be used to indicate rejection and how conflicting defaults from epistemic inference rules are resolved in the inference of rejection.

Contributions to the formalization of Grice's manner maxims have been proposed in Marcu and Hirst's work (1996), where pragmatic inferences, having to do with these maxims are treated in terms of their stratified logic (Marcu and Hirst 1995). Other logic formalism, like Perlis's active logic (Elgot-Drapkin and Perlis 1990) were proposed to handle implicatures that assume the quality and relation maxims. To our knowledge, no other formalism considers all maxims and relates them to a formal theory of contexts.

Context Specialization and Generalization

The goal of the path-finding algorithm is to reveal the web of concepts and interrelating links that draw the context of a text. Testing the Gricean maxims on these structures brings forward the focal concepts of the text. When one of the focal concepts is explicit in the text, we can extract a pattern of textual concepts and relations that may be associated with that concept on a general basis. To extract the pattern of focal concept C_f we use the following rule: (a) if C_f is a verb, all the other concepts of the pattern are text concepts directly linked to C_f via textual relations, else (b) if C_f is directly linked to a verb concept C_v, then the pattern shall contain all the text concepts directly linked to C_v. In the case when any of the other concepts linked to C_v is also a verb, the pattern will contain all text concepts directly linked to it as well. For example, for the text illustrated in figure 8, one focal concept is {car, auto, automobile, machine, motorcar}. The extracted pattern is illustrated in figure 9a.

The pattern from figure 9a holds valid properties in the context of the text illustrated in figure 8, but in order to know whether it is a pattern characteristic of the concept *car*, we need, first, to evaluate it against other patterns extracted from texts focusing on cars and second, integrate it in the WordNet knowledge base by assessing its compatibility with the glosses of the concepts sharing common properties with the concept *car*. When doing so, we found that the pattern illustrated in figure 9a is a specialization of the pattern from figure 9b, a combination of the gloss of {produce, make} and a pattern extracted from other *Wall Street Journal* articles.

The evaluation of the patterns extracted from texts is done by classifying these patterns based on their commonalities. Figure 10 illustrates the three methods we have considered to classify patterns. The methods are applied successively to the patterns and divided into sets of ordered patterns, based on an induced specialization order relation.

Method 1 finds two patterns that belong to the same class when (a) the two verb concepts belong to the same WordNet verb hierarchy and there are relations used by the second pattern included in the relations utilized by the first one and (b) the address concepts of identical relations belong to the same WordNet hierarchy. The first pattern is a generalization of the second one when its concepts subsume the concepts of the second pattern.

The second method relaxes the requirement of having identical relations by considering two patterns in the same class when a semantic path exists between the context of the first pattern to the second pattern. This path contains relations r_c, absent from *Pattern*$_1$ but employed in

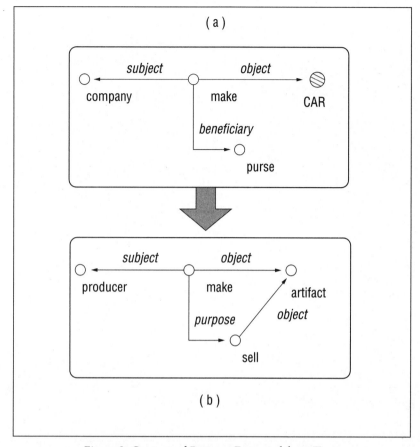

Figure 9. Contextual Patterns Extracted from Texts

Pattern$_2$. Moreover, the arguments of relations r_c from the path and from *Pattern$_2$* must belong to the same WordNet class.

In the third method, the search for the unmatched relations r_c is performed along the gloss transformations. If relation r_c is found in any gloss and its arguments belong to the same WordNet hierarchy as the arguments of r_c in *Pattern$_2$*, then *Pattern$_1$* and *Pattern$_2$* belong to the same class.

Next, we integrate into WordNet only those patterns that are universal subsumers in their class and can be coherently used in conjunction with the information that already exists in WordNet. Testing the integration capabilities of a pattern is performed using another set of three procedures, illustrated in figure 11. It is a search for similar partial patterns in the existing glosses of WordNet.

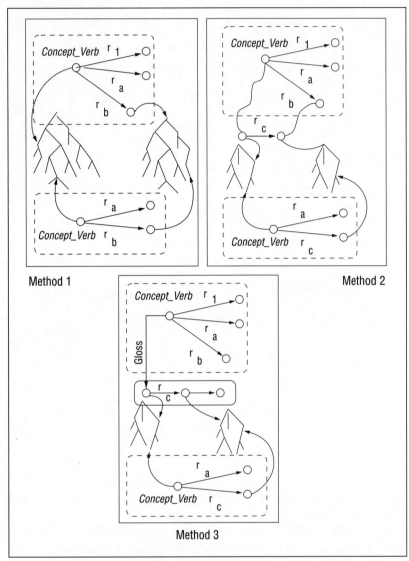

Figure 10. Methods of Classifying Contextual Patterns

The first method looks for relations from the pattern in the glosses of the subsuming (hypernym) verb concepts, and validates the pattern if at least one relation initiating at a gloss genus is matched. The gloss relation is relevant only if the arguments also belong to the same wordNet hierarchies as those from the pattern (or at least their gloss geni do).

For example, the pattern illustrated in figure 9a has the object rela-

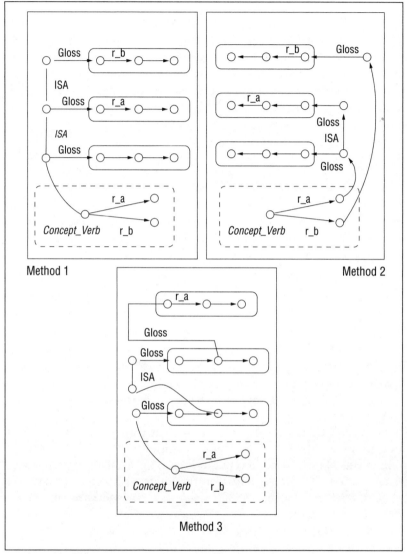

Figure 11. Three Ways of Integrating Contextual Patterns in WordNet

tion matched against the gloss of concept {produce, make, create}. The gloss is (create or manufacture a man-made product). A car is a form of artifact (i.e. man-made product). One of the other relations from the pattern, the *purpose* relation, is retrieved from the gloss of the concept {production} defined as (manufacturing or mining or growing something (usually in large quantities) for sale).

The second method integrates a pattern in WordNet when the relations are found in the glosses of the non-verbal concepts or their hypernyms, with the constraint that their arguments comply also with the requirement of being in the same WordNet hierarchies as those in the pattern. Finally the third method searches validation by discovering relations in the glosses of concepts accessed through the gloss of the verb concept (or a hypernym) and then a combination of ISA and Gloss relations.

The ISA relations create hierarchical structures in WordNet that have to be satisfied by the context patterns as well. The previous methods of integration regard only the aspects of associating the context patterns of a single concept in the knowledge base. The integration of context patterns of different concepts from a hierarchy needs further refinement, accomplished through generalization and specialization of the concepts of the pattern. The goal is to determine the optimal level in the hierarchy where these concepts should be situated.

Since verbs are central to the patterns, we look for other context patterns that use the same verbs (or their subsumers), gathering them in the collection $\{Patterns_{Verb}\}$. Given a context pattern $Pattern_k$ containing the relation ($Verb$—r_i→C_k), we collect all the concepts connected via relation r_i to the verb in the other patterns from $\{Patterns_{Verb}\}$ and consider them positive examples. The negative examples are those concepts from $\{Patterns_{Verb}\}$ that belong to the same hierarchies as the positive examples, but are connected to the verbs via different relations than r_i.

The methodology employed for the generalization and specialization of the concepts from the context patterns is similar to the one used in PALKA (Kim and Moldovan 1995). A context pattern, very much like a domain phrasal pattern from PALKA, is constrained by the semantic requirements of each of its concept elements. To generalize the patterns we use PALKA's two methods based on the inductive learning mechanism (Michalski 1983, Mitchell 1982): *single-step generalization* and *incremental generalization*.

In the single-step approach, all concepts from $\{Patterns_{Verb}\}$ are considered at the end of the acquisition of the patterns, with the purpose of detecting the most general concepts among the consistent semantic constraints. The consistent semantic constraints are those that subsume the positive examples and do not subsume the negative ones. The operation of finding the consistent semantic constraints is fully described in Kim and Moldovan (1995). Figure 12 illustrates an example of single-step generalization. P_1, P_2 and P_3 are positive examples while N_1 is a negative example.

Positive example P_3 is also the concept for which its pattern represents

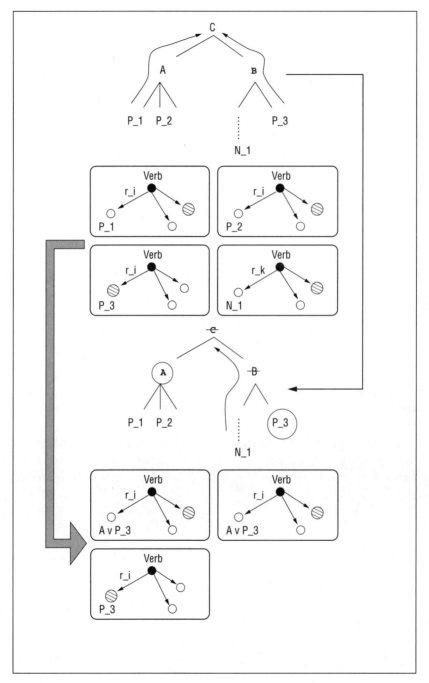

Figure 12. Single-Step Generalization of Contextual Patterns

the context approximation. The single-step generalization finds that the most consistent constraint for this set is represented by $A \lor P_3$, which replaces all positive examples. The pattern containing the negative example is discarded.

When the size of $\{Patterns_{Verb}\}$ is large, changing semantic constraints during the acquisition of the context patterns may speed up the integration process. In the incremental process, the algorithm modifies the semantic constraints as it tries to integrate the pattern in the knowledge base. Generalization and specialization are performed immediately when a new positive or negative example is encountered. A positive example determines a generalization of the semantic constraints, whereas a negative one entails a specialization of the semantic constraint.

Let S represent the current semantic constraints of the context elements from the set $\{Patterns_{Verb}\}$ linked to the verb by r_i relations. By $Inf(C)$ we denote all the subumees of a concept C, whereas $Sup(C)$ denotes the hypernyms and the subsumers of the genuses of their glosses. For the single-step generalization, the consistent semantic constraints are obtained by the operation $Sup(P) - Sup(N)$, where P and N represent the positive and the negative examples, respectively. In the incremental generalization case, whenever a new positive example is found, a new set of consistent semantic constraints is determined by computing $Sup(S \cup P_i) - Sup(N)$. A new negative example N_i determines the new consistent semantic constraints to be $Inf(S) - Sup(N \cup N_i)$. The corresponding actions taken on the contextual pattern are illustrated in figure 13.

A positive example in a context pattern may provide generalization to a superconcept as figure 13a suggests. A negative example specializes the constraint A to the disjunction $A_1 \lor A_2$ in all patterns, as illustrated in figure 13b.

Experimental Results

We have implemented the integration of WordNet with context patterns for several domains dictated by the recent MUC competitions (Sundheim 1993, 1995): the joint-venture domains, the management succession domain and the aircraft collision domain. Table 1 illustrates the number of concepts that have been enriched with contextual information, the number of texts considered, the cardinality of the semantic paths and the number of patterns extracted. The table also lists the number of generalizations and specializations.

To assess the validity of these contextual structures we have performed

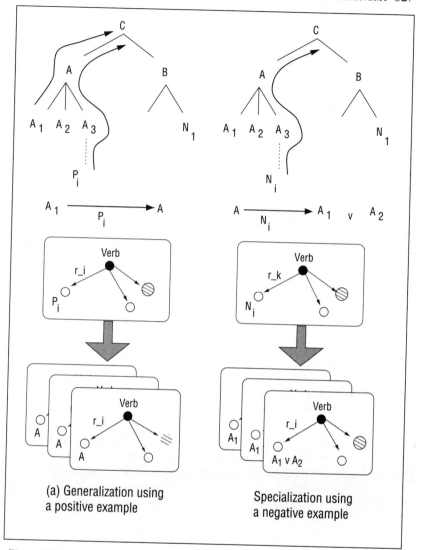

(a) Generalization using
a positive example

Specialization using
a negative example

Figure 13. Incremental Generalization and Specialization of Contextual Patterns

three different tests—involving the resolution of three diverse natural
language tasks.

Word-Sense Disambiguation

We have conceived a word-sense disambiguation procedure that selects
the senses of the words by combining the information from the glosses

Domain	Nr. WN concepts	Nr. texts	Nr.text concepts	Nr.WN paths	Nr. patterns	Nr. generalizations	Nr. specializations
joint venture	28	10	487	1853	63	27	16
management succession	19	10	376	1472	22	15	9
aircraft collision	26	10	531	2059	31	13	6

Table 1

Experimental contextual patterns acquired for WordNet 1.6.

Procedure   gloss-based_disambiguation ($word_1$, $word_2$, *lexical_relation*)

1   for each sense $s1$ of $word_1$ and for each sense s_2 of $word_2$

2   **if** (there is a lexical relation between $word_1{}^{s_1}$ and $word_2{}^{s_2}$ in gloss($s_{1/2}$)) /case 1/

3   **then** select the senses and the lexical relation from that gloss;

4   **else if** (there is a lexical relation between a hypernym/holo-nym/pertainym/similar/entailed/caused concept of $word_1$ (or $word_1$) and a /hypernym/holonym/pertainym/similar/entailed/caused concept of $word_2$ (or $word_2$) in one of the glosses of $word_1$ or $word_2$ (or any of their hypernyms/holonyms/pertainyms/simi-lar/entailed/ /caused concepts)) /case 2/

5   **then** select the senses and the lexical relation from that gloss;

6   **else if** (there is a lexical relation between the genus of a gloss reached by gloss expansion of the genuses of $word_1$ or $word_2$ and a corresponding hypernym/holonym/pertanym/similar/entailed/caused concept or genus of the other $word$)) /case 3/

7   **then** select the senses and the lexical relation from that gloss;

8   **else** select the first sense of the words and tag the lexical relation as unknown;

end;

Figure 14. Word-Sense Disambiguation Procedure

and the contextual knowledge from the patterns. Using only the gloss in-formation, we consider the disambiguation of a pair of words linked by a lexical relation in text that matches a relation from the gloss. The pro-cedure implementing this approach considers the three distinct cases de-picted in figure 14.

Texts	No. of lexical relations identified for case 1	No. of correct relations identified for case 1	No. of lexical relations identified for case 2	No. of correct relations identified for case 2	No. of lexical relations identifed for case 3	No. of crrect relations identified for case 3	No of lexical relations unidentified
w0741.par	65	56	146	104	69	50	104
w0745.par	44	38	86	55	40	32	63
w0748.par	58	49	105	76	49	36	118
w0764.par	112	98	207	150	125	83	181
w0778.par	39	31	77	55	34	24	65
Precision	85.53%		71.89%		70.97%		
Contribution	18.66%		30.19%		15.54%		

Table 2

Evaluation of the gloss-based disambiguation procedure.

	No. of lexical relations identified for case 1	No. of correct relations identified for case 1	No. of lexical relations identified for case 2	No. of correct relations identified for case 2	No. of lexical relations identified for case 3	No. of crrect relations identified for case 3	No. of lexical relations identified for case 4	No. of correct relations identified for case 4
Order 1	123	110	193	184	130	115	159	134
Order 2	76	71	108	95	85	73	152	123
Order 3	24	19	57	52	38	22	191	176
Order 4	95	88	263	243	64	51	237	215

Table 3

Evaluation of the context-based disambiguation procedure.

Table 2 illustrates the contribution of the three cases on the disambiguation process, as well as the level of correctness obtained, when applied to a group of forty *Wall Street Journal* parsed texts from the Treebank corpus (Marcus et al. 1993)

Generally, less than 70 of the lexical relations and their arguments could be disambiguated with this procedure. Far better performance is achieved when the lexical relations are matched against context patterns. Precisions levels of 96 were achieved when the matching of the arguments of the textual relations was done in the same hierarchies as the arguments of the relations from the context patterns. The case when the genuses of the arguments or their hypernyms belong to the same hierarchies was also considered. We have used the same descending order of preference for pattern matching as the one proposed in Kameyama, (1997), a method for mismatch resolution in machine translation. By doing so we match a textual relation in the following order: (Order-1) the context pattern of one of the arguments; (Order-2) the context pattern of the subsumers of the arguments or a subsuming pattern of the context patterns of the arguments; (Order-3) the context pattern of a subsumed concept of the argument or a subsumed pattern of the context patterns of the arguments; (Order-4) other context pattern that uses the relation and at least one of the arguments. Table 3 summarizes the results.

	Total	Intrasentential cases	Intersentetial cases
No. of pronoun occurrences	976	392	584
No. of pronouns for which antecedent were found	437	223	214
No. correct antecedents resolved correctly	344	176	168
Recall	44.77%	56.88%	36.64%
Precision	78.71%	78.92%	78.5%
No. of cases in which the naive algorithm correctly disagrees with the contextual structures by-product	181	66	115
No. of cases in which the by-product correctly disagrees with the naive algorithmthe contextual structures	120	36	84

Table 4

Results of pronoun resolution as by-product of contextual structures.

	Total	Intersentential cases	Intrasentential cases
No. of pronoun occurrences	976	392	584
No. correct antecedents	705	273	432
Precision	72.23%	69.64%	73.97%

Table 5

Precision of pronoun resolution enhanced with contextual knowledge.

Coreference Resolution

In Harabagiu (1997) methods for pronominal and definite coreference resolution using contextual knowledge are evaluated. For the pronominal reference, the evaluation was performed against Hobbs's naive algorithm (Hobbs 1978), that relies solely on syntactic information. Table 4 lists the results of this evaluation.

The results suggest that the by-product of contextual structures doesn't produce results as good as the naive algorithm, first of all because the recall is not very good, although the precision was better than the one obtained by Hobbs' algorithm. Therefore, we combined the two methods and obtained the results listed in table 5, which show an improvement of the precision of the pronoun resolution.

Definite coreference is solved by combining attentional and gricean constraints, an approach pioneered by Passoneau (1995). The attentional constraints are provided by the centering theory framework (Grosz et al. 1995). The gricean constraints are implemented as four semantic informativeness cases; three of them pertaining to principles derived from Grice's maxim of relevance. To define these cases, Passoneau used the principles of informational adequacy and efficiency (cf. Dale and Reiter 1996). Informational adequacy exists when sufficient unambiguous information is provided for the identification of a referent. Informational efficiency is noted when the reference is not more informative than necessary.

	Total	Case 1	Case 2	Case 3	Case 4
No. of anaphoric NPs	1264	453	279	191	341
No. correct antecedents	719	295	147	32	227
Precision	56.88%	65.12%	52.68%	16.75%	66.58%

Table 6

Precision of centering applied for NP anaphora.

	Total	Case 1	Case 2	Case 3	Case 4
No. of unresolved NPs	545	158	132	159	114
No. correct antecedents	162	58	36	27	41
Total Precision	69.69%	65.12%	77.92%	30.89%	78.59%

Table 7

Improved precision by the use of contextual knowledge.

Case 1 is characterized by a noun phrase being both informational adequate and efficient. In Case 2 the noun phrase is adequate but not efficient. The anaphoric noun phrases from the category of the Case 3 are inadequate (under-specified). The forth possibility relates the reference resolution with the identification of additional knowledge. Therefore, case 4 arises when the anaphoric noun phrase performs two functions: first, it corefers with some antecedent and second, it adds information pertaining to that antecedent. Table 6 illustrates the precision of the centering method for each category of noun phrase anaphora, while table 7 lists the precision levels obtained by making use of the contextual structures as well in the process of coreference resolution.

These results indicate that the integration of attentional constraints (used by the centering approach) with Gricean constraints (incorporated in out contextual structures) render better performance for the resolution of anaphoric noun phrases.

Domain Patterns for Information Extraction

The most immediate use of the context patterns is perhaps for the acquisition of domain patterns required by the information extraction techniques described in Appelt et al. (1993) and Kim and Moldovan (1995). Given a query template, as those defined in the MUC competitions, the contextual patterns can easily provide with the domain patterns required for the recognition of the events of interest in a text.

For every pair of concepts from the template, a search is performed for

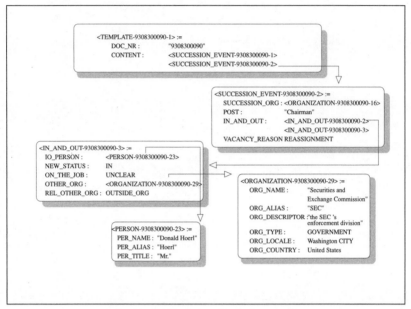

Figure 15. Template for Information
Extraction of Management Succession Events

the retrieval of the same or close relations from the contextual patterns. This search involves scanning the context patterns of the two concepts, the context patterns of their subsumers as well as all the context patterns that imply them. Whenever a hit is reached, the whole pattern is used as a domain pattern. This methodology contrasts with the approach of mining the WordNet knowledge base for domain patterns presented in Harabagiu (2000).

For example, for the template fragment illustrated in figure 15, pertaining to the information extraction task that focuses of events describing succession of management positions, we have obtained the patterns listed in table 8.

According to its developers, the quantitative enhancement of WordNet reached its end with the latest release. Before the developers and the users of WordNet stays now the goal of qualitatively enhancing it. The incorporation of contextual information in WordNet seems a natural choice, especially given the usefulness of contextual pointers proven by CYK. This enhancement may interface the integration of the two knowledge bases. The representation of the context was inspired by the experience drawn from information extraction systems. We conclude that domain and context knowledge tend to come in pattern format.

WordNet is already a semantic source for some of the most intriguing

Subject(Person)	→	Verb(be)	←	Object(Position)		
Subject(Person)	→	Verb(succeed)	←	Object(Person)	←	Prep(as,Position)
Subject(Person)	→	Verb(quit)	←	Object(Organization)	←	Prep(from,Position)
Subject(Person)	→	Verb(assume)	←	Object(Position)	←	Prep(for,organization)
Subject(Person)	→	Verb(replace)	←	Object(Person)	←	Prep(as,Position)
Subject(Person)	→	Verb(cover)	←	Object(Position)	←	Prep(at,Organization)
Subject(Person)	→	erb(control)	←	Object(Organization)		
Subject(Person)	→	Verb(join)	←	Object(Organization)	←	Prep(as,Position)
Subject(Agent)	→	Verb(promote)	←	Object(Person)	←	Prep(to,Position)
Subject(Agent)	→	Verb(appoint)	←	Object(Person)	←	Prep(to,Position)

Table 8.
Domain patterns for management succession.

and promising applications of natural language processing right now: Internet search engines and digital libraries. The extension of WordNet with contextual knowledge may benefit the aspects of knowledge discovery and knowledge federation posed by the two tasks.

10 Fully Automatic Acquisition of Taxonomic Knowledge from Large Corpora of Texts

Łucja M. Iwańska, Naveen Mata,
and Kellyn Kruger

WE PRESENT A NEW METHOD for fully automatic knowledge acquisition from large corpora of unseen texts. Our *learning from a clear-cases* approach exploits simple, efficiently, fast and reliably extractable, parsable and in-depth interpretable constructs of natural language, specialized to convey taxonomic knowledge. It includes type relations (such as type-subtype relation) and concept definitions. The approach allows the system to acquire large quantities of high quality general-purpose knowledge, which practically eliminates costly and error-prone human preprocessing, such as hand-tagging of texts prior to their use, and postprocessing, such as verification of the quality of the acquired knowledge.

Our acquisition scheme is a combination of weak and in-depth methods. For the extraction part of our acquisition scheme, the focus of this chapter—we develop weak, efficient, and computationally inexpensive methods. No natural language understanding or parsing is attempted because such automatic knowledge acquisition can be accomplished without this kind of expensive computation, many aspects of which remain open research problems. Our engineering methods take advantage of local context, including the semantics of punctuation and presence of certain keywords.

For the representation part, we use (very) in-depth methods—the UNO model of natural language, a knowledge representation system closely simulating the unique representational and inferential characteristics of natural language (Iwańska, 1992b, 1993, 1996a, 1997a, 1996b; Iwańska et al., 1995). The similarity to natural language is attractive because it results in the uniformity of representation and inference, and therefore a simple and powerful computer system architecture. No interfaces to translate between incompatible representations or interfaces to access the system knowledge bases are needed. Due to simple syntax, the natural language-based UNO representation of the extracted automatic knowledge can be generated automatically. It is used to also automatically update and access system knowledge bases via a natural languagelike mechanism.

Conjecture: *Natural Language Is a Free Lunch.* The work presented here is part of our efforts to substantiate the extremely theoretically and practically puzzling conjecture: *natural language is a free lunch.* We believe that the widely held belief in the artificial intelligence community that processing natural language necessarily requires an apriori existing knowledge is misguided. This belief is often quoted as one of the main obstacles in automatic knowledge acquisition from natural language input.

Related Work

Employing weak, local-context-based methods for processing large corpora is not a new idea (Cardie, 1997). The new aspect of our approach is that we use weak methods to bootstrap the in-depth methods. We are not aware of any approach that would resemble our limited-syntax, natural language-based knowledge representation system idea to acquire, represent, and utilize automatic knowledge from texts.

Our approach attempts to uniquely combine the advantages of the human and computer information processing—we marry the UNO framework, which allows computers to process (similarly to people) knowledge in the form of natural language, with nonhuman computer capabilities—to be precise, fast, systematic and virtually memory-unlimited.

This chapter is organized as follows: the next section discusses natural language constructs specialized to convey taxonomic automatic knowledge; we then present acquisition algorithms exploiting two such constructs, and discuss the system-acquired concepts from three different corpora. The final section contains our conclusions.

Natural Language Constructs
Conveying Taxonomic Knowledge

Certain natural language constructs convey taxonomic automatic knowledge—relations among different types and concept definitions

CONSTRUCT	KNOWLEDGE	EXAMPLES, COMMENTS
X and not Y	Related types	From r*ed and not green,* system acquires the relation between *red* and *green*
X if not Y	Scalar	From *possible if not certain,* system learns that *certain* is a stronger notion than *possible*
not only X but Y	Scalar	From *not only warm but hot,* system learns that *hot* is a stronger notion than *warm*
X—indeed Y	Scalar	From *I've seldom—indeed, hardly ever— smoked cigars,* system learns that *hardly ever* is a stronger notion than *seldom*
X, which BE Y	Definition	From *Colds are caused by viruses, which are extremely small infectious substances,* system acquires *viruses are extremely small infectious substances*
X, or Y	Definition	From *Your child probably will have more colds, or upper respiratory infections, than any other illness* system learns *colds are upper respiratory infections*
X such as Y, ..., Z	Definition	From *With a young baby, symptoms can be misleading, and colds can quickly develop into more serious ailments such as bronchiolitis, croup, or, pneumonia.* system acquires *bronchiolitis, croup, and pneumonia are serious ailments*
X rather than x	Related types	From *He fears that a heart attack or stroke could leave him 'on life support rather than kill him outright,* system learns that *life support* and *killing one outright* are related choices

Table 1
Simple, efficiently, fast and reliably extractable, parsable and in-depth interpretable constructs of natural language specialized to express taxonomic knowledge.

(see table 1). We analyze such constructs for (1) frequency of occurrences in samples of our corpora, which is indicative of the quantity of useful automatic knowledge possible to acquire via each construct, and (2) ease of eliminating construct uses that do not express the desired type of automatic knowledge, which is indicative of the quality of knowledge to be acquired via each construct.

Table 2 shows the results of the frequency analysis for the natural language constructs considered in a ten percent-sample of our *Time Magazine* corpus; this sample contains 137 articles with an average length of 930 words each.

Natural Language Construct	N_{total}	$N_{desired}$	Comments
X and not Y	10	3	
X if not Y	12	4	
not only X but Y	13	5	
X— indeed Y	8	1	
X such as Y, ..., Z	18	12	Most promising
X rather than Y	17	10	Promising

Table 2

Frequency analysis of the natural language constructs considered for small samples of textual corpora processed; N_{total} is the total number of the construct occurrences in the sample, and $N_{desired}$ is the number of the useful occurrences conveying the desired type of knowledge.

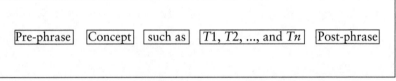

Figure 1. Structure of a Typical Sentence with the Such as *Construct*

The *Such as* Natural Language Construct for Knowledge Acquisition

A sentence with the *such as* construct has the structure depicted in figure 1. Consider the following sentences whose structures are shown in table 3.

1. Caffeine produces psychological and physical dependence, including withdrawal symptoms such as headaches, depression and fatigue.

2. Tabloid shows such as *Hard Copy* and *Inside Edition,* for all their voyeuristic overkill, have demonstrated that there is an audience for news about celebrities that isn't publicity pap.

The first major algorithm step is extraction. The boundaries of the structural elements of the *such as* construct are identified to extract the concept phrase as well as the phrase(s) that define it or relate other concepts to it. The concept resides just before the *such as* construct and is usually separated from the prephrase by a punctuation symbol. Specific elements of different syntactic categories often mark the boundary between the concept and the prephrase. They are treated as keywords and include the following.

Prephrase | Postphrase	Concept	$T1, T_2, T_3$
Caffeine produces psychological and physical dependence, including | *e*	withdrawal symptoms	headaches, depression, fatigue
e | , for all their voyeuristic overkill, have demonstrated that there is an audience for news about celebrities that isn't publicity pap	tabloid shows	*Hard Copy, Inside Edition*

Table 3

The such as structure of the sample sentences; e signifies empty phrase.

- *verbs* (is, are, will, can, might, could, should, would, shall, have, has, was, were)
- *prepositions* (in, on, out, about, for, with, of, from, at, under, including, to, by, over)
- *conjunctions* (if, and, as, or, well, whether, other, even)
- *determiners* (the, many, an, a, any, some, these, those)
- *pronouns* (while, which, that, where, who).

The concept-defining phrases are separated by commas, with the last phrase always appearing after the word *and*. Punctuation symbols usually mark the boundaries between the defining phrase(s) and the postphrase. Boundaries can also be marked by similar keywords. We found that the well-performing on a large scale keyword lists facilitating identifying different boundaries are different. Such good performance coupled with little explanatory power is typical with engineering methods.

Once all the boundaries are identified, limited post-processing is performed. If a concept phrase has more than six words, then only the first three are used. For example, if the acquired concept is a *very lively, affectionate, extremely small animal,* then the system keeps only the *extremely small animal* part as the concept phrase. If a definition phrase is more than six words long, it is excluded from the concept definition. The numbers were established experimentally.

The second major algorithm step is automatic generation of the UNO natural language-like representation of the acquired pieces of knowledge (details can be found in the publications cited earlier).

We have two implementations of the *such as* acquisition algorithm: one in Borland C++ and one in Common Lisp, both running on PC and UNIX platforms. The Lisp implementation, a much more natural choice for such a symbol processing task, is much smaller and easier to main-

Corpus	Size in KB	N_{total}	N_d	Grade A Concepts	Grade B Concepts	Grade C Concepts
Time Magazine	10,530	234	23	67%	22%	11%
Wall Street Journal	6,863	342	51	58%	22%	20%
Microbiology	6,327	335	54	68%	27%	5%
Total	23,720	911	39	64%	24%	12%

Table 4

Summary of the quantitative and qualitative evaluation of the system-acquired knowledge from three different corpora performed by human experts; N_{total} is the total number of concepts, N_d is the number of concepts per 1MB.

tain. The much larger and harder to maintain C++ implementation is four times faster.

The system handles quite limited aspects of local context, yet performs well. For example, it uses extremely crude heuristics to identify sentential boundaries. This speeds up processing tremendously, and, surprisingly, does not affect that much the precision of extraction.

Results: Quantity, Quality of System-Acquired Knowledge

We analyzed the the quantity and quality and of the system-acquired knowledge. Table 4 summarizes the quantitative aspects.

For the quality evaluation, we used human specialists. For the newspaper corpora, *Time Magazine* and the *Wall Street Journal*—which contain a lot of commonsense or generally known knowledge, a friend was the quality judge. For the *Microbiology* corpus, which contains mostly highly specialized scientific knowledge, a specialist did the quality grading. The grades were assigned as follows: An A was awarded for fully-correct knowledge; a B was assigned for mostly-correct knowledge; and a C was assigned for mostly-incorrect or inaccurate knowledge. Table 5 shows the quality evaluation.

Less than ten percent of the *Time Magazine* and *Microbiology* corpora and none of the *Wall Street Journal* corpus were used as the test and development data. This might explain why the acquisition results from *Wall Street Journal* are the worst. The *Microbiology* corpus had the best results—many more concepts were acquired and many more of them are the good ones; only about five percent are the C-grade level concepts.

Grade	Concept	$T_1 \mid T_2 \mid T_3$
A	core academic subjects	math | reading
A	big name computers	Compaq | IBM | Apple
A	human diseases	scrub typhus | spotted fever | typhus
A	crops	rice | soybeans | cotton
A	winter wheat states	Oklahoma | Kansas
A	category	history | comedy | tragedy
A	pass sensitive information	credit-card numbers safely over the network
B	volatile compounds	Diaceytl | its derivatives
B	underlying condition	alcoholism or some condition | malignancy
B	especially around feminist issues	abortion
B	tackle controversial topics	the environment | nuclear weapons
C	pay	Libya | Iran
C	established electronic concerns	Sun
C	abortion	abortion counseling | referrals
C	offer	Sony's

Table 5
Human experts graded the system-acquired knowledge.

The *Like* Natural Language Construct for Knowledge Acquisition

For a different sample of the *Time Magazine* corpus, the feasibility of the *like* natural language construct was compared with that of *such as*. In this four-issue sample, the *like* construct occurs much more frequently; (see table 6). The occurrences were judged as useful in virtually every instance—12 out of 14. Not useful occurrences were often of the easy to eliminate form *such as this*.

However, the *like* construct proved to be somewhat problematic because it is syntactically ambiguous; it can be a verb as in *We like to do this,* a noun as in *and the like,* and so on. Although the majority—roughly three quarters of instances texts—were judged not useful, 42 out of 178 were considered likely candidates, and 11 were considered possible candidates; the higher overall incidence still resulted in a considerably

Natural Language Construct	Jan94-1	Jan94-2	Jan94-3	Jan94-4	Total
X such as Y, ..., Z	4	3	5	2	14
X like Y	44	37	52	45	178

Table 6

Frequency analysis of two natural language constructs for another sample of *Time Magazine*.

Issue	Total	Eliminated	Remaining	Percentage Remaining
Jan94-1	44	27	17	38.6%
Jan94-2	37	26	9	24.3%
Jan94-3	52	35	13	25.0%
Jan94-4	45	32	12	26.7%
Total	178	127	51	28.6%

Table 7

Elimination of not useful occurrences of like in the sample of *Time Magazine*.

larger number of likely candidates than the such as instances, 53 versus 12, and therefore worth pursuing in greater depth.

In the example that follows, we outline the algorithm eliminating the not useful occurrences of like. It significantly reduces the number of likely candidates, losing relatively few "good" instances (see table 7). NSU stands for next syntactic unit, NNSU stands for *next next syntactic unit*, PW for *preceding word*, PSU for *preceding syntactic unit,* and FSU for *following syntactic unit*:

Find the next occurrence of "like"; Extract NSU;
   if (NNSU in { - " . , ; ' : }) then skip occurrence;
   else extract PSU;
      if (PW ends in { - " . , ; ' : }) or (PSU is pronoun) or (PSU is "to") or
      (PSU is adverb) or (PSU in { be, look, smell, ...}) or
      (PSU in { more, most, not, less, something, lot, anything, things,
      nothing, on, little, much })
      then skip occurrence;
      else extract FSU;
         if (FSU is pronoun) or (FSU is "to") or (FSU is adverb),
         then skip occurrence.

For this construct, the remaining part of the extraction algorithm is surprisingly simple. In most instances, extracting the single word preceding like will provide the most significant, high-level relation. For example, in the phrase *very small dogs like Pekinese and Yorkies,* taking only the immediate antecedent *dogs,* one correctly learns that *Pekinese and Yorkies are dogs.* If only one preceding word is extracted, then the more specific relation present in text is lost; here that *Pekinese and Yorkies are very small dogs.* The more antecedents considered, the more specific knowledge is acquired.

However, identifying concept and its definition boundaries in general is quite tricky. It was determined that the word immediately preceding *like* was useful 100 percent of the time, as was the word immediately following like. The second word out in each direction was useful 70 percent of the time. For antecedents, looking one word further increases desired, but not critical specificity. For the words following *like,* roughly half cases constitute is critical pieces of knowledge.

For extraction of critical words following *like,* a significant proportion may be effectively delineated by identifying the next punctuation symbol, 14 out of 17, or 82 percent, with the occurrence of that symbol no more than a relatively short distance, maximum 6-7 words from *like.* Of those remaining occurrences of like, appropriate delineation would be made with the single following word.

These extremely simple steps computed after the elimination procedure conclude the algorithm.

Conclusions

We have presented a novel method for fully automatic knowledge acquisition from large corpora of unseen texts. Our approach exploits simple, efficiently, fast and reliably extractable, parsable and in-depth interpretable constructs of natural language specialized to convey taxonomic knowledge. We have demonstrated that our natural language processing system is capable of fully automatically acquiring large quantities of high-quality knowledge from multi-domain corpora.

The importance of our results stems from: (1) our system acquires knowledge uniquely found in textual corpora, (2) our work shows that it is possible to eliminate human pre- and post-processing of the system-acquired knowledge, and (3) our system acquires both types of concept context-dependent and context-independent.
We briefly elaborate these points below.

Knowledge Uniquely Found in Textual Corpora

Knowledge acquired from texts, especially from the newspapers and magazines, cannot be found in the existing dictionaries, encyclopedias

Concept	Definition, Subtypes
definitive taxonomic studies	nucleic acid hybridizations method, placing filter paper strips
mammals	monkeys, sheep, goats, cats, dogs, swine
mineral medium	marine agar, yeast extract agar
complex medium	cells of all species, yeast extract broth
minimal medium	bma containing 0.2% glycerol
commonly used media	nutrient agar, blood agar
special selective bile-salt media	baby 4 medium, oxalate medium, cin medium, cal medium, ss-d agar
preferentially select known pathogens	shigella, salmonella
typing techniques	susceptibility, bacteriocin production
enterobacteria	hektoen enteric agars, xylose-lysine-deoxycholate, macconkey
natural environments	water, sewage, soil
immunologically compromised patients	multiply traumatized patients, burned, premature infants
human clinical specimens	sputum, nose, throat, urine
clinical specimens	wound swabs, blood, sputum, throat, urine
liquid enrichment media	tetrathionate broth, selenite broth
relatively noninhibitory medium	eosin methylene blue agar, macconkey
laboratory animals	rabbits, mice
potential terrorist targets	schools, bus stations
very fast action	football plays
strain your hands	knitting, bowling, cooking, gardening
activities	a pencil, a tennis racket, holding a steering wheel
life	loved ones, friends, jobs
describing possible side effects	facial ticks, uncontrollable jerky movements

Table 8

Sample of system-acquired concepts from the *Microbiology* corpus, Volume 1-5, and from the *Time Magazine* corpus, October 1994 issues.

and hand-crafted taxonomies. Most concepts acquired by the system are complex, multi-word concepts, not just simple single-word concepts (see table 8).

Elimination of Human Pre- and Post-Processing, Scaling Up

Overall, our system is a very useful tool for automatically acquiring large quantities of high quality general-purpose taxonomic automatic knowledge from multi-source, multi-domain large-scale corpora of texts. The system-acquired knowledge bases can subsequently support natural language understanding and other in-depth artificial intelligence tasks. In general, the larger the corpus, the better the acquisition results. It appears that the approach scales up easily.

We believe that the small percentage of incorrect or garbled pieces of knowledge acquired by our system from large-scale unseen natural language inputs justifies completely eliminating the costly, time consuming and error-prone human involvement in preprocessing of textual documents and post-processing cleanup of the acquired knowledge. Such human involvement—particularly the knowledge clean-up effort—is virtually always required by other approaches.

Context-Independent and Context-Dependent Knowledge.

Concepts found in the *Microbiology* corpus are largely context-independent. This is probably because this corpus contains mostly scientific knowledge. Concepts found in the other two corpora were much more context-dependent. This probably reflects the commonsense and temporary nature of knowledge contained in these sources.

11 A Computational Theory of Vocabulary Acquisition

William J. Rapaport and Karen Ehrlich

AS PART OF AN INTERDISCIPLINARY PROJECT to develop a computational cognitive model of a reader of narrative text (Duchan et al. 1995), we are developing a computational theory of how a natural-language–understanding system (either human or artificial) can automatically acquire new vocabulary by determining from context the meaning of words that are unknown, misunderstood, or used in a new sense (Ehrlich 1995),[1] where "context" includes surrounding text, grammatical information, and background knowledge, but no access to external sources of information (such as a dictionary or a human).

In principle, there are only a handful of ways such a system could learn the meaning of a new word (or revise its understanding of a word). First, it could look the word up (for example, in a dictionary; see Zadrozny and Jensen [1991]). Second, it could ask another system what the word means (for example, Haas and Hendrix [1983] or Zernik and Dyer [1987]). Third, it could (either by itself or with the help of another system) figure out the meaning by finding a synonym for the unknown word or by locating the meaning of the word in some taxonony or other schema (for example, Hastings [1994]). Finally, it could figure out the meaning entirely from the context in which the word was encountered, with no outside help and no pre-established schema within which to fit it. The last of these is what our system does.

As part of our goal of modeling a reader, it is important to model the ability to *learn* from reading, in particular, to expand one's vocabulary in a natural way while reading, without having to stop to ask someone or to consult a dictionary. A complete lexicon cannot be manually encoded, nor could it contain new words or new meanings (Zernik and Dyer 1987). Text-understanding, message-processing, and information-extraction systems need to be robust in the presence of unknown expressions, especially systems using unconstrained input text and operating independently of human intervention, such as "intelligent agents." For example, a system designed to locate "interesting" news items from an online information server should not be limited to keyword searches—if the user is interested in news items about a certain kind of entity, and the filter detects items about "brachets" (a term not in its lexicon), it should deliver those items as soon as it figures out that a brachet is an entity of that kind. (After reading the next section, you will know what kind of entity this is.)

The definition that our system constructs is treated as a current hypothesis about the word's meaning, which can be revised upon successive encounters with the word. Using a formal notion of what a "good" definition is (see the algorithms section), our system finds fillers for slots in a definitional frame.

An Example

Before describing our system in more detail, it will be useful to see an example of how it works. If you do not know what *brachet* means, read on; otherwise, try the following experiment with someone who doesn't know what it means.

Suppose that you are reading the fifteenth-century *Morte Darthur* (Malory 1470) and come upon the following passage (our italics):

> ... there came a white hart running into the hall with a white *brachet* next to him, and thirty couples of black hounds came running after them ....
> (p. 66.) (1)

Suppose that you have no access to a dictionary containing *brachet* and no one is around whom you can ask what *brachet* means. Can you figure it out from the context plus your current background knowledge? One subject whom we tried this with guessed

> It's an animal, "them" is plural pronoun, 30 couple hounds ran after them—hart and [brachet].[2] Human is possible, but I don't get that sense.

Another subject said:

> No strong hypothesis. Maybe something like a buckle (from the sound? brachet sounds like latchet?) Something on a harness worn by the hart?[3]

So far, so little. If you never see the word again, it probably doesn't matter whether you can figure out its meaning, or whether the meaning you figure out is correct.

But suppose that you continue reading, and come across this passage:

> ...as he [the hart] went by the sideboard, the white *brachet* bit him .... (p. 66.) (2)

Can you now say a bit more about what *brachet* means? Subject 1 now said:

Biting in the buttock and pulling out piece implies a sharp toothed animal, not human.

Subject 2 said:

Maybe ... [an] animal. It bites the hart, but that might be figurative—a pin or a buckle might "bite."

Continuing on,[4] our subjects hypothesized as follows:

... the knight arose, took up the *brachet*, ...
and rode away with the *brachet*. (p. 66.) (3)

... a lady came in ... and cried aloud to King Arthur,
"Sire, the *brachet* is mine ...." (p. 66.) (4)

... there was the white *brachet* which bayed at him fast. (p. 72.) (10)

At this point, if you already believed that an animal that bayed was probably a dog, you could be pretty sure that a brachet was a dog. Subject 1, in fact, said:

Only dogs and wolves bay, and a lady would not keep a wolf. This is definitely a dog.

Subject 2, a bit more cautious perhaps, said:

Confirmation that a brachet is an animal: it "bayed at him fast." Maybe a kind of dog? (Dogs bay). Discard buckle hypothesis.

If you next read this:

... the hart lay dead ...; a *brachet* was biting on his throat,
and other hounds came behind. (p. 86.) (18)

you can be sure that a brachet is a dog—indeed, a hound (or hunting dog)—because of the phrase *other hounds*. You have now got a pretty good hypothesis about what brachet means. Subject 1's final definition was that a brachet is "a breed of hunting dog"; subject 2's final definition was that a brachet is "a hound, a hunting dog."

Let's see how our system, named Cassie, fares. Passage 1 is too hard for her to understand, in part because the archaic English is beyond her grammatical capacities (and, in any case, we are not interested in writing a grammar for this dialect of English), and in part because, in fact, Cassie uses as input a formal-language version of a simplified English version of this passage. (The formal-language version is the intended output—i.e., the semantic interpretation, in SNePS—of a natural-language–understanding algorithm whose input will be the simplified English version.) The simplified English version of passage 1 is:

1. A hart runs into King Arthur's hall. (1S)
2. A white brachet is next to the hart.

The formal-language versions of example 1S-1 and 1S-2 consist of the following seven propositions (the expressions of the form B*n* are node labels in the SNePS semantic-network representations of these sentences, which can be thought of as Skolem constants; for more details, see Rapaport, Shapiro, and Wiebe [1997], section 3.1).

1S-1a In the story, B17 is a hart.
1S-1b In the story, B17 runs into B18.
1S-1c In the story, B18 is a hall.
1S-1d In the story, the hall (B18) is a hall of its possessor, King Arthur (B3).
1S-2a In the story, B19 is a brachet.
1S-2b In the story, the brachet has the property "white."
1S-2c Brachets are a subclass of physical object.

Proposition (1S-2c) is not part of the input, but is *deduced* by Cassie, since Cassie believes that only physical objects have color. (The hedge, "in the story," will be explained later—it is the "knowledge category" *story* (for details, see the Implementation section in this chapter; see Rapaport [1991] and Rapaport and Shapiro [1995] for some relevant discussion.)

At this point, we ask Cassie to define *brachet:*

→ (defn_noun 'brachet)

```
((CLASS INCLUSION    = (phys obj))
 STRUCTURE           = NIL
 FUNCTION            = NIL
 ACTIONS             = (NIL)
 OWNERSHIP           = NIL
 POSSIBLE PROPERTIES = ((white))
 SYNONYMS            = NIL)
```

This definition can be paraphrased as: "A brachet is a physical object that may be white."

Omitting the formal-language versions, our demonstration of Cassie trying to figure out what brachet means continues as follows:

... The *brachet* bites the hart's buttock.

→ (defn_noun 'brachet)

```
((CLASS INCLUSION    = (animal))
 STRUCTURE           = NIL
 FUNCTION            = NIL
 ACTIONS =
    ((POSSIBLE ACTIONS = (bite)))
 OWNERSHIP           = NIL
 POSSIBLE PROPERTIES = ((small white))
 SYNONYMS            = NIL)
```

This can be paraphrased as "A brachet is an animal that may bite and can be small and white."

... The lady says that she wants the brachet.

→ (defn_noun 'brachet)
```
((CLASS INCLUSION    = (animal))
```

```
STRUCTURE          = NIL
FUNCTION           = NIL
ACTIONS =
  ((POSSIBLE ACTIONS = (bite)))
OWNERSHIP          = NIL
POSSIBLE PROPERTIES = ((small valuable white))
SYNONYMS           = NIL)
```

This can be paraphrased as "A brachet is an animal that may bite and can be small, valuable, and white."

... The *brachet* bays in the direction of Sir Tor.

```
→ (defn_noun 'brachet)
(A BRACHET IS A KIND OF (dog)
ACTIONS =
  ((POSSIBLEACTIONS = (bay bite)))
FUNCTION           = ((hunt))
STRUCTURE          = NIL
OWNERSHIP          = NIL
SYNONYMS           = NIL)
```

This final definition can be paraphrased as "A brachet is a hunting dog that can bay and bite."

There are two important things to note about this demonstration. First, Cassie's behavior is very similar to those of the two human subjects whose protocols we described above. Second, all three natural-language-understanding systems (human and artificial) converged on roughly the same definition, which is not all that far from that of the *Oxford English Dictionary*, according to which a brachet (or "brach") is "a kind of hound which hunts by scent" (Compact Edition of the *Oxford English Dictionary*, volume 1, p. 261 [volume 1, p. 1043 of the original edition]). Granted, neither Cassie nor the humans included "scent" in their definitions; however, scent was not mentioned in the Malory text, so there was no reason they should have included it, nor is it necessary for understanding the text.

Fundamental Theses

We hold that linguistic contexts (and their mental counterparts) can provide meanings for expressions (Rapaport 1981). This includes nonreferential expressions: If *unicorn* is an unknown term, and we read that a unicorn looks like a horse with one horn, then we can hypothesize a meaning for *unicorn*—for example, a one-horned, horselike animal—even though the term *unicorn* does not refer (see Meinong [1910]: 25f, Rapaport [1981]). A reader understands a narrative (or other) text by interpreting the sentences of the text. The reader's interpretation is a mapping from the sentences (considered as a syntactic domain) to the reader's mental concepts (considered as the semantic domain). (In this way, semantics arises out of syntax, and Searle's Chinese-Room Argument [Searle 1980] can be refuted; see Rapaport [1988, 1995].) We can then take the meaning of a word (as understood by the reader—i.e., a cognitive agent) to be its position in a network of words, propositions, and other concepts (Quillian 1968, 1969). This gives rise to a conceptual-role semantics (see, for example, Sellars [1963]; and Harman [1974, 1982] inter alia; see Fodor and Lepore [1992] for objections).

Most importantly, we claim that a meaning for a word *can* be determined from any context, can be *revised* and refined upon further encounters with it, and *converges* to a dictionarylike definition given enough context and exposures to it. The context can be minimal, or even empty. Consider the sentence *Tommy broke a weti,* with unknown word *weti.* With some reasonable, but minimal, background knowledge, we might theorize that a weti is a breakable physical object. But even with no background knowledge or other contextual information (other than grammatical structure), we could theorize that a weti is something that Tommy broke, by "solving" the sentence for its unknown term, as in algebra (see Higginbotham [1989]).

Each encounter with the unknown word yields a definition—a hypothesis about its meaning. Of great importance, subsequent encounters provide opportunities for unsupervised revision of this hypothesis, with no (human) "trainers" or error-correction techniques. The hypothesized definitions are not guaranteed to converge to a correct meaning (if such exists) but to one stable with respect to further encounters. Finally, no *domain-specific* background information is required for developing the definition: The system need not be an expert in what it's reading.

Clearly, however, the more background knowledge it has (and the larger the textual context), the better the hypothesized definition will be. This suggests that there are two kinds of meaning that we need to consider. In an idiolectic sense, the meaning of a word for a cognitive agent is determined by idiosyncratic experience with it. The contextual meaning described above includes a word's relation to every concept in the agent's mind. Thus, the extreme interpretation of "meaning as context" defines every word in terms of every other word an agent knows. This holistic kind of meaning is circular and too unwieldy for use. In another sense, the meaning of a word is its dictionary definition, usually containing less information. Thus, we limit the connections used for the definition by selecting particular *kinds* of information. Not all concepts within a given subnetwork are equally salient to a dictionary-style definition of a word. People abstract certain conventional information about words to use as a definition.

Two features of our system mesh nicely with these desiderata, summarized as the advantages of learning over being told. First, being told requires human intervention. *Our system operates independently of a human teacher or trainer* (with one eliminable exception). Second, learning is necessary, since one can't predict all information needed to understand unconstrained, domain-independent text. *Our system does not constrain the subject matter (domain) of the text.* Although we are primarily concerned with narrative text, our techniques are general. Given an appropriate grammar, our algorithms produce domain-independent definitions, albeit ones dependent on the system's background knowledge: The more background knowledge it has, the better its definitions will be, and the more quickly they will "converge." The system does not develop correct definitions, but *dictionarylike* definitions enabling it to continue understanding the text.

Psychological Evidence

Our theory is informed and supported by psychological research on how humans store and access word meanings and expand their vocabularies once the basics of language have been acquired.

Johnson-Laird

Philip N. Johnson-Laird's (1987) theory about the mental representation of words asserts that understanding a word (and a sentence containing a word) does not imply that one has a readily accessible definition of that word stored in one's mind. Various aspects of a word's meaning may be called to mind by sentences for which those aspects are relevant, without calling the entire definition to mind. He describes experiments showing that responses to questions about specific aspects of a word's meaning come faster following a priming sentence that calls that aspect to mind than to questions where the preceding sentence uses the word, but does not call that aspect to mind. The same speed-up occurs when the priming is a result of factual inference about a word's referent as when it results from selectional restriction on the word's sense.

Linguistic context has at least three effects on the interpretation of words. It can enable selection of an appropriate sense of a truly ambiguous word. It can lead to inference of a more specific referent than is strictly warranted by the meaning of an unambiguous word. It can call to mind particular aspects of a word's meaning at the expense of other aspects. In each case, the mental representation of real or imaginary referents is important to the understanding of the word as used.

Some aspects of a word's meaning are more salient to understanding its use than others. Since the evidence indicates that we do not retrieve definitions in their entirety when understanding sentences, we may not notice gaps in our lexical knowledge, so long as we can retrieve the aspects of meaning necessary to understanding the sentence. Such gaps point to the importance of the acquisition process. One can learn a word's meaning by being told that meaning, or one can infer its meaning from encountering it in use.

Even fairly early in childhood, learning word meanings may be as much a matter of making inferences from linguistic context as of simple association. Johnson-Laird (1987) reports on experiments in which 3- and 4-year-old children listened to stories involving a novel verb. From hearing the verb used in sentences that contained other words they already understood, the children were able to perform selectional restriction on the arguments to the new verb. Children have also been shown to be able to learn aspects of the meanings of nonsense nouns from hearing them used in the context of familiar verbs.

Johnson-Laird suggests that lexical learning involves a sort of "bootstrapping" in which, once a fragment of language has been mapped onto a child's internal representation of states of affairs in the world, other words are acquired either indirectly from context or directly from explicit definition. Words may also be of mixed acquisition; different individuals will acquire a given word differently. Some words can be completely lexically specified; others (such as natural-kind terms) cannot, but instead rely in part on a schema of default information based on a prototypical exemplar.

Johnson-Laird (1987: 579) summarizes parts of his theory of lexical meanings as follows: (1) Comprehension requires the listener to construct a model of the state of affairs described by the discourse. (2) There is a mental dictionary that contains entries in which the senses of words are represented (but compare with Johnson-Laird 1987: 563). (3) A lexical entry may be incomplete as a result of ignorance or because the word is a theoretical term with an intrinsically incomplete sense. (4) The senses of words can be acquired from definitions or from encountering instances of the word in use. (5) Corresponding to the method of acquisition, elements of a lexical representation can consist of (a) relations to other words, which could be represented by a mechanism akin to a semantic network, and (b) ineffable primitives that are used in constructing and manipulating mental models of the world.

Cassie understands narrative input by building mental representations of the information contained in the narrative; forming concepts of individuals, propositions, and events described; and connecting them with her prior knowledge. Her understanding of a concept in narrative is precisely that concept's connections to the rest of the narrative, together with its connections (if any) to previously acquired knowledge.

We adopt the idea that lexical entries have aspects of meaning connected to them in a semantic network, but do not have compiled, dictionary-style definitions permanently attached. Cassie selects salient features from her knowledge of a word when asked to define it, but does not permanently store those features as a definition. Our semantic network, however, includes meaning postulates (represented as rules) that Cassie can use as part (but not all) of her knowledge for producing definitions. Some information (for example, about natural kinds) is expressed as default information. Thus, our approach is compatible with Johnson-Laird's theory and experiments.

Elshout-Mohr and van Daalen-Kapteijns

Marianne Elshout-Mohr and Maartje M. van Daalen-Kapteijns (1987) treat verbal comprehension as a mental skill involving procedural and propositional knowledge. They hold that it is useful to have a "meaning unit" that is stable across contexts, so that new contexts may provide new information at the same time that an established understanding of a word allows interpretation in a new context.

In one experiment, they chose students with high and low verbal skills as measured by standard tests. Subjects were asked to think aloud as they tried to determine from context the meanings of invented words. The neologisms filled lexical gaps, so that they would refer to things with which the subjects were familiar, but would not have direct synonyms that could be substituted for them. (For example, *kolper*: a window that transmits little light because of something outside it.) A series of sentences were presented, one per page, in which the new word was used. The first roughly indicated its superordinate:

> When you are used to a broad view it is quite depressing when you come to live in a room with one or two *kolpers* fronting on a courtyard.

The second and third distinguished it from other concepts in the same superordinate class:

> He virtually always studied in the library, as at home he had to work by artificial light all day because of those *kolpers*.

> During a heat wave a lot of people all of a sudden want to have *kolpers,* so the sales of sunblinds then reach a peak.

The fourth and fifth provided counterexamples:

I was afraid the room might have *kolpers,* but when I went and saw it, it turned out that plenty of sunlight came into it.

In those houses, you're stuck with *kolpers* all summer, but fortunately once the leaves have fallen off that isn't so any more.

Subjects were aware of the need to construct a definition rather than search for a synonym. They were asked to report on new information gained from each sentence without reviewing previous pages. It was thought that this would tax their working memory, which was considered important, because most words learned from context are not learned in situations where word acquisition is the primary focus of cognition. Rather, one usually reads for the content of a text and acquires new vocabulary incidentally (if at all).

Most subjects tried to compare the unknown word with at least one familiar word. Those with high verbal skills used the model analytically, as a group of separable components that could be individually compared with further information. New information compatible with all facets of the model could be added; conflicting facets of the model could be replaced with new information. Those with lower verbal skills tended to use the model holistically, with new compatible information broadening or restricting the domain (Kiersey 1982) and incompatible information causing the rejection of the model (and perhaps the adoption of a different model).

According to the authors, in the task of word learning, a model (1) provides a plan for knowledge retrieval; all aspects of the semantic unit of the model are accessible; (2) provides a framelike structure for the meaning to be acquired, with certain slots to fill; (3) allows conventional aspects of definitions to steer abstraction toward similar conventions in the new definition; and (4) provides default information to fill slots in the anticipated structure. The meaning of the new word is presumed to inherit aspects of meaning connected with the model unless otherwise specified.

Cassie uses her prior knowledge and the network that represents her understanding of the story (up to and including the sentence containing that word) to establish a definitional framework for the target word. This framework is not an analogical model in Elshout-Mohr and van Daalen-Kapteijns's sense, but does provide a plan for knowledge retrieval and a structure with certain slots to fill. The framework for nouns includes slots for synonyms and for hypernyms from which the target word can inherit aspects of meaning.

Because we wish our system to model an individual of high verbal ability (for general usefulness and specifically for use as a lexicographer's assistant), it does use its selected framework analytically, although new information may cause the system to select a different framework than that chosen after the first encounter with the target word.

Elshout-Mohr and van Daalen-Kapteijns suggest that children's verbal skills be developed by instruction in distinguishing between idiosyncratic experiences with a word and the more general experiences associated therewith, and in constraining the richness of individual experience by selecting a limited number of aspects of meaning. Especially important is the ability to select structural and functional aspects of a concept that are in common with and in distinction of other known concepts. Developing theory and technique for such movement from idiosyncratic understanding to conventional dictionary definitions is a central portion of our research.

Sternberg

Robert Sternberg (1987: 91) gives the following example:

> Although for the others the party was a splendid success, the couple there on the blind date was not enjoying the festivities in the least. An *acapnotic*, he disliked her smoking; and when he removed his hat, she, who preferred "ageless" men, eyed his increasing *phalacrosis* and grimaced.

It is easy to guess what *acapnotic* and *phalacrosis* might mean (although the latter is ambiguous; does it mean "baldness" or "grey hair?"). Sternberg holds that three processes are applied in acquiring words from context: (a) distinguishing irrelevant from relevant information, (b) selectively combining relevant clues, and (c) comparing what has been selected and combined with previous knowledge. These processes operate on a basis of several types of cues: (1) temporal cues regarding the duration or frequency of X, or when X can occur; (2) spatial cues regarding the location of X or possible locations where X can sometimes be found; (3) value cues regarding the worth or desirability of X, or the kinds of affects X arouses; (4) stative descriptive cues regarding the properties of X (size, color, etc.); (5) functional descriptive cues regarding possible purposes of X, actions X can perform, or potential uses of X; (6) cues regarding the possible causes of, or enabling conditions for, X; (7) cues regarding one or more classes to which X belongs, or other members of one or more classes of which X is a member; (8) equivalence cues regarding the meaning of X, or contrast (such as antonymy) to the meaning of X.

Sternberg's experiments show that readers who are trained in his three processes of recognizing relevant cues, combining cues, and comparing with known terms do better at defining new words than those who receive training only in the eight types of cues available, although any training in cue types produces better results than word memorization or no training.

Our system is designed to select certain information as most relevant, if it is present. For example, we follow Johnson-Laird as well as Elshout-Mohr and van Daalen-Kapteijns in emphasizing the structural and functional information about physical objects. If, however, such information is lacking, our system uses such other cue types as may be available. We also combine relevant information, and compare new words with known words in certain specific ways, such as possible synonymy or hyponymy.

Implementation

Our system, Cassie, consists of the SNePS-2.1 knowledge-representation and reasoning system (Shapiro 1979b; Shapiro and Rapaport 1987, 1992a, 1995), and a knowledge base representing Cassie's background knowledge. Currently, the knowledge base is hand-coded, since how she acquired this knowledge is irrelevant. Although we begin with a "toy" knowledge base, each of our tests includes all previous information, so the knowledge base grows as we test more words. Cassie's input consists of (1) information from the text being read and (2) questions that trigger a deductive search of the knowledge base (for example, "What does <word> mean?"). Output consists of a report of Cassie's current definition of the word, or answers to other queries.

SNePS has an English lexicon, morphological analyzer/synthesizer, and a generalized augmented-transition-network parser-generator that translates English input directly into a propositional semantic network without building an intermediate parse tree (Shapiro 1982, 1989; Rapaport 1988, 1991; Shapiro and Rapaport 1995). All information, including propositions, is represented by SNePS nodes; propositions about propositions can also be represented. Labeled arcs form the underlying syntactic structure of SNePS, embodied in the restriction that one cannot add an arc between two existing nodes, which would be tantamount to a proposition not represented by a node. Arc-paths can be defined for path-based inference, including property inheritance. Nodes and represented concepts are in 1–1 correspondence; this uniqueness principle guarantees that nodes are shared whenever possible and that nodes represent intensional objects (such as concepts, propositions, properties, and objects of thought including fictional entities, nonexistents, and impossible objects; [Shapiro and Rapaport 1987, 1991]).

SNePS's inference package accepts rules for deductive and default reasoning, allowing Cassie to infer "probable" conclusions in the absence of contrary information. When combinations of asserted propositions lead to a contradiction, SNeBR, the SNePS belief-revision package, allows Cassie to remove from the inconsistent context one or more of those propositions (Martins and Shapiro 1988). Once a premise is no longer asserted, the conclusions that depended on it are no longer asserted in that context. Cassie uses SNeBR and SNePSwD, a default belief-revision system that enables automatic revision (Cravo and Martins 1993; Martins and Cravo 1991), to revise beliefs about the meanings of words.

Because we wish our system to be able to revise its beliefs with a minimum of human interference, we have partially automated the selection and revision of the culprit node (i.e., the erroneous assertion that led to the contradiction); we are exploring techniques for full automation. To facilitate this process, we tag each of the asserted propositions in the knowledge base with a knowledge category. Maria Cravo and João P. Martins (1993) have developed a utility for creating orderings of propositions within the network. We use this ordering utility to build a hierarchy of certainty in which all propositions with a particular knowledge category are given higher priority than those whose knowledge category indicates less certainty of belief. Then, when SNeBR is invoked by a derived contradiction, the belief(s) with least priority (i.e., held with least certainty) in the conflict set will be selected for revision. As originally designed, once the culprit belief had been deleted, SNeBR would ask the user if she wished to add any new propositions to the network. We have modified SNeBR so that it now automatically creates a revision of the culprit belief (see Ehrlich [1995] for the algorithms).

The current version of SNePS allows ordinary deductive reasoning. SNePSWD also allows default reasoning (Cravo and Martins 1993). Default rules allow the system to infer "probable" conclusions in the absence of specific information to the contrary. For example, if the system knows that, by default, birds fly, but also knows that penguins do not fly and that Opus is a penguin, then, despite inferring that Opus is a bird, the system will not conclude that Opus flies, because the default rule is not applicable to Opus. This works well when all relevant information is known before the attempt to deduce whether Opus flies. However, if the system must make a decision before learning that penguins are flightless, it will need to revise that decision once more information is gained.

Using SNeBR for revising erroneous beliefs is not appropriate in all situations. Rather than use default rules that rely on being told in advance whether they are applicable in certain cases, we employ a method, based on theoretical work by J. Terry Nutter (1983), in which some rules have consequents marked as presumably true. Frequently, this avoids the need for nonmonotonicity. In our example above, we would have the rule that, if something is a bird, then presumably it flies. Opus the penguin, being a kind of bird, would fit the antecedent, and we would conclude that presumably Opus flies. Learning that penguins do not fly does not, then, produce a contradiction, but rather the concatenation that Opus could be presumed to fly though in fact he does not.

When a human reader encounters a discrepancy between the way a word is used in text and his previous understanding of that word, he must either assume that the word is used incorrectly or decide that his previous understanding requires revision. When our system encounters a contradiction derived from combining story information with background knowledge, it must decide which of the premises leading to the contradiction should be revised (compare with Rapaport [1991], Rapaport and Shapiro [1995]). To facilitate such decisions, each of the assertions that we build into the system's knowledge base and each of the assertions in the story is tagged with a knowledge category (*kn_cat*). Assertions having no *kn_cat* attached are beliefs that the system has derived. (SNeBR assigns each proposition an "origin tag" as either a hypothesis (a proposition received as input) or a derivation. If the proposition is derived, information about the hypotheses used in the derivation is also stored (Martins and Shapiro 1988). Our *kn_cat* tags may be considered complementary to SNeBR's origin tags, though implemented differently.) These categories are ordered in a hierarchy of certainty of belief, so that the system can restrict the field from which it chooses a belief for revision to those premises believed with the least certainty. Ideally, there would be only one such premise, but if there are more, then other means must be used to select among them (see below). Following is a description of the hierarchy of *kn_cats* ranged from greatest certainty of belief to least:

1. *kn_cat intrinsic*. Essentially, facts about language, including simple assertions, as well as some rules; background, or "world," knowledge of a very basic or fundamental sort. Intrinsic facts are found in the knowledge base, not in stories (at least, usually not). For example: The temporal relation *before* is transitive; containment of an item in a class implies containment of that item in superclasses of that class; encountering the usage <verb>(agent, object, indobj) implies that <verb> can be bitransitive.

2. *kn_cat story*. Information present in the story being read, including stated propositions and propositions implicit in the sentence (necessary for parsing the sentence); the SNePS representation that would be built on parsing a sentence in the story. For example, in the sentence "Sir Gryflette left his house and rode to town," we have the following story facts: Someone is named Sir Gryflette. That someone left his

house. That someone rode to town. (Other examples are (1S-1a)–(1S-2b) given earlier.)

3. *kn_cat life*. Background knowledge expressed as simple assertions without variables or inference. Examples of life facts include taxonomies (for example, dogs are a subclass of animals) and assertions about individuals (for example, Merlin is a wizard. Bill Clinton is a Democrat.).

4. *kn_cat story-comp*. Information not directly present in the story, but inferred by the reader to make sense of the story. This is based on Erwin M. Segal's concept of "story completion" (Rapaport et al. 1989a, b; Segal 1995). Story completion uses background knowledge, but isn't the background knowledge itself. Few (if any) assertions should be tagged with this *kn_cat*, since any necessary story completion should (ideally) be derived by the system. We include it here to cover cases where a gap in the system's knowledge base might leave it unable to infer some fact necessary to understanding the story. Using the example from the category of story facts, story completion facts might include: Sir Gryflette is a knight; Sir Gryflette mounted his horse between leaving his house and riding to town.

5. *kn_cat life-rule.1*. Background knowledge represented as rules for inference, using variables; rules reflecting common, everyday knowledge. For example: If x bears young, then x is a mammal; if x is a weapon, then the function of x is to do damage; if x dresses y, then y wears clothing.

6. *kn_cat life-rule.2*. Background knowledge represented as rules for inference, using variables, that rely on specialized, noneveryday information. For example: if x smites y, then x kills y by hitting y.

7. *kn_cat questionable*. A rule that has already been subjected to revision because its original form led to a contradiction. For example: If x smites y, then x hits y and possibly kills y. This is the only *kn_cat* that is never a part of input. The system attaches this tag when it revises a rule that was tagged as a *life-rule.2*. It is intended as a temporary classification for use while the system looks for confirmation of its revision. Once the system settles on a particular revision, the revised rule is tagged as a *life-rule.2*.

In case of contradiction, our system selects, from among the conflicting propositions, a proposition of greatest uncertainty as a candidate for revision. If the highest level of uncertainty present in the conflict set occurs in only one belief, that belief will be revised. If several alternatives exist with the same (highest present) *kn_cat*, then the system selects for the presence of a verb in the antecedent, since it seems that humans more readily revise beliefs about verbs than about nouns (Gentner 1981). If this is still insufficient to yield a single culprit, then, in the current implementation, a human user must decide among any remaining alternatives. Ideally, the system would use discourse information to make the decision between possible culprits at the same level of certainty. For example, in the case of combatants dressing shields and spears before fighting (see the dress example, later), the rule about what it means to dress something might be selected for revision because it is unrelated to the topic of fighting, whereas shields and spears are closely associated with the topic.

We have described a belief hierarchy of seven levels. In practice, it seems that four would probably suffice. We could have handled all our example revisions without separating the nonrule information into *intrinsic, story, life,* and *story-completion* information (though some intrinsic facts expressed as rules would have had to be expressed differently). A hierarchy consisting of nonrules, entrenched rules *(life-rule.1),* nonentrenched rules *(life-rule.2),* and rules under revision *(questionable)* would be enough to cover the cases with which we have dealt, since we have never had to revise a nonrule belief. However, it is at least possible that a contradiction might arise between two or more beliefs, none of which are rules.

As mentioned above, story-completion information is something of a special case, and will usually be derived; that is, it will be a conclusion based on background information and story information. When SNeBR detects a contradiction, it assembles a conflict set consisting of those *premises* that led to the contradiction. Derived conclusions are not part of the conflict set. Therefore, except where story-completion information is directly input, we need not be concerned about selecting it as the culprit whose error led to a contradiction.

So, if we were to encounter a contradiction whose conflict set contained no rules, we would need some method for selecting a culprit from among various nonrule facts. Our approach assumes that words in the story are used correctly and that information presented in the story is true, at least within the context of the story. Therefore, it makes sense to distinguish between story facts and background facts. But not all background facts are equally entrenched. Some, such as the examples of *kn_cat intrinsic* given above, seem so basic to our understanding that they should be immune from revision (even if they happen to be expressed as rules). Others seem less basic, and may be revised if they conflict with story facts. The distinction between assertions tagged *intrinsic* and those tagged *life* is not exactly analogous to distinctions between necessary and contingent properties, or between analytic and synthetic definitions, but a loose analogy to such distinctions may capture some sense of the distinction being drawn here (compare with Rapaport [1991], Rapaport and Shapiro [1995]).

At present, all the *kn_cats* (except for *questionable*) are assigned by a human at the time the proposition is input. The assignment of the *kn_cat story* could be handled automatically: The system would simply include it as a part of each proposition built from the parse of a sentence in a story (as in Rapaport [1991], Rapaport and Shapiro [1995]). Since *story-comp* is only a stop-gap measure, we need not worry about how the system might assign it: Either it wouldn't make any such assignment, or it would tag all derived propositions as being derived. (The latter is already done by SNeBR, but invisibly; compare with Martins Shapiro [1988].) This leaves us with the question of how the system might categorize the nonderived assertions in its knowledge base. Rules can be readily distinguished from nonrules, so the question breaks down into two parts: How do we tell an entrenched rule *(life-rule.1)* from a less-entrenched rule *(life-rule.2)*, and how do we tell an entrenched fact (intrinsic) from a less-entrenched fact *(life)?* We make the distinction based on an intuitive feeling for how basic a concept is, or how familiar we are with a concept. How such intuitions can be formalized and automated is an open question. We may have to continue for a while to tell Cassie how strongly she holds her beliefs.

Once a contradiction is detected and a culprit proposition selected, if it is a rule (as it usually is), then it may be necessary to select which of several consequents actually produced the contradiction. The system checks each consequent against the justification support (the premises from which a proposition is derived) of the deduced propositions that are in direct conflict with each other to find the culprit consequent within the culprit rule (i.e., the rule that has been determined to be in error).

Algorithms

Our algorithms hypothesize and revise meanings for nouns and verbs that are unknown, misunderstood, or being used in a new way. Applying the principle that the meaning of a term is its location in the network of background and story information, our algorithms deductively search the network for information appropriate to a dictionarylike definition, assuming our grammar has identified the unknown word as a noun or a verb. The algorithms (Ehrlich 1995) are shown in the Algorithm section at the end of this chapter, and are illustrated by example here.

Cassie was provided with background information for understanding King Arthur stories (Malory 1470). As we saw above, when presented with a sequence of passages containing the unknown noun *brachet,* Cassie developed a theory that a brachet was a dog whose function is to hunt and that can bay and bite. However, based on the first context in which the term appeared ("... there came a white hart running into the hall with a white brachet next to him, ..."), her initial hypothesis was that a brachet was a physical object that may be white. Each time *brachet* appeared, Cassie was asked to define it. To do so, she deductively searched her background knowledge base, together with the information she had read in the narrative to that point, for information concerning (1) direct class inclusions (especially in a basic-level category), (2) general functions of brachets (in preference to those of individuals), (3) the general structure of brachets (if appropriate, and in preference to those of individuals), (4) acts that brachets perform (partially ordered in terms of universality: probable actions in preference to possible actions, actions attributed to brachets in general in preference to actions of individuals, etc.), (5) possible ownership of brachets, (6) part-whole relationships to other objects, (7) other properties of brachets (when structural and functional description is possible, less salient "other properties" of particular brachets are not reported, although we do report properties that apply to brachets in general), and (8) possible synonyms for *brachet* (based on similarity of the above attributes). Some of these are based on the psycholinguistic studies of the sort of vocabulary expansion we are modeling (discussed above). In the absence of any of this information, or in the presence of potentially inconsistent information (for example, if the text says that one brachet hunts and another doesn't), Cassie either leaves certain "slots" in her definitional framework empty, or includes information about particular brachets. Such information is filled in or replaced upon further encounters with the term.

Each query for a definition begins the search from scratch; different information is reported depending on the kind of background information available at the time the query is made. Thus, by querying Cassie after each occurrence of *brachet,* we can see the definition frame "develop" dynamically. However, if we only queried Cassie at the last occurrence of *brachet,* then we would only see the "final" definition frame.

Although the current implementation outputs different definition frames depending on which branch of the algorithm has been taken (see the Algorithm section), a "unified" definition frame could be used, as shown in table 1. Each row is a slot. Each column represents a kind of term; for example, (1) a term that is a basic-level category, such as *dog,* (2) a term that is a subclass of a basic-level category, such as *brachet,* and so on. (See Rosch [1978] for the notion of "basic-level categories.") A check-mark means that a slot-filler is reported if it is known. A circle

Slot	Basic-Level Category	Subclass of Basic-Level Category	Subclass of Animal	Subclass of Physical Object	Subclass of Abstract Object	No Class Inclusions
actions	√	√	√	√	√	√
ownership	√	√	√	√	√	√
function	√	√	√	√	√	√
structure	√	√	√	√	⊗	√
immediate superclass	√	√	√	√	√	⊗
general stative properties	√	√	√	√	√	⊗
synonyms	√	√	√	√	√	⊗
possible properties	O	O	O	√	√	√
object of act	O	O	O	√	√	√
named individuals	O	O	O	O	O	√

Table 1. Unified Definition Frame
√ = reported if known
O = not reported (even if known)
⊗ = can't be reported

means that it is not reported, even if it is known, because it is superseded by other slot-fillers. A circled X means that that slot cannot be filled (hence, will not be reported) for that kind of term.

Other Examples of Vocabulary Acquisition

We have been investigating three types of vocabulary acquisition:

1. *Constructing* a new definition of an *unknown* word (for example, brachet)
2. *Correcting* a definition of a *misunderstood* word (see the discussion of smite that follows)
3. *Expanding* the definition of a word *being used in a new sense* (see the discussion of *dress* later in this section).

All three can be thought of as revision: (1) revision from an empty definition, (2) revision of an incorrect definition, and (3) revision of an incomplete definition. Alternatively, (3) can be thought of as adding (disjoining) a new definition to an already-established one (see the *dress* example).

Smite

Cassie was told that *to smite* meant "to kill by hitting hard" (a mistaken belief actually held by one of us [Rapaport] before reading Malory [1470]). Passages in which various characters were smitten but then continued to act triggered SNeBR, which asks Cassie which of several possible "culprit" propositions in the knowledge base to remove in order to block inconsistencies. Ideally, Cassie then decides which belief to revise. A set of rules for replacing discarded definitions with revised definitions is being developed. For example, suppose the culprit were:

If x smites y, then: x hits y & y is dead & x hitting y causes y to be dead.

On first encountering a smitee who survives, substitute these rules:

If x smites y, then: x hits y & possibly y is dead;
If x smites y & y is dead, then x hitting y causes y to be dead.

If asked for a definition of *smite* now, Cassie will report that the result of smiting is that x hits y and possibly y is dead. The only human intervention is to tell Cassie to order her beliefs (she does the ordering, based on the knowledge categories, but has to be nudged to "do it now") and to tell Cassie to *assert* the revised belief she has *already automatically* generated from the lowest-ranked belief in the conflict set.

Here, we sketch Cassie's handling of smite, with this background information in the knowledge base:

There is a king named King Arthur.
There is a king named King Lot.
There is a sword named Excalibur.
Excalibur is King Arthur's sword.
Horses are animals.
Kings are persons.
Knights are persons.
Dukes are persons.
"Person" is a basic-level category.
"Horse" is a basic-level category.
"Before" and "after" are transitive relations.
If x is dead at time t, x can perform no actions at t
   or at any subsequent time.
If x belongs to a subclass of person, x is a person.
If a person acts, the act performed is an action.
If an agent acts on an object, and there is an indirect object of the action,
   then the action is bitransitive.
If an agent acts on an object, then the action is transitive.
If an agent acts on itself, then the action is reflexive.
If x is hurt at time t, then x is not dead at t.
If x is not dead at time t, then x was not dead at any prior time.
If x smites y at time t, then x hits y at t, and y is dead at t,
   and the hitting caused the death.

Note that the last is the only information about *smite* in the knowledge base.

Cassie is then given a sequence of passages containing *smite* (adapted from Malory [1470]: 13ff), interspersed with questions and requests for definitions:

Passage S1: King Arthur turned himself and his horse. He smote before and behind. His horse was slain.   King Lot smote down King Arthur.

Definition S1: A person can smite a person. If x smites y at time t, then x hits y at t, and y is dead at t.

Question S1: What properties does King Arthur have?

Reply S1: King Arthur is dead.

Passage S2: King Arthur's knights rescued him. They sat him on a horse. He drew Excalibur.

Question S2: When did King Arthur draw [Excalibur]?

The inference required to reply to Question S2 triggers SNeBR, which reports that King Arthur's drawing (i.e., acting) is inconsistent with his being dead. Cassie automatically removes the proposition reporting her belief that smiting entails killing, which is replaced with two beliefs: that although smiting entails hitting, it only possibly entails killing, and that if smiting results in a death, then the hitting is the cause of death. These rules are *not* built in; they are *inferred* by revision rules. This results in:

Definition S2: A person can smite a person. If x smites y at time t, then x hits y at t and possibly y is dead at t.

Passage S3: Two of King Claudas's knights rode toward a passage. Sir Ulfyas and Sir Brastias rode ahead. Sir Ulfyas smote down one of King Claudas's two knights. Sir Brastias smote down the other knight. Sir Ulfyas and Sir Brastias rode ahead. Sir Ulfyas fought and unhorsed another of Claudas's knights. Sir Brastias fought and unhorsed the last of Claudas's knights. Sir Ulfyas and Sir Brastias laid King Claudas's last two knights on the ground. All of King Claudas's knights were hurt and bruised.

The information that the knights were hurt was added in forward-chaining mode to allow Cassie to notice that that they were still alive at the time they were hurt and therefore could not have died earlier at the time they were smitten. Cassie has now heard of two cases in a row (King Arthur, and the two knights) where a smitee has survived being smitten, with no intervening cases of death by smiting, yielding:

Definition S3: A person can smite a person. If x smites y at time t, then x hits y at t.

Further encounters with smite cause no further revisions. The definition has stabilized ("converged") in a manner similar to the human protocols on the same passages.

Dress

A third case is exemplified by *dress*, which Cassie antecedently understood to mean "put clothes on (something)," a well-entrenched meaning that should not be rejected. Thus, her background knowledge for this example included the following two beliefs whose *kn_cat = life-rule.1*.

1. dresses(x, y) $\Rightarrow$ $\exists z[\text{clothing}(z)$ & wears$(y, z)]$.
2. Spears don't wear clothing.

Again, Cassie was given a sequence of passages containing *dress* (adapted from Malory [1470]) interspersed with questions and requests for definitions:

Passage D1: King Arthur dressed himself.

Definition D1: A person can dress itself; result: it wears clothing.

Passage D2: King Claudas dressed his spear....

At this point, Cassie infers that King Claudas's spear wears clothing.

Question D2: What wears clothing?

This question invokes SNeBR, which detects a contradiction and automatically replaces background belief (1), not background belief (2), because of the occurrence of a verb in the antecedent, following Gentner 1981 (see the Implementation section earlier). There follow several passages in the text in which dressing spears precedes fighting. Rather than rejecting the prior definition, we add to it. Cassie decides that to dress is either to put clothes on or to prepare for battle:

Definition D3: A person can dress a spear or a person; result: the person wears clothing or the person is enabled to fight.

Admittedly, this is not perfectly satisfactory. Among the improvements we are planning are a better way of expressing such disjunctive definitions and a method to induce a more general definition. In the present case, further experience with such phrases as *salad dressing, turkey dressing,* and so on, might lead one to decide that *dress* more generally means something like "prepare" (for the day, by putting on clothes; for battle, by preparing one's spear; for eating, by preparing one's salad; for cooking, by preparing one's turkey; and so on).

Related Work

We begin with a review of some classic work along these lines, and then turn to more recent work.

Some Classic Work

Granger

Richard H. Granger's Foul-Up (1977) was designed specifically to work in conjunction with a Script Applier Mechanism (Schank and Abelson 1977) to allow stories of events to be understood in terms of stereotypical event sequences despite the presence of unknown words. Granger used the syntactic expectations generated by a parser and script-based expectations generated by the currently active script to create a partial definition of an unknown word. For example, if the currently active script is *vehicular accident,* if there is input to the effect that the car struck an elm, and if the word *elm* is unknown, Foul-Up would deduce that elm is a noun that represents something that can fill the "obstruction slot" in a script for a single-car accident (and therefore must be a physical object).

Once our grammar is in place, we also will use syntactic expectations and morphology to allow the determination of an unknown word's role in a given sentence (for example, subject, direct object, verb, and so on) as well as its part of speech. We can make deductions similar to Granger's, but in terms of sentences instead of scripts. We also use such background knowledge as is available, even though that knowledge isn't organized into scripts. We would deduce that *elm* is a noun and that an elm is a thing that can be struck by a car. For us, as for Granger, the single occurrence of the word is not enough to allow any useful inference beyond what is immediately present in the text (although background knowledge might be available about the probable size, location, etc., of objects that a car might be said to strike).

We adopt Granger's use of parsing expectations to begin hypothesizing word definitions. However, the rest of his approach, which involved the use of standard scripts, is less general than our approach. Unknown words do not always occur in the context of a story that fits a standardized script. Furthermore, even if a standardized script may apply to the text overall, the unknown term may not occur as the filler of a standard slot. This does not mean, however, that the context in which the word occurs may not yield useful information in attempting to hypothesize a definition.

Our research also differs from Granger's in that we store the knowledge acquired from reading various texts in a single, general knowledge base, and use this stored knowledge as source of information for definitions. Thus, a definition may be synthesized from several encounters.

Haas and Hendrix

Norman Haas and Gary Hendrix (1983) developed a system in which a tutor specifically gives the system a new concept, and refines it by adding further facts in response to queries from the system as it seeks to relate the new concept to previously acquired knowledge. Although asking questions is a good way to learn, the major focus of our research is to allow the system to learn from context without specific queries or direct instruction. We explore what the system learns when left to read "on its own," and allow it to include only information it can deduce in its definitions. In future work, as already noted in connection with *dress,* we may explore ways in which the system can generate *inductive* hypotheses, which might be used to generate questions to put to a human user, or might simply be kept as questions in the "mind" of our system until more evidence can be found.

Berwick

Another approach to learning verbs (and perhaps other words) was developed by Robert C. Berwick (1983), who attempted to extend the process of analogical learning (as in Patrick Henry Winston's [1975] arch-learning algorithm) to the domain of natural language. Causal networks are created to represent the events in different stories. It is assumed that a word's meaning is known by its position in such a net. A new word, then, is held to be most similar to those known words which play the most similar roles. For example, if murder and assassination both cause their objects to be dead, but love does not cause such an outcome, then *murder* and *assassinate* are closer in their meaning than either is to *love.* Berwick's work, as implemented, required the input of story outlines in specific form, with all relevant causal information explicitly present in the outlines, rather than straight narrative as it occurs in published stories.

While the notion of synonymy (or near synonymy) and similar causes producing similar effects is a useful one, our desire to test our theories on natural text would require that our system infer causal relationships in order to make the sort of comparisons that Berwick's system made. For example, were the system to read that Macbeth assassinated Duncan and then to read that Duncan was dead, it would have to infer that the one fact was the cause of the other. This done, it might use a system similar to Berwick's to infer that *assassinate* is close to *murder* in meaning (assuming, of course that it already knew that "A murdering B" causes B to be dead). Unfortunately, giving our system the ability to make such causal inferences is beyond the scope of this project, although given the presence of certain specific causal information in the knowledge base, comparisons between verbs can be made.

We do make use of the notion that words with similar meanings have similar connections in an agent's network of knowledge. The framework we use for defining nouns includes a slot for potential synonyms. The synonym-finding algorithm compares the other definitional information (such as class inclusion, structure, and function) that has been discovered about the new word with the same information about a candidate synonym. If they have more in common than iñ contrast, the system lists them as possible synonyms.

Some More Recent Work

Zernik and Dyer

Uri Zernik and Michael G. Dyer (1987) compile definitions of words and figurative phrases from conversation into a hierarchical lexicon, using a pattern constructor that analyzes parsing failures to modify its patterns and a concept constructor that selects a strategy according to background information about the goals and plans a person is likely to have in various situations. If the first interpretation of a phrase is inconsistent with that information, the system queries the user, suggesting various interpretations more consistent with the goals of persons in the story until the user confirms that a correct interpretation has been reached.

However, since we focus on literary, not conversational, discourse, Cassie is not informed by a human user when she misunderstands. As long as the misunderstanding is compatible with further encounters with the word and with her general knowledge, there is no reason for Cassie to revise her understanding. If further reading leads to the conclusion that a previous definition was wrong, Cassie revises her understanding without explicit instruction.

Hastings

Peter M. Hastings (Hastings 1994; Hastings and Lytinen 1994a, 1994b) presents several versions of a system, Camille, that uses knowledge of a given domain to infer a word's meaning. Hastings's approach is like ours: The goal is to allow the system to read and acquire word meanings without the intervention of a human tutor. His approach differs, however, in the types of information sought as the meaning of a word, and in the nature of the knowledge base. For each domain, the initial knowledge base consisted of a taxonomy of relevant objects and actions. Camille attempts to place the unknown word appropriately in the domain hierarchy. To this basic system, Hastings has added: a mutual exclusivity constraint; a script applier allowing Camille to match the unknown word with a known word that has filled the same slot in a particular script, or, for a verb, with a known word whose arguments match those of the target word; and an ability to recognize the existence of multiple senses for a word. In most instances, the meaning sought appears to be synonymy with a known word, unlike Cassie, which can create new concepts (defined in terms of preexisting ones). In one version, however, Camille is given the capacity to create a new node, and insert it into the domain hierarchy. This, however, is only available for unknown nouns. Verbs can be "defined" only by mapping them to their closest synonyms. Hastings's evaluation of Camille's performance is given in terms of "correctness" of word meaning. His focus is on the comparative precision and accuracy of the various versions of Camille as they attempt to map unknown terms onto known nodes. For us, such a notion of "correctness" does not apply.

Siskind

Jeffrey Mark Siskind's (1996) focus is on first-language acquisition during childhood, whereas ours is on mature cognitive agents who already know a large part of their language and are (merely) expanding their vocabulary. Siskind takes as given (1) an utterance; (2) a simultaneous visual perception; (3) a mental representation of the situation perceived, which is caused by it; and (4) an assumption that the utterance means that mental representation. His algorithms assign parts of the mental-representation meaning to parts (words) of the utterance. Given "multiple situations," these algorithms "converge" to "correct word-to-meaning mappings."

Although we also assume an utterance and a mental representation that the utterance means, Cassie does not use visual perception to produce the mental representation. In most cases of reading, any mental representation (including imagery) would be produced by the text, so visual perception of a real-world situation does not arise, except for illustrated texts. Although Cassie does not use illustrations, she could in principle (Srihari and Rapaport 1989, Srihari 1991). Siskind's system begins with a mapping between a whole meaning and a whole utterance, and infers mappings between their parts. Cassie already has both of those mappings and seeks to infer definition-style relations between the unknown word and the rest of the knowledge base. Moreover, it does not make sense in our theory to speak of correct word-to-meaning mappings. Finally, Siskind claims that his theory provides evidence for "semantic bootstrapping"—using semantics to aid in learning syntax. In contrast, Cassie uses *syntactic* bootstrapping (using syntax to aid in learning semantics; Gleitman [1990, 1994]), which seems more reasonable for our situation.

Campbell and Shapiro

A related project is Ontological Mediation, being conducted by Alistair E. Campbell and Stuart C. Shapiro in the SNePS Research Group at SUNY Buffalo. Suppose a speaker uses a word unknown to the listener. An "ontological mediator" agent determines the word's meaning by querying the speaker and listener concerning ontological relations, such as subclass, parts, ownership, or skills, and then defines the word for the listener in terms of the listener's already-known words. (See Campbell and Shapiro [1995], Campbell [1996], and www.cse.buffalo.edu/~aec/OM/index.html.)

Future Work

Much remains to be done. We are now developing and using a grammar for natural-language input and output (Hunt and Koplas 1997), as well as for potential use in determining meanings via morphological (and perhaps etymological) information. We plan to expand our algorithms for verb acquisition, and to investigate adjective acquisition. We need to decide under what conditions to represent the definition in the knowledge base; despite Johnson-Laird's findings, discussed previously, it is nevertheless true that eventually we do memorize definitions of words after encountering them often enough. We plan to apply our algorithms to proper names: Can we decide who someone is by using our techniques? Finally, to what extent are we developing a formal model of category-definition by exemplars, where we take as input information about a (single) individual, and output a description of a category that that individual falls under?

Algorithms

We now present the algorithms for noun definition and verb definition.

Algorithm for Noun Definition

Input unknown noun "N."
procedure Make-List1 ::=
  list (1) structure of Ns,
       (2) functions of Ns,
       (3) stative properties of Ns only if there are general rules about them.
end; {procedure Make-List1}

procedure Make-List2 ::=
  list (1) direct class inclusions of N,
       (2) actions of Ns that can't be deduced from class inclusions,
       (3) ownership of Ns,
       (4) synonyms of "N."
end; {procedure Make-List2}

procedure Make-List3 ::=
  begin
    Make-List2;
    if there is structural or functional info about Ns, **then** Make-List1
  end
end; {procedure Make-List3}

begin {defn_noun}
  if N represents a basic-level category, **then** Make-List3
  elsif N represents a subclass of a basic-level category, **then**
    begin
      report that N is a variety of the basic-level category that includes it;
      if Ns are animals, **then** list nonredundant acts that Ns perform;
      list if known:
        functions of Ns,
        structural information about Ns,
        ownership of Ns,
        synonyms of "N";
      list stative properties only if there are general rules about them
  end
  elsif N represents a subclass of animal, **then** Make-List3
  elsif N represents a subclass of physical object, **then**
    begin
      Make-List2;
      if system finds structural or functional information about Ns,
        then Make-List1
      elsif system finds actions of N or synonyms of "N," **then**
        begin
          list them;
          list possible properties of Ns
        end
      elsif N is an object of an act performed by an agent, **then**
        begin
          report that;
          list possible properties of Ns
        end
    end
  elsif N represents a subclass of abstract object, **then**
    begin
      list direct class inclusions of N & ownership of Ns;
      if system finds functional information about Ns,
        then list:
          function,
          actions of Ns that can't be deduced from class inclusions,
          stative properties only if there are general rules,
          synonyms for "N"
      else begin
        list possible properties of Ns;
        if system finds actions of N or synonyms for "N,"
          then list them
        elsif N is an object of an act performed by an agent,

```
                then report that
            end
    end
else {we lack class inclusions, so:}
    begin
        list:
            named individuals of class N,
            ownership,
            possible properties;
            if system finds information on structure, function, actions, then list
it
            elsif N is object of act performed by agent, then report that
    end
end.
```

Algorithm for Verb Definition

Input unknown verb "V."

```
begin {defn_verb}
    report on cause & effect;
    categorize the subject;
    if V is used with an indirect object,
        then categorize objects & indirect object
    elsif V is used with a direct object distinct from its subject,
        then categorize the object
    elsif V is used with its subject as direct object,
        then list the object as "itself"
end.
```

Notes

1. An earlier version of the present chapter appeared as Ehrlich and Rapaport (1997).

2. The nonsense word *arigosin* replaced the word *brachet* for this subject, since he already knew the term *brachet*.

3. The full protocols for brachet and other words are in Ehrlich (1995).

4. Here, we omit passages that do not contain the word *brachet*.

Appendices

A Propositional, First-Order, and Higher-Order Logics
Basic Definitions, Rules of Inference, and Examples

Stuart C. Shapiro

LOGIC IS THE STUDY OF CORRECT REASONING. It is not a particular knowledge representation and reasoning language. Thus, it is not proper to say "We are using (or not using) logic as our knowledge representation and reasoning language." There are, indeed, many different logics. For more details on logics, see Haack (1978), McCawley (1981), and the various articles on logic in Shapiro (1992) beginning with Rapaport (1992).

Requirements to Define a Logic

A logic consists of two parts, a language and a method of reasoning. The logical language, in turn, has two aspects, syntax and semantics. Thus, to specify or define a particular logic, one needs to specify three things: syntax, semantics, and syntactic inference method.

Syntax: The atomic symbols of the logical language, and the rules for constructing well-formed, nonatomic expressions (symbol structures) of the logic.

Semantics: The meanings of the atomic symbols of the logic, and the rules for determining the meanings of nonatomic expressions of the logic.

Syntactic inference method: The rules for determining a subset of logical expressions, called theorems of the logic.

CarPool World

I will use CarPool World as a simple example. In CarPool World, Tom and Betty carpool to work. On any day, either Tom drives Betty or Betty drives Tom. In the former case, Tom is the driver and Betty is the passenger. In the latter case, Betty is the driver and Tom is the passenger.

Propositional Logic: Propositional CarPool World

Propositional logics (sometimes called sentential logics) conceptualize domains at, but not below the level of sentences (or propositions). So the finest analysis of CarPool World is that there are six sentences:

Betty drives Tom.	*Tom drives Betty.*
Betty is the driver.	*Tom is the driver.*
Betty is the passenger.	*Tom is the passenger.*

Syntax

The syntactic expressions of propositional logics consist of atomic propositions and nonatomic, well-formed propositions (wfps).

Syntax of Atomic Propositions

- Any letter of the alphabet, e.g.: P;
- Any letter of the alphabet with a numeric subscript, e.g.: Q_3;
- Any alphanumeric string, e.g.: *Tom is the driver*

is an atomic proposition.

Syntax of Well-Formed Propositions

1. Every atomic proposition is a well-formed proposition.
2. If P is a well-formed proposition, then so is $\neg P$.
3. If P and Q are well-formed propositions, then so are
   (a) $(P \land Q)$ (b) $(P \lor Q)$ (c) $(P \Rightarrow Q)$ (d) $(P \Leftrightarrow Q)$
4. Nothing else is a well-formed proposition.

We will not bother using parentheses when there is no ambiguity, in which case $\land$ and $\lor$ will have higher priority than $\Rightarrow$, which, in turn will have higher priority than $\Leftrightarrow$. For example, we will write $P \land Q \Leftrightarrow \neg P \Rightarrow Q$ instead of $((P \land Q) \Leftrightarrow (\neg P \Rightarrow Q))$.

An example well-formed proposition in CarPool World is

Tom is the driver $\Leftrightarrow \neg$*Betty is the driver*

Semantics

To specify the semantics of a propositional logic, we must give the semantics of each atomic proposition and the rules for deriving the semantics of the well-formed propositions from their constituent propositions.

There are actually two levels of semantics we must specify: extensional semantics and intensional semantics.

The *extensional semantics* (value or *denotation*) of the expressions of a logic are relative to a particular interpretation, model, or situation. The extensional semantics of CarPool World, for example, are relative to a particular day. The denotation of a proposition is either true or false. If P is an expression of some logic, we will use $[P]$ to mean the denotation of P. If we need to make explicit that we mean the denotation relative to situation S, we will use $[P]_S$.

The *intensional semantics* (or *intension*) of the expressions of a logic are independent of any specific interpretation, model, or situation, but are dependent only on the domain being conceptualized. If P is an expression of some logic, we will use $[P]$ to mean the intension of P. If we need to make explicit that we mean the intension relative to domain D, we will use $[P]_D$. Many formal people consider the intension of an expression to be a function from situations to denotations. For them, $[P]_D(S) = [P]_S$. However, less formally, the intensional semantics of a well-formed proposition can be given as a statement in a previously understood language (for example, English) that allows the extensional value to be determined in any specific situation. Intensional semantics are often omitted when a logic is specified, but they shouldn't be.

Intensional Semantics of Atomic Propositions. The intensional semantics of atomic propositions must be specified for each particular propositional logic. For example, the intensional semantics of the atomic propositions of CarPool World are:

[*Betty drives Tom*]	= The person named "Tom" gets a ride in to work with the person named "Betty."
[*Tom drives Betty*]	= The person named "Betty" gets a ride in to work with the person named "Tom."
[*Betty is the driver*]	= The person named "Betty" is the driver of the car.
[*Tom is the driver*]	= The person named "Tom" is the driver of the car.
[*Betty is the passenger*]	= The person named "Betty" is a passenger in the car.
[*Tom is the passenger*]	= The person named "Tom" is a passenger in the car.

Note that each atomic proposition is a single indivisible symbol; the fact that the atomic propositions look like English sentences whose meanings are paraphrases of the intensional semantics is purely for mnemonic purposes. One should never rely on "pretend it's English" semantics.

Intensional Semantics of Well-Formed Propositions

Since the logical connectives ¬, $\wedge$, $\vee$, $\Rightarrow$, and $\Leftrightarrow$ are commonly used, the following clauses are the standard ones for deriving the intensional se-

	Denotation in Situation				
Proposition	1	2	3	4	5
Betty drives Tom	True	True	True	False	False
Tom drives Betty	True	True	False	True	False
Betty is the driver	True	True	True	False	False
Tom is the driver	True	False	False	True	False
Betty is the passenger	True	False	False	True	False
Tom is the passenger	True	False	True	False	False

Table 1
CarPool World situations.

mantics of well-formed propositions from the intensional semantics of their constituents:

- $[\neg P]$ = It is not the case that $[P]$.
- $[P \land Q]$ = $[P]$ and $[Q]$.
- $[P \lor Q]$ = Either $[P]$ or $[Q]$ or both.
- $[P \Rightarrow Q]$ = If $[P]$ then $[Q]$.
- $[P \Leftrightarrow Q]$ = $[P]$ if and only if $[Q]$.

Extensional Semantics of Atomic Propositions

The denotation of an atomic proposition is a truth value, true or false. Each way of assigning a truth value to each atomic proposition forms one situation. For example, each column of table 1 gives one situation of CarPool World.

Table 1 shows 5 situations. Since there are 6 propositions, and each one can have either of 2 truth values, there are $2^6 = 64$ different situations in CarPool World. We will see below how to limit these to the two that make sense.

Extensional Semantics of WFPs

Just as there is a standard way to derive the intensional semantics of well-formed propositions from their constituents, so is there a standard way to compute the denotations of well-formed propositions from their constituents. These are:

- $[\sim P]$ is true if $[P]$ is false. Otherwise, it is false.
- $[P \land Q]$ is true if $[P]$ is true and $[Q]$ is true. Otherwise, it is false.
- $[P \lor Q]$ is false if $[P]$ is false and $[Q]$ is false. Otherwise, it is true.
- $[P \Rightarrow Q]$ is false if $[P]$ is true and $[Q]$ is false. Otherwise, it is true.
- $[P \Leftrightarrow Q]$ is true if $[P]$ and $[Q]$ are both true, or both false. Otherwise, it is false.

P	True	False	
$\neg P$	False	True	

P	True	True	False	False
Q	True	False	True	False
$P \wedge Q$	True	False	False	False
$P \vee Q$	True	True	True	False
$P \Rightarrow Q$	True	False	True	True
$P \Leftrightarrow Q$	True	False	False	True

Table 2
Truth tables.

P	True	True	False	False
Q	True	False	True	False
$\neg P$	False	False	True	True
$Q \Rightarrow P$	True	True	False	True
$P \Rightarrow (Q \Rightarrow P)$	True	True	True	True
$P \wedge \neg P$	False	False	False	False

Table 3
Truth table for several well-formed propositions.

These can also be shown in the truth tables in table 2. Notice that each column of these tables represents a different situation.

Semantic Properties of WFPs

A well-formed proposition is either satisfiable, contingent, valid, or contradictory according to the situations in which it is true. A well-formed proposition is *satisfiable* if it is true in at least one situation, *contingent* if it is true in at least one situation and false in at least one situation, *valid* if it is true in every situation, and *contradictory* if it is false in every situation. For example, as table 3 shows, $\neg P$, $Q \Rightarrow P$, and $P \Rightarrow (Q \Rightarrow P)$ are satisfiable, $\neg P$ and $Q \Rightarrow P$ are contingent, $P \Rightarrow (Q \Rightarrow P)$ is valid, and $P \wedge \neg P$ is contradictory.

If A is a well-formed expression of a logic $\mathcal{L}$, it is standard to write $\models_{\mathcal{L}} A$ (The symbol "$\models$" is called a "double turnstyle") to indicate that A is valid in logic $\mathcal{L}$. The subscript may be omitted if it is clear from context. Thus, the above truth table shows that $\models P \Rightarrow (Q \Rightarrow P)$. Valid well-formed propositions are also called *tautologies*.

Related to the notion of validity is the notion of *logical implication*.

Proposition	Denotation in Situation 3	4
Betty drives Tom	True	False
Tom drives Betty	False	True
Betty is the driver	True	False
Tom is the driver	False	True
Betty is the passenger	False	True
Tom is the passenger	True	False

Table 4

The only two situations in which all five well-formed propositions are true.

The set of well-formed propositions $\{A_1, ..., A_n\}$ logically implies the well-formed proposition B in logic $\mathcal{L}$ (written $A_1, ..., A_n \vDash_{\mathcal{L}} B$) if and only if B is true in every situation in which every A_i is true. This is how domain knowledge can be used to reduce the set of situations to only those that make sense. For example, in CarPool World, we want to specify that

- Betty is the driver or the passenger, but not both:
  Betty is the driver $\Leftrightarrow$ ¬*Betty is the passenger*
- Tom is the driver or the passenger, but not both:
  Tom is the driver $\Leftrightarrow$ ¬*Tom is the passenger*
- If Betty drives Tom, then Betty is the driver and Tom is the passenger:
  Betty drives Tom $\Rightarrow$ *Betty is the driver* $\wedge$ *Tom is the passenger*
- If Tom drives Betty, then Tom is the driver and Betty is the passenger:
  Tom drives Betty $\Rightarrow$ *Tom is the driver* $\wedge$ *Betty is the passenger*
- Finally, either Tom drives Betty or Betty drives Tom:
  Tom drives Betty $\vee$ *Betty drives Tom*

Table 4 shows the only two situations of CarPool World (numbered as in table 1) in which all five of these well-formed propositions are true. Notice that these are precisely the two commonsense situations.

Logical implication and logical validity are related by the following

Metatheorem 1: $A_1, ..., A_n \vDash_{\mathcal{L}} B$ if and only if $\vDash_{\mathcal{L}} A_1 \wedge ... \wedge A_n \Rightarrow B$

The significance of this is that if one is interested in determining either logical validity or logical implication, one may solve the other problem instead.

Inference in Propositional Logics

There are two basic varieties of inference methods in propositional logics, Hilbert-style methods, and natural deduction methods. *Hilbert-style inference methods* use a large number of (logical) axioms and a small number of rules of inference, whereas *natural deduction methods* use a small number of (logical) axioms (or even none at all) and a large number of rules of inference. Usually there are two rules of inference for each logical connective, ¬, ∧, ∨, ⇒, and ⇔, an introduction rule, and an elimination rule. These are usually abbreviated by writing the logical connective before "I" or "E," respectively. For example ¬I is the "negation introduction" rule, and ∧E is the "and elimination" rule. The rule ⇒ E is also often called modus ponens.

In Hilbert-style methods, a *derivation* of a well-formed proposition, *A*, from a set of assumptions (or nonlogical axioms,) Γ, is a list of well-formed propositions in which each well-formed proposition in the list is either a logical axiom, or a nonlogical axiom, or follows from previous well-formed propositions in the proof according to one of the rules of inference. A Hilbert-style proof of a well-formed proposition, *A*, is a derivation of *A* from an empty set of assumptions. If *A* can be derived from Γ in the logic $\mathscr{L}$, we write Γ ⊢ $\mathscr{L}$ *A*, (The symbol "⊢" is called a *turnstyle*) while if *A* can be proved in $\mathscr{L}$, we write ⊢$_{\mathscr{L}}$ *A*. If *A* can be proved in $\mathscr{L}$, *A* is called a *theorem* of $\mathscr{L}$.

I will present a natural deduction inference method in more detail. This method is based on methods due to Gentzen, Kleene, and Fitch (see (Kleene 1950, 86-99, 442-443 and Fitch 1952). In this presentation, *A* and *B* will stand for any well-formed propositions of some propositional logic, Γ, Δ, Θ, Λ, and Φ will stand for any (possibly empty) sets of well-formed propositions of this logic, and "," will stand for set union, where if either argument of "," is *A* or *B*, the singleton set {*A*} or {*B*}, respectively, should be understood instead. A derivation in this method is a list of expressions of the form Γ ⊢$_{\mathscr{L}}$ Δ, where each expression in the list is either an instance of the axiom Γ, Δ ⊢$_{\mathscr{L}}$ Δ or follows from previous expressions according to one of the following rules of inference. (I will omit the subscript, since all these rules deal with the same logic.)

Hyp: If Γ ⊢ Θ then Γ, Δ ⊢ Θ
Thin: If Γ ⊢ Φ, Θ then Γ ⊢ Θ
Cut: If Γ ⊢ Φ, Λ and Δ, Φ ⊢ Θ then Γ, Δ ⊢ Λ, Θ
∧I: If Γ ⊢ *A*, *B*, Θ then Γ ⊢ *A* ∧ *B*, Θ
∧E: If Γ ⊢ *A* ∧ *B*, Θ then Γ ⊢ *A*, *B*, Θ or Γ ⊢ *A*, Θ or Γ ⊢ *B*, Θ
∨I: If Γ ⊢ *A*, Θ then Γ ⊢ *A* ∨ *B*, Θ or Γ ⊢ *B* ∨ *A*, Θ
∨E: If Γ, *A* ⊢ Θ and Γ, *B* ⊢ Θ then Γ, *A* ∨ *B* ⊢ Θ
¬I: If Γ, *A* ⊢ *B*, ¬*B*, Θ then Γ ⊢ ¬*A*
¬E: If Γ ⊢ ¬¬*A*, Θ then Γ ⊢ *A*, Θ
⇒I: If Γ, *A* ⊢ Δ, *B* then Γ ⊢ *A* ⇒ *B*
⇒E: If Γ ⊢ *A*, *A* ⇒ *B*, Δ then Γ ⊢ *B*, Δ
⇔I: If Γ ⊢ *A* ⇒ *B*, *B* ⇒ *A*, Δ then Γ ⊢ *A* ⇔ *B*, Δ
⇔E: If Γ ⊢ *A*, *A* ⇔ *B*, Δ then Γ ⊢ *B*, Δ and if Γ ⊢ *B*, *A* ⇔ *B*, Δ then Γ ⊢ *A*, Δ

Every line of such a derivation of the form $\Gamma \vdash_{\mathscr{L}} \Delta$ indicates that every well-formed proposition in the set Δ can be derived in the logic $\mathscr{L}$ from the set of assumptions Γ, and every line of the form $\vdash_{\mathscr{L}} \Delta$ indicates that every well-formed proposition in Δ is a theorem of $\mathscr{L}$. The expression $\Gamma \vdash_{\mathscr{L}} \Delta$ may also be interpreted as a knowledge base in which the well-formed propositions in Γ are assumptions, or domain rules and the well-formed propositions in $\Delta - \Gamma$ are derived propositions.

As for logical implication and logical validity, derivation and proof in either Hilbert-style or natural deduction inference methods are related by the following

Metatheorem 2: $A_1, ..., A_n \vdash_{\mathscr{L}} B_1, ..., B_m$
  if and only if $\vdash_{\mathscr{L}} A_1 \wedge ... \wedge A_n \Rightarrow B_1 \wedge ... \wedge B_m$

Again, the significance of this is that if one is interested in finding either a derivation or a proof, one may solve the other problem instead.

Example Derivation

As an example, I'll show a derivation from the CarPool World domain knowledge (nonlogical axioms) of the proposition Tom drives Betty $\Rightarrow$ ¬Betty drives Tom. To save space, I'll use the following abbreviations.

BdT:	*Betty drives Tom*
TdB:	*Tom drives Betty*
Bd:	*Betty is the driver*
Td:	*Tom is the driver*
Bp:	*Betty is the passenger*
Tp:	*Tom is the passenger*

1. $TdB, TdB \Rightarrow Td \wedge Bp, Td \Leftrightarrow \neg Tp \vdash TdB, TdB \Rightarrow Td \wedge Bp, Td \Leftrightarrow \neg Tp$ Axiom
2. $TdB, TdB \Rightarrow Td \wedge Bp, Td \Leftrightarrow \neg Tp \vdash Td \wedge Bp, Td \Leftrightarrow \neg Tp$ $\Rightarrow$ E, 1
3. $TdB, TdB \Rightarrow Td \wedge Bp, Td \Leftrightarrow \neg Tp \vdash Td, Td \Leftrightarrow \neg Tp$ $\wedge$ E, 2
4. $TdB, TdB \Rightarrow Td \wedge Bp, Td \Leftrightarrow \neg Tp \vdash \neg Tp$ $\Leftrightarrow$ E, 3
5. $BdT, BdT \Rightarrow Bd \wedge Tp \vdash BdT, BdT \Rightarrow Bd \wedge Tp$ Axiom
6. $BdT, BdT \Rightarrow Bd \wedge Tp \vdash Bd \wedge Tp$ $\Rightarrow$ E, 5
7. $BdT, BdT \Rightarrow Bd \wedge Tp \vdash Tp$ $\wedge$ E, 6
8. $TdB, TdB \Rightarrow Td \wedge Bp, Td \Leftrightarrow \neg Tp, BdT, BdT \Rightarrow Bd \wedge Tp \vdash \neg Tp, Tp$ Cut, 4, 7
9. $TdB, TdB \Rightarrow Td \wedge Bp, Td \Leftrightarrow \neg Tp, BdT \Rightarrow Bd \wedge Tp \vdash \neg BdT$ ¬I, 8
10. $TdB \Rightarrow Td \wedge Bp, Td \Leftrightarrow \neg Tp, BdT \Rightarrow Bd \wedge Tp \vdash TdB \Rightarrow \neg BdT$ $\Rightarrow$I, 9

This derivation actually only uses three of the five assumptions. The others may be added by the rule of *Hyp*.

First-Order Predicate Logic—Predicate CarPool World

First-order predicate logics (FOPLs) conceptualize domains at and below the level of propositions, down to the level of individuals, properties, and relations. In FOPL CarPool World, there are two individuals, Betty and Tom, two unary properties, being a driver and being a passenger, and one binary relation, drives.

Syntax

The syntactic expressions of first-order predicate logics consist of terms, atomic formulas, and nonatomic, well-formed formulas. Terms, in turn, consist of individual constants, variables, arbitrary individuals, undetermined individuals and functional terms. Functional terms, atomic formulas, and well-formed formulas are nonatomic symbol structures. The atomic symbols of first-order predicate logics are individual constants, variables, arbitrary individuals, undetermined individuals, function symbols, and predicate symbols. (Arbitrary individuals and undetermined individuals are not usually mentioned, but I introduce them so that every formula in a derivation can have a clear semantics.)

Syntax of Atomic Symbols

Individual Constants: Any letter of the alphabet (preferably early), any (such) letter with a numeric subscript, any character string not containing blanks nor other punctuation marks is an *individual constant,* for example, a, B_{12}, *Betty, Tom's_mother_in_law.*

Variables: Any letter of the alphabet (preferably late), and any (such) letter with a numeric subscript is a *variable,* for example, x, y, u_6.

Arbitrary Individuals and Undertermined Individuals: Any symbol that could be used as an individual constant or as a variable could also be used as an *arbitrary individual* or an *undetermined individual,* for example, *someone, a_driver, someone's_mother.*

Function Symbols: Any letter of the alphabet (preferably early middle), any (such) letter with a numeric subscript, and any character string not containing blanks is a *function symbol,* for example: f, g_2, *mother_of.*

Predicate Symbols: Any letter of the alphabet (preferably late middle), any (such) letter with a numeric subscript, and any character string not containing blanks is a *predicate symbol,* for example: P, Q_4, *odd, Driver.*

Each function symbol and predicate symbol must have a particular arity, which may be shown explicitly as a superscript, for example: *mother_of^1*, *Drives^2*, g_2^3. The arity need not be shown explicitly if it is understood. In any specific predicate logic language individual constants, variables, arbitrary individuals, undetermined individuals, function symbols, and predicate symbols must be disjoint.

Syntax of Terms

- Every individual constant, every variable, every arbitrary individual, and every undetermined individual is a term.
- If f^n is a function symbol of arity n, and $t_1, ..., t_n$ are terms, then $f^n(t_1, ..., t_n)$ is a (functional) term (the superscript may be omitted if no confusion results); for example, $Drives^2(Tom, mother\_of^1(Betty))$.
- Nothing else is a term.

Syntax of Atomic Formulas

- If P^n is a predicate symbol of arity n, and $t_1, ..., t_n$ are terms, then $P^n(t_1, ..., t_n)$ is an atomic formula.

For example, $child\text{-}in^2(Sally, family\text{-}of^2(John, mother\text{-}of^1(Sally)))$ (The superscript may be omitted if no confusion results.)

Syntax of Well-Formed Formulas

- Every atomic formula is a well-formed formula.
- If P is a well-formed formula, then so is $\neg P$.
- If P and Q are well-formed formulas, then so are $(P \wedge Q)$, $(P \vee Q)$, $(P \Rightarrow Q)$, and $(P \Leftrightarrow Q)$.
- If P is a well-formed formula and x is a variable, then $\forall x(P)$ and $\exists x(P)$ are well-formed formulas. $\forall$ is called the *universal quantifier*. $\exists$ is called the existential quantifier. P is called the scope of quantification.
- Nothing else is a well-formed formula.

We will not bother using parentheses when there is no ambiguity, in which case $\forall$ and $\exists$ will have the highest priority, then $\wedge$ and $\vee$ will have higher priority than $\Rightarrow$, which, in turn will have higher priority than $\Leftrightarrow$. For example, we will write $\forall x P(x) \wedge \exists y Q(y) \Leftrightarrow \neg P(a) \Rightarrow Q(b)$ instead of $((\forall x(P(x)) \wedge \exists y(Q(y))) \Leftrightarrow (\neg P(a) \Rightarrow Q(b)))$.

Every occurrence of x in P, not in the scope of some occurrence of $\forall x$ or $\exists x$, is said to be free in P and bound in $\forall x\ P$ and $\exists x P$. Every occurrence of every variable other than x that is free in P is also free in $\forall x P$ and $\exists x P$.

A well-formed formula with at least one free variable is called *open*. A well-formed formula with no free variables is called *closed*. An expression with no variables, arbitrary individuals, or undetermined individuals is called *ground*.

Syntax of FOPL CarPool World

In FOPL CarPool World, we will use the following atomic symbols:

Individual constants: *Betty, Tom*
Variables: x, y
Arbitrary individuals: *anyone*
Undetermined individuals: *someone*

Unary predicate symbols: *Driver, Passenger*
Binary predicate symbol: *Drives*

In FOPL CarPool World, the six atomic propositions of propositional CarPool World become the six well-formed formulas:

Drives(Betty, Tom) *Drives(Tom, Betty)*
Driver(Betty)   *Driver(Tom)*
Passenger(Betty)   *Passenger(Tom)*

Substitutions

A *substitution* is a set of pairs, $\{t_1/v_1, \ldots, t_n/v_n\}$ where the t_i are terms, the v_i are variables, arbitrary individuals, or undetermined individuals, and $\forall i, j \, [i \neq j \Rightarrow v_i \neq v_j]$. The result of applying a substitution to a well-formed formula A, written $A \{t_1/v_1, \ldots, t_n/v_n\}$ is obtained by simultaneously replacing every occurrence of each arbitrary or undetermined individual v_i in A by t_i, and every free occurrence of each variable v_i in A by t_i, as long as any variable that occurs in t_i or t_j remains free in the result. For example,

■ $P(x, y) \{x/y, y/x\} = P(y, x)$

■ $(Drives(x, someone) \Rightarrow \exists x \, Passenger(x))\{Betty/x, Tom/someone\} = (Drives(Betty, Tom) \Rightarrow \exists x \, Passenger(x))$

Semantics

Although the intensional semantics of a first-order predicate logic depends on the domain being formalized, and the extensional semantics depends also on a particular situation, we can specify the types of the entities usually given as the intensional and as the extensional semantics of first-order predicate logics expressions.

Semantics of the "Standard" Predicate Logic

The usual semantics of first-order predicate logics assumes a **Domain**, $\mathcal{D}$, of individuals, functions on individuals, sets of individuals, and relations on individuals. Let $\mathcal{I}$ be the set of all individuals in the domain $\mathcal{D}$.

Semantics of Atomic Symbols

Individual constants: If a is an individual constant, $[a]$ is some particular individual in $\mathcal{I}$.

Function symbols: If f^n is a function symbol of arity n, $[f^n]$ is some particular function in $\mathcal{D}$,

$$[f^n]: \underbrace{\mathcal{I} \times \ldots \times \mathcal{I}}_{n \text{ times.}} \to \mathcal{I}$$

Predicate symbols: If P^1 is a unary predicate symbol, $[P^1]$ is some particular subset of $\mathcal{I}$.

If P^n is a predicate symbol of arity n, $[P^n]$ is some particular subset of the relation $\underbrace{\mathcal{I} \times \ldots \times \mathcal{I}}_{n \text{ times.}}$

Semantics of Ground Terms

Individual constants: If a is an individual constant, $[a]$ is some particular individual in $\mathcal{I}$.

Functional terms: If f^n is a function symbol of arity n, and $t_1, \ldots, t_n$ are ground terms, then $[f^n(t_1, \ldots, t_n)] = [f^n]([t_1], \ldots, [t_n])$.

Semantics of Ground Atomic Formulas

- If P^1 is a unary predicate symbol, and t is a ground term, then $[P^1(t)]$ is true if $[t] \in [P^1]$, and false otherwise.
- If P^n is an n-ary predicate symbol, and $t_1, \ldots, t_n$ are ground terms, then $[P^n(t_1, \ldots, t_n)]$ is true if $<[t_1], \ldots, [t_n]> \in [P^n]$, and false otherwise.

Semantics of Well-Formed Formulas

- If P is a ground well-formed formula,
  then $[\neg P]$ is true if $[P]$ is false, otherwise, it is false.
- If P and Q are ground well-formed formulas,
  then $[P \wedge Q]$ is true if $[P]$ is true and $[Q]$ is true, otherwise, it is false.
- If P and Q are ground well-formed formulas,
  then $[P \vee Q]$ is false if $[P]$ is false and $[Q]$ is false, otherwise, it is true.
- If P and Q are ground well-formed formulas,
  then $[P \Rightarrow Q]$ is false if $[P]$ is true and $[Q]$ is false, otherwise, it is true.
- If P and Q are ground well-formed formulas,
  then $[P \Leftrightarrow Q]$ is true if $[P]$ and $[Q]$ are both true or both false, otherwise, it is false.
- If P is a well-formed formula containing the arbitrary individual x,
  then $[P]$ is true if $[P\{t/x\}]$ is true for every ground term, t.
  Otherwise, it is false.
- If P is a well-formed formula containing the undetermined individual x,
  then $[P]$ is true if there is some ground term, t such that $[P\{t/x\}]$ is true.
  Otherwise, it is false.
- $[\forall x\, P]$ is true if $[P\{t/x\}]$ is true for every ground term, t. Otherwise, it is false.
- $[\exists x\, P]$ is true if there is some ground term, t such that $[P\{t/x\}]$ is true. Otherwise, it is false.

Recall that the intensional semantics of an expression can be given as an English statement that allows the extensional value to be determined in any specific situation. In this presentation, I do not give semantics to nonground expressions. Some people do, but I think that is confusing.

Expression	Denotation in Situation (Day)			
	1	2	3	4
Driver	{Betty, Tom}	{Betty}	{Tom}	{}
Passenger	{Betty, Tom}	{Tom}	{Betty}	{}
Drives	{<Betty, Tom>, <Tom, Betty>}	{<Betty, Tom>}	{<Tom, Betty>}	{}
Driver(Betty)	True	True	False	False
Driver(Tom)	True	False	True	False
Passenger(Betty)	True	False	True	False
Passenger(Tom)	True	True	False	False
Drives(Betty, Tom)	True	True	False	False
Drives(Tom, Betty)	True	False	True	False

Table 5

The extensional semantics of some expressions in
FOPL CarPoolWorld on four different days.

Intensional Semantics of FOPL CarPool World

The intensional semantics of the atomic symbols of first-order predicate logic CarPool World are as follows.

The individual constants are:

Betty: The individual named Betty.
Tom: The individual named Tom.

The unary predicate symbols are:

Driver: The set of drivers on a given day.
Passenger: The set of passengers on a given day.

The binary predicate symbol is:

Drives: The relation that holds between a driver and a passenger when the former drives the latter to work on a given day.

The intensional semantics of other ground expressions in FOPL CarPool World can be derived from these according to the format of the previous subsection.

Extensional Semantics of FOPL CarPool World

The extensional semantics of some expressions in first-order predicate logic CarPool World in four different situations (that is, on four different days) are displayed in table 5.

Semantic Properties of Well-Formed Formulas

Just as for well-formed propositions, a well-formed formula is satisfiable if it is true in at least one situation, contingent if it is true in at least one situation and false in at least one situation, valid if it is true in every situation, and contradictory of it is false in every situation. The terms *tautology* and *logical implication* are also defined for well-formed formulas as they are for well-formed propositions, as is the notation $\vDash_{\mathscr{L}} A$ and A_1, ..., $A_n \vDash_{\mathscr{L}} B$. Metatheorem 1 also applies to first-order predicate logics as well as to propositional logic.

In a logical language without function symbols, with n individual constants and k_j predicates of arity j, there are $\Sigma_j(k_j \times n^j)$ ground atomic propositions, and $2^{\Sigma_j(k_j \times n^j)}$ situations. In CarPool World, this comes to $2^{2 \times 2^1 + 1 \times 2^2} = 256$ situations. If we add even one function symbol, we get an infinite number of ground terms, and, therefore, an infinite number of situations. For example, if we add the unary function symbol mother_of to CarPool World, we get the ground terms, *mother_of(Tom)*, *mother_of(mother_of(Tom))*, *mother_of(mother_of(mother_of(Tom)))*, ... and so on.

Domain Rules of FOPL CarPool World

In Propositional CarPool World five sentences were needed to constrain the situations to the two commonsense ones. In first-order predicate logic CarPool World, only three domain rules are needed:

- Each person is the driver or the passenger, but not both:

  $\forall x\ (Driver(x) \Leftrightarrow \neg Passenger(x))$

- If one person drives the other, then the former is the driver and the latter is the passenger:

  $\forall x \forall y\ (Drives(x, y) \Rightarrow Driver(x) \wedge Passenger(y))$

- And again, either Tom drives Betty or Betty drives Tom:

  $Drives(Tom, Betty) \vee Drives(Betty, Tom)$

One can (relatively) easily verify that, of the 256 situations of first-order predicate logic CarPool World, only situations 2 and 3 of table 5 make all these three well-formed formulas true.

Inference

Inference in predicate logics is just like inference in propositional logics, with the addition of axioms and/or rules of inference for the universal and existential quantifiers. For the natural deduction system given above, the additional rules of inference are

∀I   If $\Gamma \vdash A\{t/x\}$, where t is any arbitrary individual that does not occur in Γ, then $\Gamma \vdash \forall x A$.

∀E   If $\Gamma \vdash \forall x A$ then $\Gamma \vdash A\{t/x\}$, where t is any term.

∃I   If $\Gamma \vdash A\{t/x\}$, where t is any term, then $\Gamma \vdash \exists x A$.

∃E   If $\Gamma \vdash \exists x A$ then $\Gamma \vdash A\{t/x\}$,

    where t is any undetermined individual that does not occur in Γ.

Confusingly, as is shown in table 6, each of these four rules commonly goes by two different names. Metatheorem 2 applies to first-order predicate logic as well as it does to propositional logic.

Abbreviation	Our Name	Other Common Name
∀I	Universal Introduction	Universal Generalization
∀E	Universal Elimination	Universal Instantiation
∃I	Existential Introduction	Existential Generalization
∃E	Existential Elimination	Existential Instantiation

Table 6

Each of these four rules commonly goes by two different names.

Example Proof

In this example proof of the theorem $\neg\forall x A(x) \Rightarrow \exists x \, \neg A(x)$, the following atomic symbols are used:

Variable: x
Arbitrary individual: b
Predicate symbol: A

1. $\neg\forall x \, A(x)$	$\vdash \neg\forall x A(x)$	*Axiom*
2. $\neg\exists x \, \neg A(x)$	$\vdash \neg\exists x \neg A(x)$	*Axiom*
3. $\neg A(b)$	$\vdash \neg A(b)$	*Axiom*
4. $\neg A(b)$	$\vdash \exists x \, \neg A(x)$	*∃I, 3*
5. $\neg\exists x \, \neg A(x), \neg A(b)$	$\vdash \exists x \, \neg A(x), \neg\exists x \, \neg A(x)$	*Cut, 2, 4*
6. $\neg\exists x \, \neg A(x)$	$\vdash \neg\neg A(b)$	*¬I, 5*
7. $\neg\exists x \, \neg A(x)$	$\vdash A(b)$	*¬E, 6*
8. $\neg\exists x \, \neg A(x)$	$\vdash \forall x \, A(x)$	*∀I, 7*
9. $\neg\forall x \, A(x), \neg\exists x \, \neg A(x)$	$\vdash \forall x \, A(x), \neg\forall x \, A(x)$	*Cut, 1, 8*
10. $\neg\forall x \, A(x)$	$\vdash \neg\neg\exists x \, \neg A(x)$	*¬I, 9*
11. $\neg\forall x \, A(x)$	$\vdash \exists x \, \neg A(x)$	*¬E, 10*
12.	$\vdash \neg\forall x \, A(x) \Rightarrow \exists x \, \neg A(x)$	*⇒I, 11*

Example Derivation

As an example, I'll present the first-order predicate logic version of the derivation in the propositional logics section of

$Drives(Tom, Betty) \Rightarrow \neg Drives(Betty, Tom)$

from the CarPool World domain rules. To save space, I'll use the following abbreviations.

B: *Betty*
T: *Tom*
Dr: *Driver*
Pr: *Passenger*
D: *Drives*

1. $D(T, B) \vdash D(T, B)$ *Axiom*
2. $\forall x \forall y(D(x, y) \Rightarrow Dr(x) \wedge Pr(y)) \vdash \forall x \forall y(D(x, y) \Rightarrow Dr(x) \wedge Pr(y))$ *Axiom*
3. $\forall x \forall y(D(x, y) \Rightarrow Dr(x) \wedge Pr(y)) \vdash \forall y(D(T, y) \Rightarrow Dr(T) \wedge Pr(y))$ *∀E, 2*
4. $\forall x \forall y(D(x, y) \Rightarrow Dr(x) \wedge Pr(y)) \vdash D(T, B) \Rightarrow Dr(T) \wedge Pr(B)$ *∀E, 3*
5. $D(T, B), \forall x \forall y(D(x, y) \Rightarrow Dr(x) \wedge Pr(y))$
     $\vdash D(T, B), D(T, B) \Rightarrow Dr(T) \wedge Pr(B)$ *Cut, 1, 4*

6. $D(T, B), \forall x \forall y(D(x, y) \Rightarrow Dr(x) \wedge Pr(y)) \vdash Dr(T) \wedge Pr(B)$ $\Rightarrow E, 5$

7. $D(T, B), \forall x \forall y(D(x, y) \Rightarrow Dr(x) \wedge Pr(y)) \vdash Dr(T)$ $\wedge E, 6$

8. $\forall x(Dr(x) \Rightarrow \neg Pr(x)) \vdash \forall x(Dr(x) \Rightarrow \neg Pr(x))$ *Axiom*

9. $\forall x(Dr(x) \Rightarrow \neg Pr(x)) \vdash Dr(T) \Rightarrow \neg Pr(T)$ $\forall E, 8$

10. $D(T, B), \forall x(Dr(x) \Rightarrow \neg Pr(x)), \forall x \forall y(D(x, y) \Rightarrow Dr(x) \wedge Pr(y))$
$\vdash Dr(T), Dr(T) \Rightarrow \neg Pr(T)$ *Cut*, 7, 9

11. $D(T, B), \forall x(Dr(x) \Rightarrow \neg Pr(x)), \forall x \forall y(D(x, y) \Rightarrow Dr(x) \wedge Pr(y))$
$\vdash \neg Pr(T)$ $\Rightarrow E, 10$

12. $D(B, T) \vdash D(B, T)$ *Axiom*

13. $\forall x \forall y(D(x, y) \Rightarrow Dr(x) \wedge Pr(y)) \vdash \forall y(D(B, y) \Rightarrow Dr(B) \wedge Pr(y))$ $\forall E, 2$

14. $\forall x \forall y(D(x, y) \Rightarrow Dr(x) \wedge Pr(y)) \vdash D(B, T) \Rightarrow Dr(B) \wedge Pr(T))$ $\forall E, 13$

15. $D(B, T), \forall x \forall y(D(x, y) \Rightarrow Dr(x) \wedge Pr(y))$
$\vdash D(B, T), D(B, T) \Rightarrow Dr(B) \wedge Pr(T))$ *Cut*, 12, 14

16. $D(B, T), \forall x \forall y(D(x, y) \Rightarrow Dr(x) \wedge Pr(y)) \vdash Dr(B) \wedge Pr(T)$ $\Rightarrow E, 15$

17. $D(B, T), \forall x \forall y(D(x, y) \Rightarrow Dr(x) \wedge Pr(y)) \vdash Pr(T)$ $\wedge E, 16$

18. $D(B, T), D(T, B), \forall x(Dr(x) \Rightarrow \neg Pr(x)),$
$\forall x \forall y(D(x, y) \Rightarrow Dr(x) \wedge Pr(y)) \vdash Pr(T), \neg Pr(T)$ *Cut*, 10, 17

19. $D(T, B), \forall x(Dr(x) \Rightarrow \neg Pr(x)), \forall x \forall y(D(x, y) \Rightarrow Dr(x) \wedge Pr(y))$
$\vdash \neg D(B, T)$ $\neg I, 18$

20. $\forall x(Dr(x) \Rightarrow \neg Pr(x)), \forall x \forall y(D(x, y) \Rightarrow Dr(x) \wedge Pr(y))$
$\vdash D(T, B) \Rightarrow \neg D(B, T)$ $\Rightarrow I, 19$

Again, the final domain rule may be added by the rule of Hyp.

Some Properties of Logics

Three important properties of logics are soundness, consistency, and completeness.

- A logic $\mathcal{L}$ is *sound* if $\Gamma \vdash_{\mathcal{L}} A$ implies $\Gamma \models_{\mathcal{L}} A$. This also implies that $\vdash_{\mathcal{L}} A$ implies $\models_{\mathcal{L}} A$. That is, every theorem is valid.

- A logic $\mathcal{L}$ is *consistent* if there is no well-formed formula A for which both $\vdash_{\mathcal{L}} A$ and $\vdash_{\mathcal{L}} \neg A$. That is, there is no well-formed formula such that both it and its negation are provable. If at most one of A and $\neg A$ can be valid, soundness implies consistency.

- A logic $\mathcal{L}$ is *complete* if, for every well-formed formula A, $\models_{\mathcal{L}} A$ implies $\vdash_{\mathcal{L}} A$. That is, every valid well-formed formula is provable.

It is the essence of what we mean by correct reasoning that any logic we use be sound. Completeness, however, is less important because it says nothing about how long a proof will take. We might give up on a proof that is taking too long, and then we will not know if the well-formed formula we were trying to prove is a theorem or not. Nevertheless, all propositional logics, as well as FOPL CarPool World are both sound and complete. The famous Gödel incompleteness theorem says that any formal system that is strong enough to represent arithmetic is either inconsistent or incomplete. However, none of these logics is that strong.

Type Theory and Higher-Order Logics

Type theory was developed by Bertrand Russell (Russell 1908) in order to ban such paradoxical formulas as $\exists x\, \forall y\, [x(y) \Leftrightarrow \neg y(y)]$ which may be read as "There is a property, x, which holds of every property, y, that does not hold of itself" or as "there is a set, x, that contains all sets that don't contain themselves." Note that an instance of this formula is $R(R) \Leftrightarrow \neg R(R)$. That is, the Russell Set is a member of itself if and only if it isn't a member of itself.

In type theory, terms denoting individuals are assigned the type 0. A predicate symbol, P, may take terms and other predicate symbols as arguments, but there must be some positive integer, i such that P takes at least one argument that is of type i and no argument of type greater than i. P is then assigned the type $i + 1$. n^{th}-order predicate logic allows the use of predicate symbols of type at most n, and allows variables to range over terms of type at most $n - 1$. Thus, both $\exists R$ [Kinship(R) $\wedge$ R(Lou, Stu)] and $\forall R$ [Symmetric(R) $\Leftrightarrow$ $\forall x \forall y (R(x, y) \Leftrightarrow R(y, x))$] are second-order formulas. Ω-order predicate logic does not limit the size of n, but still requires that a predicate of type i take one argument of type $i - 1$ and no argument of type i or greater. So the Russell paradox is not well-formed in n^{th}-order predicate logic for any n.

Acknowledgments

The material in this appendix is based on the tutorial, "Foundations of Logic and Inference" given at the Fourteenth International Joint Conference on Artificial Intelligence, August 20, 1995, and the course, Reasoning in Artificial Intelligence, given at the First International Summer Institute on Cognitive Science (FISI), University at Buffalo, Buffalo, New York, July, 1994.

B Relations, Lattices, Algebras, Generalized Quantifier: Definitions and Theorems

Łucja M. Iwańska

THIS APPENDIX PROVIDES DEFINITIONS of standard sets, relations and functions, lattices and Boolean algebras, and generalized quantifiers.

Sets

This section contains definitions for set, cardinality of set, set union, set intersection, set difference, Cartesian product, and powerset of set.

Definition 1 (Set)

Sets is a no-repetition collection of objects.
$S_1 = \{a, aa, aaa\}$ is a set
$S_2 = \{b, c\}$ is another set

Definition 2 (Cardinality of Set)

$|S|$, cardinality (size) of finite set S: number of its elements.
Cardinality of infinite sets: $|A| = |B|$ if $\exists f\, f: A \to B$ one-to-one mapping of A onto B
$|S_1| = 3$
$|S_2| = 2$
I integers I_e even integers: $|I_e| = |I|$ but $I_e \subset I$

Definition 3 (Set-Union)

$A \cup B = \{x \mid x \in A \text{ or } x \in B\}$
$S_1 \cup S_2 = \{a, aa, aaa, b, c\}$

Definition 4 (Set-Intersection)

$A \cap B = \{x \mid x \in A, x \in B\}$

$S_1 \cap S_2 = 0$

Definition 5 (Set-Difference)

$A - B = \{x \mid x \in A, x \notin B\}$

$S_1 - S_2 = \{a, aa, aaa\}$

Definition 6 (Cartesian Product)

$A \times B = \{(a, b) \mid a \in A, b \in B\}$

$S_1 \times S_2 = \{(a, b), (a, c), (aa, b), (aa, c), (aaa, b), (aaa, c)\}$

Definition 7 (Powerset of Set)

Set of all subsets of a set: $2^S = \{S_i \mid S_i \subseteq S\}$

For finite sets: $|2^S| = 2^{|S|}$

$2^{S_1} = \{\emptyset, \{a\}, \{aa\}, \{aaa\}, \{a, aa\}, \{a, aaa\}, \{aa, aaa\}, \{a, aa, aaa\}\}$

Relations, Functions

In this section, definitions are provided for relation, properties of relations, inverse of relation, composition of relations, function, composition of functions, kernel of function, algebra, and right-invariant relation.

Definition 8 (Relation)

Relation is a set of ordered N-tuples, subsets of Cartesian product $A_1 \times A_2 \times \ldots \times A_N$.

Binary relation- subsets of Domain × Range.

The aRb notation: $23 < 45$

The $(a, b) \in R$ notation: $(23, 45) \in <$

Definition 9 (Properties of Relations)

Reflexive $\forall a \in S$ aRa

Irreflexive $\forall a \in S$ aRa is false

Transitive $\forall a, b, c \in S$ if aRb and bRc then aRc

Symmetric $\forall a, b \in S$ if aRb then bRa

Asymmetric $\forall a, b \in S$ if aRb then bRa is false

Equivalence reflexive, symmetric and transitive. Equivalence relation partitions set S into disjoint subsets S_i (equivalence classes) such that $\forall i, j$:

$\forall a, b \in S_i$ aRb is true

$\forall a \ e \ S_i, b \in Sj$ aRb is false

Definition 10 (Inverse of Relation)
The inverse of a relation α, $\alpha^{-1} = \{ <x, y>, y\alpha x \}$.

Definition 11 (Composition of Relations)
The composition of a relation α from A to B, and β from B to C, $\alpha \cdot \beta = \{ <x, y>, \exists z \in B, x\alpha z, z\beta y \}$.

Definition 12 (Function)
Function $f: A \to B$ is a binary relation such that $\forall a \in A, \exists!(a, x) \in R, x \in B$

Definition 13 (Composition of Functions)
The composition of a function $f: B \to C$ with a function $g: A \to B$, $(f \circ g)(x) = f(g(x)): A \to C$.
$\quad f \circ g = g \cdot f$

Definition 14 (Kernel of Function)
The kernel of a function $f: A \to B$ is the relation on A such that: $Ker(f) = \{(a_i, a_j), f(a_i) = f(a_j), a_i, a_j \in A \}$.
$\quad$ The kernel of $f: A \to B$ is an equivalence relation on A.

Definition 15 (Algebra)
An algebra is a tuple $<S, o_1^{k_1}, ..., o_n^{k_n}>$, where S is a set of elements, and $o_i^{k_i}$ are k_i-nary operations on S.

Definition 16 (Right-Invariant Relation)
Let $<A, \cdot>$ be an algebra. An equivalence relation p is right-invariant iff $\forall u, v, w \in A, u \, p \, v$ implies $u{\cdot}w \, p \, v{\cdot}w$.

Lattices, Boolean Algebras

This section provides definitions of homomorphism, monomorphism, isomorphism, partially ordered set, greatest lower bound, least upper bound, lattice, complete lattice, modular lattice, distributive lattice, inverval of lattice, complementary elements, Boolean algebra, complete Boolean algebra, atom of algebra, individual of complete atomic Boolean algebra, and restricting function on a Boolean algebra.

Definition 17 ((Order) Homomorphism, Monomorphism, Isomorphism)
Let $<A_1, \wedge_1>$ and $<A_2, \wedge_2>$ are algebras, and $\wedge_1$ and $\wedge_2$ are of the same order. The function f from A_1 into A_2 is (order) homomorphism iff for all $x_1, ..., x_n, f(\wedge_1 (x_1, ..., x_n)) = \wedge_2 (f(x_1), ... , f(x_n))$.
$\quad$ If f is an injection from A_1 into A_2 then it is called monomorphism; if

it is bijection from A_1 onto A_2 then it is called isomorphism.

Homomorphism is an operation preserving mappings.

Definition 18 (Partially Ordered Set (Poset))

A partially ordered set (poset) is a dublet $<P, \leq >$, where P is a set of elements, and $\leq$ is a binary relation on P such that it is reflexive, transitive, and antisymmetric.

Definition 19 (Greatest Lower Bound (GLB))

Let x and y be elements of a poset P with the ordering relation $<$. The greatest lower bound of x and y is an element z of P such that

1. $z \leq x, z \leq y$,
2. $\forall u \in P$, if $u \leq x \, u \leq y$ then $u \leq z$.

Definition 20 (Least Upper Bound)

Let x and y be elements of a poset P with the ordering relation $\leq$. The least upper bound of x and y is an element z of P such that

1. $x \leq z, y \leq z$,
2. $\forall u \in P$, if $x \leq u \, y \leq u$ then $z \leq u$.

Definition 21 (Lattice)

Lattice is a triple $<L, \wedge, \vee>$, where L is a set of elements, $\wedge$ (meet) and $\vee$ (join) are binary operations on L such that for any elements x and y of L, $x \wedge y \in L$, $x \vee y \in L$, and the following holds:

idempotency $x \wedge x = x$, and $x \vee x = x$

commutativity $x \wedge y = y \wedge x$, and $x \vee y = y \vee x$.

absorption $x \wedge (x \vee y) = x$, and $x \vee (x \wedge y) = x$

associativity $x \wedge (y \wedge z) = (x \wedge y) \wedge z$, and $x \vee (y \vee z) = (x \vee y) \vee z$

The operations meet and join induce the ordering relation $\leq$ on L: $x \leq y$ iff $x \wedge y = x$ iff $x \vee y = y$. With respect to the $<$, $\wedge$ and $\vee$ yield greatest lower bounds and least upper bounds of any pair of elements of L.

Definition 22 (Complete Lattice)

A lattice $<L, \wedge, \vee>$ is complete if all its subsets have a unique least upper bound and greatest lower bound.

Definition 23 (Modular Lattice)

A lattice $<L, \wedge, \vee>$ is modular if for any $x, y, z \in L$ such that $x \leq z$, the following equation holds $x \vee (y \wedge z) = (z \vee x) \wedge y$.

Definition 24 (Distributive Lattice)

A lattice $<L, \wedge, \vee>$ is distributive if for any $x, y, z \in L$, the following equation holds $x \vee (y \wedge z) = (x \vee y) \wedge (x \vee z)$.

Definition 25 (Interval of Lattice)
An interval of a lattice $<L, \leq>$, $[a, b]$, where $a \leq b$, is the subset of L such that: $[a, b] = \{x \in L, a \leq x \leq b\}$.

Definition 26 (Complementary Elements)
Two elements x and y of an interval $[a, b]$ of a lattice $<L, \wedge, \vee>$ are complementary if $x \wedge y = a$, $x \vee y = b$.

Theorem 1 A lattice is distributive iff no two distinct elements in an interval $[a, b]$ of L share a common complement.

Theorem 2 Every distributive lattice is modular.

Definition 27 (Boolean Algebra)
Boolean algebra is a six-tuple $<B, 0, 1, \wedge, \vee, not>$, where B is nonempty set, $0, 1 \in B$, $\wedge$ (meet), $\vee$ (join) are binary operations (functions from $B \times B$ to B), not is a unary operation (complement) such that $\forall x, y, z \in B$
$0 \neq 1$

commutativity laws

$x \wedge y = y \wedge x$
$x \vee y = y \vee x$

distributivity laws

$x \wedge (y \vee z) = (x \wedge y) \vee (x \wedge z)$
$x \vee (y \wedge z) = (x \vee y) \wedge (x \vee z)$

complement laws

$x \wedge not\ x = 0$
$x \vee not\ x = 1$

laws of 0 and 1 $x \wedge 1 = x$

$x \vee 0 = x$

Example of a Boolean algebra: $B = 2^P$, P is a finite set, $0 = \varnothing$, $1 = P$, set-intersection, set-union, set-complement.

Definition 28 (Complete Boolean Algebra)
A Boolean algebra $<B, 0, 1, \wedge, \vee, not>$ is complete iff for every subset D of B there is an element $x \in B$ such that x is greatest lower bound for D, and there is an element $y \in B$ such that y is greatest lower bound for D.

Definition 29 (Atom of Algebra, Atomic Boolean Algebra)
For a Boolean algebra $<B, 0, 1, \wedge, \vee, not>$, an element $x \in B$ is an atom iff (1) $x \neq 0$, and (2) for all $y \in B$, if $y \leq x$ then either $y = 0$ or $y = x$. The algebra B is atomic iff for all nonzero elements x in B there is an atom $y \in B$ such that $y \leq x$.

Definition 30 (Individual of Complete Atomic Boolean Algebra)
If x is an atom of $\mathcal{P}$ then $I_x = \{p \in \mathcal{P}, x \subset p\}$ is an individual. If a property

$p \in I$, and $p \leq q$, then the property $q \in I$; a property $p \in I$ iff its complement (not p) $\notin I$.

Definition 31 (Restricting Function on a Boolean Algebra)
A function f is a restricting function on a Boolean algebra $<B, 0, 1, \wedge, \vee,$ not> iff for any element $x \in B$ $f(x) \leq x$, where $\leq$ is the ordering relation on B induced by the operations of $\wedge$ and $\vee$.

Generalized Quantifiers

In this final subsection, definitions are supplied for generalized quantifier, external negation of a quantifier, internal negation of a quantifier, dual of quantifier, left monotonicity of quantifier, and right monotonicity of quantifier.

Definition 32 (Generalized Quantifier)
A generalized quantifier is the denotation of a noun phrase. For quantified noun phrases, NP = determiner N, it is a set of subsets of U, where U is a set of objects (universe of discourse), computed according to the semantics of determiner.

Definition 33 (External Negation of a Quantifier)
External negation of a quantifier Q, $\neg Q = \{X \subseteq U, X \nsubseteq Q\}$.

Definition 34 (Internal Negation of a Quantifier)
Internal negation of a quantifier Q, $Q\neg = \{X \subseteq U, (U - X) \subseteq Q \}$.

Definition 35 (Dual of Quantifier)
The dual of a quantifier Q, $Q_d = \{X \subseteq U, (U - X) \nsubseteq Q\}$.

Definition 36 (Left Monotonicity of Quantifier)
Let $S_1 = Det\ Noun_1\ VP$ and $S_2 = Det\ Noun_2\ VP$ be any sentences.
1. $Det\ Noun_1$ is left monotone increasing if $Noun_1 \subseteq Noun_2$ and S_1 entails S_2
2. $Det\ Noun_1$ is left monotone decreasing if $Noun_2 \subseteq Noun_1$ and S_1 entails S_2
3. Otherwise $Det\ Noun_1$ is left nonmonotone

Definition 37 (Right Monotonicity of Quantifier)
Let $S_1 = NP\ Verb_1$ and $S_2 = NP\ Verb_2$ be any sentences.
1. NP is right monotone increasing if $Verb_1 \subseteq Verb_2$ and S_1 entails S_2
2. NP is right monotone decreasing if $Verb_2 \subseteq Verb_1$ and S_1 entails S_2
3. Otherwise NP is right nonmonotone.

C Representational and Inferential Challenges of Natural Language: Examples and Data

Łucja M. Iwańska

THIS APPENDIX CONTAINS plausible, artificial as well as real-life data illustrating the complexities of the computational modeling of natural language. These data exemplify some of the greatest representational and inferential challenges of natural language. These challenges constitute the original motivation of the formal, computational models of natural language presented in this book.

The significance of the examples below, the details of the phenomena involved and computational approaches to handling them are discussed in the authors' individual chapters and their publications cited in the combined book bibliography.

We believe that these data will facilitate the readers' task of the cross-comparison of different computational models of natural language, revealing their respective strengths and weaknesses. Readers could also use these data to evaluate some other representations and natural language processing systems aiming to more fully and correctly reflect the meaning of natural language. These examples can also be used to assess the representational and inferential weaknesses of knowledge representation and reasoning systems not motivated by natural language.

The electronic version of this section, including the SGML-coded data below, can be downloaded from www.cs.wayne.edu/~lucja/book-nlkr.html and www.cse.buffalo.edu/~shapiro/KRNLBook/.

Boolean Semantics of Natural Language: Structure at All Syntactic Levels

Boolean structure: negations, conjunctions, disjunctions, adjectival modification and quantifiers at all syntactic levels, not just sentential;

All boys like but not love Mary.
Some boys like but not love Mary.
No boy hates Mary.
Not all boys hate Mary.
Not many dogs like cats.
Not very many dogs like cats.
Some but not many students smoke.
Not many students smoke.
Three indecisive women were killed.
Two indecisive women were killed.
Some men love Mary.
Some men don't hate Mary.
Some men neither love nor hate Mary.
Some men neither love nor hate Mary a lot.
Many sick dogs don't walk.
Many sick dogs don't walk very fast.
John speaks very slowly.
John sings or speaks.
Not all children like cookies.
Not all children love cookies.
All children loath Mary.
Some children hate Mary.
Many but not all children hate Mary a lot.
Some children hate Mary.
No woman hates Mary.
Not all women hate Mary a lot.
John dances.
John or Mary dances.
Every student works hard.
Every smart student works hard.

Ira dresses very well.
Ira or Marina dresses well.
Every student works hard.
Every smart student works.
Not many dogs like cats.
Not very many dogs love cats.
Mark is extremely unhappy.
Mark is unhappy.
Polish ballet dancers are excellent.
Polish ballet dancers are good.
Bob is very stupid.
Bob is not smart.
Tom is extremely modest.
Tom is very modest.
Tom is small but not very small.
Tom is small but not extremely small.
Tom is in Warsaw.
Tom is near Warsaw.
John and not Mary walks.
John sings or speaks.
John walks fast but speaks slowly.
John doesn't walk very fast.
Does John walk fast?
Does Mary walk fast?
Does John sing?
Does John sing or speak?
Does John walk very fast?
Every smart student works.
Every student works hard.
Does every smart student work hard?
Does every student work?
Does every student work hard?
Not very many dogs like cats.
Not many dogs like cats.
Not many dogs love cats.
Is it true that not many dogs

like cats?
Is it true that not many dogs love cats?
Every student works hard.
Every student works.
Every smart student works hard.
Every smart student works.
Every extremely smart student works.
Every not very happy student works.
Some very smart students don't work.
Some smart students don't work.
Some smart students don't work hard.
Some students don't work hard.
Some students don't work.
Some people work.
Some, but not many, people work.
Not many people work.
Not very many people work.
He is extremely happy.
He is very happy.
He is happy.
He is not very unhappy.
He is not very sad.
John doesn't walk.
John doesn't walk fast.
John doesn't walk very fast.
John doesn't walk his dog.
John doesn't walk late at night.
John or Mary doesn't walk.
John or Mary doesn't walk fast.
I like it.
I love it.
I don't hate it.
I don't hate it very much.

Figure 1. Data on Boolean Semantics of Natural Language
Source: Łucja M. Iwańska.

Semantics of general negation, conjunction, disjunction, quantifiers, adjectival modification and their convoluted interaction;

Universally shared, easily computable, fast inferences licensed by complex expressions computed in order to account for the literal meaning of natural language; Literal meaning is reflected by the knowledge gained from the utterance;

Question answering revealing inference and understanding literal meaning of natural language; Compactness of the natural languagelike representation- high information (knowledge) content of natural language utterances (messages).

Figure 1 displays examples; each utterance is a multi-sentence or multi-paragraph text or dialog.

Everything is an animal, a vegetable, or a mineral.	If a relation is symmetric, then whenever it holds between *A* and *B*, it also holds between *B* and A.
For every object, the following statements are equivalent: It is human; It is a featherless biped; It is a rational animal.	Bob believes anything Bill believes.
	George IV didn't know that Scott was the author of *Waverly*.
If someone votes for *X* and someone votes for *Y*, one of them will be disappointed.	If I have a quarter, I'll put it in the parking meter.
Mary, Sue, and Sally are sisters.	

Figure 2. Data on Inappropriateness of Classical Logics for Representing Boolean Connectives in Natural Language
Source: Stuart C. Shapiro.

Inappropriatness of Classical Logics for Representing Boolean Connectives in Natural Language

Boolean connectives in natural language are not represented well by classical logic. Examples are provided in figure 2.

Requirements for a Semantic Representation of Natural Language

There are various requirements for a semantic representation of natural language. The following list delineates these requirements. Example are given in figure 3.

1. Predicate modifiers such as "almost" and "very"; adjective phrases in attributive position, such as "very nice"
2. Eventualities described by quantified sentences, and anaphoric reference to such eventualities
3. Causal connections between episodes (eventualities, events, situations, etc.) described by separate sentences
4. Belief, telling, and other attitudes
5. Anaphoric reference to actions (as opposed to events—note that the second sentence cannot properly be "It was a very wicked event"):
6. Kinds of actions
7. Kinds of episodes (events): specific versus generic
8. Action-modifying and event-modifying verb phrase adverbials — in the surface semantics, as predicate modifiers, but after "deindexing" they come out as predications about actions or about events.
9. Complex tenses and modifiers
10. Question answering
11. Probabilistic conditionals (generic sentences that intuitively supply some lower bound on the frequency of a certain kind of eventuality, under stated or implied circumstances)
12. Explanatory axioms (a certain kind of general conditional statement, often expressible as a generic conditional)
13. Sentences whose understanding requires inferring likely consequences (e.g., about damage, injuries, hostilities, ...)

The wolf almost killed two very nice people

Little Red Riding Hood chased every butterfly that she saw. It made her tired. That made her tired.

Little Red Riding Hood chased a butterfly, and (as a result) lost her way.

Mother told Little Red Riding Hood that Grandmother was ill.

The wolf gobbled up Grandmother. It was a very wicked deed. That was a very wicked deed.

Little Red Riding Hood likes to visit Grandmother. Little Red Riding Hood like animals, What Little Red Riding Hood likes best is visiting Grandmother. Little Red Riding Hood likes playing and visiting Grandmother.

For Little Red Riding Hood to talk to a stranger is not unusual. Gray wolves are not unusual.

The wolf politely greeted Little Red Riding Hood in the forest.

In the forest, she met a wolf who had not eaten for three days.

Who met whom? Was the wolf ever enraged?

If a predatory animal finds a nonpredatory creature of modest size, he may attack it. Creatures are very hungry when they have not eaten for more than a day. If an aircraft that is less than 3 years old has a crack, usually the crack is not due to corrosion.

A predatory animal attacks a nearby creature only when it is hungry or enraged. If a predatory animal springs upon a nonpredatory creature, that probably is part of an attack intended to subdue the creature, allowing it to be killed and eaten.

An explosives-laden car blew up near the office of an Afghan guerrilla group in a crowded Shiite Moslem neighborhood in Beirut.

In the forest, Little Red Riding Hood met a wolf. The wolf would have very much liked to eat her, but he dared not do so on account of some woodcutters nearby. The wolf drew out the peg and the door flew open. Then he sprang upon the poor old lady and ate her up in less than no time, for he had been more than three days without food.

Company ABC has been manufacturing product X for three months.

Every company in region XYZ laid off some workers in May 1990, causing the level of unemployment in XYZ to rise by 3%.

Company ABC sold no supercomputers in May 1990, causing a drop in the value of its shares.

Company XYZ is likely to fold next month (July 1990). If company ABC has no sales this month (June 1990), it will probably fold next month.

When a company releases a new product, it usually advertises it. Computer programs with more than 2000 lines of code almost always contain bugs.

Most/many/few of the subsidiaries of ABC_CORP are located in California.

A dodo is a kind of flightless bird. This kind of bird was sometimes sighted in Mauritius, but is now extinct. Some makes of automobiles with rotary engines are popular. The cloth on this sofa is no longer being manufactured.

Smith, Green, and 18 other individuals pooled their assets and formed a company. The "nuclear club" (the set of nations possessing nuclear weapons) has at least 6 and at most 10 members. The known members are the USA, the USSR, France, (etc.) The actual number of people carrying the HIV virus is at least twice the number of known carriers.

Concealing profits is illegal. To conceal profits is illegal. For a company to conceal profits is illegal.

User interface X degrades gracefully on mildly faulty inputs. The interlingua is a highly expressive knowledge representation. A new highway runs through the ABC mountains, alongside a much older railroad track.

Company ABC suspects that a competitor obtained a copy of its (ABC's) unreleased product X. Company ABC intends to force company XYZ to sell its assets. If company ABC had not sold its subsidiary XYZ, it would have gone bankrupt.

Company ABC is seeking new customers. Company ABC is designing a new supercomputer. The new memory chip X resembles a 128-level Mayan pyramid.

Figure 3. Data on a Semantic Representation of Natural Language
Source: Lenhart K. Schubert.

14. Narrative sentences whose understanding requires inferring explanations and causal connections
15. Uncertainty
17. Generalized quantifiers
19. Sets
21. Modifiers
23. Other intensionality

16. Unreliable generalizations
18. Kinds
20. Nominalization
22. Modals

never	He named ambassador to New Zealand Takeo Iguchi to serve concurrently as ambassador to western Samoa.	sation.	It did not take a long time
rarely		He fell asleep not very long after the meeting.	It took him one week.
sometimes		The arrest immediately followed his confession.	It took him two days.
often			second
always	The announcement of the pact coincided with the release by Volkswagen of its second-quarter earnings report.	Five or six days before the trial, he confessed.	minute
very often		He gave me these papers shortly before or after the meeting.	day
not very often			week
not always			year
sometimes, but not always		after the meeting.	century
very often, but not always	His talk starts the conference.	It didn't happen immediately after the exam.	instant
before	The conference starts with his talk.	John came home not much earlier than Mark.	while
after			eon
precedes	His talk ends the conference.	The announcement was made earlier this month.	eternity
follows	The conference ends with his talk.		one year, three weeks, and five hours
later		Two years later, she was married.	
earlier	Operations came to a halt during the Cultural Revolution.	Dancing followed shortly.	Instant— a point or very short space of time.
prior			
between	Dancing was after singing.	It didn't happen during the party.	
overlap	After singing they danced.		It happened in the morning.
some overlap		not in the immediate future	
no overlap	Singing was before dancing.	It did not happen April 22, 1992	It did not happen in the evening.
coincide	Before dancing, they sang.	X and Y happened at the same time	It happened during the day.
when	Dancing followed singing.	The time of these events overlaps.	X happened early in the morning.
begin			
end	First it was singing; then dancing followed.	X happened, but not long before Y.	Very early summer the beginning of the second quarter
during	Singing preceded dancing.	X happened many years after Y.	Late May
coincide	Singing was prior to dancing.	X happened before, but not long before, Y.	6.05.95
concurrent	First it was singing; dancing was later.	a very good time	April 22, 1992, 1:09
simultaneous	Now they dance; singing was earlier.	not a bad time	April 22, 1992, 1309
since	He was born sometimes between the First and Second World Wars.	a terrible time	April, 1992
until		not a very good time	X took place sometimes in April
five or six days before	Five months or so after the treatment, he was fully recovered.	It took an extremely long time	X did not happen in early May
long before	It happened a few minutes after their conver-	It took a very short time	X happened in April, 1992
not long before		It did not take a long time	X happened in May, but not early May, 1992
not immediately after		It took a very short time	It is very likely that X happened shortly before or after Y
shortly before or after			
immediately precedes			
does not immediately follow			
The meetings took place at the same time.			
These simultaneous events surprised many.			
The same basic machines will be sold simultaneously in the United States, Europe and Japan.			

Figure 4. Data on Real Life Explicit Temporal Expressions.
Source: Łucja M. Iwańska.

Explicit Temporal Expressions of Natural Language

The following are sample artificial and real-life explicit temporal expressions of natural language that constitute references to various time entities (data on real life explicit temporal expressions are provided in figure 4):

on Monday	time of innocence	past couple of years	23 hours 50 minutes
January 12, 1993	that sunny day	on 6 january at 1625	10 seconds
early winter		hours	23 hrs 50 mins 10 secs
Monday morning	new day		1300 GMT today
between early March	same time	a century	
and late June	different week	five years	on 23-rd monday
in August	different times	very many weeks	1990
in recent years	former	several months	21/7/93
		approximately two	21 July, 1993
shortly before mid-	moment	months	7.21.93
night	century	almost entire year	July 21, 1993
after yesterday's	four or five seconds		5:30 pm, Monday, Ju-
breakfast	very many days	Thursday, May 19,	ly 21-st, 1992
on the sixth day of	three weeks or so	1994	
March	all these years		five minutes before
while we were in Rus-	this coming week	5 O'clock	midnight
sia	not a very long time	10:35:55	long before the end of
last ten years		at approximately	the month
	early winter	5:30pm	three weeks or so after
sometimes today	very late morning		Christmas
yesterday morning	early this month	in an instant	in the early 2000 BC
no more than five days	the end of summer	in a flash	between the end of the
from now		just one moment	semester and Christ-
	spring of 1993	twinkle	mas
once per week	summer 94	a little while	at sometime between
many times	Monday, 5 pm		1991 and 1993
sometimes, but no		about 2 months	from one to four pm
more often than every	on tuesday	two days or so	Monday through Fri-
other week	in two months		day
	over the past 25 years	once at 2:30	throughout October
very rapid	at the beginning of the	10:30:35 AM	throughout the season
almost immediately	19th century	2:30 Am	after yesterday's
	in the early 19 century	at 12:30 hours	breakfast
extremely happy time	at present	at 11:00 hrs	

*Figure 5. Temporal Expression Samples Extracted by
the UNO Natural Language Processing System*
Source: Łucja M. Iwańska.

1. Temporal quantifiers

2. Basic and complex temporal relations: Boolean and adjectival structure at all syntactic levels allows one to refer to an infinite number of temporal relations

3. Temporal expressions referring to absolute time, duration;

4. Time-related uncertainties: (a) explicit natural language expressions of uncertainty, (b) disjunction, (c) quantifiers, (d) underspecificity.

A sample of real-life explicit temporal expressions of natural language extracted automatically by the UNO natural language processing system from large corpora of newspaper articles (*Time Magazine, Newsweek, Wall Street Journal,* various dailies). The system automatically generates their UNO representation, which allows it to compute answers to the simulated time-related queries. These examples are shown in figure 5.

shortly before
while

following winter
the first day of the second week of June
1993
the last five days
half decade of the century

as long as needed
as long as the curfew lasts

today morning
yesterday late evening
five days after tomorrow
a month before then

long ago
three months later
a century ago
a year earlier

that sunny day

much earlier

about 2 months ago
today morning

sometimes, but not always
very often
every other day
five times per week
daily at 2:30 am

50-th anniversary

around the clock
at no time
for the time being
in the blink of an eye
in the course of time
in the near future
may day
now and then
nowadays
olden times
right away
sooner or later
up to date
from time to time
sooner and earlier
long way to go before

point of time
duration

half an hour

quite some time
closing months of

1994
a brief moment
not too long
at holidays or birthdays

for a while
as recently as a year ago
every other year
8:30-5 p.m. weekdays
after six months of
two months later
in January 1991
10 years ago
on Friday
today at 9 p.m.
at 9 tonight
for a long time
then one day
at night
three years later in 1981
in the spring of 1992
not too long ago
five days a week
one day a few months ago
in a few minutes
in the last two years
10 years later
by now
before the dawn of Aug. 20
from noon to 5 p.m.
at holidays or birthdays
until about 1984
during the 1992
since fall of 1991
since the early 1960s

last year
next year
last Christmas
two days ago
next week
in a day or so
a year earlier
a day ago
a year ago
a year later
a day later
two days ago
five days later
six months earlier
last April
next April
last January
sooner or later
most recently
in 1994
in the late 1100's
in the early 1500's

last Ground Hog Day
next Fourth of July
seconds ago
minutes ago
years ago
20 days later
five days later
the 1980's
eleven days ago

on Oct. 2
in the 1980s
this past winter
in late June
from 6:30pm to 8:30pm
Monday through Friday
this month
on the day of the concert
during the last 10 years
last May
late this year
early 1980s
in the summer of 1963
since 1993
from Dec. 1
next five years
between Nov. 1,1994 and April 1, 1995
as soon as possible
during bad weather
after 11 o'clock
in the moring
until next spring
twice a week
very recently

for the time being
18 weeks
good old days
at the beginning
every Friday afternoon
long before

one year later
3-year-old
year one
two years old
one night
previous night's
for about two seconds
for two hours
couple of weeks
ahead
last year
last week
at the weekend
since 1938
this week
in 1876
before and since

this year
from time to time
during the 1992 campaign
in June
for the 50th anniversary
for months
late last year
early this month
former
a recent
in 1975
in '79
in early 1982
more than an hour
the next day
at 80
to 94
in 1923
ever since
at the age of 79
for years
tomorrow
as long as
every day
80-year-old
last month
a day
in time
last week's
biggest Night
a week before
someday
someday soon
35 years
8 A.M. Saturday
less than 48 hours
since
later in the day
in 20 years
this minute
some time
in 10 days
over a period of about two weeks
the sooner
5-year-old
over the past five years
every day
long time
for the weekend
that night
43, so young
future
Feb 28
young years
childhood
6 years old
at night
during the second world war
overnight

Figure 5 (Continued)

13-year-old	season	the last days of	for 21/2 years
everyday	over last week	in the past	last August
years ago	in late 1992	in 1996	within a month
4-week-old	two weeks ago	for long	in November
at any time	in 1987	overnight	Saturday-night
in last week's	on the afternoon	forever	the next day
the recent	after his mother died	twice last week	after years
for years	in the late 1970's	after weeks	one day
in the afternoon	so far	about 30 seconds	soon after
today - 2	that same day	over the age of 15	weekday evenings
by the end of the year	a third	the past few weeks	from 5 to 7
the nightly	first	ten years ago	in the summer of 1990
today's	his first	in 1991 and 1992	a month after
day-to-day	a nine-term	since 1987	for 10 years
in recent years	eight months	last week's rally	72 hours after
in today's world	over the years	three years ago	at 7:02 p.m.
for 12 years	at the age of 23	this spring	on Feb. 8 1991
24 hours a day	meanwhile	in the past few years	before it began
in 1970	in November	a long time off	72-hour
from Monday	two weeks ago	by the end of the year	after 40 hours
today - 2	to November	for the first time	soon after
stretch of days	since its inception in	last April	early
76-year-old	1981	last Christmas	nineteen days after
two days	past	next December	two days after
by the weekend	future	two years ago	3 1/2 weeks old
16 years ago	long-term	how much longer	later that month
several years ago	on the day	in 1988	so long
by the end of the week	a tense half day	about 18 months	last July
the 1994 midterm	three days of	on a stormy evening	for 29 months
last Thursday	within three months	34-year-old	for nine days
the 1987 crash	in the last two years	at 3 p.m.	last summer
three days after	on the eve of	every two hours	two days after
last Friday	for six months	at 1 p.m.	for a two-hour
on Wednesday	five times	since 3 a.m.	someday
at the time of	in the last six months	at 2:30	next August
after March 1992	at a time when	on a tuesday	older
after June 1	five years ago	on a Thursday	two years of
next week's	a year later	later	one Friday
in March 1992	last November	55-mile-an-hour	nearly every day
by the summer of	this time	monthly	all night
1992	earlier this month	for 1989	most recently
in early October 1992	10 years ago	58-year-old	at a time when
in March 1993	8-year-old	in 1935	for the past two
several months	in 1967	yesteryear's	decades
a generation ago	by March 15	in 1925	a 1989 case
as soon as	in February	for 1920s murderers	a few months later
for three years	more recently	in the 1960s	in the 1980s
as expeditiously as	for another two years	late nights	each year
today's	more	lost weekends	in June 1992
since Vince's death	meantime	during the first 10	from 1982
sooner and earlier	in 1389	months of 1993	at least two years
every three months	500 years of	from 1991	nearly 10 years
in September 1993	these days	last March	forty years ago
nearly three quarters	before the massacre	part of the year	in the 1990s
long way to go before	in later february	during 1993	1 1/2 hours
short term	for now	by 1992	15 seconds
for too long	by two years	once a year	one night last month
last spring	before the war	four-year	for months
in January	recently	50th anniversary	a decade from now
recent	15-month	last fall	one day
in December	next month	2 o'clock in the after-	15 years ago
for weeks	as night fell	noon	couple of weeks ago
younger	last October	3-year-old	in November
this year's legislative	by the weekend	eight months ago	ever since

Figure 5 (Continued)

two weeks	an 18-month study	by the time	the future
later this year	over five years	seven to eight years	
23-year-old	last fall	seventh year	
since 1990	someday	early	
an hour	this year	on Saturday	
after four to eight	last month	on the same day	
weeks	a few years ago	in last year's	
each year	a second	last weekend	
more than twice	past 100	months in advance	
more than a decade	in 1985	460-year history	
ago	the very week	from 1200 B.C.	
by 1992	for 30 years	last Summer	
several months	moments later	since the early decades	
last August	seven-minute miles	of this century	
in January	in the summer of 1984	in recent months	
this month	for years	in recent years	
24-hour time	the night he died	meanwhile	
after March 24	25-year old	on Sundays	
the last time	long in advance	in 1534	
five days before	the past decade	about time	
these days	at 40	until recently	
last years	this week	all the time	
77th birthday	seven consecutive	in the preceding year	
for half a century	weeks	at some time between	
tomorrow	after a mid-February	1991 and 1993	
three minutes	week	since 1991	
42 minutes	22 hours before	at 1:30 p.m. on a	
after years	momentarily	school day	
at the same time	beginning this week	after three years	
70 years ago	on April 2 to 4	three days after	
this year	on jan. 29	a 1992 poll	
in February	different weeks	in 2005	

Figure 5 (Continued)

Explicit Expressions of Natural Language: Uncertainty, Intensionality, Proposition and Type Qualifiers

Figure 6 provides samples of real life explicit natural language expressions of uncertainty, intensionality, proposition and type qualifiers extracted from large corpora of newspaper articles (*Time Magazine, Newsweek, Wall Street Journal,* various dailies).

We are finalizing the design and implementation of the in-depth and weak methods that would allow the UNO natural language processing system to automatically extract all such expressions from large corpora, and automatically generate their UNO representation, which would allow it to compute answers to the simulated uncertainty-related queries.

a debate over	assert	considered	evidence	incredible
a feeling	assert that	contend	exclaimed	indefinitely
a justification for	assertion	contended	exclaims	indicate
a prediction	asserts	contradicted	expect	indicated
a snowball's	assess	convicted of	expectation	inevitably
chance in hell	assume	correct	expected	insist
absolutely	assure	could	expecting	insist that
accepts	assured	could anticipate	explainable	intended
acclaim	at least thought	could claim	explained	interpreted
accused	attempt	could have been	explained apolo-	it is clear that
accused of	aware	true	getically	it is hard to trace
acknowledges	bad bet	could hope	fact	it is hardly sur-
acquittal	become aware	could make sure	false	prising
acquittal of	belief	could not know	fantasy	it is likely
acquitted of	believe	could not seem	feared	it is not explicitly
charges of	believed to be	could possibly	feel	acknowledged
actual	best bet	could scarcely	felt	it is unimaginable
actually	best information	declared	firmly believes	it remains to be
adds	best known	declaring	for sure	seen
adjudged to be in-	best possible	deduces	found	it was hard to
nocent	best-known	definitely	found that	imagine
admit	blames	delivered that	gloomy prediction	it's clear
admits that	call	opinion	got no reason to	it's hard to imag-
admitted	called	depict	think	ine
agree	can	described	great hope	it's possible
agreed with	can and will	did not contest	guess	kind of
aimed	can believe	did not expect	hard information	knew
all but certain	can foresee	did not know	hardly likely	knew in advance
all but impossible	can seem	disbelief	has claimed	of
all doubt	can you believe it	disclaimer	have no idea what	know
alleged	can't	discovered	heard	know
allegedly	can't believe	dislike	heavy implications	know that
almost certainly	cannot	do not know	high hopes	knowing
almost impossible	cannot predict	do not seem to be	highest possible	knowingly
almost inconceiv-	cast doubt	do think	highly speculative	knowledge
able	certain	doable	hint	knowledgeable
almost inevitably	certainly	does not know	hinting	known
almost, though	certainly know	does not seem	hints	learned
not quite, impossi-	certainly not	doesn't know	hope	learned that
ble	certainty	don't believe	hope for	least likely
already know	chances of	don't believe	hope of	less clarity
ambivalent feel-	charge that	don't expect	hope to	less likely
ings	cited	don't hold people	ideas	lies
announced	claim	responsible	ideas to be ex-	likely
anticipate	claimed dubiously	don't know	plored	likely to be
anticipated	claimed that	don't think that	imaginable	little doubt
anticipation	claiming	doubt	imaginary	little hope
apparent	claims	doubtless	imagined	little known
apparently	clear	dubious	imperfect	little-known
appear	cleared	earliest known	implausible	little wonder
appear to be	clearly	entirely unexpect-	implicate	made their case
appeared likely	complaining, cor-	ed	implies	makes clear that
approved	rectly, that	especially true	impossible	may appear
are considered	conceivable	essentially	impression	may be
arguably	concluded	estimate	improbable	may be found
argue that	concluded that	estimated	improbably	may be possible
argues that	confesses	even argued that	in an attempt to	may be true
arguing that	confidential	even assuming	in their view	may feel
as confident	confirmed that	that	incomplete	may have known
as far as possible	confirms	ever more likely	inconceivable	may hold
as likely as	consider	every possible	inconclusive	may indeed be

Figure 6. Data on Explicit Expressions of Natural Language:
Uncertainty, Intensionality, Proposition, and Type Qualifiers
Source: Łucja M. Iwańska.

may instead be	planned	saying that	the challenge of	unmistakably
may not	plausible	says	proving	unpredictability
may not know	plausibly	second-guessing	the facts	unpredictable
may prove to be	politically correct	see	the information	unthinkable
may provide	possibilities	seem	the intention	untrue
may relieve	possibility	seem to be	the point of view	vagueness
may seem	possible	seem to have	of	verdict
may want	possibly	seemed almost as	the possibility	very clear
maybe	possibly	if	the possibility that	very uncertain
meant to suggest	potential	seemed certain	the presumption	view
mention	potentially	seemed to expect	the ultimate ar-	virtually impossi-
might	predict	seeming	biter	ble
might expect	predictable	seemingly	the wrongfulness	warned
might suggest	predictably	seems	of	warned that
might ultimately	predicting	seems likely	there are two sides	well knew
be	predictions	seems unlikely	to a story	well-known
misunderstanding	present that evi-	shaky	there is no reason	wildly unpre-
more likely	dence	show that	to believe that	dictable
most likely	presumably	shows	there is no reason	will
must surely	presumed guilty	so sure	to suppose	will think
nearly impossible	pretend	so-called	there's absolutely	willing to concede
needless to say	prevented	sought to convince	no question	with their full
never in doubt	probability	speaks from some	think	knowledge
never know	probable	experience	thinks	without question
never quite sure	probably	speculated	thought to be	wondering
never really ex-	probably not	speculation	threatened	worried that
pected	proclaiming	state	to be sure	would
never thought	promise to	statement	to be sure	would be sure
no doubt	pronounce	still believe	to blame	would have been
no doubt	properly known	still likely	to emphasize that	unthinkable
no evidence	proposition	still possible	to the best of my	would have to as-
no hope	prove	stressing	knowledge	sume
no reason	proved	strong feelings	tried to prove	would imply that
no wonder	proved them right	strongly believe	true	would not
not believe	provisionally	strongly feel	true that	would not neces-
not clear	quite clear	strongly oppose	truer	sarily
not entirely accu-	quite likely	such tales	truly believe	would probably
rate	quite so	such unlikely	truly understood	would say
not justified	raise much suspi-	suggest	trust	would seem
not know	cion	suggested	truth	would suddenly
not likely	rarely possible	support	truths	appear
not likely	real	suppose	twice as likely	would suggest
not possible	real suspicion	supposed	unbelievable	would think
not sure	realized	supposedly	uncertain	would-be
not true	really	sure	uncertainties	wouldn't
obscure	reasonable	surely	uncertainty	writes
obscured	recalled	suspect	uncertainty	wrong
obviously	referred	suspected	unclear	
occurred	refused to admit	suspicious	understand	
of course	reliable	taking a chance	understand	
on the verge of a	reported to be	tend to	understanding	
crisis of credibility	reportedly	tentative	undoubtedly	
one thing is cer-	rethinking	tentatively	unexpected	
tain	revealed	testified	unimaginable	
one thing is sure	right	testifying that	unknowability	
ought to know	said	testimony that	unknown	
perhaps	say	that's ridiculous	unlikely	

Figure 6 (Continued)

Bibliography

Abeille, A. 1988. A French Tree Adjoining Grammar. Technical Report, Department of Computer and Information Science, University of Pennsylvania.

Ackerman, M.; Billsus, D.; Gaffney, S.; Hettich, S.; Khoo, G.; Kim, D. J.; Klefstad, R.; Lowe, C.; Ludeman, A.; Muramatsu, J.; Omori, K.; Pazzani, M. J.; Semler, D.; Starr, B.; and Yapp, P. 1997. Learning Probabilistic User Profiles. *AI Magazine* 18(2): 47–66.

Adjukiewicz, K. 1935. Die Syntaktische Konnexitat (Syntactic Connection). Translated in 1976. McCall, S., ed. *Polish Logic: 1920–1939.* Oxford, U.K.: Oxford University Press.

Aït-Kaci, H. 1986. An Algebraic Semantics Approach to the Effective Resolution of Type Equations. *Journal of Theoretical Computer Science* 45:193–251.

Aït-Kaci, H.; Meyer, R.; and Van Roy, P. H. 1993. WILD LIFE: A User Manual (Preliminary Report). Preliminary Research Report, Paris Research Laboratory, Digital Equipment Corporation.

Alchourrón, C. E.; Gärdenfors, P.; and Makinson, D. 1985. On the Logic of Theory Change: Partial Meet Contraction and Revision Functions. *The Journal of Symbolic Logic* 50(2): 510–530.

Ali, S. S. 1994a. A Logical Language for Natural Language Processing. Paper presented at the Tenth Biennial Canadian Artificial Intelligence Conference, Banff, Alberta, Canada, 16–20 May..

Ali, S. S. 1994b. A "Natural Logic" for Natural Language Processing and Knowledge Representation. Ph.D. thesis, Technical Report, 94-01, Department of Computer Science, State University of New York at Buffalo.

Ali, S. S. 1993. A Structured Representation for Noun Phrases and Anaphora. In *Proceedings of the Fifteenth Annual Conference of the Cognitive Science Society,* 197–202. Hillsdale, N.J.: Lawrence Erlbaum.

Ali, S. S., and Shapiro, S. C. 1993. Natural Language Processing Using a Propositional Semantic Network with Structured Variables. *Minds and Machines* 3(4): 421–451.

Allen, J. F. 1984. Toward a General Theory of Action and Time. *Artificial Intelligence* 23(2):123–155.

Allen, J. F. 1983. Maintaining Knowledge about Temporal Intervals. *Communications of the ACM* 26(11): 832–843.

Allen, J. F., and Schubert, L. K. 1993. Language and Discourse in the TRAINS Project. In *Communication from an Artificial Intelligence Perspective,* eds. A. Ortony, J. Slack, and O. Stock, 91–120. Heidelberg, Germany: Theoretical Springer-Verlag.

Almeida, M. J. 1995. Time in Narratives. In *Deixis in Narrative: A Cognitive Science Perspective,* eds. J. F. Duchan, G. A. Bruder, and L. E. Hewitt, 159–189. Hillsdale, N.J.: Lawrence Erlbaum.

Alshawi, H., and Van Eijck, J. 1989. Logical Forms in the CORE Language Engine. In Proceedings of the Twenty-Seventh Annual Meeting of the Association for Computational Linguistics (ACL-89), 25–32. New Brunswick, N.J.: Association for Computational Linguistics.

Amit Bagga, J. Y. C., and Biermann, A. W. 1997. The Role of WORDNET in the Creation of a Trainable Message Understanding System. In Proceedings of the Fourteenth National Conference on Artificial Intelligence (AAAI-97), 941–948. Menlo Park, Calif.: American Association for Artificial Intelligence.

Anderson, J. 1971. *The Grammar of Case: Toward a Localist Theory.* Cambridge, U.K.: Cambridge Univesity Press.

Anderson, A. R., and Belnap, Jr., N. D. 1975. *Entailment, Volume 1.* Princeton, N.J.: Princeton University Press.

Anderson, A. R.; Belnap, Jr., N. D.; and Dunn, M. 1992. *Entailment, Volume 2.* Princeton, N.J.: Princeton University Press.

Appelt, D.; Hobbs, J. R.; Israel, D.; and Tyson, M. 1993. FASTUS: A Finite-State Processor for Information Extraction from Real-World Text. In Proceedings of the Thirteenth International Joint Conference on Artificial Intelligence (IJCAI-93), 277–285. Menlo Park, Calif.: International Joint Conferences on Artificial Intelligence.

Appelt, D.; Hobbs, J.; Bear, J.; Israel, D.; Kameyama, M.; Keller, A.; Martin, D.; Myers, K.; and Tyson, M. 1995. SRI International FASTUS System MUC-6 Test Results and Analysis. In *Proceedings of the Sixth Message-Understanding Conference,* 237–248, ed. B. Sundheim. San Francisco, Calif.: Morgan Kaufmann.

Asher, N., and Morreau, M. 1991. Commonsense Entailment: A Modal Theory of Nonmonotonic Reasoning. In Proceedings of the Twelfth International Joint Conference on Artificial Intelligence (IJCAI-91), 387–392. Menlo Park, Calif.: International Joint Conferences on Artificial Intelligence.

Bacchus, F.; Grove, A. J.; Halpern, J. Y.; and Koller, D. 1996. From Statistical Knowledge Bases to Degrees of Belief. *Artificial Intelligence* 87(1–2):75–143.

Bach, E. 1988. Categorical Grammars as Theories of Language. In *Categorical Grammars and Natural Language Structures,* eds. R. Oehrle, E. Bach, and D. Wheeler, 17–34. Studies in Linguistics and Philosophy 32. Dordrecht, The Netherlands: D. Reidel.

Ballim, A., and Wilks, Y. 1991. *Artificial Believers: The Ascription of Belief.* Hillsdale, N.J.: Lawrence Erlbaum.

Barnett, J.; Mani, I.; Martin, P.; and Rich, E. 1994. Reversible Machine Translation: What to Do When the Languages Don't Match Up. In *Reversible Grammar in Natural Language Processing,* ed. T. Strzalkowski. Norwell, Mass.: Kluwer Academic.

Barwise, J. 1989. *The Situation in Logic.* Stanford, Calif.: Center for the Study of Language and Information.

Barwise, J., and Cooper, R. 1981. Generalized Quantifiers and Natural Language. *Linguistics and Philosophy* 4:159–219.

Barwise, J., and Perry, J. 1983. *Situations and Attitudes.* Cambridge, Mass.: MIT Press.

Beaven, J. 1992. Shake and Bake Machine Translation. Paper Presented at the Fourteenth International Conference on Computational Linguistics, Nantes, France, July 20–28, 603–609.

Beek, P. V. 1988. Reasoning about Qualitative Temporal Information. *Artificial Intelligence* 36:375–387.

Berwick, R. C. 1983. Learning Word Meanings from Examples. In Proceedings of the Eighth International Joint Conference on Artificial Intelligence (IJCAI-83), 459–461. Menlo Park, Calif.: International Joint Conferences on Artificial Intelligence.

Bobrow, D., and Winograd, T. 1977. An Overview of KRL, A Knowledge Representation Language. *Cognitive Science* 1(1): 3–46.

Brachman, R. J. 1983. What Is-A Is and Isn't: An Analysis of Taxonomic Links in Semantic Networks. *IEEE Computer* 16(10): 30–36.

Brachman, R. J. 1979. On the Epistemological Status of Semantic Networks. In *Associative Networks: The Representation and Use of Knowledge by Computers,* ed. N. V. Findler, 3–50. San Diego, Calif.: Academic.

Brachman, R. J., and Levesque, H. J., eds. 1985. *Readings in Knowledge Representation.* San Francisco, Calif.: Morgan Kaufmann.

Brachman, R. J., and Schmolze, J. G. 1985. An Overview of KL-ONE Knowledge Representation System. *Cognitive Science* 9(2): 171–216.

Brachman, R. J.; Fikes, R. E.; and Levesque, H. J. 1985. KRYPTON: A Functional Approach to Knowledge Representation. In *Readings in Knowledge Representation,* 411–430. San Francisco, Calif.: Morgan Kaufmann.

Brachman, R. J.; Fikes, R. E.; and Levesque, H. J. 1983. KRYPTON: A Functional Approach to Knowledge Representation. *IEEE Computer* 16(10): 63–73.

Brachman, R. J.; McGuinness, D.; Patel-Schneider, P.; Resnick, L.; and Borgida, A. 1991. Living with CLASSIC: When and How to Use a KL-ONE–Like Language. In *Principles of Semantic Networks: Explorations in the Representation of Knowledge,* ed. J. Sowa, 401–456. San Francisco, Calif.: Morgan Kaufmann.

Briscoe, T. J.; Copestake, A.; and Lascarides, A. 1995. Blocking. In *Computational Lexical Semantics,* eds. P. Saint-Dizier and E. Viegas, 15–67. Cambridge, U.K.: Cambridge University Press.

Bunt, H., and Tomita, M., eds. 1996. *Recent Advances in Parsing Technology.* Dordrecht, The Netherlands: Kluwer Academic.

Buvač, S. 1996. Quantificational Logic of Context. In Proceedings of the Thirteenth National Conference on Artificial Intelligence (AAAI-96), 600–606. Menlo Park, Calif.: American Association for Artificial Intelligence.

Buvač, S.; Buvač, V.; and Mason, I. A. 1995. Metamathematics of Contexts. *Fundimenta Informaticae* 23(3): 263–304.

Campbell, A. E. 1996. Resolution of the Dialect Problem in Communication through Ontological Mediation. Paper presented at the AAAI-96 Workshop on Detecting, Preventing, and Repairing Human-Machine Miscommunication, 4 August. Available at www.cs.uwm.edu/~mcroy/mnm.html.

Carlson, G. N. 1982. Generic Terms and Generic Sentences. *Journal of Philosophical Logic* 11(2): 145–181.

Carlson, G. N., and Pelletier, F. J. 1995. *The Generic Book.* Chicago: University of Chicago Press.

Carlson, G. N., and Spejewski, B. 1997. Generic Passages. *Natural Language Semantics* 5(1): 1–65.

Carpenter, B. 1992. *The Logic of Typed Feature Structures.* Cambridge Tracts in Theoretical Computer Science 32. Cambridge, U.K.: Cambridge University Press.

Chalupsky, J. 1996. SIMBA: Belief Ascription by Way of Simulative Reasoning. Ph.D. dissertation, Technical Report, 96–18, Department of Computer Science and Engineering, University of Buffalo at New York.

Chalupsky, H., and Shapiro, S. C. 1996. Reasoning about Incomplete Agents. Paper presented at the Fifth International Conference on User Modeling, 2–5 January, Kailua-Kona, Hawaii.

Chalupsky, H., and Shapiro, S. C. 1994. SL: A Subjective, Intensional Logic of Belief. In *Proceedings of the Sixteenth Annual Conference of the Cognitive Science Society*. Hillsdale, N.J.: Lawrence Erlbaum.

Charniak, E. 1988. Motivation Analysis, Abductive Unification, and Nonmonotonic Equality. *Artificial Intelligence* 34(3):275–295.

Charniak, E., and Goldman, R. 1988. A Logic for Semantic Interpretation. In Proceedings of the Twenty-Sixth Annual Meeting of the ACL, 87–94. New Brunswick, N.J.: Association of Computational Linguistics.

Chierchia, G. 1995. *Dynamics of Meaning*. Chicago: University of Chicago Press.

Chierchia, G. 1993. Questions with Quantifiers. *Natural Language Semantics* 1(2): 181–234.

Chierchia, G. 1985. Formal Semantics and the Grammar of Predication. *Linguistic Inquiry* 16(3): 417–443.

Chierchia, G., and Turner, R. 1988. Semantics and Property Theory. *Linguistics and Philosophy* 11:261–302.

Chun, S. A. 1987. SNEPS Implementation of Possessive Phrases. SNERG Technical Note, 19, Department of Computer Science and Engineering, University of Buffalo at New York.

Clark, K. L. 1978. Negation as Failure. In *Logic and Data Bases,* eds. H. Gallaire and J. Minker. New York: Plenum.

Cohen, A. 1997. Default Reasoning and Generics. *Computational Intelligence* 13(4): 506–533.

Cravo, M. R., and Martins, J. P. 1993. SNEPSWD: A Newcomer to the SNEPS Family. *Journal of Experimental and Theoretical Artificial Intelligence* 5:135–148.

Creary, L. G. 1979. Propositional Attitudes: Fregean Representation and Simulative Reasoning. In Proceedings of the Sixth International Joint Conference on Artificial Intelligence, 176–181. Menlo Park, Calif.: International Joint Conferences on Artificial Intelligence.

Cullingford, R. 1981. SAM. In *Inside Computer Understanding,* eds. R. C. Schank and C. K. Riesbeck, 75–119. Hillsdale, N.J.: Lawrence Erlbaum.

Dahlgren, K.; McDowell, J.; and Stabler, Jr., E. P. 1989. Knowledge Representation for Commonsense Reasoning with Text. *Computational Linguistics* 15(3): 149–170.

Dale, R., and Reiter, E. 1996. The Role of the Gricean Maxims in the Generation of Referring Expressions. Paper presented at the AAAI-96 Spring Symposium on Computational Approaches to Interpreting and Generating Conversational Implicature, 25–27 March, Stanford, California.

Davidson, D. 1967. The Logical Form of Action Sentences. In *The Logic of Grammar,* eds. D. Davidson and G. Harman, 235–245. Encino, Calif.: Dickenson.

Davis, E. 1990. *Representations of Commonsense Knowledge*. San Francisco, Calif.: Morgan Kaufmann.

Davis, W., and Carnes, J. 1991. Clustering Temporal Intervals to Generate Reference Hierarchies. In *Proceedings of the Second International Conference on Principles of Knowledge Representation and Reasoning (KR91)*, 111–117. San Francisco, Calif.: Morgan Kaufmann.

Dawar, A., and Vijay-Shanker, K. 1990. An Interpretation of Negation in Feature Structure Description. *Computational Linguistics* 16(1): 11–21.

Dean, T. L., and McDermott, D. V. 1987. Temporal Data Base Management. *Artificial Intelligence* 32(1):1–55.

Dechter, R.; Meiri, I.; and Pearl, J. 1991. Temporal Constraint Networks. *Artificial Intelligence* 49(1):61–96.

De Haan, J., and Schubert, L. K. 1986. Inference in a Topically Organized Semantic Net. In Proceedings of the Fifth National Conference on Artificial Intelligence (AAAI-86), 334–338. Menlo Park, Calif.: American Association for Artificial Intelligence.

Devlin, K. 1991. *Logic and Information*. Cambridge, U.K.: Cambridge University Press.

DiMarco, D.; Hirst, G.; and Stede, M. 1993. The Semantic and Stylistic Differentiation of Synonyms and Near Synonyms. Paper presented at the AAAI Spring Symposium on Building Lexicons for Machine Translation, 23–25 March, Stanford, California.

Donini, F.; Lenzerini, M.; Nardi, D.; and Nutt, W. 1991. The Complexity of Concept Languages. In *Proceedings of KR91*, 151–162. San Francisco, Calif.: Morgan Kaufmann.

Dorr, B. J. 1994. Machine Translation Divergences: A Formal Description and Proposed Solution. *Computational Linguistics* 20(4): 597–633.

Dorr, B. 1993. *Machine Translation: A View from the Lexicon*. Cambridge, Mass.: The MIT Press.

Dorr, B. J., and Voss, C. R. 1996. A Multilevel Approach to INTERLINGUAL MT: Defining the Interface between Representational Languages. *International Journal of Expert Systems* 9(1): 15–51.

Dorr, B., and Voss, C. 1993. Machine Translation of Spatial Expressions: Defining the Relation between an Interlingua and a Knowledge Representation System. In Proceedings of the Twelfth Conference of the American Association for Artificial Intelligence, 374–379. Menlo Park, Calif.: American Association for Artificial Intelligence.

Dorr, B.; Garman, J.; and Weinberg, A. 1995. From Syntactic Encodings to Thematic Roles: Building Lexical Entries for Interlingual MT. *Machine Translation* 9(3): 221–250.

Dorr, B.; Hendler, J.; Blanksteen, S.; and Migdalof, B. 1995. On beyond Syntax: Use of Lexical Conceptual Structure for Intelligent Tutoring. In *Intelligent Language Tutors: Balancing Theory and Technology*, 289–309, eds. M. Holland, J. Kaplan, and M. Sams. Hillsdale, N.J.: Lawrence Erlbaum.

Dorr, B.; Lin, D.; Lee, J.; and Suh, S. 1995. Efficient Parsing for Korean and English: A Parameterized Message-Passing Approach. *Computational Linguistics* 21(2): 255–263.

Dorr, B.; Voss, C.; Peterson, E.; and Kiker, M. 1994. Concept-Based Lexical Selection. Paper presented at the AAAI 1994 Fall Symposium on Knowledge Representation for Natural Language Processing in Implemented Systems, 4–6 November, New Orleans, Louisiana.

Downey, P. J.; Sethi, R.; and Tarjan, R. E. 1980. Variations on the Common Subexpression Problem. *Journal of the Association for Computing Machinery* 27(4): 758–771.

Dowty, D. R. 1982. Tenses, Time Adverbs, and Compositional Semantic Theory. *Linguistics and Philosophy* 5(1): 23–55.

Duchan, J. F.; and Bruder, G. A., eds. 1995. *Deixis in Narrative: A Cognitive Science Perspective.* Hillsdale, N.J.: Lawrence Erlbaum.

Earley, J. 1985. An Efficient Context-Free Parsing Algorithm. In *Readings in Natural Language Processing*, 25–33. San Francisco, Calif.: Morgan Kaufmann.

Ehrlich, K. 1995. Automatic Vocabulary Expansion through Narrative Context. Technical Report, 95-09, Department of Computer Science, State University of New York at Buffalo.

Ehrlich, K., and Rapaport, W. J. 1997. A Computational Theory of Vocabulary Expansion. In *Proceedings of the Nineteenth Annual Conference of the Cognitive Science Society*, 205–210. Hillsdale, N.J.: Lawrence Erlbaum.

Elgot-Drapkin, J., and Perlis, D. 1990. Reasoning Situated in Time: Basic Concepts. *Journal of Experimental and Theoretical Artificial Intelligence* 2(2): 75–98.

Elshout-Mohr, M., and Van Daaleen-Kapteijns, M. M. 1987. Cognitive Processes in Learning Word Meanings. In *The Nature of Vocabulary Acquisition*, eds. M. G. McKeown and M. E. Curtis, 53–71. Hillsdale, N.J.: Lawrence Erlbaum.

Fahlman, S. E. 1979. NETL: *A System for Representing Real-World Knowledge.* Cambridge, Mass.: MIT Press.

Feigl, H., and Sellars, W., eds. 1949. *Readings in Philosophical Analysis.* New York: Appleton-Century-Crofts.

Fellbaum, C.; Gross, D.; and Miller, G. A. 1991. WORDNET: A Lexical Database Organized on Psycholinguistic Principles. In *Lexical Acquisition: Exploiting Online Resources to Build a Lexicon*, ed. U. Zernik. Hillsdale, N.J.: Lawrence Erlbaum.

Ferrari, G. 1997. Types of Contexts and Their Role in Multimodal Communication. *Computational Intelligence* 13(2): 90–102.

Ferrari, G. 1995. Types of Contexts and Their Role in Multimodal Communication. Paper presented at the IJCAI-95 Workshop on Context in Natural Language Processing, 20–25 August, Montreal, Quebec, Canada.

Fitch, F. B. 1952. *Symbolic Logic: An Introduction.* New York: Ronald.

Fodor, J., and Lepore, E. 1992. *Holism: A Shopper's Guide.* Cambridge, Mass.: Basil Blackwell.

Fodor, J. D., and Sag, I. A. 1982. Referential and Quantificational Indefinites. *Linguistics and Philosophy* 5(3): 355–398.

Frederking, R. E. 1996. Grice's Maxims: Do the Right Thing. Paper presented at the AAAI-96 Spring Symposium on Computational Approaches to Interpreting and Generating Conversational Implicature, 25–27 March, Stanford, California.

Geach, P. T. 1962. *Reference and Generality.* Ithaca, N.Y.: Cornell University Press.

Gentner, D. 1981. Some Interesting Differences between Nouns and Verbs. *Cognition and Brain Theory* 4:161–178.

Gerevini, A., and Schubert, L. K. 1995. The Temporal Reasoning Tools Timegraph I–II. *International Journal of Artificial Intelligence Tools* 4(1–2): 281–299.

Gerevini, A., and Schubert, L. K. 1993. Efficient Temporal Reasoning through Timegraphs. In Proceedings of the Thirteenth International Joint Conference on Artificial Intelligence (IJCAI-93), 649–654. Menlo Park, Calif.: International Joint Conferences on Artificial Intelligence.

Givan, R.; McAllester, D.; and Shalaby, S. 1991. Natural Language–Based Inference Procedures Applied to Schubert's Steamroller. In Proceedings of the Ninth Conference of the American Association for Artificial Intelligence, 915–920. Menlo Park, Calif.: American Association for Artificial Intelligence.

Gleitman, L. 1994. A Picture Is Worth a Thousand Words—But That's the Problem. In *Proceedings of the Sixteenth Annual Conference of the Cognitive Science Society,* 965. Hillsdale, N.J.: Lawrence Erlbaum.

Gleitman, L. 1990. The Structural Sources of Verb Meanings. *Language Acquisition* 1:1–55.

Golding, J.; Magliano, J.; and Hemphill, D. 1992. WHEN: A Model for Answering When Questions about Future Events. In *Questions and Information Systems,* eds. T. Lauer, E. Peacock, and A. Graesser. Hillsdale, N.J.: Lawrence Erlbaum.

Granger, R. H. 1977. FOUL-UP: A Program That Figures Out Meanings of Words from Context. In Proceedings of the Fifth International Joint Conference on Artificial Intelligence (IJCAI-77), 67–68. Menlo Park, Calif.: International Joint Conferences on Artificial Intelligence.

Green, N., and Carberry, S. 1994. A Hybrid Reasoning Model for Indirect Answers. In *Proceedings of the Thirtieth Annual Meeting of the Association for Computational Linguistics (ACL-94),* 58-65. San Francisco, Calif.: Morgan Kaufmann.

Green, N., and Lehman, J. F. 1996. Goals for Future Computational Models of Computational Implicature—Grice's Maxims: Do the Right Thing. Paper presented at the AAAI-96 Spring Symposium on Computational Approaches to Interpreting and Generating Conversational Implicature, 25–27 March, Stanford, California.

Grice, H. P. 1978. Further Notes in Logic and Conversation. In *Lecture 3 of Grice in Knowledge Representation,* eds. Cole and Morgan, 113–128.

Grice, H. P. 1975. Logic and Conversation. In *Speech Acts, Volume 3,* eds. P. Cole and J. L. Morgan, 41–58. Syntax and Semantics Series. San Diego, Calif.: Academic.

Groenendijk, J., and Stokhof, M. 1991. Dynamic Predicate Logic. *Linguistics and Philosophy* 14(1): 39–100.

Grosz, B. J., and Sidner, C. L. 1986. Attention, Intentions, and the Structure of Discourse. *Computational Linguistics* 12(3): 175–204.

Grosz, B. J.; Joshi, A. K.; and Weinstein, S. 1995. Centering: A Framework for Modeling the Local Coherence of Discourse. *Computational Linguistics* 21(2): 203-225.

Guha, R. V. 1991. Contexts: A Formalization and Some Applications. Ph.D. dissertation, Department of Computer Science, Stanford University.

Guralnik, D. B., ed. 1982. *Webster's New World Dictionary, The American Language*. New York: Simon and Schuster.

Haack, S. 1978. *Philosophy of Logics*. New York: Cambridge University Press.

Haas, A. R. 1986. A Syntactic Theory of Belief and Action. *Artificial Intelligence* 28(3): 245–292.

Haas, N., and Hendrix, G. 1983. Learning by Being Told: Acquiring Knowledge for Information Management. In *Machine Learning: An Artificial Intelligence Approach*, eds. R. S. Michalski, J. G. Carbonell, and T. M. Mitchell, 405–428. San Francisco, Calif.: Morgan Kaufmann.

Haddawy, P.; Jacobson, J.; and C. E. K, Jr. 1997. BANTER: A Bayesian Network Tutoring Shell. *Artificial Intelligence in Medicine*. 10(2):177–200.

Haller, S. 1996. Planning Text about Plans Interactively. *International Journal of Expert Systems* 9(1): 85–112.

Hamm, F. 1989. Natürlich-Sprachliche Quantoren. (Natural Language Quantifiers) Tübingen, Germany: Max Niemeyer Verlag.

Harabagiu, S. M. 2000. Knowledge-Based Information Extraction and Question Answering. *IEEE Transactions on Knowledge and Data Engineering*. Forthcoming.

Harabagiu, S. M. 1997. WORDNET-Based Inference of Textual Context, Cohesion, and Coherence. Ph.D. dissertation, University of Southern California, Dept. of Electrical Engineering Systems, Los Angeles, Calif.

Harabagiu, S. M., and Moldovan, D. I. 1997. TEXTNET—A Text-Based Intelligent System. *Natural Language Engineering* 3(2): 171–190.

Harabagiu, S. M.: Moldovan, D. I.; and Yukawa, T. 1996. Testing Gricean Constraints on a WORDNET-Based Coherence Evaluation System. Paper presented at the AAAI-96 Spring Symposium on Computational Approaches to Interpreting and Generating Conversational Implicature, 25–27 March, Stanford, California.

Harman, G. 1982. Conceptual Role Semantics. *Notre Dame Journal of Formal Logic* 23:242–256.

Harman, G. 1974. Meaning and Semantics. In *Semantics and Philosophy*, eds. M. K. Munitz and P. K. Unger, 1–16. New York: New York University Press.

Hastings, P. M. 1994. Automatic Acquisition of Word Meanings from Natural Language Contexts. Ph.D. dissertation, Department of Computer Science and Engineering, University of Michigan.

Hastings, P. M., and Lytinen, S. L. 1994a. Objects, Actions, Nouns, and Verbs. In *Proceedings of the Sixteenth Annual Conference of the Cognitive Science Society*, 397–402. Hillsdale, N.J.: Lawrence Erlbaum.

Hastings, P. M., and Lytinen, S. L. 1994b. The Ups and Downs of Lexical Acquisition. In Proceedings of the Twelfth National Conference on Artificial Intelligence (AAAI-94), 754–759. Menlo Park, Calif.: American Association for Artificial Intelligence.

Heine, B.; Claudi, U.; and Huennemeyer, F. 1991. *Grammaticalization: A Conceptual Framework*. Chicago: University of Chicago Press.

Higginbotham, J. 1989. Elucidations of Meaning. *Linguistics and Philosophy* 12:465–517.

Hinkelman, E. A. 1990. Linguistic and Pragmatic Constraints on Utterance Interpretation. Ph.D. dissertation, Technical Report, 288, Department of Computer Science, University of Rochester.

Hirschberg, J. B. 1985. A Theory of Scalar Implicature. Ph.D. dissertation, Technical Report, MS-CIS-85-56, Department of Computer and Information Science, University of Pennsylvania.

Hirst, G. 1988. Semantic Interpretations and Ambiguity. *Artificial Intelligence* 34(2): 131–177.

Hirst, G. 1991. Existence Assumptions in Knowledge Representation. *Artificial Intelligence* 49(1–3): 199–242.

Hirst, G., and Ryan, M. 1992. Mixed-Depth Representations for Natural Language Text. In *Text-Based Intelligent Systems,* 59–82, ed. P. Jacobs. Hillsdale, N. J.: Lawrence Erlbaum.

Hobbs, J. R. 1978. Resolving Pronoun References. *Lingua* 44(4): 311–338.

Hobbs, J. R. 1985a. On the Coherence and Structure of Discourse. Lecture Notes, 37, Center for the Study of Language and Information, Stanford University.

Hobbs, J. R. 1985b. Ontological Promiscuity. In Proceedings of the Twenty-Third Annual Meeting of the Association of Computational Linguistics, 61–69. New Brunswick, N.J.: Association of Computational Linguistics.

Hobbs, J. R.; Stickel, M. E.; Appelt, D. E.; and Martin, P. 1993. Interpretation as Abduction. *Artificial Intelligence* 63(1–2): 69–142.

Hobbs, J. R.; Croft, W.; Davies, T.; Edwards, D.; and Laws, K. 1986a. Commonsense Metaphysics and Lexical Semantics. *Computational Linguistics* 13(3–4): 241–250.

Hobbs, J. R.; Croft, W.; Davies, T.; Edwards, D.; and Laws, K. 1986b. Commonsense Metaphysics and Lexical Semantics. In the Proceedings of the Twenty-Eighth Annual Meeting of the Association of Computational Linguistics. New Brunswick, N.J.: Association of Computational Linguistics.

Horacek, H. 1996. Commonalities and Differences in Two Approaches Dealing with Conversational Implicature. Paper presented at the AAAI-96 Spring Symposium on Computational Approaches to Interpreting and Generating Conversational Implicature, 25–27 March, Stanford, California.

Horn, L. R. 1989. *A Natural History of Negation.* Chicago: University of Chicago Press.

Horn, L. R. 1972. *On the Semantic Properties of Logical Operators in English.* Bloomington, Ind.: IULC Publications.

Huet, G. P. 1975. A Unification Algorithm for Typed Lambda-Calculus. *Theoretical Computer Science* 1:27–57.

Hunt, A., and Koplas, G. D. 1997. Definitional Vocabulary Acquisition Using Natural Language Processing and a Dynamic Lexicon. Technical SNERG Note, 29, Department of Computer Science, SNEPS Research Group, State University of New York at Buffalo.

Hwang, C. H. 1992. A Logical Approach to Narrative Understanding. Ph.D. dissertation, University of Alberta, Dept. of Computer Science.

Hwang, C. H., and Schubert, L. K. 1994. Interpreting Tense, Aspect, and Time Adverbials: A Compositional, Unified Approach. In *Proceedings of the First International Conference on Temporal Logic (ICTL94),* eds D. M. Gabbay and H. J. Ohlbach, 238–264. Bonn, Germany: Springer-Verlag.

Hwang, C. H., and Schubert, L. K. 1993a. Episodic Logic: A Comprehensive, Natural Representation for Language Understanding. *Minds and Machines* 3(4): 381–419.

Hwang, C. H., and Schubert, L. K. 1993b. Episodic Logic: A Situational Logic for Natural Language Processing. In Situation Theory and Its Applications, Volume 3, eds. P. Aczel, D. Israel, Y. Katagiri, and S. Peters, 303–338, Center for the Study of Language and Information, Stanford, California.

Hwang, C. H., and Schubert, L. K. 1993c. Interpreting Temporal Adverbials. In Proceedings of the ARPA Workshop on Human Language Technology, 138–143. Washington, D.C.: Defense Advanced Research Projects Agency.

Hwang, C. H., and Schubert, L. K. 1992. Tense Trees as the "Fine Structure" of Discourse. In Proceedings of the Thirtieth Annual Meeting of the Association for Computational Linguistics, 232–240. New Brunswick, N.J.: Association for Computational Linguistics.

Iwańska, L. 1997a. Reasoning with Intensional Negative Adjectivals: Semantics, Pragmatics, and Context. *Computational Intelligence* 13(3): 348–390.

Iwańska, L. 1997b. Recovering Nonlinearly Distributed Knowledge: Computing Discourse Structure in Factual Reports. *Natural Language Engineering* 4(4): 60–85.

Iwańska, L. 1996a. Natural (Language) Temporal Logic: Reasoning about Absolute and Relative Time. *International Journal of Expert Systems* 9(1): 113–149.

Iwańska, L. 1996b. Toward a Formal Account of Context-Dependency and Underspecificity of Natural Language. Paper presented at the AAAI-96 Spring Symposium on Computational Approaches to Interpreting and Generating Conversational Implicature, 25–27 March, Stanford, California.

Iwańska, L. 1993. Logical Reasoning in Natural Language: It Is All about Knowledge. *Minds and Machines* 3(4): 475–510.

Iwańska, L. 1992a. A General Semantic Model of Negation in Natural Language: Representation and Inference. In *Proceedings of the Third International Conference on Principles of Knowledge Representation and Reasoning (KR92)*, 357–368. San Francisco, Calif.: Morgan Kaufmann.

Iwańska, L. 1992b. A General Semantic Model of Negation in Natural Language: Representation and Inference. Ph.D. dissertation, Technical Report UIUCDCS-R-92-1775, Technical Report UILU-ENG-92-1755, Department of Computer Science, University of Illinois at Urbana-Champaign.

Iwańska, L. 1991. Discourse Processing Module. Technical Report 91CRD180, Artificial Intelligence Laboratory, GE Research and Development Center, Schenectady, New York.

Iwańska L. 1989. Automated Processing of Narratives Written by 6–12 Grade Students: The BILING Program. Technical Report, UIUCDCS-R-89-1508, Department of Computer Science, University of Illinois at Urbana-Champaign.

Iwańska, L., and Kruger, K. 1996. Natural Language for Knowledge Acquisition: Learning from Definite Anaphora. Paper presented at the AAAI Fall Symposium on Knowledge Representation Systems Based on Natural Language, 9–11 November, Cambridge, Massachusetts.

Iwańska, L., and Zadrozny, W. 1997. Context in Natural Language Processing. *Computational Intelligence* 13(2): 1–12.

Iwańska, L.; Kruger, K.; and Mata, N. 1998. Generating and Recognizing Abbreviations: English and Beyond. *Computational Linguistics.* 13(3): 301–308.

Iwańska, L.; Croll, M.; Yoon, T.; and Adams, M. 1995. Wayne State University: Description of the UNO Natural Language Processing System as Used for MUC-6. In *Proceedings of the Sixth Message-Understanding Conference (MUC-6),* ed. B. Sundheim, 263–277. San Francisco, Calif.: Morgan Kaufmann.

Iwańska, L.; Appelt, D.; Ayuso, D.; Dahlgren, K.; Stalls, B. G.; Grishman, R.; Krupka, G.; Montgomery, C.; and Riloff, E. 1991. Computational Aspects of Discourse in the Context of MUC-3. In *Proceedings of the Third Message-Understanding Conference (MUC-3),* 256–282. San Francisco, Calif.: Morgan Kaufmann.

Jackendoff, R. 1992. What Is Semantic Structures About? *Computational Linguistics* 18(2): 240–242.

Jackendoff, R. 1991. Parts and Boundaries. In *Lexical and Conceptual Semantics,* eds. B. Levin and S. Pinker. Cambridge, Mass.: Blackwell.

Jackendoff, R. 1990. *Semantic Structures.* Cambridge, Mass.: MIT Press.

Jackendoff, R. 1983. *Semantics and Cognition.* Cambridge, Mass.: MIT Press.

Jenkins, T.; Gaillard, A.; Holmback, H.; Namioka, A.; Darvish, J.; Harrison, P.; and Lorbeski, M. 1990. Automated Message Understanding: A Real-World Prototype. In Proceedings of the IEA/AIE-90, 15–18 July, Charleston, South Carolina.

Johnson, M. 1990. Expressing Disjunctive and Negative Feature Constraints with Classical First-Order Logic. Paper presented at the Twenty-Eighth Annual Meeting of the Association of Computational Linguistics. New Brunswick, N.J.: Association of Computational Linguistics.

Johnson, M. 1988. Attribute-Value Logic and the Theory of Grammar. Lecture Notes 16, Center for the Study of Language and Information, Stanford University.

Johnson, M. 1987. Attribute-Value Logic and the Theory of Grammar. Ph.D. dissertation, Department of Linguistics, Stanford University.

Johnson, S. D.; Constable, R. L., and Eichenlaub, C. D. 1982. *An Introduction to the PL/CV2 Programming Logic.* Lecture Notes in Computer Science Volume 135. Berlin: Springer-Verlag.

Johnson-Laird, P. N. 1987. The Mental Representation of the Meanings of Words. In *Readings in Philosophy and Cognitive Science,* ed. A. I. Goldman, 561–583. Cambridge, Mass.: MIT Press.

Joshi, A. K. 1985. How Much Context Sensitivity Is Required to Provide Reasonable Structural Descriptions: Tree-Adjoining Grammars. In *Natural Language Processing,* eds. D. et al. Cambridge, U.K.: Cambridge University Press.

Kadmon, N. 1987. On Unique and Nonunique Reference and Asymmetric Quantification. Ph.D. dissertation, University of Massachusetts at Amherst, Dept. of Linguistics.

Kahn, K., and Gorry, G. A. 1977. Mechanizing Temporal Knowledge. *Artificial Intelligence* 9(1): 87–108.

Kameyama, M. 1997. Resolving Translation Mismatches with Contextual Inferences. Paper presented at the AAAI-97 Fall Symposium on Context in Knowledge Representation and Natural Language, 8–10 November, Cambridge, Massachusetts.

Kamp, H. 1981. A Theory of Truth and Semantic Representation. In *Formal Methods in the Study of Language*, eds. J. Groenendijk, T. Janssen, and M. Stokhof, 277–320. Amsterdam, The Netherlands: University of Amsterdam.

Kant, I. 1992. *Lectures on Logic*. Cambridge, U.K.: Cambridge University Press.

Kaplan, A. N. 1998. Simulative Inference about Nonmonotonic Reasoners. In Proceedings of the Seventh Conference on Theoretical Aspects of Rationality and Knowledge (TARK VII), 22–24 July, Evanston, Illinois.

Kaplan, A. N., and Schubert, L. K. 1997. Simulative Inference in a Computational Model of Belief. In IWCS II: Second International Workshop on Computational Semantics, eds. H. Bunt, L. Kievit, R. Muskens, and M. Verlinden. Tilburg, The Netherlands: Tilburg University.

Kasper, R. T., and Rounds, W. C. 1986. A Logical Semantics for Feature Structures. In Proceedings of the Twenty-Fourth Annual Meeting of the Association for Computational Linguistics. New Brunswick, N.J.: Association for Computational Linguistics.

Kay, M.; Gawron, J. M.; and Norvig, P. 1994. VERBMOBIL: A Translation System for Face-to-Face Dialog, Lecture Notes 33, Center for the Study of Language and Information, Stanford University.

Kearney, G. D., and McKenzie, S. 1993. Machine Interpretation of Emotion: Design of a Memory-Based Expert System for Interpreting Facial Expressions in Terms of Signaled Emotions. *Cognitive Science* 17:589–622.

Keenan, E. L., and Faltz, L. M. 1985. *Boolean Semantics for Natural Language*. Dordrecht, The Netherlands: D. Reidel.

Kiersey, D. M. 1982. Word Learning with Hierarchy-Guided Inference. In Proceedings of the Second National Conference on Artificial Intelligence (AAAI-82), 172–178. Menlo Park, Calif.: American Association for Artificial Intelligence.

Kim, J.-T., and Moldovan, D. I. 1995. Acquisition of Linguistic Patterns for Knowledge-Based Information Extraction. *IEEE Transactions on Knowledge and Data Engineering* 7(2): 713–724.

Kinoshita, S.; Phillips, J.; and Tsujii, J. 1992. Interaction between Structural Changes in Machine Translation. In Proceedings of the Fourteenth International Conference on Computational Linguistics, 679–685. New Brunswick, N.J.: Association of Computational Linguistics.

Kleene, S. C. 1950. *Introduction to Mathematics*. Princeton, N.J.: Van Nostrand.

Kolodner, J. L. 1981. Organization and Retrieval in a Conceptual Memory for Events or CON54, Where Are You? In Proceedings of the Seventh Joint International Conference on Artificial Intelligence, 227–233. Menlo Park, Calif.: International Joint Conferences on Artificial Intelligence.

Konolige, K. 1986. *A Deduction Model of Belief*. San Francisco, Calif.: Morgan Kaufmann.

Kozen, D. C. 1977. Complexity of Finitely Presented Algebras. In Proceedings of the Ninth Annual ACM Symposium on the Theory of Computation, 164–177. New York: Association for Computing Machinery.

Kronfeld, A. 1996. The Role of Gricean Implicature in Computational Models of Speech Acts. Paper presented at the AAAI-96 Spring Symposium on Computational Approaches to Interpreting and Generating Conversational Implicature, 25–27 March, Stanford, California.

Kumar, D. 1996. The SNEPS BDI Architecture. *Decision Support Systems* 16:3.

Kumar, D., and Shapiro, S. C. 1994. Acting in Service of Inference (and Vice Versa). In Proceedings of the Seventh Florida AI Research Symposium (FLAIRS 94), 207–211. Gainesville, Fla.: Florida AI Research Society.

Lambek, J. 1958. The Mathematics of Sentence Structure. American Mathematical Monthly 65(3): 154–169.

Langacker, R. 1987. Foundations of Cognitive Grammar, Volume 1: Theoretical Prerequisites. Stanford, Calif.: Stanford University Press.

Lascarides, A., and Asher, N. 1991. Discourse Relations and Defeasible Knowledge. In Proceedings of the Twenty-Ninth Annual Meeting of the Association of Computational Linguistics (ACL '91), 55–62. New Brunswick, N.J.: Association of Computational Linguistics.

Lascarides, A., and Copesake, A. 1995. The Pragmatics of Word Meaning. Paper presented at the SALT V Conference, Ithaca, New York.

Lascarides, A.; Asher, N.; and Oberlander, J. 1992. Inferring Discourse Relations in Context. In Proceedings of the Thirtieth Annual Meeting of the Association for Computational Linguistics (ACL '92), 1–8. New Brunswick, N.J.: Association for Computational Linguistics.

Leech, G. 1987. Meaning and the English Verb. 2d ed. London: Longman.

Lehmann, F., ed. 1992. Semantic Networks in Artificial Intelligence. Oxford, U.K.: Pergamon.

Lenat, D. B. 1995. CYC: A Large-Scale Investment in Knowledge Infrastructure. Communications of the ACM 38(11): 33–38.

Lenat, D. B., and Guha, R. V. 1990a. Building Large Knowledge Bases. Reading, Mass.: Addison-Wesley.

Lenat, D., and Guha, R. V. 1990b. Representation and Inference in the CYC Project. Reading, Mass.: Addison-Wesley.

Levin, B. 1993. English Verb Classes and Alternations: A Preliminary Investigation. Chicago, Ill.: University of Chicago Press.

Levin, L., and Nirenburg, S. 1994. The Correct Place of Lexical Semantics in Interlingual MT. Paper presented at the Fifteenth International Conference on Computational Linguistics, August, Kyoto, Japan, August 5–9.

Levin, L., and Nirenburg, S. 1993. Principles and Idiosyncracies in MT Lexicons. Paper presented at the AAAI Spring Symposium on Building Lexicons for Machine Translation, 23–25 March, Stanford, Calif.

Levin, B., and Rappaport-Hovav, M. 1995a. The Elasticity of Verb Meaning. Paper presented at the Tenth Annual Conference of the Israel Association for Theoretical Linguistics and the Workshop on the Syntax-Semantics Interface, June 12–13, Haifa, Israel.

Levin, B., and Rappaport-Hovav, M. 1995b. Unaccusativity: At the Syntax-Semantics Interface. Cambridge, Mass.: MIT Press.

Levinson, S. 1983. Pragmatics. Cambridge, U.K.: Cambridge University Press.

Lewis, D. 1969. Convention. Cambridge, Mass.: Harvard University Press.

Lindop, J., and Tsujii, J. 1991. Complex Transfer in MT: A Survey of Examples. Technical Report, CCL/UMIST 91/5, Center for Computational Linguistics, University of Science and Technology in Manchester.

Link, G. 1983. The Logical Analysis of Plurals and Mass Terms: A Lattice-Theoretical Approach. In Meaning, Use, and Interpretation of Language, eds. R.

Bäuerle, C. Schwarze, and A. von Stechow, 302–323. Berlin: Walter de Gruyter.

Lytinen, S., and Schank, R. 1982. Representation and Translation. Technical Report, 234, Department of Computer Science, Yale University.

Maida, Anthony S., and Shapiro, Stuart C. 1982. Intensional Concepts in Propositional Semantic Networks. *Cognitive Science* 6(4): 291–330.

Maida, A. S., and Shapiro, S. C. 1985. Intensional Concepts in Propositional Semantic Networks. In *Readings in Knowledge Representation*, 170–189. San Francisco, Calif.: Morgan Kaufmann.

McAllester, D. A. 1989. ONTIC: *A Knowledge Representation System for Mathematics*. Cambridge, Mass.: MIT Press.

McAllester, D., and Givan, R. 1993. Taxonomic Syntax for First-Order Inference. *Journal of the ACM* 40(2): 246–283.

McAllester, D. A., and Givan, R. 1992. Natural Language Syntax and First-Order Inference. *Artificial Intelligence* 56(1): 1–20.

McCarthy, J. 1993. Notes on Formalizing Context. In Proceedings of the Thirteenth International Joint Conference on Artificial Intelligence (IJCAI-93), 555–560. Menlo Park, Calif.: International Joint Conferences on Artificial Intelligence.

McCarthy, J. 1979. First-Order Theories of Individual Concepts and Propositions. In *Machine Intelligence 9*, eds. J. E. Hayes, D. Michie, and L. I. Mikulich, 129–147. Chichester, U.K.: Ellis Horwood.

McCawley, J. D. 1981. *Everything That Linguists Have Always Wanted to Know about Logic— But Were Ashamed to Ask*. Chicago: University of Chicago Press.

McDonald, D. D. 1998. Controlled Realization of Complex Objects by Reversing the Output of a Parser. Paper presented at the Ninth International Conference on Natural Language Generation, St. Catherines, Ontario, Canada.

McDonald, D. D. 1996. Internal and External Evidence in the Identification and Semantic Categorization of Proper Names. In *Corpus Processing for Lexical Acquisition*, eds. B. Boguraev and J. Pustejovsky, 21–39. Cambridge, Mass.: MIT Press.

McDonald, D. D. 1994. KRISP: A Representation for the Semantic Interpretation of Texts. *Minds and Machines* 4(1): 59–73.

McDonald, D. D. 1993. Reversible NLP by Deriving the Grammars from the Knowledge Base. In *Reversible Grammar in Natural Language Processing*, ed. T. Strzalkowski. Norwell, Mass.: Kluwer Academic.

McDonald, D. D. 1992. An Efficient Chart-Based Algorithm for Partial Parsing of Unrestricted Texts. Paper presented at the Third Conference on Applied Natural Language Processing, Trento, Italy.

McDonald, D. D.; Meteer, M.; and Pustejovsky, J. 1987. Factors Contributing to Efficiency in Natural Language Generation. In *Natural Language Generation: Recent Advances in Artificial Intelligence, Psychology, and Linguistics*, 159–181. Dordrecht, The Netherlands: Kluwer Academic.

MacGregor, R. 1991. The Evolving Technology of Classification-Based Knowledge Representation. In *Principles of Semantic Networks: Explorations in the Representation of Knowledge*, ed. J. Sowa, 385–400. San Francisco, Calif.: Morgan Kaufmann.

McKay, D. P., and Shapiro, S. C. 1981. Using Active Connection Graphs for Reasoning with Recursive Rules. In Proceedings of the Seventh International Joint Conference on Artificial Intelligence, 368–374. Menlo Park, Calif.: International Joint Conferences on Artificial Intelligence.

McRoy, S. 1998. Achieving Robust Human-Computer Communication. International *Journal of Human-Computer Studies* 48(5): 681-704.

McRoy, S. W. 1995. Misunderstanding and the Negotiation of Meaning. *Knowledge-Based Systems* 8(2–3):126–134.

McRoy, S. W., and Hirst, G. 1995. The Repair of Speech Act Misunderstandings by Abductive Inference. *Computational Linguistics* 21(4): 435–478.

McRoy, S. W.; Haller, S. M.; and Ali, S. S. 1997. Uniform Knowledge Representation for Language Processing in the B2 System. *Journal of Natural Language Engineering* 3(2): 123–145.

Malory, S. T. 1982. Le Morte D'Arthur. New York: Collier.

Mani, I. 1995. An Integrative, Layered Approach to Lexical Semantics and Its Application to Machine Translation. Paper presented at the AAAI Spring Symposium on Representation and Acquisition of Lexical Knowledge: Polysemy, Ambiguity, and Generativity, 27–29 March, Stanford University.

Mann, W., and Thompson, S. 1986. Rhetorical Structure Theory: Description and Construction of Text Structures. In *Natural Language Generation,* ed. G. Kempen, 279–300. Boston: Kluwer Academic.

Marcu, D., and Hirst, G. 1996. Detecting Pragmatic Infelicities. Paper presented at the AAAI-96 Spring Symposium on Computational Approaches to Interpreting and Generating Conversational Implicature, 25–27 March, Stanford, California.

Marcu, D., and Hirst, G. 1995. A Uniform Treatment of Pragmatic Inferences in Simple and Complex Utterances and Sequences of Utterances. In *Proceedings of the Thirty-Third Annual Meeting of the Association for Computational Linguistics,* 144–150. San Francisco, Calif.: Morgan Kaufmann.

Marcus, M.; Santorini, B.; and Marcinkiewicz, M. A. 1993. Building a Large Annotated Corpus of English: The Penn TREEBANK. *Computational Linguistics* 19(2): 313–330.

Martins, J. P., and Cravo, M. R. 1991. How to Change Your Mind. *Noûs* 25:537–551.

Martins, J. P., and Shapiro, S. C. 1988. A Model for Belief Revision. *Artificial Intelligence* 35 (1): 25–79.

Masuko, M. 1996. Sorting Out the Inventory. Paper presented at the AAAI-96 Spring Symposium on Computational Approaches to Interpreting and Generating Conversational Implicature, 25–27 March, Stanford, California.

Meinong, A. 1928. *Über Annahmen.* 3d ed. Leipzig: Verlag von Johann Ambrosius Barth.

Melby, A. 1986. Lexical Transfer: Missing Element in Linguistic Theories. Paper presented at the Eleventh International Conference on Computational Linguistics, August 25–29, Bonn, Germany.

Mellish, C. S. 1985. *Computer Interpretation of Natural Language Descriptions.* Chichester, U.K.: Ellis Horwood.

Michalski, R. 1983. A Theory and Methodology of Inductive Learning. *Artifi-

cial Intelligence 20:1–41.

Miller, G. A. 1995. WORDNET: A Lexical Database for English. *Communications of the ACM* 38(11): 39–41.

Miller, G. A., and Charles, W. G. 1991. Contextual Correlates of Semantic Similarity. *Language and Cognitive Processes* 36(3): 1–28.

Miller, S. A., and Schubert, L. K. 1988. Using Specialists to Accelerate General Reasoning. In Proceedings of the Seventh National Conference on Artificial Intelligence (AAAI-88), 161–165. Menlo Park, Calif.: American Association for Artificial Intelligence.

Miller, S.; Hwang, C. H.; de Haan, J.; and Schubert, L. K. 1991. The User's Guide to EPILOG. Boeing Co., Edmonton, Alberta, Canada.

Minsky, M. 1975. A Framework for Representing Knowledge. In *The Psychology of Computer Vision,* ed. P. H. Winston, 211–277. New York: McGraw-Hill.

Mitchell, T. 1982. Generalization as Search. *Artificial Intelligence* 18(5): 23–78.

Moens, M., and Steedman, M. 1988. Temporal Ontology and Temporal Reference. *Computational Linguistics* 14(2): 15–28.

Montague, R. 1974a. The Proper Treatment of Quantification in Ordinary English. In *Formal Philosophy: Selected Papers of Richard Montague,* ed. R. H. Thomason. New York: Yale University Press.

Montague, R. 1974b. Universal Grammar. In *Formal Philosophy: Selected Papers of Richard Montague,* ed. R. H. Thomason, 222-246. New York: Yale University Press.

Montague, R. 1973. The Proper Treatment of Quantification in Ordinary English. In *Approaches to Natural Language,* eds. J. Hintikka, J. Moravcik, and P. Suppes, 221–242. Dordrecht, The Netherlands: Reidel.

Montague, R. 1970a. The Proper Treatment of Quantification in Ordinary English. In *Approaches to Natural Language: Proceedings of the 1970 Stanford Workshop on Grammar and Semantics.* Dordrecht, The Netherlands: D. Reidel.

Montague, R. 1970b. Universal Grammar. *Theoria* 36:373–398.

Moore, J. D., and Paris, C. L. 1993. Planning Text for Advisory Dialogues: Capturing Intentional and Rhetorical Information. *Computational Linguistics* 19(4): 651–695.

Moore, R. C. 1977. Reasoning about Knowledge and Action. In Proceedings of the Fifth International Joint Conference on Artificial Intelligence (IJCAI-77), 223–227. Menlo Park, Calif.: International Joint Conferences on Artificial Intelligence.

Moshier, M. D., and Rounds, W. C. 1987. A Logic for Partially Specified Data Structures. In Proceedings of the Fourteenth ACM Symposium on Principles of Programming Languages, 156–167. New York: Association of Computing Machinery.

Namioka, A.; Hwang, C. H.; and Schaeffer, S. 1992. Using the Inference Tool EPILOG for a Message-Processing Application. *International Journal of Expert Systems* 5(1): 55–82.

Neal, J. G., and Shapiro, S. C. 1994. Knowledge-Based Multimedia Systems. In *Multimedia Systems,* ed. J. F. K. Buford, 403–438. Reading, Mass.: Addison-Wesley.

Neal, J. G., and Shapiro, S. C. 1991. Intelligent Multimedia Interface Technology. In *Intelligent User Interfaces,* eds. J. W. Sullivan and S. W. Tyler, 11–43. Reading, Mass.: Addison-Wesley.

Neal, J. G., and Shapiro, S. C. 1987. Knowledge-Based Parsing. In *Natural Language Parsing Systems,* ed. L. Bolc, 49–92. Berlin: Springer Verlag.

Nebel, B. 1988. Computational Complexity of Terminological Reasoning in BACK. *Artificial Intelligence* 34(3): 371–384.

Nelson, G., and Oppen, D. 1979. Simplification by Cooperating Decision Procedures. *ACM Transactions on Programming Languages and Systems* 1(2): 245–257.

Ng, H. T., and Lee, H. B. 1996. Integrating Multiple Knowledge Sources to Disambiguate Word Sense: An Exemplar-Based Approach. In *Proceedings of the Thirty-Fourth Annual Meeting of the Association for Computational Linguistics (ACL-96),* 40–47. San Francisco, Calif.: Morgan Kaufmann.

Nirenburg, S., and Nirenburg, I. 1988. A Framework for Lexical Selection in Natural Language Generation. Paper presented at the Twelfth International Conference on Computational Linguistics, August 22–27, Budapest, Hungary.

Nirenburg, S.; Carbonell, J.; Tomita, M.; and Goodman, K. 1992. *Machine Translation: A Knowledge-Based Approach.* San Francisco, Calif.: Morgan Kaufmann.

Nutter, J. T. 1983. Default Reasoning Using Monotonic Logic: A Modest Proposal. In Proceedings of the Third National Conference on Artificial Intelligence (AAAI-83), 297–300. Menlo Park, Calif.: American Association for Artificial Intelligence.

OED. 1971. *Compact Edition of the Oxford English Dictionary.* New York: Oxford University Press.

Palmer, M., and Wu, Z. 1995. Verb Semantics for English-Chinese Translation. *Machine Translation* 10(1/2): 59–92.

Palmer, M.; Passonneau, R.; Weir, C.; and Finin, T. 1993. The KERNEL Text-Understanding System. *Artificial Intelligence* 63:17–69.

Partee, B. H. 1984. Compositionality. In *Varieties of Formal Semantics,* eds. Landman and Veltman, 281–331. Dordrecht, The Netherlands: Foris.

Passonneau, R. 1995. Integrating Gricean and Attentional Constraints. In Proceedings of the Fourteenth International Joint Conference on Artificial Intelligence (IJCAI-95), 1267–1273. Menlo Park, Calif.: International Joint Conferences on Artificial Intelligence.

Pearl, J. 1988. *Probabilistic Reasoning in Intelligent Systems.* San Francisco, Calif.: Morgan Kaufmann.

Pereira, F. 1987. Grammars and Logics of Partial Information. In *Proceedings of the International Conference on Logic Programming, Volume 2,* 989–1013.

Perrault, C. 1961 (trans. by A. E. Johnson). *Perrault's Complete Fairy Tales.* New York: Dodd, Mead.

Peters, S. L., and Rapaport, W. J. 1990. Superordinate and Basic Level Categories in Discourse: Memory and Context. In *Proceedings of the Twelfth Annual Conference of the Cognitive Science Society.* Hillsdale, N.J.: Lawrence Erlbaum.

Peters, S. L., and Shapiro, S. C. 1987. A Representation for Natural Category Systems. In Proceedings of the Tenth International Joint Conference on Artificial Intelligence, 140–146. Menlo Park, Calif.: American Association for Artificial

Intelligence.

Peters, S. L.; Shapiro, S. C.; and Rapaport, W. J. 1988. Flexible Natural Language Processing and Roschian Category Theory. In *Proceedings of the Tenth Annual Conference of the Cognitive Science Society,* 125–131. Hillsdale, N.J.: Lawrence Erlbaum.

Pinker, S. 1989. *Learnability and Cognition.* Cambridge, Mass.: MIT Press.

Pugeault, F.; Saint-Dizier, P.; and Monteil, M. 1994. Knowledge Extraction from Texts: A Method for Extracting Predicate-Argument Structures from Texts. Paper presented at the Fifteenth International Conference on Computational Linguistics, August 5–9, Kyoto, Japan.

Pustejowsky, J. 1995. The Generative Lexicon. Cambridge, Mass.: MIT Press.

Quantz, J., and Schmitz, B. 1994. Knowledge-Based Disambiguation for Machine Translation. *International Journal of Minds and Machines* (Special Issue on Knowledge Representation for Natural Language) 4(1): 39–57.

Quillian, M. R. 1969. The Teachable Language Comprehender: A Simulation Program and Theory of Language. *Communications of the ACM* 12:459–476.

Quillian, M. R. 1968. Semantic Memory. In *Semantic Information Processing,* ed. M. Minsky, 227–270. Cambridge, Mass.: MIT Press.

Rapaport, W. J. 1995. Understanding Understanding: Syntactic Semantics and Computational Cognition. In *Philosophical Perspectives, Volume 9: AI, Connectionism, and Philosophical Psychology,* ed. J. E. Tomberlin, 49–88. Atascadero, Calif.: Ridgeview.

Rapaport, W. J. 1994. Syntactic Semantics: Foundations of Computational Natural Language Understanding. In *Thinking Computers and Virtual Persons: Essays on the Intentionality of Machines,* ed. E. Dietrich, 225–273. San Diego, Calif.: Academic.

Rapaport, W. J. 1992. Logic. In *Encyclopedia of Artificial Intelligence,* 851–853, ed. S. C. Shapiro. 2d ed. New York: Wiley.

Rapaport, W. J. 1991. Predication, Fiction, and Artificial Intelligence. *Topoi* 10:79–111.

Rapaport, W. J. 1988. Syntactic Semantics: Foundations of Computational Natural Language Understanding. In *Aspects of Artificial Intelligence,* ed. J. H. Fetzer, 81–131. Dordrecht, The Netherlands: Kluwer Academic. Reprinted in 1994. Dietrich, E., ed. *Thinking Computers and Virtual Persons: Essays on the Intentionality of Machines,* 225–273. San Diego, Calif.: Academic.

Rapaport, W. J. 1981. How to Make the World Fit Our Language: An Essay in Meinongian Semantics. *Grazer Philosophische Studien* 14:1–21.

Rapaport, W. J., and Shapiro, S. C. 1995. Cognition and Fiction. In *Deixis in Narrative: A Cognitive Science Perspective,* eds. J. F. Duchan, G. A. Bruder, and L. E. Hewitt, 107–128. Hillsdale, N.J.: Lawrence Erlbaum.

Rapaport, W. J.; Shapiro, S. C.; and Wiebe, J. M. 1997. Quasi-Indexicals and Knowledge Reports. *Cognitive Science* 21:63–107.

Rapaport, W. J.; Segal, E. M.; Shapiro, S. C.; Zubin, D. A.; Bruder, G. A.; Duchan, J. F.; and Mark, D. M. 1989a. Cognitive and Computer Systems for Understanding Narrative Text. Technical Report, 89-07, Department of Computer Science, State University of Buffalo at New York.

Rapaport, W. J.; Segal, E. M.; Shapiro, S. C.; Zubin, D. A.; Bruder, G. A.;

Duchan, J. F.; Almeida, M. J.; Daniels, J. H.; Galbraith, M. M.; Wiebe, J. M.; and Yuhan, A. H. 1989b. Deictic Centers and the Cognitive Structure of Narrative Comprehension. Technical Report, 89-01, Department of Computer Science, State University of New York at Buffalo.

Reichenbach, H. 1947. *Elements of Symbolic Logic.* New York: MacMillan.

Reiter, R. 1985. On Reasoning by Default. In *Readings in Knowledge Representation,* 402–410. San Francisco, Calif.: Morgan Kaufmann.

Rips, L. J. 1983. Cognitive Processes in Propositional Reasoning. *Psychological Review* 90(1): 38–71.

Robin, J., and McKeown, K. R. 1995. Empirically Designing and Evaluating a New Revision-Based Model for Summary Generation. *Artificial Intelligence* 85(1–2): 1–41.

Rosch, E. 1978. Principles of Categorization. In *Cognition and Categorization,* eds. E. Rosch and B. B. Lloyd, 27–48. Hillsdale, N.J.: Lawrence Erlbaum.

Rosetta, M. T. 1994. *Compositional Translation.* Dordrecht, The Netherlands: Kluwer Academic.

Rounds, W. C., and Kasper, R. T. 1986. A Complete Logical Calculus for Record Structures Representing Linguistic Information. In *Symposium on Logic in Computer Science.* Washington, D.C.: IEEE Computer Society.

Rupp, C. J.; Johnson, R.; and Rosner, M. 1992. Situation Schemata and Linguistic Representation. In *Computational Linguistics and Formal Semantics,* eds. M. Rosner and R. Johnson, 191–221. Cambridge, U.K.: Cambridge University Press.

Rusiecki, J. 1985. *Adjectives and Comparison in English.* LOCATION: Longman.

Russell, B. 1949. On Denoting. In *Readings in Philosophical Analysis,* eds. H. Feigel and W. Sellars. New York: Appleton-Century-Crofts.

Russell, B. 1906. On Denoting. *Mind* 14.

Russell, B. 1908. Mathematical Logic as Based on the Theory of Types. *American Journal of Mathematics* 30:222–262.

Schank, R., ed. 1975. *Conceptual Information Processing.* Amsterdam, The Netherlands: Elsevier Science.

Schank, R. 1973. Identification of Conceptualizations Underlying Natural Language. In *Computer Models of Thought and Language,* eds. R. C. Schank and K. M. Colby, 187–247. San Francisco, Calif.: Freeman.

Schank, R. C., and Abelson, R. P. 1977. *Scripts, Plans, Goals, and Understanding.* Hillsdale, N.J.: Lawrence Erlbaum.

Schank, R. C., and Leake, D. B. 1989. Creativity and Learning in a Case-Based Explainer. *Artificial Intelligence* 40(1–3): 353–385.

Schank, R. C.; Goldman, N. M., IRieger, C. J. III; and Riesbeck, C. K. 1975. *Conceptual Information Processing.* New York: North Holland.

Schmidt-Schaub, M., and Smolka, G. 1991. Attributive Concept Descriptions with Complements. *Artificial Intelligence* 48(1): 1–26.

Schmolze, J. 1989. Terminological Knowledge Representation Systems Supporting *n*-Ary Terms. In *Proceedings of the First International Conference on Knowledge Representation and Reasoning.* San Francisco, Calif.: Morgan Kaufmann.

Schrag, R.; Boddy, M.; and Carciofini, J. 1992. Managing Disjunction for Practical Temporal Reasoning. In *Proceedings of the Third International Conference on Principles of Knowledge Representation and Reasoning (KR92),* 36–46. San Francisco, Calif.: Morgan Kaufmann.

Schubert, L. 1991. Semantic Nets Are in the Eye of the Beholder. In *Principles of Semantic Networks,* 95–108, ed. J. Sowa. San Francisco, Calif.: Morgan Kaufmann.

Schubert, L. K. (forthcoming). The Situations We Talk About. In *Logic-Based Artificial Intelligence,* ed. Jack Minker. Dordrecht: Kluwer.

Schubert, L. K. 1999. Dynamic Skolemization. In *Computing Meaning,* vol. 1, eds. H. Bunt and R. Muskens, 219–253. Studies in Linguistics and Philosophy Series. Dordrecht, The Netherlands: Kluwer Academic.

Schubert, L. K. 1996. Framing the Donkey: Toward a Unification of Semantic Representations with Knowledge Representations. Paper presented at the AAAI Fall Symposium on Knowledge Representation Systems Based on Natural Language, 9–11 November, Cambridge, Massachusetts.

Schubert, L. K. 1994. Explanation Closure, Action Closure, and the Sandewall Test Suite for Reasoning about Change. *Journal of Logic and Computation* 4(5): 679–799.

Schubert, L. K. 1990. Monotonic Solution of the Frame Problem in the Situation Calculus: An Efficient Method for Worlds with Fully Specified Actions. In *Knowledge Representation and Defeasible Reasoning,* eds. H. E. Kyburg, R. Loui, and G. N. Carlson, 23–67. Dordrecht, The Netherlands: Kluwer Academic.

Schubert, L. K. 1986. Are There Preference Trade-Offs in Attachment Decisions? In Proceedings of the Fifth National Conference on Artificial Intelligence (AAAI-86), 601–605. Menlo Park, Calif.: American Association for Artificial Intelligence.

Schubert, L. K. 1984. On Parsing Preferences. In Proceedings of the Tenth International Conference on Computational Linguistics (COLING-84), 247–250. Stanford, Calif.: Stanford University.

Schubert, L. K., and Hwang, C. H. 1989. An Episodic Knowledge Representation for Narrative Texts. In *Proceedings of the First International Conference on the Principles of Knowledge Representation and Reasoning (KR'89),* 444-458. San Francisco, Calif.: Morgan Kaufmann.

Schubert, L. K., and Pelletier, F. J. 1989. Generically Speaking, or Using Discourse Representation Theory to Interpret Generics. In *Property Theory, Type Theory, and Semantics, Volume 2: Semantic Issues,* eds. G. Chierchia, B. H. Partee, and R. Turner, 193–268. Boston: Kluwer Academic.

Schubert, L. K., and Pelletier, F. J. 1986. From English to Logic: Context-Free Computation of "Conventional" Logical Translations. In *Readings in Natural Language Processing,* eds. B. Grosz, K. S. Jones, and B. Webber, 293–311. San Francisco, Calif.: Morgan Kaufmann.

Schubert, L. K., and Pelletier, F. J. 1982. From English to Logic: Context-Free Computation of "Conventional" Logical Translations. *American Journal of Computational Linguistics* 8(1): 26–44.

Schwartz, D. G. 1989. Outline of a Naive Semantics for Reasoning with Qualitative Linguistic Information. In Proceedings of the International Joint Conference on Artificial Intelligence, Menlo Park, Calif.: International Joint Conferences on Artificial Intelligence.

Searle, J. 1992. *The Rediscovery of the Mind*. Cambridge, Mass.: MIT Press.

Searle, R. 1980. Minds, Brains, and Programs. *Behavioral and Brain Sciences* 3:417–457.

Segal, E. M. 1995. A Cognitive-Phenomenological Theory of Fictional Narrative. In *Deixis in Narrative: A Cognitive Science Perspective*, eds. J. F. Duchan, G. A. Bruder, and L. E. Hewitt, 61–78. Hillsdale, N.J.: Lawrence Erlbaum.

Sellars, W. 1963. Some Reflections on Language Games. In *Science, Perception, and Reality*, 321–358. London: Routledge and Kegan Paul.

Shapiro, S. C. 1998. Embodied CASSIE. In *Cognitive Robotics: Papers from the 1998 AAAI Fall Symposium*, Technical Report FS-98-02, 136–143. Menlo Park, Calif.: AAAI Press.

Shapiro, S. C. 1996. Formalizing English. *International Journal of Expert Systems* 9(1): 151–171.

Shapiro, S. C. 1993. Belief Spaces as Sets of Propositions. *Journal of Experimental and Theoretical Artificial Intelligence (JETAI)* 5(2–3): 225–235.

Shapiro, S. C., ed. 1992a. *Encyclopedia of Artificial Intelligence*. 2d ed. New York: Wiley.

Shapiro, S. C. 1992b. Relevance Logic in Computer Science. In *Entailment*, eds. A. R. Anderson, N. D. Belnap, Jr., and M. Dunn, 553–563. Princeton, N.J.: Princeton University Press.

Shapiro, S. C. 1991. Cables, Paths, and "Subconscious" Reasoning in Propositional Semantic Networks. In *Principles of Semantic Networks: Explorations in the Representation of Knowledge*, 137–156. San Francisco, Calif.: Morgan Kaufmann.

Shapiro, S. C. 1989. The CASSIE Projects: An Approach to Natural Language Competence. In *EPIA 89: Fourth Portuguese Conference on Artificial Intelligence Proceedings*, eds. J. P. Martins and E. M. Morgado, 362–380. Lecture Notes in Artificial Intelligence 390. Berlin: Springer-Verlag.

Shapiro, S. C. 1986. Symmetric Relations, Intensional Individuals, and Variable Binding. In Proceedings of the IEEE 74(10): 1354–1363. Washington, D.C.: IEEE Computer Society.

Shapiro, S. C. 1982. Generalized Augmented Transition Network Grammars for Generation from Semantic Networks. *American Journal of Computational Linguistics* 8(1): 12–25.

Shapiro, S. C. 1979a. Numerical Quantifiers and Their Use in Reasoning with Negative Information. In Proceedings of the Sixth International Joint Conference on Artificial Intelligence, 791–796. Menlo Park, Calif.: International Joint Conferences on Artificial Intelligence.

Shapiro, S. C. 1979b. The SNEPS Semantic Network Processing System. In *Associative Networks: Representation and Use of Knowledge by Computers*, ed. N. Findler, 179–203. San Diego, Calif.: Academic.

Shapiro, S. C., and McKay, D. P. 1980. Inference with Recursive Rules. In Proceedings of the First Annual National Conference on Artificial Intelligence, 151–153. Menlo Park, Calif.: American Association for Artificial Intelligence.

Shapiro, S. C., and Rapaport, W. J. 1995. An Introduction to a Computational

Reader of Narrative. In *Deixis in Narrative: A Cognitive Science Perspective,* eds. J. F. Duchan, G. A. Bruder, and L. E. Hewitt, 79–105. Hillsdale, N.J.: Lawrence Erlbaum.

Shapiro, S. C., and Rapaport, W. J. 1992a. The SNEPS Family. *Computers and Mathematics with Applications* 23(2–5): 243–275.

Shapiro, S. C., and Rapaport, W. J. 1992b. The SNEPS Family. In *Semantic Networks in Artificial Intelligence,* ed. F. Lehmann, 243–275. Oxford, U.K.: Pergamon.

Shapiro, S. C., and Rapaport, W. J. 1991. Models and Minds: Knowledge Representation for Natural Language Competence. In *Philosophy and AI: Essays at the Interface,* eds. R. Cummins and J. Pollock, 215–259. Cambridge, Mass.: MIT Press.

Shapiro, S. C., and Rapaport, W. J. 1987. SNEPS Considered as a Fully Intensional Propositional Semantic Network. In *The Knowledge Frontier: Essays in the Representation of Knowledge,* eds. N. Cercone and G. McCalla, 262–315. New York: Springer-Verlag.

Shapiro, S. C., and the SNEPS Implementation Group. 1998. SNEPS 2.4 User's Manual. Department of Computer Science, State University of New York at Buffalo.

Shapiro, S. C., and the SNEPS Implementation Group. 1992. SNEPS-2.1 User's Manual. Department of Computer Science, State University of New York at Buffalo.

Shapiro, S. C.; McKay, D. P.; Martins, J.; and Morgado, E. 1981. SNEPSLOG: A "Higher-Order" Logic Programming Language. SNERG Technical Note, 8, Department of Computer Science, State University of New York at Buffalo.

Shapiro, S.; Rapaport, W.; Cho, S.-H.; Choi, J.; Feit, E.; Haller, S.; Kankiewicz, J.; and Kumar, D. 1994. A Dictionary of SNEPS Case Frames. Unpublished ms. available at www.cse.buffalo.edu/sneps/manuals.

Shelov, S. P., ed. 1991. *Caring for Your Baby and Young Child.* New York: Bantam.

Shoham, Y. 1987. Temporal Logics in AI: Semantical and Ontological Considerations. *Artificial Intelligence* 33(1): 89–104x.

Siskind, J. M. 1996. A Computational Study of Cross-Situational Techniques for Learning Word-to-Meaning Mappings. *Cognition* 61:39–91.

Slobin, D. 1996. Two Ways to Travel. In *Grammatical Constructions: Their Form and Meaning,* 195–219, eds. M. Shibatani and S. Thompson. Oxford, U.K.: Oxford University Press.

Smith, B. C. 1996. *On the Origin of Objects.* Cambridge, Mass.: MIT Press.

Sondheimer, N.; Cumming, S.; and Albano, R. 1990. How to Realize a Concept: Lexical Selection and the Conceptual Network in Text Generation. *Machine Translation* 5(1): 57–78.

Sowa, J., ed. 1991a. *Principles of Semantic Networks.* San Francisco, Calif.: Morgan Kaufmann.

Sowa, J., ed. 1991b. Toward the Expressive Power of Natural Language. In *Principles of Semantic Networks,* ed. J. Sowa, 157–189. San Francisco, Calif: Morgan Kaufmann.

Spector, L.; Hendler, J.; and Evett, M. 1990. Knowledge Representation in

PARKA. Technical Report, UMIACS TR 90-23, CS TR 2410, Department of Computer Science, University of Maryland at College Park.

Srihari, R. K. 1991. PICTION: A System That Uses Captions to Label Human Faces in Newspaper Photographs. In Proceedings of the Ninth National Conference on Artificial Intelligence (AAAI-91), 80–85. Menlo Park, Calif.: American Association for Artificial Intelligence.

Srihari, R. K., and Rapaport, W. J. 1989. Extracting Visual Information from Text: Using Captions to Label Human Faces in Newspaper Photographs. In Proceedings of the Eleventh Annual Conference of the Cognitive Science Society, 364–371. Hillsdale, N.J.: Lawrence Erlbaum.

Steedman, M. 1996. Surface Structure and Interpretation. Cambridge, Mass.: MIT Press.

Steedman, M. 1987. Combinatory Grammars and Parsitic Gaps. Natural Language and Linguistics 5:403–439.

Sterling, L., and Shapiro, E. 1986. The Art of Prolog. Cambridge, Mass.: MIT Press.

Sternberg, R. J. 1987. Most Vocabulary Is Learned from Context. In The Nature of Vocabulary Acquisition, eds. M. G. McKeown and M. E. Curtis, 89–105. Hillsdale, N.J.: Lawrence Erlbaum.

Stickel, M. 1986. Schubert's Steamroller Problem: Formulations and Solutions. Journal of Automated Reasoning 2:89–101.

Strzalkowski, T., ed. 1994. Reversible Grammar in Natural Language Processing. Dordrecht, The Netherlands: Kluwer Academic.

Sundheim, B. 1995a. Overview of Results of the MUC-6 Evaluation. In DARPA, 13–32. Washington, D.C.: Defense Advanced Research Projects Agency.

Sundheim, B., ed. 1993. Proceedings of the Fifth Message-Understanding Conference (MUC-5). San Francisco, Calif.: Morgan Kaufmann.

Sundheim, B., ed. 1995b. Proceedings of the Sixth Message-Understanding Conference (MUC-6). San Francisco, Calif.: Morgan Kaufmann.

Talmy, L. 1987. The Relation of Grammar to Cognition. In Topics in Cognitive Linguistics, ed. Rudzka-Ostyn. Erdenheim, Pa.: John Benjamins.

Talmy, L. 1985. Lexicalization Patterns: Semantic Structure in Lexical Forms. In Language Typology and Syntactic Description 3: Grammatical Categories and the Lexicon, ed. T. Shopen, 57–149. Cambridge, U.K.: Cambridge University Press.

Talmy, L. 1983. How Language Structures Space. In Spatial Orientation: Theory, Research, and Application, eds. H. Pick and L. Acredolo, 225–282. New York: Plenum.

Tarski, A. 1956. Logic, Semantics, Metamathematics. Oxford, U.K.: Clarendon.

Thomason, R. H. 1997. The Theoretic Foundations for Context. Paper presented at the AAAI-97 Fall Symposium on Context in Knowledge Representation and Natural Language, 8–10 November, Cambridge, Massachusetts.

TIPSTER. 1993. Proceedings of the TIPSTER Text Program (Phase 1). San Francisco, Calif.: Morgan Kaufmann.

Traugott, J. 1986. Nested Resolution. In Proceedings of the Eighth Conference on Automated Deduction (CADE-8), 394–402. Oxford, U.K.: Springer-Verlag.

Traum, D.; Schubert, L.; Poesio, M.; Martin, N.; Light, M.; Hwang, C. H.; Hee-man, P.; Ferguson, G.; and Allen, J. 1996. Knowledge Representation in the TRAINS-93 Conversation System. *International Journal of Expert Systems* (Special Issue on Knowledge Representation and Inference for Natural Language Processing) 9(1): 173–223.

Verrière, G. 1994. Manuel d'utilisation de la structure lexicale conceptuelle (LCS) Pour Représenter des Phrases en Français. (Instruction Manual of the Lexical Conceptual structure (LCS) for Prepresenter of the Frence Sentences). Research Note, Institut de Recerche en Informatique de Toulouse, Université Paul Sabatier.

Voss, C.; Dorr, B.; and Şencan, M. Ü. 1995. Lexical Allocation in Interlingua-Based Machine Translation of Spatial Expressions. Paper presented at the IJCAI-95 Workshop on the Representation and Processing of Spatial Expressions, August 20–25, Montreal, Quebec, Canada.

Walker, M. A. 1996. Inferring Rejection by Default Rules of Inference. Paper presented at the AAAI-96 Spring Symposium on Computational Approaches to Interpreting and Generating Conversational Implicature, 25–27 March, Stanford, California.

Walker, M. A. 1992. Redundancy in Collaborative Dialogue. In *Proceedings of the Twenty-Eighth Annual Meeting of the Association for Computational Linguistics (ACL-92)*, 29–39. San Francisco, Calif.: Morgan Kaufmann.

Webber, B. L. 1988. Tense as Discourse Anaphor. *Computational Linguistics* 14(2): 61–73.

Whitelock, P. 1992. Shake-and-Bake Translation. In Proceedings of the Fourteenth International Conference on Computational Linguistics, 784–791. Grenoble, France: International Committee on Computational Linguistics.

Wilensky, R.; Chin, D. N.; Luria, M.; Martin, J.; Mayfield, J.; and Wu, D. 1988. The Berkeley UNIX Consultant Project. *Computational Linguistics* 14(1): 35–84.

Winograd, T. 1983. *Language as a Cognitive Process.* Reading, Mass.: Addison Wesley.

Winograd, T. 1972. *Understanding Natural Language.* San Diego, Calif.: Academic.

Winston, P. H. 1985. Learning Structural Descriptions from Examples. In *Readings in Knowledge Representation,* 141–168. San Francisco, Calif.: Morgan Kaufmann.

Winston, P. H. 1975. Learning Structural Descriptions from Examples. In *The Psychology of Computer Vision,* ed. P. H. Winston, 157–209. New York: McGraw-Hill.

Woods, W. A. 1973. An Experimental Parsing System for Transition Network Grammars. In *Natural Language Processing,* ed. R. Rustin, 111–154. New York: Algorithmics.

Woods, W., and Brachman, R. 1978. Research in Natural Language Understanding. Quarterly Technical Progress Report, 1, Bolt, Beranek, and Newman, Cambridge, Massachusetts.

Wu, Z., and Palmer, M. 1994. Verb Semantics and Lexical Selection. In Proceedings of the Association of Computational Linguistics, 133–138. New Brunswick, N.J.: Association of Computational Linguistics.

Zadeh, L. A. 1975. The Concept of a Linguistic Variable and Its Application to Approximate Reasoning. *Information Sciences* 8–9: 199–249, 301–357, 43–80.

Zadrozny, W., and Jensen, K. 1991. Semantics of Paragraphs. *Computational Linguistics* 17(2): 171–209.

Zernik, U., and Dyer, M. G. 1987. The Self-Extending Phrasal Lexicon. *Computational Linguistics* 13(3–4): 308–327.

Zwarts, J., and Verkuyl, H. 1994. An Algebra of Conceptual Structure: An Investigation into Jackendoff's Conceptual Semantics. *Linguistics and Philosophy* 17(1): 1–24.

Index

About the Editors

Lucja M. Iwańska is Assistant Professor of Computer Science at Wayne State University. She is also founder and President of LuxLink Inc., a startup company developing state-of-the-art natural language processing, knowledge representation and machine learning technologies.

Iwańska, a native of Poland, received her M.S. in computer science from Moscow Institute of Technology in 1982, and her Ph.D in computer science from University of Illinois at Urbana-Champaign in 1992. Her research focuses on natural language processing and involves the other areas of artificial intelligence, particularly knowledge representation and machine learning. Her specific research interests, contributions and published results include: (1) formal, computational models of semantics, pragmatics and context-dependency of natural language; (2) knowledge representation and automated reasoning systems based on natural language; (3) fully automatic knowledge acquisition from large corpora of texts, query and update via natural language-like mechanism; and (4) learning motivated by natural language.

Iwańska chaired a number of successful conferences on natural language processing. She also served as guest editor of special issues of *Computational Intelligence, International Journal of Expert Systems,* and *Natural Language Engineering.* She speaks English, French, German, Polish and Russian.

Stuart C. Shapiro has been publishing in the area of knowledge representation for natural language understanding for over thirty years. His Ph.D. dissertation (University of Wisconsin—Madison, 1971) is considered to be one of the seminal works in the development of semantic networks as a representation of knowledge. With various colleagues and students, he also did pioneering research in natural language help systems, natural language generation, SCRABBLE Crossword Game-playing programs, intelligent multi-modal interfaces, and assumption-based truth maintenance systems. Shapiro is editor-in-chief of *The Encyclopedia of Artificial Intelligence* (John Wiley & Sons, First Edition, 1987, Second Edition, 1992), author of *Techniques of Artificial Intelligence* (D. Van Nostrand, 1979), *LISP: An Interactive Approach* (Computer Science Press, 1986), *Common Lisp: An Interactive Approach* (Computer Science Press, 1992), and author or coauthor of over 170 technical articles and reports.

Shapiro is currently Professor of Computer Science and Engineering at the State University of New York at Buffalo, where he was Department Chair 1984-1990 and 1996-1999. He has served on the editorial board of the American Journal of Computational Linguistics, and as guest editor of special issues of *Minds and Machines,* and of the *International Journal of Expert Systems.* He is currently on the editorial board of the *International Journal of Applied Software Technology* (IJAST), and on the Advisory Board of *Intelligence: New Visions of AI in Practice.* Shapiro is a member of the ACM, the ACL, the Cognitive Science Society, and Sigma Xi. He served as chair of ACM/SIGART 1991-1995, and as president of KRR, Inc., 1998-2000. He is a Senior Member of the IEEE, and a Fellow of the American Association for Artificial Intelligence. He is listed in *Who's Who in America, Who's Who in the East, Who's Who in the Media and Communications, American Men and Women of Science, Contemporary Authors, Who's Who in Technology* and *Who's Who in Artificial Intelligence.*